Economic Commission for Europe
Geneva

ECONOMIC SURVEY OF EUROPE

2001 No. 1

Prepared by the
SECRETARIAT OF THE
ECONOMIC COMMISSION FOR EUROPE
GENEVA

UNITED NATIONS
New York and Geneva, 2001

NOTE

The designations employed and the presentation of the material in this publication do not imply the expression of any opinion whatsoever on the part of the Secretariat of the United Nations concerning the legal status of any country, territory, city or area, or of its authorities, or concerning the delimitation of its frontiers or boundaries.

UNITED NATIONS PUBLICATION

Sales No. E.01.II.E.14

ISBN 92-1-116780-9
ISSN 0070-8712

Copyright © United Nations, 2001
All rights reserved
Printed at United Nations, Geneva (Switzerland)

CONTENTS

Page

Explanatory notes x
Abbreviations xi
Preface xiii

Part One

RECENT ECONOMIC DEVELOPMENTS AND THE SHORT-RUN OUTLOOK IN THE ECE REGION

Chapter 1   THE ECE ECONOMIES IN SPRING 2001: AN OVERVIEW OF THE CURRENT SITUATION AND SELECTED POLICY ISSUES 3

    1.1   Introduction 3

    1.2   The market economies of western Europe and North America 4
        (i)   Recent developments and the current outlook 4
        (ii)   Is European monetary policy too cautious? 5
        (iii) Raising western Europe's growth rate: are labour markets a constraint? 7

    1.3   The transition economies 9
        (i)   Recent developments and the current outlook 9
        (ii)   The Yugoslav economy and stability in south-east Europe 12

Chapter 2   THE GLOBAL CONTEXT AND WESTERN EUROPE 15

    2.1   World economy 15
        (i)   Overview 15
        (ii)   North America 19

    2.2   Western Europe 25
        (i)   Euro area 25
        (ii)   Other western Europe 35

    2.3   United States current account deficit, saving-investment balances and capital mobility 41
        (i)   Current account developments 41
        (ii)   Saving-investment balances 44
        (iii) Financial account developments 46
        (iv)   Saving-investment balances and capital mobility 48
        (v)   Conclusions 51

    2.4   Factor incomes and labour market performance 52
        (i)   Introduction 52
        (ii)   The econometric model 56
        (iii) Conclusion 58

    2.5   Inflation and interest rate differentials in the euro area 59
        (i)   Inflation differentials in the euro area 59
        (ii)   Nominal and real interest rate differentials 61
        (iii) Economic implications 62

    2.6   Ireland: regional economic adjustment in a monetary union 64

			Page
Chapter 3	THE TRANSITION ECONOMIES		69
	3.1	Expectations and outcomes	69
	3.2	Macroeconomic policy	73
		(i) Monetary policy	74
		(ii) Fiscal policy	83
		(iii) Seigniorage and the inflation tax in the transition economies	92
		(iv) Reforming Yugoslavia's economy	97
	3.3	Output and demand	101
		(i) The pattern of output and demand in 2000-early 2001	101
		(ii) Eastern Europe and the Baltic states	103
		(iii) Commonwealth of Independent States	109
		(iv) Investment	112
	3.4	Costs and prices	114
		(i) Overview	114
		(ii) Consumer prices in 2000	114
		(iii) Producer prices and labour costs in industry in 2000	120
		(iv) Structure and change in manufacturing industry wages during transition	122
	3.5	Labour markets – employment and unemployment	131
		(i) Changes in employment in 2000	131
		(ii) Unemployment	133
	3.6	Foreign trade and payments	137
		(i) Current account developments	137
		(ii) International trade	140
		(iii) External financing and CIS debt issues	155

Part Two

ASPECTS OF STRUCTURAL CHANGE AND ADJUSTMENT IN TRANSITION ECONOMIES

			Page
Chapter 4	DOMESTIC SAVINGS IN THE TRANSITION ECONOMIES		167
	4.1	Introduction	167
	4.2	Savings, investment and growth	167
	4.3	The patterns of savings and investment in the ECE transition economies	170
	4.4	The determinants of private saving in the transition economies	177
	4.5	Policy implications and conclusions	182
Chapter 5	ECONOMIC GROWTH AND FOREIGN DIRECT INVESTMENT IN THE TRANSITION ECONOMIES		185
	5.1	Introduction: theoretical aspects of FDI and economic growth	185
		(i) The role of transnational corporations (TNCs) in facilitating technological and organizational change	186
		(ii) The role of FDI in economic growth: theoretical and empirical considerations	187
	5.2	Principal determinants of FDI flows	188
	5.3	The development of FDI flows, 1990-2000	193

			Page
5.4	FDI and the balance of payments		198
5.5	The direct effect of FDI on economic growth		202
	(i)	Evidence from the developing economies	203
	(ii)	Direction of causation	204
	(iii)	FDI and growth in the transition economies	204
5.6	FDI and productivity spillovers in the transition economies		207
	(i)	FDI in east European manufacturing industry	209
	(ii)	A simple test for productivity spillovers at the industry level	211
	(iii)	Testing for productivity spillovers at the enterprise level	213
5.7	Does FDI facilitate catching up with the European Union?		216
5.8	Concluding comments and policies		218
	Annex to chapter 5: Measuring technology transfer and spillovers		223

Chapter 6 ECONOMIC TRANSFORMATION AND REAL EXCHANGE RATES IN THE 2000s: THE BALASSA-SAMUELSON CONNECTION ... 227

6.1	Introduction		227
6.2	The choice of an exchange rate regime in the 2000s		228
	(i)	General principles	228
	(ii)	Historical overview of exchange rate arrangements	229
	(iii)	The challenges of accession to the European Union	229
6.3	The implications of catch up		231
6.4	A first look at the evidence		232
	(i)	Relative wages	232
	(ii)	Relative productivity	232
	(iii)	Relative prices	234
6.5	Formal evidence		234
	(i)	Sectoral productivity	236
	(ii)	Sectoral real product wages	236
	(iii)	Sectoral real wages	237
	(iv)	Sectoral growth	237
	(v)	The Balassa-Samuelson effect	237
6.6	Policy implications		239

Part Three

STATISTICAL APPENDIX

STATISTICAL APPENDIX ... 241

LIST OF TABLES

Table		Page
1.1.1	Annual changes in real GDP in the ECE region, 1998-2001	4
2.1.1	World commodity prices, 1997-2000	19
2.1.2	Contribution of main expenditure items to the annual change in real GDP in North America, 1998-2000	23
2.1.3	Accounting for changes in labour productivity in the United States, 1973-2000	24
2.2.1	Quarterly changes in real GDP and main expenditure items in western Europe, 1999 QIV-2000 QIV	26
2.2.2	Annual changes in real GDP in western Europe, North America and Japan, 1998-2001	30
2.2.3	Annual changes in major expenditure items on GDP in western Europe, North America and Japan, 1999-2000	33
2.2.4	Consumer price indices in western Europe, North America and Japan, 1997-2000	34
2.2.5	Employment and unemployment in western Europe, North America and Japan, 1998-2000	36
2.2.6	Unemployment by gender in the European Union, North America and Japan, 1991 and 2000	36
2.2.7	Unemployment by age in the European Union, North America and Japan, 1991 and 2000	38
2.2.8	General government financial balances and gross debt in western Europe, North America and Japan, 1998-2000	39
2.3.1	Current account balances, 1997-2000	42
2.3.2	Main components of the United States current account balance, 1970-2000	42
2.3.3	Composition of United States goods imports, 1990-2000	44
2.3.4	Gross investment and gross savings in the United States, 1980-1999	46
2.3.5	Gross savings and gross investment in the euro area, 1980-2000	46
2.3.6	Gross savings and gross investment in the European Union, 1980-2000	47
2.3.7	Gross savings and gross investment in Japan, 1980-1999	47
2.3.8	Composition of capital flows in the United States balance of payments, 1985-2000	48
2.3.9	Changes in the relationship between national savings and domestic investment, 1960-1997	50
2.4.1	European unemployment equation, 1971-1999	58
2.4.2	North American unemployment equation, 1971-1999	58
2.5.1	Annual inflation differentials vis-à-vis average euro area rates, 1997-2000	60
2.5.2	Ratios of non-euro area goods imports to total goods imports and of imports to GDP in 1999	61
2.5.3	Changes in nominal effective exchange rates, January 1999 to February 2001	62
2.5.4	Price level and GDP per capita indices in the euro area, 1998	63
2.5.5	Interest rates in the euro area, 1996-2000	64
3.1.1	Basic economic indicators for eastern Europe, the Baltic states and the CIS, 1998-2001	70
3.1.2	International trade and external balances of eastern Europe, the Baltic states and the CIS, 1998-2000	71
3.2.1	Short-term interest rates in selected east European, Baltic and CIS economies, 1996-2000	79
3.2.2	Monetization in selected east European, Baltic and CIS economies: share of monetary aggregates in GDP, 1996-2000	82
3.2.3	Monetary ratios for selected east European, Baltic and CIS economies, 1996-2000	83
3.2.4	Consolidated general government deficits and their sources of financing in eastern Europe, the Baltic states and the CIS, 1997-2001	84
3.2.5	Consolidated general government current revenue in eastern Europe, the Baltic states and the CIS, 1998-2000	86
3.2.6	Consolidated general government expenditure in eastern Europe, the Baltic states and the CIS, 1998-2000	89
3.2.7	Seigniorage and the inflation tax in selected east European, Baltic and CIS economies, 1995-2000	94
3.3.1	GDP and industrial output in eastern Europe, the Baltic states and the CIS, 1999-2000	102
3.3.2	Contribution of final demand components to real GDP growth in eastern Europe, the Baltic states and the CIS, 1999-2000	105
3.3.3	GDP by kind of activity in eastern Europe, the Baltic states and the CIS, 1993 and 1999	106
3.3.4	Growth of industrial output by NACE categories in eastern Europe and the Baltic states, 1999-2000	108
3.3.5	Growth of industrial output by branch in the CIS, 1999-2000	110
3.3.6	Annual changes in major final expenditure items in eastern Europe, the Baltic states and the CIS, 1999-2000	112
3.3.7	Retail trade in eastern Europe, the Baltic states and the CIS, 1999-2000	113
3.3.8	Gross investment outlays in the CIS, 1996-2000	113
3.4.1	Consumer prices in eastern Europe, the Baltic states and the CIS, 1999-2000	115
3.4.2	Producer prices in industry in eastern Europe, the Baltic states and the CIS, 1999-2000	121
3.4.3	Wages and unit labour costs in industry in eastern Europe, the Baltic states and the CIS, 1999-2000	122
3.4.4	Relative average gross wages in manufacturing branches in selected east European and Baltic economies, 1999	125
3.4.5	Relative average gross wages in manufacturing branches in selected east European and Baltic economies, 1993 and 1999	127
3.5.1	Total and industrial employment in eastern Europe, the Baltic states and the CIS, 1999-2000	132
3.5.2	Registered unemployment in eastern Europe, the Baltic states and the CIS, 1999-2001	134
3.6.1	Current account balances of eastern Europe, the Baltic states and the CIS, 1997-2000	138
3.6.2	Current account balances, by country group and composition, 1997-2000	139
3.6.3	Foreign trade of eastern Europe, the Baltic states and the CIS by direction, 1998-2000	143
3.6.4	Trade balances of eastern Europe, the Baltic states and the CIS, 1995-2000	144
3.6.5	Changes in the volume of foreign trade in selected east European and Baltic countries and the Russian Federation, 1997-2000	145
3.6.6	Changes in commodity composition of foreign trade in eastern Europe and the Baltic states, 1996-2000	146
3.6.7	Average import prices in dollars and volumes, Russian Federation, 2000	150

Table		Page
3.6.8	CIS countries' trade with CIS and non-CIS, 1998-2000	151
3.6.9	A sample of energy related disputes among the members of the CIS	153
3.6.10	Trade in energy products in selected CIS economies, January-September 2000	154
3.6.11	Net capital flows into eastern Europe, the Baltic states and the CIS, 1997-2000	156
3.6.12	Net capital flows into eastern Europe, the Baltic states and selected CIS, by type of capital, 1998-2000	157
3.6.13	Selected external financial indicators for eastern Europe, the Baltic states and the CIS, 1997-2000	158
3.6.14	Selected inter-CIS debt operations, 1995-2000	161
4.3.1	Saving-investment balances in selected east European and Baltic countries, 1994-1999	173
4.3.2	Saving-investment balances in selected countries of the CIS, 1994-1999	174
4.4.1	The main determinants of private savings in eastern Europe, the Baltic states and the CIS, 1995-1998: descriptive statistics	179
4.4.2	Regression analysis of the determinants of private savings in eastern Europe, the Baltic states and the CIS, 1995-1998: ordinary least squares estimations on panel data	181
5.2.1	Foreign direct investment in eastern Europe, the Baltic states and the CIS, 1990-2000	189
5.2.2	Foreign direct investment inflows in eastern Europe, the Baltic states and the CIS, 1988-2000	190
5.3.1	FDI inflows as a percentage of GDP(PPP), 1993-1999	197
5.4.1	Ratio of FDI inflows to current account deficits, 1993-1999	198
5.4.2	Coefficients of variation of FDI inflows and other capital flows, 1990-1999	199
5.4.3	Direct effect of FDI on the balance of payments in Hungary, 1996-1999	201
5.4.4	Direct effect of FDI on the balance of payments of the oil sector in Azerbaijan, 1995-2000	201
5.4.5	FDI penetration and exports in selected east European and Baltic economies, 1996-1998	202
5.6.1	Distribution of total manufacturing sales by industry in selected east European and Baltic economies, 1993 and 1998	210
5.6.2	Share of FIEs in total sales by industry in selected east European and Baltic economies, 1993 and 1998	210
5.6.3	Convergence of gross output per employee in DEs and FIEs in selected east European and Baltic economies, 1993 and 1998	212
5.6.4	Convergence of value added per employee in DEs and FIEs in selected east European and Baltic economies, 1993 and 1998	212
5.6.5	Comparison of capital intensity (capital assets per employee) in DEs and FIEs in selected east European and Baltic economies, 1993 and 1998	213
5.6.6	Regression analysis I of productivity convergence between DEs and FIEs in selected east European economies, 1993-1998	214
5.6.7	Regression analysis II of productivity convergence between DEs and FIEs in selected east European economies, 1993-1998	214
5.6.8	Impact of FDI: direct effects and spillovers in Slovenia (1994-1998) and Estonia (1995-1998)	215
5.6.9	Impact of R&D: importance of innovative and absorptive capacity in Slovenia (1994-1998) and Estonia (1995-1998)	216
5.6.10	Impact of R&D and international knowledge spillovers through trade in Slovenia and Estonia	216
5.7.1	International comparisons of labour productivity, 1998	217
5.7.2	Regression analysis of productivity convergence between selected east European and Baltic economies and EU industries, 1993-1998	218
5.8.1	Obstacles to foreign direct investment in Estonia, 1997 and 1998	221
6.1.1	Per capita GDP (PPP-adjusted) in relation to the EU average, 1991 and 1998	228
6.2.1	Exchange rate arrangements in eastern Europe, the Baltic states and the Russian Federation, 1990-2000	230
6.5.1	Estimated regressions results for sectoral productivity	236
6.5.2	Estimated regressions results for sectoral real product wages	236
6.5.3	Estimated regressions results for sectoral real wage	237
6.5.4	Estimated regressions results for sectoral output growth	238
6.5.5	Estimated results on service-to-consumer goods price ratio	238
A.1	Real GDP in western Europe, North America and Japan, 1986-2000	243
A.2	Real private consumption expenditure in western Europe, North America and Japan, 1986-2000	244
A.3	Real general government consumption expenditure in western Europe, North America and Japan, 1986-2000	245
A.4	Real gross domestic fixed capital formation in western Europe, North America and Japan, 1986-2000	246
A.5	Real total domestic expenditures in western Europe, North America and Japan, 1986-2000	247
A.6	Real exports of goods and services in western Europe, North America and Japan, 1986-2000	248
A.7	Real imports of goods and services in western Europe, North America and Japan, 1986-2000	249
A.8	Industrial output in western Europe, North America and Japan, 1986-2000	250
A.9	Total employment in western Europe, North America and Japan, 1986-2000	251
A.10	Standardized unemployment rates in western Europe, North America and Japan, 1986-2000	252
A.11	Consumer prices in western Europe, North America and Japan, 1986-2000	253
B.1	Real GDP/NMP in eastern Europe, the Baltic states and the CIS, 1980, 1987-2000	254
B.2	Real total consumption expenditure in eastern Europe, the Baltic states and the CIS, 1980, 1987-2000	255
B.3	Real gross fixed capital formation in eastern Europe, the Baltic states and the CIS, 1980, 1987-2000	255
B.4	Real gross industrial output in eastern Europe, the Baltic states and the CIS, 1980, 1987-2000	256
B.5	Total employment in eastern Europe, the Baltic states and the CIS, 1980, 1987-2000	257
B.6	Employment in industry in eastern Europe, the Baltic states and the CIS, 1989-2000	258
B.7	Registered unemployment in eastern Europe, the Baltic states and the CIS, 1990-2000	259
B.8	Consumer prices in eastern Europe, the Baltic states and the CIS, 1990-2000	260

Table		Page
B.9	Producer price indices in eastern Europe, the Baltic states and the CIS, 1990-2000	261
B.10	Nominal gross wages in industry in eastern Europe, the Baltic states and the CIS, 1990-2000	262
B.11	Merchandise exports of eastern Europe, the Baltic states and the CIS, 1980, 1988-2000	263
B.12	Merchandise imports of eastern Europe, the Baltic states and the CIS, 1980, 1988-2000	264
B.13	Balance of merchandise trade of eastern Europe, the Baltic states and the CIS, 1980, 1988-2000	265
B.14	Merchandise trade of eastern Europe and the Russian Federation, by direction, 1980, 1988-2000	266
B.15	Exchange rates of eastern Europe, the Baltic states and the CIS, 1980, 1988-2000	267
B.16	Current account balances of eastern Europe, the Baltic states and the CIS, 1990-2000	268
B.17	Inflows of foreign direct investment in eastern Europe, the Baltic states and the CIS, 1990-2000	269

LIST OF CHARTS

Chart		Page
1.1.1	Real GDP growth in the ECE region in 2001: changes in consensus forecasts, January 2000-March 2001	3
1.3.1	Real west European imports and real exports of central Europe and the Baltic states, 1995-2001	10
2.1.1	Industrial production and unemployment in Japan, January 1997-January 2001	16
2.1.2	International share prices, January 1995-February 2001	17
2.1.3	Bilateral exchange rates between the euro, the dollar and the yen, January 1998-February 2001	18
2.1.4	World commodity prices, January 1991-February 2001	18
2.1.5	Quarterly changes in real GDP in North America, 1996-2000	20
2.1.6	Consumer confidence and retail sales in the United States, January 1995-February 2001	21
2.1.7	Manufacturing output, capacity utilization and the purchasing managers' index in the United States, January 1988-January 2001	21
2.1.8	Employment and unemployment in the United States, January 1995-January 2001	22
2.1.9	Consumer prices in the United States, January 1995-January 2001	22
2.1.10	Nominal short-term and long-term interest rates in the United States, January 1995-February 2001	22
2.1.11	The old and new productivity trends in the United States, 1973 QI-2000 QIV	23
2.2.1	Quarterly changes in real GDP in the industrialized countries, 1996-2000	26
2.2.2	Industrial confidence and industrial production in the European Union, January 1995-February 2001	27
2.2.3	Quarterly changes in real GDP and main expenditure items in western Europe, 1996 QI-2000 QIII	28
2.2.4	Consumer confidence and retail sales in the European Union, January 1995-February 2001	29
2.2.5	Quarterly changes in real gross fixed capital formation, 1996 QI-2000 QIII	29
2.2.6	Consumer prices in the euro area, January 1997-January 2001	34
2.2.7	Employment and unemployment in the euro area and western Europe, 1995 QI-2000 QIV	35
2.2.8	Unemployment rates by sex and age group in the European Union, euro area and the United States, 1991-2000	37
2.2.9	Short-term and long-term interest rates in the euro area, January 1997-February 2001	38
2.2.10	Interest rate differentials between the United States and the euro area, January 1997-February 2001	38
2.3.1	Current account balance of the United States, 1970-2000	42
2.3.2	Private sector and government financial balances and the current account balance in the United States, 1980-2000	45
2.3.3	Private sector savings and investment in the United States, 1980-1999	45
2.3.4	Private sector and government financial balances and the current account balance in the euro area, 1980-2000	47
2.3.5	Private sector and government financial balances and the current account balance in Japan, 1980-1998	48
2.3.6	The changing relationship between national savings and domestic investment, 1960-1997	51
2.3.7	Savings retention coefficients, 1960-1997	51
2.4.1	Unemployment rates and wage shares of output, 1970-1999	53
2.4.2	Real long-term interest rates, 1970-1999	55
2.4.3	Unemployment rates and wage shares, 1970-1999	57
2.5.1	Dispersion of inflation rates in the euro area, January 1997-January 2001	60
2.5.2	Nominal effective exchange rates, January 1999-February 2001	62
2.6.1	Real GDP, consumer prices and unemployment in Ireland, 1990-2000	65
2.6.2	Consumer price inflation in Ireland, January 1997-January 2001	66
3.2.1	Real effective exchange rates in selected east European and Baltic economies, 1995-2000	78
3.2.2	Real short-term interest rates in selected east European, Baltic and CIS economies, 1997-2000	80
3.2.3	Fiscal balance and its change from the previous year in eastern Europe, the Baltic states and the CIS, 1999-2000	87
3.2.4	Changes in the fiscal balance and domestic absorption in eastern Europe, the Baltic states and the CIS, 1999-2000	88
3.2.5	General government balance in the Russian Federation, 1996-2000	91
3.2.6	General government revenue and expenditure in the Russian Federation, 1996-2000	91
3.2.7	Average levels of seigniorage by regional groups, 1994-2000	95
3.2.8	Average levels of inflation tax by regional groups, 1994-2000	95
3.2.9	Fiscal deficits and the inflation tax in selected east European, Baltic and CIS economies, 1995-2000	96
3.2.10	Monetization and seigniorage in selected east European, Baltic and CIS economies, 1993-1999	97

Chart		Page
3.3.1	Gross output in the electrical and optical equipment industry in central Europe, 1996-2000	103
3.3.2	Gross output in the transport equipment industry in central Europe, 1996-2000	103
3.3.3	Gross output in the electrical and optical equipment industry in Hungary by branch, 1996-2000	106
3.3.4	Industrial production and wage arrears in the Russian Federation and the international oil price, 1998-2000	109
3.4.1	Consumer prices in eastern Europe, the Baltic states and the CIS, 1997-2001	116
3.4.2	Relative average gross wages in manufacturing branches: unweighted average of 11 east European and Baltic economies and Germany, 1999	126
3.4.3	Relative average gross wages in manufacturing branches: unweighted average of seven east European and Baltic economies, 1993 and 1999	128
3.4.4	Change in relative average gross wages by manufacturing branches in selected east European and Baltic economies and Germany, 1993 and 1999	129
3.4.5	Growth rates of wages, labour productivity and output, by manufacturing branch, in selected east European and Baltic economies, 1993-1999	130
3.5.1	Registered unemployment rates in selected east European, Baltic and CIS economies, 1993-2000	136
3.6.1	Specific western demand for exports from selected east European and Baltic economies and the Russian Federation, 1998-2001	142
4.3.1	Investment ratios and rates of growth of GDP per capita in selected east European, Baltic and CIS economies, 1995-1999	171
4.3.2	Saving and investment ratios in selected east European and CIS economies, 1990-1999	175
4.3.3	Gross domestic savings and gross investment in selected east European, Baltic and CIS economies, 1991-1999	176
4.3.4	Private savings and fixed investment in selected east European, Baltic and CIS economies, 1995-1999	177
4.4.1	Current account balance and private savings in selected east European, Baltic and CIS economies, 1995-1998	180
4.4.2	GDP per capita and private savings in selected east European, Baltic and CIS economies, 1995-1998	180
4.4.3	Monetization and private savings in selected east European, Baltic and CIS economies, 1995-1998	180
5.2.1	Cumulative FDI inflows as a percentage of current year GDP in eastern Europe, the Baltic states and the CIS, 1990-1999	191
5.2.2	Ratio of cumulative FDI inflows in GDO(PPP) and progress in reform	192
5.3.1	Annual FDI inflows as a percentage of GDP, 1990-1999	194
5.3.2	Cumulative FDI inflows per capita and GDP(PPP) per capita, 1999	197
5.3.3	Annual FDI inflows as a percentage of nominal GDP, 1985-1999	197
5.3.4	Cumulative FDI inflows as a percentage of current year GDP, 1985-1999	198
5.4.1	Export growth and ratio of cumulative FDI inflows to GDP(PPP)	201
5.5.1	GDP growth and FDI flows as a per cent of nominal GDP in selected east European and Baltic economies, 1991-1999	205
5.5.2	Growth of GDP and ratio of cumulative FDI inflows to GDP(PPP)	207
5.6.1	Productivity convergence between DEs and FIEs in total manufacturing in selected east European and Baltic economies, 1993-1998	213
6.2.1	Consumer price inflation in Estonia and the euro area, January 1994-January 2001	231
6.4.1	Relative wages in industry and services, 1992-1999	233
6.4.2	Relative productivity in industry and services, 1992-1998	234
6.4.3	Relative prices of services and non-food manufactures, 1989-1999	235

LIST OF BOXES

Box		Page
2.2.1	Greece joins the EMU	31
2.2.2	Universal Mobile Telecommunication System (UMTS) license sales	40
3.2.1	Dynamic equilibrium during a process of catch up in productivity and price levels: policy implications for the acceding countries	75
3.3.1	Structure and change in east European manufacturing industry	104
3.4.1	NACE Rev. 1 classification of economic activities in manufacturing	124
4.3.1	The arithmetic of the national saving-investment balance	172
5.3.1	FDI indicators and their interpretation	195
6.2.1	The exchange rate mechanism-2	229

EXPLANATORY NOTES

The following symbols have been used throughout this *Survey*:

    .. = not available or not pertinent

    – = nil or negligible

    * = estimate by the secretariat of the Economic Commission for Europe

    | = break in series

In referring to a combination of years, the use of an oblique stroke (e.g. 1998/99) signifies a 12-month period (say, from 1 July 1998 to 30 June 1999). The use of a hyphen (e.g. 1998-2000) normally signifies either an average of, or a total for, the full period of calendar years covered (including the end-years indicated).

Unless the contrary is stated, the standard unit of weight used throughout is the metric ton. The definition of "billion" used throughout is a thousand million. The definition of "trillion" used throughout is a thousand billion. Minor discrepancies in totals and percentages are due to rounding.

References to dollars ($) are to United States dollars unless otherwise specified.

The membership of the United Nations Economic Commission for Europe (UN/ECE) consists of all the states of western Europe, eastern Europe and the territory of the former Soviet Union, North America and Israel.

The term *transition economies*, as used in the text and tables of this publication, refers to the formerly centrally planned economies of the ECE regions. *Eastern Europe* refers to the economies of Albania, Bosnia and Herzegovina, Bulgaria, Croatia, the Czech Republic, Hungary, Poland, Romania, Slovakia, Slovenia, The former Yugoslav Republic of Macedonia and Yugoslavia. The *Baltic states* refers to Estonia, Latvia and Lithuania and the *CIS countries* refers to Armenia, Azerbaijan, Belarus, Georgia, Kazakhstan, Kyrgyzstan, Republic of Moldova, Russian Federation, Tajikistan, Turkmenistan, Ukraine and Uzbekistan.

ABBREVIATIONS

BBC	British Broadcasting Corporation
BIS	Bank for International Settlements
BNA	Bureau of National Affairs
BSE	bovine spongiform encephalopathy
CEECs	central and east European countries
CEFTA	Central European Free Trade Agreement
CETE	central European transition economies
c.i.f.	cost, insurance and freight
CIS	Commonwealth of Independent States
CMEA	(former) Council for Mutual Economic Assistance
CPI	consumer price index
DE	domestically owned enterprise
EBRD	European Bank for Reconstruction and Development
ECB	European Central Bank
ECLAC	Economic Commission for Latin America and the Caribbean
ECOFIN	Council of Economic and Financial Ministers
ECP	European Comparison Programme
ECU	European currency unit
EFF	Extended Fund Facility (of IMF)
EFTA	European Free Trade Association
EIB	European Investment Bank
EIU	Economist Intelligence Unit
EMS	European Monetary System
EMU	economic and monetary union
ERM-2	exchange rate mechanism-2 (replaces the EMS)
ESA	European System of Integrated Economic Accounts
EU	European Union
EURIBOR	euro interbank offered rate
FDI	foreign direct investment
FIE	foreign investment enterprise
G-7	Group of Seven
G-24	Group of Twenty-four
GDFCF	gross domestic fixed capital formation
GDP	gross domestic product
GDR	(former) German Democratic Republic
GLS	generalized least squares
HICP	Harmonized Index of Consumer Prices
HWWA	Hamburg Institute for Economic Research
IFI	international financial institutions
IFTZ	industrial foreign trade zone

IIF	Institute of International Finance, Inc.
ILO	International Labour Office
IMF	International Monetary Fund
ISIC	International Standard Industrial Classification
IT	information technology
M&As	mergers and acquisitions
NACE	Nomenclature générale des activités économiques dans les Communautés européennes (General Industrial Classification of Economic Activities within the European Communities)
NAIRU	non-accelerating inflation rate of unemployment
NATO	North Atlantic Treaty Organization
NBER	National Bureau of Economic Research, Inc.
n.e.c.	not elsewhere classified
NMP	net material product
OECD	Organisation for Economic Co-operation and Development
OLS	ordinary least squares
OPEC	Organization of the Petroleum Exporting Countries
OPT	outward processing trade
PECA	Protocols on European Conformity Assessment
PHARE	Assistance programmes for the countries of central and eastern Europe (of the EU)
PPI	producer price index
PPP	purchasing power parity
PRGF	Poverty Reduction and Growth Facility (of IMF)
PSA	production sharing agreement
R&D	research and development
RFE/RL	Radio Free Europe/Radio Liberty
RPIX	retail price index excluding mortgage interest payments
SDR	special drawing right
SETE	south-east European transition economies
SITC	Standard International Trade Classification
SNA	System of National Accounts
TACIS	Technical Assistance for the Commonwealth of Independent States (of the EU)
TFP	total factor productivity
TNC	transnational corporation
ULC	unit labour costs
UNCTAD	United Nations Conference on Trade and Development
UN/ECE	United Nations Economic Commission for Europe
USSR	(former) Union of Soviet Socialist Republics
VAT	value added tax
WTO	World Trade Organization

PREFACE

The present *Survey* is the fifty-fourth in a series of annual reports prepared by the secretariat of the United Nations Economic Commission for Europe to serve the needs of the Commission and of the United Nations in reporting on and analysing world economic conditions.

Until 1997 the *Economic Survey of Europe* was issued once a year as was the *Economic Bulletin for Europe*, the secretariat's second publication which focused on trade and payments issues. At its 52nd Session, in April 1997, the Commission decided to replace these two publications with an annual *Survey* of several issues. In 1998 and 1999 there were three issues each year. There are now two issues a year published in April and November.

The Survey is published on the sole responsibility of the Executive Secretary of ECE and the views expressed in it should not be attributed to the Commission or to its participating governments.

The analysis in this issue is based on data and information available to the secretariat in late-March 2001.

Economic Analysis Division
United Nations Economic Commission for Europe
Geneva

PART ONE

RECENT ECONOMIC DEVELOPMENTS AND THE SHORT-RUN OUTLOOK IN THE ECE REGION

CHAPTER 1

THE ECE ECONOMIES IN SPRING 2001: AN OVERVIEW OF THE CURRENT SITUATION AND SELECTED POLICY ISSUES

1.1 Introduction

The fragility of economic forecasts has again been highlighted by developments over the last six months. Last October global economic prospects looked better than at any time in the previous 10 years: forecasts for the world economy in 2000 were being raised to some 4¾ per cent and, despite some slowing down associated with the anticipated rebalancing of output towards Europe and away from the United States, growth was expected to remain at around 4¼ per cent. It is now apparent, however, that the world economy peaked in the first half of 2000. One negative factor was the higher price of oil but the forecasters were correct in forecasting that this would fall back to the OPEC target range in early 2001. The major downside risk had been recognized for some time but was essentially unpredictable as to scale and timing – and that concerned the inevitable correction of the United States stock market bubble and of the "irrational exuberance" about the future prospects for the United States economy.

At the end of the first quarter of 2001, the short-term economic outlook for the western market economies looks much less favourable than in the autumn of 2000. The main factor behind this is the unexpectedly sharp slowdown in economic growth in the United States since the second half of 2000 and the stalled recovery in Japan. Activity in the two largest economies in the world is thus weakening rapidly or continuing to stagnate. This has started to feed through changes in net exports to other regions of the world economy. As a result, there has been a progressive lowering of growth forecasts, especially for the United States, since late 2000 (chart 1.1.1).

In the United States, real GDP is now expected to increase by only some 1¾ per cent in 2001, a very abrupt deceleration from an average growth rate of 5 per cent in 2000. In Japan, economic growth is expected to only slightly exceed 1 per cent in 2001, and even that is uncertain given disagreements over economic policy and delays in introducing another economic emergency programme. Growth forces are seen to hold up somewhat better in western Europe. In the euro area, real GDP is currently forecast to increase by some 2.5 per cent in 2001, down from 3.4 per cent in 2000 and half a percentage point less than was being forecast last autumn. Broadly similar changes are expected for the European Union and for western Europe as a whole (table 1.1.1). For the industrialized economies in aggregate, the average rate of economic growth is likely to be only some 2 per cent in 2001, down from 3.8 per cent in 2000 and the smallest annual increase since 1993. As a result, the prospects for economic growth in the central and east European economies, as well as the CIS and other parts of the world economy, will also be adversely affected, leading to a mutually reinforcing process which will amplify the direct trade effects of the cyclical downturn in the United States. The upshot is that world output might now grow by only some 2.5-3 per cent in 2001, down from 4.7 per cent in 2000 and considerably less than was expected in the autumn of 2000.[1]

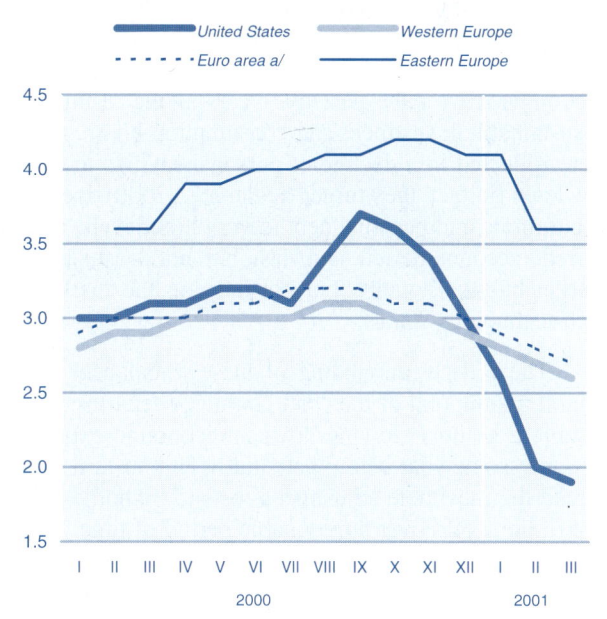

CHART 1.1.1

Real GDP growth in the ECE region in 2001: changes in consensus forecasts, January 2000-March 2001
(Percentage change over previous year)

Source: Consensus Forecast.

ᵃ From January 2001 Greece is included.

---

[1] The IMF was forecasting 4.2 per cent in October of last year. IMF, *World Economic Outlook* (Washington, D.C.), October 2000.

TABLE 1.1.1

Annual changes in real GDP in the ECE region, 1998-2001
(Percentage change over previous year)

	1998	1999	2000 [a]	2001 [b]
Western Europe	2.8	2.2	3.5	2.5
European Union	2.8	2.6	3.3	2.6
Euro area	2.8	2.6	3.4	2.6
North America	4.3	4.3	5.0	1.8
United States	4.4	4.2	5.0	1.7
Eastern Europe [c]	2.0	1.1	3.9	4.2
CIS	-3.0	3.2	7.4	4.2
Russian Federation	-4.9	3.5	7.7	4.0
Memorandum items:				
Europe (east and west)	2.7	2.1	3.5	2.7
Europe (east and west) and **CIS**	2.0	2.2	4.0	2.9

Source: This *Survey*, tables 2.2.2 and 3.1.1.

[a] Preliminary estimates.

[b] Forecast.

[c] Including the Baltic states.

1.2 The market economies of western Europe and North America

(i) Recent developments and the current outlook

In the United States, the long economic expansion, which, if maintained in the first quarter of 2001 will have lasted for 10 years, was expected to slow down in 2001 against the background of tighter monetary policy and the real income effects of higher energy prices. In fact, a slowdown was seen as highly desirable, given that actual output had grown at a rate significantly above potential for quite some time with increasing risks of overheating and a hard landing. There were, moreover, mounting concerns about the huge imbalances which had accumulated over the past five years as the result of an unsustainable investment and consumption boom. These were reflected in a decline of personal savings to a very low level (in fact, they turned negative in 2000), increases in corporate and personal debt to very high levels, a huge current account deficit and, last but not least, a stock market bubble, notably, but not only, in the market for high-technology shares.

The orderly unwinding of these imbalances is the central assumption of the "soft landing" scenarios, which assume a gradual slowing down in economic expansion to a rate somewhat below potential. This in turn would spread the inevitable adjustment costs to be borne by the rest of the world over a reasonable period of time. In the event, however, there was an unanticipated abrupt cyclical downswing in the United States economy after the second quarter of 2000, a development which serves as a sharp reminder of the inherent difficulties of forecasting cyclical turning points. The investment boom in information technology equipment, a major force behind the long expansion, petered out in the face of growing excess capacity in the manufacturing sector. To this was added a sharp fall in the demand for consumer durables and for exports in the last quarter of 2000, which led to a build-up of excess inventories and a weakening of industrial activity. The reaction of the United States monetary authorities to the deteriorating economic conditions was very swift. The target for the federal funds rate was lowered in three steps by 1.5 percentage points between January and March of 2001. Against this background and the decline in actual and expected business profits, there has been a sharp decline in equity prices for a broad range of stocks in the first quarter of 2001, with adverse consequence for households' net wealth and the debt-equity ratios of the corporate sector.

While imbalances are more or less typical of any strong and sustained cyclical upswing – largely a reflection of overly optimistic production and profit expectations – there has been a degree of excess in the United States, especially in the financial markets, which would not have been possible without the generous credit expansion allowed by the United States Federal Reserve. But these kind of miscalculations are always easier to diagnose *post facto* and can often only be avoided *ex ante* by stifling the expansion itself.[2]

In Japan, against a background of deflationary tendencies and increasingly pessimistic business assessments of the country's short-term prospects, the monetary authorities reverted to the "zero interest rate" policy in March 2001, a policy which had been abandoned in the second half of 2000. This shift in monetary policy has been accompanied by a marked depreciation of the yen which should, in principle, support exports and increase imported inflation. In the face of deteriorating export prospects, notably to the United States market, the corporate sector is cutting back on planned investments. Given the limited room for manoeuvre left by the near-zero interest rates, the Bank of Japan has decided that it will target the inflation rate, i.e. it will inject liquidity – using outright purchases of government bonds – until the year-on-year rate of consumer price inflation has become slightly positive again. The government also intends to launch a new package of measures designed to prevent the economy sliding back into recession, but this had still not been introduced by the end of the first quarter of 2001.

In western Europe, the cyclical recovery held up relatively well in the second half of 2000, but there was also a noticeable slowing in the rate of economic expansion. The optimistic view that the European economies would be largely immune to the deterioration in the rest of the global economy, however, has been overtaken by events as evidenced by the significant lowering of forecasts for GDP in 2001. This is also reflected in the sharp drop in business confidence in Germany, the largest west European economy. Many forecasters now expect real GDP in Germany to increase by only 2 per cent in 2001, down from the 2¾ per cent forecast in the autumn of 2000.

---

[2] G. Haberler, *Prosperity and Depression*, New Edition (Cambridge, MA, Harvard University Press, 1964), pp. 471-472.

above, the sudden and rapid deceleration of the United States economy in the second half of 2000 and early 2001 has triggered a gradual lowering of the forecasts for economic growth in western Europe as well. In addition, oil prices have been falling since the last quarter of 2000 and it seems likely that their average level in 2001 will be below that in 2000 (although still higher than in 1999). The first of these developments will have a serious impact on all the transition economies, increasing the downside risks to their short-term prospects, but the second will affect net oil importers and exporters differently.

The recent and rapid changes in the world economy do not appear to have been always taken into account in the official forecasts for eastern Europe and the Baltic states, most of which were made in the context of the budgetary preparations for 2001 when the global slowdown was not yet visible (table 3.1.1). These forecasts indicate that governments throughout eastern Europe and the Baltic area were generally expecting a further strengthening of the recovery in 2001 and, in many cases, an acceleration of their rates of economic growth.[24] In fact, the most recent data indicate that, in a number of east European and Baltic economies, the growth of output was already decelerating in the closing months of 2000 and at the beginning of 2001.

Against this background, the actual short-term outlook for eastern Europe and the Baltic area largely depends on the success or failure of western Europe in countering the weakening of its own prospects for output growth. A benign scenario (along the lines of the official forecasts in eastern Europe and the Baltic states) is conditional on success in arresting the slowdown in western Europe and, especially, in Germany.[25] A significant deceleration of growth in western Europe (involving a deceleration in import growth from around 10 per cent to 7 per cent) would have highly detrimental consequences for eastern Europe and the Baltic area, which could effectively translate into a reduction of their average GDP growth by 1-2 percentage points.

The unprecedented growth of Russia's GDP in 2000 reflected the combination of a low base (due to the 1998 crisis) and an extremely favourable external environment which is unlikely to be sustained. Indeed, all the indications are that the Russian economy (in particular industrial output) was also slowing down at the beginning of 2001. If oil prices continue to fall, domestic demand in Russia will be negatively affected and the official forecast for the year as a whole (GDP growth of 4 per cent) will be difficult to achieve. The prospects for most of the other CIS economies are conditional both on the outlook for world oil and commodity prices and on the performance of the Russian economy, including the development of rouble exchange rate. Hence, the uncertainties concerning the outlook for Russia are largely translated into uncertainties for the Commonwealth as a whole.

This uncertain outlook, and the increasing downside risks, implies the need for a more active role of economic policy in the transition economies in 2001 and modifications to the policy stances embodied in government budgets already adopted for the year. Policy makers will have to maintain a close monitoring not only of their own economic performance but also of current developments in their main trading partners and on the world markets. If external conditions continue to deteriorate, policy makers in the transition economies will have to be prepared to act swiftly with counter cyclical measures in order to offset, at least partly, an eventual negative shock. Although a full offset may not be in their power, given the risk of aggravating existing imbalances, timely policy responses may help to dampen its negative repercussions.

A prolonged slowdown, first in western Europe and then in the transition economies as well, would pose significant risks for the process of economic transformation and the future prospects of these economies. A slowdown will undoubtedly have a strong negative impact on the labour markets of the transition economies which are already in distress. At the end of 2000 the average unemployment rate in eastern Europe was still around 15 per cent: despite the high rate of economic growth, enterprise restructuring was still releasing more labour than was being employed in new jobs. A slowdown in economic growth will not only worsen unemployment but the likely social tensions may put a brake on the necessary but painful process of economic restructuring and systemic reform.

As seen from recent experience, growth in the most successful transition economies has been based on the expansion of exports and the upgrading of their commodity structure, both of which are conditional on large amounts of fixed investment, and especially of FDI. A slowdown of output growth in western Europe (which is a major source of FDI for the transition economies) may also lead to the weakening of direct investment in the transition economies. All these increasing downside risks in the transition economies, together with those in western Europe, reinforce the case for a counter cyclical policy stance.

A slowdown in western Europe also carries risks for the prospects of EU enlargement. As repeatedly stressed in this *Survey*, if the transition economies are to catch up with the industrialized west European economies in terms of per capita incomes and levels of development (an important condition for a smooth accession to the EU),

---

[24] Aggregate GDP in eastern Europe was expected to grow by some 4.2 per cent in 2001 (0.3 percentage points more than in 2000) while the forecast for the Baltic states was an average 4.7 per cent, slightly below the 2000 outcome (table 3.1.1).

[25] The share of Germany in the trade of most east European and Baltic economies is much larger than the share of Germany in the aggregate output of the EU.

they need to sustain high rates of economic growth (of the order of 5-6 per cent per annum, or even more) for a sufficiently long period of time. The candidate countries from eastern Europe and the Baltic area are crucially dependent on robust import demand in the west European markets for making a reality of such a strategy. Hence, if the eastern enlargement of the EU is to occur sooner rather than later, the EU and its policy makers have a double responsibility in maintaining steady growth in the Union: this is not only in its own self-interest but even more so in the interest of its potential future members and, therefore, in the broader, regional interest of a future, United Europe.

(ii) The Yugoslav economy and stability in south-east Europe

The new, democratically elected government of Yugoslavia is facing one of the most complex and serious set of economic problems to be faced by any transition economy since 1989. The 1980s were already problematic for the former SFR of Yugoslavia, a lost decade in terms of development; but the 1990s were disastrous, a decade of economic regress. Yugoslavia's GDP per head was some 46 per cent of the EU average in 1980; in 1990 it had fallen to some 34 per cent, and rough estimates put it at somewhat under 25 per cent in 2000.[26] Devastated by a series of wars culminating in the Kosovo conflict of 1999, by the chronic misallocation of resources under authoritarian rule, by economic sanctions and isolation from the international community, and debilitated by extensive corruption among the ruling elite which appropriated a considerable proportion of the state's resources to itself, the present government is faced with an economy wracked by macroeconomic imbalances which are far greater than those encountered in any other transition economy, including Russia. Many of these imbalances were hidden by the previous regime in the form of suppressed inflation and hidden subsidies to the enterprise sector.

An enormous quasi-fiscal deficit – swollen by the losses of publicly owned firms, which amounted to 123 per cent of GDP at the end of 1998 – has accumulated as an alternative to confronting the structural causes of the hyperinflation of 1992-1994 and is the largest single imbalance facing the government. The government debt and the country's foreign debt, which amounts to some $12.2 billion, are both equivalent to well over 100 per cent of GDP.[27] But attempts to correct these imbalances quickly run into a series of connected problems. Dealing with the stock of enterprise debt will require large-scale public funding to restructure their balance sheets, while stopping the further accumulation of debt will require hard budget constraints in a market environment. But hard budget constraints will threaten at least 30 per cent of the total employed labour force, which are estimated to be underemployed in state owned firms, in a country where registered unemployment is already running at some 27 per cent of the labour force. Enterprise restructuring, in turn, will require a reform of the complicated system of social and public ownership, and the highly distorted structure of relative prices will have to be liberalized if there is to be any significant movement to a more efficient allocation of resources.

At the same time the government will have to confront two other major tasks: the reform of the public finances and the tax system, and the restructuring of the banks. The net worth of the banks is probably close to zero and so huge amounts of fresh funds will be needed to recapitalize them.

The government must attempt to introduce this major programme of reform in a country where the population, after more than a decade of drastically falling living standards and the loss of a major part of its savings through hyperinflation and government sequestration, has little or no confidence in the country's financial institutions, is distrustful of state institutions, and is resentful of what it sees as excessive foreign interference. Whatever reforms are introduced further hardship for many groups in Serbian society seems inevitable. In these circumstances it may be dangerously counter-productive to withhold assistance to the Yugoslav government until international demands are met for the former President to be handed over to the International War Crimes Tribunal in The Hague. As stressed in previous issues of this *Survey*, the economic recovery of Yugoslavia is essential for the peace, prosperity and stability of south-east Europe as a whole. The stability of the region remains highly fragile as recent events in The former Yugoslav Republic of Macedonia and Bosnia and Herzegovina have underlined. Without in any way compromising Yugoslavia's legal obligations to the Tribunal in The Hague, the immediate priority is for the Yugoslav government to get a comprehensive programme of reforms underway and to bring about some improvement in the living standards of the population. But it will not be able to do this without massive help from abroad. There are signs that the international financial institutions are now acting more rapidly and effectively in south-east Europe than they did in central Europe in the 1990s,[28] but they are unlikely to be able to

---

[26] UN/ECE, *Economic Survey of Europe, 2000 No. 1*, chap. 5.

[27] A foreign debt to GDP ratio of 118 per cent is based on a GDP figure of $10.3 billion, which is an estimate adjusted for the multiple exchange rates (official, black market and inter-enterprise) existing during most of 2000. P. Petrovic, D. Dragutinovic and M. Arsic, *The FRY Economy: Macroeconomic Developments and Main Imbalances* (Belgrade), February 2001. Use of a dollar GDP, based on the unrealistically high official exchange rate, yields a debt-to-GDP ratio of 49 (table 3.6.13). The foreign debt-export ratio of Yugoslavia was some 500 per cent in 2000, far beyond the 200-220 range that is normally taken to signal debt sustainability. Foreign exchange reserves amounted to only 1.6 months of import coverage (imports themselves being very depressed).

[28] PlanEcon, *Monthly Report* (Washington, D.C.), 23 February 2001, pp. 2-6.

It is therefore fortunate that a number of European governments had already decided some time ago to shift to more expansionary fiscal policies, mainly by cutting income taxes in 2001. In the United Kingdom and Switzerland, the central banks also lowered interest rates in early 2001 to support economic activity.

In contrast, in the euro area, despite deteriorating growth prospects, the ECB has left its main refinancing rate unchanged at 4¾ per cent since October 2000, when it was raised by a ¼ of a percentage point, just at the time when the evidence of the slowdown was becoming available.

A major source of downside risks to the current growth forecasts are – apart from developments in Japan – the uncertainties surrounding future economic developments in the United States. The expected annual growth rate of some 1¾ per cent implies a moderate upturn in economic activity in the course of 2001, given a statistical carry-over effect of 0.8 percentage points from the final quarter of 2000.[3] The current consensus of forecasts is that this will be followed by a further strengthening of growth in 2002.

But this scenario could well turn out to be too optimistic and the cyclical downturn could well be more protracted. Much will depend on the extent to which private households desire, or are forced, to adjust their expenditures (and savings) in response to the deterioration in economic conditions and the loss of financial wealth implied by the marked decline in equity prices (a fall which had still not bottomed out at the time of writing). Also the response of business investment to the cyclical downturn is currently difficult to gauge. Relatively large margins of excess capacity in the manufacturing sector will tend to weaken the accelerator principle which links net investment to changes in output. This will add to the dampening effects of falling profits, higher financing costs associated with lower share prices and the need to reduce high levels of corporate debt. More generally, the effectiveness of the more expansionary monetary policy in the United States may be reduced in an environment dominated by excess capacity and the need for balance sheet adjustments in the private sector.

The need to rebuild private sector savings is the counterpart to the required United States current account adjustment given that the very large deficit ($435 billion or some 4.4 per cent of GDP in 2000) cannot be sustained.[4] It depends crucially on the willingness of foreigners to hold dollar-denominated assets. In a deteriorating economic environment this willingness is likely to become increasingly stretched with increased downside risks for the dollar exchange rate. There are mixed opinions as to whether the continued strength of the dollar, so far, reflects its "safe haven" properties in a more uncertain world outlook or expectations that the loosening of monetary policy will lead to a rapid recovery of domestic demand. But neither scenario bodes well for the stability of the world economy. A quick recovery based on domestic demand would only postpone the inevitable reduction of the domestic and external imbalances. This is a necessary condition for laying the foundations of a new sustainable upswing. The longer these adjustments are delayed the greater is the probability that when they do eventually occur they will involve very abrupt changes in behaviour with a much greater risk of international financial turmoil. A reduction of the United States external deficit implies a correspondingly smaller external surplus in the rest of the world, and the major policy challenge is to reduce these imbalances with as little disruption as possible to global economic activity.

Given the current cyclical weakness in the United States and the chronic weakness in Japan, this adjustment process will largely depend on a strengthening of economic growth in western Europe. This will not only help to reduce the downside risks to global economic activity but would match regional ambitions to turn Europe into the world's strongest economy.[5]

(ii) Is European monetary policy too cautious?

The ECB is now[6] the only central bank among the G-7 not to lower interest rates in the wake of the cuts made by the Federal Reserve. The reason for this is that the bank still believes that the balance of risks facing the euro area, between higher inflation and lower growth, are "evenly balanced" even though the economic environment is now very different from when it first set its key interest rate at 4.75 per cent in October 2000. Since then activity has slowed sharply, especially in Germany, where the prospective stimulus of tax cuts has been somewhat offset by the weakness of net exports and construction activity. Forecasts for 2001 have been generally lowered and business confidence has fallen. Most observers and forecasters are unable to see any serious inflation threat. The prospect of the large rise in oil prices triggering an upturn in inflation was dismissed by most forecasters and their prediction that the risk in oil prices would be temporary proved to be correct. Indeed the impact of higher oil prices in lowering effective demand seems to have been more important than its effect on the underlying inflation rate.[7]

---

[3] This is the difference between the fourth quarter 2000 real GDP and the average annual GDP. In other words, real GDP will increase by 0.8 per cent in 2001 compared with 2000, even if it remains at the fourth quarter 2000 level throughout 2001. For comparison, the statistical carry-over effect for 2000 was 2.3 per cent, which is another way of illustrating the considerable loss of momentum in the United States economy.

[4] See sect. 2.3 of this *Survey*.

[5] The French Prime Minister noted that "Europe is the main zone for stability and growth in the world". Mr. Solbes, the EU's commissioner for economic and monetary affairs stated that "Europe is by definition the economic safe haven of the developed world at the moment ...", *Financial Times*, 24 March 2001.

[6] The position of "wait and see" with regard to its monetary policy stance was confirmed at the meeting of the ECB's Governing Council on 29 March 2001.

[7] This is the reverse of the situation in 1973 when many governments concentrated on the demand effect and neglected the impact on prices.

There can be little doubt that a lowering of interest rates will be a help for economic growth. Neither of the two pillars of the ECB's monetary policy strategy stand in the way of a reduction in the interest rates. Money supply growth has been slowing down and was approaching the reference value of 4.5 per cent in the first quarter of 2001. In any case, it can be argued that the derivation of the reference value is based on rather cautious estimates of potential output growth and the trend decline in money velocity.[8] Inflationary expectations are, moreover, quite moderate. The ECB's own Survey of Professional Forecasters shows that inflation is expected to average 2 per cent in 2001 declining to 1.7 per cent by December 2001 and remaining at an average of 1.7 per cent in 2002.[9] Long-term inflationary expectations are even lower. Thus, the inflation rate implied by the difference between yields on French nominal and real (i.e. price index linked) bonds which mature in 2009 was only 1.4 per cent at the end of February 2001.[10] It is true that the actual inflation rate was about half a percentage point above the ECB's target rate of 2 per cent in February 2001, but the underlying, core rate of inflation is well below that and there is no sign of any acceleration in prices or in average wages.

It may be argued that the current situation constitutes a dilemma for monetary policy because a lowering of interest rates when inflation is above target could compromise the ECB's efforts to establish its credibility. On the other hand, there is general awareness that this overshooting of the inflation target reflects specific circumstances, mainly the sharp rise in oil prices, the effects of which have already started to diminish. And in view of the deteriorating external environment, the risks to both output and inflation are tilted to the downside.

In any case, given the long and variable lags with which monetary policy affects inflation, the actual inflation rate is not the appropriate focus for monetary policy. The objective is to maintain price stability in the medium term and this implies the need for a forward-looking, medium-term orientation of monetary policy, which the ECB itself correctly emphasized in its first monthly report at the beginning of 1999.[11] This provides at the same time a degree of discretion for the conduct of monetary policy to react to specific shocks in the short term without losing sight of the general objective of price stability. It goes without saying that this also requires the provision of clear explanations to the public as to why certain actions are taken or not. But, in practice, the bank's actions appear to many observers to be more backward than forward looking, and too sensitive to fluctuations in monthly price changes.

The apparent deflationary bias of the ECB arises not only from its actions but also from its terms of reference. Its target of 2 per cent inflation is asymmetric in that it is not required to take any action when the actual rate is below it for a sustained period of time (unlike the Bank of England, for example). Secondly, it has no formal responsibility for other policy objectives such as growth or employment (unlike the Federal Reserve, for example). Thirdly, there is no political influence on the setting of the inflation target, which could provide such a broader view of policy. Finally, the bank's target rate of 2 per cent inflation is very low, especially when the upward bias due to quality improvements and the effects of fixed base weights are taken into account.

In their public pronouncements ECB officials also give the impression that they believe nothing much has changed in the past two decades as regards inflationary expectations and wage-setting behaviour. At the end of January the bank's focus was said to be "on avoiding possible second-round effects of the temporary increase in inflation".[12] These fears would appear to discount heavily the many structural changes which have occurred in the world and European economies in the last two decades. As a result disinflationary pressures are now greater than at any time since the 1930s and there is no sign of the struggle over functional income shares that triggered the wage-price spirals of the 1970s. In Europe wage indexing has disappeared, union membership and strength have fallen drastically, and all economies are vulnerable to the intense competitive pressures from the global economy. The relation between inflation and the labour markets now appears to have returned to that prevailing before the oil crises of the 1970s, or even earlier given that perceptions of job insecurity in Europe seem to be greater than in the 1950s and 1960s. The examples of the United States and the United Kingdom, as well as a number of smaller European economies, suggest that expansionary policies can reduce unemployment now without setting off a new inflation. But the key appears to be the need to have a coherent mix of policies for employment and growth, not just a one-dimensional monetary policy.

There would now appear to be a strong case for a sharp reduction in euro area interest rates in order to tip the balance towards stronger growth in Europe and offset the effects of weaker net exports to the rest of the world. The behaviour of the euro exchange rate against the dollar over the last two years seems to be largely explained by capital flows responding to relative growth prospects in Europe and the United States and, hence, to expectations of relative stock prices. A large cut in euro interest rates is therefore likely to lead to an appreciation of the euro, encourage investment and growth, and dampen further any residual inflationary pressures in the system. (This goes against the view that it is the weakness of the euro that is inhibiting the willingness of

---

[8] DIW, *Die Lage der Weltwirtschaft und der deutschen Wirtschaft im Herbst 2000*, Wochenbericht 43/2000, 26 October 2000, pp. 728-729.

[9] ECB, *Monthly Report* (Frankfurt am Main), March 2001, pp. 28-29, box 3.

[10] Ibid., p. 19.

[11] ECB, *Monthly Report* (Frankfurt am Main), January 1999, p. 47.

[12] Speech of the President of the ECB to the Parliamentary Assembly of the Council of Europe, Strasbourg, 24 January 2001.

the ECB to lower interest rates.) But, as mentioned below, raising the growth rate and lowering unemployment will also require special attention to improving workforce skills, especially among the young. This in turn will probably require an increase in government spending, but this is likely to be a good investment, not least for ageing populations. One of the key lessons to be learned from the performance of the United States economy over the last decade is for policy to recognize the dynamic interactions between growth expectations, fixed investment, rising productivity and employment – and mild or falling inflation rates. This is not the new economy, but an older one that was lost sight of during the crises of the 1970s and the disinflation of the 1980s.

(iii) Raising western Europe's growth rate: are labour markets a constraint?

Whenever suggestions are made for faster growth in western Europe official discussions invariably stress that this will only be possible if further supply-side improvements are made. The pessimism about the potential for growth in Europe is particularly focused on the alleged lack of flexibility of European labour markets. This leads to the conclusion that any aggressive lowering of euro interest rates would simply renew inflation rather than promote growth. For a decade or more unfavourable comparisons have been made between the United States and the European economies in their ability to generate employment and lower unemployment rates: in the United States, the average unemployment rate was only 4 per cent in 2000, down from a peak of 7.4 per cent in 1992. In contrast, in western Europe, unemployment was nearly twice as high at 7.9 per cent in 2000, but down from a peak of 10.5 per cent in 1994. Employment rose by some 15 per cent in the United States between 1991 (the cyclical trough) and 2000 (the cyclical peak). Over the same period, there was only a meagre increase in west European employment, by 5¼ per cent, although this is influenced by the difference in cyclical positions. Compared with the cyclical low point in 1993, employment was some 8 per cent higher in 2000.

The standard explanation for these differences is that the United States labour market is much more "flexible" than those in Europe. In the United States hiring and firing is not hampered by complicated rules and regulations, whereas in Europe social protection and an array of various labour market institutions create rigidities and resistance to necessary adjustments to market forces and changes in the global economy. In Europe gains in productivity quickly translate into higher wages for those already with jobs at the expense of profits, investment and increased employment for those unemployed. According to this view, which is shared by most of the international economic institutions, the problem in Europe is not one of macroeconomic policy but of supply-side rigidities, not only but especially in the labour market. Hence the stress in official briefings at the recent Stockholm Summit of EU leaders on the urgency for European countries to "bite the bullet of reform".[13]

Although this "story" about the differences between the United States and Europe is constantly repeated, it is badly flawed because it appears to be at variance with a number of key facts: in the first place, it is misleading to treat western Europe as a homogenous whole.[14] Labour market performance varies considerably and there are several smaller economies (e.g. Denmark, Finland, Ireland, the Netherlands, Portugal) which have performed as well or even better than the United States in the second half of the 1990s. Indeed these economies (among others) have also outperformed the "new economy" of the United States in terms of labour productivity and multi-factor productivity growth in the business sector.[15]

Secondly, labour market institutions are also very heterogeneous (including among the countries just mentioned). Although some of these arrangements are associated with higher levels of unemployment – for example, high levels of benefit paid indefinitely and with no pressure on recipients to seek work or high levels of unionization with no coordinated wage bargaining[16] – many of the institutions and practices blamed for higher unemployment turn out to have little effect either way and in some cases may even have a positive effect.[17] Thirdly, there is little evidence in Europe that productivity gains have been captured by employed workers in the form of higher wages. In fact wages in Europe, as in the United States, have lagged behind the growth of productivity in the 1990s. As is shown in chapter 2 of this *Survey*, the share of wages in national output has fallen in favour of gross profits on both sides of the Atlantic, but whereas the falling share in the United States has been associated with falling unemployment, in Europe the reverse has been the case.

Why should a falling wage share be associated with large increases in employment and falling unemployment in the United States and with only marginal

---

[13] Apart from making labour markets more flexible, another major current concern is to liberalize the gas, electricity and postal markets of the EU. This is part of the programme for completing the Single Market, although failure to push ahead is seen by the Single Market Commissioner, Frits Bolkestein, as sending an empty signal to investors. He also sees the reluctance of some EU governments to speed up reform of the public sector utilities as a "fear of modernity ... a mental block" that must be overcome. *Financial Times*, 24/25 March, p. 2.

[14] See also UN/ECE, *Economic Survey of Europe, 1998 No. 1*, pp. 24-25.

[15] S. Scarpetta, A. Bassanini, D. Pilat and P. Schreyer, *Economic Growth in the OECD Area: Recent Trends at the Aggregate and Sectoral Level*, OECD, Economics Department Working Papers, No. 248 (Paris), June 2000, p. 47, table 10.

[16] In fact a *coordinated* wage bargaining process is a feature of Austria, Denmark and the Netherlands. Ireland has had a series of incomes policies since the late 1980s (see below chap. 2.6).

[17] S. Nickell, "Unemployment and labour market rigidities: Europe versus North America", *Journal of Economic Perspectives*, Vol. 11, No. 3, Summer 1997, pp. 55-74.

improvements in Europe? A plausible explanation is that the stance of macroeconomic policy in the United States has provided a more supportive environment for the growth of domestic demand, and especially of fixed investment. Confident expectations of sustained output growth created a virtuous circle of rising investment and productivity which in turn led to rising levels of real wages, profits and employment. Part of the gains in productivity was also distributed to consumers via price reductions (or smaller price increases than might otherwise have occurred). In western Europe, in contrast, much of the 1990s were marked by fairly restrictive macroeconomic policies: fiscal policy was tight as the future members of the EMU strove to meet the Maastricht convergence criteria and real long-term interest rates were also relatively high, falling below those in the United States only in 1997. Fixed investment did occur in Europe but it was very weak in comparison with the United States[18] and much of it was focused on rationalization rather than capacity expansion (or employment creation). The gains from productivity that did occur in western Europe, which in terms of GDP per head were not very different from those in the United States (around 13-14 per cent between 1991 and 1999), went to profits (either retained by enterprises or distributed to shareholders) or to consumers in the form of lower prices (or smaller price increases than might have otherwise occurred).

The "defensive" nature of much European investment in the 1990s is understandable given the disappointment of expectations in the early years of the decade – when the Single Market programme was forecast to deliver an average annual rate of growth of 3 per cent over the decade – and continuing uncertainty as to whether a faster rate of growth would be cut short by an excessive concern with short-run fluctuations in the inflation rate. A key difference between the performance of the United States and that of Europe therefore lies both in the stronger rate of growth of domestic demand in the United States and greater confidence that the Federal Reserve would not bring it to a premature halt.

The need for increased "flexibility" and structural change is often presented, in both western and eastern Europe, as an institutional or behavioural problem which must be solved as a *pre-condition* for faster rates of output growth and employment. But this approach ignores three important points. The first is that a crucial requirement for a flexible economy and a fast rate of structural change is a high rate of gross investment. At any given time the structure of output and employment is fixed by the existing capital stock; the rate of structural change thus depends on rates of gross investment in new equipment sufficient to employ in new sectors the labour released by declining industries or activities, to maintain reduced numbers in the latter, and to provide jobs for new entrants to the labour force.[19] In an open, global economy there will anyway be pressure on traditional industries to "downsize" and release labour, but without gross investment in new activities there will be a rise in unemployment (an example of passive or negative structural change). Second, the movement of labour into new jobs will also depend on the skills (human capital) of those who are forced to move or who are entering the labour market for the first time. Weak educational levels are recognized as a significant feature of European labour markets,[20] but this is more a failure of government policies and insufficient spending on education than a labour market rigidity per se. The admission of a serious shortage of IT skills in western Europe alongside a youth (under 25 years) unemployment rate in the EU of 16.4 per cent only serves to underline the deficiencies in European education systems.[21] And thirdly, economic growth and rising levels of GDP per head are, in themselves, powerful solvents of traditional rigidities and modes of behaviour. It is in periods of slow growth and uncertain prospects that attachment to existing practice is greatest – what is criticised by the policy maker as a rigidity is seen by those fearful of losing their jobs as perhaps their only chance for some hope of security.[22]

High rates of unemployment alter the balance of power in favour of employers (corporations and shareholders) and this affects not only functional income shares but also working conditions and the way most people live. Both anecdotal and survey evidence point to increasing hours of work, increasing levels of stress, more disruption of family life and leisure, and other welfare reducing features, as a result of the increasingly liberalized economies of the 1990s. Most of these changes were made under the duress of the high unemployment of the 1980s and the increased sense of

---

[18] Between 1991 and 1999 real gross domestic capital formation increased by some 19 per cent in western Europe (some 13.5 per cent in the euro area) against 95 per cent in the United States (appendix table A.4.)

[19] A declining industry does not necessarily have to disappear. It may just have to adjust to a lower level, and different composition, of output. But different *levels* of output invariably involve different methods of production and hence will also require gross investment.

[20] S. Nickell, loc. cit.

[21] Some European governments are attempting to make up for these deficiencies by encouraging a brain drain of people with IT skills from poorer countries in eastern Europe and Asia, which can ill afford to lose them. Similar encouragement to immigration is being given to other professions, such as nurses and teachers, which have been hit by European fiscal restraint over the past decade. The ethics of such policies by the governments of some of the richest countries in the world are questionable, to say the least. Investment in European education to ease such skill shortages should not only focus on school-leavers but also on the lower-paid and part-time workers, many of whom are women who have suffered various forms of discrimination in their schooling. American Association of University Women, *Tech-Savvy: Educating Girls in the New Computer Age* (www.aauw.org).

[22] Adam Smith understood this very well: "... it is in the progressive state, while the society is advancing to the further acquisition, rather than when it has acquired its full complement of riches, that the condition of the labouring poor, of the great body of the people, seems to be the happiest and the most comfortable. It is hard in the stationary, and miserable in the declining state." Adam Smith, *An Inquiry into the Nature and Causes of the Wealth of Nations*, Vol. 1, edited by R. Campbell and A. Skinner (Oxford, Clarendon Press, 1976), p. 99.

insecurity of those still in work. The spread of a more aggressive management culture in Europe has not led to better economic performance than in the period before 1973, although it has produced large returns to shareholders and very large salaries for the leaders of business and those engaged in financial intermediation. At the same time many of the social programmes and legislation introduced by governments in the 1990s are basically a response to high unemployment and an attempt to compensate for the relatively weak power of labour. However, their effect is limited when employees fear for their jobs because the prospects of getting another one is low. The best way to empower employees is to make enterprises compete for their services – without the pressure of full employment, employers will resist or evade concessions on greater flexibility in working hours and leisure, in providing support for working mothers, in reducing onerous working hours and conditions, and in general creating a more civilized working environment. In such circumstances, employees can thus do much to improve their own working conditions without the need for excessive help and legislation (and expenditure) from the state. Tight labour markets can also stimulate enterprises to increase fixed investment and, as has been happening in parts of the United States, to train not only their existing staff but also the young unemployed.

1.3 The transition economies

(i) Recent developments and the current outlook

For the first time since the start of their economic and political transformation, the former centrally planned economies of eastern Europe and the former Soviet Union were all growing in 2000: their aggregate GDP increased by 6 per cent, significantly more than the world economy as a whole. This very high rate of economic growth was largely due to the unexpectedly strong recovery in Russia where GDP increased by 7.7 per cent, its highest growth rate in more than 30 years. After a weak performance in 1999, output also recovered strongly in eastern Europe and in the Baltic states, their aggregate GDP increasing by 3.9 per cent and 5 per cent, respectively.

These outcomes suggest that after 10 years of painful reforms, the prolonged and deep transformational recession in these economies has for the most part come to an end. Divergent experiences in coping with this difficult phase, as well as in the deepening and widening of the reform process, has left the region much more heterogeneous than it was 10 years ago. Most central European and Baltic states have already made considerable progress in instituting a functioning market economy and have enjoyed several years of strong economic growth which has placed them among the leading candidates for EU membership. At the same time, in a number of other countries the transformational recession and the process of introducing basic reforms has turned out to be much longer and much more strenuous than initially expected: for some CIS economies 2000 was the first year of positive growth in a decade while in Yugoslavia real market reforms can only now get underway with the new, democratically elected government.

The strong growth in the transition economies in 2000 is a positive and encouraging outcome; at the same time, however, it must be borne in mind that for a number of countries this represents only a meagre recovery after a long economic slump. In fact, after 10 years of reform only four economies (Hungary in 2000, Poland in 1995, Slovakia in 1999 and Slovenia in 1998) have managed to surpass their levels of GDP prevailing before the start of transformation.[23] On average, the CIS economies are still some 40 per cent below their GDP levels of 1989 and in a number of individual countries GDP in 2000 was less than half of what was being produced a decade ago (appendix table B.1).

It should also be emphasized that, with the exception of a few central European economies, domestic demand generally remains weak despite its moderate recovery in 2000. This reflects the fact that in a number of countries, especially in south-east Europe, central Asia and Caucasus, large sections of the population have suffered considerable impoverishment during the prolonged recession, while investment fell dramatically in the face of highly uncertain economic prospects. The falls in output and incomes in these economies are of such magnitude that it will probably take many years, if not decades, before the population at large begins to sense the positive outcomes of the reform process.

Nevertheless, as a result of the sweeping reforms of the past decade, most transition economies have established most of the basic institutions of a market economy and have liberalized their domestic markets and foreign trade (admittedly, to widely varying degrees). With the exception of a few CIS countries, the transition economies can now be considered as open economies that have the potential to benefit from their increased trade with the rest of the world. In fact, the growth figures for 2000 underline the gains from trade that are now possible for the transition economies.

Thus, in 2000, many transition economies benefited from strong and diversified demand in their major export markets, principally for manufactured goods but also for services and a wide range of primary commodities and semi-manufactures. In particular, the east European and the Baltic economies capitalized on the sharp rebound in west European import demand while the recovery in Russia stimulated exports from neighbouring CIS countries. In addition, the commodity exporting countries (and especially the oil and natural gas exporters in the CIS) benefited from the upsurge in world market prices which led to a considerable improvement in their trade and current account balances.

---

[23] According to the available statistics (appendix table B.1), Albania's GDP in 2000 may also have regained its 1989 level; however, it is difficult to be sure of this given the poor quality of Albanian statistics.

The EU is now the main trading partner for all the east European and Baltic economies, accounting for about two thirds of their exports and imports. Due to their differences in size, the exposure of the transition economies to the EU in terms of the relative importance of these trade flows, is much greater than the exposure of the EU to eastern Europe and the Baltic states. Hence, eastern Europe and the Baltic area are extremely susceptible (in both positive and negative directions) to changes in west European import demand. Another element in their greater sensitivity is the fact that supply-side constraints in the transition economies have been generally low in recent years due to the availability of underutilized resources (labour and, to a lesser extent, physical capital) and the start-up of large new capacities thanks to greenfield investments, usually involving FDI, and especially in those countries bordering the EU. This, in turn, has amplified the gearing effect of west European demand, on the one hand allowing eastern manufacturers to export even more during periods of boom but on the other hand reinforcing the probability of negative shocks during the downturn. During the second half of the 1990s the approximate elasticity of total central European and Baltic exports with respect to total west European import demand has been roughly of the order of 2 to 3 (chart 1.3.1).

The contrast between the development of trade in 1999 and 2000 is especially revealing. In 1999 total west European imports rose by just 6 per cent which contributed to an increase in central European and Baltic exports by a little over 7 per cent, which for the latter was one of the smallest increases during the second half of the 1990s (chart 1.3.1). Given the persistence of weak domestic demand, aggregate GDP in eastern Europe rose by a meagre 1.3 per cent, while the Baltic area as a whole went into recession (the aftershocks of the Russian crisis reinforcing the general economic weakness in 1999). In contrast, the acceleration in the volume of west European imports in 2000 (increasing in aggregate by a little over 10 per cent) was the major factor behind central European and Baltic exports increasing by some 20 per cent in volume. This strong export performance made a major contribution to the recovery of output in eastern Europe and the Baltic area in 2000.

The upsurge in world market prices of oil and other primary commodities, coupled with a stronger dollar in which most commodities are traded, provided a substantial terms of trade gain for the commodity exporting transition economies that underpinned their growth in 2000. As discussed in chapter 3 of this *Survey*, the effect of such a terms of trade gain is indirect: in the first place it helps to raise final domestic demand and imports; and subsequently, the increase in demand may lead to higher domestic output as well. When such a transmission channel is functioning in a large economy, the increase in its import demand can boost the exports of its main suppliers: this is how Russia's terms of trade gains in 2000 not only contributed to the strong recovery of the Russian economy but also served as an engine of growth for a number of neighbouring CIS economies.

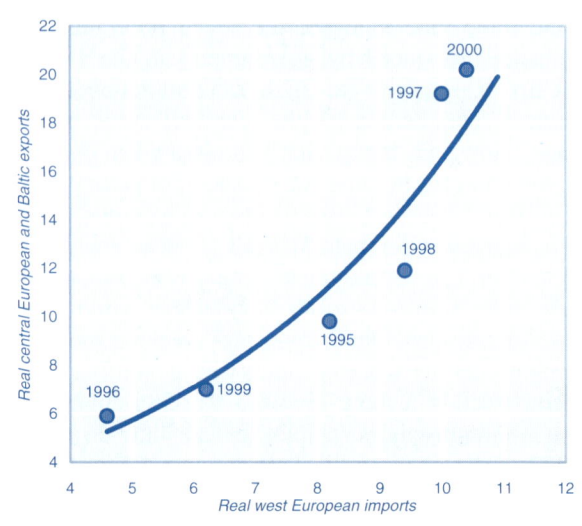

CHART 1.3.1

Real west European imports and real exports of central Europe and the Baltic states, 1995-2001
(Annual percentage change)

Source: UN/ECE secretariat calculations, based on national data.
Note: Real imports of west European countries (goods and services); real exports of central Europe and Baltic countries does not include Slovakia, for which data are not available.

Indeed, the Commonwealth of Independent States was the fastest growing regional group among the transition economies in 2000: in nine of the 12 CIS economies GDP growth was 5 per cent or more, resulting in an average of 7.4 per cent for the Commonwealth as a whole.

Despite the generally favourable outcome for economic growth in 2000, there are no grounds for complacency among policy makers. The fact is that most transition economies, including those most advanced in the reform process, are still rather fragile and vulnerable to external and other disturbances that are capable of causing painful setbacks in economic performance. Indeed, as already emphasized, the strong performance in 2000 underlines the considerable sensitivity of these economies to changes in the external environment, not least in the short run. Commodity exporters and economies specializing in exports of resource intensive, low value added goods are especially vulnerable. Given their large exposure to west European demand, the more advanced economies of central Europe and the Baltic area are also very susceptible to changes in demand in their major external markets. Thus, as the favourable external trends of 2000 are likely to be reversed, the transition economies may well suffer a negative external shock.

Due to their high degrees of export concentration, whether by commodities or export markets, the short-term outlook for the transition economies hinges on the two main factors that contributed to strong growth in 2000: west European import demand and world commodity prices (especially for oil). As discussed provide all that is needed. A large and generous – and prompt – effort will also be required from the EU, which should include a significant proportion of non-debt finance in its assistance, as well as efforts to prepare Yugoslavia for eventual accession to the Union. A rescheduling and reduction of the country's foreign debt is also urgent. So far the sums being discussed by the international community fall far short of the Yugoslav government's estimates of its needs. Without speedy and adequate assistance there is a considerable risk that support for the government's liberal reforms will evaporate into outright opposition and that the economy will collapse into chaos with the risk of a renewed hyperinflation. The crisis in Yugoslavia and the threat of further instability in south-east Europe, together with the programme for its eastward enlargement, present two major challenges to the capacity of the European Union to act as the major economic power in the region.

CHAPTER 2

THE GLOBAL CONTEXT AND WESTERN EUROPE

The overall economic performance in western Europe was quite favourable in 2000. The annual growth of real GDP was the highest since 1988, leading to substantial gains in employment. The average annual unemployment rate fell to its lowest level since 1990. Inflationary pressures remained moderate despite the sharp rise in oil prices. The external economic environment, however, deteriorated markedly in the second half of 2000, when an unexpectedly abrupt cyclical downturn in the United States and a faltering recovery in Japan started to weaken global economic growth. Economic growth also started to slow down in western Europe in the second half of 2000, largely because of the negative effects on real incomes stemming from the latest oil price shock and the lagged effects of tighter monetary policy. Forecasts for growth in 2001 have been progressively lowered since late 2000. On the west European periphery, Turkey experienced a financial-cum-exchange rate crisis in late 2000, which culminated in the floating of the lira in early 2001. Greece became a member of the euro area at the beginning of 2001.

2.1 World economy

This section provides a broad overview of recent tendencies in the global economy and of economic developments in North America. There is also a brief discussion of factors that have contributed to the new productivity trend in the United States and how it might be affected by the cyclical downturn.

(i) Overview

The global business cycle reached a peak in the first half of 2000, but instead of the moderate deceleration that had been generally forecast there was an unexpectedly pronounced slowdown of economic growth in the second half of 2000. This development reflected to a large degree the abrupt cyclical downswing in the United States, and prompted the Federal Reserve to swiftly cut interest rates in January 2001. The effects of the cyclical downturn in the United States on world output growth were accentuated by the faltering recovery in Japan. These adverse developments have started to feed through via international trade to emerging markets in Asia and Latin America. In Europe, economic growth has held up relatively well so far, but there is also increasing evidence of a slowdown in economic growth in the final months of 2000. Against this background, there has been a general lowering of growth forecasts for 2001. World output is now expected to increase by some 2.5-3 per cent in 2001, which compares with an earlier forecast of 4.2 per cent made in the autumn of 2000.[29] But the short-run outlook for the world economy is surrounded by a considerable margin of uncertainty. Much will depend on whether or not the United States economy moves into recession ("hard or soft landing") and how rapidly the forces of domestic growth will strengthen again. Given the large share of the United States economy in world demand and output, any sharp and extended cyclical downturn is bound to have, directly or indirectly, considerable adverse effects on the rest of the world.

A slowdown in global output growth, although not a pronounced one, had been largely expected. Monetary policies in the United States and other industrial countries had been progressively tightened between mid-1999 and May 2000 and the associated higher bank lending rates were bound to restrain, after the normal lag, the interest-sensitive components of domestic demand. To this was added the adverse effects of the surge in oil prices on real incomes in the net oil importing countries, which was not offset by higher spending of oil exporting countries. For the industrialized countries combined this real income loss amounted to about half a percentage point of GDP in 2000. This was much less than during the oil price shocks of 1974 and 1979-1980, when the real income loss was within the range of 2½-2¾ per cent of GDP. The smaller impact of the latest oil price shock largely reflects the substantial decline in the oil intensity of production, by some 50 per cent since the 1970s.[30] However, the increase in the headline rate of inflation caused by the rise in oil prices probably led to a tighter stance of monetary policy than was really justified.

The cyclical weakening in the second half of 2000 is not apparent from the annual figures for world

---

[29] IMF, *World Economic Outlook* (Washington, D.C.), October 2000.

[30] OECD, *Economic Outlook* (Paris), December 2000.

economy. World output rose by some 4.5 per cent in 2000, nearly 1 percentage point higher than in 1999, and the best performance for more than a decade. As in 1999, the United States was again the main engine behind this acceleration in global economic activity. Stronger output growth was accompanied by a more rapid expansion of international trade. World merchandise trade rose in volume by some 10 per cent in 2000, double the rate in 1999. This reflected both the cyclical upturn in western Europe and Latin America and the continued strong demand for foreign goods in North America and in the emerging markets of Asia.

In *Latin America and the Caribbean*, economic activity picked up in 2000 after the adverse effects on the region's performance of the international financial crises in 1998-1999. Real GDP is estimated to have increased by 4 per cent in 2000, up from a small increase of just 0.3 per cent in 1999.[31] This upturn was to a large extent export driven. The average outcome for 2000, however, hides wide differences among individual countries. Vigorous growth in Mexico, which benefited from the United States economic boom and the surge in oil prices, together with a higher rate of expansion in Brazil were the main factors behind the improved performance of the region. This contrasts with a disappointing performance in Argentina, where real GDP broadly stagnated in 2000, following a decline by nearly 4 per cent in 1999. Against this background, Argentina was faced with a progressive decline in investors' confidence in the second half of 2000. This was reflected in tighter borrowing conditions on the international financial markets and high domestic interest rates designed to prevent capital outflows and to sustain the currency board, which links the national currency, the peso, to the dollar. In early January 2000, agreement was reached with the IMF and other lenders on a financial package to ease the government's financing constraint in 2001.

There was strong economic growth in the *east Asian emerging markets* in 2000, with annual growth rates of GDP ranging from some 8 per cent in China and the Republic of Korea to some 4 per cent in Indonesia. Exports were the main source of economic growth, reflecting both increased intraregional trade and robust demand from western Europe and the United States. Rising domestic activity levels stimulated private consumption in most countries and business fixed investment also picked up. Activity was also supported by a loosening of fiscal policies and a generally accommodating stance of monetary policy. The latter helped to ease the debt-servicing burdens on the high levels of private sector debt in many countries. Progress in corporate and financial restructuring – required as a result of the financial crisis – has been uneven among countries, but achieving it is important if long-term growth prospects are to be improved. Short-term prospects are clouded by the economic slowdown in the

---

[31] ECLAC, *Preliminary Overview of Latin America and the Caribbean 2000* (Santiago), December 2000 (www.eclac.cl).

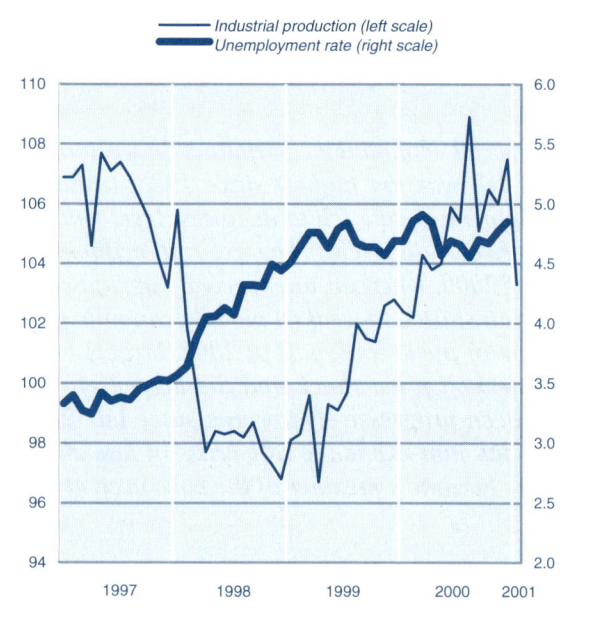

CHART 2.1.1

Industrial production and unemployment in Japan, January 1997-January 2001
(1995=100, per cent)

Source: OECD, *Main Economic Indicators* (Paris), various issues.

United States and the weakening global demand for electronic products.

In *Japan*, a moderate cyclical upturn was not sustained in the second half of 2000. Real GDP fell between the second and third quarters and was only half a percentage point above its level of a year earlier. Industrial production turned increasingly sluggish in the second half of 2000 and unemployment continued to rise (chart 2.1.1). Real GDP is estimated to have increased by about 1.7 per cent in 2000. The overall weakness of domestic demand reflects to a large degree the continued sluggishness of private consumption expenditure against a background of persistent job insecurity. Confidence in the recovery may have also been affected by the chronic weakness of the financial sector, which is related to the huge stock of non-performing loans. The bleakness of the overall picture, however, masks a pickup in business investment. Improved corporate profits, associated with stronger demand for exports, and the process of restructuring underway in the corporate sector has especially stimulated demand for IT capital goods. But the overall growth of business investment continues to be restrained by the scrapping of excess capacity in many parts of the corporate sector. Public investment declined in 2000. Exports were buoyant in the first half of 2000, but faced a weakening of foreign demand in the second half. This may eventually have adverse effects, via weaker profit growth, on fixed investment. Deflationary tendencies continue to prevail: consumer prices fell (year-on-year) by 0.7 per cent in 2000 despite rising energy prices and following a decline of 0.3 per cent in

1999. But the decline in wholesale prices has bottomed out and there were small increases in the second half of 2000.

Following 14 months of a near zero interest rate policy, the Bank of Japan raised the target for its overnight lending rate to 0.25 per cent in August 2000, on the basis of more optimistic expectations of a recovery and an associated easing of deflationary pressures. But in the face of a pronounced weakening of economic activity this move was reversed at the end of February 2001, when this key interest rate was lowered to 0.15 per cent. At the same time the discount rate was reduced to 0.25 per cent, a record low. It is difficult to see, however, how such small changes in interest rates can stimulate economic activity. The weakening growth prospects led to a marked depreciation of the yen against the dollar in early 2001 and the Nikkei share price index fell to its lowest level since December 1985. Fiscal policy had a slight contractionary effect in 2000 judging by the decline of the large structural budget deficit from 1999. Although the very high level of government debt has largely exhausted the scope for expansionary policy, lingering doubts about the underlying strength of economic growth led the government to launch another small fiscal stimulus (equivalent to half a per cent of GDP) in October 2000, which is intended to stimulate infrastructure investment in the first half of 2001. Nevertheless, this new package of measures should leave fiscal policy in a broadly neutral stance.

In the major *international equity markets* there was a marked shift in investors' sentiment in the second half of 2000. From late summer, the lowering of forecasts of economic growth for 2001 coincided with disappointing announcements of corporate profit developments, notably in the high-technology sector. This highlighted increasing concerns about the extraordinarily high valuation of stocks in this sector and triggered a massive sell-off. In the United States, the NASDAQ had fallen by some 50 per cent in February 2001 from its peak 12 months earlier. Also, the development of other broader sectoral indices point to increasingly cautious behaviour by investors (chart 2.1.2). Prices in the major equity markets have risen to historically high levels since 1994, a process characterized as "irrational exuberance" with attendant risks of a sharp downward correction.[32] Even after their recent fall, however, stock markets still appear to be overvalued when judged on the basis of long-term price earnings ratios.[33]

The pattern of *exchange rates* among the three main world currencies has changed somewhat in recent months (chart 2.1.3). Against the backdrop of weakening growth expectations for the United States and relatively better prospects for the euro area, the fall in the eurodollar was arrested and has been partly reversed since late 2000.

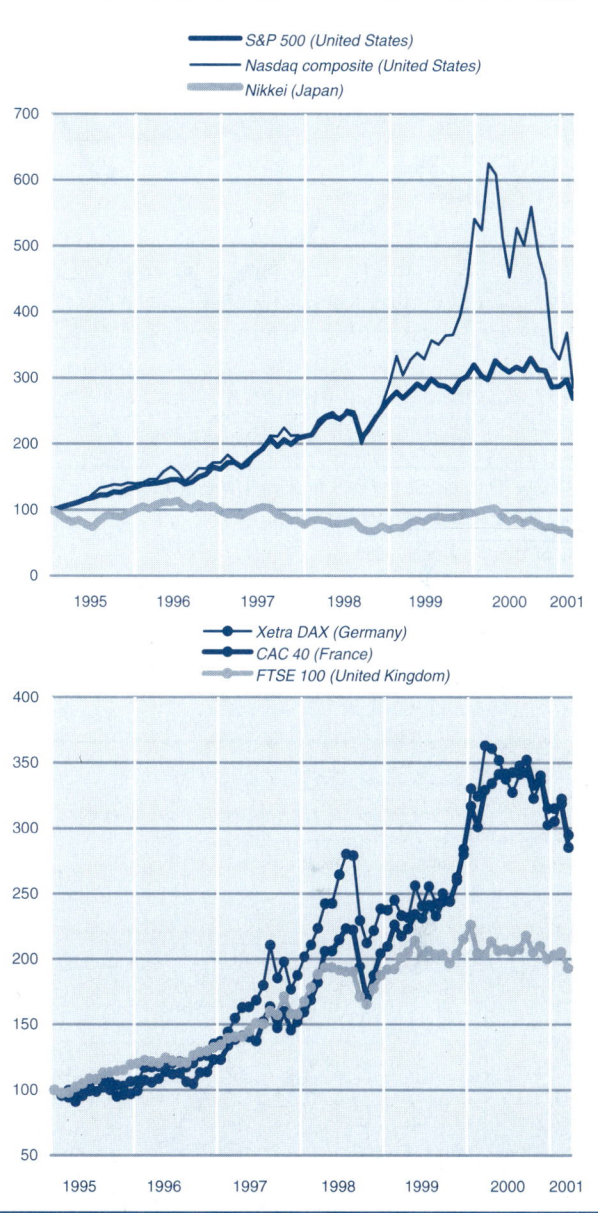

CHART 2.1.2

International share prices, January 1995-February 2001
(Indices, January 1995=100)

Source: Reuters Business Briefing (www.rbb.reuters.com).
Note: Data refers to end of month.

This process was supported by the narrowing of yield differentials in favour of dollar-denominated financial assets. The strength of the dollar in foreign exchange markets in the past year has also been closely associated with sizeable long-term capital inflows from overseas, including the euro area. In February 2001, the euro had appreciated against the dollar on average by some 7.5 per cent from its recent trough in October 2000. But compared with the average exchange rate in January 1999, there was still a sizeable depreciation of 21 per cent. The euro has strengthened also against the yen in recent months. In February 2001, the euro reached its highest level against the yen since October 1999, a reflection of the worsening

---

[32] For a general discussion, see R. Shiller, *Irrational Exuberance* (Princeton, Princeton University Press, 2000).

[33] BIS, *70th Annual Report* (Basle), June 2000, p. 107.

CHART 2.1.3
Bilateral exchange rates between the euro,ᵃ the dollar and the yen, January 1998-February 2001
(Dollar, euro, yen)

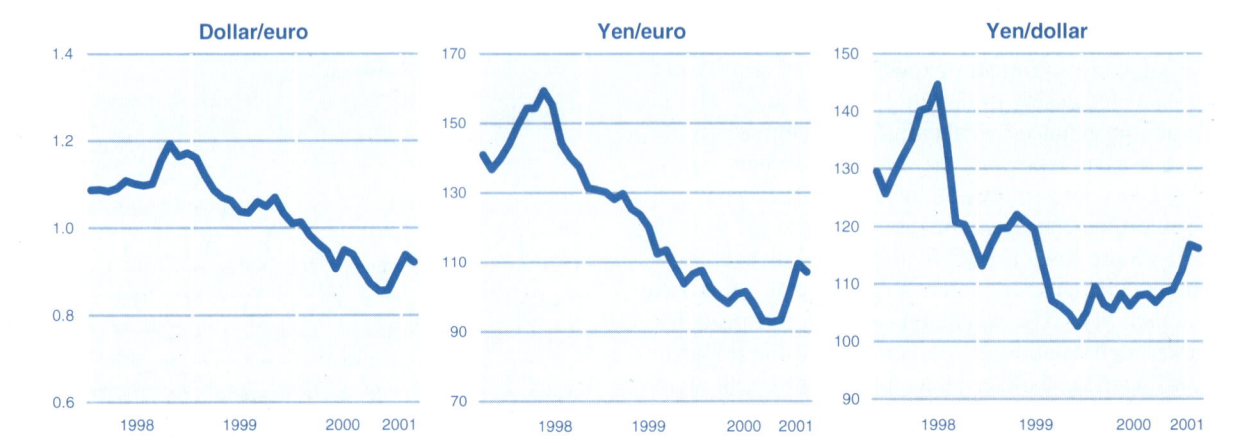

Source: European Central Bank (Frankfurt) (www.ecb.de).
Note: Average monthly exchange rates.

a ECU before January 1999.

CHART 2.1.4
World commodity prices, January 1991-February 2001
(Indices, 1990=100)

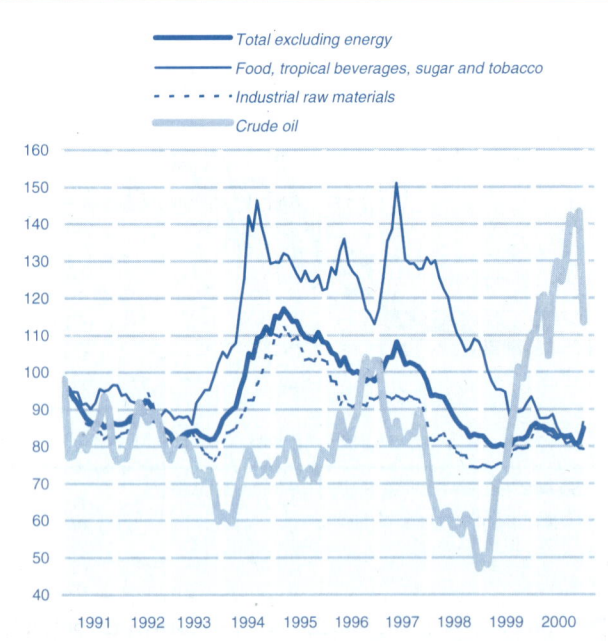

Source: Hamburg Institute for Economic Research (HWWA).
Note: Indexes calculated on the basis of current dollar prices.

economic outlook for Japan. For the same reason, the yen has also depreciated significantly against the dollar since the final months of 2000.

In the *international oil market*, the price of Brent crude rose to some $37 per barrel in early September 2000, its highest level in more than a decade. But since then, the trend has been downward (chart 2.1.4), although volatility continued to be high. Between the last quarter of 2000 and February 2001 the price of Brent crude has fluctuated within a band of just under $12. The average price for the first two months of 2001 was some $26.5 per barrel, broadly unchanged from the same period of 2000 but about 5 per cent below the average price of $28 assumed in the central growth forecasts for 2001 in the OECD area.[34] Downward pressure on prices was probably accentuated in January 2001 by the increase in supply from Iraq where it had been sharply curtailed in the preceding month. Prices edged up temporarily when OPEC members agreed to reduce production quotas by 1.5 million barrels per day, effective from 1 February 2001. This reversed production increases decided upon in 2000. Additional cuts are expected to be discussed at OPEC's March 2001 meeting, but increases in non-OPEC production in 2001, mainly from the former Soviet Union, could partly offset these.

The steep fall in oil prices since September 2000 is largely due to the changing outlook for the world economy. The economic slowdown in the United States and the world economy as a whole are expected to have a negative effect on demand throughout the current year. This is reflected in lower projections by the International Energy Agency of the growth in oil demand in 2001 and 2002.[35] Most of the reduction in demand is centred in Asia. Market sentiment may have also been influenced by the United States administration's announcement in early December 2000 that it would coordinate with the

---

[34] OECD, *Economic Outlook* (Paris), December 2000, p. 31, table 1.8.

[35] As reported by the United States Energy Information Administration, *Short-Term Energy Outlook*, February 2001, p. 2. Also OPEC has lowered its estimate of world oil demand, but still expects an annual increase of nearly 2 per cent in 2001 compared with 2000. OPEC, *Monthly Oil Market Report*, January 2001, p. 11.

TABLE 2.1.1

World commodity prices, 1997-2000

(Percentage change over previous year)

	Weights [a]	1997	1998	1999	2000
Total	100.0	-1.7	-22.3	11.8	31.7
Total, excluding energy	39.5	0.9	-13.8	-7.6	2.5
Industrial raw materials	29.5	-1.5	-14.5	-2.2	7.9
Food and beverages	9.9	5.9	-12.3	-18.7	-10.5
Energy	60.5	-3.6	-29.0	30.1	50.9
Crude oil	55.5	-3.6	-31.1	35.7	55.9

Source: Hamburg Institute for Economic Research (HWWA).

Note: Growth rates calculated on the basis of current dollar prices.

[a] Weights refer to average commodity shares in total imports of western industrialized countries in 1989-1991.

International Energy Agency to counteract any possible disruption to supplies from the Middle East.

Prices of *commodities* have also responded to changes in world demand. So-called "hard" commodities such as metals are highly sensitive to fluctuations in economic activity, especially in industry. The downward trend of world commodity prices (excluding energy) was partly reversed in 2000 (chart 2.1.4) and for the year as a whole, the annual increase was 2.5 per cent (table 2.1.1). Prices for industrial raw materials increased by as much as 8 per cent (year-on-year) but food prices (in nominal dollar terms) including tropical beverages, sugar and tobacco continued their decline (which began in 1997) albeit at a lower rate. The prices of these "soft" commodities are less sensitive to changes in economic activity than industrial raw materials and more strongly influenced by seasonal factors.

(ii) North America

(a) Current developments

In the *United States*, real GDP rose by 5 per cent in 2000. This was the highest annual growth rate since 1978, when the increase was 5.5 per cent. But this very favourable outcome for the year as a whole masks a sharp deceleration in the rate of economic expansion in the second half of the year (chart 2.1.5). Real GDP rose by only 0.3 per cent the final quarter, equivalent to a seasonally adjusted annual rate of 1.4 per cent. This slowdown was mainly due to a considerable weakening of private domestic demand, which was only partly offset by increased government spending. Against a background of only small gains in employment and higher inflation, real personal disposable incomes hardly increased at all in the final quarter. Although there was a further fall in the savings rate (which turned negative) the net effect was still a relatively pronounced slowdown in the growth of real personal consumption expenditures. Real expenditures on consumer durables fell in the final quarter. The scope for increased consumer spending was also reduced by debt service payments which rose to their highest levels since the late 1980s, a reflection of the rapid rise in household debt that has occurred during the long expansion. To some extent consumer demand may have also been affected by the substantial loss in financial wealth associated with the decline of share prices. "The broad decline in equity prices last year is estimated to have lopped more than $1¾ trillion from household wealth, or more than 4 per cent of the total net worth of households. Nevertheless, the level of household net worth is still quite high – about 50 per cent above its level at the end of 1995."[36] Stock market volatility, the deteriorating short-run outlook and the expected consequences for the labour market all contributed to a sharp drop in consumer confidence in the final months of 2000 and in early 2001. In February 2001, consumer confidence fell to its lowest level since October 1996 (chart 2.1.6).

Business confidence also weakened considerably in the final quarter against a background of deteriorating sales and profit prospects and tighter financing conditions. In fact, the Conference Board's business confidence index fell to its lowest level since the second quarter of 1980. Faced with increasing excess capacity and tighter terms and standards of bank lending, firms reacted by cutting their spending on equipment and software. Purchases of computers, for long the most dynamic component of investment, increased only marginally in the final quarter of 2000. Falling share prices, via higher refinancing costs, may have also affected business investment.

The weakening of business spending on equipment and software was partly offset by the continuing strong growth of outlays on structures, although residential investment continued to fall under the impact of high mortgage rates. Changes in business inventories subtracted from economic growth in the last two quarters of 2000, and the weakening of domestic demand was accentuated by a pronounced fall in exports in the fourth quarter of 2000, following very strong growth in the preceding quarters. The adverse effects of weaker exports on domestic output, however, were offset by a similarly abrupt slowdown in import demand. In the event, changes in real net exports subtracted about one quarter of a percentage point from economic growth in the final quarter, broadly unchanged from the preceding quarter.

Inventory adjustments and the overall slowdown in demand led to a fall in manufacturing activity in the final months of 2000 that continued in January 2001. The Purchasing Managers' Index fell below the 44.5 per cent threshold in December 2000, which is traditionally taken to indicate that economic activity is contracting. Capacity utilization fell close to levels previously experienced in August 1992 (chart 2.1.7), but it is noteworthy that during this long expansion capacity

---

[36] Testimony of Chairman Alan Greenspan, Federal Reserve Board's Semi-annual Policy Report to the Congress Before the Committee on Banking, Housing and Urban Affairs, United States Senate, 13 February 2001 (www.federalreserve.gov/boarddocs/hh/2001/February/Testimony.htm).

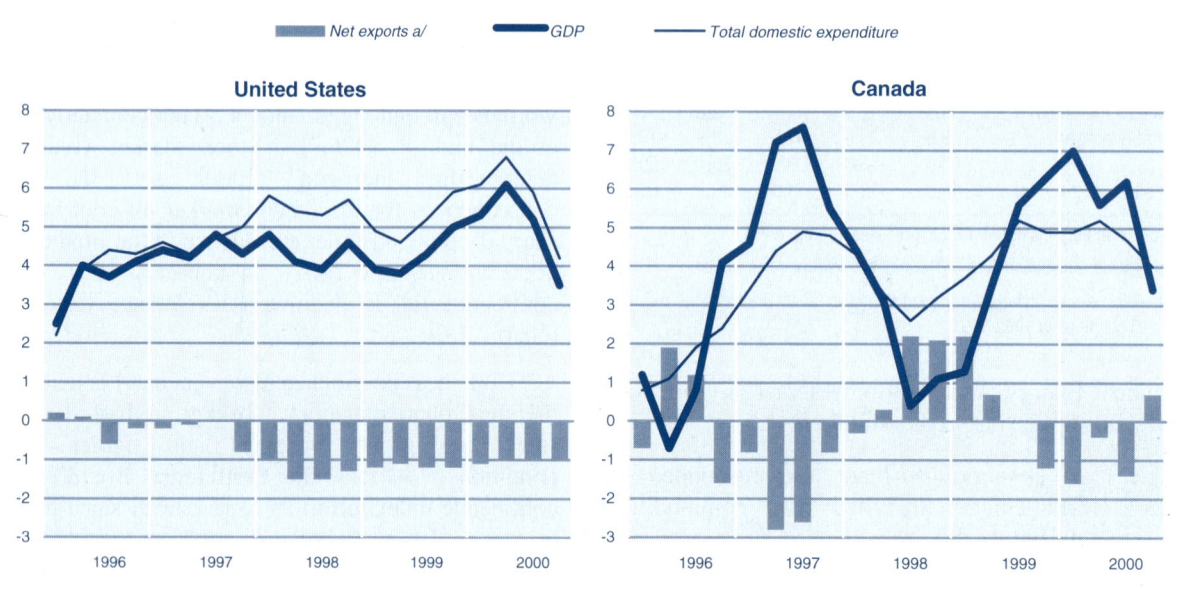

CHART 2.1.5

Quarterly changes in real GDP in North America, 1996-2000
(Percentage change over same period of preceding year)

Source: United States Department of Commerce, Bureau of Economic Analysis (Washington D.C.); Statistics Canada (Ottawa).

a Growth contribution (percentage points).

utilization rates in the manufacturing industry have remained significantly below their previous high in 1988-1989. In fact, the growth in capacity output has significantly exceeded actual output since about 1995.

The sharp weakening of economic growth has so far not fed through to the labour market, which is not surprising given the lagged adjustment of labour to changes in output. But non-farm employment growth slowed down markedly in the second half of the year to near stagnation. In the face of slowing output growth firms reduced weekly hours worked in the final quarter of 2000 rather than shedding labour; this is the normal cyclical response in view of the costs of hiring in the tight labour markets. In fact, non-farm payrolls edged up strongly in January 2001, but this total masked the sixth consecutive monthly decline in manufacturing employment and large employment gains in services. The unemployment rate rose to 4.2 per cent in January 2001, up from 4 per cent in December but still close to its historic low of 3.9 per cent seen in some months of 2000 (chart 2.1.8). Labour cost pressures increased in the final two quarters of 2000 as large increases in the cost of employment were no longer offset by productivity gains, which were getting smaller as a result of sluggish output growth.

Inflation edged up in 2000 largely because of higher prices for energy. Core inflation (which excludes prices of food and energy products) remained moderate but with a slight upward tendency. For the year as a whole the consumer price index rose by 3.4 per cent, but core inflation was much lower at 2.4 per cent. Data for January 2001 show some stronger upward pressures on inflation, largely a reflection of energy prices (chart 2.1.9): the CPI edged up by 0.6 percentage points over December and was 3.7 per cent higher than in January 2000. Core inflation rose 2.6 per cent over the same period. There were also upward pressures on producer prices of finished goods, which rose by 1.1 percentage points in January 2001 compared with December and were 4.8 per cent higher than a year earlier.

The progressive tightening of monetary policy since mid-1999 continued in early 2000 when the target for the federal funds rate was raised in three steps (a quarter of a percentage point each) to 6.5 per cent in May. Monetary policy remained on hold for the rest of the year but with a bias towards tightening in the face of very tight labour markets. But, faced with the unexpectedly sharp slowdown in economic activity in the final months of 2000, the target for the federal funds rate was cut swiftly in two steps by a full percentage point to 5.5 per cent in the course of January 2001. The first cut, by half a percentage point at the beginning of January, may have been partly motivated by adverse conditions in the financial markets in late 2000, such as widening credit spreads for corporate bonds which restrained corporate borrowing. In any case, capital market conditions improved considerably in the course of January 2001.

As a result of the recent changes in monetary policy, the real federal funds rate (the nominal rate less core inflation) is now close to 3 per cent, equal to its long-run average over the period since 1980. This could suggest that monetary policy has shifted to a broadly

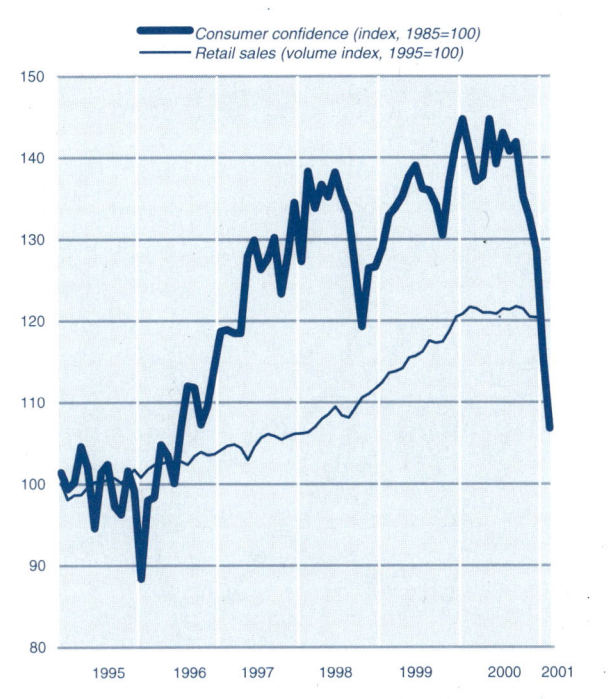

CHART 2.1.6

Consumer confidence and retail sales in the United States, January 1995-February 2001
(Indices)

Source: United States Conference Board (New York) (www.conference-board.org); Federal Reserve Bank of St. Louis (www.stls.frb.org).

CHART 2.1.7

Manufacturing output, capacity utilization and the purchasing managers' index in the United States, January 1988-January 2001
(1992=100, per cent)

Source: United States Federal Reserve Board (Washington, D.C.) (www.federalreserve.gov); National Association of Purchasing Management (Arizona) (www.napm.org).

neutral stance.[37] Short-term interest rates, which had been relatively steady at some 6.6-6.7 per cent since May 2000, fell in January 2001 in response to the monetary easing by about 1 percentage point. This was their lowest level since September 1999. Nominal long-term interest rates continued to fall, reflecting the "scarcity premium" on treasury bills which has arisen because of their reduced supply, due in turn to large government fiscal surpluses (chart 2.1.10). But another factor contributing to declining yields was the flight of investors from the increased downside risks in the equity markets to the "safe haven" of the government bond market. The flattening of the yield curve – approximated by the difference between long-term and short-term interest rates – also reflects the more accommodative stance of monetary policy.

Buoyant growth in federal government receipts by far outpaced growth in its expenditures in 2000. The surplus on the unified budget rose to $236 billion in fiscal 2000, about twice that in fiscal 1999. The financial surplus of the general government corresponded to 2¼ per cent of GDP in 2000, up from 1 per cent in the preceding year. Buoyant domestic demand for most of the year, together with the strong dollar, led to further rise in the merchandise trade deficit to $450 billion in 2000. This is the largest deficit on record, corresponding to 4.5 per cent of GDP. The current account deficit was broadly similar and also at a record level.[38]

In Canada, the economic boom continued in 2000 but the sharp slowdown in the United States economy started to have adverse effects on manufacturing activity in the final months of the year. Real GDP rose by 5 per cent in 2000, up from 4.2 per cent in 1999, but in the United States, there was a sharp slowdown in the rate of economic expansion in the second half of the year (chart 2.1.5). Exports were the main source of growth, reflecting the expansion of demand in the United States for most of the year and the rising global demand for energy products and other commodities (table 2.1.2).

---

[37] WEFA, *US Financial Markets Outlook*, 5 February 2001.

[38] See sect. 2.3 for a more detailed analysis of United States current account developments.

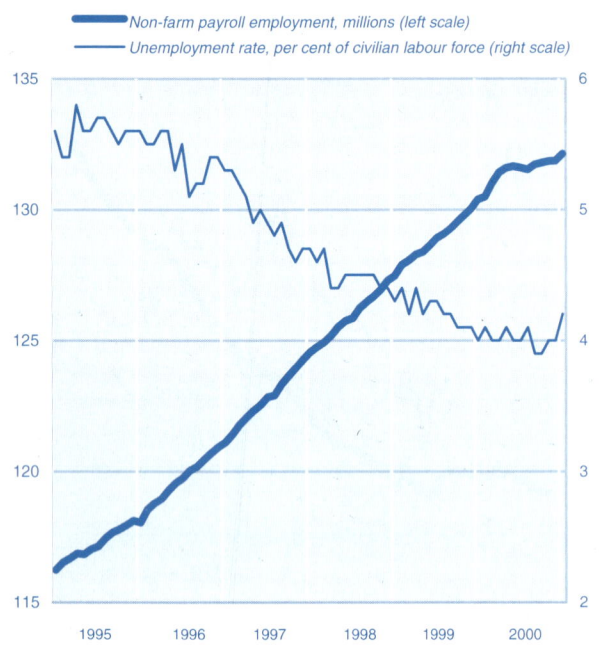

CHART 2.1.8

Employment and unemployment in the United States, January 1995-January 2001
(Millions, per cent of civilian labour force)

Source: Bureau of Labor Statistics (Washington, D.C.) (www.bls.gov).

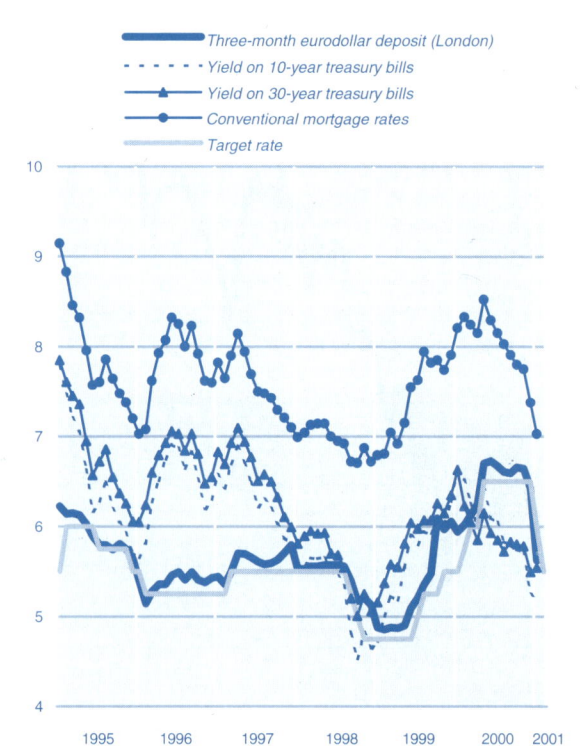

CHART 2.1.10

Nominal short-term and long-term interest rates in the United States, January 1995-February 2001
(Per cent per annum)

Source: United States Federal Reserve Board (Washington, D.C.) (www.federalreserve.gov).

Note: Average monthly values.

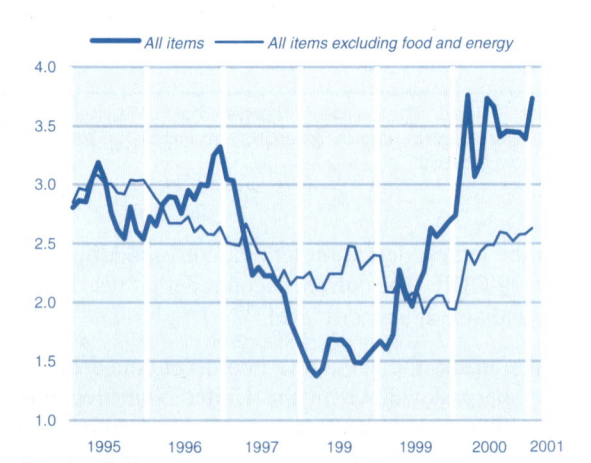

CHART 2.1.9

Consumer prices in the United States, January 1995-January 2001
(Percentage change over same month of preceding year)

Source: Bureau of Labor Statistics (Washington, D.C.) (www.bls.gov).

Business investment responded favourably to rising profits and capacity utilization levels, while private consumption was stimulated by gains in employment and aggregate incomes.

Although the Canadian economy has been operating close to full capacity, inflationary pressures have remained moderate. Higher prices of energy products drove the consumer price index slightly above the central bank's inflation target range of 1.5-3 per cent, but core inflation remained below 2 per cent. Strong productivity gains offset to a large extent the increases in labour costs. The Bank of Canada had followed the tightening of monetary policy in the United States from mid-1999 to May 2000 and held rates steady for the rest of the year. Given their strong trade links, the abrupt weakening of economic growth in the United States is bound to have adverse effects on economic growth in Canada. Consequently, the monetary authorities followed the Federal Reserve and lowered the key official interest rate by 0.25 percentage points to 5.5 per cent in late January 2001. Buoyant government receipts, a result of the economic boom, have led to a comfortable budget surplus. At the same time, favourable changes in terms of trade contributed to a swing in the current account balance from a small deficit in 1999 to a large surplus in 2000.

(b) The new productivity trend in the United States and the business cycle

The astonishing performance of the United States economy over the past 10 years has been largely associated with the development and diffusion of information and communications technology (ICT). A

TABLE 2.1.2

Contribution of main expenditure items to the annual change in real GDP in North America, 1998-2000
(Percentage points)

	Canada			United States		
	1998	1999	2000	1998	1999	2000
Private consumption.............	1.7	2.0	2.3	3.1	3.5	3.6
Government consumption	0.3	0.3	0.4	0.4[a]	0.6[a]	0.5[a]
Gross fixed capital formation ...	0.7	2.0	2.3	1.9[b]	1.6[b]	1.7[b]
Changes in inventories	-0.5	-0.2	0.3	0.2	-0.4	0.2
Total domestic expenditures	2.2	4.1	5.4	5.6	5.3	5.9
Net exports	1.1	0.4	-0.7	-1.3	-1.2	-1.0
Exports of goods and services .	3.3	3.9	3.9	0.3	0.3	1.1
Imports of goods and services .	2.2	3.4	4.6	1.6	1.5	2.1
GDP	3.3	4.5	4.7	4.4	4.2	5.0

Source: National statistics.

[a] Total government expenditures (consumption and investment).

[b] Private sector only.

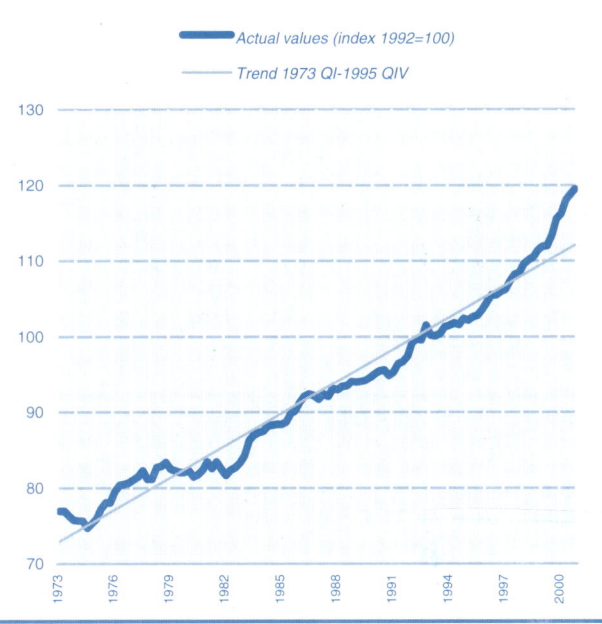

CHART 2.1.11

The old and new productivity trends in the United States, 1973 QI-2000 QIV
(1992=100)

Source: Bureau of Labor Statistics (Washington, D.C.) (www.bls.gov).

major feature of the recent investment boom was the large rise in the proportion of information processing equipment in total real capital formation in the private business sector. There was also a considerable acceleration in labour productivity growth in the second half of the 1990s, which has been hailed as a significant deportive from the previous trend (chart 2.1.11). The average annual growth rate of labour productivity (in the private non-farm business sector) rose to some 3 per cent in 1995-2000, about twice the rate over the period 1973-1975. These two features, the increasing role of ICT equipment and the acceleration in trend productivity growth, constitute the key elements of the so-called "new economy".[39]

A standard growth accounting framework[40] can be used to assess the role of ICT capital and the computer producing sector in the recent acceleration of productivity growth. In this framework an increase in labour productivity can result from an increase in the amount of capital per worker (i.e. in increase in capital intensity or capital deepening) and/or from technical progress. The latter is derived as a residual after the contribution of capital intensity to labour productivity growth has been calculated. This residual is also known as total factor productivity (TFP), i.e. it is the change in output which cannot be directly attributed to changes in the two main factor inputs, namely, capital and labour. More generally, TFP is a broad measure of improvements in productive efficiency for a given level of resource endowments. In order to estimate the role of IT equipment, the total business capital stock is split into two parts, the IT capital stock and the remaining non-IT stock. The TFP residual is also split into two parts, one accounted for directly by the sector producing computers and the remainder "originating" in the rest of the economy. The reason for taking this approach is that there is strong evidence that computer production has gone through a very rapid period of technical progress, with associated positive effects on labour productivity in the sector. The rapid rate of technical progress in the computer producing sector is also reflected in a sharp decline in the prices of computer equipment in recent years.

New estimates prepared by the United States Council of Economic Advisers (CEA) show that about a quarter of the change in United States productivity growth between 1973-1995 and 1995-2000 is accounted for by capital deepening, i.e. a rise in capital per worker (table 2.1.3). This is the traditional "old economy" mechanism for raising labour productivity. What is new is the larger contribution of IT capital to labour productivity growth; but this is also not surprising since IT capital now accounts for a larger proportion of the total capital stock.[41] In fact, the aggregate contribution of capital deepening to labour productivity growth masks the considerable importance of IT capital, which contributed some 40 per cent to the improved productivity performance. But this was partly offset by the negative contribution of other types of capital. There was little growth in non-IT capital per worker in 1995-2000 with a concomitantly very small contribution to total labour productivity growth, and, importantly, a much smaller contribution than in 1973-1995.

---

[39] UN/ECE, *Economic Survey of Europe, 2000 No. 1*, pp. 2 and 23.

[40] This is based on neoclassical growth theory and the use of a Cobb-Douglas production function with constant returns to scale.

[41] B. Bosworth and J. Triplett, "What's new about the new economy? IT, economic growth and productivity", Brookings Institution, 12 December 2000, mimeo.

TABLE 2.1.3

Accounting for changes in labour productivity in the United States, 1973-2000

(Average annual percentage rates of change)

	CEA			Gordon
	1973-1995	1995-2000	Change[a]	Change[b]
Labour productivity	1.39	3.01	1.63	1.33
Cycle	–	0.04	0.04	0.50
Trend	1.39	2.97	1.58	0.83
Growth contributions[a]				
Capital deepening	0.70	1.09	0.38	0.33
IT capital	0.41	1.03	0.62	..
Other capital	0.30	0.06	-0.23	..
Labour quality	0.27	0.27	–	0.05
Total factor productivity	0.40	1.59	1.19	0.45
Computer sector TFP	0.18	0.36	0.18	0.29
Other sectors	0.22	1.22	1.00	0.16[c]

Source: The Executive Office of the President, Council of Economic Advisors, *Economic Report of the President. Transmitted to the Congress January 2001* (Washington, D.C.), p. 28, table 1-1. R. Gordon, "Does the 'new economy' measure up to the great inventions of the past?", *Journal of Economic Perspectives*, Vol. 14, No. 4, Fall 2000, p. 49, table 2.

Note: Private non-farm business sector. Labour productivity is defined as output per hour worked.

[a] Percentage points.

[b] 1995 QIV-1999 QIV compared with 1972 QII-1995 QIV.

[c] In Gordon's study this residual reflects mainly the effects of changes in price measurement between the two periods.

The upshot, therefore, is that more rapid TFP growth explains some three quarters of the acceleration in labour productivity growth since 1995 (table 2.1.3). The interesting question is to what extent the acceleration in TFP can be associated with the growth of the IT capital stock and technical progress in the sector producing computers. The estimates show that the more rapid rate of technical change in the computer producing sector contributed some 20 per cent of the acceleration in TFP growth. In other words, the by far larger part of the acceleration in TFP growth occurred in the sectors *using* computers. This large unexplained residual may to some extent reflect an underestimation of the contribution of IT capital to labour productivity growth within the traditional accounting framework. One reason for this could be that there are favourable spillover effects (network effects) from IT capital, which improve the overall organization of the production process.[42] But quantitative evidence on this at the macroeconomic level is hard to come by.

Changes in labour productivity, however, can also be influenced by changes in the composition of the labour force. Thus, a rapidly increasing share of skilled labour in total employment will tend to be associated with a rise in average labour productivity in the economy. Conversely, a larger increase in young and less experienced workers will tend to reduce average labour productivity. As can be seen from table 2.1.3, however, adjustments for labour quality do not reduce the relative importance of capital deepening and TFP for the acceleration of productivity growth.

But labour productivity is also sensitive to cyclical fluctuations. Labour hoarding and other factors explain why productivity (growth) tends to fall in a period of cyclical downswing and recession and increase in a cyclical upswing. More generally, this reflects the fact that labour is partly a quasi-fixed factor rather than a variable input.[43] This can be explained, *inter alia*, by the complementarity of capital and labour (in the short run) and costs of hiring and training. A strong expansion can therefore add a "bonus" to average labour productivity because the existing "overhead labour" is spread over a larger output. Another explanation for an acceleration in productivity growth could be economies of scale and dynamic learning processes associated with sustained rates of high output growth. This is also known as the Verdoorn Law.[44]

To what extent does the measured increase in labour productivity reflect this sensitivity to cyclical fluctuations? This is a controversial issue because both the cyclical effect as well as the trend cannot be directly measured but have to be estimated. The CEA estimates point to only a minor cyclical effect. This could be explained by the mature stage that the United States economic expansion had already reached in 1995, when productivity growth started to accelerate. But another study by R. Gordon[45] found a relatively large cyclical effect (table 2.1.3). The two studies differ slightly with regard to the period covered, but while this can explain the small difference in the aggregate productivity growth rates it cannot account for the large discrepancy between the estimated cyclical effects. Given that the contribution of capital deepening to the change in productivity growth is broadly similar in both studies, the implication is that the Gordon study shows a correspondingly smaller improvement in TFP growth. In fact, there is virtually no acceleration of TFP outside the computer-producing sector which is in marked contrast to the CEA study. This is obviously an important issue that will have to be explored in future research.

The other interesting question is how productivity growth will hold up during the current cyclical downturn of the United States economy. This has direct

---

[42] Ibid.

[43] W. Oi, "Labour as a quasi-fixed factor", *Journal of Political Economy*, Vol. 70, December 1962, pp. 538-555. For a more general treatment of labour as a quasi-fixed factor, see A. Okun, *Prices and Quantities* (Oxford, Oxford University Press, 1981).

[44] P. Verdoorn, "Fattori che regolano lo sviluppo della produttività del lavora", *L'industria*, No. 1, 1949, pp. 45-53; R. Rowthorne, "A note on Verdoorn's Law", *The Economic Journal*, Vol. 89, March 1979, pp. 131-133; P. Rayment, "Structural change in manufacturing industry and the stability of the Verdoorn Law", *Economia Internazionale*, Vol. 34, No. 1, 1981, pp. 104-123.

[45] R. Gordon, "Does the 'new economy' measure up to the great inventions of the past?", *Journal of Economic Perspectives*, Vol. 14, No. 4, Fall 2000, pp. 49-74.

implications for the labour market because a better than normal cyclical behaviour would *ceteris paribus* be reflected in larger layoffs. It is, however, still too early to judge this issue given the present stage of the downswing. In any case, as the "old economy" experience would suggest, the sharp deceleration in output growth in the final two quarters of 2000 was accompanied by a deceleration in productivity growth. Productivity growth slowed down to 2.4 per cent (seasonally adjusted annual rate) in the fourth quarter, down from 3.4 per cent in the preceding quarter and 6.3 per cent in the second. The still strong productivity growth in the final two quarters reflects a sharp fall in total hours worked which, in turn, was entirely due to reduced hours per work week. The number of persons employed actually increased slightly in the third and fourth quarters.

The apparent cyclical productivity slowdown in the second half of 2000, however, does not allow any conclusions to be drawn about the role of cyclical effects in the productivity performance for the whole period since 1995. The current cyclical downswing is not yet an occasion to test the sustainability of the new productivity trend; this can only be done once the next upswing has reached an advanced stage.

2.2 Western Europe

The overall economic performance in western Europe in 2000 was quite favourable if the year is taken as a whole. Real GDP rose by 3.5 per cent compared with 2.2 per cent in 1999. This was the best performance since 1988, when it increased by 3.6 per cent. Robust economic growth led to strong gains in employment and declining rates of unemployment, while inflationary pressures remained very weak despite a sharp rise in oil prices. But the very good average outcome masks a slowdown in the pace of expansion in the second half of the year (table 2.2.1). In the four major economies, real GDP rose at a quarterly rate of only 0.5 per cent in the last two quarters of 2000, equivalent to a seasonally adjusted annual rate of some 2 per cent. This compares with an average annual rate of some 3.5 in the first two quarters. Short-term economic prospects have become much more uncertain in early 2001: the outlook increasingly depends on the resilience of domestic growth forces to the deteriorating external economic environment and on west European policy responses.

(i) Euro area

In the euro area, the cyclical upswing which started in 1997 peaked in the first half of 2000. Real GDP rose by 0.5 per cent in the third quarter of 2000 compared with an equivalent increase of 0.7 per cent in the previous quarter (table 2.2.1). Incomplete data available at the time of writing suggest that the third quarter rate of expansion was maintained in the final quarter of 2000. There were, however, opposing tendencies in the three main economies. Relatively robust economic growth in France and Italy contrasts with an abrupt deceleration in Germany in the second half of the year. Growth also held up quite well in Spain and some of the smaller economies. The slowdown in the rate of expansion also dampened the year-on-year changes in real GDP: there was an increase of 3.2 per cent in the third quarter of 2000 compared with 3.6 per cent in the second quarter.[46] Year-on-year growth rates of the major economies have converged in the second half of 2000 (chart 2.2.1).

Recent monthly economic indicators confirm the tendency for a weakening of growth forces in the final months of 2000. The growth of manufacturing output slowed down in the second half of 2000 and capacity utilization rates in January 2001 had fallen, albeit only slightly, from the very high levels attained in October 2000. Less optimistic expectations about future production and assessments of order books contributed to a weakening of industrial confidence in early 2001 from its recent peak in November 2000 (chart 2.2.2). In Germany, the ifo Institute business climate index, a key cyclical indicator for the assessment of the current and expected business situation, fell sharply in February 2001. This resumed a steady decline of the index in the second half of last year, which had been temporarily interrupted by a small increase in January 2001.

The slowdown in the euro area in the third quarter of 2000 was entirely due to a weakening of domestic demand, which was partly offset by real net exports. The main factor behind the slowdown was the increasing sluggishness of private consumption expenditures due to the real income losses associated with higher oil prices. The weaker growth of employment has also tended to restrain gains in aggregate factor incomes. To some extent, the deterioration in the general economic situation may have also dampened households' spending propensity and led to some rebuilding of savings. Real private consumption rose by only 0.2 per cent between the second and third quarters of 2000, the corresponding year-on-year increase being only about 2¼ per cent (table 2.2.1 and chart 2.2.3). The volume of retail sales in October/November 2000 (the last months for which data are available at the time of writing) was only 1¼ per cent higher than a year earlier. This compares with an average increase of 2¾ per cent in July/September 2000. Consumer confidence has been volatile since late summer 2000 but the underlying tendency till February 2001 has been for a decline (chart 2.2.4). The weaker growth of private consumption expenditures was accompanied by a similarly strong slowdown in government consumption expenditures. Changes in stockbuilding subtracted from overall growth in the third quarter of 2000.

---

[46] These data exclude Greece and Ireland, for which seasonally adjusted quarterly GDP data are not available. The Irish central statistical office has started to publish a quarterly GDP series as from 1998, but it is not adjusted for seasonal factors because the number of observations is still too small. At the time of writing, non-seasonally adjusted GDP data for Ireland are available only up to the second quarter of 2000. Including Ireland, real GDP rose year-on-year by 3.8 per cent in the second quarter of 2000, i.e. 0.2 percentage points more than the aggregate excluding Ireland.

TABLE 2.2.1

Quarterly changes in real GDP and main expenditure items in western Europe, 1999 QIV-2000 QIV
(Percentage change over preceding quarter)

	Western Europe[a]					Four major economies[b]					Euro area[c]				
	1999	2000				1999	2000				1999	2000			
	QIV	QI	QII	QIII	QIV	QIV	QI	QII	QIII	QIV	QIV	QI	QII	QIII	QIV
Private consumption	0.8	0.7	0.8	0.3	..	0.8	0.6	1.0	0.3	0.3	0.7	0.8	0.8	0.2	..
Government consumption	0.4	0.5	0.5	0.3	..	0.4	0.6	0.4	0.2	0.5	0.4	0.7	0.3	0.1	..
Gross fixed capital formation	0.9	1.5	0.7	1.0	..	1.2	1.1	0.9	1.0	0.8	0.8	1.8	0.6	1.1	..
Changes in stockbuilding[d]	0.3	-0.1	0.1	-0.2	..	0.5	-0.3	0.2	-0.1	–	0.3	-0.3	0.1	-0.1	..
Total domestic expenditures	1.0	0.7	0.8	0.3	..	1.2	0.4	1.0	0.3	0.4	1.0	0.7	0.7	0.2	..
Net exports[d]	–	0.1	-0.1	0.3	..	-0.3	0.3	-0.2	0.2	0.1	0.1	0.2	–	0.3	..
Exports	2.5	2.3	2.5	3.1	..	1.8	2.6	2.9	3.4	2.9	3.0	2.6	2.6	3.6	..
Imports	2.9	1.9	2.8	2.4	..	3.1	1.7	3.6	2.7	2.6	3.3	1.9	2.8	2.8	..
GDP	1.0	0.8	0.7	0.6	..	0.9	0.8	0.8	0.5	0.5	1.0	0.9	0.7	0.5	..

Source: National statistics.

[a] 14 countries: European Union (excluding Greece and Ireland) plus Norway and Switzerland.
[b] France, Germany, Italy and the United Kingdom.
[c] Excluding Greece and Ireland.
[d] Contribution to quarterly change in real GDP (percentage points).

CHART 2.2.1

Quarterly changes in real GDP in the industrialized countries, 1996-2000
(Percentage change over same period of previous year)

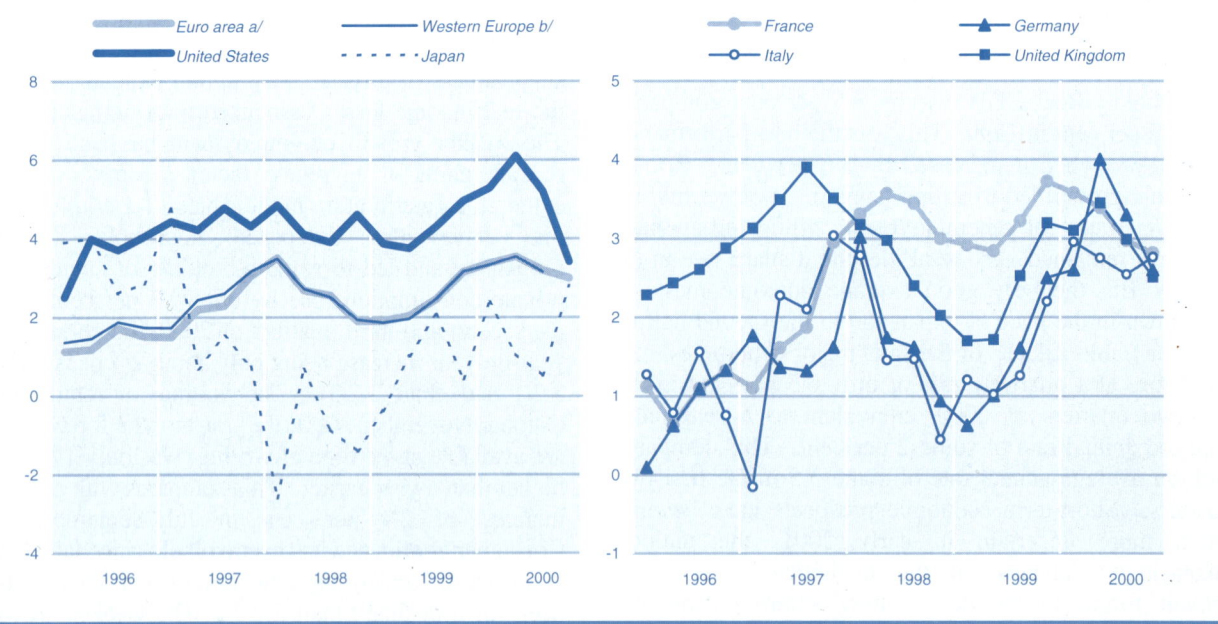

Source: Eurostat; OECD National Accounts; national statistics.

[a] Excluding Greece and Ireland.
[b] Euro area plus Denmark, Norway, Sweden, Switzerland and the United Kingdom.

There was some slight offset to these dampening factors from gross fixed capital formation, mainly reflecting increased business expenditures on machinery, equipment and software. Partial data suggest that they rose by some 7-8 per cent in the third quarter of 2000 over the same period of 1999. Business investment had been stimulated by the rise in capacity utilization rates to high levels, favourable financing conditions and by earlier expectations of good sales and profit. Construction investment slowed down considerably in the course of 2000 (chart 2.2.5).

Real exports of goods and services remained the mainstay of domestic economic activity in the second half of 2000. This reflected in part the gains in price competitiveness resulting from the depreciation of the euro but also the mutually reinforcing effects of strong intraregional trade, as well as demand from central and

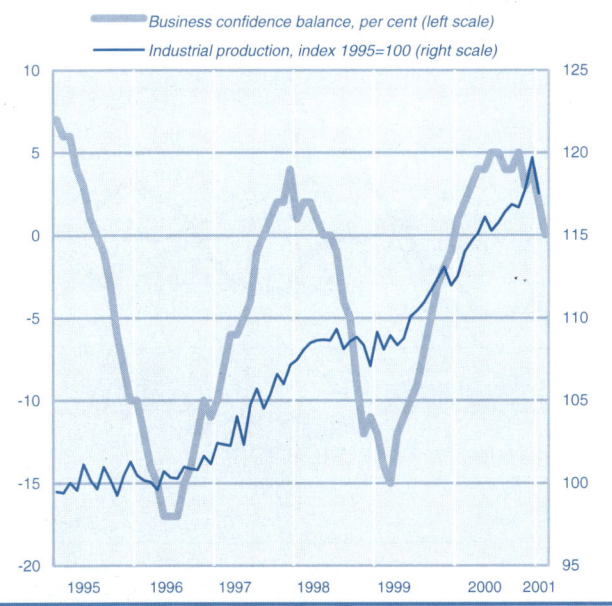

CHART 2.2.2

Industrial confidence and industrial production in the European Union, January 1995-February 2001
(Per cent, 1995=100)

Source: Eurostat, New Cronos Database; Commission for the European Communities (Brussels) (www.europa.eu.int).

eastern Europe. The expansion in domestic output and incomes led to a considerable increase in imports of final and intermediate products, and this offset to a large extent the considerable stimulus to domestic economic activity from foreign demand. Nevertheless, the change in real net exports contributed 0.3 percentage points to the overall increase in real GDP by 0.5 per cent in the third quarter of 2000 (table 2.2.1).

For the year as a whole, real GDP in the euro area[47] rose by 3.4 per cent, up from 2.6 per cent in 1999. This was the largest annual increase for this group of countries since 1990, when the German unification boom drove up the annual growth rate to 3.7 per cent (table 2.2.2). The pervasiveness of growth in the euro area in 2000 is underlined by the fact that no member country had an annual growth rate below 3 per cent. Most of them were within a range of 3-4 per cent, but some were significantly higher – Finland (5.7 per cent), Ireland (10 per cent) and Luxembourg (8.1 per cent).

The relatively short cyclical upswing phases for the euro area (and for western Europe) as a whole disguises much longer periods of expansion in some of the smaller economies. Thus, Finland, Ireland, the Netherlands, Portugal and Spain were all in the seventh consecutive year of a strong economic expansion in 2000, probably the strongest boom period in the postwar period. In Finland and Ireland, economic activity continued to be supported by extraordinarily strong growth in the high-tech electronics sector. Real GDP in Ireland rose at an average annual rate of about 10 per cent in 1995-2000 with associated risks of overheating.[48] In Greece, which joined the euro area at the beginning of 2001, there has also been above average growth since 1997 (box 2.2.1). Growth differentials among the three major economies have narrowed significantly since 1999, when activity was still much more sluggish in Germany and Italy compared with France.[49] The stronger average annual growth rate of GDP in the euro area in 2000 was due to the growth in real net exports, which more than offset a slowdown in the growth of total domestic expenditures. This represented a marked swing from 1999 when net exports had a negative impact on GDP, of about the same magnitude (table 2.2.3).

Sharp increases in energy prices in 2000 were the main factor which drove *consumer price inflation* above the 2 per cent ceiling fixed by the ECB. The average annual inflation rate was 2.4 per cent in 2000, up from 1.2 per cent in 1999 (table 2.2.4.) This average, however, conceals some large differences among the members of the euro area, which can be explained by a combination of cyclical and other factors.[50] Headline inflation peaked at 2.9 per cent in November 2000, but was down to 2.4 per cent (excluding Greece) by January 2001 (chart 2.2.6). Including Greece, the latter inflation rate was somewhat higher at 2.5 per cent.[51] The fall in the inflation rate reflects lower increases in prices for energy products, which, however, were partly offset by higher prices for unprocessed food. Underlying inflationary pressures remained, however, relatively subdued. Core inflation edged upward in the course of 2000, but was only 1.7 per cent in January 2001 compared with 1.2 per cent 12 months earlier. The implicit GDP deflator, the broadest measure of inflation, rose by only about 1 per cent in 2000. These moderate rates of inflation largely reflect the continued weaknesses of labour cost pressures. Compensation per employee in the whole economy rose by 2.3 per cent in the first three quarters of 2000 (over the same period of 1999). But because of higher productivity this translated into an increase in unit labour costs of only 0.8 per cent.

The cyclical upswing in 2000 led to a significant improvement in *labour market* conditions in the euro area (chart 2.2.7). Employment rose for the year as a whole by nearly 2 per cent, the third consecutive year in which it has increased by more than 1.5 per cent (table 2.2.5). Within the average there have been large above average gains in employment in Ireland, Luxembourg, the

---

[47] Including Greece, which joined EMU at the beginning of 2001.

[48] For a brief review of recent economic developments in Ireland see sect. 2.6 below.

[49] See below for a brief account of recent developments in these three countries.

[50] Sect. 2.5.

[51] Inflation rate calculated by including Greece in the base period, i.e. January 2000.

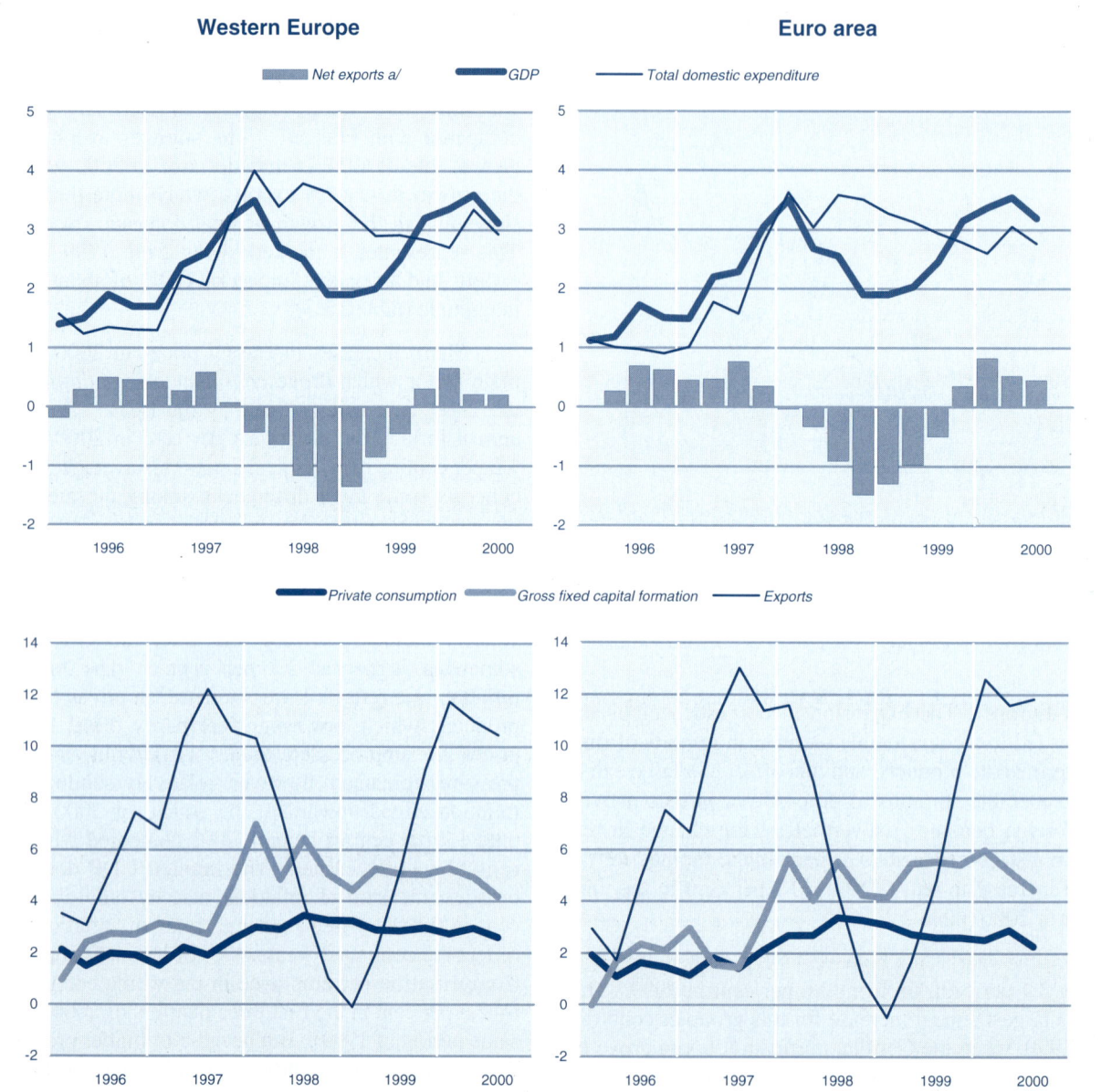

CHART 2.2.3

Quarterly changes in real GDP and main expenditure items in western Europe, 1996 QI-2000 QIII
(Percentage change over same period of previous year)

Source: National statistics.
Note: See chart 2.2.1.
a Growth contributions to percentage change of GDP (percentage points).

Netherlands, Portugal and Spain in recent years. The average annual unemployment rate fell to 9.1 per cent in 2000, down from 10 per cent in 1999 and the lowest rate since 1992. But employment growth slowed down and the fall in the monthly employment rates bottomed out in the second half of 2000. In January 2001, the average unemployment rate in the euro area rose slightly to 8.8 per cent, up from 8.7 per cent in the preceding month, although still well below its previous peak of 11.6 per cent in January 1997.

The decline in unemployment has benefited both male and female members of the labour force, but the female unemployment rate still averaged 11.3 per cent in 2000, some 4 percentage points more than for males (table 2.2.6). This "gender gap" has narrowed slightly since the beginning of the 1990s, when it was some 4.5 percentage points (chart 2.2.8), but the difference between the two is strongly influenced by the persistence of large gender gaps in the three Mediterranean countries. Thus, in Greece and Spain the female unemployment rate was more than 10 percentage points higher than for males and some 6 percentage points more in Italy. This contrasts with a difference of some 3.5 percentage points or less in the remaining countries. Only in Ireland was female unemployment, albeit only slightly, lower than

CHART 2.2.4

Consumer confidence and retail sales in the European Union, January 1995-February 2001
(Per cent, 1995=100)

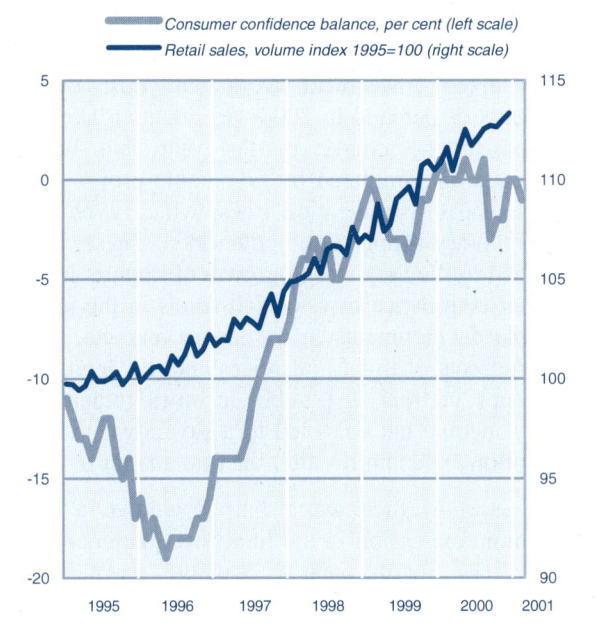

Source: Eurostat (www.europa.eu.int).

male unemployment in 2000. Outside the euro area this was also the case in Sweden and the United Kingdom. In the United States there has been virtually no difference between male and female unemployment rates over the past decade.

More important than gender differences are the differences in unemployment by age groups, particularly for persons below the age of 25 (the so-called youth unemployment). The youth unemployment rate was some 17.7 per cent in the euro area in 2000, nearly 10 percentage points more than the rate for persons in the higher age group (table 2.2.7). The incidence of youth unemployment is typically inversely related to the level of education, but it is also dependent on the strength of economic growth forces in the region of residence and the differential development of sectoral labour markets. Youth unemployment rose markedly in the early 1990s but has declined in recent years and by more than that of older persons (chart 2.2.8). At the beginning of the 1990s young unemployed persons accounted for about one third of total unemployment, but this share was down to about one quarter in 2000. While the youth unemployment rate has also fallen in the United States during the long economic expansion, the share of young persons in total unemployment rose to 37 per cent in 2000, compared with 33 per cent in 1991.

As in the case of unemployment by gender, there are some considerable differences in the relative importance of youth unemployment across countries, which translate into above average "age gaps". In Greece and Italy nearly every third young person, and in Spain every fourth, was unemployed in 2000. Youth unemployment was also above average in Finland and

CHART 2.2.5

Quarterly changes in real gross fixed capital formation, 1996 QI-2000 QIII
(Percentage change over same period of preceding year)

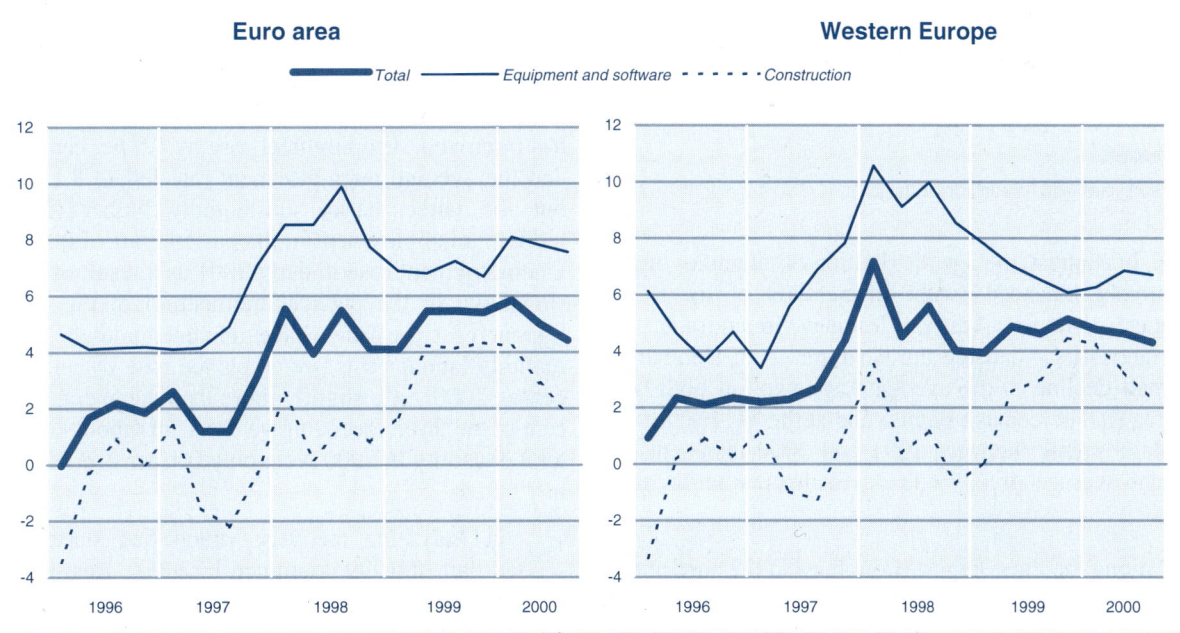

Source: Eurostat; OECD, *National Accounts;* national statistics.

Note: Euro area: nine countries (excluding Greece, Ireland and Portugal). Western Europe: euro area plus Denmark, Norway, Sweden, Switzerland and the United Kingdom.

TABLE 2.2.2

Annual changes in real GDP in western Europe, North America and Japan, 1998-2001

(Percentage change over previous year)

	1998	1999	2000 [a]	2001 [b]
France	3.3	3.2	3.2	2.7
Germany	2.1	1.6	3.0	2.1
Italy	1.8	1.6	2.9	2.5
Austria	3.3	2.8	3.3	2.6
Belgium	2.4	2.7	3.9	2.5
Finland	5.3	4.2	5.7	4.0
Greece	3.1	3.4	4.0	4.0
Ireland	8.6	9.8	10.0	7.5
Luxembourg	5.0	7.5	8.1	6.2
Netherlands	4.1	3.9	3.9	3.3
Portugal	3.6	3.0	3.2	2.6
Spain	4.3	4.0	4.1	3.0
Euro area	2.8	2.6	3.4	2.6
United Kingdom	2.6	2.3	3.0	2.5
Denmark	2.8	2.1	2.4	1.8
Sweden	3.6	4.1	3.6	2.5
European Union	2.8	2.6	3.3	2.6
Cyprus	5.0	4.5	4.9	4.1
Iceland	4.5	4.3	3.6	1.3
Israel	2.2	2.3	3.0	3.0
Malta	3.4	4.0	4.3	4.3
Norway	2.0	0.9	2.2	1.5
Switzerland	2.3	1.5	3.3	2.1
Turkey	3.1	-5.0	7.0	–
Western Europe	2.8	2.2	3.5	2.5
Canada	3.3	4.5	4.7	2.4
United States	4.4	4.2	5.0	1.7
North America	4.3	4.3	5.0	1.8
Japan	-1.1	0.8	1.7	1.2
Total above	2.8	2.8	3.8	2.0
Memorandum items:				
4 major west European economies [c]	2.4	2.1	3.0	2.5
Western Europe and North America	3.6	3.2	4.2	2.1

Source: National statistics and national economic reports.

Note: All aggregates exclude Israel. Growth rates of regional aggregates have been calculated as weighted averages of growth rates in individual countries. Weights were derived from 1996 GDP data converted from national currency units into dollars using purchasing power parities.

[a] Preliminary estimates or forecasts.

[b] Forecasts.

[c] France, Germany, Italy and United Kingdom.

France. In contrast, the age distribution of unemployment is relatively balanced (with differentials of up to 3 percentage points) in Austria, Germany, Ireland and the Netherlands and – outside the euro area – in Denmark. The small decline in the average "age gap" in both the euro area (0.8 percentage points) and at the EU level (0.4 percentage points) between 1991 and 2000 represents a statistical average of opposite developments across the Union.

Among the three largest economies in the euro area, the pace of economic activity maintained a high momentum in *France* in the course of 2000. Real GDP rose by 3.2 per cent in 2000, the same as in 1999. Robust growth has been accompanied by large gains in employment, which were also helped by continuing wage moderation, reductions in social security contributions for unskilled workers and the development of more flexible labour contracts. The unemployment rate was 8.7 per cent in January 2001, its lowest rate for 10 years and down from its previous peak of 12.5 per cent in June 1997. Consumer price inflation remained moderate and significantly below the euro area average. Exports and business fixed investment were the most dynamic components of demand in 2000. Residential investment weakened in the course of the year, but business investment was stimulated by favourable profits growth and high capacity utilization rates, which even led to some temporary supply-side bottlenecks. These, in turn, contributed to the very strong growth of imports in 2000. Consumer confidence rose to high levels in the wake of favourable developments in the labour markets, but the negative effects of higher oil prices and the depreciation of the euro on real disposable incomes (albeit partly offset by income tax cuts) led to a slowdown in private consumption expenditures after the first quarter of 2000.

In *Germany*, there was a sharp slowdown in the rate of economic expansion in the final two quarters of 2000 (table 2.2.1). For the year as a whole, real GDP still increased by 3 per cent, the largest increase rate since 1990. The slowdown in the second half of 2000 reflects to a large degree the dampening effects of the higher prices for energy products on households' purchasing power. Business investment in equipment and software continued to rise and in the final quarter of 2000 they were some 10.5 per cent higher than in the same period of 1999. Weak construction activity continues to dampen overall economic growth: for 2000 as a whole, construction investment fell by 2.5 per cent, the net effect of declines of 8 per cent in eastern Germany and only 0.5 per cent in west Germany. The sharp fall in construction investment in east Germany mainly reflects the large excess supply of buildings created in the aftermath of unification, a process which was stimulated by overly generous government subsidies. Against the background of stronger output growth, the demand for labour demand has improved. Employment rose by 1.5 per cent in 2000, and the average unemployment rate fell to 8.1 per cent, but the latter masks substantially higher (open and hidden) unemployment in the eastern part of the country. Unemployment rose in early 2001 as a result of the sharp slowdown in the cyclical momentum of the economy. Labour cost pressures have remained muted. Average monthly labour costs per employee rose by only 1.2 per cent in 2000, only slightly more than the average of 1 per cent in the three preceding years. Unit labour costs in the total economy in 2000 were only 0.1 per cent higher than in 1999.

In *Italy,* the recovery which had started in the second half of 1999 continued in 2000. Real GDP rose by 2.9 per cent, up from 1.6 per cent in 1999, the improvement entirely due to favourable changes in net exports. Total domestic expenditure growth actually slowed down in 2000, although business investment was

BOX 2.2.1

Greece joins the EMU

Greece became the twelfth member country of the European Monetary Union on 1 January 2001. Greece was the only country in the European Union which did not meet any of the Maastricht convergence criteria when 11 EU member countries adopted the single currency in 1999. But with a rate of economic growth considerably above the euro area average since 1997, it has made significant progress in nominal convergence (see chart below) and this led the European Council to accept Greece's application for membership of EMU in June 2000. In fact, the successful compliance with the Maastricht convergence criteria resulted from the continuation of a stability-oriented economic policy, which started in the early 1990s. This policy was reinforced by the government's revised convergence plan of December 1997, which aimed at achieving Greek entry into the EMU by 2001.

A stringent fiscal consolidation, reflecting a combination of expenditure retrenchment and revenue-enhancing measures, was amplified by the favourable effects of stronger economic growth on government net revenues. This led to a reduction of the government deficit from 4.6 per cent of GDP in 1997 to 0.9 per cent in 2000. Over the same period, the level of government debt was reduced from 108.3 per cent of GDP to 103.9 per cent. The latter is still well above the 60 per cent Maastricht reference value, but as in the case of Belgium and Italy, which both have debt levels higher than Greece, it was the declining trend in the debt ratio that counted in the assessment of whether the convergence criteria had been fulfilled. Relatively tight monetary policy contributed to a steady decline in inflation, which fell from an average rate of 5.4 per cent in 1997 to 2.9 per cent in 2000, just 0.5 percentage points above the euro area average.

An important role in the reduction of inflation was played by incomes policy, which, from 1998, secured a pronounced degree of wage moderation in the public and private sectors. From the early 1990s, the central bank had used the exchange rate against the ECU as a nominal anchor to limit inflation, but this "hard drachma policy" encountered difficulties after 1996 when rapid wage growth led to a sharp real appreciation of the exchange rate and a loss of competitiveness. To achieve convergence with the euro area rate of inflation in a short period, the government also reduced indirect taxes in the final months of 1998 and in 1999. These were passed through into lower retail prices and contributed significantly to the decline in the inflation rate in these two years.

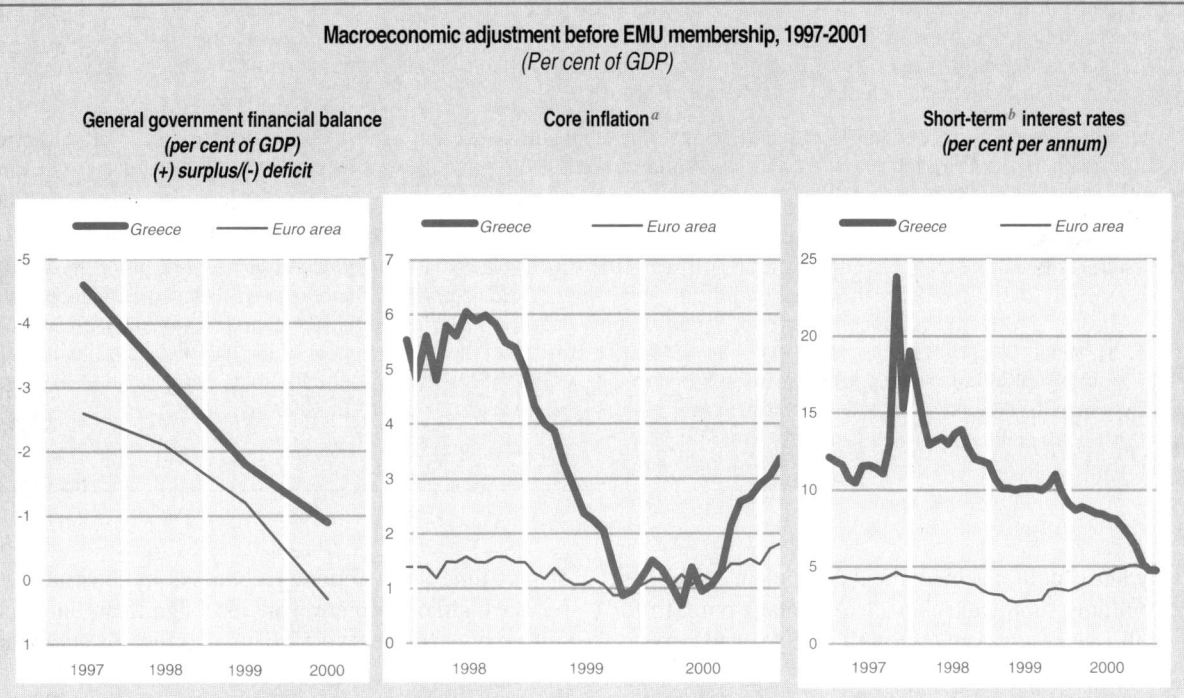

Macroeconomic adjustment before EMU membership, 1997-2001
(Per cent of GDP)

Source: Eurostat.

a Harmonized Index of Consumer Prices, excluding food and energy (monthly).
b Three-month interest rates.

The reliance on incomes policy to reduce inflation to low rates was also motivated by the need to meet the exchange rate criterion for EMU membership. This implied a commitment to broad exchange rate stability within the ERM, into which the drachma entered in March 1998 and which was followed by participation in the ERM-2 from the beginning of 1999. Since the second half of 1999, the drachma has converged steadily onto its ERM-2 central rate, a process which was supported by its revaluation against the euro (i.e. an effective lowering of the central rate) in January 2000.

> **BOX 2.2.1 (concluded)**
>
> **Greece joins the EMU**
>
> The stability-oriented economic policy was part and parcel of a wider programme of structural reforms aimed at reducing labour market rigidities, privatizing state owned enterprises and deregulating the markets for utilities and telecommunications. Although progress in these various areas has been uneven, supply-side reforms in combination with sound macroeconomic policies have created an economic environment which is more conducive to growth. Rapid economic expansion since 1997 was also supported by sharply falling long-term interest rates, largely a reflection of reduced inflationary expectations and anticipations of EMU membership. Yields on 10-year government bonds fell from 10.5 per cent in December 1997 to 5.3 per cent in December 2000. Over the same period, the differential over yields on benchmark German bonds fell from 5.2 percentage points to 0.7 percentage points. In February 2001, this yield differential had fallen to 0.5 percentage points and Greeks yields were only 0.3 percentage points higher than the average rate in the euro area. The stimulus of falling long-term interest to consumption and investment was amplified during 2000 by the progressive easing of monetary policy required to reduce official interest rates to the much lower level in the euro area. As a result, short-term interest rates (three month Athibor) fell from 9.1 per cent in January 2000 to 5.2 per cent in December 2000.
>
> Apart from lower interest rates due to the elimination of exchange rate risk, membership in the monetary union should provide the traditional benefits of savings in transaction costs for intra-euro area trade. EMU membership is also expected to foster closer trade and investment links with the rest of the European Union. The single currency should also increase price transparency and intensify competition, which should lead to efficiency gains. But EMU membership also constitutes a great challenge for Greece. The significant difference between its economic structure and the euro area average and its much lower degree of integration in European product markets compared with the other members, leaves Greece more vulnerable to country-specific shocks for which the exchange rate is no longer available as an instrument for adjustment. Also, the appreciation of the real exchange rate associated with the convergence of real incomes and prices to euro area levels will need to be controlled in order to avoid a loss of competitiveness (see also section 2.5 below).
>
> The immediate concern of Greek policy makers is to stem inflationary pressures arising from the continued rapid rate of economic expansion in 2001 which is fuelled by the monetary stimulus originating in the convergence of domestic interest rates to euro area levels. The collective wage agreements concluded in May 2000 ensure a moderate rate of labour cost growth until 2001, but wage drift has already increased in some sectors. Since June 2000, the core inflation rate has been diverging steadily from the euro area average and in February 2001 the differential was 1.5 percentage points. The headline inflation rate in 2000 was increasing as a result of the oil price increases, the decline of the effective exchange rate and the vanishing statistical base effects stemming from the reduction of indirect taxes in 1998-1999.
>
> More generally, sustaining economic growth and maintaining competitiveness will require further progress in structural reforms in a large number of areas such as public sector administration, taxes, privatization, deregulation of the gas and electricity sectors and of labour markets.
>
> While the potential effects of EMU membership will be considerable for Greece, the country's impact on the average economic performance of the euro area, including inflation, is likely to be small. Greece accounted for only 1.9 per cent of the enlarged euro area's GDP in 1999, broadly the same as Finland and Portugal. But entry into the euro area means that Greece is now represented on the Governing Council of the ECB, its supreme decision-making body with regard to monetary policy. The Governing Council comprises the six members of the Executive Board and the 12 Governors of the national central banks. If a "small economy" is defined as one with a share in the euro area's GDP of less than 5 per cent, then there are now seven such small economies in the euro area with a combined share of 14.1 per cent of total GDP in 1999 and with 7 out of 18 seats (or some 40 per cent) on the Governing Council.

relatively buoyant in machinery and equipment. Changes in stockbuilding subtracted about 1 percentage point from the overall rate of economic growth in 2000 and private consumption was relatively sluggish in the face of only moderate growth in real disposable incomes. The surge in real exports by some 10 per cent in 2000 is attributed to the euro depreciation and the overall strength of the world economy. The growth of exports to markets outside the EU was much stronger than to the euro area and other EU markets. Italian exports rose broadly in line with world trade in 2000 thus arresting a declining trend in Italy's share of world exports, which had been underway since 1996 as a result of weakening competitiveness. Developments in the labour market were favourable in 2000: employment rose on average by 1.4 per cent, to a large degree reflecting the strong growth of part-time and temporary contracts in construction and services, although there were also significant increases in full-time, permanent jobs. This was the third consecutive year that annual employment gains exceeded 1 per cent. The unemployment rate fell to 10.1 per cent in December 2000, down by 1 percentage point from its level a year earlier. The average figure, however, masks very tight labour markets in the northern part of the country. Unit labour costs edged up only slightly, by some 1¼ per cent in 2000, with stronger increases in labour costs per employee being offset by productivity gains. Unit labour costs in industry (excluding construction) broadly stagnated in 2000. Adverse changes in the terms of trade in 2000 led to a swing in the current account from a surplus of 0.75 per cent of GDP in 1999 to a deficit of some 0.5 per cent of GDP.

TABLE 2.2.3

Annual changes in major expenditure items on GDP in western Europe, North America and Japan, 1999-2000
(Percentage change over preceding year)

	Private consumption		Government consumption		Gross fixed capital formation		Changes in stockbuilding[a]		Total domestic expenditures		Exports of goods and services		Imports of goods and services		Net exports[a]	
	1999	2000	1999	2000	1999	2000	1999	2000	1999	2000	1999	2000	1999	2000	1999	2000
France	2.7	2.4	2.5	1.5	7.3	6.7	-0.3	0.2	3.2	3.2	4.0	13.6	4.0	14.7	0.1	0.1
Germany	2.6	1.6	-0.1	1.4	3.3	2.4	0.2	0.2	2.4	2.1	5.1	13.2	8.1	10.2	-0.8	1.0
Italy	2.3	2.2	1.5	1.6	4.6	6.1	0.4	-1.0	3.0	2.3	–	10.2	5.1	8.3	-1.3	0.6
Austria	2.3	2.7	3.2	2.5	3.2	3.7	-0.3	-0.2	2.6	2.7	7.6	7.5	7.1	6.3	0.2	0.6
Belgium	1.9	2.9	3.4	2.1	4.8	4.2	-0.7	0.1	2.1	3.1	5.2	10.6	4.5	9.9	0.7	1.0
Finland	3.7	3.0	2.0	0.4	2.7	4.8	-0.5	0.3	2.5	3.0	7.1	17.7	4.3	12.8	1.6	3.5
Greece	2.9	2.9	-0.1	0.8	7.3	7.8	-0.4	–	3.0	3.7	6.5	12.5	3.9	8.7	0.2	–
Ireland	7.8	9.1	5.2	4.5	12.5	11.0	-1.8	-0.8	6.0	9.0	12.4	16.2	8.7	16.3	4.5	2.3
Luxembourg	4.1	3.5	12.8	3.9	26.6	0.1	0.1	-0.1	11.3	2.5	7.9	15.0	11.2	11.2	-1.9	6.0
Netherlands	4.4	3.7	2.5	3.1	6.5	4.3	-0.2	-0.2	4.2	3.5	5.6	9.1	6.3	8.9	-0.1	0.6
Portugal	4.8	3.3	3.4	3.0	6.0	5.8	-0.1	-0.2	4.7	3.7	4.8	8.9	8.8	8.7	-2.2	-0.9
Spain	4.7	4.0	2.9	2.6	8.9	5.9	0.2	-0.1	5.5	4.1	6.6	10.8	11.9	10.4	-1.5	-0.1
Euro area	3.0	2.5	1.6	1.8	5.5	4.9	–	-0.1	3.2	2.9	4.3	12.0	6.6	10.6	-0.6	0.6
United Kingdom	4.4	3.6	4.0	2.6	5.4	2.3	-0.8	0.5	3.7	3.7	4.0	7.4	8.1	8.9	-1.5	-0.9
Denmark	0.5	0.2	1.4	0.8	1.5	8.4	-1.6	0.3	-0.6	2.4	9.7	5.4	2.2	5.8	2.8	0.1
Sweden	3.8	3.0	1.7	0.1	8.1	4.5	-0.5	0.2	3.4	2.7	5.9	9.8	4.3	9.7	1.1	0.9
European Union	3.2	2.6	2.0	1.8	5.5	4.6	-0.2	–	3.2	3.0	4.3	11.1	6.7	10.2	-0.6	0.4
Cyprus	3.1	5.5	-5.0	2.8	-1.2	2.9	-0.3	0.1	0.7	4.7	6.5	6.6	-3.3	5.4	4.6	0.3
Iceland	6.9	4.0	4.9	3.5	-0.8	11.1	-0.3	–	4.6	5.3	5.5	2.6	6.1	7.0	-0.6	-2.1
Israel	3.4	3.6	2.9	2.1	0.6	-2.6	2.6	-0.3	5.1	1.7	10.1	9.5	14.6	4.8	-3.4	1.0
Malta	5.9	5.8	-1.1	3.6	0.8	18.7	1.6	3.8	5.0	11.9	8.1	5.6	9.1	13.9	-1.1	-8.1
Norway	2.4	2.1	2.7	1.4	-5.6	-2.7	-1.3	0.8	-1.0	1.6	1.7	2.8	-3.1	1.2	1.8	0.7
Switzerland	2.2	2.3	-0.4	0.5	1.8	4.7	-0.2	-0.2	1.4	2.5	5.9	8.4	5.5	6.4	0.1	0.8
Turkey	-3.1	6.0	6.5	5.0	-16.0	16.2	2.1	-0.3	-4.0	8.0	-7.0	15.0	-3.7	18.0	-0.9	-1.7
Western Europe	2.9	2.8	2.1	2.0	4.2	5.0	-0.1	–	2.8	3.2	3.8	11.1	6.1	10.4	-0.6	0.3
Canada	3.5	4.0	1.3	2.4	10.1	11.2	-0.2	0.3	4.2	5.5	10.0	9.6	9.4	12.0	0.4	-0.7
United States	5.3	5.3	3.3	2.8	9.2	9.2	-0.4	0.2	5.2	5.7	2.9	9.2	10.7	13.7	-1.2	-1.0
North America	5.1	5.2	3.2	2.8	9.2	9.4	-0.4	0.2	5.1	5.7	3.5	9.2	10.6	13.5	-1.1	-1.0
Japan	1.2	0.5	4.0	3.6	-0.9	1.2	-0.2	0.1	0.9	1.3	1.4	12.0	3.0	9.7	-0.1	0.4
Total above	3.6	3.4	2.9	2.6	5.5	6.3	-0.2	0.1	3.5	4.0	3.3	10.4	7.5	11.6	-0.7	-0.2
Memorandum items:																
4 major west European economies	3.0	2.3	1.7	1.7	5.0	4.2	-0.1	–	3.0	2.8	3.4	11.4	6.5	10.5	-0.9	0.3
Western Europe and North America	4.0	4.0	2.7	2.4	6.7	7.2	-0.2	0.1	3.9	4.5	3.7	10.1	8.3	11.9	-0.8	-0.4

Source: OECD national accounts and national statistics.

Note: All aggregates exclude Israel. Growth rates of regional aggregates have been calculated as weighted averages of growth rates in individual countries. Weights were derived from 1996 GDP data converted from national currency units into dollars using 1996 purchasing power parities. 1993 SNA/ESA 95 definitions except for Iceland, Malta, Switzerland and Turkey.

[a] Percentage point contribution to annual GDP growth.

(a) Monetary policy

The stance of monetary policy in the euro area has remained unchanged since early October 2000, when the main refinancing rate was raised by a quarter of a percentage point to 4¾ per cent. Against a background of weakening output growth in the final months of the year, this appears to have been the end of a period of tightening monetary policy, which had led since early November 1999 to a progressive increase in the main refinancing rate, in seven steps, by a cumulative 2¼ percentage points. The restraining effects of higher interest rates were accentuated by the nominal and real effective appreciation of the euro between October 2000 and February 2001. The growth in the money supply (M3) slowed down since last spring and was 4.7 per cent in January 2001, close to the ECB's reference value of 4.5 per cent. This reflects in part a shift in portfolios towards higher interest bearing financial assets (outside M3) in response to higher money market rates since autumn 2000 and a lower rate of growth of bank lending to the private sector.

The marked rise in short-term interest rates in response to the monetary tightening in most of 2000 was partly reversed at the end of the year. Three-month EURIBOR fell from 5.1 per cent in November to 4.8 per cent in January 2001 and had remained broadly stable at that level by mid-March 2001 (chart 2.2.9). The decline in money market interest rates reflects the expectations of

TABLE 2.2.4

Consumer price indices in western Europe, North America and Japan, 1997-2000
(Percentage change over previous year)

	1997	1998	1999	2000
France	1.3	0.7	0.5	1.9
Germany	1.5	0.6	0.7	2.0
Italy	1.9	2.0	1.7	2.6
Austria	1.2	0.8	0.5	2.0
Belgium	1.5	0.9	1.2	2.9
Finland	1.2	1.4	1.3	3.0
Greece	5.4	4.6	2.2	2.8
Ireland	1.2	2.2	2.5	5.2
Luxembourg	1.4	1.0	1.0	3.8
Netherlands	1.9	1.8	2.0	2.3
Portugal	1.9	2.3	2.1	2.8
Spain	1.9	1.8	2.2	3.5
Euro area	1.7	1.3	1.2	2.4
United Kingdom	1.8	1.6	1.4	0.8
Denmark	1.9	1.4	2.0	2.8
Sweden	1.9	1.0	0.5	1.4
European Union	1.7	1.3	1.2	2.1
Cyprus	3.6	2.2	1.7	4.3
Iceland	1.8	1.4	2.1	4.4
Israel	9.0	5.4	5.2	1.1
Malta	3.2	2.2	2.1	2.3
Norway	2.6	1.9	2.1	3.0
Switzerland	0.5	–	0.8	1.5
Turkey	84.8	86.2	64.9	48.8
Western Europe	1.7	1.3	1.2	2.1
Canada	1.6	0.9	1.7	2.7
United States	2.3	1.6	2.2	3.4
North America	2.2	1.5	2.2	3.3
Japan	1.8	0.6	-0.3	-0.7
Total above	2.0	1.3	1.5	2.3
Memorandum items:				
4 major west European economies	1.6	1.1	1.0	1.8
Western Europe and North America	2.0	1.4	1.8	2.8

Source: National statistics.

Note: Harmonized Index of Consumer Prices (HICP) for the 15 member countries of the EU and for Iceland and Norway. Consumer price index according to national definition for other countries. All aggregates exclude Israel and Turkey.

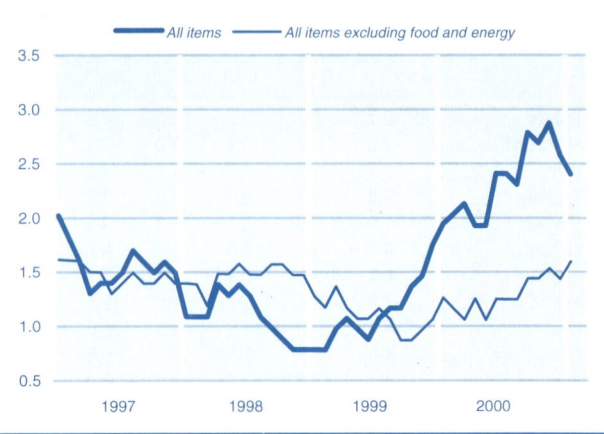

CHART 2.2.6

Consumer prices [a] in the euro area, January 1997-January 2001
(Percentage change over same month of preceding year)

Source: Eurostat.

[a] Harmonized Index of Consumer Prices (HICP).

falling interest rates associated with the outlook for reduced growth in 2001. In the capital markets, long-term bond yields also started to fall in the final months of 2000. By mid-March 2001, the average yield on 10-year government bonds was 4.9 per cent, down from their previous peak of 5.7 per cent in January 2000. Falling bond yields reflected not only low long-term inflationary expectations but also the reaction of investors to the heightened risks of falling stock markets and the associated flight of funds to safe havens. This put upward pressure on bond prices with a corresponding decline in yields. The maturity spread – the difference between long-term and short-term interest rates – fell steadily in the course of 2000 (chart 2.2.9), and by mid-March 2001, it had fallen to slightly more than 10 basis points. As a result, the slope of the yield curve in early 2001 was very flat. But the overall stance of monetary policy is now probably broadly neutral. Real short-term interest rates were relatively low at 2.3 per cent in January 2001. In Germany, they were 2.6 per cent in the final quarter of 2000, in line with their long-term average for the period 1992-2000.[52] As a result of changes in monetary policy and market tendencies, short-term interest rate differentials in favour of dollar-denominated financial assets (compared with euro-denominated assets) have fallen markedly in the course of 2000, a tendency which was accentuated in early 2001 by the substantial cut in the target for the federal funds rate in the United States. The differential amounted on average to ¼ of a percentage point in February 2001, down from a peak of 2.8 percentage points in September 1999 (chart 2.2.10), and by mid-March it had fallen further to 0.2 percentage points. At the long end of the maturity spectrum, the differential in favour of yields on 10-year bonds in the United States had vanished by mid-March 2001, having been at a peak of 2.7 percentage points in October 1999.

(b) Fiscal policy

There was a small surplus on the aggregate government financial balances in the euro area in 2000 corresponding to 0.3 per cent of GDP; in 1999 there had been a deficit equivalent to 1.2 per cent of GDP (table 2.2.8). This was the first surplus for this aggregate of countries since the early 1970s.[53] It partly reflected the working of automatic stabilizers: higher growth rates boosted tax revenues and improved labour market conditions led to reduced spending on unemployment and other social benefits. In addition, declining debt levels curbed interest payments. But the main factor behind the marked improvement in government financial balances

---

[52] Including 1991, when monetary policy was very tight, the average monthly real short-term interest rate was 3.1 per cent. The average for the 1980s was 3.9 per cent.

[53] There was a surplus in 1970 and 1973. For the EU-15, there was an aggregate budget surplus in 1970, 1971 and 1973.

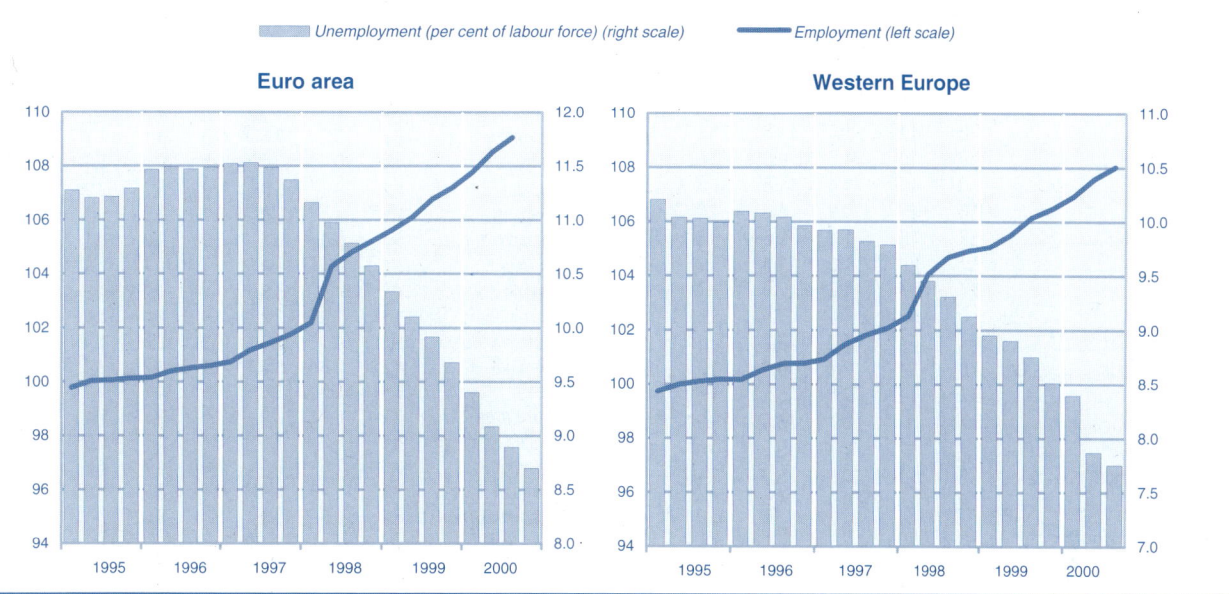

CHART 2.2.7

Employment and unemployment in the euro area and western Europe, 1995 QI-2000 QIV
(Index, 1995=100, per cent)

Source: OECD, *Main Economic Indicators* and *Quarterly Labour Force Statistics*; Eurostat, New Cronos Database; national statistics.

was the revenue from the Universal Mobile Telecommunication System (UMTS) licence sales. Excluding these, there was still a small budget deficit corresponding to 0.8 per cent of GDP in 2000, although this is still a considerable improvement on 1999. The importance of UMTS revenues differed significantly among those countries that sold these licences, in part because of different sales methods. There is, moreover, some controversy as to whether all these proceeds should have been included in the government financial accounts for 2000 (box 2.2.2). It is estimated that the structural (or cyclically adjusted) budget deficit corresponded to only 0.6 per cent of GDP in 2000, unchanged from 1999 but down from 4 per cent in 1995.[54] This reflects the overall restrictiveness of fiscal policy in the second half of the 1990s, which petered out into a broadly neutral stance in 2000. In general, the UMTS fees were used to redeem government debt. General government gross debt fell to 69.7 per cent of GDP in 2000, down from 72 per cent in 1999. Most countries in the euro area now have debt levels below or only slightly above the Maastricht threshold of 60 per cent of GDP. Debt levels have declined in Belgium, Greece and Italy in recent years but they still correspond to more than 100 per cent of GDP.

(ii) Other western Europe

Outside the euro area, growth has also tended to weaken in the other countries of western Europe in the second half of 2000. For the year as a whole, real GDP in these countries rose on average by 3.7 per cent compared with only 1 per cent in 1999. Both figures are influenced by the rapid change in economic conditions in Turkey, where there was a marked rebound in economic activity in 2000 following a slump in 1999 due to the effects of the Russian crisis of August 1998 and the Marmara earthquake of August 1999. As in the euro area, stronger economic growth led to an improved labour market performance in a context of relatively moderate inflation.

In the *United Kingdom*, the rate of economic expansion slowed down markedly in the second half of 2000, with real GDP rising only 0.3 per cent in the final quarter of 2000 compared with 0.8 per cent in the third. The main factor behind this deceleration was a pronounced inventory adjustment, which subtracted about half a percentage point from the quarterly GDP growth rate, but there was also some weakening in consumption expenditures. There was some offset, however, from a rebound in export growth. The resilience of exports in the face of a strong pound sterling suggests that firms may have accepted lower profit margins to maintain price competitiveness. For the year as whole, real GDP rose by 3 per cent. Robust private consumption, supported by a sharp drop in the savings rate, was the mainstay of economic growth in 2000 as a whole. Gross fixed capital formation was relatively weak following large increases in the three preceding years. Changes in real net exports subtracted 0.9 percentage points from overall economic growth in 2000, much less than in 1999, when the negative impact amounted to 1.5 percentage points of GDP. Recent developments in the labour market suggest that the pace of economic expansion may have strengthened again in early 2001.

---

[54] OECD, *Economic Outlook* (Paris), December 1999.

TABLE 2.2.5

Employment and unemployment in western Europe, North America and Japan, 1998-2000

(Per cent)

	Employment (percentage change over preceding year)			Unemployment (per cent of civilian labour force)		
	1998	1999	2000	1998	1999	2000
France	1.2	1.8	1.9	11.8	11.2	9.5
Germany	0.9	1.1	1.5	9.3	8.6	8.1
Italy	1.0	1.2	1.4	11.8	11.3	10.5
Austria	0.8	1.4	0.9	4.5	4.0	3.7
Belgium	1.2	1.3	1.3	9.5	8.8	7.0
Finland	2.1	2.1	1.5	11.4	10.2	9.8
Greece	3.4	-0.7	1.2	10.9	11.7	11.1
Ireland	5.0	6.4	5.0	7.5	5.6	4.2
Luxembourg	4.4	5.1	5.2	2.7	2.3	2.2
Netherlands	3.0	2.8	2.7	4.0	3.3	2.8
Portugal	2.7	1.8	1.5	5.2	4.5	4.2
Spain	3.7	3.5	3.1	18.8	15.9	14.1
Euro area [a]	1.7	1.7	1.8	10.9	10.0	9.1
United Kingdom	1.2	1.0	0.6	6.3	6.1	5.6
Denmark	1.2	1.1	0.9	5.2	5.2	4.7
Sweden	1.2	2.3	2.0	8.3	7.2	5.9
European Union	1.6	1.6	1.6	9.9	9.2	8.3
Cyprus [b]	1.2	0.8	..	3.3	3.8	3.5
Iceland [b]	3.4	2.7	2.0	2.7	2.1	2.3
Israel	1.6	3.1	4.0	8.5	8.9	8.8
Malta [c]	0.4	0.6	2.1	5.1	5.3	4.5
Norway	2.3	0.7	0.5	3.3	3.3	3.5
Switzerland	1.2	0.6	1.4	3.5	3.0	2.7
Turkey	2.8	2.2	2.7	6.8	7.6	6.6
Western Europe	1.7	1.6	1.7	9.3	8.8	7.9
Canada	2.6	2.8	2.6	8.3	7.6	6.8
United States	1.5	1.5	1.3	4.5	4.2	4.0
North America	1.6	1.7	1.4	4.9	4.5	4.3
Japan	-0.7	-0.8	-0.5	4.1	4.7	4.7
Total above	1.2	1.2	1.3	6.9	6.6	6.1
Memorandum items:						
4 major west European economies [d]	1.1	1.2	1.3	9.6	9.1	8.3
Western Europe and North America	1.6	1.6	1.6	7.4	7.0	6.4

Source: OECD, *Main Economic Indicators, National Accounts, Economic Outlook and Quarterly Labour Force Statistics*; Eurostat, New Cronos Database; national statistics.

Note: All aggregates exclude Israel. Employment is defined according to national account definitions with the exception of Canada, Israel, Turkey, the United Kingdom and the United States, which follow the labour force survey definition.

[a] Euro area includes Greece.
[b] Employment: full-time equivalent.
[c] End of year.
[d] France, Germany, Italy and the United Kingdom.

TABLE 2.2.6

Unemployment by gender in the European Union, North America and Japan, 1991 and 2000

(Per cent of civilian labour force)

	1991				2000			
	Total	Male	Female	Gender gap [a]	Total	Male	Female	Gender gap [a]
France	9.5	7.3	12.1	4.8	9.5	7.8	11.5	3.7
Germany [b]	6.6	5.2	8.5	3.3	8.1	7.7	8.5	0.8
Italy	8.6	6.1	13.0	6.9	10.5	8.1	14.4	6.3
Austria [c]	4.0	3.1	5.0	1.9	3.7	3.2	4.4	1.2
Belgium	6.6	4.3	10.0	5.7	7.0	5.7	8.8	3.1
Finland	6.6	8.0	5.1	-2.9	9.8	9.1	10.6	1.5
Greece [d]	7.0	4.4	11.8	7.4	11.7	7.5	17.8	10.3
Ireland	14.7	14.2	15.8	1.6	4.2	4.3	4.2	-0.1
Luxembourg	1.7	1.3	2.3	1.0	2.2	1.6	3.0	1.4
Netherlands	5.8	4.1	8.4	4.3	2.8	1.9	3.9	2.0
Portugal	4.2	2.8	5.9	3.1	4.2	3.4	5.2	1.8
Spain	16.4	12.3	23.8	11.5	14.1	9.8	20.6	10.8
Euro area	8.2	6.3	10.9	4.6	9.1	7.4	11.3	3.9
United Kingdom	8.8	9.9	7.5	-2.4	5.6	6.0	5.0	-1.0
Denmark	8.4	7.5	9.4	1.9	4.7	4.2	5.3	1.1
Sweden	3.1	3.4	2.8	-0.6	5.9	6.0	5.8	-0.2
European Union	8.2	6.9	10.0	3.1	8.3	7.1	9.9	2.8
United States	6.7	7.0	6.3	-0.7	4.0	3.9	4.1	0.2
Canada	10.3	10.9	9.7	-1.2	6.8	6.9	6.7	-0.2
Japan	2.1	2.0	2.2	0.2	4.7	4.9	4.5	-0.4

Source: Eurostat, New Cronos Database.

[a] Difference between female and male unemployment rates (percentage points).
[b] 1992 instead of 1991.
[c] 1993 instead of 1991.
[d] 1999 instead of 2000.

Growth in average earnings in the whole economy strengthened in the second half of 2000, the so-called headline earnings rate[55] rising 4.4 per cent in January 2001, up from 3.9 per cent in July 2000 but still below the increase of 5.7 per cent in January 2000. Growth in unit wage costs was only moderate as a result of productivity growth in 2000. The average annual inflation rate (RPIX) was only 2.1 per cent in 2000, well below the target of 2.5 per cent to be attained by the Bank of England. Inflation dropped to 1.8 per cent in January 2001. Against this background, together with concerns about the likelihood of adverse spillover effects from the sharp cyclical downturn in the United States, the Bank of England lowered its base lending rate by 0.25 percentage points to 5.75 per cent in early February 2001. Strong economic growth led to increased government revenues in 2000 but, as in the euro area, the overriding factor was the proceeds from the sales of UMTS licences. The surplus on the general government financial balance corresponded to 4.4 per cent of GDP in 2000, up from 1.3 per cent in 1999. Excluding the revenues from the UMTS licence sales, the surplus corresponded to 2 per cent of GDP in 2000. The current account deficit increased slightly to 1.5 per cent of GDP in 2000, up from 1.3 per cent in 1999.

The growth in the number of persons in employment slowed down during the first 10 months of 2000 but edged up again in the following three months. Between November 2000 and January 2001, total employment rose on average by 0.4 per cent compared with the preceding three months and was 1.2 per cent higher than one year earlier. The standardized unemployment rate fell to 5.2 per cent in November 2000-January 2001, down from 5.5 per cent in the preceding three months.

---

[55] This is the change in the seasonally adjusted earnings over the last three months compared with the same period one year earlier.

CHART 2.2.8

Unemployment rates[a] by sex and age group in the European Union, euro area and the United States, 1991-2000
(Per cent)

A: Total unemployment

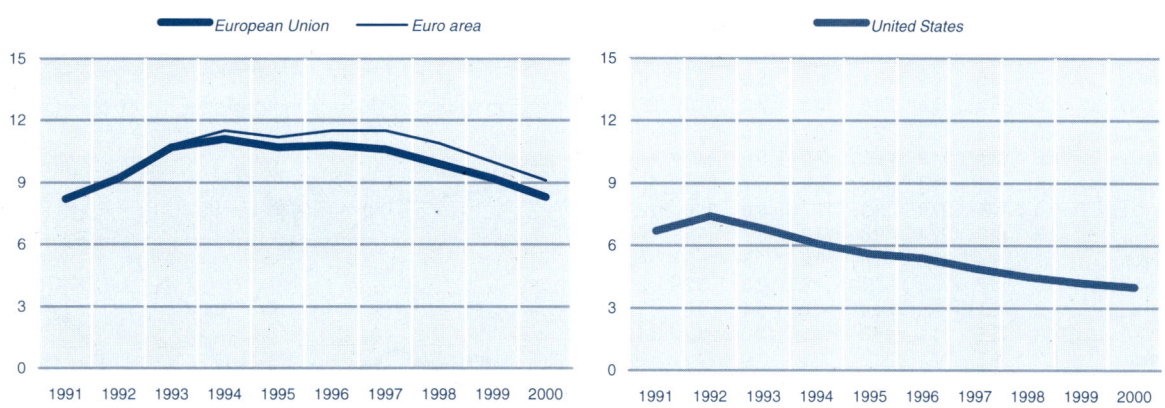

B: Unemployment by sex

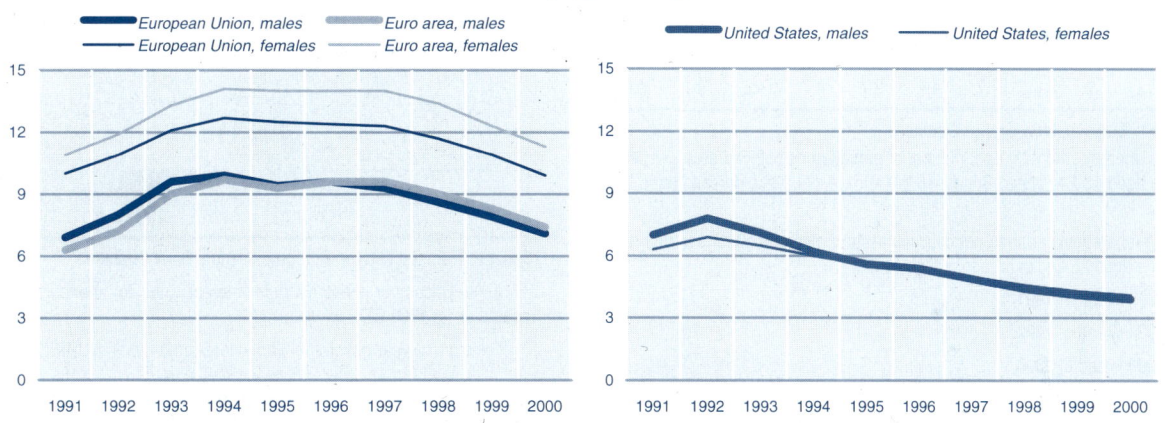

C: Unemployment by age group

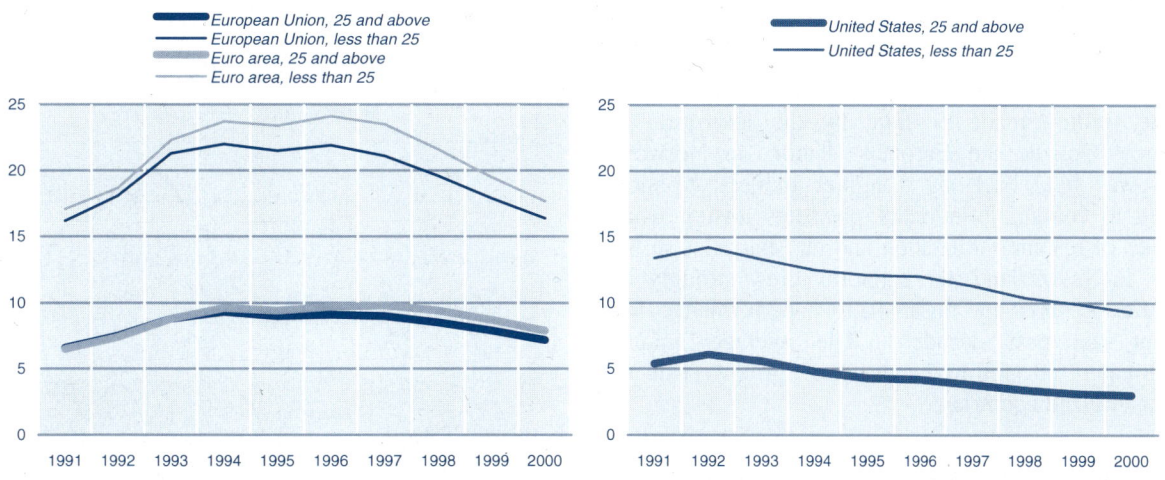

Source: Eurostat, New Cronos Database.

[a] As per cent of labour force in relevant category. Annual averages.

TABLE 2.2.7

Unemployment by age in the European Union, North America and Japan, 1991 and 2000

(Per cent of civilian labour force)

	1991				2000			
	Total	25+	<25	Age gap[a]	Total	25+	<25	Age gap[a]
France	9.5	7.7	21.3	13.6	9.5	8.4	20.1	11.7
Germany[b]	6.6	6.6	6.5	-0.1	8.1	8.0	8.8	0.8
Italy	8.6	5.3	25.9	20.6	10.5	8.0	31.0	23.0
Austria[c]	4.0	3.5	6.3	2.8	3.7	3.5	5.3	1.8
Belgium	6.6	5.4	14.9	9.5	7.0	5.8	17.7	11.9
Finland	6.6	5.1	16.3	11.2	9.8	8.1	21.4	13.3
Greece[d]	7.0	4.6	22.9	18.3	11.7	8.9	31.6	22.7
Ireland	14.7	12.6	22.4	9.8	4.2	3.7	6.5	2.8
Luxembourg	1.7	1.4	3.2	1.8	2.2	1.8	6.0	4.2
Netherlands	5.8	5.2	8.3	3.1	2.8	2.3	5.2	2.9
Portugal	4.2	3.1	9.5	6.4	4.2	3.4	9.0	5.6
Spain	16.4	12.8	31.1	18.3	14.1	12.0	26.2	14.2
Euro area	8.2	6.5	17.1	10.6	9.1	7.9	17.7	9.8
United Kingdom	8.8	7.5	14.4	6.9	5.6	4.3	12.8	8.5
Denmark	8.4	7.7	11.6	3.9	4.7	4.3	7.3	3.0
Sweden	3.1	2.3	7.6	5.3	5.9	5.3	11.3	6.0
European Union	8.2	6.6	16.2	9.6	8.3	7.2	16.4	9.2
United States	6.7	5.4	13.4	8.0	4.0	3.0	9.3	6.3
Canada	10.3	9.1	15.8	6.7	6.8	5.7	12.6	6.9
Japan	2.1	1.7	4.4	2.7	4.7	4.2	9.1	4.9

Source: Eurostat, New Cronos Database.

Note: Unemployment by age: number of persons unemployed as a per cent of persons aged 15-24 (United States: 16-24) and, respectively, persons aged 25 and above.

[a] Difference between the unemployment rate of persons aged less than 25 and persons aged 25 and over (percentage points).

[b] 1992 instead of 1991.

[c] 1993 instead of 1991.

[d] 1999 instead of 2000.

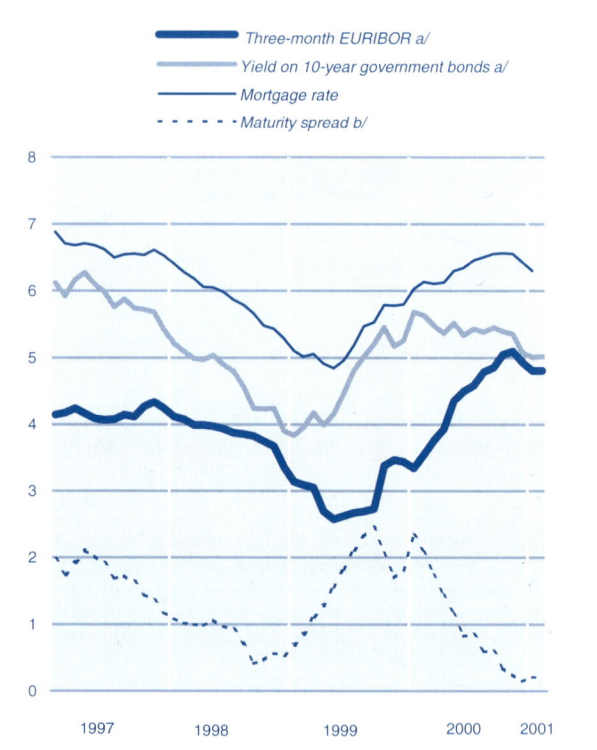

CHART 2.2.9

Short-term and long-term interest rates in the euro area, January 1997-February 2001

(Average monthly rates, per cent per annum)

Source: Eurostat and the European Central Bank (Frankfurt).

[a] Up to December 1998 average interest rates for the euro area were aggregated using 1995 GDP weights.

[b] Yields on 10-year government bond less three-month EURIBOR.

CHART 2.2.10

Interest rate differentials between the United States and the euro area, January 1997-February 2001

(Average monthly rates; per cent)

Source: European Central Bank (Frankfurt).

Note: United States yields less euro area yields.

In the two other EU countries which are outside the monetary union, economic activity picked up in Denmark, supported by buoyant fixed capital formation and export growth. In Sweden, rapid economic growth continued in 2000 supported by an accommodative monetary policy made possible by the low rate of inflation. Outside the European Union, in Norway, growth was held back by a tighter monetary policy designed to contain inflationary pressures arising from high rates of resource utilization and the sharp rise in oil prices. In Switzerland, the economy grew strongly in 2000 after a relatively unsatisfactory performance for most of the past decade. The average annual unemployment rate fell to 2.7 per cent, the lowest of all the industrialized countries.

Among the other economies, economic growth remained significantly above the west European average in Cyprus, Iceland and Malta. Economic growth picked up in Israel, but this was essentially due to favourable changes in real net exports as there was a significant slowdown in total domestic expenditures on account of falling investment.

In Turkey, the government had announced a Three-year Stabilization Programme, which was supported by the IMF within the framework of a stand-by arrangement in December 1999. The objective of the programme was

TABLE 2.2.8

General government financial balances and gross debt in western Europe, North America and Japan, 1998-2000

(Per cent of GDP)

	Financial balances (+)surplus/(-)deficit			Gross debt		
	1998	1999	2000	1998	1999	2000
France	-2.7	-1.6	-1.3	59.7	58.7	58.0
Germany	-2.1	-1.4	1.3	60.7	61.1	60.2
Italy	-2.8	-1.8	-0.3	116.2	114.5	110.2
Austria	-2.3	-2.1	-1.1	63.9	64.7	62.8
Belgium	-0.9	-0.7	–	119.8	116.4	110.9
Finland	1.3	1.8	6.7	48.8	46.9	44.0
Greece	-3.2	-1.8	-0.9	105.5	104.6	103.9
Ireland	2.1	2.1	4.5	55.0	50.1	39.1
Luxembourg	3.2	4.7	5.3	6.4	6.0	5.3
Netherlands	-0.7	1.0	2.0	66.8	63.2	56.3
Portugal	-2.2	-2.0	-1.4	55.3	55.0	53.8
Spain	-2.6	-1.2	-0.3	64.7	63.4	60.6
Euro area	-2.1	-1.2	0.3	73.5	72.0	69.7
United Kingdom	0.4	1.3	4.4	48.1	45.7	42.9
Denmark	1.1	3.1	2.5	55.8	52.6	47.3
Sweden	1.9	1.8	4.0	71.8	65.2	55.6
European Union	-1.5	-0.6	1.2	68.9	68.0	64.2
Canada	0.2	2.2	2.5	116.2	111.6	105.9
United States	0.3	1.0	2.3	68.4	65.3	59.5

Source: Eurostat and OECD.

to reduce the traditionally very high Turkish inflation rate to a single digit figure by 2002. The main pillar of the ambitious disinflation strategy was a crawling exchange rate peg, which linked the lira to a currency basket composed of the dollar and the euro. The crawl involved a pre-announced monthly rate of depreciation in line with the inflation target. The programme was supported by an incomes policy which limited wage growth in the government sector, but this arrangement was not extended to the private sector and public sector enterprises where wage bargaining outcomes "have been slow to adjust to the inflation target".[56] The stabilization programme was embedded in a wider programme of economic reforms designed, *inter alia*, to privatize state owned companies, increase competition in product markets and improve fiscal transparency. The announcement of the agreement with the IMF led to a sharp fall in interest rates in early 2000 while the deceleration in actual and expected inflation was much less. As a result there was a marked decline in real interest rates, which stimulated consumer and business expenditures. In addition, exports strengthened markedly on the back of the marked upturn in world output growth. As a result, there was a considerable rebound in economic activity in 2000: real GDP rose by about 7 per cent in 2000, more than reversing the sharp fall in output by 5 per cent in 1999. The average annual inflation rate fell to some 49 per cent in 2000, down from 65 per cent in 1999, but the 25 per cent inflation target for December 2000 (year-on-year) was overshot by nearly 10 percentage points. Tight fiscal policies contributed to a substantial decline in the government budget deficit, with the primary balance moving into a considerable surplus compared with a deficit in 1999. The main blot on this favourable macroeconomic performance was a sharp rise in the current account deficit to some 5 per cent of GDP in 2000, up from 0.8 per cent in 1999. This rapid deterioration in the external balance reflects the high import content of domestic demand, the sharp rise in oil prices and the pronounced real appreciation of the lira. In fact, the real effective exchange rate rose by 14.1 per cent in the 12 months to September 2000.[57]

For most of 2000 there were no problems in financing the large current account deficit with short-term private capital inflows and government borrowing abroad. Local commercial banks borrowed abroad in foreign currency to exploit the arbitrage opportunities provided by the differential with foreign interest rates, which was not covered by the pre-announced nominal depreciation of the currency.[58] Tensions appeared in November 2000 when foreign investors started to worry about the fragility of the Turkish banking sector, delays in structural reforms and the sustainability of the exchange rate peg, and consequently cut back their lending. The result was turmoil in the financial markets associated with capital outflows (i.e. a loss of foreign reserves), liquidity problems in highly indebted banks, sharply rising domestic interest rates and falling equity prices.

To prevent the stabilization and reform programme from faltering the IMF provided additional resources to alleviate the balance of payments difficulties in December 2000. A domestic political conflict, however, triggered a renewed and sharper financial crisis on 19 February 2001. Considerable capital outflows drove up domestic interest rates to extraordinary levels as the monetary authorities tried to stem the loss of foreign reserves and defend the exchange rate peg, while the banks faced mounting balance sheet problems. In the overnight market, interest rates temporarily reached 7500 per cent. A refinancing of maturing government debt on the basis of one-month treasury bills was only possible at an effective interest rate of 144 per cent per annum. Prices in the equity markets plummeted by 18 per cent on 21 February 2001, and the next day the Turkish government decided to abandon the crawling peg policy and to let the exchange rate float. This led to a sharp depreciation of the lira, by some 30 per cent in the following days, but it also triggered a substantial fall in the very high interest rates and some recovery in share prices. The devaluation has created considerable problems for banks, which had borrowed funds abroad at low interest rates in order to invest them with the prospect of higher returns in the domestic economy. The sharp depreciation has led to a corresponding increase in the amount of domestic currency required to repay the foreign debt and this in turn accentuated the selling pressure on the lira, a process that is reminiscent of the Asian financial crises of 1997.

---

[56] OECD, *Economic Outlook* (Paris), December 1999, p. 175.

[57] This was the last observation available at the time of writing.

[58] UNCTAD, *Trade and Development Report 2001*, box 2.2, forthcoming.

Box 2.2.2
Universal Mobile Telecommunication System (UMTS) licence sales

UMTS is one of the major new third-generation mobile communication systems, which will progressively supplant the current standard, the Global System for Mobile Communication (GSM) as from 2002. UMTS will, *inter alia,* increase the capacity and speed of data transmission, deliver video communications and other wide-band information and allow for more rapid access to the internet from mobile phones.

Two different mechanisms have been used for awarding UMTS licences, namely auctions and tenders, the latter also being referred to as "beauty contests" where governments compare the offers made by candidates. The process of issuing these licences is already well advanced and as regards the EU member states is to be completed by 1 January 2002. In western Europe, the countries in which UMTS licences have already been issued by governments are Austria, Belgium, Finland, Germany, Italy, the Netherlands, Norway, Portugal, Spain, Sweden, Switzerland and the United Kingdom.

Revenues from licence auctions were relatively large in Germany and the United Kingdom, corresponding to 2.5 per cent of GDP in 2000. This revenue constitutes a considerable windfall for the treasuries. In other countries, these windfall gains were smaller although, in general, still relatively large. The outcome was below expectations, however, in Switzerland. Among the four major west European economies only France has opted for a "beauty contest": licences will be awarded at a relatively high fixed cost, which contrasts with the nominal fees charged in Norway, Portugal and Sweden. In Finland, the government decided to award the four national licences free of charge in 1999.

There are some quite large differences in the price charged per licence among the countries within the European Union (see table). It has been suggested that this variation reflects an average degree of implicit subsidization, which would be in conflict with existing EU regulations. Another matter of concern is the considerable amount of debt which telecommunication companies have contracted in order to obtain a licence and which could affect their ability to invest in the infrastructure required for UMTS and to compete with the United States.

UMTS licence sales
(Euros, per cent)

	Method	Revenue (billion euros)	Revenue (per cent of GDP)	Average price per licence[a] (million euros)	Number of licences	Licence awarded
Austria	Auction	0.71	0.3	118	6	QIV 2000
Belgium	Auction	0.45	0.2	113	4	QI 2001
Germany	Auction	50.5	2.5	8 417	6	QIII 2000
Italy	Auction	12.2	1.1	2 440	5	QIV 2000
Netherlands	Auction	2.7	0.7	540	5	QIII 2000
Switzerland	Auction	0.1	–	34	4	QIV 2000
United Kingdom	Auction	36.3	2.5	7 260	5	QIII 2000
Finland	Beauty contest	–	–	–	4	QI 1999
France	Beauty contest	19.8	1.4	4 950	4	QII 2001[b]
Norway	Beauty contest	–	–	0.6[c]	4	QIV 2000
Portugal	Beauty contest	0.1	–	25	4	QIV 2000
Spain	Beauty contest	0.5[d]	–	130	4	QI 2000
Sweden	Beauty contest	–	–	0.01	4	QIV 2000

Source: The UMTS forum website (umts-forum.org) and national statistics.

[a] Revenue divided by number of licences.
[b] Expected date.
[c] Starting fee only. In addition there will be an annual licence fee of 12.3 million euros.
[d] Starting fee only. In addition there will be an annual licence fee of 150 million euros.

Another important issue is the treatment of mobile phone licences and the associated sales revenues in the national accounts as this can affect significantly all the key fiscal indicators, including the government net borrowing/net lending and the international comparability of these indicators. The 1993 SNA and the 1995 European System of Accounts (ESA) do not specifically address this question, for the simple reason that the third generation mobile phone technology was not available at the time the relevant manuals were revised.

The main question to be decided is the nature of the asset which is involved and whether it is leased or sold by the government. It is clear that the transactions involve a non-produced asset, that is, they are assets that are needed for economic activity but which have not themselves been produced. The typical example is land. But mobile phone licences involve two assets: one is the spectrum which is owned by the government, and the other is the licence, an intangible non-produced asset, which is sold by the government to the licence-holder in the corporate sector. The controversial issue concerns the classification of government receipts from allowing use of the radio spectrum. The two main options being discussed are whether to treat the proceeds as a result of (i) rent of the spectrum, or (ii) the sale of an intangible asset (the licence). Depending on the choice, the impact on government finances will differ.

> **Box 2.2.2 (concluded)**
>
> **Universal Mobile Telecommunication System (UMTS) licence sales**
>
> Eurostat has decided that for the EU member states the transactions involved have to be treated as sales of non-financial assets. The proviso is that the licence has to run for more than five years and that the full purchase price is agreed at the time of the transaction. In line with the accrual accounting principle – which, put simply, means that flows are recorded at the time economic value is created – all the proceeds from the licence sales are recorded in the government financial accounts at the time the licence is awarded, irrespective of when payments are actually received. This has led to a significant impact of UMTS licence sales on government finances in some of the EU member countries in 2000.
>
> The alternative approach is to treat the electromagnetic spectrum as a tangible non-produced asset, which is rented from the government for a given period of time. This procedure was suggested by the United Kingdom's National Statistical Office. In line with accrual accounting, this rent would be treated as accruing continuously to the government over the length of the rental contract, independently of the timing of the actual payments made. The impact on the government finances would then be spread out over a longer period of time rather than being concentrated in a single year. The issue remains controversial and a continuing subject for discussion among national income accounting experts.

In mid-March 2001, the government announced a package of structural reforms designed to salvage the economy. These involved, *inter alia*, the consolidation of three loss-making state owned banks under a single supervisory board, the granting of central bank independence, measures to facilitate the liquidation of loss-making banks and a renewed effort to privatize the state telecommunication company. All these measures still have to be approved by parliament. On 19 March 2001, the government reached a framework agreement with the IMF designed to revitalize the stabilization programme of December 1999, but there was no agreement on increased financial support which will depend on the progress with structural reform.

More generally, the Turkish crisis is yet another illustration of the fact that an exchange rate peg is virtually impossible to sustain in the presence of a significant real exchange rate appreciation and a large current account deficit. Doubts about the sustainability of the exchange rate policy are the trigger for capital outflows and associated selling pressure on the domestic currency, which generate the depreciation that investors fear (the well-known process of self-fulfilling expectations) and the monetary authorities want to avoid. But the domestic economic costs associated with the sharp rise in interest rates required to defend the peg can be too high, especially in the presence of a fragile banking sector. The short-term economic outlook for Turkey is now very uncertain and largely depends on the government's ability to forge and maintain a policy consensus on structural reforms, including the consolidation of the banking sector, and the continuation of disinflationary policies.

2.3 United States current account deficit, saving-investment balances and capital mobility

This subsection examines the recent sharp rise in the United States current account deficit and its counterparts, namely changes in national saving-investment balances and associated changes in net international capital flows. This is followed by an examination of the relation between national saving rates and domestic investment in a cross-section of countries in order to gauge the degree of capital mobility.

(i) Current account developments

The record long economic expansion in the United States has been associated with a progressive deterioration in its current account, which has accelerated in the last few years. In 2000, the current account deficit rose above $400 billion, equivalent to some 4.5 per cent of GDP. This unprecedented level of the deficit, both in absolute value and relative terms, compares with a broadly balanced current account in 1991, when the economy started to emerge from recession. It is generally acknowledged that such a large deficit is not sustainable: how long the present situation can last depends essentially on the willingness of foreign countries to invest in dollar-denominated assets. The possibility of a rapid shift of investor sentiment away from United States assets has been a major downside risk to short-term prospects for the world economy over the last two years.[59]

The progressive widening of the current account deficit implies that the United States economy is absorbing an increasingly large share of excess foreign savings (i.e. current account surpluses) in the rest of the world, notably in Japan and western Europe (table 2.3.1). Large current account surpluses have also developed in the Asian emerging markets since 1998, as a result of the economic adjustments made after the financial crises of 1997, and which involved sharply reduced domestic absorption and a shift of resources into the export sector. Last year's surge in oil prices also led to sizeable current account surpluses in the oil exporting developing countries which more than offset the deficit of non-oil exporters. In the event, the United States economy fully absorbed the aggregate current account surpluses of the rest of the world in 2000.

---

[59] UN/ECE, *Economic Survey of Europe, 2000 No. 1*, p. 35.

TABLE 2.3.1

Current account balances, 1997-2000 [a]

(Billion dollars)

	1997	1998	1999	2000 [a]
United States	-140.5	-217.1	-331.5	-418.5
European Union	124.9	90.6	25.1	38.7
Euro area	110.3	87.2	39.9	55.6
Japan	94.1	121.0	106.8	121.2
Industrial countries	85.8	-15.8	-194.1	-224.7
Developing countries	-57.7	-93.6	-24.1	21.1
Newly industrialized Asian economies	9.7	67.9	62.5	51.1
Countries in transition	-20.4	-26.4	-3.8	6.9
World [a]	13.8	-68.8	-162.1	-148.0

Source: IMF, *World Economic Outlook* (Washington, D.C.), October 2000, p. 233, table 27.

[a] Projections.

[b] Reflects mainly errors, omissions and asymmetries in balance of payments statistics.

By definition, current account surpluses of countries or regions must be offset by corresponding deficits in other countries and regions and the world current account balance should therefore be zero. But as can be seen in table 2.3.1 this is not the case. There is a huge world current account discrepancy, which corresponded to some 3 per cent of world imports in 1999.[60] This does not alter the basic fact, however, that there exist considerable external imbalances among the main regions of the world economy. But it does mean that the individual orders of magnitudes should be treated with some circumspection.

The United States current account has been in deficit for most years since the early 1980s.[61] A large deficit developed for the first time in the mid-1980s, reaching a peak of 3.4 per cent of GDP in 1987. Subsequently there was a progressive decline and even a swing into small surplus in 1991 after the economy had moved into recession (chart 2.3.1). The long and robust expansion of the 1990s was then associated with a more or less steady deterioration in the current account, a process which accelerated from 1997. The development of the current account during the past two decades largely reflects variations in the persistent United States deficit in goods trade. Thus, the trade deficit rose from 2.4 to 4.5 per cent of GDP between 1997 and 2000, whereas the current account deficit rose from 1.7 to 4.3 per cent of GDP (table 2.3.2).

---

[60] The main causes of the discrepancy are the recording of exports and imports at different times due to transportation delays, different valuation of the same goods in the country of origin and the country of destination, and underreporting of investment income. But these factors alone cannot explain the sharp rise in the world current account discrepancy in 1999. IMF, *World Economic Outlook* (Washington, D.C.), October 2000, chap. I, appendix II, pp. 46-47.

[61] For a detailed analysis of United States current account developments since 1980, see C. Mann, *Is the United States Trade Deficit Sustainable?* (Washington, D.C., Institute for International Economics, 1999).

CHART 2.3.1

Current account balance of the United States, 1970-2000 [a]

(Billion dollars)

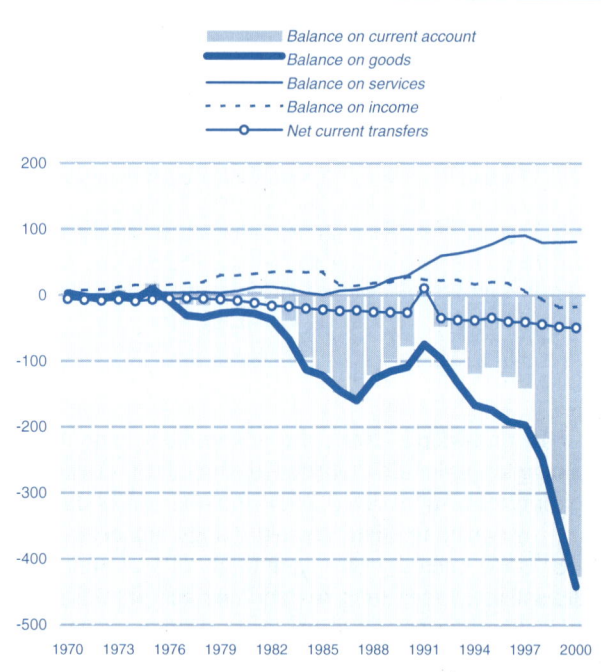

Source: The Executive Office of the President, Council of Economic Advisors, *Economic Report of the President. Transmitted to the Congress January 2001* (Washington, D.C.), pp. 392-393, table B-103.

[a] Annualized data for the first three quarters of 2000.

TABLE 2.3.2

Main components of the United States current account balance, 1970-2000

(Per cent of GDP)

	Goods	Services	Income	Transfers	Total [a]
1970-1979 [b]	-0.5	0.1	0.8	-0.5	–
1980-1989 [b]	-2.2	0.2	0.7	-0.5	-1.7
1990-1999 [b]	-2.3	0.9	0.2	-0.4	-1.6
1990-1995 [b]	-1.9	0.9	0.4	-0.4	-1.1
1996	-2.4	1.1	0.2	-0.5	-1.6
1997	-2.4	1.1	0.1	-0.5	-1.7
1998	-2.8	0.9	-0.1	-0.5	-2.5
1999	-3.7	0.9	-0.2	-0.5	-3.6
2000 [c]	-4.5	0.8	-0.2	-0.5	-4.3

Source: The Executive Office of the President, Council of Economic Advisors, *Economic Report of the President. Transmitted to the Congress January 2001* (Washington, D.C.), pp. 392-393, table B-103.

[a] Differences between totals and the sum of components are due to rounding.

[b] Period averages.

[c] Annualized data for the first three quarters.

The trade deficit has been partly offset by the traditional surplus in services. But the steady rise in this surplus since the mid-1980s has petered out into broad stagnation since 1998. The balance on investment income, moreover, has swung from the traditional surplus into a small deficit since 1998. Net investment income is the difference between the receipts of United States residents from direct[62] and portfolio investments abroad less the corresponding income of foreign investors in the United States. The aggregate deficit since 1998 comprises a (declining) surplus on direct investment income, which is more than offset by an increasing deficit on portfolio investment income. This deterioration reflects the cumulative effects of the persistent current account deficits on the United States net international investment position. Over time, there has been an increasing gap between the market value of foreign owned assets in the United States and the corresponding value of United States owned assets abroad. The difference amounted to some 16 per cent of GDP in 1999, up from some 6 per cent in 1995. The United States net foreign investment position had already turned negative in 1989,[63] but net investment income remained positive until recently on account of the higher returns which United States investors earned on direct investment abroad compared with the far lower return on foreign direct investment in the United States.[64] It can be expected that net investment income will continue to add to the current account deficit given that there is now quite a large gap between the value of United States assets owned by foreigners and the value of overseas assets owned by United States residents. Another burden on the current account has been the traditional deficit on the United States unilateral transfers abroad, but this has remained relatively small and stable, corresponding to some 0.5 per cent of GDP (table 2.3.2).

There are a number of factors that have contributed to the surge in the United States foreign trade deficit since 1991. On the demand side, the more rapid rate of economic expansion of the United States economy compared with its main trading partners led to a strong demand for foreign goods, which by a considerable margin outpaced the demand for United States goods abroad.[65] Protracted stagnation in Japan, moderate growth in Europe for most of the past decade, and adjustments in the Asian emerging markets following the 1997 crises have all tended to restrain foreign demand for United States goods. At the same time, the strong United States demand for imports helped to sustain world output growth. The rising trade deficit was also a "safety valve" which helped to keep inflation at moderate levels despite an increasingly high degree of domestic factor utilization. A specific feature of the United States economy, however, is that its income elasticity for imports is much larger than the response of United States exports to changes in economic activity abroad.[66] In addition, price competitiveness in the tradeables sector was weakened by the real appreciation of the dollar. The real effective exchange rate rose by nearly 20 per cent between 1995 and 2000, and there is wide agreement that the dollar is overvalued.

The strong economic expansion in the United States in the 1990s largely reflected an investment boom. This was driven by a rapid diffusion of information and communications equipment, a process which increased the flexibility of production processes and raised productivity (the "new economy").[67] This surge in demand for investment goods was to a large degree met by imports,[68] the share of capital goods in total imports (at constant prices) rising from 18 per cent in 1990 to 35 per cent in 2000.[69] Just over 70 per cent of this increase was accounted for by IT equipment. The degree to which demand for capital goods imports, notably computers, outpaced the demand for other items is more clearly visible in the very large changes of volume indices (table 2.3.3). When measured at current values, the rise in the share of capital goods is much smaller but it is still substantial. The difference between the changes in real and nominal terms reflects mainly the steep fall in prices for IT equipment and, partly, the appreciation of the dollar. This surge in imports of investment goods has contributed to the overall growth of production capacity, which, in turn, is expected to yield a return on United States assets held by foreign investors.

The economic boom has also stimulated the growth of employment and incomes and a sharp rise in asset prices, the combined effect of which has been to boost consumer demand. Imports of consumer goods were buoyant but more or less in line with the overall volume growth of merchandise imports, their share of the total in both constant and current prices remaining rather stable over the past decade (table 2.3.3).

A broader measure of capital goods that is sometimes used also includes automotive products (cars etc.) and consumer durables. These three categories combined accounted for some 60 per cent of total import volumes in 2000 compared with 50 per cent in 1990 and nearly 55 per cent in 1995. Thus changes in the composition of United States imports during the long cyclical upswing are not, in

---

[62] The purchase of equity by a single owner or affiliated group is recorded as direct investment if it amounts to at least 10 per cent of the voting equity in a company.

[63] This holds when the direct investment position is measured at market values. On a current cost basis, the net foreign investment position turned negative in 1986.

[64] F. Warnock, "U.S. international transactions in 1999", *Federal Reserve Bulletin* (Washington, D.C.), May 2000, pp. 309-310.

[65] This cyclical desynchronization also helps to explain the rapid rise in the trade deficit in the early 1980s, when the United States economy emerged earlier from the global recession of 1981-1982 than its major trading partners.

[66] C. Mann, op. cit., p. 124, table 8.2. The OECD has estimated that the United States has an import elasticity of demand of 2.25. This is much higher than the corresponding values for Japan and the European Union, which fall within a range of 1.5 to 1.75. OECD, *Economic Outlook* (Paris), June 1999, p. 199.

[67] UN/ECE, *Economic Survey of Europe, 2000 No. 1*, sects. 1.1 and 2.2.

[68] M. Pakko, "The United States trade deficit and the 'new economy'", *Federal Reserve Bank of St. Louis Review*, September/October 1999, pp. 11-19.

[69] These figures for shares are only approximate because the use of chain-weighted deflators implies that the sum of components can deviate from the total.

TABLE 2.3.3

Composition of United States goods imports, 1990-2000

(Total=100, indices 1995=100)

	Value			Volume			Volume indices 1995=100		
	1990	1995	2000	1990	1995	2000	1990	1995	2000
Foods, feeds and beverages	5.2	4.4	3.7	6.1	4.4	3.8	93.5	100	152.9
Industrial supplies and materials	15.4	15.8	13.7	16.8	16.0	12.6	70.7	100	140.8
Petroleum and products	12.3	7.4	9.5	12.0	9.1	6.4	88.0	100	126.2
Capital goods, except automotive	22.9	29.2	28.2	17.8	26.2	34.8	45.8	100	237.3
of which:									
Computers and parts	4.5	7.4	7.2	2.3	6.5	11.7	24.0	100	320.5
Automotive vehicles and parts	17.4	16.3	15.8	20.4	16.9	14.6	81.5	100	155.5
Consumer goods, except automotive	20.7	21.1	22.1	22.7	21.7	21.7	70.2	100	179.2
of which:									
Durable goods	11.0	11.1	11.5	12.0	11.3	11.6	71.1	100	183.7
Other	6.2	5.7	7.0	7.1	5.8	6.6	81.5	100	202.1
Total	100	100	100	100	100	100	67.4	100	179.1

Source: United States Department of Commerce, Bureau of Economic Analysis, *National Income and Product Accounts Tables* (www.bea.doc.gov).

principle, unfavourable, but the key question is to what extent the imports of capital goods have contributed to creating economically viable capacity.

(ii) Saving-investment balances

The United States current account deficit implies that total domestic spending on final goods and services (absorption) is higher than total national income or, in other words, that national savings are lower than domestic investment. This follows from the financing constraint of open economies, which is defined by the following national accounts identity:

$$(Sp-Ip) + (T-G) = (X-M) - Tr \quad \ldots (1)$$

where Sp = private saving, Ip = private investment, T = taxes, G = government expenditures, X (M) = exports (imports) of goods and services including factor payments and Tr = net transfer payments paid to the rest of the world. The second term on the left hand side of equation (1) is government savings (Sg), i.e. the general government budget surplus or deficit. The term on the right hand side is equal to the current account balance (CA). Since total national saving (S) is equal to the sum of private sector and government saving:[70]

$$S-I = CA \quad \ldots (2)$$

A country with a current account surplus has more savings than required to finance its domestic investment, the surplus being invested abroad (i.e. there is an export of capital). Conversely, in a case of a current account deficit, national saving is smaller than domestic investment, and capital is imported to finance the shortfall. Given that the current account balance is equal to the change in claims or liabilities against the rest of the world it is also referred to as net foreign investment. It also follows from equation (1) that private savings can be invested at home (to finance domestic investment and a government budget deficit) or abroad.

Equation (1) is a mathematical identity which always holds. The mechanism of balances[71] implies that the magnitude of a change in any one of them must have an exact counterpart in a change of either one or both of the other two. Thus, for a given private sector financial balance, an increase in the government budget deficit has to be matched by a deterioration in the current account position. Of course, private sector and government financial balances are not independent since a change in one can affect the other. In fact, all three balances are determined simultaneously. More generally, this means that it is important to understand the factors which influence saving and investment decisions in both the private and public sectors at home and abroad. This is briefly illustrated by a comparison of changes in the domestic financial balances, which were associated with the emergence of the large current account deficits in the 1980s and 1990s.

In the early 1980s, a domestic investment boom led the United States cyclical upswing from the global recession of 1981-1982. As is normal at such a stage in the upswing, private investment rose faster than private saving leading to a fall in the financial surplus of the private sector (chart 2.3.2). Already at that time the personal savings rate was tending to decline, in contrast with the broadly stable rate for business savings (chart 2.3.3).[72] What was untypical in this earlier period of

---

[70] Note the distinction between *national* saving and *domestic* investment. The first is defined as the difference between national disposable income and consumption. Gross national disposable income is defined as gross incomes from domestic production plus net factor incomes and net transfers received from abroad. Domestic investment refers to gross investment in the domestic economy.

[71] The term is borrowed from W. Stützel, *Volkswirtschaftliche Saldenmechanik* (J.C.B. Mohr (Paul Siebeck), Tübingen, 1958). There is also an intertemporal mechanism of balances, given that a current account deficit, for example, cannot be sustained forever.

[72] Business savings are defined as retained corporate earnings, i.e. after-tax profits less distributed dividends.

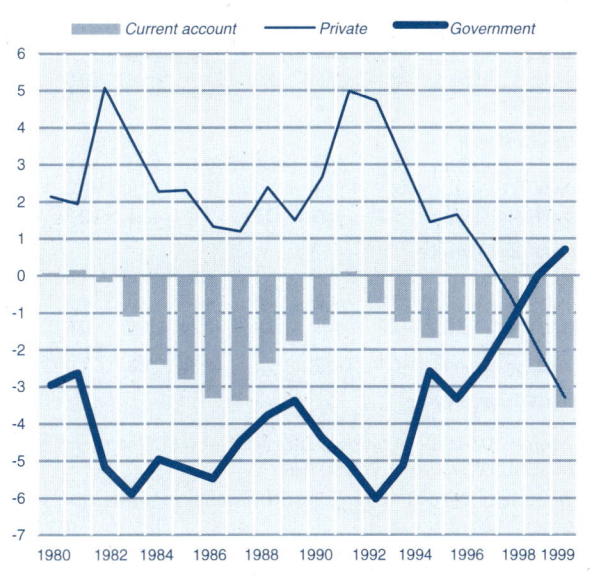

CHART 2.3.2

Private sector and government financial balances and the current account balance in the United States, 1980-2000
(Per cent of GDP)

Source: The Executive Office of the President, Council of Economic Advisors, *Economic Report of the President*. Transmitted to the Congress January 2001 (Washington, D.C.). Also see text table 2.1.2.

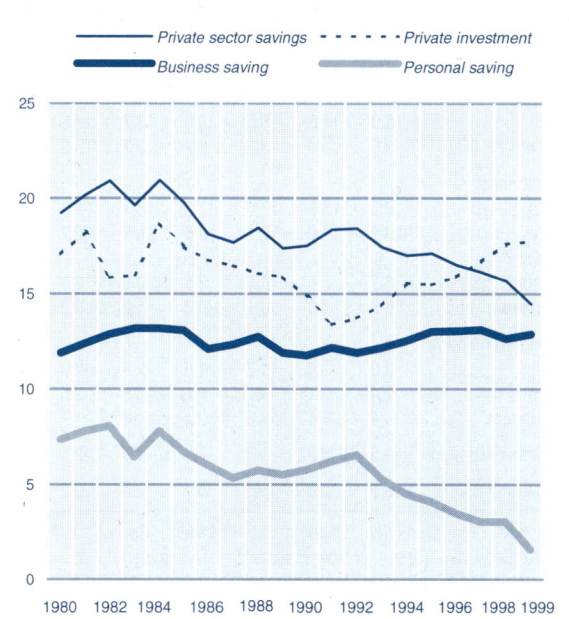

CHART 2.3.3

Private sector savings and investment in the United States, 1980-1999
(Per cent of GDP)

Source: The Executive Office of the President, Council of Economic Advisors, *Economic Report of the President*. Transmitted to the Congress January 2001 (Washington, D.C.).

expansion was that instead of a cyclical improvement of the government finances, which would have tended to offset the fall in the private sector savings-investment balance, there was a sharp rise in the general government budget deficit that more than offset the financial surplus of the private sector. This was reflected in a progressive widening of the current account deficit, which peaked at a level corresponding to 3.4 per cent of GDP in 1987.[73] More generally, this outcome reflected a combination of fiscal stimulus (the Economic Recovery Tax Act of 1981) and high real interest rates, which were partly a reflection of tight monetary policy. This does not necessarily mean that the government was financing its budget deficit with funds from abroad. In fact, the budget deficit was absorbing a large part of private savings, which meant that part of domestic investment was financed by capital inflows, attracted by high real interest rates.

The close association between changes in the budget and current account deficits became known as the "twin deficit" problem, because of the perception that the reduction of the budget deficit would translate into a corresponding improvement in the current account. There was, of course, never an automatic link between these two deficits, and in the late 1980s and early 1990s the current account improved whereas the budget deficit increased. The other important factor which played a role in this development was the sharp rise in the private sector surplus of savings over investment due to increasingly sluggish investment as mirrored in the marked decline of the investment rate (chart 2.3.3).

In the second half of the 1990s there was again an investment boom, but it was sustained for much longer than in the 1980s. The gross investment rate rose from some 15 per cent of GDP in 1990 to about 18.5 per cent in 2000, close to its previous peak of 18.7 per cent in 1984 (chart 2.3.3). There was also a concomitant fall in private savings, largely driven by a steep decline in the personal savings rate (table 2.3.4). In fact, personal savings as a per cent of personal disposable income became slightly negative in 2000. This sharp fall in United States personal savings has been largely associated with the wealth effects of the rise in asset prices, especially real estate and equities, and easy access to mortgages and loans. Consequently, the financial surplus of the private sector fell rapidly and swung into deficit after 1996. This deterioration in the private sector's financial balance contrasts with a steady improvement in the financial position of the federal government, which led to very large budget surpluses in 1999 and 2000. The latter reflected a relatively tight fiscal policy and buoyant tax revenues associated with the cyclical boom, which was sustained by an accommodating monetary policy. The overall improvement of the government financial balance, however, was not sufficient to offset the shortfall of savings in the private sector. The investment boom was therefore increasingly financed by capital inflows, i.e. foreign savings, a process which culminated in the record current account deficit in 2000.

---

[73] The Executive Office of the President, Council of Economic Advisors, *Economic Report of the President*. Transmitted to the Congress January 1987 (Washington, D.C.), p. 110.

TABLE 2.3.4

Gross investment and gross savings in the United States, 1980-1999
(Per cent of GDP)

	1980-1989[a]	1990-1995[a]	1995	1996	1997	1998	1999
Gross investment							
Total	20.5	18.0	18.7	19.1	19.9	20.8	21.1
Private	16.9	14.6	15.5	15.9	16.7	17.6	17.7
Government	3.6	3.4	3.2	3.2	3.2	3.2	3.3
Gross savings							
Total	18.5	16.5	17.0	17.3	18.1	18.8	18.5
Private	19.2	17.6	17.1	16.5	16.2	15.7	14.4
of which:							
Personal savings	6.7	5.4	4.1	3.5	3.0	3.0	1.6
Government	-0.8	-1.0	-0.1	0.8	1.9	3.2	4.0
Savings - investment							
Total	-2.0	-1.5	-1.7	-1.8	-1.8	-2.0	-2.6
Private	2.4	3.1	1.7	0.6	-0.6	-2.0	-3.3
Government	-4.4	-4.4	-3.3	-2.4	-1.3	–	0.7
Net foreign investment	-1.5	-0.9	-1.3	-1.4	-1.5	-2.3	-3.4
Statistical discrepancy	0.5	0.6	0.4	0.4	0.4	-0.3	-0.8

Source: The Executive Office of the President, Council of Economic Advisors, *Economic Report of the President. Transmitted to the Congress January 2001* (Washington, D.C.), pp. 288 and 298, tables B-10 and B-20.

[a] Period averages.

TABLE 2.3.5

Gross savings and gross investment in the euro area, 1980-2000
(Per cent of GDP)

	1980-1989[a]	1990-1995[a]	1996	1997	1998	1999	2000
Gross savings							
Total	21.8	21.7	21.4	21.9	21.9	21.9	22.4
Private	22.1	22.8	22.2	21.7	21.0	20.0	19.9
Government	-0.4	-1.2	-0.8	0.2	1.0	1.9	2.4
Gross investment							
Total	21.9	21.9	20.3	20.1	20.4	20.9	21.4
Private	18.7	18.8	17.7	17.7	17.9	18.4	18.9
Government	3.2	3.1	2.6	2.4	2.4	2.5	2.5
Savings - investment							
Total	-0.1	-0.2	1.1	1.8	1.6	1.0	1.0
Private	3.4	4.0	4.5	4.0	3.0	1.6	1.1
Government	-3.5	-4.3	-3.4	-2.2	-1.5	-0.6	-0.1
Net foreign investment[b]	-0.1	-0.2	1.1	1.8	1.6	1.0	1.0
Statistical discrepancy	..	..	..	..	..	..	..

Source: Direct communications between the UN/ECE secretariat and the Commission of the European Communities.

Note: 1968 SNA until 1994 and 1993 SNA from 1995 onwards.

[a] Period averages.

[b] Difference between gross savings and gross investment.

By definition, the counterpart to the United States current account deficit is a corresponding surplus on the aggregate current account of the rest of the world. The main contributors to this aggregate surplus were the European Union and Japan.

In the *euro area*, the financial surplus of the private sector fell markedly in the second half of the 1990s, the combined effect of rising investment and a falling savings rate. At the same time, restrictive fiscal policies and, in some countries, the favourable development of revenues due to strong economic growth, led to a progressive decline of government financial deficits to near zero in the course of the second half of the 1990s (table 2.3.5). But it should be underlined that the progress in fiscal consolidation was at the expense of a declining public investment rate. In sum, the reduced net borrowing of the government only partly offset the reduced net saving of the private sector (chart 2.3.4).[74] But there still remained a sizeable surplus of national saving over domestic investment, corresponding to some 1 per cent of GDP in 2000, which added to the global pool of excess savings. In contrast, in the 1980s and the first half of the 1990s the euro area had to attract foreign savings to finance a small current account deficit, since at that time a private sector surplus was offset by relatively large government budget deficits. This pattern was broadly the same for all 15 member countries of the European Union, but their aggregate current account surplus was somewhat larger than that of the euro area (table 2.3.6).

In *Japan*, the national savings and investment rates have been traditionally much higher than in the United States and western Europe (table 2.3.7). The high private saving rate reflects to a large degree the strong savings propensity of private households. This has been generally associated with "consumption smoothing" by an ageing population but in recent years it may also reflect the impact of the protracted economic crisis on public finances and the associated uncertainty regarding future incomes. Against a background of relatively sluggish investment, there was a marked rise in the financial surplus of the private sector in the second half of the 1990s (chart 2.3.5). This contrasts with a large swing into deficit of the government financial balance, reflecting the effects of sluggish economic activity on tax revenues and the series of fiscal measures designed to stimulate economic activity. But the government deficit only partly offset the private sector surplus, and so the current account remained in comfortable surplus corresponding to just under 3 per cent of GDP in 2000. The upshot is that Japan has been the largest net provider of financial funds to the rest of the world, especially the United States.

(iii) Financial account developments

The relation between current account balances and national saving-investment balances points directly to the role of international capital markets and capital flows in current account developments. The counterpart to the current account is the financial account[75] and if one is in surplus the other must be in deficit.

---

[74] This recalls the Ricardian equivalence between government debt and taxes, i.e. national savings are not affected by changes in government financial balances because there is an offsetting change in private sector (net) savings.

[75] Traditionally the balance of payments was divided into two accounts, the current and the capital accounts. Recent changes in the methodology for balance of payments statistics has led to a regrouping of international

CHART 2.3.4

Private sector and government financial balances and the current account balance [a] in the euro area, 1980-2000
(Per cent of GDP)

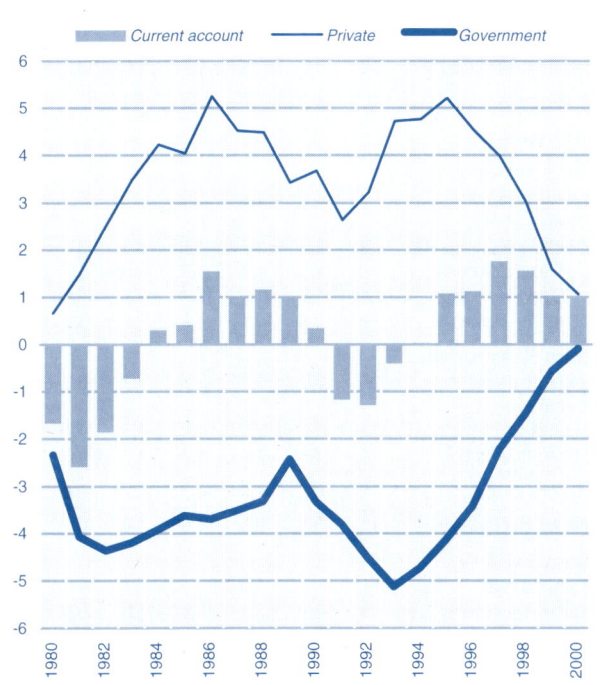

Source: Direct communications to the UN/ECE secretariat from the Commission of the European Communities.

[a] Calculated as the difference between gross savings and gross investment.

TABLE 2.3.6

Gross savings and gross investment in the European Union, 1980-2000
(Per cent of GDP)

	1980-1989[a]	1990-1995[a]	1996	1997	1998	1999	2000
Gross savings							
Total	20.9	20.6	20.9	21.5	21.5	21.4	22.0
Private	21.1	22.1	22.0	21.4	20.3	19.2	19.3
Government	-0.3	-1.5	-1.1	0.1	1.2	2.2	2.8
Gross investment							
Total	21.3	21.1	19.6	19.4	19.8	20.2	20.6
Private	18.3	18.2	17.1	17.2	17.5	17.9	18.3
Government	3.0	3.0	2.4	2.2	2.2	2.3	2.3
Savings - investment							
Total	-0.5	-0.5	1.3	2.1	1.8	1.2	1.4
Private	2.8	3.9	4.9	4.2	2.8	1.3	0.9
Government	-3.3	-4.4	-3.5	-2.1	-1.0	-0.1	0.5
Net foreign investment[b]	-0.5	-0.5	1.3	2.1	1.8	1.2	1.4
Statistical discrepancy	..	..	..	..	..	..	..

Source: Direct communications between the UN/ECE secretariat and the Commission of the European Communities.

Note: 1968 SNA until 1994 and 1993 SNA from 1995 onwards.

[a] Period averages.

[b] Difference between gross savings and gross investment.

TABLE 2.3.7

Gross savings and gross investment in Japan, 1980-1999
(Per cent of GDP)

	1980-1989	1990-1995	1996	1997	1997[a]	1998[a]	1999
Gross savings							
Total	31.7	32.8	31.6	31.0	31.0	29.6	..
Private	26.8	25.7	27.6	27.4	27.4	27.3	..
Government	4.9	7.1	3.9	3.6	3.6	2.3	..
Gross investment							
Total	29.5	30.4	30.0	28.7	29.1	26.7	..
Private	22.9	22.9	21.9	21.7	23.4	20.9	..
Government	6.2	7.0	7.7	6.7	5.7	5.8	..
Savings - investment							
Total	2.1	2.4	1.6	2.3	1.9	2.9	..
Private	3.9	2.8	5.7	5.7	4.0	6.4	..
Government	-1.3	0.1	-3.8	-3.1	-2.1	-3.5	..
Net foreign investment	2.1	2.4	1.4	2.3	1.9	2.9	..
Statistical discrepancy	–	–	-0.2	–	–	–	..

Source: OECD, *National Accounts of OECD Countries: Detailed Tables*, Vol. 2, 1960-1997, 1999 Edition and Vol. 2, 1988-1998, 2000 Edition (Paris).

[a] 1993 SNA. Private sector obtained as the difference between total and government sector.

These two accounts are mutually dependent and the direction of causality can run either way. However, a current account deficit can only arise if foreign investors are willing to extend loans to domestic agents. The strength of the United States economy and expectations of high rates of return provided a conducive environment for private capital inflows to finance the United States' foreign trade deficit. On the other hand, the increasing demand for dollar-denominated assets in the United States also affected the current account via its impact on domestic interest rates and the dollar exchange rate.

Private foreign purchases of United States assets corresponded to nearly 7 per cent of GDP in 2000, twice as large as in 1995 (table 2.3.8). There was a surge in demand for corporate bonds and stocks, partly reflecting the sharp rise in equity prices. In contrast, foreign investors were net sellers of government securities in 1999 and 2000. Over the same period the importance of foreign direct investment (FDI), triggered by expectations of higher rates of return than in other regions of the world economy, increased considerably. Direct investment flows from abroad corresponded to some 3 per cent of GDP in the late 1990s, up from slightly less than 1 per cent in 1995 (table 2.3.8). But this should be kept in perspective. The share of direct investment in total private capital inflows was 43.5 per cent in 1998-2000, which is not substantially higher than the share 38.5 per cent in 1985-1987 when there was also a large current account deficit.

Most of the recent FDI originated in western Europe and has consisted of mergers and acquisitions rather than

---

transactions into three accounts, the current account, the capital account and the financial account. The new financial account records all transactions of the former capital account. The new capital account records a small subset of unilateral transfers (mainly debt forgiveness and transfers of goods and financial assets by migrants as they enter or leave the country), that were previously in the current account. IMF, *Balance of Payments Manual*, Fifth Edition (Washington, D.C.), 1993.

CHART 2.3.5

Private sector and government financial balances and the current account balance in Japan, 1980-1998
(Per cent of GDP)

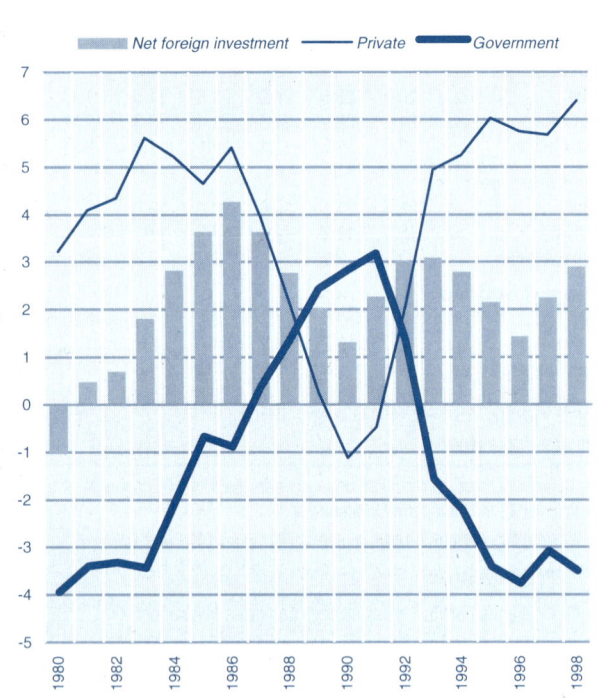

Source: OECD, *National Accounts of OECD Countries: Detailed Tables,* Vol. 2, 1960-1997, 1999 Edition and Vol. 2, 1988-1998, 2000 Edition (Paris).

TABLE 2.3.8

Composition of capital flows in the United States balance of payments, 1985-2000
(Per cent of GDP)

	1985-1988[a]	1995	1996	1997	1998	1999	2000[b]
Current account balance	-3.0	-1.5	-1.6	-1.7	-2.5	-3.6	-4.3
Official capital	0.6	1.3	1.7	0.2	-0.3	0.6	0.5
Private capital, net	2.2	0.2	0.3	3.0	2.0	2.9	3.9
Foreign purchase of United States assets, net	2.2	3.4	4.8	5.4	5.2	6.3	6.9
of which:							
Portfolio	1.3	2.6	3.7	4.1	3.0	3.3	4.0
Treasury security	0.2	1.3	2.0	1.8	0.6	-0.2	-0.6
Corporate bonds	1.1	1.3	1.7	2.4	2.5	3.6	4.6
Direct investment	0.9	0.8	1.1	1.3	2.1	3.0	2.9
United States purchase of foreign assets, net	-0.7	-3.0	-3.1	-2.7	-3.2	-3.0	-2.9
of which:							
Portfolio	-0.1	-1.7	-1.9	-1.4	-1.5	-1.4	-1.3
Direct investment	-0.5	-1.3	-1.2	-1.3	-1.7	-1.6	-1.6
Others	0.7	-0.2	-1.4	0.3	-0.2	-0.4	-0.1
Statistical discrepancy	0.1	-0.1	-0.5	-1.5	0.8	0.1	-0.2
Memorandum item:							
Net international investment position	1.4	-5.7	-6.9	-12.8	-16.0	-15.8	..

Source: United States Department of Commerce, Bureau of Economic Analysis, *Survey of Current Business,* July 2000 and January 2001.

[a] Period averages.
[b] Annualized data for the first three quarters.

greenfield investment.[76] These mergers are not only reflected in the direct investment account but also in the portfolio account in the event they are financed by swapping equity in the foreign acquiring (usually European) firm for equity in the United States firm.[77] The recent financial crises in emerging markets, moreover, led to a (temporary) massive (albeit temporary) "flight to quality" of capital to United States financial markets. All these large net capital inflows, in turn, put downward pressure on interest rates and upward pressure on the dollar exchange rate. While lower interest rates tended to stimulate economic activity and the demand for imports, the appreciation of the dollar restrained export growth. Thus the net effect of the surge in capital inflows was a larger deficit in the current account, which was matched by a correspondingly larger surplus in the financial account (i.e. the former capital account).

At the same time that foreigners were making huge purchases of United States assets, United States residents continued to purchase foreign assets on a considerable scale. These capital outflows were relatively stable, corresponding to some 3 per cent of GDP in every year between 1995 and 2000. The volume of gross flows (the sum of inflows and outflows) was equivalent on average to some 12 per cent of GDP in 1998-2000, more than three times the size of the current account deficit (i.e. the net flows). This compares with gross flows of some 6.5 per cent of GDP in 1985-1987 (the previous episode of a very large external imbalance), which were slightly more than twice the volume of net flows.

(iv) Saving-investment balances and capital mobility

The mutual dependence of the current and financial accounts points to the important role of world capital markets for matching the excess demands for capital in some countries with the excess supply in others. Domestic saving-investment balances must, by definition, be associated with compensating net international capital flows. This suggests that the strength of the correlation between national saving and domestic investment can be interpreted as a measure of international capital mobility.[78]

---

[76] The total value of inward FDI in 1999 is strongly influenced by the Vodafone AirTouch deal and in 2000 by the Daimler Chrysler transaction.

[77] It has been estimated that United States residents acquired $114 billion of foreign equities through this mechanism in 1999. F. Warnock, op. cit., p. 314.

[78] M. Feldstein and C. Horioka, "Domestic saving and international capital flows", *The Economic Journal,* Vol. 90, June 1980, pp. 314-329. The most common alternative measure of capital mobility are interest rate parity tests which, however, are generally only applied to a small subset of financial assets, namely highly liquid short-term financial assets. Also, interest parity tests provide no information per se about the volume of

The basic approach is to estimate the following regression equation for a cross-section of countries for a given time period:

$$(I/Y)_i = a + b(S/Y)_i + e_i \quad \ldots (3)$$

where I/Y = the investment rate, S/Y = savings rate, e is a random error term and i is a country subscript. The estimated coefficient on the saving rate (b) is a "savings retention coefficient" – it measures what proportion of an autonomous increase in savings remains in the domestic economy to finance investment rather than adding to the supply of financial funds in the rest of the world. (Alternatively, b can be regarded as a measure of the proportion of domestic investment that is crowded out by a fall in national saving). In other words, b is an indicator of the degree of international capital mobility. The closer b is to unity, the lower the degree of capital mobility (and the higher the degree of crowding out in case of a fall in national savings). Conversely, in the presence of very high capital mobility b would tend to be closer to zero (and there would be correspondingly only little crowding out). In a world of perfect capital mobility there would be no significant association between national savings and domestic investment: domestic investment would not vary with national saving because there would be an infinitely elastic supply of foreign capital to finance domestic investment.[79]

For a cross-section of 16 OECD countries, Feldstein and Horioka estimated that the savings retention coefficient for the period 1960-1974 was 0.89 and not statistically different from one. The implication is that national borders are major barriers to international capital flows, a finding which has since been known as the "Feldstein-Horioka puzzle" and which has stimulated a plethora of research.[80] Broadly speaking, this research confirms the existence of a robust empirical regularity but also finds evidence for a declining savings retention coefficient in the 1980s and early 1990s (see below). The finding that there is still a strong correlation between rates of national saving and domestic investment, however, is striking as it appears to conflict with the evidence of high capital mobility due to international interest rate arbitrage, the progressive removal of capital controls, and a series of technical and institutional innovations. An important benchmark for assessing the strength of the international saving-investment correlation was the finding that this correlation is very low across regions within an individual country, suggesting that intranational capital mobility is much higher than international mobility.[81]

Critical assessments of this approach to measuring international capital mobility have focused on the role of "omitted variables" such as productivity shocks and demographic factors which could simultaneously affect both savings and investment and therefore explain the long-run correlation of savings and investment even in a context of high capital mobility. Also, if government policies aim to prevent large and persistent external imbalances then this should lead to a close association of saving and investment over the long run. Another factor could be "home market bias", i.e. the propensity of financial institutions to hold a disproportionately high share of domestic financial assets. This could partly reflect asymmetric information between investors.[82] Capital mobility may also be restrained by political and exchange rate risk, although the former is hardly important for industrial countries. It should also be noted that the measure of capital mobility based on savings-investment balances refers to net capital flows; increasing gross flows need not necessarily be accompanied by proportional changes in net flows[83] although the question remains as to why "substantial gross capital flows produce relatively small net capital flows."[84]

To examine changes in saving-investment correlations over time, cross-country regressions of investment rates on saving rates are estimated here using average values of saving and investment rates for various subperiods between 1960 and 1997.[85] The rationale is that

---

international capital flows. For a discussion of different measures of capital mobility, see M. Obstfeld, *International Capital Mobility in the 1990s*, NBER Working Paper, No. 4534 (Cambridge, MA), November 1993.

[79] Ibid. In an environment of high capital mobility there should be a tendency for the marginal product of capital to converge over time across countries. The corollary is that countries where capital is relatively more productive would attract correspondingly more savings and investment. If the determinants of national savings are not related to the productivity of capital then again there should be no systematic relation between national savings and domestic investment provided capital is internationally mobile.

[80] For example, M. Obstfeld, op. cit.; M. Baxter and M. Crucini, "Explaining saving-investment correlations", *The American Economic Review*, Vol. 83, No. 3, 1993, pp. 416-436; J. Coakley, F. Kulasi and R. Smith, "The Feldstein-Horioka puzzle and capital mobility", *International Journal of Finance and Economics*, No. 3, 1998, pp. 169-188; M. Dooley, F. Frankel and D. Mathieson, "International capital mobility – what do saving-investment correlations tell us?", *IMF Staff Papers*, Vol. 34, No. 3, September 1987, pp. 503-530; L. Tesar, "Savings, investment and international capital flows", *Journal of International Economics*, Vol. 31, 1991, pp. 55-78.

[81] J. Helliwell and R. McKitrick, "Comparing capital mobility across provincial and national borders", *Canadian Journal of Economics*, Vol. 32, No. 5, 1999, pp. 1164-1173T (a study on Canada); T. Bayoumi and A. Rose, "Domestic savings and intranational capital flows", *European Economic Review*, Vol. 37, 1993, pp. 1197-1202 (a study on Great Britain); S. Sinn, "Saving-investment correlations and capital mobility: on the evidence from annual data", *The Economic Journal*, Vol. 102, September 1992, pp. 1162-1170 (a study on the United States).

[82] R. Gordon and A. Bovenberg, "Why is capital so immobile internationally? Possible explanations and implications for capital income taxation", *The American Economic Review*, Vol. 86, No. 5, 1996, pp. 1057-1075.

[83] Gross financial flows have tended to remain relatively small in relation to gross domestic asset creation for OECD countries, but it was found that on the basis of this measure the degree of capital mobility has also increased in the 1980s. S. Golub, "International capital mobility: net versus gross stocks and flows", *Journal of International Money and Finance*, Vol. 9, No. 4, 1990, pp. 424-439.

[84] M. Feldstein, "Domestic saving and international capital movements in the long run and the short run", *European Economic Review*, Vol. 21, 1983, p. 150.

[85] The estimates do not cover more recent years because of a break in the series introduced by the recent change in national accounts methodology. Historical time series for savings and investment based on the 1993 SNA are currently available for only a few countries.

TABLE 2.3.9

Changes in the relationship between national savings and domestic investment, 1960-1997

(Regression analysis)

Country group (number of countries)	Industrialized countries (22)		Major economies (7)		Smaller economies (15)		European Union (14)		Euro area (11)		Western Europe (17)	
	b	R^2	b	R^2	b	R^2	b	R^2	b	R^2	b	R^2
1960-1973	0.834 (0.063)	0.897 A/B	0.935 (0.06)	0.980 A	0.715 (0.085)	0.844 A/B	0.740 (0.095)	0.835 A/B	0.633 (0.115)	0.790 A/B	0.786 (0.08)	0.866 A/B
1974-1989	0.658 (0.114)	0.623 A/B	0.789 (0.023)	0.999 A/B	0.582 (0.160)	0.505 A/B	0.726 (0.203)	0.515 A	0.525 (0.353)	0.216	0.656 (0.150)	0.560 A/B
1990-1997	0.565 (0.099)	0.619 A/B	0.753 (0.067)	0.962 A/B	0.389 (0.151)	0.337 A/B	0.607 (0.210)	0.414 A	0.552 (0.411)	0.184	0.491 (0.131)	0.483 A/B
1960-1997	0.713 (0.075)	0.819 A/B	0.831 (0.055)	0.979 A/B	0.591 (0.109)	0.694 A/B	0.760 (0.138)	0.716 A	0.624 (0.234)	0.472 A	0.684 (0.095)	0.776 A/B

Source: UN/ECE secretariat.

Note: Cross country regression analysis. Equation: $(I/Y)_i = a + b(S/Y)_i + e_i$, where I = gross investment, S = gross savings, Y = GDP, e_i = error term. Figures in brackets below the estimated coefficient b are standard errors. A(B) indicates a coefficient which is statistically significantly different from zero (one) at the 5 per cent significance level (t-test). Western Europe: 17 countries, namely EU-15 (excluding Luxembourg) plus Iceland, Norway and Switzerland. Industrialized countries: western Europe plus Australia, Canada, Japan, New Zealand and the United States. Major seven economies: Canada, France, Germany, Japan, United Kingdom and the United States.

long-term averages avoid problems of pro-cyclical movements in the savings and investment rates and possible biases due to a lack of close synchronization of the business cycles of individual countries. Estimates based on long-term averages should therefore provide a measure of the response of investment to a sustained change in savings.[86]

The estimated saving retention coefficients (table 2.3.9) show that there is indeed a strong correlation between saving and investment rates across different groupings of industrialized countries over the period 1960-1997. But there is also evidence that the strength of the relation has become weaker over time. This suggests a greater role of net international capital flows in offsetting a shortfall of national savings for financing domestic investment. Nevertheless, the general result is that the correlation is much stronger than would be expected in a world of very high capital mobility.

There are some interesting variations in the results for different country groupings. For the 22 industrial countries, the savings retention coefficient has fallen from 0.834 in the period 1960-1973 to 0.565 in 1990-1997 (chart 2.3.6).[87] The high coefficient for the period 1960-1973 can be partly associated with the Bretton Woods fixed exchange rate system and the presence of capital controls which limited capital mobility. Similarly, the fall in the coefficient can be explained by the removal of capital controls and increased integration of international financial markets. The results for the sample of 17 west European countries are similar to those for the total sample, the savings retention coefficient falling from 0.79 in 1960-1973 to 0.49 in 1990-1997.

The estimates also point to a stronger association between saving and investment in the major seven economies compared with the group of 15 smaller economies, but in both cases capital mobility has increased between 1960-1973 and 1990-1997. The weaker relation between saving and investment in the smaller economies points to their relatively greater reliance on foreign capital markets for channelling savings to profitable investment opportunities. A possible explanation for this is that smaller economies tend to have a relatively smaller "supply" of profitable investment projects than larger economies, which leads to a proportionately larger outflow of capital.[88] Taken at face value, the results suggest that in the period 1990-1997 an increase in the national savings of the smaller economies by 1 percentage point was associated with an increase in domestic investment by only 0.4 per cent. The resulting excess saving was channelled to the international capital market. Conversely, a fall in national saving by 1 percentage point was associated with a decline in investment by only 0.4 percentage points, suggesting that foreign capital markets represented a ready source of financing for a shortfall in domestic savings.[89]

---

[86] M. Feldstein and C. Horioka, loc. cit.

[87] The difference between both coefficients is statistically significant, corresponding to more than twice their respective standard errors. But the coefficients for 1974-1989 and 1990-1997 differ by less than twice their respective standard errors. For all regressions the null hypothesis of zero correlation between savings and investment is rejected.

[88] A. Harberger, "Vignettes on the world capital market", *The American Economic Review*, Vol. 70, May 1980, pp. 331-337. Harberger argued that the original Feldstein-Horioka finding reflected a large country bias rather than low capital mobility. On the other hand, two of the major economies (Japan and the United States) are counter-examples to this in the 1980s and 1990s.

[89] This does not necessarily apply to the transition economies of eastern Europe and the CIS. In a world of highly integrated capital markets the pool of global savings should be available to finance investment projects anywhere in the world provided, of course, that the

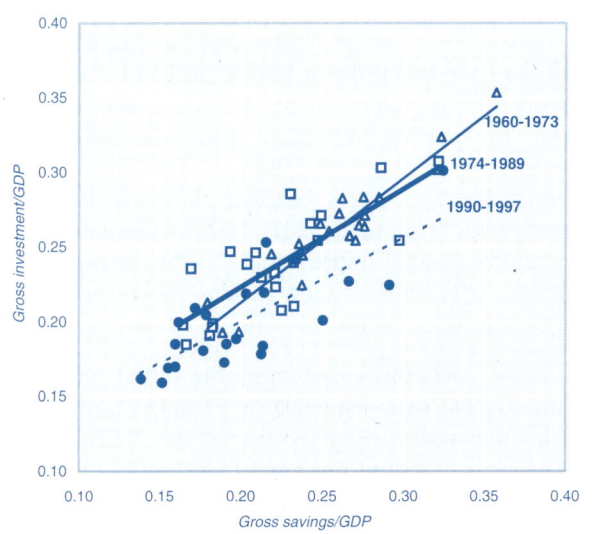

CHART 2.3.6

The changing relationship between national savings and domestic investment, 1960-1997
(Per cent of GDP)

Source: UN/ECE secretariat.

Note: Cross-country regression analysis based on annual data for 22 industrialized countries (see table 2.3.9).

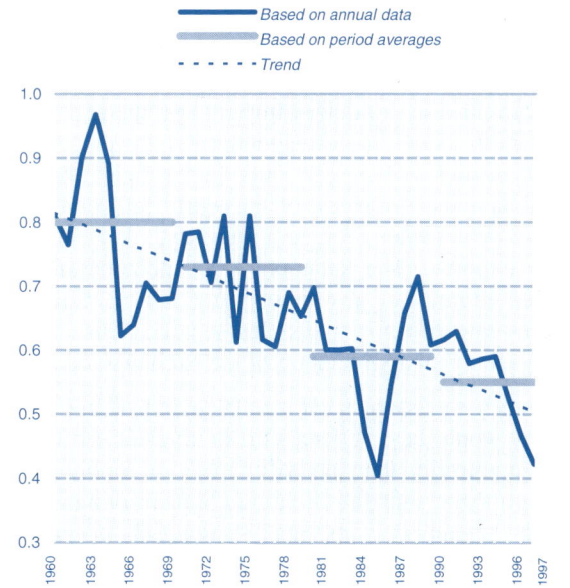

CHART 2.3.7

Savings retention coefficients, 1960-1997

Source: UN/ECE secretariat estimates.

Note: Pooled cross-country regression analysis based on annual data for 22 industrialized countries (see table 2.3.9.) Equation: $(I/Y)_i = a + b\,(S/Y)_i$.

For the member states of the European Union (excluding Luxembourg) there is quite a close relationship between domestic savings and investment for the period 1960-1997 as a whole, but again the correlation has weakened markedly in the post-1973 period, a pointer to increased capital mobility. However, the estimated savings coefficients for the post-1973 period have quite large standard errors which do not support this conclusion. As regards the euro area (11 countries) the correlation between investment and saving for the whole period 1960-1997 is relatively weak, but the estimated coefficient is statistically not significantly different from one. After 1973 the standard errors are so large that neither of the hypotheses that its true value is one or zero can be rejected.[90]

It can be argued that the use of long-term averages for saving and investment rates will tend to impart a downward bias to estimates of capital mobility (i.e. a tendency for b to be closer to one).[91] This is so because the external financing constraint on any economy implies that in the long run the annual current account deficits must sum to zero, because any deficit or surplus will not be sustained indefinitely.[92] The alternative is to use annual data, but these may also impart a downward bias if countries do not have closely synchronized business cycles. The intertemporal approach to the balance of payments, however, would suggest that the use of annual data will yield higher estimates of capital mobility than estimates based on long-term averages of saving and investment. Cross-country estimates for each year of the period 1960-1997 show large fluctuations in the annual savings retention coefficients, but there is a clear underlying downward trend (chart 2.3.7), which broadly matches the same tendency of the coefficients based on the long-term averages of savings and investment rates.[93]

(v) Conclusions

Putting the current account deficit into the broader perspective of national savings-investment balances enables a better understanding of the likely adjustments to be faced by the United States economy and the rest of the world. In the United States, these adjustments involve a combination of increased private savings (mainly a higher personal savings rate), relative to domestic investment and/or a strengthening of exports relative to import demand. The former implies reduced domestic

---

risk adjusted rate of return is competitive. But de facto the role of (net) foreign savings inflows relative to domestic investment is likely to be more limited than for the established market economies given, *inter alia*, the higher risk premia and, partly related to that, the still relatively weak state of financial institutions. See also chap. 4 below.

[90] The estimated coefficients measure the degree of capital mobility between the individual EU (or euro area) member states and the rest of the world, not the degree of capital mobility within the EU or the euro area.

[91] S. Sinn, loc. cit.

[92] The theoretical framework is the intertemporal approach to the balance of payments.

[93] This essentially updates the study by S. Sinn, who estimated these regressions for each year of the period 1960-1988 for 23 OECD countries.

absorption while the latter points to the need to shift resources into the tradeables sector. Both processes will require a real depreciation of the dollar. To the extent that there is spare capacity in the export sector, this adjustment process will be facilitated if supported by strong demand abroad for United States goods and services.

In any case, a significant reduction in the United States current account deficit implies that the rest of the world must have a correspondingly lower current account surplus. This can only be brought about if national savings in the rest of the world fall relative to domestic investment, or, equivalently, that imports outpace exports. The latter points to the necessity for increased domestic absorption and for a shift of resources into the non-tradeables sector. This in turn will require a real appreciation of the exchange rate.

The main risk to such a rebalancing of the world economy would be a sudden shift in investor sentiment, i.e. the possibility that the willingness of foreigners to make up for the shortfall of United States savings could suddenly evaporate, putting substantial downward pressure on the dollar and upward pressure on interest rates.[94] The high proportion of direct investment in the financing of the current account deficit can, in principle, be viewed as a positive development insofar as it signals a long-term commitment to the recipient country. But the recent surge of direct investment in the United States also appears to have been driven by special factors and cannot be expected to continue at the same rate. Much will depend on the longer-term expectations of investors about the relative rates of return in different parts of the global economy.

Looking at the relative size of saving and investment rates in industrial countries it was found that by far the larger part of domestic investment is financed from national savings. There is evidence of some weakening in the relationship between domestic investment and national saving in a cross-section of countries, suggesting that capital mobility has increased since the 1960s. But the fact that the saving-investment correlations are still close also point to the conclusion that international capital markets are characterized by various imperfections and are not as highly integrated as is often assumed.

2.4 Factor incomes and labour market performance

(i) Introduction

This section analyses unemployment in ECE countries from an international perspective, focusing on its relationship to the distribution of the national income between labour and capital. Traditional analysis focuses on the behaviour of wage rates, an important price in the overall economy, in relation to equilibrium or disequilibrium in the labour market. The alternative approach here looks at the share of wages in output as a source of information about the response of the demand for labour to different shocks that remain essentially unmeasurable.

After 1980 unemployment rates increased sharply in all the ECE countries, reaching peaks of 10 per cent or more of the labour force in most countries (chart 2.4.1). In some of them there were twin peaks in the mid-1980s and the mid-1990s. The Scandinavian countries fared relatively better in the early 1980s, but faced a major crisis in the early 1990s. Thereafter, there was a fairly general improvement in the unemployment position, with the United States and the United Kingdom leading the recovery in the labour markets.

Most economists explained the initial increase in unemployment by a sequence of adverse supply shocks that hit the world economy during the 1970s. Many explanations highlight the impact of the oil price shock in the presence of sticky wages.[95] Notwithstanding this explanation, Blanchard and Wolfers[96] argue that the initial increase in unemployment in the period 1973-1985 was essentially due to the sharp decline in the growth rate of total factor productivity (TFP). According to their estimates, the growth of TFP in the five largest European economies (France, Germany, Italy, Spain, United Kingdom) was around 5 per cent in the 1960s; it fell to some 2 per cent at the end of the 1970s and failed to recover thereafter. How does such a productivity slowdown translate into higher unemployment? If, for some time, wage increases keep pace with *previous* rates of TFP growth, and if these exceed the current TFP growth rate, then the demand for labour may well decline, a result of what Stiglitz calls the "wage-aspiration effect".[97] Of course, this effect can be only temporary: at some moment in time, the rate of wage increase should fall in line with that of TFP variation, and unemployment will fall to its "normal" rate. By contrast, when productivity growth exceeds the aspiration growth rate of wages, unemployment will temporarily fall (this may well have occurred in the late 1990s in the United States).[98]

---

[94] See also the discussion of the short-run outlook in sect. 2.2 above.

[95] See the pioneering text by M. Bruno and J. Sachs, *Economics of Worldwide Stagflation* (Cambridge, MA, Harvard University Press, 1985) and E. Phelps, *Structural Slumps. The Modern Equilibrium Theory of Unemployment, Interest and Assets* (Cambridge, MA, Harvard University Press, 1994).

[96] O. Blanchard and J. Wolfers, "The role of shocks and institutions in the rise of European unemployment: the aggregate evidence", *The Economic Journal*, Vol. 110, March 2000, pp. C1-C33. See also O. Blanchard, "The medium run", *Brookings Papers on Economic Activity*, 2:1997 (Washington, D.C.), pp. 89-157 and "Revisiting European unemployment. Unemployment, capital accumulation and factor prices", ESRI, *Twenty-eighth Geary Lecture* (Dublin), 1997, mimeo.

[97] J. Stiglitz, "Reflections on the natural rate hypothesis", *Journal of Economic Perspectives*, Vol. 11, No. 1, 1997, pp. 3-10.

[98] UN/ECE, *Economic Survey of Europe, 2000 No. 1*, pp. 26-29.

CHART 2.4.1

Unemployment rates and wage shares of output, 1970-1999
(Per cent of labour force, per cent of GDP)

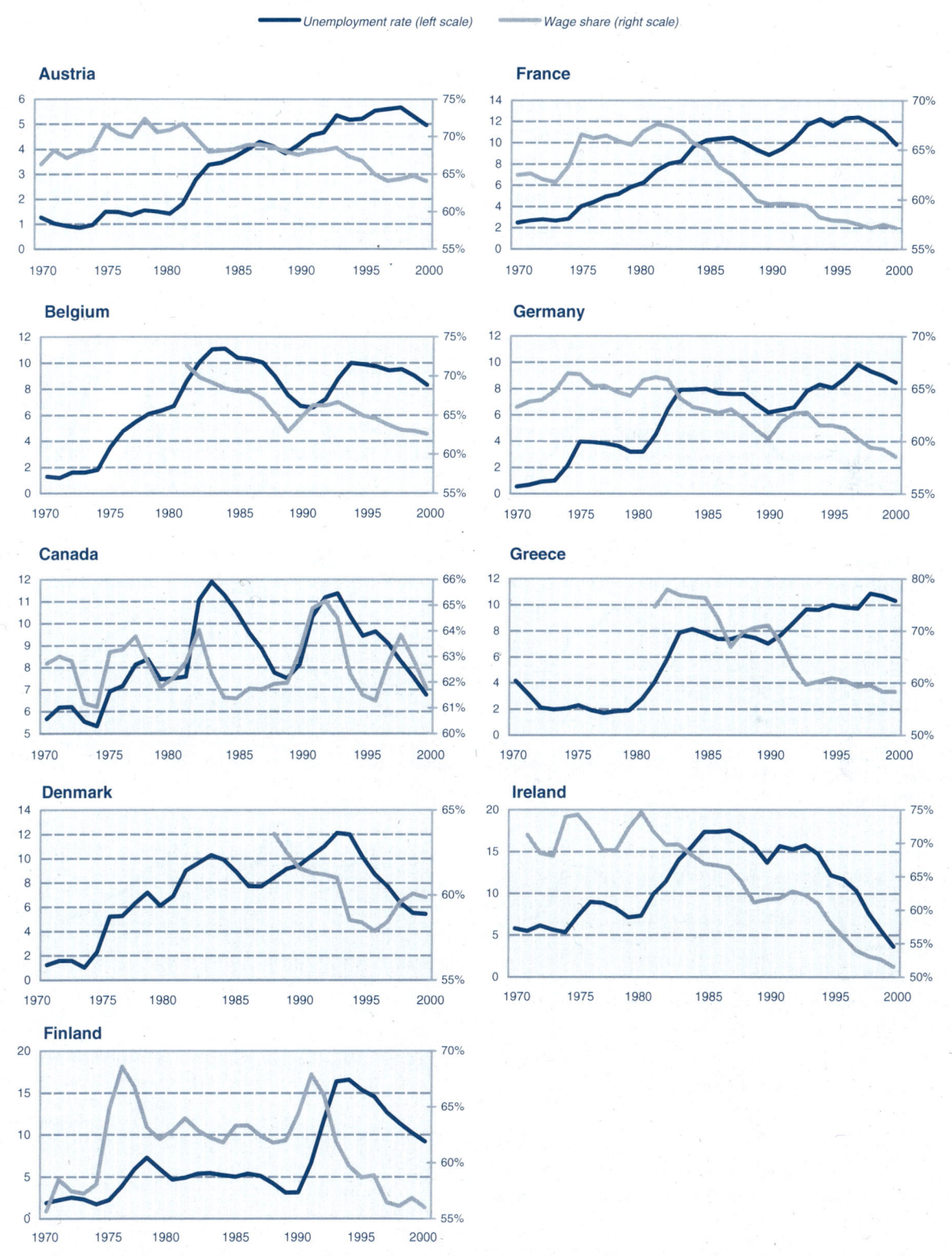

(For source see end of chart.)

CHART 2.4.1 (concluded)

Unemployment rates and wage shares of output, 1970-1999
(Per cent of labour force, per cent of GDP)

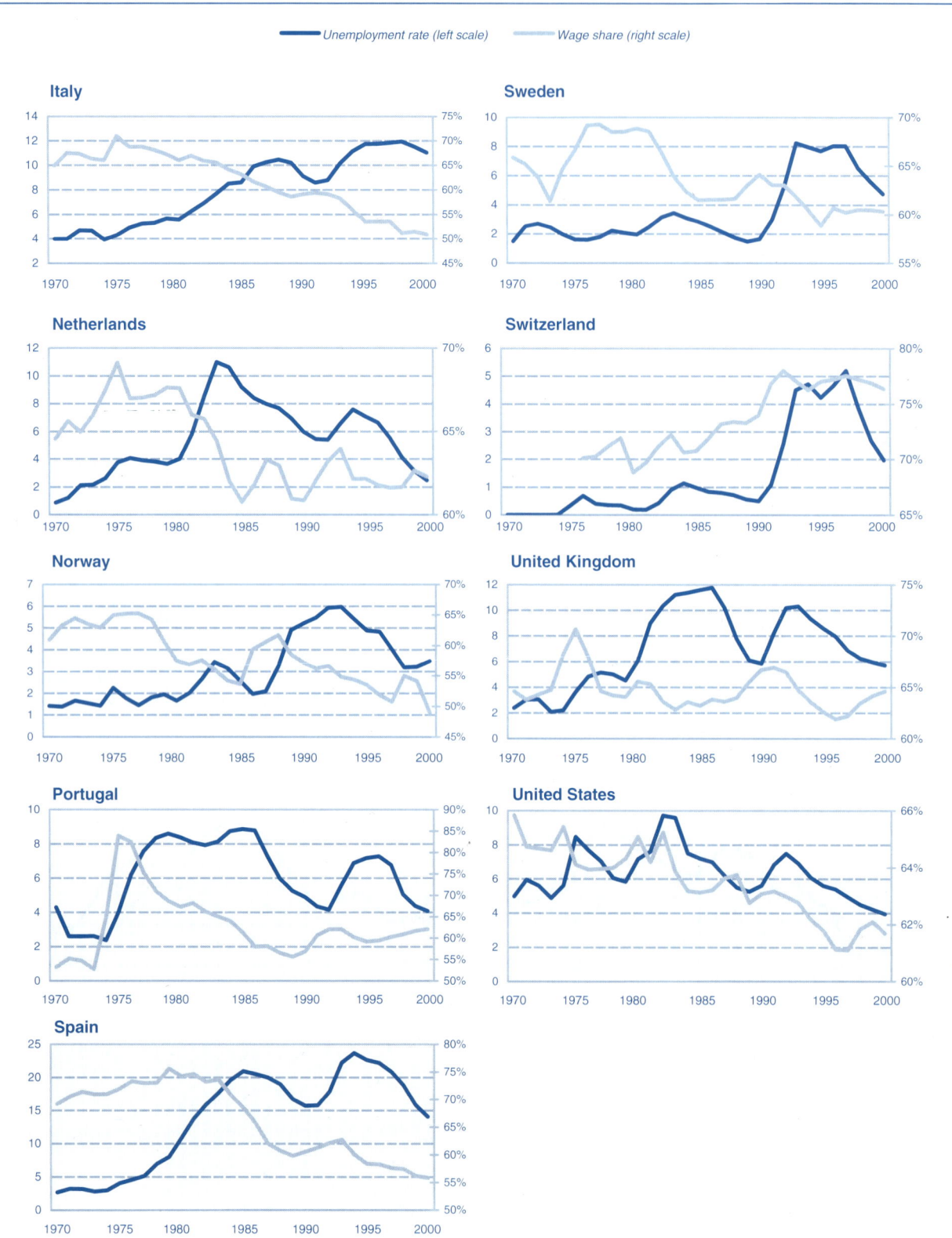

Source: OECD Database; UN/ECE secretariat calculations.

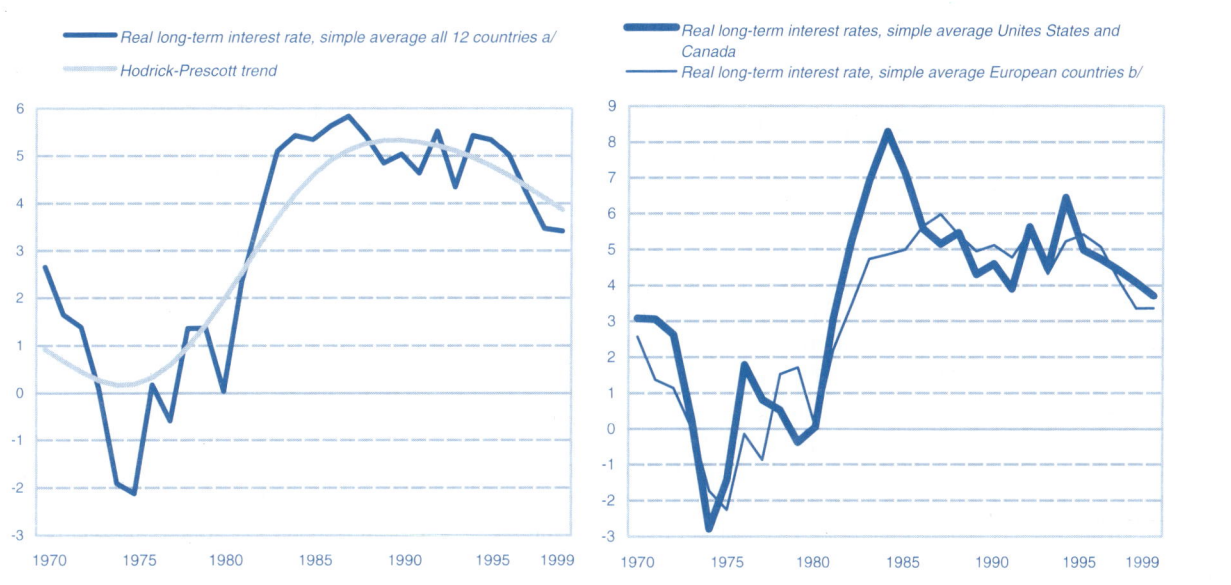

CHART 2.4.2

Real long-term interest rates, 1970-1999
(Per cent)

Source: OECD Database; UN/ECE secretariat calculations.
Note: Interest rates on 10-year treasury bonds less annual inflation.

a Austria, Canada, France, Germany, Italy, Netherlands, Norway, Spain, Sweden, Switzerland, United Kingdom and United States.

b Selected European countries: Austria, France, Germany, Italy, Netherlands, Norway, Spain, Sweden, Switzerland and United Kingdom.

The post-shock persistence of high unemployment in Europe is widely associated with an assumed high degree of institutional rigidity in the region's labour markets and a consequential slow response of wages to adverse shocks, what Giersch once termed as *Eurosclerosis*.[99] However, other adverse macroeconomic developments may have sustained the high levels of unemployment. For instance, high interest rates and a cyclical fall in the demand for labour could also be responsible for the persistence of high rates of European unemployment during the 1980s and the first half of the 1990s.

Chart 2.4.2 displays the simple average of real long-term interest rates in 12 ECE countries: Austria, Canada, France, Germany, Italy, the Netherlands, Norway, Spain, Sweden, Switzerland, the United Kingdom and the United States.[100] The interest rate increases of the early 1980s affected most of these economies in much the same way.

Given that long-term and short-term interest rates are correlated, the pattern observed in chart 2.4.2 is consistent with what we know about monetary policy over this period. In the 1970s, many governments tried to accommodate the oil shocks with a loosening of the monetary stance. But in the early 1980s, high rates of inflation forced most policymakers to tighten monetary policy and to raise interest rates. In the second half of the 1990s, an improved performance in terms of inflation allowed a reduction in short-term rates.[101]

Why should high real interest rates bring about increased unemployment? In the textbook model of a demand-constrained economy, higher interest rates entail lower rates of investment, which in turn adversely affect aggregate demand and the derived demand for labour. Higher real rates will also discourage investment, thus harming job creation if capital and labour are perfectly complementary. In an economy where firms are free to adjust output, and capital and labour are substitutes, for a constant wage rate, an increased cost of capital will induce labour/capital substitution in favour of labour, but the increase in the price of output may offset the first favourable effect.

In most European countries wage shares increased in the 1970s and then fell back in the 1980s (chart

---

[99] H. Giersch, "Eurosclerosis", in H. Giersch (ed.), *The World Economy in Perspective: Essays on International Trade and European Integration* (Aldershot, Edward Elgar, 1991), pages 260-274 (previously published 1985). See also H. Siebert, "Labor market rigidities: at the root of unemployment in Europe", *Journal of Economic Perspectives*, Vol. 11, No. 3, Summer 1997, pp. 37-54. The usual suspects behind this market failure are efficiency wage considerations, the self-interest of trade unions, overly generous unemployment benefits and separation costs, and excessive minimum wages.

[100] These were obtained by subtracting actual inflation from the nominal yield on 10-year treasury bonds. For these countries a complete set of indicators is available and the following econometric analysis concentrates on this group.

[101] Phelps argues that the increase in world real interest rates in the period 1979-1989 is associated with the increase in oil prices until 1982 but thereafter the link is more with increasing government expenditures and public debt. E. Phelps, op. cit.

2.4.1).[102] In North America, fluctuations in the wage share have been much less significant, and only in the 1990s was a decline clearly evident. What is intriguing is that, while wage shares and unemployment rates increased simultaneously in the 1970s, in the 1980s European unemployment remained high despite falling wage shares. Blanchard argues that a low wage share signals a reduced demand for labour and may therefore be associated with a higher unemployment rate. Why would the demand for labour have declined in the 1980s? He suggests that, in this period, European firms may have at last decided to reduce labour hoarding or to introduce labour saving technologies. In the same vein, increased openness to trade with low-wage regions may have also contributed to boost production in capital-intensive industries and reduced the demand for (less qualified) workers. Of course, for a reduced demand for labour to translate into higher levels of unemployment, some degree of wage stickiness is necessary. In the opposite case of highly flexible labour markets, a reduced demand for labour would bring about lower wage rates and a lower wage share, but not necessarily more unemployment. If a country increases the flexibility of its labour markets, wage rates may decline while employment increases along the labour demand curve. The decline in wage rates would thus be accompanied by a decline in the unemployment rate and, under plausible assumptions about the elasticity of output with respect to labour and the wage elasticity of the demand for labour, by a fall in the share of wages in total factor incomes.[103]

The direct relationship between the unemployment rate and the wage share is shown in detail in chart 2.4.3, which contains scatter diagrams of the two variables for the 18 countries for which the data are available. Also displayed is the regression line when the relationship is significant. It is difficult to discern a clear pattern from direct inspection of these plots. In three countries (Canada, Switzerland, United States) the relationship appears to be positive; it is not significant in three of them (Denmark, Ireland, Portugal), while it is negative in the remaining 11. The wide dispersion of observations around the regression lines indicates that other variables have contributed to the changes in unemployment.

(ii) **The econometric model**

In order to assess the contributions of other factors to unemployment, a panel data analysis was made of a pool of 12 countries for the period 1970-1999. This period contains enough variation in both the explained and explanatory variables to provide for valid estimates. The methodology builds on a fixed effects model that assumes that differences across countries are captured by the country-specific constant term. The dependent variable is the unemployment rate (UR). The selected explanatory variables are total factor productivity (TFP),[104] the real long-term interest rate (IRR), the wage share of output (WS), and the first difference in the inflation rate (DINF), which is taken as a proxy for unexpected inflation.[105]

The general equation is:

$$UR_{tk} = a_{0,k} + a_1 TFP_{tk} + a_2 IRR_{tk} + a_3 WS_{tk} + a_4 DINF_{tk} + e_{tk}$$

where e_{tk} is an error term.

The regression was first estimated by treating wage shares as a country-specific variable in the pool of 12 countries. The signs of the coefficients ($a_{3,k}$) were found to be negative for all the countries, except Canada, the United States and Switzerland (which is consistent with the stylized facts displayed in chart 2.4.3). The basic equation was re-estimated twice, one for just the European countries (excluding Switzerland) and the other for North America (Canada and the United States).

Table 2.4.1 displays the results of the European equation. High real interest rates do have a negative impact on unemployment: an increase in real interest rates by 3 percentage points increases the unemployment rate by about 1.5 percentage points. Thus, following the Phillips curve approach, an inflation shock may stimulate employment. A high rate of TFP growth is associated with a low unemployment rate and vice versa. The regressors include a dummy variable (DUMGER) for German reunification (1 for Germany after 1991, 0 elsewhere), which is also significant. Wage shares and unemployment are negatively correlated: a 5 percentage point reduction in wage shares is associated with a 1.5 percentage point increase in the unemployment rate.

These results are similar to those of Blanchard and Wolfers,[106] who studied the impact of these factors on unemployment in 15 European countries over the period

---

[102] The OECD reports on the average compensation of wage earners, so-called dependent workers. Thus, an approximation of the total wage bill of the business sector (for dependent and self-employed workers) may be obtained by assuming that the self-employed earn roughly the same wages as the dependent ones. To find total compensation the average compensation (of the dependent workers) is multiplied by the total number of workers, to which is added the compensation of government workers, also available in the OECD database. The wage share is obtained by dividing total compensation by nominal GDP.

[103] Denoting the wage share elasticity with respect to wage rates by η_w^{WS}, the output elasticity with respect to labour by η_L^y, and the wage elasticity of the demand for labour by η_w^L, the wage share elasticity can be written as $\eta_w^{WS} = 1 + (1 + \eta_L^y)\eta_w^L$, which is positive for the standard values ($\eta_L^y = 0.6$, $\eta_w^L = -0.5$).

[104] Usually, the TFP growth rate is estimated by the so-called Solow residual, which is the difference between the growth rate of real output and the weighted growth rates of labour and capital, where the weights correspond to the respective shares of the two factors in total income. The formula is $\Delta A/A = \Delta Y/Y - \alpha(\Delta L/L) - (1-\alpha)(\Delta K/K)$, where output Y, labour L and capital K are real variables and $\Delta A/A$ is the variation in total factor productivity. Under the assumption that the production function is homogenous of degree one, the weight α is the wage share of output.

[105] A similar methodology was used by E. Phelps, op. cit., and O. Blanchard and J. Wolfers, loc. cit. Phelps's model focuses on the interest rate impact and does not include the wage share as an explanatory variable. Blanchard and Wolfers' model includes wage shares and interest rates, but not the inflation differential.

[106] O. Blanchard and J. Wolfers, loc. cit.

The Global Context and Western Europe

CHART 2.4.3

Unemployment rates and wage shares, 1970-1999
(Per cent of labour force, per cent of GDP)

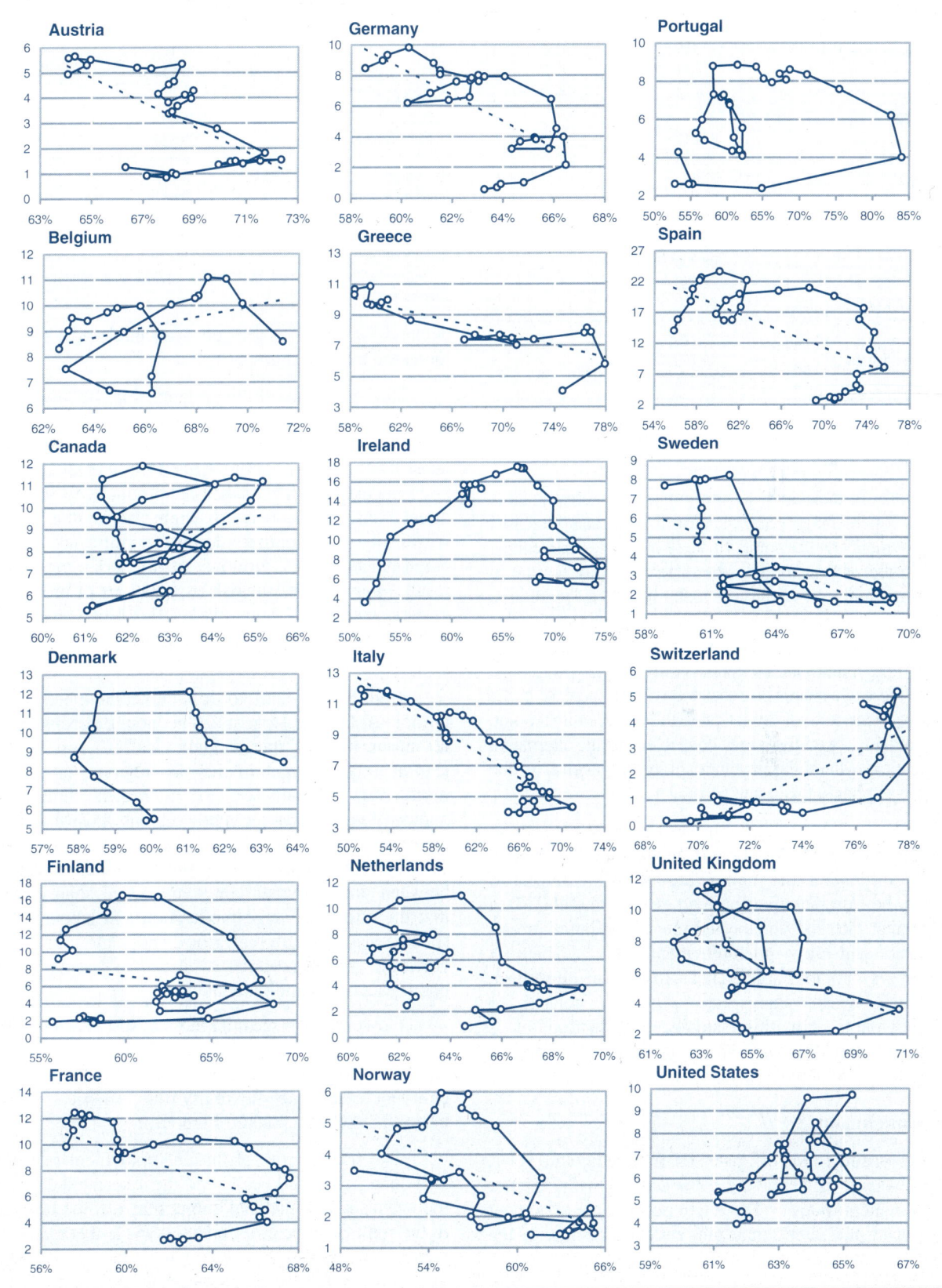

Source: OECD Database; UN/ECE secretariat calculations.

TABLE 2.4.1

European unemployment equation, 1971-1999

Variable	Coefficient	t-Statistic
IRR	0.397	6.48
DINF	-0.175	-2.39
TFP	-0.189	-2.25
WS	-0.321	-6.64
DUMGER	2.513	2.71
Fixed effects		
Austria	23.312	
Spain	35.034	
France	27.029	
Germany	24.007	
Italy	27.243	
Netherlands	25.067	
Norway	20.929	
Sweden	22.950	
United Kingdom	27.300	
R-squared	0.775	
Adjusted R-squared	0.763	
F-statistic	212.814	

Source: UN/ECE secretariat estimates, based on OECD statistics.

Note: Estimation method: pooled least squares; total panel (balanced): 261 observations.

TABLE 2.4.2

North American unemployment equation, 1971-1999

Variable	Coefficient	t-Statistic
IRR	0.288	4.39
DINF	-0.267	-2.98
TFP	-0.199	-2.03
WS	0.459	3.27
Fixed effects		
Canada	-21.250	
United States	-23.384	
R-squared	0.709	
Adjusted R-squared	0.681	
F-statistic	42.194	

Source: UN/ECE secretariat estimates, based on OECD statistics.

Note: Estimation method: pooled least squares; total panel (balanced): 58 observations.

1960-1998. In their analysis, the impact of interest rates is larger: a 3 percentage point increase in real rates increases unemployment by 1¾ points (instead of the 1.5 percentage points in the present model); the difference may be due to their omission of inflation shocks in their regression equation.[107] The Blanchard-Wolfers analysis also emphasizes the negative relationship between wage shares and unemployment, but the impact is smaller: a 5 percentage point fall in wage shares is associated with an increase in the unemployment rate of less than half a percentage point. (They obtain a slightly larger coefficient in an alternative specification where the institutional heterogeneity of the sample is explicitly taken into account.)

Table 2.4.2 presents the estimate of the basic equation for North America (Canada and the United States). In general, the main relationships are similar to those in the European pool: a high growth rate of TFP, a low interest rate and unexpected rates of inflation are all associated with low unemployment rates. There is however a notable difference from the European experience: wage shares are *positively* related to unemployment. In this sample, a reduction of 2 percentage points in wage shares is associated with a 1 percentage point decline in the unemployment rate.

(iii) Conclusion

According to the estimates for Europe in table 2.4.1, lower wages shares are associated with higher unemployment rates. The increase in unemployment rates during the 1980s may thus reflect a decline in the demand for labour as a result of technological shocks or increased trade openness.

But why should the relationship be reversed in Canada and the United States? One explanation points to the outstanding degree of wage moderation during the latest United States boom. After 1995 increases in wage rates persistently lagged behind productivity gains, the direct consequence being a slight fall in the share of wages in total output despite significant gains in employment. This virtuous wage inertia may be the result, *inter alia*, of sluggish expectations of productivity growth, increased labour market flexibility or increased competitive pressures stemming from market deregulation and liberalization of international trade.

Both Europe and North America have been subject to more or less the same macroeconomic shocks; there is no reason to think that technological progress has been significantly different in the two regions; or that they react very differently to increased international competition. Moreover, both regions have extensively deregulated their goods and labour markets since 1980. The opposite signs of the two regional correlations between unemployment rates and wage shares suggest that the effects of wage moderation and labour demand shocks may be different from one region to another. However, further research is needed to disentangle their net impact on unemployment.

However, if wage stickiness is still prevalent in the European economies then, in the light of the above analysis, the fight against unemployment will require either increased wage flexibility (the "American way") or a stimulus to the demand for labour.

The rise and fall of the unemployment rate over a very long period (30 years) and the associated changes in the wage share of national output may also be interpreted in the light of some older business cycle theories. In the well-known model by Goodwin,[108] the unemployment

---

[107] Phelps's analysis refers to 17 countries over the interval 1957-1989. In his equation, a 5 percentage point increase in real interest rates leads ultimately to an increase in the unemployment rate by 1.1 percentage points, E. Phelps, op. cit.

[108] R. Goodwin, "A growth cycle", in C. Feinstein (ed.), *Socialism, Capitalism and Economic Growth* (Cambridge, MA, Cambridge University Press, 1967). See also M. Jarsulic, "Growth cycles in a

rate and the wage share chase each other in a cyclical movement. High rates of unemployment entail low wage shares and large profits that stimulate investment. In turn, more investment creates new jobs, thus reducing unemployment. At some point, the wage share will start to increase following the gains in employment.[109] As profits weaken, investment is reduced, jobs are lost, unemployment rises, wage rates fall and income shares shift again in favour of capital. During the 1980s, western Europe may have been in a phase of the cycle where high unemployment pushed down wages and turned income distribution in favour of capital; today, increased capacity leads to significant employment gains and a reduction in unemployment. However, the North American experience, where unemployment rates fell dramatically despite relatively stable wage shares is at odds with this explanation. If both shocks and cycle theories can account for the observed patterns in Europe, policy recommendations would however differ: in the first analysis, greater flexibility in the labour market or a demand stimulus would help reduce European unemployment; in the second, the cycle is, by assumption, endogenous and little can be done.

2.5 Inflation and interest rate differentials in the euro area

The existence of EMU since the start of 1999 has not eliminated differences in rates of inflation among the participating countries. Controlling inflation differentials is important for individual countries because the exchange rate can no longer be used as an instrument to maintain international competitiveness. This section provides an empirical account of inflation differentials and related differences in real interest rates among countries in the euro area. There is also a discussion of the main factors behind such differentials and their economic implications.

(i) Inflation differentials in the euro area

Inflation differentials among the member states of EMU have persisted since the launch of the euro in January 1999 (table 2.5.1). Differentials in rates of consumer price inflation (relative to the average rate in the euro area) ranged on average from some -0.5 per cent in Austria, France and Germany to nearly 3 per cent in Ireland in 2000. Luxembourg and Spain also had considerably higher than average rates during the past year. The pattern is broadly similar with regard to core inflation (i.e. the consumer price index excluding prices of food and energy products). In Ireland, Portugal and Spain core inflation rates were considerably higher than in other EMU countries. Moreover, these differentials, ranging from 1.6 to 2.6 percentage points above the average rate in 2000, have widened since the launch of the euro. In Greece, which joined the euro area at the beginning of 2001, there has been pronounced convergence of its inflation rate on the euro area average over the past three years. Inflation differentials are particularly large for services, where they range from some -1 percentage point in France to 4 percentage points in Ireland.

Although the range (the difference between largest positive and largest negative) of annual inflation differentials has widened sharply over the past two years, the standard deviations (which take all the values into account, except Greece), generally show only a slight upward tendency (table 2.5.1). The annual averages, however, conceal quite a large degree of volatility in the monthly dispersion of inflation of differentials (chart 2.5.1). In fact, the feature was for a clear upward tendency for both headline and core inflation rates in the course of 2000.

There are a number of factors that can explain the inflation differentials among the member countries of EMU.[110] These include short-term cyclical influences, policy measures, structural factors such as the difference in economic output and trade structures and the associated asymmetric impact of common shocks and, last but not least, differences in real income per capita.

A simple statistical reason is due to differences in the pattern of consumption across countries: these mean that the weights used for aggregating the price changes of the various expenditure items vary from country to country so that even if the price changes for each product category are similar in all countries, the total inflation rates can still diverge. Another reason is that price differentials across countries for internationally traded products do not always reflect factors such as transport costs or indirect taxes. To the extent that fixing exchange rates at the start of monetary union did not fully equate price levels across the common currency area, scope for further price convergence remained after January 1999. The increased price transparency associated with the common currency, in combination with the removal of barriers to trade implied by the Single Market, should via intensified competition lead to a more complete price convergence of tradeables. This process of convergence could also contribute to a temporary divergence of inflation rates, although the overall importance of this factor is likely to be small.

Changes in individual member state's indirect taxation, in administrative pricing or liberalization measures can also lead to inflation differentials. Recent examples are the inflation reducing effects of deregulation of national electricity, gas or telecommunications markets. Changes in indirect taxes (e.g. the introduction of an ecological tax ("eco tax") in Germany or the sharp increase in the tobacco excise duty in Ireland) will have temporary effects on the inflation rate which, on account of the statistical base effect, will disappear one year after

---

classical-Keynesian model", in W. Semmler (ed.), *Competition, Distribution and Non-linear Cycles* (Berlin, Springer-Verlag, 1986) for a standard non-linear model inspired by Goodwin's analysis.

[109] In keeping with traditional Phillips curve logic, as the economy gets closer to full-employment wage increases will accelerate.

[110] ECB, *Monthly Bulletin*, October 1999, pp. 35-44.

TABLE 2.5.1

Annual inflation differentials vis-à-vis average euro area rates, 1997-2000
(Per cent)

	Total				Core				Non-energy				Services			
	1997	1998	1999	2000	1997	1998	1999	2000	1997	1998	1999	2000	1997	1998	1999	2000
Weight in total *(per cent)*	100	100	100	100	86.4	86.3	86.9	87.1	56.7	56.4	55.9	53.4	34.0	34.3	35.3	37.6
France	-0.3	-0.4	-0.6	-0.6	-0.7	-0.6	-0.7	-0.9	0.2	-0.4	-0.5	0.1	-1.0	-0.5	-0.4	-1.1
Germany	-0.1	-0.5	-0.4	-0.4	-0.2	-0.3	-0.7	-0.4	-0.1	-0.4	-0.6	-0.9	-0.1	-0.6	-1.0	-0.4
Italy	0.3	0.9	0.7	0.1	0.9	1.1	0.7	0.8	0.3	0.7	0.7	0.8	0.9	0.8	0.9	0.6
Austria	-0.4	-0.3	-0.6	-0.5	-0.6	-0.3	-0.4	-0.2	-0.8	-0.5	-0.7	-0.4	-0.2	–	-0.3	0.2
Belgium	-0.1	-0.2	0.1	0.5	-0.6	–	0.1	0.2	0.2	-0.1	-0.1	-0.2	-0.7	0.2	0.2	0.6
Finland	-0.4	0.3	0.2	0.6	-0.6	0.2	0.3	0.9	–	-0.4	-0.3	–	-0.7	0.9	0.9	1.8
Greece	3.8	3.5	1.1	0.4	5.2	4.2	1.2	0.4	3.9	3.4	0.9	0.9	6.6	4.4	2.2	0.9
Ireland	-0.4	1.1	1.4	2.8	-0.8	0.3	0.9	2.6	-0.5	0.9	1.0	2.4	-0.1	1.1	2.3	4.0
Luxembourg	-0.2	-0.1	-0.1	1.4	-0.3	-0.2	-0.5	0.8	-0.4	0.2	-0.1	0.3	0.1	-0.2	–	0.8
Netherlands	0.3	0.7	1.0	-0.1	-0.4	0.4	0.9	-0.1	-0.1	0.4	1.0	-0.1	-0.3	0.5	1.0	-0.2
Portugal	0.3	1.2	1.0	0.4	1.0	0.4	1.2	1.7	–	0.5	1.5	0.8	1.7	1.6	1.8	2.3
Spain	0.3	0.7	1.1	1.1	1.0	1.2	1.1	1.6	0.2	0.3	0.9	1.5	1.2	1.6	1.7	1.8
Dispersion measures:																
SD	0.3	0.6	0.7	0.9	0.7	0.5	0.7	1.0	0.3	0.5	0.7	0.9	0.8	0.7	1.0	1.4
WSD	0.2	0.6	0.6	0.6	0.6	0.7	0.7	0.8	0.2	0.5	0.7	0.8	0.8	0.8	1.0	1.0
Range	0.7	1.7	2.0	3.3	1.8	1.7	1.9	3.4	1.1	1.4	2.3	3.3	2.7	2.2	3.2	5.1

Source: Eurostat; UN/ECE secretariat calculations.

Note: Inflation as measured by the HICP. (W)SD – (weighted) standard deviation; range – maximum value less minimum value.

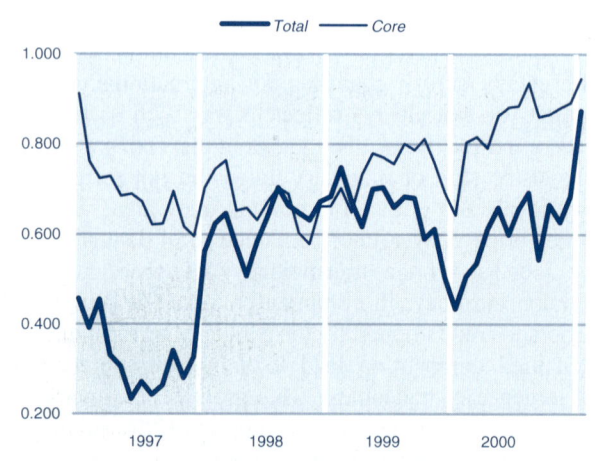

CHART 2.5.1

Dispersion of inflation rates in the euro area, January 1997-January 2001
(Standard deviation)

Source: Eurostat; UN/ECE secretariat calculations.

Note: Weighted standard deviations of year-over-year inflation rates across 11 euro area member states (excluding Greece).

its introduction. Another example is the change in administrative energy prices in Portugal in April 2000, which reduced the domestic inflationary impact of the sharp rise in international oil prices.

A country that is growing more rapidly than other members of EMU can, in general, be expected to have a higher than average inflation rate and vice versa. This points to the importance of cyclical factors, i.e. the level and rate of change of demand relative to capacity output in individual countries. Different positions in the business cycle automatically give rise to differences in the scope for passing on price increases. A major influence is the degree of tightness of the labour market. Increased labour scarcity will tend to put upward pressure on consumer prices through wage inflation. In view of the intense competition in the market for tradeables, this effect will be transmitted mainly via the prices of non-tradeables. A good measure of the cyclical position of a country is the output gap, i.e. the ratio of actual to potential output. In Ireland there is currently a large and positive output gap, which is much larger than that in other euro zone countries. This was reflected in an above average rate of inflation in Ireland in 2000. However, the association between the output gap and inflation is by no means perfect as illustrated by recent developments in the United States, where moderate inflation went along with actual output significantly above potential for quite a long time.

Countries differ with regard to their economic structures, notably their dependence on trade with non-euro area countries. Common shocks, such as the sharp depreciation of the euro against the dollar (or the oil shock), therefore affect individual euro economies asymmetrically. This, in turn, can increase inflation differentials in the short term. These can be accentuated by differential second-round effects, such as wage-bargaining outcomes in response to such shocks. As economies become more integrated, these differences are likely to diminish.

There are some large differences among the EMU member states with regard to their exposure to non-euro area trade (table 2.5.2). The share of non-euro area goods in total imports ranged from about 78 per cent in Ireland to 35 per cent in Portugal in 1999, but this exposure is also quite high (within a range of 40-50 per cent) in most

TABLE 2.5.2

Ratios of non-euro area goods imports to total goods imports and of imports to GDP in 1999
(Per cent)

	Ratio of non-euro area imports to total imports	Ratio of non-euro area imports to GDP
Ireland	77.7	38.8
Finland	61.3	15.2
Netherlands	57.9	29.9
Germany	52.9	11.9
Euro area	48.6	12.7
Italy	48.3	8.9
France	44.2	9.7
Greece	41.8	9.4
Belgium-Luxembourg	40.1	26.3
Austria	32.4	11.0
Portugal	30.8	10.8

Source: Eurostat.

of the other countries. To some extent therefore, the observed inflation differentials across the euro area can be partly explained by the depreciation of the euro.[111]

A good measure of imported inflationary pressures are changes in nominal effective exchange rates. These are trade-weighted bilateral exchange rate indices with a country's major trading partners and they mirror differences in the effective depreciation of the euro in each country since the beginning of 1999 (chart 2.5.2). By far the largest effective depreciation of all the euro area countries is in Ireland, a reflection of its much greater reliance on trade with the United Kingdom and the United States. This indicates that exchange rate developments have a proportionately larger impact on domestic prices in Ireland than in the other countries. In contrast, the smallest decline in the nominal effective exchange rate was in Austria, a reflection of its reliance on intra-area trade (table 2.5.3). Clearly the ultimate direct effect of exchange rate developments on consumer prices will be a function of the share of imports in total output and in the consumer basket and of pricing power in a given market.

While the above-mentioned factors impinging on inflation are not generally persistent over time, there are also longer-term structural influences making for differences in inflation rates across countries. It is well known from economic theory that poorer countries have lower price levels for non-traded goods (e.g. housing and personal services) than richer countries. It is also an empirical regularity that countries which tend to have more rapid productivity growth, and therefore relatively more rapid growth in real incomes per capita, will tend to have higher rates of inflation than other countries. Given that price changes for tradeables will be broadly the same across countries (as a result of international competition), the differential increase in price levels must therefore reflect more rapid rates of increase in the prices of non-tradeables. The mechanism behind this is that an increase in productivity in the tradeable sector will lead to at most a proportional increase in wages and therefore leave the prices of tradeables unaffected. But competition in labour markets will drive up wages in the non-tradeable sector which, in general, will not be matched by corresponding productivity gains. The result is an increase in the prices of non-tradeables and in the overall price level in the economy. Put differently, if the nominal exchange rate is fixed the country experiences a real appreciation. This mechanism is known as the Balassa-Samuelson effect.[112]

The potential for the Balassa-Samuelson effect to operate in individual countries of the euro area depends on the degree of real convergence already achieved at the introduction of the euro among the various countries. Table 2.5.4 suggests that this "catch-up inflation" should be concentrated mainly in Greece, Italy, Portugal and Spain. It has been estimated that 1999 price level differences explain between 7-13 per cent of the cross-country variation in inflation within the euro area in 2000.[113] Another study found that almost 50 per cent of the change in inflation differentials in the euro area is explained by the variation of the relative price levels in recent years.[114]

(ii) Nominal and real interest rate differentials

Convergence in nominal short-term and long-term interest rates across the euro area began with the run-up to EMU. The start of EMU brought perfect convergence of short-term interest rates (three-month EURIBOR) due to financial arbitrage in the money markets. Longer-term nominal rates (yields on 10-year government bonds) did not mirror quite the same degree of convergence as shorter-term nominal rates, but the remaining differentials are now rather small (table 2.5.5). Long-term rates in the traditional high interest rate countries (Ireland, Italy, Portugal, Spain) fell progressively with the approach of EMU. The difference between the highest and lowest (German) annual average rates among the euro area member countries dropped from 3.1 percentage points in 1996 to only 0.3 percentage points in 1998. Since then, their dispersion has remained more or less constant. On average, the difference between the highest and the lowest monthly nominal long-term interest rate in the euro area was 0.35 per cent from January 1999 to December 2000. Italy, Portugal and Spain have dominated the high end of the long-term interest rate range in the euro

---

[111] Bank of England, *Quarterly Bulletin* (London), August 2000, p. 240.

[112] B. Balassa, "The purchasing power parity doctrine: a reappraisal", *Journal of Political Economy*, Vol. 72, 1964 and P. Samuelson, "Theoretical notes on trade problems", *Review of Economics and Statistics*, Vol. 46, 1964.

[113] J. Rogers, G. Hufbauer and E. Wada, *Price Level Convergence and Inflation in Europe*, Institute for International Economics Working Paper, No. 01-1 (Washington, D.C.), January 2001. The study covered 17 western European countries and Israel. The 1999 price level indices were constructed from the raw price data for 165 goods and services from 26 cities in 18 countries, including the euro area.

[114] J. Pelkmans, D. Gros and J. Ferrer, *Long-run Economic Aspects of the European Union's Eastern Enlargement*, WRR Scientific Council for Government Policy, Working Documents W 109 (The Hague), September 2000.

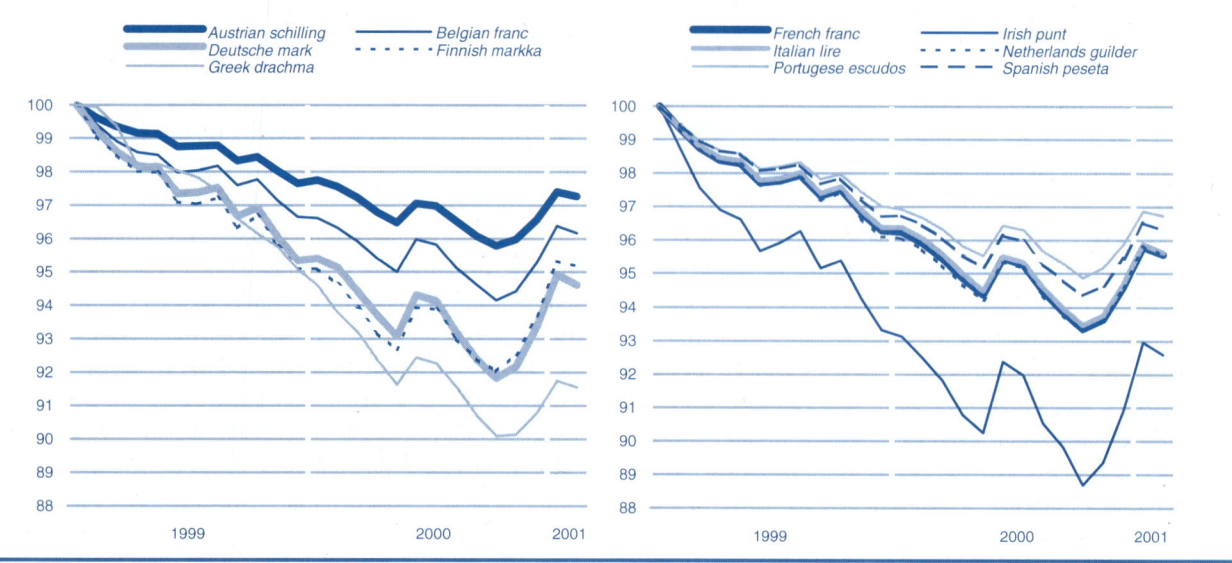

CHART 2.5.2

Nominal effective exchange rates, January 1999-February 2001
(Monthly averages, January 1999=100)

Source: Bank of England website (www.bankofengland.co.uk/mfsd/rates/index.htm#monthly).

TABLE 2.5.3

Changes in nominal effective exchange rates, January 1999 to February 2001
(Per cent)

	Per cent
Greek drachma	-8.4
Austrian schilling	-2.7
Belgian franc	-3.8
Deutsche mark	-5.4
Finnish markka	-4.8
French franc	-4.4
Irish punt	-7.4
Italian lire	-4.4
Netherlands guilder	-4.4
Portugese escudos	-3.3
Spanish peseta	-3.7

Source: Eurostat; UN/ECE secretariat calculations.

area, with average monthly rates within a narrow range of 5.1-5.2 per cent.

The remaining nominal long-term interest rate differentials suggest that the much larger differentials observed within the ERM largely reflected a risk premium for expected depreciation. Given that this risk has been removed with the adoption of the common currency, there now remains only a country risk premium which, however, is rather small. This suggests that formerly high interest rate countries have effectively imported credibility by joining the euro area. It is noteworthy that interest rate convergence has occurred independently of the level of government debt in the various countries. Thus, for Italy, a country with a government debt significantly higher than stipulated in the Maastricht Treaty, the differential over German long-term rates fell, on average, from 3 percentage points in 1996 to only 0.3 percentage points in 2000.

The result is that differences in real short-term interest rates are now only reflecting inflation differentials among the countries of the euro area. Every percentage point of inflation above the euro area average translates one-to-one into a correspondingly below average real short-term interest rate. Since the start of monetary union, Ireland has persistently had the lowest real short-term interest rates and in 2000 the annual average rate was even negative (-1.0 per cent). Similarly, Spain has enjoyed low real rates, its annual average in 2000 being only 0.9 per cent. This contrasts with much higher, positive real short-term rates of 2¼-2½ per cent in Austria, France and Germany in 2000 (table 2.5.5). Given the small country risk premia, differences in the levels and rates of change of contemporaneous real long-term interest rates also reflect predominantly inflation differentials. In 1999, the difference between the lowest and highest annual real long-term interest rate averaged 2.05 per cent and by 2000 this had risen to 3.38 per cent. In view of its high rate of inflation, real long-term interest rates fell, on average, to 0.3 per cent in Ireland in 2000. As in the case for real short-term rates, in Spain contemporaneous real long-term interest rates since the start of EMU have been significantly below average. Conversely, moderate rates of inflation meant that real long-term interest rates in most of the other member countries of the euro area exceeded those in Ireland by 3 percentage points and more.

(iii) Economic implications

What are the implications of inflation and real interest rate differentials for individual countries and for

TABLE 2.5.4

Price level and GDP per capita indices in the euro area, 1998
(EU-15=100)

	Price level index	GDP per capita (in PPP terms)
EU-15	100	100
Germany	109	106
Luxembourg	109	176
Finland	109	101
France	108	99
Austria	105	110
Belgium	98	112
Ireland	97	112
Netherlands	96	114
Italy	88	104
Spain	83	79
Greece	76	68
Portugal	68	72

Source: Eurostat.

the euro area as a whole? Given that monetary policy in the euro area is focusing on the average inflation rate, differentials that do not significantly affect the (weighted) average rate, or do not risk potential inflationary spillovers to other member states, are not a concern for the ECB. This would, in general, be the case for asymmetric inflationary shocks experienced by a smaller economy such as Ireland.[115] But it could become a problem if such an inflationary shock were to hit one or more of the three larger economies or several small economies. Depending on the magnitude of the inflation differentials, therefore, the stance of monetary policy may be too loose for some and too tight for other members of the euro area. In any case, countering idiosyncratic inflationary pressures is left to domestic economic policies in the various member states.

At the individual country level it is important to draw a distinction between temporary and sustained inflation differentials. Concern over differentials is not warranted as long as these remain relatively small and temporary. Also inflation differentials which reflect the productivity gains associated with real convergence, i.e. an appreciation of the equilibrium real exchange rate, can be sustained without a loss of external competitiveness. (The same holds, *mutatis mutandis*, for inflation differentials resulting from favourable productivity shocks in the technologically leading country, which drives up its general price level.) More generally, however, any sustained inflation differential which reflects the unbalanced growth of labour costs and productivity in the tradeable sector will be harmful for a country's competitiveness. If such a higher rate of inflation reflects mainly the increased pressure on resources due to higher activity levels, falling or even negative real interest rates could have a procyclical effect and accentuate inflationary pressures, with the attendant risks of a wage-price spiral. Over time, however, these effects should be offset by a deterioration in competitiveness associated with above average increases in wages and prices. Changes in the real effective exchange rate will therefore act as a self-correcting mechanism which, via adverse changes in real net exports, will lead to a slowdown in economic growth and a reduced rate of inflation.

The problem of inflation differentials may be potentially more important for those member countries of the euro area with real incomes per capita which are significantly below the euro area average, i.e. Greece, Portugal and Spain. This is so, because the Balassa-Samuelson mechanism implies that a sustained, above-average rate of economic growth, which is required for a successful catching up, will be associated with a higher inflation rate than in the rest of the monetary union.[116] On the one hand, the lower real interest rate implied by an above average inflation rate can be expected to stimulate fixed capital formation and thus promote the process of real income convergence. On the other hand, catching up implies that the domestic price of tradeables falls *relative* to the price of non-tradeables. If this spills over into a more generalized increase in wages and prices in the tradeables sector then the result is a real appreciation, which damages international competitiveness with the consequence of a rising current account deficit, falling employment and rising unemployment. The real appreciation could be accentuated by foreign capital inflows, attracted by rapid economic growth, which would further increase the risk of inflation in a context of increasingly scarce domestic resources.

One way to attenuate the real exchange rate effects of a rapid expansion of domestic demand and output is to introduce a restrictive fiscal policy. This faces, however, the traditional problems of timeliness, lags in effectiveness and the redistributive effects of higher taxes and lower government expenditures.[117] Another possibility is an incomes policy designed to restrain wage increases in order to maintain international competitiveness. This has been adopted in several small open economies in western Europe such as Belgium, Ireland and the Netherlands.[118] Moreover, structural reforms in the product, labour and capital markets to enhance the overall flexibility of the economy can help

---

[115] For a more detailed analysis of recent developments in Ireland see sect. 2.6.

[116] This is, of course, a long-run tendency which can be masked temporarily by cyclical factors and monetary shocks.

[117] W. Corden, *Economic Policy, Exchange Rates and the International System* (Oxford, Oxford University Press, 1994), pp. 64-65.

[118] In Belgium a law on international competitiveness stipulates that wage increases in a given period cannot exceed the weighted average of wage increases in three main trading partners, i.e. France, Germany and the Netherlands. F. Abraham, K. de Bruyne and I. van der Auwera, "Will wage policy succeed in euroland? The case of Belgium", *Cahiers Economiques de Bruxelles*, No. 168, 4eme trimestre 2000, pp. 441-480.

TABLE 2.5.5

Interest rates in the euro area, 1996-2000
(Per cent per annum)

	Short-term rates										Long-term rates									
	Nominal					Real					Nominal					Real				
	1996	1997	1998	1999	2000	1996	1997	1998	1999	2000	1996	1997	1998	1999	2000	1996	1997	1998	1999	2000
Euro area	4.7	4.2	3.9	3.0	4.3	2.6	2.6	2.8	1.9	2.0	7.0	5.9	4.7	4.6	5.5	4.9	4.3	3.6	3.5	3.2
Austria	3.4	3.5	3.6	3.0	4.3	1.6	2.3	2.8	2.5	2.3	6.3	5.7	4.7	4.7	5.6	4.6	4.5	3.9	4.2	3.7
Belgium	3.2	3.4	3.6	3.0	4.3	1.5	1.9	2.7	1.8	1.4	6.5	5.8	4.8	4.8	5.6	4.7	4.3	3.9	3.6	2.8
Finland	3.6	3.2	3.6	3.0	4.3	2.5	2.0	2.2	1.7	1.3	7.1	6.0	4.8	4.7	5.5	6.0	4.8	3.4	3.5	2.6
France	3.9	3.5	3.6	3.0	4.3	1.9	2.2	2.9	2.5	2.5	6.3	5.6	4.6	4.6	5.5	4.3	4.3	3.9	4.1	3.7
Germany	3.3	3.3	3.5	3.0	4.3	2.1	1.8	2.9	2.3	2.3	6.2	5.7	4.6	4.5	5.3	5.0	4.2	4.0	3.8	3.3
Ireland	5.4	6.1	5.4	3.0	4.3	3.3	4.9	3.3	0.4	-1.0	7.3	6.3	4.8	4.7	5.6	5.1	5.1	2.6	2.2	0.3
Italy	8.8	6.9	5.0	3.0	4.3	4.9	5.0	3.0	1.2	1.7	9.2	6.7	4.9	4.7	5.6	5.3	4.8	2.9	3.0	3.1
Netherlands	3.0	3.3	3.5	3.0	4.3	1.6	1.4	1.7	0.9	2.0	6.2	5.6	4.6	4.6	5.5	4.7	3.6	2.9	2.6	3.2
Portugal	7.4	5.7	4.3	3.0	4.3	4.5	3.8	2.1	0.8	1.7	8.6	6.4	4.9	4.8	5.7	5.7	4.5	2.6	2.7	3.1
Spain	7.5	5.4	4.2	3.0	4.3	4.0	3.5	2.5	0.7	0.9	8.7	6.4	4.8	4.8	5.6	5.2	4.5	3.1	2.5	2.2
Dispersion measures																				
SD	2.1	1.3	0.7	–	–	1.2	1.2	0.5	0.7	1.0	1.1	0.4	0.1	0.1	0.1	0.5	0.4	0.5	0.7	0.9
Range	5.8	3.7	2.0	–	–	3.4	3.6	1.6	2.0	3.5	3.1	1.2	0.3	0.3	0.4	1.7	1.4	1.4	2.1	3.4

Source: Eurostat; UN/ECE secretariat calculations.

Note: See table 2.5.1. Real interest rates – nominal interest rates less the annual inflation rate.

to create an environment which would allow an economy to absorb shocks less disruptively and to better respond to country-specific shocks.

Finally, inflation differentials are likely to be of greater concern, when countries from central and eastern Europe, with average real incomes per capita substantially below the EU average, eventually join the monetary union. Their accession to the EU is likely to result in greater dispersion of inflation rates than at present, which could complicate the task of monetary policy. Rough estimates suggest that the "equilibrium inflation differential" as a result of the very low price levels in the candidate countries joining the euro area could be some 3.5 to 4 percentage points.[119] Given that the ECB is focusing on the average euro area inflation rate, the implication is that monetary policy would tend to become more restrictive for the core countries with concomitant adverse effects on their economic growth, though these could be partly offset by the increasing trade flows to the periphery and fiscal policy measures. Conversely, given the relatively greater importance of the structural-cum-catch-up component of their aggregate inflation rates, the economically less advanced countries may find the stance of monetary policy required to keep average inflation at its current target level of 2 per cent also inadequate for their own economic conditions; if such is the case, the adjustment burden will have to be borne largely by wage and fiscal policies if the new members are to avoid a decline in competitiveness.[120]

2.6 Ireland: regional economic adjustment in a monetary union

The Irish economy has boomed in the second half of the 1990s. Increasingly tight labour markets have contributed to a sharp rise in inflation in 2000. The combination of unanticipated high inflation and tight labour markets has led to tensions in the long-standing consensual approach to wage policy in Ireland and presented a major policy dilemma for the government. Ireland is facing a regional economic adjustment problem, which cannot be addressed with classical short-run demand management tools (domestic interest rates and the exchange rate) because control over these was lost with entry into EMU at the beginning of 1999. Ireland was reprimanded by the ECOFIN for its 2001 Budget and the associated continuation of pro-cyclical fiscal policy in February 2001. This episode raises some wider issues of policy-making at the broader euro area level, and especially concerns fiscal policy coordination and the need and scope for euro area-wide wage policy. But this section is only concerned with the adjustment problems faced by the Irish economy and possible domestic policy options.

The Irish economy has undergone a fundamental transformation over the last few decades. In the early 1960s, the economy was underdeveloped and dominated by agricultural activity. Today, it is dominated by an export-oriented high-tech sector, which has been the main source of growth over the past decade. High and above average rates of economic growth have led to convergence on the average real per capita income in the European Union.[121] Obviously, catch up is not an

---

[119] J. Pelkmans et al., op. cit., p. 120.

[120] Chap. 3.2 below.

[121] UN/ECE, *Economic Survey of Europe, 2000 No. 1*, chap. 5.

automatic process for a poorer country. The Irish success story reflects the interplay of a host of factors, the relative importance of which is difficult to quantify.[122] These include the progressive opening of the economy, amplified by EU membership and the Single Market process; the attraction of foreign direct investment in the fast-growing high-tech sectors with tax incentives; agglomeration economies and demonstration effects; investment in human capital and the upgrading of physical infrastructure with the support of generous EU structural funds; sound macroeconomic management (since the mid-1980s); the advantages of the English language for multinational companies; and, last but not least, a consensual approach to wage setting which kept wages low compared with the rest of western Europe.

It has been argued that Ireland's success can best be understood when it is viewed not as a national economy but rather as a regional economy[123] with a very elastic supply of labour provided by migration.[124] Put simply, labour was very responsive to the changing economic conditions in the domestic economy. In bad times, part of the surplus labour traditionally emigrated to the United Kingdom and the United States, and in good times this outflow was reversed. The end result was that the rapidly growing export sector could for a long time draw on a pool of surplus labour at home (as long as unemployment was high) and abroad.

The long economic boom has led to markedly improved labour market conditions. This reflected not only the strong growth of the foreign owned manufacturing sector but also the fact that economic activity was increasingly supported by the rapid expansion of the tradeable segment of market services and tourism. Higher real incomes, falling real interest rates and the return of labour from abroad also stimulated housing construction. All these developments led to a substantial increase in employment and a pronounced fall in unemployment. The unemployment rate was 3.6 per cent in December 2000, down from a peak of 15.9 per cent in May 1993 (chart 2.6.1). Such a low rate is probably equivalent to the NAIRU, i.e. the rate of unemployment at which inflation can be expected to accelerate.

As Ireland is a small open economy, inflation is typically influenced by external factors, i.e. changes in

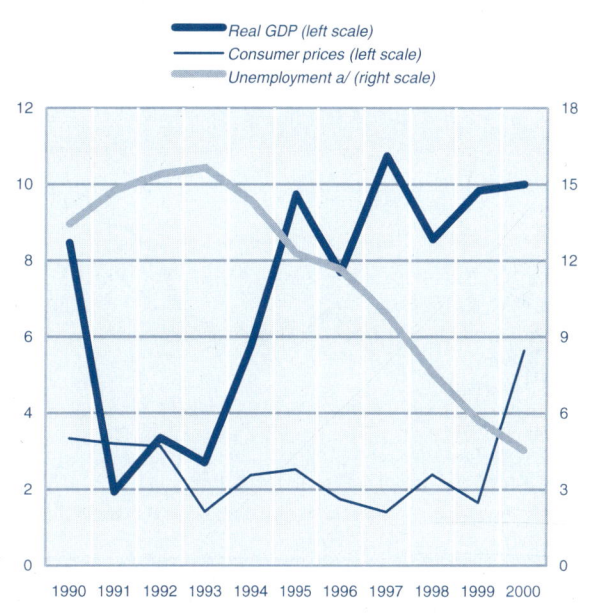

CHART 2.6.1

Real GDP, consumer prices and unemployment in Ireland, 1990-2000
(Percentage change over previous year)

Source: Central Statistical Office of Ireland (Dublin).

a Per cent of labour force.

world market prices of goods and services and the exchange rate. Indeed, as in other member states of the euro area, the surge in oil prices and the sharp depreciation of the euro led to imported inflationary pressures. But buoyant domestic demand and mounting wage pressures throughout the economy also contributed to the sharp rise in consumer prices in 2000. In the fast growing export sector, the higher wages resulting from higher demand for labour were offset by a high rate of productivity growth. But, given the generally tight labour markets, these wage increases raised the pressure for similar rises in the non-tradeable sector, where productivity gains are generally lower. The result was an acceleration in the rate of services inflation, which rose to above 6 per cent during 2000 and was the main factor behind the rise in the core inflation rate (chart 2.6.2). Other indications of strain produced by the boom are increasing transport bottlenecks, a surge in house prices, and growing job vacancies.

In principle, an increase in the relative prices of services and other non-tradeables is the expected result of the Balassa-Samuelson effect.[125] Rising real incomes in the total economy lead to a relatively stronger demand for services,[126] which, in turn, bids up wages and prices in this sector. But Ireland could well be on the verge of a process of unbalanced, rapid economic

---

[122] For a detailed analysis of Ireland's economic growth see A. Gray (ed.), *International Perspectives on the Irish Economy* (Dublin, Indecon Consultants, 1999); F. Barry (ed.), *Understanding Ireland's Economic Growth* (London, MacMillan, 1999); T. Baker, "The Irish economy: then, now and next", ESRI, *Quarterly Economic Commentary* (Dublin), December 1999, pp. 1-12.

[123] A region is generally far more open and therefore much more dependent on foreign trade than a small open economy. In Ireland, real exports of goods and services accounted for some 95 per cent of GDP in 1999. The corresponding import share was 82 per cent.

[124] P. Krugman, "Good news from Ireland: A geographical perspective", in A. Gray (ed.), op. cit, pp. 38-51.

[125] Sect. 2.5 above.

[126] That is, the income elasticity of demand for services is larger than unity.

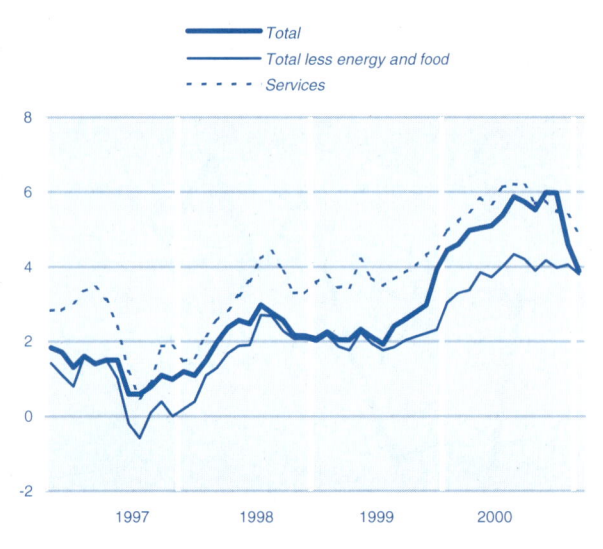

CHART 2.6.2

Consumer price [a] inflation in Ireland, January 1997-January 2001
(Percentage change over same month of previous year)

Source: Eurostat.

[a] Harmonized Index of Consumer Prices (HICP).

growth in which rising prices of non-tradeables spill over to the tradeables sector (as workers' real incomes are eroded) leading to a more generalized wage-price spiral in the economy as a whole. If sustained for a longer period, the resulting real exchange rate appreciation will damage international competitiveness with adverse consequences for the country's long-term growth potential. This is the principal reason why after a long period "of exceptional growth with stable prices, inflation has emerged ... as a pressing policy concern."[127]

Since the late 1980s, the partnership approach to incomes policy has led to series of national agreements[128] that have aimed to ensure rising employment through wage restraint, which, in turn, was rewarded with income tax cuts. Combined with large increases in productivity and favourable changes in the nominal effective exchange rate this policy led to large gains in competitiveness. The mirror image of this was the rising trend in the share of profits in national income. These national agreements covered all pay in the public sector and most pay in the private sector. Although market forces inevitably created wage drift across industrial sectors,[129] the agreements provided an anchor which prevented the stronger wage growth in the tradeable sector (made possible by corresponding productivity gains) from pulling up wages beyond what was regarded as justified by the lower productivity gains in the non-tradeable sector.

This policy of wage moderation, organized in a centralized bargaining framework, was effective with relatively slack labour market conditions and an elastic labour supply. Not surprisingly, it was weakened by market forces once the economy was running up against the constraints of limited labour supply. Not only has unanticipated inflation eroded much of the expected real income gains from the agreed nominal wage growth in 2000, but labour scarcity has driven wage increases in the private sector well above the limit set in the new national agreement which started in 2001.[130]

Full employment has also changed the context for fiscal policy, which besides incomes policy is the only instrument available to *governments* for demand management in a monetary union. At times of lower resource utilization, cuts in income tax (the counterpart to wage moderation) supported not only domestic demand but also – together with the improvement in the overall economic outlook – had a significant supply-side effect in the labour market. This, in turn, dampened the inflationary impact of lower taxes and rising demand. Similarly, rising public capital expenditures, supported by EU grants, increased both supply potential and domestic demand in a context of low and stable inflation. But with the economy reaching a cyclical peak in 2000 and the pool of unemployed labour virtually dried out, an anti-cyclical fiscal policy seemed to be required to avoid overheating. Instead, the Irish government adhered to its pro-cyclical budget for 2001 (while preserving a comfortable financial surplus) and this led to it being reprimanded by the ECOFIN.

Nevertheless, the Irish authorities were faced with a dilemma. Adhering to the terms of the partnership agreement and lowering taxes was likely to add to inflation; but the cancellation of promised tax cuts could also be expected to lead to demands for higher wages to achieve the expected increase in standards of living. The impact on demand of holding back the tax cuts, moreover, would depend on the decision being perceived as permanent and not as a postponement. But if it were perceived as permanent then one of the pillars of the partnership agreements, designed to ensure wage moderation and external competitiveness, would have been effectively removed and the government's credibility seriously compromised.

The effectiveness of demand management will also depend on its supply-side effects. Tax cuts stimulated an increase in labour supply in the past; postponing tax cuts

---

[127] J. McHale, "Options for inflation control in the Irish economy", ESRI, *Quarterly Economic Commentary* (Dublin), September 2000, pp. 43-58.

[128] There have been five agreements so far concluded for a period of three to four years. The latest is the Programme for Prosperity and Fairness for the period 2001-2004.

[129] J. FitzGerald, "Wage formation and the labour market", in F. Barry (ed.), op. cit, pp. 137-166.

[130] The implication is that wages in sectors where the agreement is binding will fall behind. This pertains notably to the public sector and, if not corrected, can be expected to have adverse effects on the supply of skilled labour. ESRI, *Quarterly Economic Commentary* (Dublin), December 2000, p. 38.

could therefore have adverse effects on labour supply and thereby accentuate inflationary pressures. But it is not clear to what extent such an effect is likely in a situation where the unemployment rate is already very low. More generally, this underlines the uncertainties surrounding the effectiveness of discretionary fiscal policy in a very open economy such as Ireland's.[131] The government also faced a dilemma over its commitments to infrastructure spending in the National Development Plan. Supply constraints, notably in the areas of transport and housing, have been accentuating inflationary pressures, but attempts to relieve them with government expenditure will add to effective demand in the short run and thereby raise the inflation rate in the short run whereas the benefits of removing the bottlenecks will appear only in the medium run.

While the inflationary effects of the income tax cuts are estimated to be relatively small, they may be much larger for the planned increases in direct government spending.[132]

While the inflationary pressures arising from increasingly scarce labour resources are generally characteristic of the final phase of a cyclical upswing, it has been suggested that this episode can also be interpreted in terms of the "transitional dynamics" from a lower to a higher growth path[133] which will lead to a "soft landing" once diminishing returns start to set in. But this is very uncertain. If this is indeed the case then the higher levels of infrastructure investment could be seen to support this process rather than accentuating the risks of overheating.[134]

More generally, the achievement of full employment puts into focus the need for greater wage flexibility across sectors in response to market forces and more decentralized wage bargaining. The rigidity of relative wages built into the social partnership programmes seems likely to have restrained the movement of labour from less to more efficient uses. Certainly, the current cyclical position is not the moment to relax the incomes policy as such a move would risk aggravating a wage-price spiral which, in turn, could trigger a "hard landing". From the Irish vantage point there is also another consideration, which argues against the idea of completely abandoning the social partnership programme. This has to do with the central concern about preserving the competitiveness of the export base and, related to that, retaining the attractiveness of Ireland for FDI. It could be argued that these concerns are much better accommodated in a coordinated, economy-wide, centralized, wage-bargaining process.[135] It remains unclear, however, whether this can be reconciled with the recognized need for more wage flexibility to ensure that goods and factor prices can better fulfil their resource-allocating function. But the open question is to what extent the long-standing consensus on economic strategy can be maintained in a fully-employed economy given a "widespread and justified perception that the benefits of success have not been equitably distributed."[136] It also remains to be seen to what extent the still very favourable short-term outlook for the Irish economy will be affected if there is a sharper and more prolonged cyclical downturn in the United States and in the global market for electronic products than currently expected. It should be recalled that Ireland, of all the EMU economies, is the most open to the non-EMU world (see table 2.5.2 in the preceding section) and therefore much more vulnerable to external shocks.

---

[131] OECD, *Ireland, Economic Surveys 1999* (Paris), pp. 94-96.

[132] The effective tax cuts of I£1.2 billion are estimated to add a cumulative 0.3 percentage points to consumer price inflation over a period of three years. A similar increase in government spending would, however, have an inflationary impact, which is about three times as large. ESRI, *Quarterly Economic Commentary* (Dublin), December 2000, p. 36, table C1.

[133] ESRI, *Quarterly Economic Commentary* (Dublin), September 2000, p. 37.

[134] This is part of the "disagreement [between the Irish government on the one hand and the European Commission and ECOFIN on the other hand] which arises from different interpretations of the small, open economy model within the EU economy". M. Harney, "Ireland's misunderstood budget", *Financial Times*, 5 February 2001 (the author is deputy prime minister of Ireland).

[135] J. McHale, loc. cit., p. 54.

[136] T. Baker, loc. cit., p. 9.

CHAPTER 3

THE TRANSITION ECONOMIES

For the first time in a decade all ECE transition economies reported positive rates of economic growth in 2000. The very high average rate of GDP growth for the region as a whole was largely due to the unexpectedly strong recovery in Russia; economic growth rates were at their highest in a decade in a number of other countries as well. All transition economies benefited from the strong demand in their major export markets, and commodity exporters had windfall gains from the surge in world market prices and the improvement in their terms of trade. Most CIS economies benefited from the recovery in Russia's domestic demand, which gave a strong impetus to their exports and contributed to a general revival of intra-CIS trade. While the outcomes in 2000 were rather favourable for the transition economies, their very high dependence on external demand and world markets also point to the potential risks of adverse shocks.

3.1 Expectations and outcomes

The year 2000 was the most successful year for the ECE transition economies since the start of economic transformation in 1989. For the first time in a decade all the transition economies in the region were growing and their average rate of GDP growth was quite impressive: at 6 per cent (table 3.1.1) it was 1.5 percentage points higher than the rate of growth of world output. Also for the first time since the start of their market reforms, the Commonwealth of Independent States (CIS) was the fastest growing regional group among the transition economies: nine out of the 12 CIS economies had rates of GDP growth of 5 per cent or more, resulting in an average of 7.4 per cent for the Commonwealth as a whole. The main engine of the robust recovery in the CIS was the Russian economy where GDP grew by an unprecedented 7.7 per cent in 2000. After a weak performance in 1999, output also recovered strongly in eastern Europe and in the Baltic states, their aggregate GDP increasing by 3.9 per cent and 5 per cent, respectively.

In general these outcomes exceeded (in some cases considerably) the expectations of policy makers in the transition economies: in 19 of the 26 countries for which official forecasts had been published at the beginning of the year (usually in the context of the budgetary process), GDP grew more strongly in 2000 than had been envisaged (table 3.1.1). Part of the explanation lies in the fact that most of the official forecasts for 2000 had been made in autumn 1999 when the robust recovery had not yet started. But, nevertheless, the strength of the economic upturn (especially in Russia and some of the CIS economies) came as a surprise both to the governments of these countries and to independent analysts.

While the strong recovery in the transition economies was a positive and encouraging outcome, their performance in 2000 was largely driven by a sharp and externally driven cyclical component. The ECE transition economies benefited significantly – although to varying degrees – from the strong and diversified demand in their major markets, in the first place for manufactured goods but also for a wide range of primary commodities and semi-manufactures. Competitive exchange rates and, more selectively, favourable world market price conditions added to this positive impact (section 3.6). Although basically all the transition economies enjoyed favourable external conditions in 2000, there were important differences among groups of countries both in the specificity of the external effects and in the ways in which they were channelled into their economies.

Thus the primary impetus for the east European and Baltic economies came from the acceleration in the demand of western Europe for manufactured and semi-manufactured goods, which accompanied the economic upturn in that part of the continent. This was an example of a positive real external shock, which fed directly into the manufacturing sectors of the east European and Baltic countries and boosted the volume of their exports. In addition, as discussed in more detail in sections 3.2 and 3.6, those east European and Baltic economies whose currencies are pegged to the euro also benefited from its depreciation vis-à-vis the dollar: the latter gave an additional boost to the price competitiveness of their exporters, especially for goods that are traded in dollars. As a result, the total volume of merchandise exports from this group of countries increased by some 20 per cent in 2000,[137] which was undoubtedly a major contribution to

---

[137] Statistics for the volume of trade are not available for all the east European and Baltic countries; however the partial data in table 3.6.5 outline the main trends in the aggregate real flows.

TABLE 3.1.1

Basic economic indicators for eastern Europe, the Baltic states and the CIS, 1998-2001

(Rates of change and shares, per cent)

	GDP (growth rates)					Industrial output (growth rates)			Inflation (per cent change, Dec./Dec.)			Unemployment rate (end of period, per cent)		
			2000		2001									
	1998	1999	Ex-ante forecast	Actual outcome	official forecast	1998	1999	2000	1998	1999	2000	1998	1999	2000
Eastern Europe	1.8	1.3	4	3.9	4.2	1.4	-0.1	8.3	..	..	..	12.6	14.6	15.1
Albania	8	7.3	8	8*	5-7	21.8	16	12*	7.8	-1.0	4.2	17.6	18.2	16.9
Bosnia and Herzegovina [a]	..	..	12	10*	7-9	23.8	10.6	8.8	2.2	-0.4	3.4	38.7	39.0	39.4
Bulgaria	3.5	2.4	4	5.0*	5	-7.9	-12.3	2.3	0.9	6.2	11.2	12.2	16.0	17.9
Croatia	2.5	-0.4	2.6	3.7	3-4	3.7	-1.4	1.7	5.6	4.6	7.5	18.6	20.8	22.6
Czech Republic	-2.2	-0.8	1.5	3.1	3	1.6	-3.1	5.1	6.7	2.5	4.1	7.5	9.4	8.8
Hungary	4.9	4.4	5	5.2	4.5-5	12.5	10.4	18.3	10.4	11.3	10.1	9.1	9.6	8.9
Poland	4.8	4.1	5.2	4.1	4.5	3.5	4.8	7.1	8.5	9.9	8.6	10.4	13.0	15.0
Romania	-5.4	-3.2	1.3	1.6	4.1	-13.8	-7.9	8.2	40.7	54.9	40.7	10.3	11.5	10.5
Slovakia	4.1	1.9	2	2.2	3.2	3.8	-3.6	9.1	5.5	14.2	8.3	15.6	19.2	17.9
Slovenia	3.8	5.2	3.75	4.8	4.5	3.7	-0.5	6.2	6.6	8.1	9.0	14.6	13.0	12.0
The former Yugoslav Republic of Macedonia	2.9	2.7	6	5.1	6	4.5	-2.6	3.5	-1.1	2.3	10.8	41.4	43.8	44.9
Yugoslavia [b]	2.5	-19.3	14	10.0	5	3.6	-23.1	10.9	45.7	54.0	115.1	27.2	27.4	26.6
Baltic states	4.7	-1.8	3	5.0	4.7	6.0	-7.6	6.7	..	..	..	7.3	9.1	10.0
Estonia	4.7	-1.1	3.8-4.0	6.4*	6	4.1	-1.7	9.1	6.8	3.9	4.9	5.1	6.7	7.3
Latvia	3.9	1.1	3.5	6.6	5-6	3.1	-5.4	3.2	2.8	3.3	1.9	9.2	9.1	7.8
Lithuania	5.1	-3.9	2	3.3	3.7	8.2	-11.2	7.0	2.4	0.3	1.5	6.9	10.0	12.6
CIS	-3.0	3.2	2.3	7.4	4.2	-3.1	7.3	9.6	..	..	..	9.0	8.3	6.9
Armenia	7.3	3.3	5.6	6.0	6.5	-2.1	5.2	6.4	-1.2	2.1	0.4	8.9	11.5	10.9
Azerbaijan	10.0	7.4	8	11.4	8.5	2.2	3.6	6.9	-7.6	-0.5	2.1	1.4	1.2	1.2
Belarus	8.4	3.4	2-3	5.8	3-4	12.4	10.3	8.0	181.6	251.3	108.0	2.3	2.0	2.1
Georgia	2.9	3.0	4.2-4.8	1.9	3-4	-1.8	7.4	6.1	13.4	11.1	4.6	4.2	5.6	..
Kazakhstan	-1.9	2.7	3	9.6	4	-2.4	2.7	14.6	1.9	18.1	10.0	3.7	3.9	3.7
Kyrgyzstan	2.1	3.7	4-5	5.0	5	5.3	-4.3	6.0	16.6	39.8	9.5	3.1	3.0	3.1
Republic of Moldova [c]	-6.5	-3.4	2	1.9	5	-15.0	-9.0	2.3	18.2	43.8	18.5	1.9	2.1	1.8
Russian Federation	-4.9	3.5	1.5-2.5	7.7	4	-5.2	8.1	9.0	84.5	36.6	20.1	13.3	12.2	9.7
Tajikistan	5.3	3.7	..	8.3	6.7	8.2	5.6	10.3	2.7	30.1	60.6	2.9	3.1	3.0
Turkmenistan	5.0	16.0	12	17.6	16	0.2	15.0	25*	19.8	..	..	..	..	..
Ukraine	-1.9	-0.4	1	6.0	3-4	-1.0	4.3	12.9	20.0	19.2	25.8	4.3	4.3	4.2
Uzbekistan	4.4	4.4	5	4.0	4.4	3.6	6.1	6.4	25.9	26.0	..	0.4	0.5	0.6
Total above	-1.1	2.4	3	6.0	4.2	-0.9	3.7	9.0	..	..	..	..	..	..
Memorandum items:														
CETE-5	3.2	3.0	4.1	4.0	4.1	4.5	2.9	8.7	..	..	..	10.2	12.5	13.3
SETE-7	-1.5	-3.0	3.6	3.6	4.5	-7.3	-9.9	6.6	..	..	..	15.4	16.5	17.8
Former GDR	2.0	..	..	..	..	7.6	4.8	..	1.1	0.2	..	17.4	17.7	17.2

Source: National statistics; CIS Statistical Committee; direct communications from national statistical offices to UN/ECE secretariat (IMF and World Bank data for Albania).

Note: Aggregates are UN/ECE secretariat calculations, using PPPs obtained from the 1996 European Comparison Programme. Output measures are in real terms (constant prices). Forecasts are those of national conjunctural institutes or government forecasts associated with the central budget formulation. Industrial output refers to gross output, not the contribution of industry to GDP. Inflation refers to changes in the consumer price index. Unemployment generally refers to registered unemployment at the end of the period (with the exceptions of the Russian Federation where it is the Goskomstat estimate according to the ILO definition, and Estonia where it refers to job seekers). Aggregates shown are: *Eastern Europe* (the 12 countries below that line), with sub-aggregates *CETE-5* (central European transition economies: Czech Republic, Hungary, Poland, Slovakia, Slovenia) and *SETE-7* (south-east European transition economies: Albania, Bosnia and Herzegovina, Bulgaria, Croatia, Romania, The former Yugoslav Republic of Macedonia and Yugoslavia); *Baltic states* (Estonia, Latvia, Lithuania); and *CIS* (12 member countries of the Commonwealth of Independent States).

[a] Data reported by the Statistical Office of the Federation; these exclude the area of Republika Srpska.

[b] Data for 1999 and 2000 exclude Kosovo and Metohia.

[c] Excluding Transdniestria.

their high rates of output growth. At the same time, most of these economies suffered a loss (although not large) in their terms of trade in 2000; consequently, although real imports grew more slowly than real exports (by some 15 per cent in aggregate), there were no, or only marginal, improvements in their trade balances (table 3.1.2).

In contrast, the primary impetus for the commodity exporting countries (in the first place, the oil and natural gas exporters in the CIS) originated in the upsurge in world market prices coupled with a stronger dollar (since most commodities are traded in dollars). The combined effect of the two was equivalent to a substantial terms of

TABLE 3.1.2

International trade and external balances of eastern Europe, the Baltic states and the CIS, 1998-2000
(Rates of change and shares, per cent)

	Merchandise exports in dollars (growth rates)			Merchandise imports in dollars (growth rates)			Trade balances (per cent of GDP)			Current account (per cent of GDP)		
	1998	1999	2000[a]	1998	1999	2000[a]	1998	1999	2000[a]	1998	1999	2000[a]
Eastern Europe	9.3	-1.2	12.9	9.0	-2.5	11.0	-9.9	-9.6	-9.8	-4.6	-5.6	-5.1
Albania	50.9	28.3	-10.0	28.2	11.3	14.0	-19.2	-16.9	-20.6	-1.5	-4.2	-13.4
Bosnia and Herzegovina	82.7	47.3	30.2	36.4	14.7	-5.8	-41.7	-42.1	-32.6	-18.6	-21.4	-17.7
Bulgaria	-15.1	-4.5	20.0	0.5	11.3	17.6	-6.2	-12.2	-13.6	-0.5	-5.3	-5.6
Croatia	8.9	-5.3	3.0	-7.9	-7.0	1.6	-17.8	-17.4	-18.3	-7.1	-7.6	-3.9
Czech Republic	15.7	-0.4	10.4	4.4	-2.5	14.9	-4.3	-3.5	-6.6	-2.4	-3.0	-4.8
Hungary	20.4	8.7	12.3	21.1	9.0	14.5	-5.7	-6.2	-8.5	-4.9	-4.3	-3.7
Poland	2.6	-2.9	15.5	10.9	-2.4	6.6	-11.9	-11.9	-10.9	-4.3	-7.4	-6.3
Romania	-1.5	2.4	21.9	4.9	-12.2	25.6	-8.5	-5.6	-7.3	-7.2	-3.8	-3.8
Slovakia	11.8	-4.6	15.8	11.9	-13.4	12.5	-10.5	-5.0	-4.0	-9.7	-5.5	-3.7
Slovenia	8.1	-5.6	2.2	7.8	-0.2	0.3	-5.4	-7.7	-7.6	-0.8	-3.9	-3.2
The former Yugoslav Republic of Macedonia	6.0	-9.1	11.3	7.7	-7.2	16.3	-17.2	-17.0	-21.0	-8.8	-3.9	-5.7
Yugoslavia	6.8	-47.6	15.1	0.1	-31.8	12.6	-11.8	-10.9	-7.9	-7.4	-8.7	-5.6
Baltic states	3.5	-12.5	24.9	7.5	-13.7	15.0	-22.7	-18.8	-17.5	-11.0	-9.5	-6.2
Estonia	10.3	-9.2	33.2	7.8	-14.2	23.7	-29.7	-22.8	-22.5	-9.2	-5.7	-6.8
Latvia	8.3	-4.9	8.1	17.1	-7.6	8.1	-22.6	-18.4	-19.0	-10.7	-9.7	-7.2
Lithuania	-3.9	-19.0	28.1	2.6	-16.6	13.0	-19.4	-17.2	-14.4	-12.1	-11.2	-5.3
CIS[b]	-15.2	-1.1	46.0	-14.0	-23.8	15.6	6.0	14.9	22.0	-1.7	8.3	14.8
Armenia	-5.2	5.4	22.5	1.1	-11.2	10.9	-36.0	-30.9	-33.3	-21.3	-16.6	-16.0
Azerbaijan	-22.4	53.3	235.7	35.6	-3.9	10.3	-10.6	-2.4	19.3	-30.7	-13.3	1.9
Belarus	-3.2	-16.2	29.4	-1.6	-22.1	36.5	-12.4	-6.7	-11.6	-7.3	-1.8	-2.8
Georgia	-19.7	23.7	50.3	-6.3	-31.9	7.1	-19.0	-12.8	-9.9	-11.4	-6.9	-7.5
Kazakhstan	-16.3	2.9	76.7	1.1	-15.3	30.5	4.9	11.3	21.3	-5.6	-1.4	4.8
Kyrgyzstan	-15.0	-11.6	10.6	18.7	-28.7	-6.1	-20.5	-11.9	-0.9	-23.2	-15.1	-4.0
Republic of Moldova	-27.8	-26.9	2.9	-12.6	-44.0	39.0	-23.1	-9.5	-24.4	-19.3	-2.9	-7.9
Russian Federation	-16.3	0.5	49.5	-17.9	-29.5	9.3	10.2	22.4	28.7	0.3	13.4	19.3
Tajikistan	-20.0	15.4	13.5	-5.2	-6.7	1.0	-8.7	2.4	12.7	-9.1	1.6	10.4
Turkmenistan	-20.9	99.9	92.0	-14.9	46.7	36.9	-14.6	-8.9	12.4	-33.0	-26.0	1.5
Ukraine	-11.2	-8.4	23.9	-14.3	-19.3	21.3	-5.0	-0.9	1.8	-3.2	2.8	7.0
Uzbekistan	-20.1	-9.0	-2.9	-25.4	-9.1	-5.6	0.6	0.5	0.8	-0.7	-1.0	0.2
Total above	-3.5	-1.8	28.2	0.4	-10.2	13.3	-2.7	-0.1	4.7	-3.4	–	4.3
Memorandum items:												
CETE-5	11.6	0.1	12.2	11.1	-1.0	10.3	-9.0	-8.7	-9.1	-4.2	-5.8	-5.3
SETE-7	-0.1	-6.8	16.2	2.2	-7.9	13.8	-12.7	-12.5	-12.4	-6.0	-5.1	-4.7

Source: National statistics; CIS Statistical Committee; direct communications from national statistical offices to UN/ECE secretariat; UN/ECE secretariat calculations.

Note: Foreign trade growth is measured in current dollar values. Trade and current account balances are related to GDP at current prices, converted from national currencies at current dollar exchange rates. Current price GDP values for 2000 are in some cases estimated from reported real growth rates and consumer price indices. On regional aggregates, see the note to table 3.1.1.

[a] Full year 2000 provisional results for eastern Europe and the Baltic states; January-September for CIS and "Total above".

[b] Including intra-CIS trade.

trade gain (that is, a nominal shock) for these economies, leading to an improvement in their merchandise trade balances. Consequently, in virtually all the commodity exporting countries (Azerbaijan, Russia and the central Asian CIS countries) there was a substantial improvement in both their trade and current account balances in 2000 (table 3.1.2), despite a relatively modest growth in the volume of exports.[138]

The effect of such a nominal shock on the real economy is indirect: the increased revenue of exporters allows them to increase investment and to pay higher wages, both of which add to domestic demand and, consequently, to domestic output. Another transmission channel is fiscal: as exporters' profits swell, they pay larger amounts of tax and contribute to increased fiscal revenue; governments may also collect higher revenue from export tariffs where applicable (such as those imposed on the exports of oil and natural gas in some CIS countries). In turn, increased revenue may allow higher

---

[138] Volume trade data are even more scarce for the CIS countries than for central Europe. To the extent that some partial data exist, they indicate that the volume of commodity exports of these countries increased little in 2000 (section 3.6). The trade data for Russia suggest that the volume of imports increased much faster than the volume of exports in 2000 (table 3.6.5); nevertheless there was a substantial improvement in the Russian merchandise trade balance (table 3.1.2).

levels of public expenditure without endangering the fiscal balance thus giving further impetus to domestic demand. In sum, in the case of a positive terms of trade shock, the induced effect on domestic output is likely to occur primarily through its indirect effect on domestic demand, while the real net trade effect may not necessarily be substantial.[139]

Although some transition economies (particularly in the CIS) were not directly affected by any of these positive shocks, they nevertheless benefited from their secondary effects due to the strong recovery in neighbouring economies. Thus, most CIS economies benefited from the recovery in Russia's domestic demand, which gave a strong impetus to their exports to Russia and contributed to a general revival in intra-CIS trade. Mutual trade was recovering among the east European and Baltic countries as well.

In many transition economies, their strong growth in 2000 was accompanied by higher rates of inflation, although in general there were no obvious signs of a direct link between the dynamics of output and prices (such as overheating). In most cases where inflation was higher than expected (or higher than in 1999), this was largely due to higher import prices, especially for oil, and the subsequent general rise in energy and fuel prices (section 3.4). In some transition economies, however (mostly in the CIS and in south-east Europe), high rates of inflation continued to be fuelled by chronic macroeconomic imbalances.

In general, the strong economic upturn in 2000 did not bring about a matching improvement in the labour markets of the transition economies. Due to the continuing process of microlevel restructuring and rationalization in eastern Europe and the Baltic states (a process which in general tends to be protracted due to the social costs involved), many firms are continuing to shed excessive labour, adding to the large pools of long-term unemployed (section 3.5). At the same time, the corporate sector in these countries (including the local operations of foreign firms) appears to be mostly investing in modern and efficient (hence, labour saving) technologies; while this type of investment is essential for the upgrading of production structures in the transition economies, it does not lead to job creation on a large scale at least in the short run.

While labour market statistics for most of the CIS countries remain quite unreliable, the available data for Russia indicate that the recent strong recovery led to a notable reduction in the rate of unemployment, which is in contrast to developments in other transition economies.

Part of the explanation may be related to the fact that the upturn in Russia was largely based on a reversal in the rates of utilization of existing capacities, which allowed firms to re-employ workers who were laid off during the previous downturn.

In general, the external position of the transition economies improved in 2000, although the changes varied considerably from country to country. Given their large terms of trade gains, the oil exporting economies and others specializing in commodity exports improved their current accounts, in some cases, dramatically (table 3.1.2). In eastern Europe and the Baltic economies, the changes in current account balances were more heterogeneous: while some reduced their current account deficits in 2000 (often as a result of restrictive domestic policy), others slipped further into the red. In most cases, however, the current accounts of these economies appear to be manageable, at least in the short run. In particular, the conditions on the international financial markets also improved in 2000 and remain attractive for most of the east European and Baltic economies, while inflows of FDI in some cases continued to cover a large proportion of their current account deficits.

A worrying recent development has been the rapid growth in the foreign indebtedness of some CIS countries. In some of them the level of foreign debt has already reached alarming proportions (section 3.6); the implied balance of payment constraints are likely to curb the future growth potential of these economies. In addition, as the bulk of this debt is incurred by governments, it also creates a serious burden on the public finances in these countries and threatens their long-term fiscal sustainability. The recent borrowing patterns of these economies do not appear to be sustainable and they will be faced with the need for major policy adjustments in the not too distant future.

Overall, external conditions in 2000 were favourable for the majority of the ECE transition economies. However, the patterns of economic performance and the dynamics of output growth in this benign environment at the same time point to the potential risks for these economies, even in the short run. The strong impact of the favourable changes in the external environment in 2000 also underlines the high degree of sensitivity of these economies to external shocks. Commodity exporters and economies specializing in exports of resource intensive, low value added goods are especially vulnerable to such shocks (section 3.3). However, due to their large exposure to west European demand, the more advanced economies of central Europe and the Baltic area are also very susceptible to changes in demand in their major external markets.

Such an extreme cyclical dependence on the external economic environment in these economies is not abnormal given the usually small size and generally low per capita income levels. However, their vulnerability to external shocks may be amplified by unnecessary policy austerity, for example, by targeting a faster rate of

---

[139] The preliminary national account statistics for Russia provide strong evidence in support of this conjecture despite the relatively restrictive stance of fiscal policy (section 3.2.2); in 2000, the main contribution to growth came from domestic consumption (4.5 percentage points) and fixed investment (2.2 percentage points), while the net trade effect accounted for just 0.6 per cent of GDP growth (table 3.3.3). Due to the absence of adequate data it is not possible to test this hypothesis for all the commodity exporting countries.

disinflation than is feasible in a process of fast catching up (section 3.2). Therefore, more realistic fine-tuning is needed in setting and pursuing inflation targets especially in those economies where the annual rate has already fallen to single or low double digits. Too ambitious a target may not only impede the productivity catch up but may also slow down the process of price liberalization as has been the case in some of these economies in 2000.

Thus, should the favourable external trends of 2000 be reversed, the transition economies might be subject to a negative external shock which could mirror that in 2000. Indeed, in the closing months of 2000 and the opening months of 2001 there has been a widespread weakening of output in virtually all the transition economies, which is already more pronounced than the current slowdown in western Europe. A further deterioration in the latter is therefore likely to have a considerably amplified effect on economic activity in the transition economies. Should developments in North America and western Europe take such a turn, the currently envisaged rates of economic growth for 2001 (table 3.1.1) may turn out to be very optimistic.

3.2 Macroeconomic policy

The macroeconomic environment and external conditions in 2000 were generally favourable for the transition economies: the waning of the aftershocks from the Russian crisis and the considerable strengthening of global demand helped to reduce financial and macroeconomic volatility and to revive or accelerate economic activity in most of them. This favourable environment was beneficial for the policy process in that it allowed some reordering of priorities and an extension of the policy horizon. In most transition economies policy makers refocused their attention from responding to the crises (mainly external) that had occupied a great deal of their time and effort in recent years to the pursuit of their longer-term goals. However, the positive influence of favourable external conditions is likely to be a one-off effect for the transition economies, as the growth in global demand started to slow down in the final months of 2000, and macroeconomic policies will need to be retuned accordingly.

As the heterogeneity of the different groups of transition economies continues to grow, so do the differences in their macroeconomic policy objectives. The start of accession negotiations with the European Union by a group of 10 transition economies (plus Cyprus and Malta) has had enormous impact on the economic policy process in this region. The accession agenda has already become the centrepiece of economic policy in these countries, especially in those central European and Baltic countries which are most advanced in the reforms and which aspire to early membership. The policy implications of the drive towards EU accession are diverse and wide-ranging and they affect not only the process of legislative and regulatory harmonization with the EU but also important aspects of the conduct of day-to-day economic policy. The declared goal of policy synchronization with the EU is highly beneficial and stimulating for the acceding countries in that it acts both as a catalyst for speeding up the reform process and as a source of discipline on policy. However, such sychronization also places constraints on the policy agenda and on the freedom of policy makers in the acceding countries to deal with the often unpredictable transitional environment.

The change of political regime in Yugoslavia has transformed the political and economic situation in the whole of south-east Europe. The new Yugoslav government is now facing the daunting task of carrying out a plethora of difficult reforms after a decade of delays in the process (these issues are discussed in more detail in section 3.2(iv)). Nevertheless, the lifting of the outer wall of sanctions that followed the elections in Yugoslavia last December has improved the outlook for all the neighbouring countries which had suffered their side effects for a number of years. The EU has also signalled that all the successor states of the former SFR of Yugoslavia as well as Albania will now be considered as potential candidates for future EU membership. It is hoped that this clear signal might have the stimulating effect on the policy process in south-east Europe that it has had in the other candidate countries.

There has also been some progress in the conduct of macroeconomic policy in some of the CIS countries as well. With the change of administration, the Russian authorities have announced an ambitious long-term plan for comprehensive economic reform. This process is likely to be long and difficult, and the record of reform in Russia has not been so encouraging. However, the external environment in 2000 was extremely favourable for the Russian economy and the large windfall gains from high oil prices provide an opportunity for making a decisive break with the past. In these circumstances, and despite the progress made, the Russian authorities might have done more and taken bolder steps in the reform process.[140]

Thanks to the upturn in world commodity prices in 2000, most commodity-exporting CIS economies have been able to recover from the damaging impact of the Russian crisis in 1998. Moreover, there are signs that policy makers in some of these countries are paying more attention to the need for domestic and external equilibrium and to the general consistency of their conduct of macroeconomic policy (Kazakhstan is a case in point). In general, however, the macroeconomic stabilization and policy reforms in the CIS are being pursued at a much slower speed than in the other transition economies (and especially in comparison with the advanced central European and Baltic countries), and this is leading to a further widening of the differences in income and development levels among the transition economies as a whole.

---

[140] The failure to capitalize fully on this window of opportunity has been admitted by high-level Russian officials such as Andrei Illarionov, the chief economic adviser to the Russian president. *The Economist*, 27 January 2001, p. 85.

(i) Monetary policy

The conditions for the conduct of monetary policy in the transition economies in 2000 were considerably better than in the previous two years. With the main stimulus to final demand coming from abroad and confidence returning to the international financial markets, the monetary authorities in most countries were relieved both from political pressures to stimulate domestic demand and from the need to counterbalance financial disturbances. The unprecedented export-led boom in many transition economies in 2000 allowed the monetary authorities to focus more closely on the improvement of domestic and external equilibrium and on the pursuit of some longer-term goals.

The generally strong demand from international markets in 2000 was nevertheless accompanied by some adverse developments, in the first place the soaring prices of crude oil. Most of the transition economies are small and open and as a result are especially vulnerable to such external price shocks. Consequently, in a number of these economies in 2000, there was a reversal of the disinflationary trend of previous years (section 3.4).

Thus, as regards the external factors, the stance of monetary policy in the transition economies in 2000 was affected by the simultaneous impact of increased demand and an adverse inflationary shock. Such a combination does not in general lead to unsolvable policy dilemmas as it leaves sufficient room for manoeuvre in setting the monetary targets. The increase in prices was closely monitored by the central banks, which are keen to avoid a reversal in the overall decline of inflationary expectations in the transition economies. Nevertheless, the central banks in most transition economies apparently regarded the inflationary effect of rising import prices for fuel to be transitory and with limited consequences for the underlying rate of core inflation. Thus, in general, their reaction to the unanticipated upsurge in domestic prices was more or less neutral.

Most of the transition economies in accession negotiations with the EU have openly shifted their monetary policy priorities towards harmonizing their regulations with those of the EU and achieving nominal convergence with the Union within a relatively short period. A number of these countries have adopted medium-term policy programmes for monetary integration with the EU, goals which are operationalized in the setting of the annual policy targets and in the conduct of day-to-day policy. This shift in priorities often has direct macroeconomic implications; hence considerable care and prudence are required in setting specific policy goals (particularly those related to the synchronization of monetary policy and monetary convergence) at the different stages of the accession process (box 3.2.1).

Before accession, the candidate countries will have to harmonize their banking and financial regulations with those in the EU. This concerns a wide range of legislative and regulatory norms including central bank independence, prudential banking regulations, banking supervision, protection of bank customers, and the regulation of financial markets, including the gradual liberalization of domestic financial markets and the external capital account. Probably the most sensitive element of the pre-accession strategy are the preparations for joining the Economic and Monetary Union (EMU) and, eventually, for the future introduction of the single currency. In this respect, the declared long-term accession strategies of the candidate countries vary substantially, due to the differences in their current monetary and exchange rate regimes but, nevertheless, two general types of strategy can be identified. Those countries with floating, quasi-pegged or pegged exchange rate regimes apparently are opting for greater flexibility in their exchange rate regimes during the pre-accession phase in order for them to become gradually compatible with the ERM-2 exchange rate mechanism at the moment of joining the EMU. Countries with currency boards or rigidly fixed exchange rate regimes (Bulgaria, Estonia, Latvia, Lithuania) all seem to be inclined to maintain these arrangements[141] not only until they join the EMU but also until they adopt the single currency.[142]

A number of technical monetary policy regulations, such as the required reserve ratio,[143] also fall into the category of norms that must be harmonized. Since 1999, the central banks in a number of acceding countries have taken a more active stance towards the reserve ratio after a fairly long period when monetary policy took a more neutral stance towards it.[144] One of the reasons for these changes is the fact that the reserve ratio in most transition economies is higher than in the EMU (which is 2 per cent for all types of deposit). In the earlier phases of the transition, the monetary authorities in a number of

---

[141] See the proceedings of the seminar, *Currency Boards – Experience and Prospects*, organized by the Bank of Estonia (Tallinn), 5-6 May 2000 (www.ee/epbe/en/monetary_policy.html).

[142] This is not fully in line with the current framework of the European Monetary System, which requires a minimum adjustment period of two years under the ERM-2 exchange rate mechanism before eventually introducing the single currency. However, it can be argued that the EMU norms do not preclude such a transitory arrangement. A.-M. Gulde, J. Kahkonen and P. Keller, *Pros and Cons of Currency Board Arrangements in the Lead-Up to EU Accession and Participation in the Euro Zone*, IMF Policy Discussion Papers PDP/00/1 (Washington, D.C.), February 2000. The practical feasibility of such a policy remains an open question.

[143] The required reserve ratio defines a portion of the liabilities (in the first place deposits of clients) of commercial banks and other financial institutions subject to reserve requirements that have to be set aside in a special account kept with the central bank. The required reserves serve as a precaution against withdrawals of deposits but they are also used by central banks as a tool of monetary policy (as the reserve ratio affects money supply).

[144] In February 2001 the reserve ratio in Hungary was reduced from 11 to 7 per cent, after a 1 percentage point cut in 2000; further cuts are in the pipeline for 2001. During 2000, the ratio in Latvia was lowered from 8 per cent to 6 per cent. In Poland it had been reduced to 5 per cent already in July 1999 and a further gradual lowering to 2 per cent is envisaged in the next few years. In Estonia, a gradual unification of existing reserve requirements (in line with EU norms) is underway. The reserve ratio in Bulgaria was reduced from 11 to 8 per cent in July 2000. In the Czech Republic it was set at 2 per cent (equal to the EU norm) in October 1999.

> **BOX 3.2.1**
>
> **Dynamic equilibrium during a process of catch up in productivity and price levels: policy implications for the acceding countries**
>
> One of the central macroeconomic aspects of the preparation for EU accession and monetary integration in the EMU is the attainment of nominal convergence (that is, convergence of inflation rates with the EU) in the acceding countries, which is often treated as an immediate policy goal. Despite the significant progress with disinflation in the transition economies, the process is difficult not only because of the ongoing adjustment of relative prices (including the removal of administrative controls over a range of prices) but also because the fundamental structural changes that these economies are undergoing require a sufficient degree of freedom for nominal adjustments.
>
> One of the problems that may result from striving for a rapid rate of convergence to the inflation rates prevailing in the EU, arises from the fact that the goals for disinflation and for quickly catching up with the income levels in the EU may be to some extent mutually exclusive. The main reason for this is that at present there exist substantial gaps between both the productivity and domestic price levels in the candidate countries (notably in the non-tradeables sector) vis-à-vis the EU, while closing these gaps involves a dynamic and interactive process of changes in both productivity and prices. If the transition economies are to reduce the gap in per capita income levels vis-à-vis the EU, their economies will have to grow faster than the EU, which in turn implies faster productivity growth in their tradeable sectors. However, as is well known both from theory and from past experience, an inherent feature of a productivity catch up is that inflation will be higher in the catching-up economy due to wage increases in the tradeable sector being matched by the non-tradeable sector, where higher rates of increase in prices spill over to the whole economy.[1] This is a fundamental feature of economic structural change and policy cannot prevent it from happening if a fast catch-up process is underway. The higher rate of inflation in the catching-up country is in no way linked to macroeconomic disequilibria or to lax policy; it simply reflects and registers the fact that productivity convergence brings about convergence in wage and price levels as well. Or, in other words, a process of productivity catch up implies a dynamically changing macroeconomic equilibrium which entails a catch up in price levels.
>
> If macroeconomic policy is about equilibrium, then it should aim at sustaining equilibrium in dynamics; hence, if a process of productivity catch up is underway then policy should target rates of change in the price level that are consistent with the underlying catch-up process. Any attempt by policy to hold rates of inflation below those implied by the underlying process of productivity-cum-price catch up may in fact push the economy below its equilibrium performance path. The danger of such a policy is that it may brake the very process of productivity catch up (and fast growth) that produced the relatively faster growth of prices in the first place.[2] Thus, from the point of view of social welfare in the acceding countries, the wisdom of a policy aimed at premature inflation convergence with the EU (that is, at convergence in rates of inflation before convergence in productivity and price levels is achieved) is questionable.
>
> ---
>
> [1] This is due to the so-called Balassa-Samuelson effect. For more details and discussion on its implications for the transition economies, see UN/ECE, *Economic Survey of Europe, 2000 No. 1*, pp. 54-59; R. Corker, C. Beaumont, R. van Elkan and D. Iakova, *Exchange Rate Regimes in Selected Advanced Transition Economies – Coping with Transition, Capital Inflows and EU Accession*, IMF Policy Discussion Papers PDP/00/3 (Washington, D.C.), April 2000; P. Masson, *Monetary and Exchange Rate Policy of Transition Economies of Central and Eastern Europe after the Launch of EMU*, IMF Policy Discussion Papers PDP/99/5 (Washington, D.C.), July 1999.
>
> [2] This by no means implies that macroeconomic policy should not aim at disinflation, especially when inflation is still at moderate (double-digit) levels. The pro-inflationary impact of a productivity catch up may surface only when inflation is generally low (at single-digit levels) and this is when more fine-tuning is needed in setting the inflation targets. Another policy implication for the acceding countries is that policy should distinguish between the relative price of tradeables (which should be close to zero, relative to EU) and the relative price of non-tradeables.

countries had opted for high reserve ratios, either to curb liquidity in the banking system (and hence to check money supply) or to strengthen the banks against the risk of volatile withdrawals (due to the instability of money demand). In preparing for EU accession, the monetary authorities in most candidate countries have started to lower the reserves ratios, a process which was helped by the generally favourable macroeconomic environment in 2000.[145]

In pursing their main policy goal of price stability, the authorities in the transition economies, depending on the exchange rate regime, select a monetary target and tune the available policy tools in the pursuit of this target. The majority of the transition economies apply various forms of exchange rate targeting[146] in which they aim at a pre-specified nominal exchange rate which is expected to provide the principal monetary anchor for the economy. More recently, the central banks in some countries (Czech Republic, Poland, Slovakia) have reverted to inflation targeting, a regime in which the central bank

---

[145] It should be noted that it is not only accession candidates which have lowered reserve requirements. In 2000 the central banks in several other transition economies (Croatia and Russia, for example) also lowered the ratio, taking advantage of the improved macroeconomic conditions and the greater stability of their banking systems.

[146] The transition economies apply a wide variety of monetary and exchange rate regimes ranging from currency boards (Bosnia and Herzegovina, Bulgaria, Estonia, Lithuania) to a more or less free float (most of the CIS countries). Some of them have intermediate exchange rate regimes such as a crawling peg with a band (Hungary), implicit peg (Croatia) or variations of the managed float (for example, based on inflation targeting as in the Czech Republic, Poland and partly Slovakia, or on a money supply target as in the case of Slovenia). The monetary and exchange rate regimes largely predefine the instruments available to policy makers in the pursuit of both their long-term and day-to-day goals.

sets a specific inflation rate as its policy target. Depending on the degree of convergence or deviation from the targeted inflation rate, the authorities then implement policy adjustments.

Direct targeting of the money supply was widely used in the early phases of transition but has been losing ground in many transition economies. This shift has been prompted, on the one hand, by the instability of money demand in a transitional environment (which creates difficulties for the operationalization of this approach) and, on the other, by the growing sophistication of financial intermediation in many transition economies (which reflects the fact that, with the increasing complexity of the monetary transmission mechanism, the efficiency of the policy tools to control monetary expansion tend to weaken). Among the transition economies, only Slovenia still adheres to direct targeting of the money supply,[147] apparently thanks to the relative stability of money demand in this country. After the financial crisis of 1998, Russia's central bank also introduced elements of monetary targeting.[148]

While the main goal of the central banks is in principle price stability, the emergence of other concerns may and does affect the conduct of monetary policy. The actual conduct of monetary policy in individual transition economies in 2000 was affected by a number of additional factors such as the existence of internal imbalances as well as the concern of the authorities about growth and growth prospects, the degree of which differs from country to country. Thus, variations in the mix of outstanding issues and problems were reflected in significant differences in the stance of monetary policy in the transition economies.

During 2000 and early 2001, a number of changes in the *monetary and exchange rate* regimes and regulations of the transition economies were introduced or initiated. In April, Poland implemented the planned transition from a crawling peg with a band to a free float; however, given that monetary policy is governed by the inflation target, the central bank continued to closely monitor changes in the exchange rate, so that the current regime is closer to a managed float. In Hungary, the monthly devaluation rate of the forint (in the framework of the crawling band) was reduced in April from 0.4 per cent to 0.3 per cent. This move was in line with the long-term national monetary strategy, but the rise in imported inflation also prevented further intended cuts in the rate of crawl. In January 2001, Lithuania announced that the re-pegging of the currency from the dollar to the euro (initially envisaged for the year 2001) would take place at the beginning of 2002, without any further changes in the monetary and exchange rate regimes.[149]

Belarus and Russia have concluded a preliminary agreement on a currency union between the two states which is to enter into effect in 2005. In preparation for that, the authorities in Belarus announced that, as of 1 January 2001, the Belarussian currency would be pegged to the Russian rouble within a pre-set fluctuation band.[150] In Uzbekistan, which has a rather rigid exchange rate regime (the non-convertibility of the currency has given rise to multiple exchange rates), there were some first steps towards currency liberalization: in May 2000 the "official" exchange rate was abolished by unifying it with the so-called "interbank" rate,[151] and in July, the authorities established a limited market where the currency would be allowed to be traded freely.[152] At the end of October 2000, a new currency, the somoni, was introduced in Tajikistan replacing the Tajik rouble at the rate of 1000 roubles per somoni. The introduction of the new currency (which is pegged to the dollar) in Tajikistan is a key element of a new programme of economic reforms supported by IMF funding.[153]

In general, the currencies of the transition economies were less subject to pressure in 2000 than during the previous two years. In the course of the year there was only one forced devaluation, namely in Yugoslavia, where the artificially low official rate of 6 dinars to the deutsche mark was initially raised to 20 dinars in June and then to 30 dinars in December.[154]

The substantial appreciation of the dollar in 2000, together with generally higher than expected domestic inflation, had a significant impact on *real exchange rates* in the transition economies. With the start of negotiations with the EU, a number of candidate countries have increased the greater weight of the euro in their exchange rate targets or have pegged directly to the euro.[155] The weakening of the euro in 2000 eased somewhat the pressure for real exchange rate appreciation in those

---

[147] The intermediate monetary target in Slovenia is broad money (M3).

[148] After the August 1998 financial crisis, Russia reinforced administrative controls over its foreign exchange market, which were equivalent to restrictions on convertibility (in particular exporters are required to sell between 50 and 75 per cent of their proceeds through highly regulated exchanges). Some of these restrictions are expected to be scrapped in 2001.

[149] Statement by central bank governor R. Sarkinas, as reported in Oxford Analytica, *EEDB Executive Summaries*, 22 January 2001.

[150] RFE/RL *Newsline*, Vol. 4, No. 249, Part II, 29 December 2000.

[151] The interbank market is also tightly regulated; although the May move was equivalent to a devaluation of some 50 per cent, the interbank rate remained three times higher than the black market exchange rate.

[152] *Reuters News Service*, 1 July 2000.

[153] IMF, "IMF management welcomes Tajikistan's currency reform", *News Brief No. 00/97*, 26 October 2000.

[154] The first change was in fact a palliative measure as the so-called "incentive" rate of 20 dinars was introduced in parallel with the official rate; in contrast, the December change was the first step towards internal convertibility of the currency as the multiple exchange rates were abolished.

[155] Thus, at the beginning of 2000 Hungary exchanged the previous eurodollar currency basket for a direct peg to the euro. The currencies of Bulgaria and Estonia are also directly pegged to the euro. The euro is also the reference currency for the Czech Republic, Poland and Slovakia where the monetary authorities have inflation targets (previously they targeted currency baskets).

countries targeting the euro; at the same time they were exposed to greater exchange rate volatility caused by the fluctuation of the eurodollar exchange rate. By contrast, in countries where the exchange rate was targeted on the dollar, the effect of the eurodollar fluctuations in 2000 had the opposite effect on the real exchange rate.

The different development of the real exchange rate in these two groups of countries is shown in chart 3.2.1.[156] Thus, the trend towards real exchange rate appreciation, which was quite marked in Bulgaria, the Czech Republic, Estonia, Slovakia and Slovenia between 1996 and 1999, subsided or was even reversed in 2000. The reverse happened in Lithuania where the currency is pegged to the dollar, in Romania where the implicit exchange rate target is set in dollars, and partly in Latvia where the currency is pegged to the SDR (in which the dollar has a large weight).

The particular mix of external disturbances in 2000 (positive for the real economy and adverse for inflation) had a specific impact on *interest rates* and on the interest rate policies followed by the central banks. As noted above, in terms of interest rate policy, central banks generally reacted in a rather neutral manner towards the unexpected rise in domestic prices. Thus, the central banks' intervention rates continued to be dominated by the expectation of a further moderation in the rate of inflation and interest rates were lowered in many transition economies.[157] There were practically no cases of monetary tightening in 2000 in response to imported inflation. Consequently, nominal interest rates in the banking sectors of most transition economies declined in 2000 (table 3.2.1); this was the case also in economies with currency boards (Bulgaria, Estonia, Lithuania) where the central banks have no direct leverage on interest rates.

There were a few exceptions to this general pattern of lower nominal interest rates, among them Poland and Slovenia.[158] Since the last quarter of 1999, Poland's Monetary Policy Council has been tightening monetary policy.[159] Although the inflation trend in Poland in this period has not been significantly different from those in neighbouring countries, the stance of monetary policy was largely a response to delays in some structural reforms and some fiscal loosening which resulted in the widening of Poland's current account deficit. In the absence of an appropriate policy response by the government, the concern about external equilibrium probably outweighed any worries about inflation, and so the Monetary Policy Council reacted with a very tight policy in order to check the external imbalance. The tightening of monetary policy in Slovenia (including increases in the central bank's interest rates) was prompted by a rapid growth of wages and a credit expansion in 1999-2000 that led to fears of a possible overheating of the economy. An additional factor was the surge in domestic (rather than imported) inflation, a reaction to the introduction of VAT in 1999, which led to an acceleration of core inflation in 2000.

Due to a combination of falling nominal interest rates and higher than anticipated inflation, *real interest rates* in most transition economies were declining in 2000 and in some the fall was substantial (chart 3.2.2).[160] The lowering of real borrowing costs for businesses was another favourable factor which contributed to the robust economic performance in most transition economies in 2000. At the same time, consumers were generally at a disadvantage, as the low (sometimes negative) real interest rates on deposits implied a transfer of real resources from households to the banks and to the corporate sector.[161]

---

[156] The reference here is to the price-deflated real effective exchange rates shown in chart 3.2.1. The changes in real effective rates deflated by unit labour costs were quite different, depending on the changes in productivity and wages (discussed in sect. 3.4).

[157] During the course of 2000, the key central bank refinancing rates were substantially reduced in Albania (from 17.6 to 10.8 per cent), Kazakhstan (from 18 to 14 per cent), Slovakia (from 12 to 9.25 per cent), Russia (from 55 to 25 per cent) and Ukraine (from 45 to 27 per cent). Between January 2000 and February 2001 the central bank's two-week deposit rate in Hungary was reduced from 12.25 to 11.25 per cent. In March 2000 the Bank of Latvia cut all its intervention rates (among them the 60-day discount rate was reduced from 4 to 3.5 per cent). In April, the Croatian National Bank reduced all its key rates (the Lombard rate from 13 to 12 per cent and the discount rate from 7.9 to 5.9 per cent), the central bank of The former Yugoslav Republic of Macedonia cut its refinancing rate from 8.9 to 7.9 per cent, while the National Bank of Romania lowered its Lombard rate from 95 to 75 per cent. The intervention rates of the Czech National Bank have remained unchanged since mid-1999.

[158] The central bank in Belarus also raised its intervention rates in 2000 in an attempt to counter the continuing macroeconomic instability in the country; however the overall stance of macroeconomic policy in Belarus remains precariously inconsistent and unbalanced.

[159] Between October 1999 and August 2000 the central bank's main interest rates increased by some 600 basis points (for example, the 60-day discount rate increased from 15.5 to 21.5 per cent and the Lombard rate from 17 to 23 per cent).

[160] In principle, what matters for the financial decisions taken by economic agents is the expected real interest rate because when businesses and households make decisions about borrowing or saving/consumption, they factor in not only the current nominal interest rate but also the expected rate of price change. However, this "true" real interest rate is not measurable as there are no adequate indicators of expected price changes. Consequently, numerous approximate (but measurable) definitions of the true real interest rates have been suggested and are being used in applied research (for a discussion, see National Bank of Hungary, *Quarterly Report on Inflation* (Budapest), December 2000, p. 27). The *ex-post* forward looking short-term real interest rates shown in chart 3.2.2 are the nominal rates discounted by the prevailing rate of inflation (PPI and CPI, respectively) over the life of the loan or deposit. So defined, the real interest rate measures the actual real return on the financial asset (real costs borne by firms or real income accruing to depositors). Such quantitative assessments can only be performed *ex post*, as they imply knowledge of the future inflation rate (hence, forward-looking), but it may be different from the *ex-ante* judgment of economic agents.

[161] For a discussion of the implication of different combinations of real interest rates see UN/ECE, *Economic Survey of Europe, 2000 No. 1*, pp. 50-54.

CHART 3.2.1

Real effective exchange rates in selected east European and Baltic economies, 1995-2000

(Indices, first quarter 1995=100)

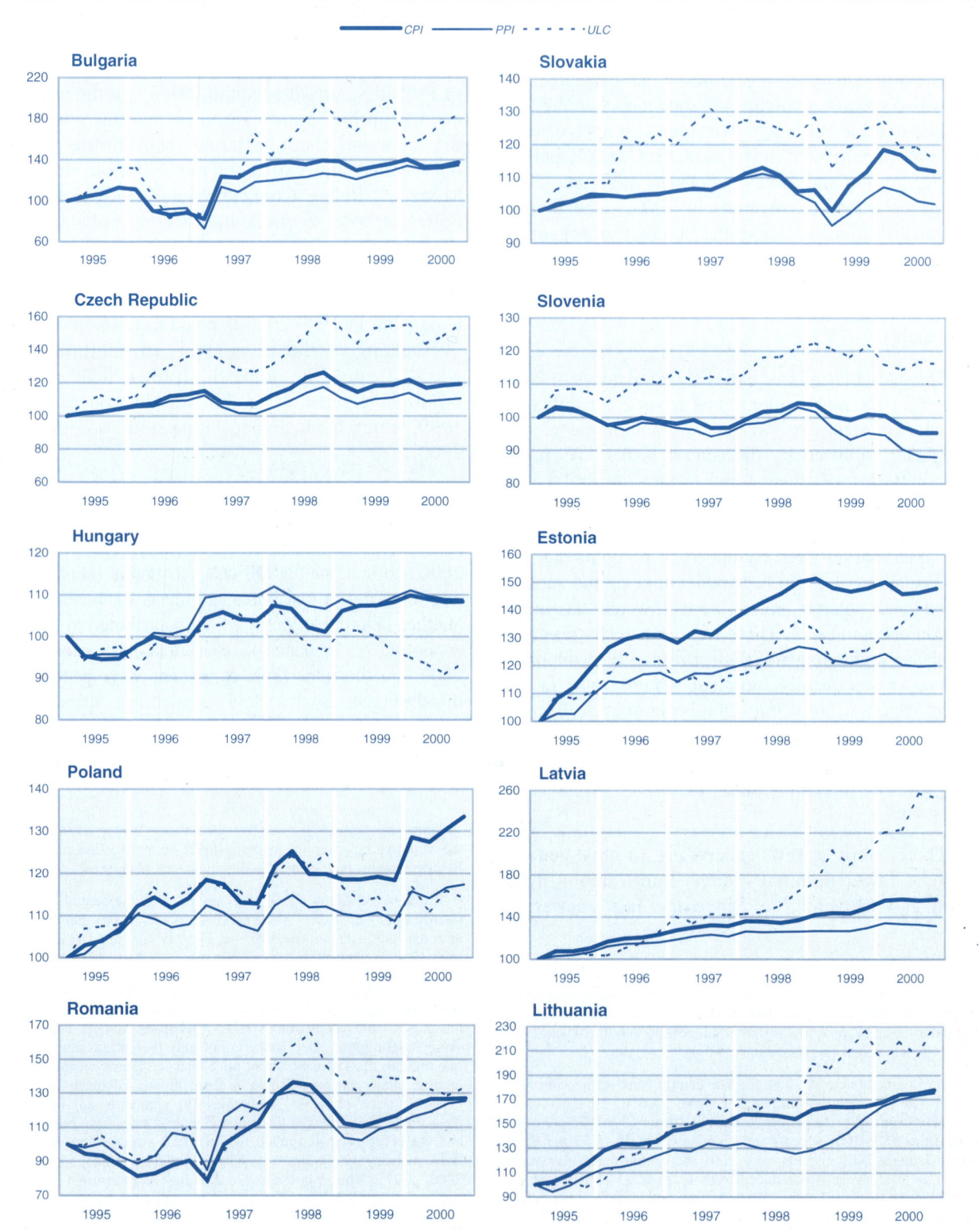

Source: National statistics and UN/ECE secretariat Common Database.

Note: The real effective exchange rate indicators were computed from the nominal exchange rates against the deutsche mark and the dollar, deflated respectively by the domestic and German or United States consumer and producer price indices, indices of estimated unit labour costs in industry, while the shares of the EU and the rest of the world in total exports of individual transition economies were used to determine the deutsche mark and the dollar trade weights, respectively. Indices of unit labour costs in industry are computed from seasonally adjusted indices of average quarterly gross wages in industry and of estimated labour productivity. Unit labour costs for Germany and the United States are from the OECD Database. Unit labour cost deflator for the fourth quarter 2000 is based on preliminary employment and/or wage data for Bulgaria, the Czech Republic, Romania, Slovenia, Latvia and Lithuania.

TABLE 3.2.1

Short-term interest rates in selected east European, Baltic and CIS economies, 1996-2000

(Per cent)

	Short-term credits					Short-term deposits (domestic currency)					Average yield on short-term government securities				
	1996	1997	1998	1999	2000[a]	1996	1997	1998	1999	2000[a]	1996	1997	1998	1999	2000
Albania	24.0	..	..	21.6	21.9	16.8	..	..	12.9	8.4	17.7	32.6	27.5	17.5	10.7
Bulgaria	300.3	209.8	14.1	13.6	12.2	146.4	80.8	3.0	3.3	3.2	278.7	200.8	6.2	5.5	4.3
Croatia	22.5	15.5	15.8	14.9	12.1	5.6	4.3	4.6	4.3	3.7	18.1	8.8	10.2	11.1	9.2
Czech Republic	12.5	13.2	12.8	8.7	7.2	6.8	7.7	8.1	4.5	3.4	..	..	..	..	..
Hungary	27.3	21.8	19.3	16.3	12.6	22.2	18.5	18.5	13.3	9.6	24.0	20.1	17.7	14.7	11.1
Poland	26.1	24.9	24.6	17.1	20.0	18.5	18.1	17.4	11.2	13.6	20.3	21.6	19.1	13.1	16.6
Romania	55.3	72.5	55.4	65.5	53.8	38.1	55.8	37.3	46.0	32.9	51.1	85.7	64.0	74.6	52.3
Slovakia	14.3	17.3	20.6	19.6	13.8	6.7	8.0	10.2	10.5	7.3	..	..	..	..	..
Slovenia	22.6	20.0	16.1	12.4	15.8	15.0	13.2	10.6	7.2	10.1	5.7	5.0	4.4	3.3	..
The former Yugoslav Republic of Macedonia	21.6	21.4	21.0	20.4	18.9	12.8	11.7	11.7	11.6	11.2	..	..	..	..	..
Estonia	14.9	11.8	15.0	11.1	7.8	6.1	6.2	8.1	4.2	3.8	..	..	..	..	..
Latvia	25.8	15.2	14.3	14.2	11.9	11.7	5.9	5.3	5.0	4.4	16.3	4.7	5.3	6.2	4.5
Lithuania	21.6	14.4	12.2	13.1	12.2	13.6	8.1	6.5	7.4	6.7	21.0	8.6	10.7	6.2	5.9
Armenia	66.4	54.2	48.5	38.8	31.6	32.2	26.1	24.9	26.6	18.1	41.4	55.8	45.8	53.3	23.6
Belarus	64.3	32.5	27.0	51.0	69.5	32.3	15.5	14.4	23.8	37.5	..	..	..	..	..
Georgia	58.2	50.6	46.0	33.4	32.8	31.1	13.7	17.0	14.6	..	..	..	..	..	..
Kazakhstan	..	30.9	21.4	23.7	19.4	35.9	19.5	12.4	17.0	16.5	33.2	16.3	23.6	20.7	12.3
Kyrgyzstan	63.2	63.8	57.5	59.6	57.0	30.2	35.0	31.1	31.4	23.9	40.1	35.8	43.7	47.2	32.3
Republic of Moldova	25.4	33.3	30.8	35.3	..	25.4	26.4	22.0	27.5	24.9	..	..	..	..	..
Russian Federation	146.8	46.2	43.4	39.7	25.0	55.1	16.4	16.0	13.7	6.7	85.8	26.0	45.8	..	..
Ukraine	79.9	49.1	54.5	55.0	41.5	33.6	18.2	21.9	20.7	13.7	..	..	..	..	..

Source: Central bank publications and direct communications to UN/ECE secretariat; IMF, *International Financial Statistics* (Washington, D.C.), various issues.

Note: Definition of interest rates:

Credits – Belarus: weighted average rate on short-term loans; Bulgaria: average rate on short-term credits; Croatia: weighted average rate on new credits; Czech Republic: average rate on total short-term loans; Estonia: weighted average rate on short-term loans; Hungary: weighted average rate on loans of less than one year; Latvia: average rates on short-term credits; Lithuania: average rates on loans of one to three months; Poland: median rate on low-risk short-term loans. Beginning January 1995, weighted average rate; Romania: average short-term lending rate; Kazakhstan: weighted average interest rates (for new credits); Kyrgyzstan: weighted average rate on loans in sums for one- to three-month maturities; Russian Federation: weighted average rate on loans of up to one-year maturity; Slovakia: average rate on new short-term loans; Slovenia: average rate on short-term working capital loans; The former Yugoslav Republic of Macedonia: midpoint rates for short-term loans to all sectors; Ukraine: weighted average rate on short-term loans.

Deposits – Belarus: weighted average rate on short-term deposits; Bulgaria: average rates on one-month time deposits; Croatia: weighted average rate on new deposits; Czech Republic: average rate on short-term time deposits; Estonia: weighted average rate on short-term deposits; Hungary: weighted average rate on deposits fixed for more than one month, but less than one year; Latvia: average rates on short-term deposits; Lithuania: average rates on deposits of one to three months; Poland: weighted average rate (according to information collected from 15 biggest commercial banks) on short-term household deposits in domestic currency; Romania: average short-term deposit rate; Kazakhstan: weighted average interest rates (for new deposits); Kyrgyzstan: weighted average rate offered on some time deposits of three-month maturities; Russian Federation: prevailing rate for time deposits with maturity of less than one year; Slovakia: average rate on time deposits; Slovenia: average rate on time deposits of 31-90 days; The former Yugoslav Republic of Macedonia: lowest reported interest rate on household deposits with maturities of three to six months; Ukraine: weighted average rate on short-term deposits.

Yields of government securities – Bulgaria: yield on government securities is computed as the average weighted yield of all issues during the calendar month; Croatia: interest rate on NBC bills, due in 91 days; Hungary: weighted average yield on 90-day treasury bills sold at auctions; Poland: yield on bills purchased, weighted average, 13 weeks; Romania: rate on 91-day treasury bills; Slovenia: BS tolar bills, 14 days overall nominal rate; Latvia: weighted average auction rate on 91-day treasury bills; Lithuania: average auction rate on treasury bills with maturity of 91-days; Kazakhstan: yield based on treasury bill prices established at the last auction of the month; Kyrgyzstan: weighted average rate on three-month treasury bills sold in the primary market; Russian Federation: weighted average rate on government short-term obligations (GKO) with maturities of up to 90 days. Beginning in April 1997, the rate is calculated on the basis of GKOs with remaining maturity of up to 90 days.

[a] January-November for Albania; January-October for Belarus.

Poland was a notable exception to this pattern. Monetary conditions remained rather tight until the end of 2000 (and also in the first months of 2001) which kept nominal interest rates high and little changed throughout most of this period. At the same time, the inflation rate started to slow down in the second half of the year. This combination reinforced the monetary restraint and resulted in a sharp rise in real interest rates in the second half and especially in the final months of the year (chart 3.2.2). Thus, in contrast to the rest of the transition economies, the monetary conditions in Poland are likely to have had a highly negative impact on economic activity in this period.

Money demand (apart from the demand for credit) remained relatively stable in 2000 in most of the transition economies, with rising real incomes and falling real interest rates largely offsetting each other. The main monetary aggregates in most countries moved in line with or slightly exceeded the growth of aggregate output, so there were only small (mostly positive) changes in the level of monetization in most countries (table 3.2.2). However, as regards the growth of credit, the picture in 2000 was more differentiated among the transition economies, as higher incomes and lower interest rates led to higher credit demand.

CHART 3.2.2

Real short-term interest rates in selected east European, Baltic and CIS economies, 1997-2000
(Three-month moving average of the ex-post forward-looking real rates,[a] per cent)

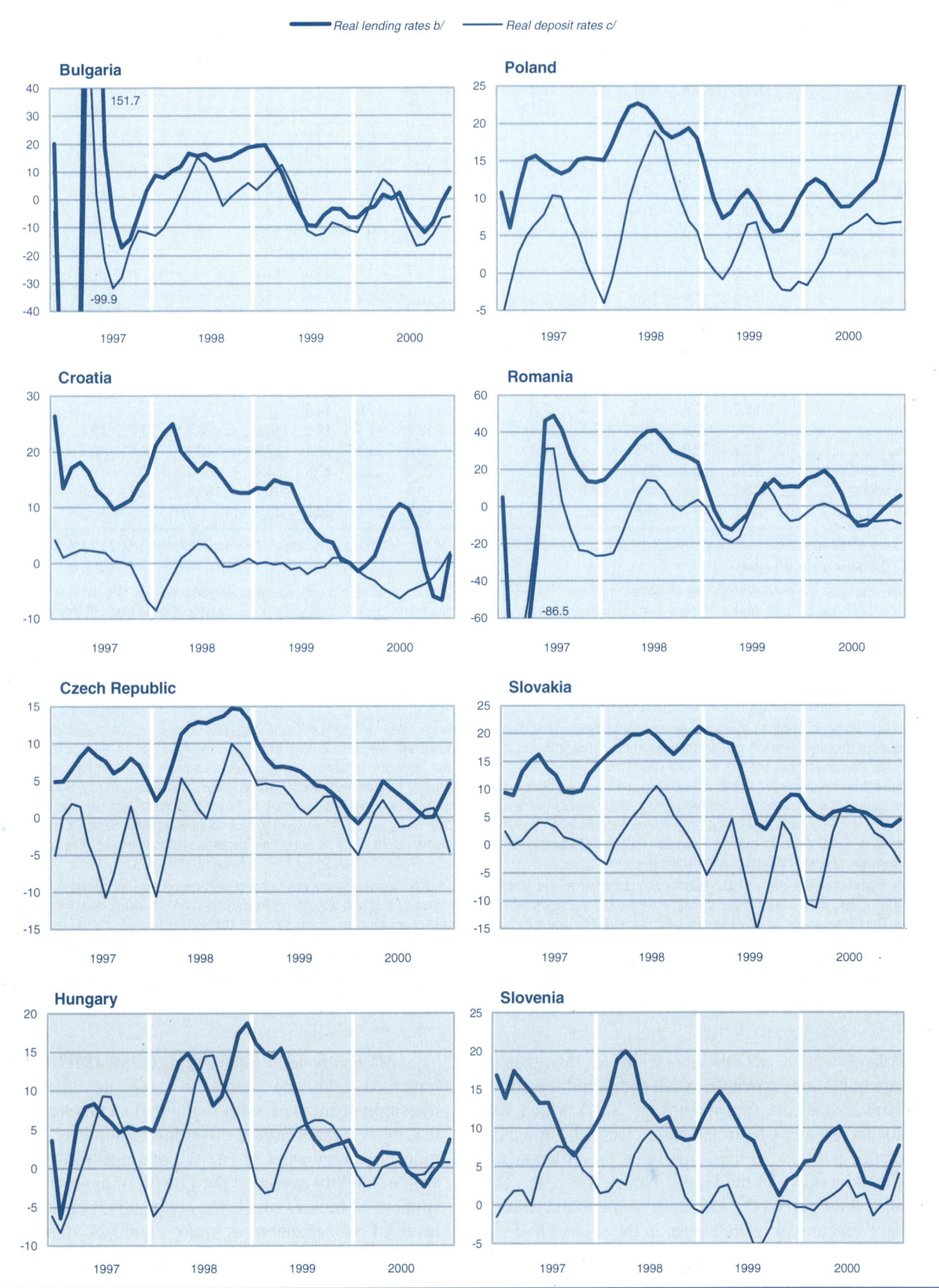

(For source and notes see end of chart.)

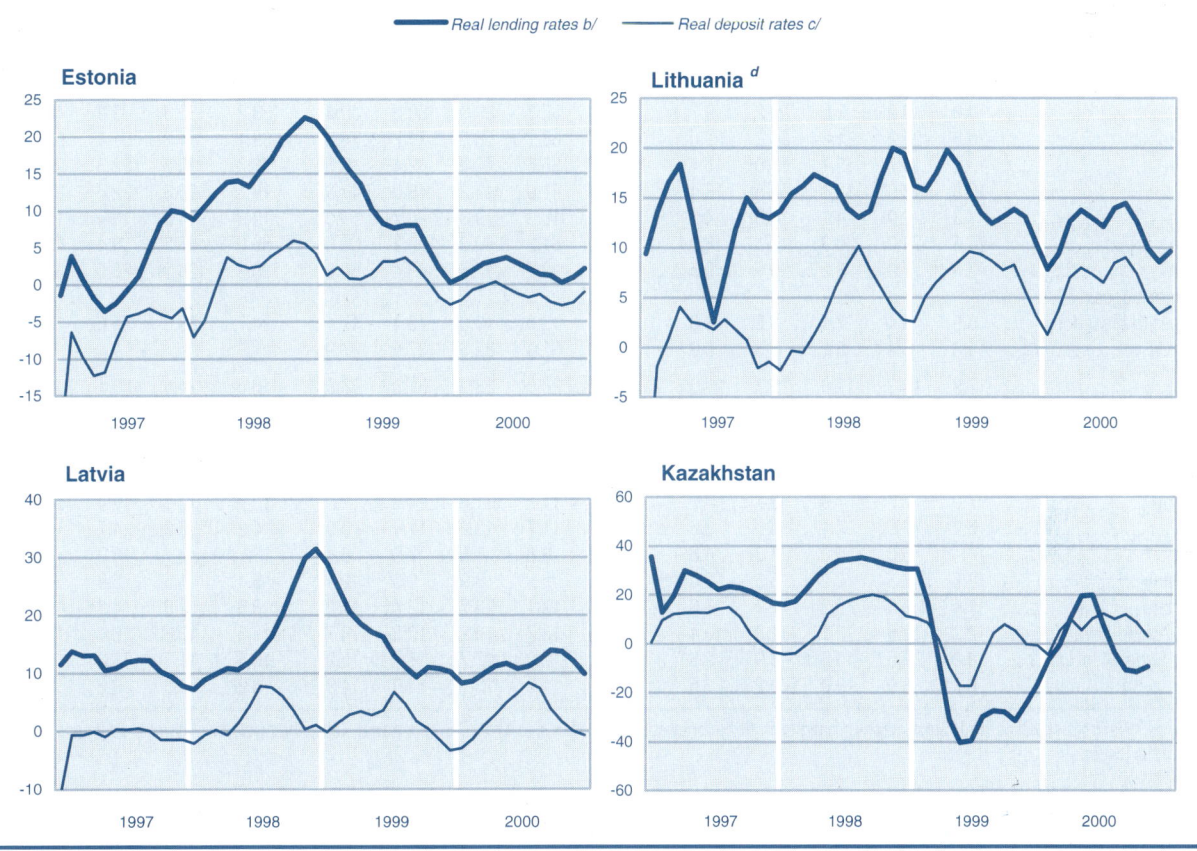

CHART 3.2.2 (concluded)

Real short-term interest rates in selected east European, Baltic and CIS economies, 1997-2000
(Three-month moving average of the ex-post forward-looking real rates, a per cent)

Source: UN/ECE secretariat calculations, based on national statistics and direct communications from central banks.

a The *ex-post* forward-looking rates are the nominal rates discounted by the rate of inflation in the following three-month period.

b Discounted by PPI.

c Discounted by CPI.

d The lending rate for Lithuania is discounted by the index of producer prices excluding the prices of petroleum products.

In recent years, credit has expanded rapidly in a number of transition economies, in some cases substantially exceeding the pace of output growth. In 2000, credit continued to grow in parts of eastern Europe and the Baltic states (Hungary, Slovenia, Estonia, Latvia) and it started to recover in some CIS countries (Armenia, Kazakhstan, Russia, Ukraine). In general, this is a positive sign of progress in economic transformation as it reflects optimistic expectations about the future by all economic agents (businesses and households, as well as the banking sector). The expansion of credit to the corporate sector has undoubtedly contributed to the strength of output growth, especially in the more advanced reform economies. However, an unbalanced credit expansion increases the risk of overheating as well as the vulnerability of still fragile financial systems to sudden reversals in economic growth or to external shocks. Hence, the monetary authorities carefully monitor credit expansion and often step in to check it.

Imprudent lending in the absence of adequate supervision has resulted in the accumulation of large amounts of substandard and non-performing loans in the Czech banking system. Although banking regulations have now been substantially tightened (leading to a net withdrawal of financial resources from the corporate sector to the banking system and a contraction of outstanding credit in recent years – table 3.2.2), the cleaning up of the loan portfolios of the troubled Czech banks will require major government intervention and will involve significant amounts of public funds.[162] A similar process of credit contraction occurred in 2000 in Romania (due to the destabilization of the banking system by risky lending which resulted in several bank failures in 2000) and in Slovakia (after the tightening of bank lending policies). In Poland, where there was

---

[162] The costs of rehabilitating two of the largest Czech banks (IPB and Komercni Banka) are estimated at some koruna 200 billion (more than 10 per cent of the Czech GDP in 1999). Overall, the stock of bad loans stemming from weak risk management in the Czech banking sector over the past 10 years is estimated at one third of GDP in 1999. *Reuters News Service*, 19 December 2000; *Reuters Business Briefing*, 12 February 2001.

TABLE 3.2.2

Monetization in selected east European, Baltic and CIS economies: share of monetary aggregates[a] in GDP, 1996-2000

(Per cent)

	M1[b]					Total broad money[c]					Total credit[d]				
	1996	1997	1998	1999	2000[e]	1996	1997	1998	1999	2000[e]	1996	1997	1998	1999	2000[e]
Albania	25.9	27.7	18.0	17.8	19.9	46.8	52.3	47.8	53.5	56.1	4.8	4.4	3.8	3.7	4.2
Bulgaria	7.4	6.5	10.1	10.7	11.7	44.4	24.9	28.1	28.3	30.8	34.5	17.4	16.4	16.8	16.0
Croatia	9.0	9.9	9.6	9.2	9.7	28.4	35.7	39.0	38.6	40.4	33.2	32.9	39.9	40.7	36.4
Czech Republic	28.5	25.2	21.8	24.2	27.0	68.3	68.1	66.3	71.7	74.2	62.1	64.0	61.4	59.0	53.5
Hungary	15.2	14.7	15.1	15.8	16.1	36.4	35.6	40.9	42.4	42.5	36.2	20.8	22.3	22.9	26.2
Poland	10.8	13.8	13.4	14.5	13.4	33.3	41.0	43.2	48.0	48.3	17.1	20.3	22.7	25.8	27.0
Romania	7.3	5.0	4.7	4.3	4.1	20.8	18.3	19.3	20.7	19.0	19.2	14.8	13.4	12.6	9.1
Slovakia	24.5	23.0	20.3	17.5	18.0	61.4	61.2	60.3	60.2	63.6	56.0	53.3	50.4	49.5	46.3
Slovenia	7.8	7.9	8.2	9.9	9.5	40.6	42.5	47.5	49.4	50.6	26.9	26.3	28.5	32.4	35.5
The former Yugoslav Republic of Macedonia	6.6	6.4	7.1	8.8	8.3	11.4	12.0	13.3	16.4	17.1	24.7	25.8	22.6	19.5	17.8
Yugoslavia	5.3	6.4	6.1	7.5	6.0	36.6	31.4	35.6	37.8	27.9	..	..	..	..	..
Estonia	17.9	19.2	17.8	19.7	23.0	23.3	26.6	28.0	31.0	36.5	16.6	24.9	33.1	32.3	36.3
Latvia	12.4	14.1	16.0	15.1	15.5	19.7	22.5	25.4	24.1	26.4	7.3	8.9	14.4	15.8	18.0
Lithuania	10.6	10.7	11.9	12.4	11.5	16.5	16.3	17.6	20.3	21.0	12.3	10.4	12.1	14.9	13.6
Armenia	5.1	5.1	4.8	4.8	5.2	7.0	7.8	8.6	10.1	11.9	5.2	5.5	6.6	8.8	9.9
Azerbaijan	7.0	7.7	7.6	6.7	..	10.0	11.2	11.6	14.8	..	13.7	12.1	12.4	14.4	.
Belarus	6.2	6.5	7.1	5.0	3.6	12.1	11.7	13.2	11.4	9.9	4.2	3.8	4.7	4.1	3.4
Georgia	..	5.0	5.0	4.6	4.8	..	6.6	7.3	7.5	8.4	..	3.7	5.2	6.9	7.6
Kazakhstan	8.6	6.3	7.2	6.5	8.0	..	..	8.9	9.5	12.4	5.4	4.5	5.9	7.5	9.2
Kyrgyzstan	11.1	9.6	9.2	7.9	6.8	12.4	12.1	13.7	12.4	11.2	8.5	2.8	4.8	4.8	4.1
Republic of Moldova	12.2	12.5	12.1	11.0	10.4	17.3	18.7	19.7	19.0	18.7	17.6	17.6	18.4	13.8	12.1
Russian Federation	8.0	9.5	10.3	8.9	9.6	15.1	17.0	17.7	16.9	18.2	10.4	11.1	11.3	9.8	10.5
Ukraine	6.7	8.5	9.0	9.2	9.5	9.5	11.8	13.1	14.0	14.9	6.2	7.5	8.2	8.6	9.6

Source: National statistics and direct communications from national statistical offices to UN/ECE secretariat; IMF, *International Financial Statistics* (Washington, D.C.), various issues.

[a] Averages of monthly or quarterly figures.

[b] Currency in circulation plus demand deposits.

[c] M1 plus time deposits in domestic currency and foreign currency deposits.

[d] Total outstanding claims on firms and households (except claims on government).

[e] January-October for The former Yugoslav Republic of Macedonia and Belarus and January-November for Albania; GDP data for (2000) are based on preliminary reports by national statistical offices, wherever available, otherwise they are based on estimates.

significant credit expansion in 1998-1999, the process slowed down considerably in 2000 as a result of the central bank's restrictive measures.

The Asian and Russian crises appear to have led to a persistent shift in financial investors' perception of risk which, in turn, has led to changes in the currency composition of their portfolios in some transition economies. In particular, there has been some reversal of the process of dedollarization and rising shares of dollar-denominated assets in the stock of broad money since 1998 (table 3.2.3).[163] This underscores the inherent fragility of the transition economies' financial systems, which are still rather vulnerable to financial disturbance.

Nevertheless, a number of transition economies have been successfully replenishing their foreign exchange reserves during the last few years. Using various measures (such as raising the proportion of reserves relative to national money stocks – table 3.2.3), official foreign exchange reserves in most of these countries are now sufficiently high to be able to serve as a cushion against random volatility on the foreign exchange markets. Although this strengthens the domestic financial systems somewhat, higher levels of foreign exchange backing to monetary stocks is no guarantee against systemic financial instability; moreover, the adequacy of foreign exchange reserves has to be judged also in relation to other indicators of the external financial position of each economy (table 3.6.13).

Macroeconomic conditions and the external environment at the beginning of 2001 have deteriorated somewhat from those prevailing in most of 2000. The expected slowdown in global demand and some signs of increasing volatility in international financial markets (for example, the financial crisis in Turkey) may have adverse repercussions for the transition economies. This will require increased attention to the changing external conditions by the monetary authorities and design of adequate policy responses.

---

[163] In fact, Hungary was the only transition economy where such a reversal did not take place.

TABLE 3.2.3

Monetary ratios for selected east European, Baltic and CIS economies, 1996-2000
(Per cent)

	Dollarization: share of foreign currency in broad money					Official foreign exchange reserves as percentage of M1					Official foreign exchange reserves as percentage of broad money, domestic currency				
	1996	1997	1998	1999	2000[a]	1996	1997	1998	1999	2000[a]	1996	1997	1998	1999	2000[a]
Albania	..	..	..	..	..	37.5	44.2	68.4	55.3	48.2	..	..	..	..	..
Bulgaria	34.8	52.5	39.2	38.0	39.7	71.3	221.7	203.9	200.9	199.2	19.7	120.1	133.5	100.2	134.2
Croatia	59.8	62.1	65.1	66.8	66.4	125.7	123.6	124.6	146.0	174.9	98.7	91.0	88.2	104.8	124.2
Czech Republic	8.0	10.3	11.2	10.8	10.5	78.2	81.5	91.6	94.4	94.2	35.5	33.6	34.3	36.3	39.6
Hungary	26.6	23.4	19.4	17.9	17.2	150.2	126.5	123.0	126.5	143.5	85.5	68.2	54.7	58.0	66.5
Poland	16.4	14.1	12.6	12.8	13.0	111.9	96.6	116.3	112.3	117.7	43.7	37.9	41.3	38.9	37.4
Romania	23.0	32.0	29.7	37.4	39.7	67.5	160.6	160.3	164.0	218.4	30.8	63.4	55.7	54.0	78.4
Slovakia	10.6	10.7	12.0	14.4	15.3	70.9	68.5	75.0	81.7	113.7	31.7	28.8	28.8	27.7	38.0
Slovenia	34.9	31.5	27.2	25.9	28.9	129.3	214.9	206.3	171.6	176.4	38.2	54.3	53.1	46.3	47.0
The former Yugoslav Republic of Macedonia	..	..	..	..	..	80.4	98.4	109.1	115.3	156.2	..	..	..	..	..
Yugoslavia	79.4	72.1	75.3	74.2	71.3	..	..	..	..	..	..	..	..	..	..
Estonia	11.1	12.7	14.9	15.9	17.2	77.0	71.7	80.4	66.1	67.6	66.4	59.4	60.1	56.8	51.6
Latvia	32.2	32.6	30.7	29.2	31.4	89.8	85.1	77.2	80.1	75.8	83.6	78.7	70.0	71.1	65.0
Lithuania	25.7	25.3	23.4	27.3	32.8	85.2	87.8	100.3	98.6	100.6	73.2	76.6	88.3	83.3	82.3
Armenia	..	..	..	..	..	66.0	74.9	90.1	112.9	123.9	..	..	..	..	..
Azerbaijan	..	..	..	..	..	92.3	104.6	138.5	228.8	..	..	..	..	..	..
Belarus	..	..	..	..	..	45.4	45.4	33.5	57.8	75.6	..	..	..	..	..
Georgia	..	..	..	..	..	..	82.2	76.6	94.6	78.7	..	..	..	..	..
Kazakhstan	..	..	..	..	..	68.2	107.0	87.5	110.8	105.8	..	..	..	..	..
Kyrgyzstan	..	..	..	..	..	47.9	74.3	111.2	205.4	264.9	..	..	..	..	..
Republic of Moldova	..	..	..	..	..	103.3	140.0	111.7	146.8	151.2	..	..	..	..	..
Russian Federation	19.5	17.9	21.7	30.5	29.7	37.5	37.7	31.9	44.9	71.8	24.5	25.7	24.1	33.9	53.8
Ukraine	19.1	14.3	18.5	22.9	24.6	33.1	53.4	40.4	30.9	30.7	44.9	44.6	33.8	26.5	26.1

Source: National statistics and direct communications from national statistical offices to UN/ECE secretariat; IMF, *International Financial Statistics* (Washington, D.C.), various issues.

[a] January-October for The former Yugoslav Republic of Macedonia and Belarus. January-November for Albania.

(ii) Fiscal policy

(a) Fiscal policy challenges in the transition economies

There was a notable improvement in the fiscal position of the ECE transition economies in 2000: the unweighted average of their consolidated general government fiscal deficits was -2.6 per cent[164] which was the best fiscal outcome for these economies since the start of economic transformation. This outcome also represented considerable progress from the situation in 1998 and 1999 when the unweighted average deficit was -3.6 per cent and -3.9 per cent, respectively. The strengthening of output in 2000 obviously contributed significantly to this outcome (in contrast to 1998 and 1999 when the cyclical influence was negative). Even if 1997 (the year before the global and Russian financial crises) is taken as a reference point, there was still a 1.1 percentage point improvement in 2000 in the average fiscal deficit for the transition economies taken as a whole, which suggests an improvement in their structural deficits.

As a further sign of the progress in fiscal consolidation in the transition economies, 15 of the 23 economies for which preliminary data for 2000 were available at the time of writing this *Survey*, reported fiscal deficits below 3 per cent and seven were below this threshold in both 1999 and 2000. In general, the transition economies are now in a more stable fiscal position than several years ago: excessive deficits and a persistent deterioration in the balance over time are becoming more the exception than the rule. Governments in most of the transition economies now seem determined to pursue generally prudent fiscal policies.

The improvement in fiscal positions reflects the progress in macroeconomic and systemic reforms as well as the increased attention of governments to issues of policy coordination. The sources of the large and chronic fiscal imbalances that fuelled persistent macroeconomic instability in the early years of the transition – when the transformation recession was coupled with a collapse of

---

[164] Calculated on the basis of the fiscal deficit data shown in table 3.2.4. Throughout this section the fiscal position in the transition economies is measured by the balance of the consolidated general government which includes the central government, the regional governments and any public ("extrabudgetary") funds. The definition of the consolidated balance (deficit or surplus) is "current revenue minus total expenditure". Hence capital receipts (including privatization revenue) do not contribute to the fiscal balance but are treated as sources of deficit financing. For more details, see UN/ECE, *Economic Survey of Europe, 2000 No. 1*, p. 51, box 3.2.1. The data for 2000 reported in table 3.2.4 are preliminary and incomplete, and are subject to revision.

TABLE 3.2.4

Consolidated general government deficits and their sources of financing in eastern Europe, the Baltic states and the CIS, 1997-2001

(Per cent of GDP)

	Consolidated general government deficit/surplus[a]					Financing of consolidated general government deficit by components								
						Borrowing			Privatization receipts			Other capital receipts		
	1997	1998	1999	2000*	2001 target	1998	1999	2000	1998	1999	2000	1998	1999	2000
Albania	-12.5	-10.6	-11.1	-9.8	-9.2	10.6	10.9	8.0	..	..	..	..	0.2	1.8
Bulgaria	-1.6	0.7	-1.6	1.0	-1.5	-2.7	-1.4	-0.3	1.7	2.3	1.3	0.4	0.6	..
Croatia	-2.2	-1.5	-6.2	-6.3	-4.9	-0.5	2.2	..	1.9	..	..	0.1	..	..
Czech Republic	-2.5	-2.9	-3.7	-5.5	-9.4	1.5	0.6	3.6	0.8	1.4	1.0	0.5	1.7	0.9
Hungary	-5.0	-7.2	-4.6	-2.5	-3.2[b]	6.0	3.5	1.8	0.2	0.1	–	1.0	1.0	0.7
Poland	-3.5	-3.2	-3.8	-2.7[b]	-1.8[b]	1.2	1.0	..	1.3	2.2	..	0.7	0.7	..
Romania	-5.2	-5.0	-3.8	-3.7	-3.7[b]	3.0	1.7	..	1.7	1.3	..	0.9	1.2	..
Slovakia	-6.1	-6.0	-4.4	-3.7[b]	-3.9[b]	4.6	3.6	..	0.7	0.3	..	0.7	0.5	..
Slovenia	-1.9	-1.2	-1.1	-1.5	-1.3	0.7	0.7	1.2	0.4	0.3	0.1	0.1	0.2	0.2
The former Yugoslav Republic of Macedonia	-0.4	-1.9	-1.6	-1.3	–	1.9	1.6	1.3	..	..	..	..	..	..
Yugoslavia	..	..	..	..	-2	..	..	..	..	..	..	..	..	..
Estonia	1.0	-1.6	-5.1	-1.9	–	0.3	4.6	1.7	..	..	..	1.3	0.5	0.2
Latvia	1.2	0.1	-3.7	-2.8[b]	-2.2[b]	-0.1	4.0	2.9	..	..	..	..	..	..
Lithuania	-2.1	-5.5	-8.4	-2.9	-1.5	0.3	7.4	..	5.2	1.0	..	–	–	..
Armenia	-2.6	-2.8	-4.2	-5.2	-4.8	0.6	4.1	5.2	2.2	0.1	..	..	..	..
Azerbaijan	-1.0	-1.9	-4.5	-2.2	-1.7	1.9	4.5	2.2	..	..	..	..	..	..
Belarus	-1.1	-1.0	-2.0	-0.2	-1.7	0.5	1.7	-0.1	0.1	–	0.1	0.3	0.2	0.3
Georgia	-7.0	-6.8	-6.1	-4.6	-4.2	6.8	6.1	..	..	..	..	..	..	..
Kazakhstan	-7.2	-7.9	-5.3	0.8	-2.2	3.9	3.5	-1.8	..	..	..	4.0	1.8	1.0
Kyrgyzstan[c]	-5.4	-2.7	-2.5	-1.2	-5.9	2.5	1.6	0.9	0.2	0.5	0.3	–	0.3	–
Republic of Moldova	-10.5	-4.1	-4.2	-1.9	-3.5	3.3	3.0	1.0	0.9	1.1	0.9	..	..	..
Russian Federation	-5.8	-6.2	-0.9[d]	2.7[e]	–[f]	6.1	0.3[d]	..	..	..	..	0.7	0.6[d]	..
Tajikistan	-1.6	-1.0	-3.1	-3.0	-0.6	1.0	3.1	3.0	..	..	..	..	..	..
Turkmenistan	-1.8	-6.0	..	..	-1.1	..	..	..	..	..	..	..	..	..
Ukraine	-5.8	-0.7	0.1	–	–[g]	..	..	..	..	..	..	..	..	..
Uzbekistan	-2.2	-3.4	-2.2	..	-1.4	..	..	..	..	..	..	..	..	..

Source: UN/ECE secretariat estimates and calculations, based on direct communications from national Ministries of Finance and IMF data.

Note: The consolidated general government deficit, or financing requirement, is defined here as (current revenue and grants) - (current and capital expenditure plus net lending for policy purposes). A deficit is negative, a surplus is positive. With this definition of the deficit, it follows that privatization and other capital receipts are components of financing, not of revenue. The three components of financing (borrowing, privatization and other capital receipts) sum to the general government deficit (or surplus) with opposite sign. Where the borrowing item is negative, this indicates net repayment of government debt. The "IMF" method of the IMF Fiscal Affairs Division is generally to treat only privatization receipts, but not other capital receipts, as financing. Thus the "IMF methodology deficit" is normally equal to the general government deficit plus other capital receipts. The general government deficit here is closest to the present definition of the "Maastricht criterion", as presently interpreted by Eurostat. The "IMF-GFS" method, frequently cited by national sources, defines the general government deficit as in the first panel of this table. Deficits projected at the start of 2001 are official budget deficits, forecast in the initial budget proposals, necessarily involving GDP and inflation projections as well as fiscal data. The definitions of the projected deficits as well as of some of the preliminary estimates of the deficits in 2000 may differ from the above definition. Sources are national Ministries of Finance, official press releases from Reuters, IMF publications and country information (www.imf.org/external/country) and official websites of ministries of finance.

[a] For some countries the deficit shown in this table may not equal the difference between the revenue and expenditures shown in tables 3.2.5 and 3.2.6. The most current aggregate information was used for table 3.2.4, while the more detailed breakdown by type of revenue or expenditure in tables 3.2.5 and 3.2.6 in some cases had to be based on more dated information.

[b] Central government deficit/surplus.

[c] The officially reported deficit for Kyrgyzstan does not include the national public investment programme. According to IMF estimates, if expenditure under this programme were included in the fiscal accounts, the consolidated government deficit would be as follows, 1997: -9.0 per cent; 1998: -9.5 per cent; 1999: 12.0 per cent; 2000 (preliminary) -8.0 per cent.

[d] Consolidated central government (including social security and extra budgetary funds) plus (without consolidation) regional and local government.

[e] Federal, regional and local governments (excluding extra budgetary funds).

[f] Federal government.

[g] Including expected privatization revenue.

the old taxation system and an upsurge in various demands on public spending, in particular, social security[165] – are gradually receding and lowering the pressure on public spending. Thanks to progress in fiscal reform (in particular, reforms in the systems of taxation and tax collection as well as the reorganization of public spending), the fiscal authorities in the transition economies have generally gained greater operational control over public finances, as regards both revenue and spending. Governments are now better equipped not only to adopt a fiscal stance (in terms of setting a target for the

---

[165] For details, see UN/ECE, *Economic Survey of Europe, 2000 No. 1*, pp. 60-63.

fiscal balance) but also to actively pursue such a target, which is notable progress compared with the early years of the transition. In this regard, the current fiscal consolidation mirrors the greater concern of governments with long-term fiscal sustainability and with the coherence of macroeconomic policy. In turn, the growing fiscal responsibility of the executive bodies has largely relieved central banks from an excessive concern about macroeconomic equilibrium (as was the case during the initial years of the transition), allowing them to pursue their main goal of ensuring price stability.

Despite the fact that all the transition economies have made progress in their fiscal reforms, the cross-country perspective is nevertheless heterogeneous and many problems remain.[166] Although the fiscal pressures related to systemic reform have generally diminished in many transition economies, they are far from being exhausted. Thus, in a number of transition economies wide-ranging reforms of the pension and health-care systems have been introduced, which are costly and have serious, long-term fiscal implications; those countries that have not yet started these reforms, will have to face their fiscal costs in the years to come. Another source of fiscal problems are various contingent liabilities of the public sector such as the quasi-fiscal operations of the central banks (involving, for example, directed or subsidized credit), or implicit guarantees to the corporate sector (the presumed commitment of governments to engage in financial rescue operations). During the past decade, the absence of proper control over contingent fiscal liabilities has sometimes led to full-blown crises (Bulgaria in 1996-1997 is a case in point) and although such claims on the public finances are generally decreasing, they can still pose threats to financial and macroeconomic stability.

Although fiscal deficits in the transition economies have on average been reduced, in a number of cases they are still precariously high from the viewpoint of long-term fiscal sustainability. At the same time, all governments are under persistent pressure to increase social spending, mostly due to the growing impatience of the population with mediocre living standards. Pensioners, who figure prominently among the losers from the transformation reforms, are also among the most active in demanding decent living conditions. A wide range of professions in the public sector (teachers, medical personnel, scientists) who view themselves as marginalized in the new society due to the fall in their incomes (both in real and relative terms), are continually voicing demands for higher wages. The sizeable stagnant pools of the unemployed are also maintaining large claims on public funds.

The transition economies that aspire to EU membership are facing additional fiscal challenges during their preparation for EU accession. The candidates are entering a period when there will be large extra claims on government expenditure in order to meet the requirements of policy harmonization with the EU. For example, complying with EU environmental norms will require massive public spending during the pre-accession period. Overall, the necessary policy measures for accession may well result in higher levels of government expenditure and, probably, larger fiscal deficits as well.

The countries that are lagging behind in the process of reform (which are also among the poorest in terms of per capita income) face different types of fiscal problems. For example, almost all the central Asian and Caucasian rim economies are locked into a vicious circle caused by their governments' inability to raise sufficient revenue. With total fiscal revenue of around or below 20 per cent of GDP (table 3.2.5), these governments face major constraints on their ability to implement much needed fiscal reforms, including the establishment of efficient tax administration and tax collecting systems. The fundamental problems in these economies are essentially developmental in nature and their solution will require persistence and long-term commitment by the governments and the international community.

Another challenge concerns the financing of budget deficits. In recent years some countries were able to maintain large fiscal deficits mostly thanks to the privatization revenues which provided a major source of government finance (table 3.2.4). However, with privatization coming to an end in most transition economies, a new round of fiscal adjustments will be needed to maintain long-term fiscal sustainability.

(b) Fiscal stance and fiscal position in 2000-early 2001

Of the 22 transition economies for which preliminary fiscal statistics were available at the time of writing this *Survey*, 17 managed to reduce their fiscal deficits (in terms of the consolidated government balance) in 2000. This was a notable improvement over 1999 when the fiscal position deteriorated in more than half of them (chart 3.2.3).[167] The *ex-ante* deficit reduction targets set in the budgets for 2000 were met or even exceeded in the majority of the transition economies.

As noted above, governments in many of these countries are facing a policy dilemma in trying to attain long-term fiscal sustainability (and hence improve their fiscal balance), while being under pressure for higher

---

[166] One outstanding problem is the basic one of being able to accurately assess the fiscal position, and especially the consolidated government balance. The absence of uniform reporting standards across countries, the persistent lack of transparency (especially as regards extrabudgetary spending), and delays in reporting fiscal statistics all create considerable difficulties – and sometimes confusion – in properly measuring the fiscal position of a country at any given time, its change over time, and its standing in cross-country comparisons. Thus, the fiscal data presented in this section should be treated with caution, especially those for the most recent period which are tentative and often incomplete.

[167] The data for Kyrgyzstan are not included in these comparisons and are not shown on charts 3.2.3 and 3.2.4 due to the absence of accurate data on the consolidated government deficit (see the note to table 3.2.4)

TABLE 3.2.5

Consolidated general government current revenue in eastern Europe, the Baltic states and the CIS, 1998-2000

(Per cent of GDP)

	Total current revenue and grants			Taxes on income, profits and capital gains			Indirect taxes and customs duties			Non-tax revenue			Social security contributions		
	1998	1999	2000	1998	1999	2000	1998	1999	2000	1998	1999	2000	1998	1999	2000
Albania	20.0	21.2	22.9	1.2	1.8	1.8	10.0	9.6	11.6	4.5	4.8	3.8	3.4	3.6	3.7
Bulgaria	39.4	39.0	42.1	8.8	7.9	6.9	13.6	12.6	13.8	7.4	7.8	8.2	7.7	7.9	11.2
Croatia	50.8	..	..	8.4	..	..	23.4	..	..	4.0	..	..	14.0	..	..
Czech Republic	38.0	39.8	39.2	8.9	9.0	8.9	11.6	12.8	12.3	2.6	2.5	2.8	14.4	14.8	14.5
Hungary	43.3	43.8	41.7	8.7	9.0	8.9	13.6	15.0	13.5	6.1	5.4	5.1	13.8	13.0	12.6
Poland	40.0	40.2	..	11.0	7.9	..	13.0	13.2	..	5.4	6.4	..	9.2	8.6	..
Romania	30.8	37.6	..	9.1	10.3	..	10.0	11.0	..	2.6	6.2	..	8.1	9.0	..
Slovakia	36.5	38.5	..	9.1	8.5	..	12.6	12.4	..	3.1	6.5	..	11.1	10.5	..
Slovenia	42.8	43.5	42.2	7.8	7.5	7.6	16.2	17.8	15.7	2.7	2.2	2.4	13.8	13.6	13.6
The former Yugoslav Republic of Macedonia	33.9	36.2	43.2	5.7	6.6	7.3	13.9	15.1	18.1	2.4	2.4	3.1	11.4	11.6	14.1
Estonia	37.1	36.5	35.8	11.1	10.8	9.0	12.7	12.3	13.4	2.6	3.0	2.7	10.2	9.6	10.1
Latvia	43.9	40.8	38.6	8.7	8.5	..	14.1	12.5	..	7.2	5.9	..	11.9	11.6	..
Lithuania	32.0	31.5	..	9.3	9.3	..	12.9	12.5	..	1.4	1.7	..	7.1	6.8	..
Armenia [a]	17.6	19.3	22.4	13.6	16.1	19.6	..	..	..	2.3	1.6	1.1	..	..	..
Azerbaijan	13.5	19.6	15.7	4.2	5.3	4.2	6.7	10.1	7.7	0.9	1.6	1.5	..	..	..
Belarus	42.9	43.7	42.9	8.0	7.8	7.9	19.8	21.3	16.1	2.9	3.0	2.0	8.7	8.7	7.6
Georgia	15.2	15.5	18.1	2.8	2.8	2.9	5.9	6.9	8.5	1.8	0.7	0.7	2.2	2.0	2.2
Kazakhstan	17.9	17.8	..	1.7	1.8	..	7.2	6.8	–	1.1	1.3	..	4.3	–	–
Kyrgyzstan	17.2	15.7	11.4	2.5	1.7	2.1	7.3	6.6	6.9	3.3	2.7	2.6	..	..	..
Republic of Moldova	37.6	30.4	30.7	4.4	3.7	3.4	17.6	13.1	13.8	4.8	3.5	4.5	8.6	6.4	6.2
Russian Federation	35.8	36.3[b]	..	6.4	7.5[b]	..	11.3	10.8[b]	..	3.4	4.5[b]	..	9.2	7.0[b]	–
Tajikistan [a]	17.6	15.9	19.5	13.3	11.7	18.3	..	..	..	4.3	4.2	0.7	..	..	..
Ukraine [a]	37.4	33.4	28.3	21.3	19.1	16.1	..	..	..	2.1	2.0	4.0	..	..	..

Source: UN/ECE secretariat estimates and calculations, based on direct communications from national Ministries of Finance and IMF data. Data not available for Yugoslavia, Turkmenistan or Uzbekistan.

[a] Total tax revenue used in place of income and profit taxes.

[b] Consolidated central government (including social security and extra budgetary funds) plus (without consolidation) regional and local government.

---

spending (which would worsen the balance). In view of this conflict, the outcome for 2000 suggests that in general the stance of fiscal policy has been moderately restrictive. Indeed, fiscal retrenchment in most countries in 2000 was associated with relatively lower levels (in proportion to GDP) of final domestic demand (the lower panel of chart 3.2.4) despite the strong growth of aggregate output.

The generally restrictive stance of macroeconomic policy was not something new for the transition economies, as many of them have been trying to contain not only domestic but also external imbalances. Thus, in 1999 domestic absorption shrank in relative terms in an even greater number of transition economies (the upper panel of chart 3.2.4). However, given the fact that the fiscal stance in 1999 was relatively looser than in 2000 (in the majority of countries there was a deterioration in the fiscal position), final domestic demand in 1999 was largely checked by monetary restrictions. In contrast, while monetary policy was broadly neutral in 2000 (as noted in section 3.2(i)), fiscal policy was more active in maintaining domestic and external equilibrium. This shift in the balance between monetary and fiscal policy was probably the most important general change in the overall stance of macroeconomic policy in the transition economies in 2000.

Despite the progress in fiscal reform and a generally tight fiscal stance, deficit reduction in 2000 was uneven and a number of countries failed to meet their *ex-ante* targets. In addition, there were notable exceptions to the general pattern of fiscal consolidation, as well as specificities in the stance of fiscal policy in individual countries. In several countries there was a deterioration in their fiscal position, including in some of the most advanced reformers of central Europe where various fiscal pressures emerged in 2000.

The Czech Republic is one of the countries where the fiscal balance has been deteriorating in recent years. The main factor behind this development is the accumulation by the public sector over the past decade, of large amounts of deferred contingent fiscal liabilities, which ultimately emerged as non-performing bank assets.[168] When the degradation in the quality of the

---

[168] Most of this quasi-fiscal deficit arose from soft bank lending to inefficient firms which, in turn, were able to survive because of the absence of proper governance in both the corporate and the banking sectors. Rapid, mass privatization did not contribute to better governance or to greater efficiency in bank lending due to the specific governance structures that emerged from the mass privatization. Cross-ownership structures bred soft budget constraints in the corporate sector and distorted incentives in the banking system; as a result, the banks continued to extend credit to enterprises not on the basis of expected returns but as an obligation of "cozy" bank-enterprise relations.

CHART 3.2.3

Fiscal balance and its change from the previous year in eastern Europe, the Baltic states and the CIS, 1999-2000
(Per cent of GDP)

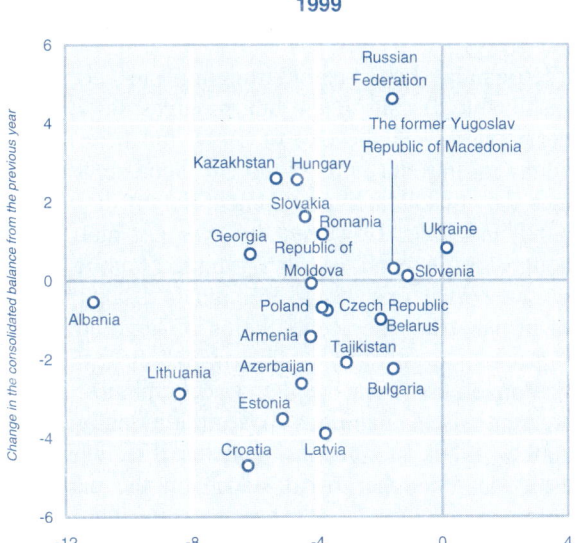

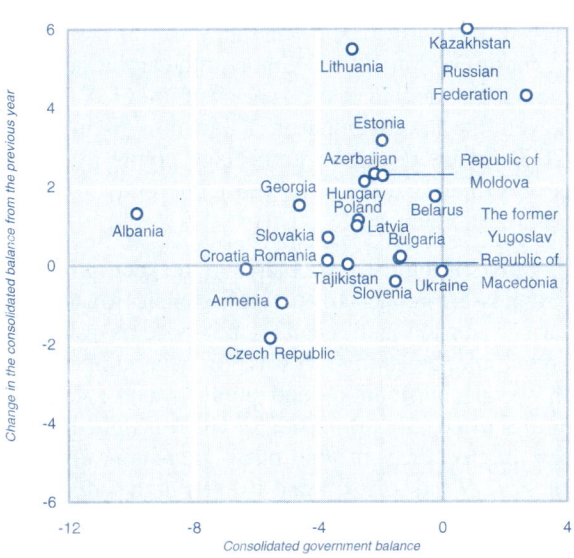

Source: UN/ECE secretariat estimates and calculations, based on direct communications from national Ministries of Finance and IMF data.

expenditure,[169] largely the result of populist measures by the previous government (such as generous increases in public sector wages as well as large transfers to the pension and health insurance funds, partly to compensate war veterans). In 2000, the newly elected Croatian government made an effort to reverse this trend, targeting a nominal reduction in central government spending by 5 per cent and a central government budget deficit (excluding privatization revenue) of 1.3 per cent. However, this ambitious target could not be achieved, in large part because of the need to settle sizeable payments arrears, amounting to some 2-3 per cent of GDP.[170] Thus the authorities were forced to revise the 2000 budget and allow central government spending to rise by 3.7 per cent. The *ex-ante* deficit target was not met either: the central budget deficit including privatization revenue reached some 4.2 per cent and with privatization revenue excluded it was 6.3 per cent.[171] However, given the fact that a large share of this deficit is due to the settlement of payments arrears, the outcome suggests a marked adjustment in the underlying fiscal situation in 2000 that will have to be consolidated in the future.

Since 1999 the authorities in Slovakia have also been trying to correct an unsustainable growth in the fiscal deficit, which was the result of a large-scale public investment programme pursued by the previous administration. In 2000 the government was aiming to reduce the consolidated government deficit to 3 per cent of GDP. However, it proved difficult to meet this target (despite the fact that total revenues were some 16 per cent higher than projected) due to the need to settle quasi-fiscal deficits accumulated in previous years.[172] In 2000 the government initiated a large-scale programme of restructuring and financial rehabilitation of the banking system, total spending on this programme in 2000 amounting to 8.5 billion koruny, or close to 1 per cent of GDP. Even more spending on bank restructuring is envisaged in 2001 and as a result a significant reduction in the Slovak fiscal deficit is unlikely in the near future.

In Poland there was a shortfall in public revenue in 2000 due to lower than expected tax collection, which was probably due to the weakening of output. In the final months of the year, the Polish government was forced to cut its planned expenditure by 5.3 billion zlotys (some 3.4 per cent of the planned expenditure of the central government) in order to achieve a central government deficit target of 2.2 per cent of GDP, as set by the budget law. Spending cuts were made across the board but the largest reductions were in regional administration (affecting mostly education and local government

---

[169] The share of total government expenditure in GDP in Croatia is the highest of all the transition economies (table 3.2.6).

[170] Zagrebačka Banka, *Croatian Economic Forecast* (Zagreb), January 2001, p. 8.

[171] Ibid.

[172] As in the Czech Republic, improper bank lending over a number of years had resulted in an escalation of bad loans, which eventually threatened the stability of the banking sector.

banks' asset portfolios reached a level that began to threaten the stability of the banking system, the Czech government intervened with a programme for the financial rehabilitation of several large banks. Part of the expenditure under this programme occurred already in 2000 but the bulk of it is envisaged for 2001 when the bailout costs are expected to raise the fiscal deficit to more than 9 per cent of GDP (table 3.2.4).

Croatia is also faced with acute fiscal problems because of an unsustainable growth in public

CHART 3.2.4

Changes in the fiscal balance and domestic absorption in eastern Europe, the Baltic states and the CIS, 1999-2000
(Per cent of GDP)

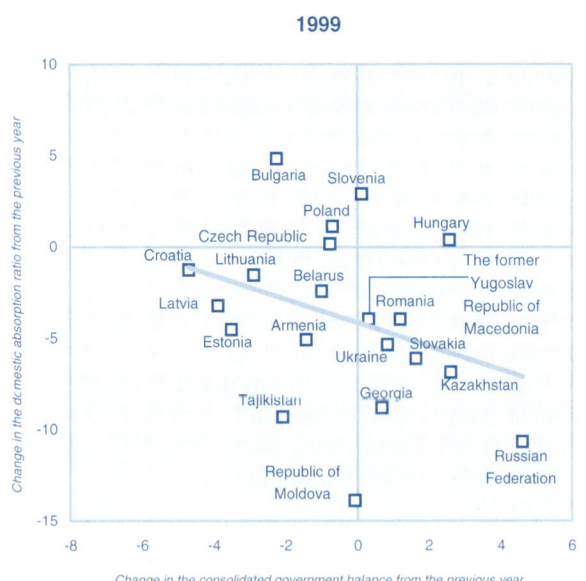

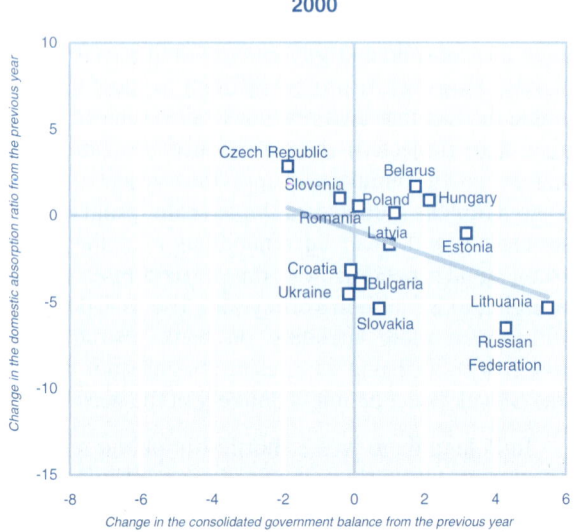

Source: UN/ECE secretariat estimates and calculations, based on direct communications from national Ministries of Finance and IMF data.

government in December to make an additional allocation of public funds, amounting to 95 billion forint (or around 0.6 per cent of annual GDP), to meet expenditure that had been initially envisaged for 2001, while keeping the state budget deficit in 2000 to its target of 3.5 per cent of GDP. Thus the actual improvement in Hungary's fiscal position in 2000 was greater than appears from the preliminary fiscal data.

Romania has been struggling to control an unsustainable fiscal deficit but progress in 2000 was rather modest. At the end of 1999, the newly elected government introduced a tax reform[173] and set a target to reduce the consolidated government deficit to 3 per cent of GDP in 2000. However, this was not met because, although total expenditure was trimmed, public revenue was lower than expected. Romania's fiscal problems stem in part from the accumulation of large amounts of tax arrears, mostly by state owned firms.[174] The toleration of tax arrears and the accumulation of other contingent fiscal liabilities have traditionally been a stumbling block in relations with the IFIs, which have insisted on a tougher fiscal stance on the part of the government.[175] Despite some progress in these areas, a number of problems clearly remain to be addressed.

A radical and painful fiscal adjustment was necessary in Lithuania in 2000 after the fiscal deficit soared in the wake of the Russian crisis to more than 8 per cent of GDP in 1999. Although the ambitious aim of reducing the deficit to 1.7 per cent of GDP was not achieved, the improvement in Lithuania's fiscal position in 2000 (by more than 5 percentage points from 1999) was nevertheless among the most impressive of all the transition economies.

Some of the fiscal problems in the central European economies are related to the inefficiencies of the social security, pension and health care systems as well as delays in implementing reforms. In general, the level of both social contributions and public social spending in central Europe, as a proportion of GDP, is quite high: it is much higher than in the other transition economies (tables 3.2.5 and 3.2.6)[176] and is even higher than that in many industrialized countries.[177] Thus the amount of income redistribution which is brought about through the system of public social funds in these countries is

administration). During the year, disagreements emerged between the monetary authorities and the executive arm of the government, mostly over the view of the Monetary Policy Council that the government was delaying important structural and systemic reforms which, in turn, prevented a more rapid rate of fiscal consolidation. In contrast to other transition economies, the National Bank of Poland maintained a relatively tight monetary policy throughout 2000 aimed at compensating for the perceived loosening of fiscal policy.

In contrast, government revenues were higher than expected in Hungary in 2000. This allowed the

---

[173] In particular, the corporate profits tax rate was cut from 38 to 25 per cent and a uniform value added tax rate of 19 per cent was introduced.

[174] Tax arrears (non-payment of taxes) are a form of implicit subsidy to the corporate sector and are widely considered as a form of soft budget constraint. They have been widespread in the transition economies but Romania is one of the countries where they have been considerable.

[175] In October 2000, the IMF suspended the release of funds under the $540 million stand-by loan agreed upon earlier in the year due to the lack of sufficient progress in dealing with tax arrears and higher than planned wages in the public sector.

[176] In table 3.2.6 social spending falls into the category "Subsidies and other current transfers".

[177] V. Tanzi and L. Schuknecht, *Public Spending in the 20th Century* (Cambridge, Cambridge University Press, 2000), pp. 32-45.

TABLE 3.2.6

Consolidated general government expenditure in eastern Europe, the Baltic states and the CIS, 1998-2000
(Per cent of GDP)

	Total expenditure including capital outlays			Current expenditure on goods and services			Subsidies and other current transfers			Interest payments			Capital outlays		
	1998	1999	2000	1998	1999	2000	1998	1999	2000	1998	1999	2000	1998	1999	2000
Albania	30.7	31.0	35.8	10.2	10.8	17.4	7.5	7.4	5.5	7.8	6.9	4.4	7.8	6.9	4.4
Bulgaria	36.8	40.8	43.1	16.5	20.3	20.2	13.3	13.2	14.5	4.4	3.9	4.1	4.4	3.9	4.1
Croatia	52.4	..	..	24.7	..	..	18.4	..	..	1.5	..	..	1.5	..	..
Czech Republic	40.1	42.1	43.7	8.0	8.5	9.1	26.6	27.9	28.6	1.2	1.1	1.0	1.2	1.1	1.0
Hungary	52.2	49.0	46.4	17.7	17.7	15.9	19.5	19.3	19.4	7.8	7.4	6.1	7.8	7.4	6.1
Poland	41.9	41.8	..	14.9	17.0	..	20.9	20.4	..	3.3	3.1	..	3.3	3.1	..
Romania	35.0	37.0	..	11.6	13.2	..	15.0	15.4	..	4.7	5.5	..	4.7	5.5	..
Slovakia	41.9	39.6	..	10.6	10.1	..	22.5	22.3	..	2.9	3.2	..	2.9	3.2	..
Slovenia	43.6	44.4	43.6	18.1	17.8	17.7	19.7	20.3	20.0	1.3	1.4	1.5	1.3	1.4	1.5
The former Yugoslav Republic of Macedonia	33.9	35.2	40.3	12.0	13.6	12.7	20.1	20.0	23.8	1.9	1.6	1.8	1.9	1.6	1.8
Estonia	38.7	41.6	37.7	18.8	20.8	18.4	14.9	16.0	15.8	0.5	0.4	0.4	0.5	0.4	0.4
Latvia	43.8	44.8	41.5	18.9	18.0	..	19.9	21.2	..	0.8	0.8	..	0.8	0.8	..
Lithuania	36.1	39.0	..	19.0	19.1	..	12.0	12.7	..	1.2	1.5	..	1.2	1.5	..
Armenia	20.4	23.5	27.6	..	..	..	..	..	..	..	..	..	..	..	..
Azerbaijan	..	24.1	17.9	..	15.0	12.1	..	4.4	3.9	..	0.5	0.4	..	0.5	0.4
Belarus	43.8	45.8	43.1	17.5	16.0	..	17.2	18.4	..	0.7	0.6	..	0.7	0.6	..
Georgia	20.1	21.9	..	9.6	14.5	..	5.5	2.8	..	2.5	2.8	..	2.5	2.8	..
Kazakhstan	23.9	21.5	..	10.0	11.1	..	11.6	8.1	..	0.8	1.1	..	0.8	1.1	..
Kyrgyzstan	20.9	19.8	17.1	15.6	13.9	12.3	3.2	2.9	2.4	1.7	3.4	1.5	1.7	3.4	1.5
Republic of Moldova	41.7	34.6	32.7	16.3	12.9	9.3	14.5	11.2	14.0	5.5	7.4	6.5	5.5	7.4	6.5
Russian Federation	38.9	37.2[a]	..	13.3	13.6[a]	..	19.6	15.2[a]	..	5.9	4.1[a]	..	5.9	3.5[a]	..
Tajikistan	18.6	18.9	22.5	..	..	..	..	..	..	..	..	..	..	..	..
Ukraine	38.6	34.2	29.8	..	..	..	..	..	..	..	..	..	..	..	..

Source: As for table 3.2.5.

[a] Consolidated central government (including social security and extra budgetary funds) plus (without consolidation) regional and local government.

relatively high and poses a serious burden on public finances. A related problem is the fact that the eligibility criteria for access to funding from some of these systems appears to be rather loose as compared with western Europe, resulting in even greater pressure on public spending.[178] Accelerating the reform of the systems of social spending in central Europe is therefore a priority for policy, especially in view of the anticipated increase in public spending which will be necessary in preparation for EU accession.

Fiscal deficits shrank in 2000 in the majority of CIS countries, most notably in Russia where this occurred for a second consecutive year. Fiscal positions have improved considerably in most CIS economies in recent years, but some of them are still facing chronic fiscal problems; among the latter are the Republic of Moldova and, more recently, Kyrgyzstan. The economy of the Republic of Moldova is slowly retreating from the twin deficit crisis, which has plagued the economy for a number of years and has blocked access to funding from the IFIs. The forced macroeconomic adjustment resulted in a sharp and protracted economic downturn which lasted for several years; despite the improvement in the fiscal position in 1999 and 2000, some further efforts in this direction are still needed.

The consolidated government deficit in Kyrgyzstan deteriorated rapidly after 1997 due to a combination of external and internal factors. The depreciation of the som that followed the Russian crisis resulted in a heavier foreign debt burden[179] while exports, heavily dependent on gold, started to fall in value. The weakening of economic activity triggered shortfalls of fiscal revenue that coincided with an accumulation of tax arrears. In addition, the government has been engaged in a large-scale public investment programme, the annual spending on which amounts to several per cent of GDP.[180] Given the size of the public debt and the magnitude of the fiscal deficit, the authorities in Kyrgyzstan will be faced with the necessity of implementing a major fiscal adjustment.

---

[178] B. Fakin and A. de Crombrugghe, *Fiscal Adjustments in Transition Economies Transfers and the Efficiency of Public Spending: A Comparison with OECD Countries*, World Bank Working Paper Series, No. 1803 (Washington, D.C.), July 1997.

[179] In Kyrgyzstan in 2000, public external debt reached 110 per cent of GDP. IMF, "IMF concludes Article IV consultation with Kyrgyz Republic", *Public Information Notice*, No. 00/87, 13 October 2000.

[180] Apparently, the programme is financed through foreign borrowing and is therefore adding to the already high level of foreign debt. However, the investment programme has not been incorporated into the official fiscal statistics (table 3.2.4) and the available information does not allow its fiscal implications to be evaluated accurately.

Among the other CIS countries, a shortfall in revenue was the main cause of the fiscal deterioration in Armenia, while a strong recovery of output in both 1999 and 2000 allowed the government of Kazakhstan to reduce substantially its fiscal deficit which had reached dangerous proportions in 1998 (table 3.2.4).

(c) Fiscal consolidation in Russia

One of the underlying causes of the 1998 financial crisis in Russia was a large and chronic fiscal deficit and the ways in which it was financed. The resort to debt financing was coupled with an excessively tight monetary policy, a combination that led to very high interest rates and depressed economic activity. The tax base was eroded by falling corporate profits and the demonetization of the payments system through the emergence of monetary surrogates (including payments to and from the budget), which resulted in an even larger fiscal imbalance. The escalation of the crisis in 1998 was considerably amplified by the fall in oil prices, which made the current account and fiscal deficits worse and further encouraged the demonetization of the economy.

Since the financial collapse of August 1998, events have taken a different course and the Russian economy has managed a remarkable recovery: in 2000, its rate of growth of GDP was one of the highest among the transition economies, the rate of inflation was falling, the current account surplus reached a record high, while investors' confidence began to improve. The fiscal consolidation which has taken place since 1998 has been one of the more surprising achievements in this period. The chronic fiscal deficit (which was in the range of 5 to 10 per cent of GDP until 1998)[181] was not only closed but the balance started to move into surplus.[182] According to preliminary estimates, the full-year primary surplus of general government in 2000 amounted to 5.2 per cent of GDP while the overall surplus was estimated at 2.7 per cent.[183] Between 1997 and 2000, the fiscal position of the Russian government has improved by 9.2 percentage points of GDP in terms of the primary balance and by 11.4 percentage points in terms of the overall balance.[184]

There are a number of factors behind the economic upturn in Russia and the dramatic reversal in the fiscal situation. The combination of rising oil prices and a strong dollar have been highly favourable for the Russian economy, which is extremely sensitive to changes in international oil prices.[185] The substantial real depreciation of the rouble after 1998 led to widespread import substitution, which boosted Russian manufacturing output. The large current account surplus contributed to the replenishment of foreign exchange reserves, which reached a record high level by the end of 2000. This combination of factors halted the devaluation of the rouble and the strengthening of the exchange rate anchor contributing to the reduction of inflationary pressures.

The active stance of economic policy also contributed significantly to the recovery of the Russian economy and the strengthening of the public sector's finances. In 2000, the government introduced an ambitious and comprehensive long-term reform programme, the central focus of which is the reform of public finance and the strengthening of the Russian financial system. Although it is still early to judge the likely effect of the programme, some of the planned measures have already entered into force either before or in parallel with the debates on the 2001 budget. Among the latter is a sweeping tax reform, which affects virtually all the major components of the tax and social security system,[186] as well as a major reform of the system of import tariffs.[187] Among the other priorities in the government's programme are the further liberalization and deregulation of the economy, coupled with the protection of ownership rights and the provision of guarantees to creditors, all of which are aimed at improving the business climate and stimulating investment activity.

The Russian government has also invested considerable effort in improving the efficiency of tax collection and streamlining budgetary procedures. One of the major changes after the 1998 crisis was a complete break with the past practice of non-monetary fiscal

---

[181] UN/ECE, *Economic Survey of Europe, 1998 No. 3*, p. 36.

[182] The primary balance of the consolidated government started to move into surplus in mid-1999 and by 2000 the overall balance also became positive (chart 3.2.5).

[183] The reports on the consolidated public finances in Russia are usually prepared and published with a considerable delay. The current (monthly) fiscal statistics reported by the Russian Ministry of Finance include a preliminary (non-consolidated) report of the federal government balance and a preliminary (consolidated) report of the balance of regional and local governments. For the purposes of the assessment reported in this section, a rough assessment of the general government balance (excluding extrabudgetary funds) has been made by summing the above two fiscal reports. Since such an operation falls short of proper consolidation, the reported results should be treated with caution and as tentative estimates. Thus, as there are transfers between federal and local government, there may be some double counting in the total government revenue and expenditure, as shown in chart 3.2.6. Such potential distortions do not, however, affect the level of the general government deficit, as shown in chart 3.2.5.

[184] UN/ECE secretariat estimates, based on Russian Ministry of Finance data.

[185] According to a statement by Prime Minister Kasyanov, Russia's earnings from the export of oil products in 2000 were 2.4 times higher than those in 1999, while one third of Russia's GDP growth reflected higher oil and gas prices. RFE/RL *Newsline*, Vol. 34, No. 1, Part I, 19 February 2001. For a discussion of the interdependence between Russia's industrial output and international oil prices see sect. 3.3(i) below.

[186] Thus, the previous progressive income tax scale with a top rate of 30 per cent was replaced by a flat, single 13 per cent tax rate; most of the numerous non-profit based taxes levied on corporate units were abolished and a uniform profits tax was established; a new unified social security tax was introduced to replace previous payments to three separate off-budget funds; the VAT system was also modified, bringing it closer to European standards.

[187] The new tariff system which entered into force on 1 January 2001 is much simpler and considerably more uniform than the previous one. It is a four-tier system (with custom duties ranging from 5 to 20 per cent) and is broadly in line with WTO norms (joining WTO is one of Russia's policy priorities). "Russia: tariff reform", *Oxford Analytica Brief*, 27 November 2000. For a discussion of some of the wider background issues to Russia's application for WTO membership, see P. Naray, *Russia and The World Trade Organization* (London, Palgrave, 2001).

CHART 3.2.5

General government[a] balance in the Russian Federation, 1996-2000
(12-month rolling averages, per cent of GDP)

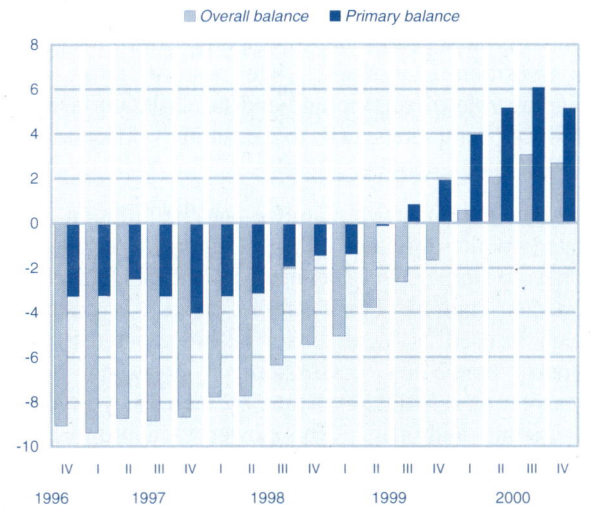

Source: UN/ECE secretariat calculations, based on national statistics.

[a] Federal, regional and local governments (excluding extrabudgetary funds).

CHART 3.2.6

General government[a] revenue and expenditure in the Russian Federation, 1996-2000
(12-month rolling averages, per cent of GDP)

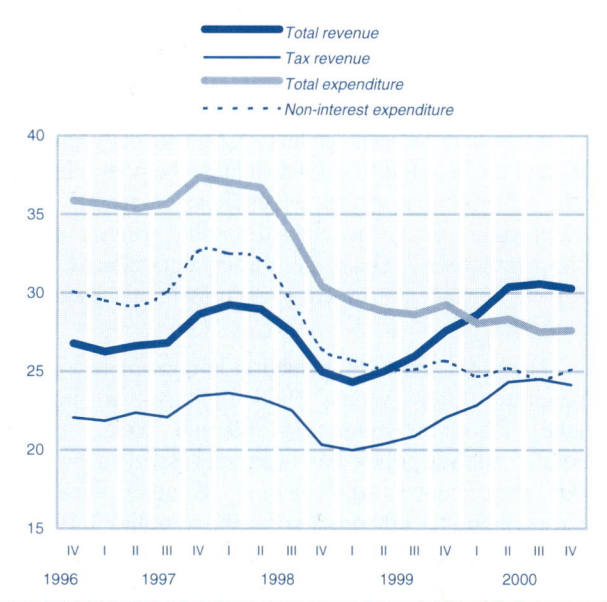

Source: UN/ECE secretariat calculations, based on national statistics.

[a] Federal, regional and local governments (excluding extrabudgetary funds).

payments: federal tax offsets were practically discontinued already in 1999 and this has had a generally beneficial effect for the remonetization of the payments system. A number of budgetary procedures have been reorganized with the aim of concentrating spending on key priority areas and reducing the amounts of inefficient expenditure. Another change, which reverses the earlier trend towards decentralization of the system of public finance, was an amendment to the Budgetary Code of the Russian Federation that calls for greater centralization of fiscal revenue and spending in the federal budget at the expense of regional and local budgets.

Although these policy measures were already in place in 2000, most of them are of a medium- and long-term nature and obviously it will take time before their full effect is seen in the behaviour of economic agents and, consequently, on economic performance. At the same time the turnround in the fiscal position started before most of these policy changes were initiated; despite the size of the Russian economy, this major turnround occurred in a very short time (in 1999-2000, as can be seen on charts 3.2.5 and 3.2.6). Thus, while some of the above policy measures helped to improve Russia's fiscal situation in this period (particularly those related to the efficiency of tax collection and the remonetization of fiscal flows) they cannot fully explain the scale of the consolidation that occurred in the period 1998-2000.

It has become fairly common for observers to ascribe the fiscal improvement in Russia mainly to the rise in international oil prices coupled with the stronger dollar in this period. As noted above, this combination was an important factor in Russia's improved economic performance and, undoubtedly, it also contributed to a sizeable increase in fiscal revenue.[188] However, higher oil prices cannot fully explain the reversal in the fiscal balance. The consolidated government revenue in mid-2000 stood at 30.5 per cent of GDP which was only 1.5 percentage points higher than its peak level before the 1998 crisis (chart 3.2.6),[189] an increase that is much smaller than the improvement in the overall fiscal position.

Changes in some of the main fiscal aggregates during the period 1996-2000 (chart 3.2.6) provide some clues as to the other determinants of fiscal consolidation. A close look at this chart reveals that the most important factor behind the improvement in the fiscal position of the general government is the reduction in public, non-interest expenditure relative to aggregate output. While interest payments also shrank in relative terms after the crisis, partly thanks to the default on public debt (from 4.6 per cent of GDP at mid-1998 to 2.5 per cent at the end of 2000), it was the major cut in non-interest expenditure that made the most dramatic contribution to the overall balance. In 2000, the non-interest component of the consolidated government expenditure fell by 7.5

---

[188] According to Yegor Gaidar, member of the State Duma and former Prime Minister, a rise in the export prices of Russian oil by $1 brings an extra R10-15 billion of revenue (or approximately 0.5 per cent of the consolidated government revenue in 2000) to the Russian budget. *TASS Energy News Service*, 7 September 2000.

[189] Note that all the fiscal indicators in the chart are 12-month rolling averages of the variables. Accordingly, the end-year values (the last quarter of the year on the charts) are identical to the full-year fiscal outcome for each year.

percentage points of GDP as compared with its share in 1997. The importance of this cut can be illustrated as follows: if non-interest public expenditure had remained at its 1997 peak level of 32.7 per cent of GDP, the primary balance would have been in deficit in 2000 to the extent of 2.4 per cent of GDP while the overall deficit would have been close to 5 per cent of GDP or, in other words, not very different from the levels prevailing before the 1998 crisis.

It can also be seen on chart 3.2.6 that between mid-1997 and the beginning of 1998 (that is, the period leading to the crisis), non-interest expenditure increased at an unsustainable rate, which added to the severity of the subsequent crisis. Thus, the subsequent reduction was partly a forced adjustment to correct this excessive expansion.

The rapid and large reduction in non-interest public expenditure after August 1998 indicates an unusual degree of fiscal restraint in 1999 and 2000. By all accounts, such a policy has been successful in bringing about the needed adjustment. Another beneficial macroeconomic outcome of this policy is the improvement in the competitive position of Russian manufacturing industry – in terms of both prices and costs via the accompanying reduction in unit labour costs – which was an important factor behind the strong recovery of domestic output in 1999-2000.

However, the austerity of fiscal policy after the crisis caused a dampening of final domestic demand, mostly through across-the-board cuts in real incomes (in the first place, of pensioners and civil servants, but eventually of the population at large).[190] Thus, despite some improvement during the year, average real per capita incomes in 2000 were still some 22 per cent lower than in 1997 while the real value of pensions were on average some 26 per cent lower.[191] It is not yet clear whether the degree of *ex-post* fiscal retrenchment was the reflection of a deliberate policy stance or whether it merely reflected the absence of an accommodating policy amendment during a period of unexpectedly high growth. Indeed, as most spending targets were fixed in the 2000 budget in nominal terms and were not revised upwards in line with the higher revenue, the government may have simply "overshot" its objectives in terms of overall fiscal balance. Given the magnitude of the fall in domestic absorption (see chart 3.2.4) and the size of the fiscal surplus in 2000, it has to be questioned whether the severity of fiscal restraint in this period was really justified.

(iii) Seigniorage and the inflation tax in the transition economies

After the turbulent macroeconomic environment that characterized the initial stages of their economic transformation, most transition economies have now entered a phase of relative stability characterized by moderate (double-digit) or, in most cases, low (single-digit) inflation. While both the disinflation strategies and their degree of success vary widely among countries, the elimination of excessively high inflation implies a number of changes in the set of policy instruments in all the transition economies. This section looks at the changing role of seigniorage and the inflation tax in the transition economies and the ensuing implications for macroeconomic policy.

The notions of seigniorage and the inflation tax are related to the privilege of the authorities issuing fiat-money to derive net revenue from the holders of such monetary claims. For example, money in circulation which is used as legal tender bears no interest for its holders, hence its possession is equivalent to the extension of zero-interest loans by the money holders to the issuing authority. The power to appropriate real resources through the issue of fiat-money stems from the monopoly of the governments of sovereign states to decree its use as legal tender or to insist on its use for certain types of transaction within the territory of the state.

Although closely related (and sometimes erroneously treated as synonyms), the notions of seigniorage and the inflation tax are not identical. While seigniorage refers to an institutional privilege of the national authorities to issue fiat-money, the notion of the inflation tax usually denotes a specific type of economic policy, namely that of financing a spending programme (usually in the presence of a fiscal imbalance or deficit) through an inflationary expansion of the money supply. Depending on the elasticity of the aggregate supply curve, an increase in money supply causes prices to rise which leads to higher inflation and this, in turn, reduces the real value of the stock of money in circulation. The reduction in the real value of the claims of money holders on the issuing authority is equivalent to an extra tax levied on the holders of fiat-money (hence the term "inflation tax").[192] The link between seigniorage and the inflation tax lies in the fact that while the monetary expansion may not necessarily be in the form of fiat-money at the moment of emission, ultimately it leads to an expansion of the amount of money in circulation and results in the appropriation of net revenue by the authorities through seigniorage.

For practical purposes it is useful to quantify the net revenue that the money issuing authority collects through seigniorage or the inflation tax. Such quantification allows a distinction to be made between different types of macroeconomic policy or to trace some of the macroeconomic implications of various disturbances and shocks. There are three main concepts – and approaches – in defining seigniorage, which may lead to different

---

[190] Although there were no incomes policies targeting the corporate sector (which is mostly private) in this period, the reduction of real wages in the public sector triggered similar falls in the private sector which preserved the prevailing structure of relative wages.

[191] UN/ECE secretariat calculations, based on Goskomstat data.

[192] It should be noted that a non-zero inflation rate always gives rise to an inflation tax even when it is not the result of a deliberate policy followed by the authorities.

estimates of its magnitude.[193] The first, referred to as "monetary seigniorage", is based on the idea that seigniorage constitutes transfer of wealth from the private sector to the government (or, more generally, to the consolidated public sector). In this context, monetary seigniorage has two aspects: on the one hand, it reflects the monopoly of the government to issue money and make it legal tender; on the other hand, it mirrors the money demand of the private sector which may change over time depending on the interplay of the principal motives for holding money (i.e. for transactions purposes, as a precaution against unforeseen spending, and as a store of wealth). This is the approach most widely used to measure seigniorage in empirical applications; the estimates of seigniorage in the transition economies reported below are also based on this concept.

For practical purposes, the flow of monetary seigniorage in period t is defined as the amount of real resources appropriated by the public sector through the emission of new money during the period and is usually calculated as $\Delta M_t/P_t$, where $\Delta M_t = M_t - M_{t-1}$ is the change in the stock of base money[194] in period t and P_t is the price index at the end of this period. This formulation reflects the real value of the new monetary issue during the specified period.

A second approach is to define seigniorage as the opportunity costs incurred by the private sector. This reflects the view that holding fiat-money is a zero-interest loan by the money holders (the private sector) to the issuing authority (the consolidated public sector). As a result, the private sector incurs an opportunity cost in terms of the foregone return on an equivalent amount of alternative monetary assets.[195] According to this concept, seigniorage in period t is usually defined as: $M_{t-1}i_t/P_t$, where M_{t-1} is the stock of base money at the beginning of the period, P_t is the price index at the end of this period and i_t is an appropriate nominal interest rate. While this approach is theoretically sound, its practical application is problematic due to the difficulties of defining a suitable interest rate to measure the foregone income of the private sector.

Yet a third approach is to define seigniorage from the institutional side, making a distinction between the issuing authority (the central bank) and the executive arm of the public sector (the government proper). From an institutional perspective, the central bank issues money and incurs operating costs; the net revenue from money creation (seigniorage) is defined as the net profit of the central bank, which is transferred to the general government as a budgetary contribution. However, from an economic point of view, this is a rather narrow interpretation of seigniorage since both the issuing authority and the executive branch belong to the consolidated public sector and so the budgetary contribution of the central bank is merely an intrasectoral transfer.[196]

As to the inflation tax, following the conceptual notion outlined above, its flow in period t can be quantified as the reduction in the real value of the stock of base money due to inflation during this period: $M_{t-1}/P_{t-1} - M_{t-1}/P_t = M_{t-1}\pi_t/P_t$, where M_{t-1} is the stock of base money at the beginning of the period and π_t is the rate of inflation in period t ($\pi_t = (P_t - P_{t-1})/P_{t-1}$). As can be seen from this definition, in the special case when the rate of inflation in period t, π_t, is equal to the nominal interest rate in the period i_t (i.e. the real interest rate is zero), the inflation tax is numerically equivalent to the opportunity cost definition of seigniorage.

Summing up the above arguments, seigniorage and the inflation tax denote different nuances of macroeconomic policy and performance. Inflation tax is a measure of the amount of real resources transferred from the private to the public sector due to the inflationary financing of public spending (or just to the incidence of inflation). Seigniorage also implies a wealth transfer from the private sector to the government, but it also measures the incidence of money demand on the part of money holders. Thus, seigniorage can be regarded as the outcome of a two-sided contractual agreement between the private and the public sectors while the inflation tax is always the result of a one-sided, distortive fiscal action on the part of the state.

The quantitative measures of seigniorage and the inflation tax in the ECE transition economies in recent years are shown in table 3.2.7 (by individual countries) and in charts 3.2.7 and 3.2.8 (weighted averages by subregions).[197] For convenience and cross-country comparison, all numerical values are presented as proportions of the corresponding GDP figures. Because of the approximate nature of some of the data used for this assessment, the estimates shown in the table and charts should be regarded as tentative,[198] and so attention here will be mostly focused on changes in them over time.

---

[193] For a more comprehensive discussion of this issue, see M. Klein and M. Neumann, "Seigniorage: what is it and who gets it?", *Weltwirtschaftliches Archiv*, Vol. 126, No. 2 (Kiel), 1990, pp. 205-221 and W. Buiter, *Aspects of Fiscal Performance in Some Transition Economies under Fund-Supported Programs*, IMF Working Paper WP/97/31 (Washington, D.C.), April 1997.

[194] Base money is usually defined as the sum of the currency (notes and coins) in circulation plus the non-interest bearing reserves of commercial banks with the central bank.

[195] Respectively, the "opportunity gain" of money issue to the public sector is the foregone interest burden on an equivalent amount of monetary assets borrowed on the market.

[196] E. Baltensperger and T. Jordan, "Seigniorage and the transfer of central bank profits to the government", *Kyklos*, Vol. 51, No. 1, 1998, pp. 73-88.

[197] Seigniorage in the table has been evaluated according to the first concept defined above (that of monetary seigniorage), which measures the transfer of wealth from the private sector to the consolidated public sector.

[198] The source data for the evaluation of both seigniorage and inflation tax is "base" or "high power" money, which defines the non-interest bearing component of the money supply. It is usually defined as the sum of notes and coins in circulation plus the required reserves of commercial banks with the central bank (which, in turn, are made against deposits collected by the commercial banks); in addition, it should be stressed that only reserves denominated in domestic currency constitute

TABLE 3.2.7

Seigniorage and the inflation tax in selected east European, Baltic and CIS economies, 1995-2000
(Per cent of GDP)

	Seigniorage						Inflation					
	1995	1996	1997	1998	1999	2000	1995	1996	1997	1998	1999	2000
Albania	5.5	2.4	8.4	-0.2	2.8	3.1	1.0	3.1	7.0	-0.2	0.8	0.8
Bulgaria	5.9	5.7	7.7	0.5	0.8	0.8	2.7	21.8	7.5	0.5	0.8	0.8
Croatia	0.8	1.1	0.9	0.2	0.2	0.2	0.1	0.1	0.2	0.2	0.3	0.3
Czech Republic	5.8	0.2	-1.5	0.3	-0.8	1.3	0.9	1.3	1.4	0.3	0.4	0.4
Hungary	1.2	-0.3	2.0	1.7	2.2	1.5	2.9	1.8	1.3	0.9	0.9	0.9
Poland	2.9	1.5	2.3	1.3	0.1	-0.1	1.2	1.3	0.9	0.8	0.6	0.6
Romania	2.2	1.7	1.5	0.7	1.2	0.9	0.9	2.0	3.5	1.3	0.9	1.0
Slovakia	0.3	2.8	1.4	0.5	0.8	1.7	0.8	0.6	0.7	1.6	0.9	0.9
Slovenia	0.6	0.5	0.6	1.0	0.8	0.1	0.3	0.3	0.3	0.3	0.4	0.4
The former Yugoslav Republic of Macedonia	1.0	–	0.9	0.3	1.1	0.1	0.4	–	0.2	0.1	0.5	0.5
Yugoslavia	0.8	1.9	1.6	0.2	0.9	0.8	2.7	1.1	0.3	1.5	2.5	1.9
Estonia	2.0	1.9	2.8	0.6	3.1	1.6	2.9	1.4	1.1	0.4	0.6	0.6
Latvia	0.4	2.0	2.7	0.7	1.1	1.7	2.3	1.1	0.6	0.4	0.2	0.2
Lithuania	2.5	0.1	2.1	1.6	-0.5	-0.5	2.4	0.9	0.5	–	0.1	0.1
Armenia	2.9	1.6	0.5	0.4	0.8	0.2	0.7	0.2	1.0	0.1	-0.1	-0.1
Azerbaijan	4.3	1.5	2.2	-1.8	1.1	..	2.4	0.4	–	–	..	0.1
Belarus	3.7	2.4	3.0	3.1	3.1	1.7	3.0	1.3	1.8	3.5	1.6	2.2
Georgia	..	1.4	1.4	-0.6	0.5	0.4	..	0.5	0.3	0.4	0.2	0.2
Kazakhstan	3.1	1.2	2.1	-1.9	2.0	1.0	1.6	1.2	0.5	0.7	0.5	0.5
Kyrgyzstan	..	2.0	1.4	0.4	1.7	1.9	..	3.0	1.2	2.5	0.6	0.7
Republic of Moldova	3.6	1.0	3.1	-1.5	2.5	1.6	1.9	1.4	1.0	3.5	1.6	1.7
Russian Federation	3.5	1.2	1.3	1.7	2.2	3.0	3.8	1.0	0.5	1.6	0.9	1.0
Ukraine	–	1.7	2.6	0.9	2.3	1.9	–	1.6	0.5	1.2	1.6	1.7

Source: UN/ECE secretariat calculations, based on national monetary statistics and data in IMF, *Staff Country Reports* (Washington, D.C.), various issues.

One clear and widespread trend during the period 1994-2000 is the declining importance of seigniorage and the inflation tax as sources of net revenue to the public sector in the transition economies. At the beginning of the period these variables typically accounted for several percentage points of GDP, but they fell dramatically in most countries in the following years: during 1998-2000, the unweighted average seigniorage in eastern Europe, the Baltic states and in the CIS was 0.8 per cent, 1.1 per cent and 1.4 per cent of GDP, respectively; the corresponding unweighted average values of the inflation tax were 0.7 per cent, 0.3 per cent and 1.4 per cent of GDP, respectively. During the initial phases of transition (1990-1994), seigniorage and the inflation tax were much higher: in many countries both variables, as proportions of GDP, were at double-digit levels for several years in a row.[199] But in recent years their average levels in the transition economies are not much different from those observed in developed market economies[200] and are generally lower than the typical levels in developing countries.[201]

---

part of the national base money. However, very few transition economies directly report base money according to this definition and there are several data-related problems in properly computing base money from other monetary aggregates. The first is that the national monetary surveys published by the central banks in the transition economies usually report the total reserves of commercial banks, which also include reserves denominated in foreign currencies. Due to the absence of accurate source statistics on domestic currency reserves, a proxy for the latter was constructed as follows: the reported total amount of reserves in each individual country was first split in proportion to the total amounts of deposits in domestic and foreign currencies, with only the first component being added to the stock of money in circulation. Admittedly, this is no more than a rough estimate of the true stock of domestic currency reserves. Another problem is related to the fact that in some cases, depending on monetary policy considerations and local regulations, central banks may choose to pay interest on the reserves collected from commercial banks. This has been the case in Hungary where such rates have tended to change in parallel with other central bank rates. For example, until 15 November 2000, the National Bank of Hungary paid 5 per cent interest on reserves in forints and 5.5 per cent on reserves in foreign currencies. As of 15 November 2000 both rates were increased by 1 percentage point, but in January, in two subsequent moves, they were reduced again to 3.5 per cent and 4 per cent, accordingly. (National Bank of Hungary, *Press Releases*, various issues.) Due to the absence of adequate data for most of the transition economies, it has been assumed that all reserves are non-interest bearing, an assumption that may add some distortion in some cases.

---

[199] A. Ghosh, *Inflation in Transition Economies: How Much? And Why?*, IMF Working Paper WP/97/80 (Washington, D.C.), July 1997 and W. Buiter, *Aspects of Fiscal Performance...*, op. cit.

[200] In 1990-1994, the unweighted average share of seigniorage in the EU member states was 0.69 per cent of GDP (ranging from -0.42 per cent of GDP in Spain to 2.93 per cent in Portugal), while the unweighted average share of the inflation tax was 0.65 per cent of GDP (ranging from 0.07 per cent of GDP in Ireland to 2.9 per cent in Portugal). W. Buiter, "Politique macroéconomique dans la période de transition vers l'union monétaire," *Revue d'Economie Politique*, Vol. 105, No. 5, September-October 1995, pp. 807-846.

[201] Seigniorage and inflation tax shares in developing countries vary widely depending on the rate of inflation; in countries with double-digit inflation rates they tend to be of the order of several percentage points of GDP. A. Jafari-Samimi, "Relationship between inflation and seigniorage in developing countries: an estimation of the 'Laffer curve'", *Indian Economic Journal*, Vol. 45, No. 1, July-September 1997-1998, pp. 67-79.

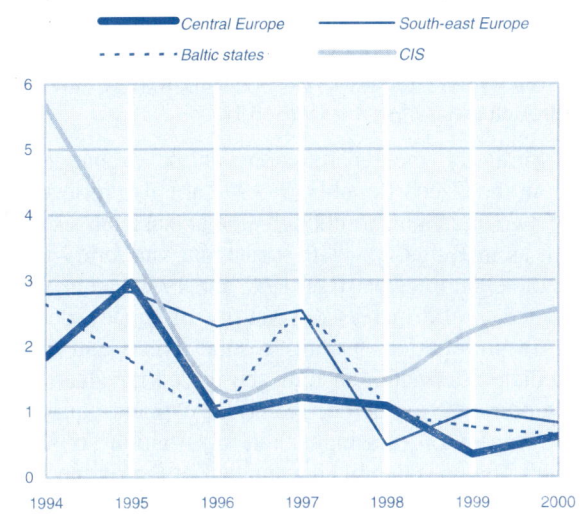

CHART 3.2.7

Average levels of seigniorage by regional groups, 1994-2000
(Weighted averages, per cent of GDP)

Source: UN/ECE secretariat calculations, based on national monetary statistics and data in IMF, *Staff Country Reports* (Washington, D.C.), various issues.

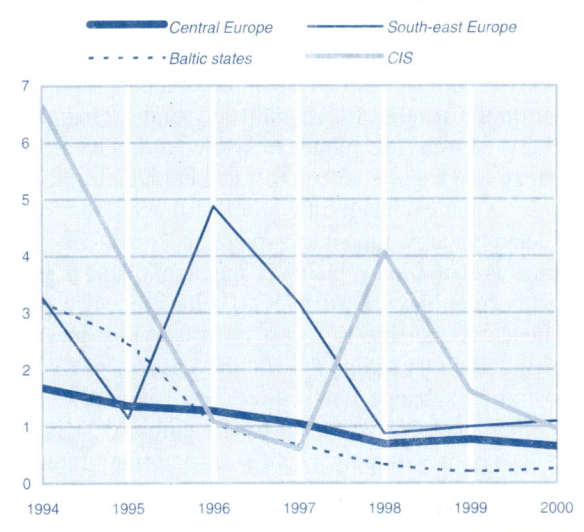

CHART 3.2.8

Average levels of inflation tax by regional groups, 1994-2000
(Weighted averages, per cent of GDP)

Source: UN/ECE secretariat calculations, based on national monetary statistics and data in IMF, *Staff Country Reports* (Washington, D.C.), various issues.

These dramatic changes reflect in the first place the recent progress in disinflation in many transition economies; at the same time they also indicate significant shifts in the stance of macroeconomic policy. Probably the most important macroeconomic factor behind these changes has been the progress in fiscal reform and the elimination of unsustainable fiscal deficits. The initial phases of economic transformation in many transition economies were marked by very large fiscal deficits. The reasons for this were numerous and complex, but the need for rapid fiscal reforms was generally underestimated at the onset of the transition process.[202] Faced with the impossibility of financing these deficits through non-inflationary sources, the authorities in many countries were forced to resort to printing money in order to close the deficits (that is, to impose the inflation tax). By monetizing the fiscal deficits, governments raised the necessary net revenue through seigniorage, which in some cases amounted to a sizeable share of GDP; however, the unpleasant side effect was an extremely high rate of inflation, sometimes reaching triple digits.

With the progress in economic transformation and in fiscal reform, the sources of the excessive fiscal imbalances started to diminish, while macroeconomic policy, especially fiscal policy, became more prudent. Thanks to the reduction of fiscal deficits, the pressures for inflationary financing also started to subside, leading to generally lower levels of the inflation tax. In particular, the generally smooth decline of the inflation tax to low levels in most central European and Baltic economies in recent years (table 3.2.7 and chart 3.2.7) can be regarded as a sign not only of greater macroeconomic stability in these economies but also of their growing maturity.

However, fiscal deficits are not entirely eliminated and some governments in the transition economies continue to resort to printing money to finance excessive spending or unexpected deficits. The recent data indicate a positive statistical association between the size of fiscal deficits and the level of the inflation tax in individual countries (chart 3.2.9). Although the direction of causality may be rather complex, this nevertheless suggests that the larger the fiscal imbalance, the more likely it is that the authorities will be inclined to monetize part of it.

As argued above, there are differences between the notions of seigniorage and the inflation tax and, not surprisingly, the two indicators for the same country can develop differently, as can be seen from the data in table 3.2.7. In particular, seiniorage reflects the outcome of a two-way quasi-contractual relation between the public and the private sector; hence higher real money demand leads to a higher level of seigniorage and vice versa. A negative side effect of the high inflation rates experienced in the initial phases of transition was a fall in real money demand in many transition economies; such demonetization, by definition, leads to lower levels of seigniorage.[203] This can be seen in chart 3.2.10, which illustrates both the downward shift in money demand between two consecutive periods (1993-1995 and 1996-1999) and the fact that lower degrees of monetization are generally associated with lower levels of seigniorage.

---

[202] For a discussion of these issues, see UN/ECE, *Economic Survey of Europe, 2000 No. 1*, pp. 60-63.

[203] Demonetization surfaced in the form of declining money to output ratios, a phenomenon which occurred in many transition economies, especially during the first half of the 1990s. Consequently, lower money stocks resulted in lower levels of seigniorage relative to output.

CHART 3.2.9

Fiscal deficits and the inflation tax in selected east European, Baltic and CIS economies, 1995-2000
(Per cent of GDP)

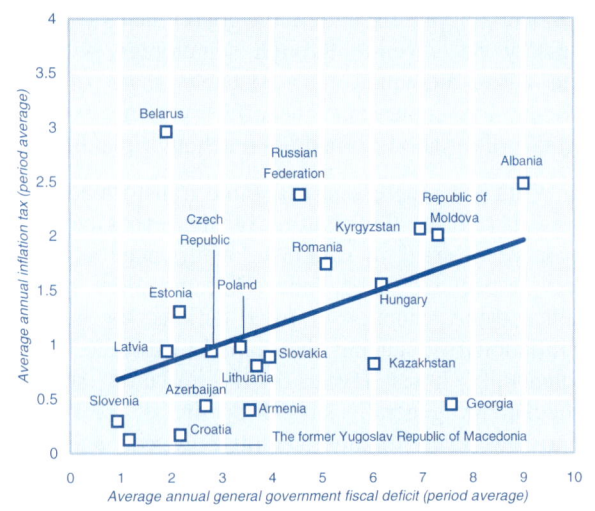

Source: UN/ECE secretariat calculations, based on national monetary statistics and data in IMF, *Staff Country Reports* (Washington, D.C.), various issues.

One problem with such changes is that the demand response to demonetization and remonetization may be asymmetric resulting in some hysteresis in money demand: while a high inflation rate may reduce money demand rapidly (hence demonetization is fast), low inflation only causes money demand to grow gradually (hence remonetization is slow); moreover, the previous levels of money demand may never be regained.[204] Consequently, there has been a once-and-for-all loss in seigniorage, at least in some transition economies, which may be permanent.

The observed levels of seigniorage and the inflation tax are not just the outcome of a deliberate policy stance; they may also reflect the macroeconomic repercussions of external or internal disturbances. As argued in previous issues of this *Survey*, the transition economies in general, and especially those that are less advanced in the reform process, are still rather vulnerable to external shocks. The considerable degree of variability over time in the observed levels of seigniorage and the inflation tax in individual countries and subregions (especially the CIS) is just another indication of both the inherent instability of their economies and their susceptibility to external or internal disturbances.

The development of these indicators in Bulgaria is a case in point. Until 1997, Bulgaria's economy was marked by chronic macroeconomic instability and large fiscal (and quasi-fiscal) deficits, which are mirrored in the high and variable levels of the inflation tax and seigniorage. The only case of a double-digit rate of the inflation tax among the transition economies in this period (that of Bulgaria in 1996) was a direct outcome of the severe economic and financial crisis that hit the country in 1996-1997. However, since the establishment of the currency board in July 1997, there has been remarkable progress towards macroeconomic stability and fiscal consolidation which, in turn, is reflected in low and relatively stable levels of seigniorage and the inflation tax in the period 1998-2000.

Similarly, the repercussions of the exchange rate crisis in the Czech Republic in 1997 are also reflected in these two indicators (although not to such an extreme extent as in Bulgaria). The substantial variability in the level of seigniorage between 1996 and 1999 can be partly attributed to the increased volatility of money demand both in the period leading to the crisis and in its immediate aftermath. In turn, the forced devaluation of the koruna was a macroeconomic adjustment equivalent to the imposition of a higher rate of inflation tax in this period. The considerable devaluation of the rouble in the wake of the Russian financial crisis in August 1998 was also equivalent to an increase in the distortionary inflation tax imposed by the government on the private sector in that year (which provided a complementary source of finance for the fiscal deficit, in addition to the default on the public debt). In turn, the subsequent strong recovery, which was accompanied by a reduction in macroeconomic imbalances, led to strong growth in base money demand which produced higher levels of seigniorage in 1999 and 2000 (table 3.2.7).

The ability of governments to resort to inflationary methods of financing their spending depends to a large extent on the nature of their monetary and exchange rate regimes. From this point of view, a freely floating exchange rate regime is the most accommodating for this purpose as the exchange rate absorbs directly and almost immediately any monetary injection. At the other extreme is a currency board arrangement, under which the authorities have no discretion over monetary policy and hence are unable to resort to inflationary means of financing their spending.[205] In the case of a fixed or quasi-fixed exchange rate regime, there is greater room for policy manoeuvre thanks to the authorities' control over the money supply: hence, a one-time monetary injection is in principle within the scope of discretionary policy. However, repeated actions of this nature may fuel inflation and result in a real appreciation of the exchange rate, which may ultimately drive the economy onto an unsustainable path. In the event, the authorities may be

---

[204] For a rationalization of this argument, see A. Ghosh, op. cit.

[205] This does not mean, however, that a currency board precludes the formation of seigniorage: as can be seen in table 3.2.7, the latter has positive values in the transition economies that adhere to such a regime (Bulgaria, Estonia, Lithuania). The source of seigniorage under a currency board is the interest that accrues on the foreign exchange reserves held by the monetary authorities (which can be redeposited with foreign banks or invested in the international financial markets). However, under a currency board, the level of seigniorage is essentially exogenous to policy, meaning that the public sector has no discretion over its level, which is solely determined by the net inflow or outflow of foreign exchange reserves to or from the monetary authority.

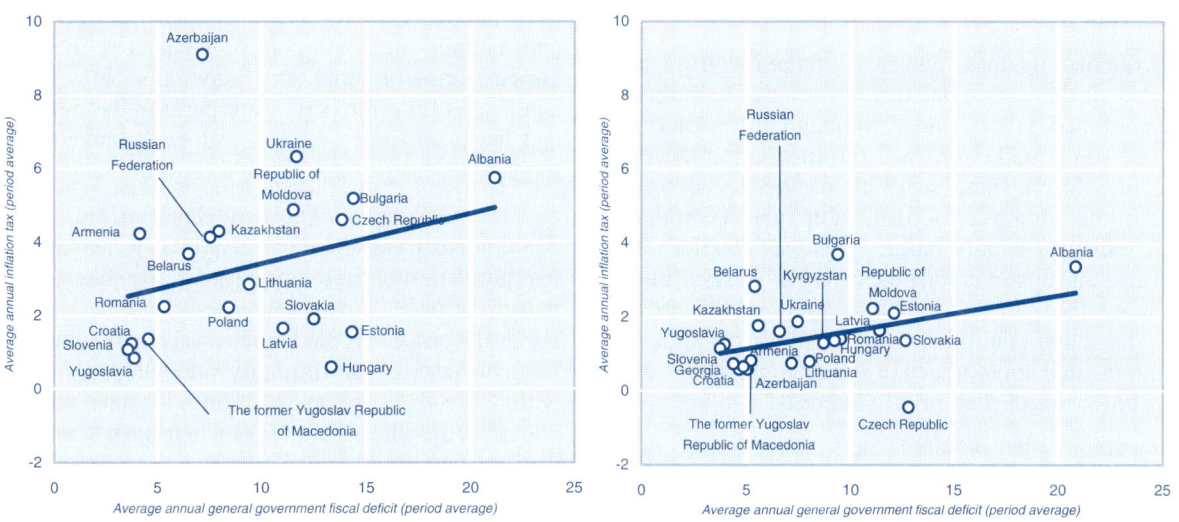

CHART 3.2.10

Monetization and seigniorage in selected east European, Baltic and CIS economies, 1993-1999
(Per cent of GDP)

Source: UN/ECE secretariat calculations, based on national monetary statistics and data in IMF, Staff Country Reports (Washington, D.C.), various issues.

forced to abandon the fixed exchange rate regime, or to introduce a one-off devaluation (there have been a number of such crises among the transition economies).

At the present stage of economic transformation, the transition economies have adjusted to lower levels of seigniorage than those observed in the early 1990s. The level of the policy-induced inflation tax has also been reduced substantially in most countries, which also constitutes a notable departure from the practices prevailing in the initial years of the transition. Further progress towards macroeconomic stability and systemic reform in the less advanced economies implies even greater macroeconomic prudence which, in turn, requires the elimination or substantial reduction of resort to the inflation tax as a source of financing public spending. Once confidence builds up, these economies can expect a gradual reversal of the past trends and higher levels of seigniorage; this process is already underway in some of the economies where the reforms are more advanced.

(iv) Reforming Yugoslavia's economy

The fall of the Milosevic regime in late 2000 not only marks the start of the transition from autocratic rule to pluralistic democracy in Yugoslavia (a process that began in most eastern European countries a decade ago), but also the beginning of real market reforms in this country. Ten years of war, dictatorial rule and international isolation resulted in economic devastation and an unprecedented fall in living standards in a country that was once considered among the most prosperous in the region. The new, democratically elected government now faces the daunting challenge to move ahead rapidly with badly needed and much delayed reforms while facing an inheritance of deep and complex economic problems which are probably unparalleled among the east European transition economies.

The causes of the economic catastrophe in Yugoslavia are numerous and diverse but they are mostly political in nature. The violent breakdown of the former SFR of Yugoslavia led to the disintegration of the regional market, which had a particularly negative impact on Serbia due to its central geographical position in the former state. The series of military conflicts – culminating in the Kosovo crisis – persistently diverted real resources from a weakening economy and generated considerable strain on the public finances. Apart from the direct economic damage, the series of military conflicts were a humanitarian disaster involving considerable loss of life as well as huge numbers of refugees and internally displaced persons on the territory of Yugoslavia.[206]

The series of external economic sanctions imposed on Yugoslavia by the international community during the past decade were the equivalent of a severe economic blockade. After the dissolution of the former SFR of Yugoslavia, Yugoslavia's membership in the IMF and the World Bank was frozen due to the refusal by the regime to honour the decisions of the IMF's Executive Board and the World Bank's Board of Directors regarding the succession to the SFR of Yugoslavia's

---

[206] Apart from the tragedy in Kosovo, which was widely publicized in the media, there are numerous war victims in other parts of the country as well: at the end of 1999, the total number of refugees in Yugoslavia (excluding Kosovo) was estimated at 600,000 persons, of which some 350,000 were refugees from Croatia and Bosnia and Herzegovina and 250,000 were internally displaced persons from Kosovo. P. Petrovic, D. Dragutinovic and M. Arsic, "The FRY economy: macroeconomic developments and main imbalances" (Belgrade), February 2001, mimeo.

membership.[207] The unsettled membership status in the IFIs precluded funding from these institutions and added to the harsh external sanctions, forcing the Yugoslav economy into autarky and turning the country into an economic pariah in an increasingly internationalized global economy.

Economic mismanagement – stemming from and embedded in the authoritarian rule over the economy – also contributed to the ruin. Although the authorities mimicked some market-oriented reforms during the past decade, the fundamental structure of the economy, in particular the structure of ownership and centralized control, remained largely intact. This was coupled with widespread corruption among the ruling elite, resulting in an extreme form of state capture by a small, corrupt clique. The latter controlled virtually all the resources of the economy and appropriated or allocated its output with a heavy bias towards their private interests.

Economic performance in this period was catastrophic, even when compared with the great economic difficulties experienced by other east European countries. Between 1989 and 1999 Yugoslavia lost some 60 per cent of its gross domestic product (appendix table B.1). In 1992-1994 there was a hyperinflation of extraordinary scale and duration: at its peak (in January 1994) the monthly inflation rate reached 313 million per cent.[208]

The former regime preserved a peculiar form of "social ownership" which is still the dominant ownership structure in the Yugoslav economy. This is a hybrid form of public and private ownership (that existed already in the SFR of Yugoslavia) under which firms are formally owned by their employees but are subject to centralized regulation and control and thus are easy to manipulate by the authorities, especially through the appointment of executive directors. In addition to the "socially owned" firms, there were traditional state owned enterprises. These ownership structures, coupled with an extraordinary high level of centralized administrative control and specific institutional arrangements run by a corrupt administration led to serious distortions in resource allocation and microeconomic behaviour and resulted in numerous macroeconomic imbalances.

The engagement in a series of military conflicts increased the distortions in resource allocation (by diverting large amounts of resources from productive use) and on incentives (by supporting the emergence of "war lords" close to the regime). It also generated a persistent and heavy financial burden on public finance, adding to the macroeconomic imbalances. In effect the Yugoslav economy throughout the 1990s closely resembled a war economy.

Until October 2000, there was direct administrative control over virtually all important economic relations. Most key prices were subject to extensive and rigid controls and the exchange rate was officially fixed to the deutsche mark while the currency was not convertible, even internally. The combination of rigid price controls and chronic macroeconomic imbalances gave rise to various forms of suppressed inflation such as widespread shortages (those for fuels were perhaps the most evident) and the emergence of black and grey markets including multiple exchange rates on the foreign exchange market.[209]

The labour market was characterized by built-in institutional rigidities most of which were equivalent to overprotection of those employed in the state and socially owned firms.[210] Over time, these rigidities have led to major distortions in the labour market, combining a large stagnant pool of the formally unemployed (table 3.5.2) with large-scale labour hoarding in state and socially owned firms (during a period when there was a sizeable drop in output),[211] and with yet a third segment of the labour market including those employed in the black or grey labour markets. One of the most damaging social features of these distortions was the barrier they created to entry into gainful employment by new job seekers (such as school leavers and university graduates).

During the past decade, Yugoslavia's public finances were chronically on the brink of collapse. The monetization of large fiscal deficits – the root cause of which were the inherent structural disequilibria in the economy, amplified by the effects of the wars and external sanctions – was the main source of the 1992-1994 hyperinflation. The stabilization programme launched in January 1994 was successful in stopping hyperinflation and temporarily curbing some of the main macroeconomic imbalances, at least in their open form. However, given the multiple macroeconomic disequilibria of the Yugoslav economy, which were not addressed in the stabilization programme, as well as the authoritarian political regime which precluded an independent central bank, these imbalances not only re-emerged but started to escalate.[212]

---

[207] IMF Staff Country Report No. 01/07, *Federal Republic of Yugoslavia: Membership and Request for Emergency Postconflict Assistance* (Washington, D.C.), January 2001.

[208] The Yugoslav hyperinflation was the second highest on record after the Hungarian hyperinflation of 1945-1946. P. Petrovic, Z. Bogetic and Z. Vujosevic, "The Yugoslav hyperinflation of 1992-1994: causes, dynamics, and money supply process", *Journal of Comparative Economics*, Vol. 27, No. 2, June 1999, pp. 335-353.

[209] The black foreign exchange market was in reality tolerated by the authorities and practically all foreign exchange transactions (including wholesale purchases and sales by corporate entities) were conducted on this market. Only a few privileged companies had access to foreign exchange at the official rate.

[210] Such as the formal and informal administrative controls over potential layoffs in such firms.

[211] According to some estimates, labour hoarding in state and socially owned firms amounted to some 30 per cent of total employment in those firms. P. Petrovic, D. Dragutinovic and M. Arsic, op. cit.

[212] The stabilization programme was based on a monetary regime that operated in the fashion of a currency board but stopped short of formally introducing a currency board arrangement. It provided for a one-to-one coverage of domestic base money by foreign exchange reserves and reduced to a minimum the monetary interventions of the central bank, including direct credit to the government. However, the absence of a legislative provision barring central bank monetary operations, coupled with the lack of a strong commitment by the authorities to deepen the reform process, brought about a gradual softening and eventual disintegration of this regime: in the course of time, the central bank resumed direct lending to the government, giving way to strong political pressure.

Consequently – and despite rigid administrative price controls – open inflation remained high in the second half of the 1990s.

The budgetary process in Yugoslavia was opaque and discretionary both in revenue collection and in public spending. The tax system was non-transparent and fragmented with built-in discriminatory arrangements; this left room for a high degree of discretion in enforcement, increasing still further its discriminatory character.[213] There was even less transparency on the expenditure side: this was subject to highly discretionary management and no official statistics were published on the composition and levels of public spending or public debt.

Since 1994, partly thanks to the measures undertaken in the context of the stabilization programme, the fiscal deficit on a cash basis appears to have been reduced (although there are still no reliable statistics for the deficit). However, as the root causes of the macroeconomic imbalances were never addressed, a chronic structural deficit continued to plague the public finances. The major policy change in this period has been in the approach to financing the structural deficit: instead of fully monetizing it, the authorities chose to close part of it by not honouring some of their liabilities, that is, by accumulating payment arrears.[214] Apart from its unilateral and discretionary character, the policy of not honouring expenditure commitments was socially unjust as those who were worst affected belonged to the weakest and poorest layers of society, pensioners and those on social benefit.

An independent central bank was never put in place in Yugoslavia and, as noted above, this was one of the reasons for the failure of the 1994 stabilization programme. Although monetary policy was officially proclaimed to be non-expansionary, de facto it was largely accommodating as the central bank bowed to pressures from the government. Thus the executive arm had a large measure of control over the money supply and often used this to close the part of the fiscal deficit that it was unable to finance from other sources and to subsidize the corporate sector through directed credit. The latter, while not contributing directly to the cash deficit, added to the growing quasi-fiscal deficit which, as discussed below, is now the most serious macroeconomic imbalance in the Yugoslav economy.

The external financial isolation was used by the regime in the early 1990s as a pretext to "freeze" household foreign exchange accounts held in local banks, funds which were then used to finance the fiscal and the current account deficits.[215] This unilateral and arbitrary seizure of private funds resulted in a catastrophic loss of confidence in the banking system, which had not recovered by the end of the regime. Private savings, if any, were stored outside the banking system, mostly in the form of foreign currency. As a result, although the banks continued to operate, financial intermediation in Yugoslavia was virtually brought to a halt; instead, the banks functioned mainly as channels through which directed central bank credit was delivered to chosen firms. This was a form of discretionary subsidy to privileged firms while the majority of enterprises had virtually no access to bank credit.

Foreign trade was closely controlled by the central authorities through administrative measures and quantitative restrictions. As with most other policy arrangements, the regulations governing foreign trade were discretionary and favoured selected firms. The outcomes were highly distorted trade flows (in addition to the effects of external sanctions) and the accumulation (and subsequent appropriation) of monopoly rents by a selected few. As to the chronic current account deficit, it was financed with the funds confiscated from households, revenue from a few large-scale privatization deals with foreign investors and from secret overseas funds controlled by the regime.

Yugoslav firms thus operated in an institutional and regulatory environment which was highly discriminatory and involved controls over prices, employed labour and international trade, non-convertibility of the currency, the absence of commercial credit and a high degree of tax discretion. Coupled with the persistent depression of final demand, it is not surprising that most social and state owned enterprises were chronic loss makers.[216] The size of the losses generated by Yugoslav firms is quite unparalleled in any other transition economy: the cumulative uncovered losses during the period 1994-1999 amounted to the equivalent of $15.4 billion, or 125 per cent of Yugoslavia's GDP in 2000.[217] These losses were highly concentrated, with almost half of them generated in a handful of industrial branches.[218]

---

[213] Some 230 different taxes were in force in the territory of Serbia alone. In addition, the actual level of taxation was regulated by numerous by-laws and instructions, institutionalizing various tax holidays and special regimes.

[214] It is estimated that at the end of 2000, the stock of non-debt budgetary payment arrears amounted to 11.2 per cent of GDP, the largest amounts being due to the pension funds and to the health insurance fund.

[215] The "freezing" of bank accounts was a form of "forced lending" by the public to the state. In 1998 the resources obtained through this unilateral operation were formally converted into public debt and the state accepted the obligation to repay it, at least partially and over an extended period of time. At present this is the largest single item of public domestic debt: at the end of 2000, public liabilities on frozen household foreign exchange accounts were $3.6 billion or 29 per cent of GDP.

[216] New private firms did emerge in Yugoslavia during the 1990s and some of them grew and performed relatively well. However, it is not yet clear to what extent they did so because of higher efficiency or of privileged treatment by the regime, the latter being equivalent to the channelling of public funds into them.

[217] M. Arsic and M. Cvetkovic, "Regulating internal short-term debt of enterprises" (Belgrade), February 2001, mimeo. The data after 1999 exclude the territory of Kosovo.

[218] Among the biggest loss-making industries in 1998 and 1999 were electric power generation (with over 16 per cent of the total), food processing (with 4.5-6 per cent) and oil and gas extraction (with 3-3.5 per

Despite their chronic losses, firms were allowed to continue to operate as going concerns. Bankruptcy procedures, although formally in place, were never initiated against big socially or state owned enterprises. As to the growing losses, they were partly covered by directed credit but mostly by the widespread non-payment by firms of their own liabilities to suppliers, banks, the budget or to their employees, an endemic practice which was tolerated by the government. Enterprises' payment arrears thus increased rapidly, almost fully matching the amount of corporate losses. At the end of 1998, the accumulated "short-term enterprise debt" amounted to some 123 per cent of GDP; presumably, a large share of this was due to arrears, although a precise estimate is not available.[219] As most of the loss-making firms were publicly owned, their losses contributed to the quasi-fiscal deficit and, as such, they constitute contingent liabilities of the public sector (see section 3.2(ii)).

If Yugoslavia's macroeconomic performance after 1994 is compared with that during the previous, hyperinflationary period, the principal difference is mainly in the approach to monetizing the overall fiscal deficit. In the earlier period, a significant portion of the deficit, generated by the structural disequilibria in the economy (including most of the inherent quasi-fiscal deficit of the corporate sector), was immediately monetized and this resulted in hyperinflation. During the second half of the 1990s, the government merely avoided the instant monetization of the imbalance; however, as most of the structural disequilibria remained intact, they continued to generate contingent liabilities for the public sector on a massive scale. Since the root causes of the structural disequilibria were never addressed by policy, this imbalance was allowed to escalate – and accumulate as hidden public debt – over many years. In other words, the regime managed to avoid open hyperinflation in this period but only by suppressing it in this disguised way. In view of its magnitude, this accumulated quasi-fiscal deficit is probably the most serious macroeconomic imbalance inherited from the Milosevic regime.

Given the multiple distortions and disequilibria, the structural rigidities and the huge macroeconomic imbalances, reforming Yugoslavia's economy presents an unprecedented policy challenge. The new government has taken some important steps towards reforming the economy but the most acute problems remain to be addressed. In should be emphasized that, due to the magnitude of the inherited problems, and the fact that most of them are interrelated, the government is facing severe and painful policy dilemmas which are not eased by the overall deficiency of resources.

For example, the inherited price structure was highly distorted by numerous administrative price controls and this was a major obstacle to efficient resource allocation. In turn, administered prices were one of the main causes of the losses in some industries, especially public utilities, where prices were kept artificially low for social reasons. The policy dilemma is how to move towards equilibrium prices, while at the same time avoiding an additional shock to the poorest layers of society who would be most affected by a rapid rise in utility prices. In the final months of 2000 the government liberalized most prices as well as the exchange rate (introducing a managed float), but it refrained from adjusting utility prices where the distortions are probably the greatest. Thus the dual task of price-cum-enterprise restructuring in the utility sector remains to be undertaken.

Reforming public finances is another daunting policy task. The Yugoslav authorities will need to introduce a comprehensive and full-scale tax reform, to reform the tax administration and to reorganize public expenditure. Fiscal reforms will also have to address the quasi-fiscal deficit: a more appropriate policy arrangement would probably be to replace the previous hidden and discretionary subsidies with open and transparent ones which, however, should be conditional on changes in enterprise behaviour and performance, and with a timetable for their eventual abolition.

The problem of enterprise debt and inter-enterprise arrears, while related to the fiscal reform, has two distinct aspects. The first is how to deal with the enterprise debt already accumulated (the "stock" problem). Although it may be possible to eliminate some of the debt by mutual write-offs, dealing with the stock is likely to require the allocation of fresh public funds to clean the enterprise balance sheets. Such an operation, however, should be designed and executed as a once-and-for-all act in order to avoid the problem of moral hazard. The second, related aspect of the debt problem, is how to avoid the accumulation of new enterprise arrears (the "flow" problem). The "flow" aspect implies instituting hard budget constraints on firms in the framework of a comprehensive effort at enterprise restructuring including the reform of ownership patterns.

The banking system is also in dire need of a complete overhaul. Apart from cleaning the banks' balance sheets, such an operation will necessitate the injection of massive amounts of fresh capital in order to recapitalize them. It will also require committed and long-term policy effort to raise public confidence in the banking system so that it will be able to resume normal financial intermediation. As the aggregate net worth of the banking system at present is probably close to zero (or even negative), a bank restructuring on this scale will only be possible with the help of foreign capital.

Given the scale of its inherited problems, both the policy effort and the amount of resources required to reform the Yugoslav economy are enormous. Even if the political will to go ahead with the necessary reforms is

---

cent). Among the other big loss makers were the chemical and engineering industries. M. Arsic and M. Cvetkovic, op. cit.

[219] Payables to suppliers accounted for 55 per cent of the total short-term debt at the end of 1998, outstanding short-term bank credit amounted to 15 per cent of the total, 6 per cent was tax arrears, wage arrears accounted for 2 per cent of the total and other payment liabilities for the remaining 20 per cent. M. Arsic and M. Cvetkovic, op. cit.

there, and even if these reforms enjoy wide public support, their success will largely depend on the amount of resources at the disposal of the authorities. Taking into account the magnitude of the macroeconomic imbalances, the financing needs of this policy effort are likely to be considerable. Thanks to the efforts of the new government, Yugoslavia has managed to regain its membership of the IMF,[220] which will undoubtedly be a key factor in raising external finance not only from the IMF but also from other sources. However, the successful implementation of the reforms in Yugoslavia will not be possible without a wider international assistance effort and a more generous approach to funding (including the provision of non-debt finance) by the international community.

3.3 Output and demand

(i) The pattern of output and demand in 2000-early 2001

Almost all of the ECE transition economies benefited greatly from the rapid expansion of international trade in 2000 and for the first time since the economic transformation began in 1989, GDP increased in all of them (table 3.3.1). The average rate of GDP growth for the transition economies (6 per cent) was well above the average increase in world output in 2000 (4.5 per cent). Gross industrial output increased on average by 9 per cent, also the largest increase in the past decade (appendix table B.4). The growth of aggregate output was highest in the oil exporting CIS countries, exceeding expectations by a wide margin. But it was also strong in countries where relatively high technology products are gaining importance and in the economies of south-east Europe, which had been most affected by the Kosovo conflict in 1999.

The rate of growth of dollar exports in 2000 was in the double digits in almost all of the transition economies (table 3.1.2). The strong growth in the demand for exports from the region had several important consequences. First, since it involved mainly tradeable goods, it stimulated growth in manufacturing output, triggering record rates of industrial output growth. Second, it stimulated higher rates of capacity utilization and fixed investment, encouraging more efficient use of existing capacities and raising expectations for future investment. Finally, strong demand generates economies of scale in production and technology spillovers. As a component of autonomous demand, export growth can induce higher productivity growth, creating a virtuous circle that can sustain growth in the long run. Over time, many local products have moved up the "quality ladder", resulting in a pronounced shift in the production structure toward high-tech products, especially in the countries closest to the EU. The main "winners" in this respect were industries such as electrical and optical equipment and transport equipment (charts 3.3.1 and 3.3.2).

The export-led growth of industrial output in central Europe and the Baltic states reflects a decade of restructuring, institution building and technology upgrading in these economies. The rapid recovery of industrial output from about 1993 encouraged enterprises in the region to be more assertive and search for new products and markets. During the initial phases of the economic transformation the traditional manufacturing industries such as food, textiles and wood products performed relatively better than the high-tech industries, but this pattern was reversed after 1993 when the science-based industries (such as electrical and optical equipment) and scale-intensive industries (in particular, the automotive industry) performed much better than the traditional industries (box 3.3.1).[221]

In contrast to these structural changes, manufacturing industry in the CIS countries has remained largely unrestructured. The volume of FDI attracted by technology intensive industries in the CIS has been much smaller (both in absolute and especially in relative terms) compared with eastern Europe and the Baltic states. The CIS economies continue to rely heavily on exports of oil, natural gas and other primary commodities or semi-manufactured goods with a low degree of processing.

There were thus two main patterns of economic growth among the transition economies in 2000: while output in central Europe and the Baltic states was mainly driven by exports of manufactured goods (with a growing share of technology-intensive products),[222] growth in the CIS economies was mainly supported by increased commodity exports, with the highest growth rates in those countries with oil and natural gas resources. Countries in the former group tended to have higher labour productivity than countries specializing in commodity exports and more resource-intensive industries. One explanation for this difference is that the production of scale-intensive and science-based technology products, particularly electronic products, has a greater scope for increasing returns and long-run sustainable growth.[223]

In terms of the contribution of final demand to growth,[224] the general trend in the east European and

---

[220] IMF, "IMF approves membership of Federal Republic of Yugoslavia and $151 million in emergency post-conflict assistance", *Press Release,* No. 00/75, 20 December 2000.

[221] M. Knell and D. Hanzl, "Technology and industrial restructuring in central Europe", in D. Dyker and S. Radosevic (eds.), *Innovation and Structural Change in Post-Socialist Countries: A Quantitative Approach* (Amsterdam, Kluwer, 1999).

[222] The south-east European transition economies are also relatively concentrated on manufactures but their exports lean more heavily towards products requiring a lower degree of processing and which are generally more labour intensive (table 3.6.6).

[223] B. Amable, "The effects of foreign trade specialization on growth. Does specialization in electronics foster growth?", paper prepared as part of the project sponsored by the EU TSER programme *Technology, Employment and European Cohesion,* November 1996, mimeo.

[224] The contributions of the final demand components to growth (table 3.3.2) are based on statistical accounting only and do not imply causality.

TABLE 3.3.1

GDP and industrial output in eastern Europe, the Baltic states and the CIS, 1999-2000
(Percentage change over the same period of the preceding year)

	GDP						Industrial output					
			2000						2000			
	1999	2000	QI	QII	QIII	QIV	1999	2000	QI	QII	QIII	QIV
Eastern Europe	1.3	3.9	..	..	..	..	-0.1	8.3	..	..	..	..
Albania	7.3	8.0	..	..	..	..	16.0	12.0	..	..	..	..
Bosnia and Herzegovina	..	..	..	..	..	..	10.6	8.8	23.3	16.1	4.8	7.1
Bulgaria	2.4	5.0	4.8	5.5	5.6	..	-12.3	2.3	5.2	1.2	3.5	-0.7
Croatia	-0.4	3.7	3.7	4.5	4.1	2.4	-1.4	1.7	3.7	2.0	2.5	-1.3
Czech Republic	-0.8	3.1	4.3	2.1	2.2	3.9	-3.1	5.1	5.3	7.5	10.0	6.3
Hungary	4.4	5.2	6.6	5.8	4.5	4.2	10.4	18.3	20.7	20.4	19.7	13.2
Poland	4.1	4.1	6.0	5.2	3.3	2.4	4.8	7.1	10.7	9.6	6.7	2.5
Romania	-3.2	1.6	0.9	3.5	1.6	..	-7.9	8.2	0.5	9.4	13.1	9.5
Slovakia	1.9	2.2	1.5	1.9	2.4	2.9	-3.6	9.1	7.3	8.6	9.0	11.4
Slovenia	5.2	4.8	6.4	3.5	5.8	3.7	-0.5	6.2	7.2	9.6	6.1	2.3
The former Yugoslav Republic of Macedonia	2.7	5.1	13.5	7.6	0.1	..	-2.6	3.5	10.3	11.0	-4.0	-1.3
Yugoslavia	-19.3	10.0	..	..	..	..	-23.1	10.9	-2.5	65.6	20.3	-8.7
Baltic states	-1.8	5.0	..	..	..	..	-7.6	6.7	..	..	..	..
Estonia	-1.1	6.4	5.2	7.5	7.0	5.9	-1.7	9.1	9.9	12.1	10.2	4.7
Latvia	1.1	6.6	6.1	5.0	6.6	8.7	-5.4	3.2	4.4	3.9	1.1	3.3
Lithuania	-3.9	3.3	4.1	0.5	5.0	3.6	-11.2	7.0	10.1	-0.6	11.0	7.4
CIS	3.2	7.4	..	..	..	..	7.3	9.6	..	..	..	..
Armenia	3.3	6.0	0.3	4.0	3.2	12.7	5.2	6.4	0.3	5.5	5.8	13.9
Azerbaijan	7.4	11.4	6.5	10.4	11.9	..	3.6	6.9	3.5	5.9	8.0	10.2
Belarus	3.4	5.8	6.5	2.3	6.4	7.9	10.3	8.0	7.3	3.5	13.0	7.0
Georgia	3.0	1.9	2.7	-4.0	1.1	8.0	7.4	6.1	14.1	4.6	3.8	3.1
Kazakhstan	2.7	9.6	9.4	11.8	11.0	6.5	2.7	14.6	15.1	17.4	11.4	12.8
Kyrgyzstan	3.7	5.0	0.6	11.5	5.0	3.4	-4.3	6.0	-1.2	10.7	10.9	4.7
Republic of Moldova	-3.4	1.9	1.0	2.3	0.1	4.3	-11.6	2.3	3.3	3.9	-1.1	3.2
Russian Federation	3.5	7.7	8.4	6.7	7.9	..	8.1	9.0	11.9	8.5	8.6	6.5
Tajikistan	3.7	8.3	..	..	..	..	5.6	10.3	8.7	9.3	12.3	10.9
Turkmenistan	16.0	17.6	..	..	..	..	15.0	28.6	14.0	14.0	..	..
Ukraine	-0.4	6.0	5.5	4.5	5.7	..	4.3	12.9	9.7	10.6	10.6	12.8
Uzbekistan	4.4	4.0	3.0	4.4	..	..	6.1	6.4	5.1	7.3	6.8	6.4
Total above	2.4	6.0	..	..	..	..	3.7	9.0	..	..	..	..
Memorandum items:												
CETE-5	3.0	4.0	..	..	..	..	2.9	8.7	..	..	..	..
SETE-7	-3.0	3.6	..	..	..	..	-9.9	6.6	..	..	..	..

Source: National statistics; CIS Statistical Committee; direct communications from national statistical offices to the UN/ECE secretariat.

Note: Industrial output figures for 2000 in table 3.3.1 are based on monthly data. Because of differences in coverage, the cumulative monthly figures for 2000 as a whole differ slightly from the reported annual figures for some countries; where this is the case, the annual figures have been used. On regional aggregates see the note to table 3.1.1. Various types of monthly and quarterly indices of industrial output (fixed-base index, month over previous month, month over corresponding month of previous year, cumulative months over cumulative months of previous year, quarter over previous quarter, quarter over corresponding quarter of previous year) published by transition countries often contradict each other. The reasons for that are perhaps related to problems in source data and to inadequate revision and dissemination practices. In the above table, officially reported quarterly indices were used for Hungary, Poland, Slovenia, Estonia, Latvia, Lithuania and the Russian Federation. Quarterly indices were calculated from fixed-base monthly indices, either reported by countries or constructed by the UN/ECE secretariat from other types of monthly indices, for Bosnia and Herzegovina, Croatia, Czech Republic, Romania, Slovakia, The former Yugoslav Republic of Macedonia, Yugoslavia, Belarus, Kazakhstan, Kyrgyzstan and the Ukraine. For Bulgaria, Armenia, Azerbaijan, Georgia, the Republic of Moldova, Tajikistan, Turkmenistan and Uzbekistan fixed-base indices are not available, but indices of cumulative months over cumulative months of the preceding year are published. For these countries a special technique was used to determine a unique decumulated index level based on criterion of minimum seasonality.

Baltic economies was that net exports and private consumption were the most important contributors to the growth of GDP in 2000 (table 3.3.2). In a few cases such as the Czech Republic, Romania and Estonia, the net trade effect was negative and in Slovakia the contribution of domestic demand as a whole was negative. Partial and incomplete data for the CIS economies, suggest that domestic demand added the most to real GDP growth in 2000.

Agriculture still accounts for a major share of GDP and exports in many of the transition economies, its share ranging from 3.6 per cent in Slovenia to over 50 per cent in Albania (table 3.3.3).[225] The share of agriculture in GDP was on average much higher in the CIS countries,

---

[225] In comparison, the average share of agriculture in GDP in the high-income economies in 1999 was 2 per cent. World Bank, *World Development Report 2000/2001: Attacking Poverty* (Washington, D.C.), p. 297.

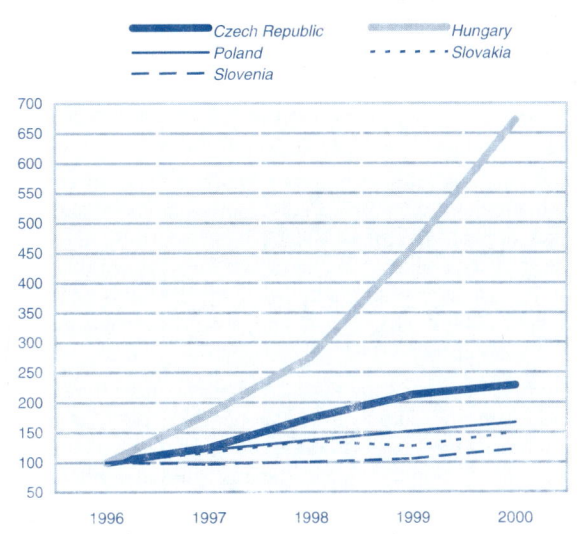

CHART 3.3.1

Gross output in the electrical and optical equipment industry in central Europe, 1996-2000
(1996=100)

Source: UN/ECE secretariat, based on national sources.

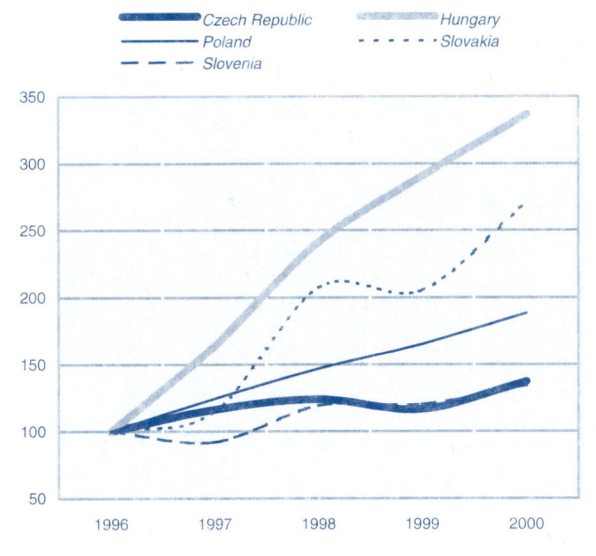

CHART 3.3.2

Gross output in the transport equipment industry in central Europe, 1996-2000
(1996=100)

Source: UN/ECE secretariat, based on national sources.

apart from Russia, than in central Europe and the Baltic states. The share has declined considerably since 1993 in most of the transition economies, particularly in those closest to the EU.[226] In most of the transition economies the contributions of industry and construction to GDP also declined between 1993 and 1999, but much more slowly than agriculture.[227] Overemphasis on the production of heavy machinery and equipment and neglect of the services sector under the previous system of central planning might explain this pattern of structural change. The services sector appears to have increased its share of GDP in almost every transition economy since 1993.

Despite the generally favourable trend of output in 2000, all of the ECE transition economies remain vulnerable to external disturbance. Although the slowdown in global growth during the second half of 2000 was not so apparent when the year is taken as a whole, it had a noticeable effect on the dynamics of output growth during the year. In many of these economies GDP and industrial output growth slowed significantly during the last quarter of 2000 (table 3.3.1). In the energy exporting CIS countries, falling oil and natural gas prices in the last quarter reduced revenues and consequently their rates of GDP growth. A weakening of external demand, perhaps triggered by the collapse in demand for high-tech products in the United States, may be having an effect on output growth in some central European countries as well. But, as suggested by the most recent business surveys in these countries, business confidence remained generally high in central Europe at the start of 2001.

(ii) Eastern Europe and the Baltic states

In 2000, the main determinant of GDP and industrial output growth in eastern Europe and the Baltic states was western European import demand. In contrast with 1999, external demand grew faster than domestic demand in every country in *eastern Europe* and the Baltic states. Real exports of goods and services increased at double-digit rates in 2000 throughout the region (except in Croatia), with increases as high as 30 per cent in Estonia (table 3.3.6). The rate of growth of exports was greater than for imports in every country except Romania. In Hungary, the exports of industrial producers grew three times faster than their domestic sales in 2000.[228] In Slovenia, the rate of growth of exports was almost seven times greater than the growth of total domestic demand, a marked break with the pattern of previous years when domestic demand played the leading role.[229] The pattern was similar in Poland and Slovakia; in the Czech Republic, however, growth in domestic demand, particularly investment, also contributed strongly to the recovery in 2000. This high growth in the demand for exports contributed to the acceleration in the growth of industrial output throughout the region during 2000 and was the main engine of high productivity growth.

---

[226] Generally, as income per capita rises, the contribution of agriculture to GDP can be expected to decline rapidly, while the contribution of industry (including construction) and services increases. H. Chenery and M. Syrquin, "Typical patterns of transformation", in H. Chenery, S. Robinson and M. Syrquin (eds.), *Industrialization and Growth: A Comparative Study* (Oxford, Oxford University Press, 1986).

[227] The percentage share of industry in GDP in most of the transition economies is similar to the average of a 30 per cent share in the high-income economies. World Bank, op. cit.

[228] The exports of industry as a whole increased by 27.4 per cent whereas domestic sales increased by 9 per cent. Hungarian central statistical office, Stadat system (www.ksh.hu).

[229] Institute for Macroeconomic Analysis and Development, *Slovenia: Analysis of Economic Developments in 2000, Prospects for 2001 and 2002 and Projections up until 2005* (Ljubljana), 2001.

Box 3.3.1

Structure and change in east European manufacturing industry

Periods of rapid change in the growth of output are invariably associated with considerable changes in the structure of industry. The *Economic Survey of Europe in 1993-1994* described how the rapid contraction of industrial output from 1990 to 1993 resulted in a similar pattern of structural change across countries. During this period, manufacturing output declined by more than 50 per cent in Bulgaria and Romania, by somewhat less in the Czech Republic and Slovakia, by one third in Hungary and Slovenia and by about one fourth in Poland. Output in virtually every industry declined, but what surprised some observers, especially in the countries affected, was that the more technology-intensive industries, such as machinery and equipment (DK) and electrical and optical equipment (DL), declined more rapidly than total manufacturing output. This was worrisome to policy makers because they considered their countries to have the necessary skill and technological endowments to be able to compete successfully in these industries.

This trend was reversed during the second phase of the economic transformation, which started roughly in 1993 in central Europe and 1995 in the Baltic states. The more advanced technological industries grew more rapidly, increasing their shares of total manufacturing output over the rest of the decade. Electrical and optical equipment (DL) led the recovery in these industries, growing much faster than total manufacturing output in almost every country. Bulgaria and Latvia were the only exceptions where they continued to decline in absolute terms. What is particularly striking is that in 1993 this industry comprised only 6.2 per cent of total manufacturing output in Hungary, but by 2000 its share was 42 per cent. But it also gained between 2 and almost 8 percentage points in the other countries.

Industries where economies of scale are important also tended to perform much better during the second phase of the transition. In particular, the transport equipment sector grew faster than total manufacturing output in every country except Bulgaria, Estonia and Latvia. In Slovakia its share of total manufacturing gained almost 17 percentage points and in Hungary more than 10 percentage points. The rubber and plastics industry also gained share in every country except Romania. In Latvia the share of basic metals and fabricated metal products increased by more than 6 percentage points.

The more traditional, labour-intensive industries were the biggest "losers" in the second phase of the economic transformation. The share of food products, beverages and tobacco declined by about 15 percentage points in Hungary and Estonia, while the food, textile and leather, and wood industries together declined by several percentage points in every country except Romania and Latvia. The wood and wood products industry gained in all of the Baltic states. All of these industries did relatively better in Bulgaria and Romania, but mainly because the manufacturing sector has still not fully recovered from the declines of the late 1990s. The machinery and equipment branch was also a "loser" during the second phase of the transition, mainly because many of its products are generally designed for specific uses and often require particular technological skills and endowments to be competitive.

The structure of manufacturing industry in selected east European and Baltic economies, 1993 and 2000

	Bulgaria	Czech Republic	Hungary	Poland	Romania	Slovakia	Slovenia	Estonia	Latvia	Lithuania
Branch share of manufacturing production, 1993 (per cent)										
D Total manufacturing	100.0	100.0	100.0	100.0	100.0	100.0	100.0	100.0	100.0	100.0
DA Food products, beverages and tobacco	24.8	19.1	28.5	26.5	21.4	19.4	16.1	37.0	40.3	35.7
DB Textiles and textile products	7.0	6.1	5.0	7.0	6.4	5.3	7.9	10.7	7.4	12.2
DC Leather and leather products	1.9	1.9	1.2	1.4	1.6	1.7	3.1	1.5	1.3	1.7
DD Wood and wood products	1.3	1.7	1.7	3.5	3.0	1.7	4.0	5.9	9.7	3.2
DE Pulp, paper & paper products; publishing & printing	3.6	4.7	5.5	5.3	2.0	5.7	8.0	6.8	5.1	3.7
DF Coke, refined petroleum products & nuclear fuel	12.4	4.6	9.4	5.6	8.3	7.9	1.4	..	..	..
DG Chemicals, chemical products and man-made fibres	7.9	9.1	12.6	7.7	12.5	9.3	9.3	9.2	7.3	7.3
DH Rubber and plastic products	2.3	2.8	3.3	3.5	3.5	3.8	4.1	1.3	0.8	0.9
DI Other non-metallic mineral products	3.6	5.2	3.9	5.0	4.9	5.3	4.2	4.9	2.7	3.8
DJ Basic metals and fabricated metal products	13.7	17.4	10.4	11.7	19.6	19.3	11.5	4.9	4.9	1.8
DK Machinery and equipment n.e.c.	7.3	9.3	5.7	6.3	5.5	8.4	8.4	2.9	5.1	4.3
DL Electrical and optical equipment	4.9	4.8	6.2	5.6	2.7	4.9	5.8	4.3	4.9	5.6
DM Transport equipment	4.9	10.3	4.7	7.3	6.2	4.8	11.1	4.2	7.6	1.7
DN Manufacturing n.e.c.	4.5	3.1	1.8	3.7	2.4	2.5	5.0	6.3	3.8	3.3
Change in branch shares, 1993-2000 (percentage points)										
DA Food products, beverages and tobacco	-2.1	-3.5	-15.2	-4.6	3.9	-5.1	-0.2	-14.6	-6.4	-5.6
DB Textiles and textile products	-0.4	-2.0	-2.1	-2.2	0.5	-2.7	-1.4	2.0	2.4	0.3
DC Leather and leather products	-0.7	-1.4	-0.7	-0.5	0.3	-0.6	-1.7	–	-1.0	-0.4
DD Wood and wood products	-0.1	-0.1	-0.6	0.5	-0.5	-0.3	-1.4	8.4	9.3	1.4
DE Pulp, paper & paper products; publishing & printing	0.2	0.5	-1.7	1.5	–	1.4	-2.8	0.8	2.1	0.2
DF Coke, refined petroleum products & nuclear fuel	6.4	-1.4	-6.3	-1.7	-0.8	–	-1.1	..	..	..
DG Chemicals, chemical products and man-made fibres	2.9	-1.2	-7.6	-1.2	-4.2	-2.0	2.6	-4.3	-4.6	3.6
DH Rubber and plastic products	0.1	1.5	-0.1	1.8	-1.8	0.1	0.7	1.0	0.6	0.6
DI Other non-metallic mineral products	0.4	0.2	-1.6	0.2	-0.1	-0.9	0.6	-0.1	0.3	-1.1
DJ Basic metals and fabricated metal products	-2.2	-4.8	-2.9	0.1	-3.0	-4.1	0.5	2.3	6.1	–
DK Machinery and equipment n.e.c.	2.1	-0.1	-2.1	-0.7	-0.3	-1.7	-0.3	0.2	-3.1	-2.0
DL Electrical and optical equipment	-0.8	7.6	35.6	2.0	1.9	2.1	3.9	3.7	-2.2	4.3
DM Transport equipment	-3.2	4.2	10.3	3.7	2.9	16.9	0.7	-0.2	-2.9	1.4
DN Manufacturing n.e.c.	-3.0	0.7	-0.6	0.9	1.5	-0.7	0.1	1.6	0.6	0.4

Source: UN/ECE secretariat calculations, based on WIIW Industrial Database Eastern Europe and national sources.

Note: The Baltic states data are for 1995-2000. Time series data may include changes in coverage and 2000 data are preliminary.

TABLE 3.3.2

Contribution of final demand components to real GDP growth in eastern Europe, the Baltic states and the CIS, 1999-2000
(Percentage points)

	Consumption		Fixed investment		Total domestic demand		Net trade		Exports of goods and services		Imports of goods and services		GDP	
	1999	2000[a]	1999	2000[a]	1999	2000[a]	1999	2000[a]	1999	2000[a]	1999	2000[a]	1999	2000[a]
Bulgaria	4.1	3.4	3.3	1.4	7.2	0.6	-5.1	3.9	-2.5	10.7	-2.6	-6.9	2.4	5.3
Croatia	-1.4	2.2	-0.3	-0.8	-2.1	2.2	1.7	1.5	0.3	3.7	1.4	-2.2	-0.4	3.7
Czech Republic	0.3	0.7	-1.4	1.6	-1.0	4.3	0.2	-1.2	3.3	13.7	-14.9	-14.9	-0.8	3.1
Hungary	3.0	2.2	1.6	1.6	4.4	5.3	0.1	-0.1	7.0	12.5	-12.7	-12.7	4.5	5.2
Poland	3.6	1.7	1.6	0.8	5.1	3.0	-1.1	1.2	-0.7	..	-0.3	..	4.1	4.1
Romania	-3.9	1.4	-2.1	1.0	-6.9	4.4	3.7	-2.8	2.1	7.2	1.6	-10.0	-3.2	1.6
Slovakia	-1.6	-1.9	-7.0	-0.2	-5.1	-1.3	7.1	3.6	2.3	10.9	4.8	-7.3	1.9	2.2
Slovenia	4.3	1.1	4.9	0.5	9.4	1.4	-4.2	3.4	1.1	7.4	-5.3	-4.0	5.2	4.8
The former Yugoslav Republic of Macedonia	0.5	..	0.2	..	-1.1	..	3.7	..	0.6	..	3.1	..	2.7	10.0
Estonia	0.2	6.1	-4.8	0.2	-4.8	9.2	4.3	-0.8	-2.1	26.6	6.4	-27.5	-1.1	6.6
Latvia	3.7	1.8	-1.7	4.3	1.1	1.2	-0.1	4.2	-3.6	6.9	3.6	-2.8	1.1	5.4
Lithuania	-3.8	..	-1.7	..	-4.8	..	0.6	..	-11.7	..	12.3	..	-4.2	2.9
Armenia	0.4	4.8	0.1	1.2	0.6	5.7	3.3	-2.6	3.3	..	–	..	3.3	2.9
Belarus	6.5	5.1	-1.0	-0.5	2.2	8.4	4.3	-2.4	4.1	..	0.1	..	3.4	5.2
Kazakhstan	5.3	..	0.1	..	5.4	..	10.2	..	3.8	..	6.4	..	9.4	9.6
Kyrgyzstan	1.0	..	3.6	..	4.6	..	-0.9	..	-3.8	..	2.9	..	3.7	5.0
Republic of Moldova	-15.9	8.2	-5.1	0.9	-21.0	8.8	17.6	-6.9	1.4	8.3	16.2	-15.2	-3.4	1.9
Russian Federation	-3.8	4.9	-0.3	2.3	-1.9	7.7	5.3	–	1.2	..	4.0	..	3.2	7.7
Ukraine	-1.1	..	–	..	-4.6	..	4.6	..	-2.8	..	7.4	..	-0.3	6.0

Source: National statistics and direct communications from national statistical offices to the UN/ECE secretariat.

Note: The sum of the component changes may not add up to the GDP change for some countries because of reported statistical discrepancies.

[a] January-September for Bulgaria, Estonia, Latvia, Armenia and Belarus.

Gross manufacturing output in Hungary increased by almost 21 per cent, the largest increase among all the transition economies (table 3.3.4). Strong demand for electrical and optical equipment and transport equipment, mainly from the EU, helped to speed up the process of industrial restructuring in the country.[230] Over the past 5 years, both of these industries in Hungary had the highest growth rates among the central European countries, and by 2000 they were contributing more than half of total manufacturing output in Hungary (chart 3.3.3).[231] The two industries are dominated by firms with foreign participation, which in 1999 accounted for 73 per cent of domestic sales and almost 89 per cent of exports.[232]

There was also strong demand from the EU for various high value added manufacturing products from the Czech Republic, Poland, Slovakia and Slovenia. Although net trade made a negative contribution to the growth of GDP in the Czech Republic, the strong growth of merchandise exports contributed toward the 4.8 per cent growth of manufacturing output, especially in the transport equipment industry. But the growth of domestic demand was the main reason for the rise in imports, which gradually overtook exports. In Slovakia, the acceleration of exports helped total manufacturing output to grow by over 10 per cent in 2000.[233] GDP, however, increased by just 2.2 per cent, mainly because of the austerity measures introduced in 1999: all the components of final domestic demand continued to decline in 2000 for the second consecutive year (table 3.3.6).

GDP and industrial output growth decelerated during the course of 2000 in Poland (table 3.3.1), mainly because of the tightening of monetary policy in late 1999. Nevertheless, the growth of GDP was over 4 per cent in 2000 and gross manufacturing output increased by almost 8 per cent. Manufacturing growth became increasingly reliant on external demand during the course of the year,

---

[230] Output increased by more than 54 per cent in the electrical and optical equipment industry as a whole. Within that group, electrical machinery and television and radio equipment were the fastest growing branches, with output increasing by more than 64 per cent and 78 per cent, respectively. Production of office machinery and computers increased by 30 per cent; this industry had the highest cumulative growth rate over the previous 5 years. Hungarian central statistical office, *Stadat system* (www.ksh.hu). Less spectacular changes occurred in Slovenia and Slovakia where the output of the industry increased by 14 and 19 per cent, respectively. In the Czech Republic and Poland its growth rate was about 8 per cent.

[231] In 2000, the share of electrical and optical equipment and transport equipment in total manufacturing output was 42 per cent and 15 per cent, respectively.

[232] In the electrical and optical equipment industry, foreign owned enterprises accounted for 89 per cent of sales from domestic production and 97 per cent of exports. Foreign owned firms also dominate the motor vehicle industry. WIIW Database on Foreign Investment Enterprises in Central European Manufacturing, Vienna Institute for International Economic Studies (Vienna).

[233] The key element here was the strong growth of output in the transport equipment industry (by 32 per cent in 2000).

TABLE 3.3.3

GDP by kind of activity in eastern Europe, the Baltic states and the CIS, 1993 and 1999
(Percentage share of GDP)

	Agriculture		Industry and construction		Services	
	1993	1999	1993	1999	1993	1999
Albania	54.6	52.6	22.9	25.4	22.5	22.0
Bosnia and Herzegovina[a]	25.0	10.0	27.4	29.4	47.6	60.6
Bulgaria	10.6	17.3	35.0	26.8	54.4	55.9
Croatia	13.3	9.2	34.4	31.6	52.3	59.2
Czech Republic	5.3	3.7	41.1	41.9	53.6	54.4
Hungary	6.6	4.9	31.6	31.2	61.9	63.9
Poland	7.2	3.9	42.7	35.8	50.0	60.2
Romania	21.6	15.5	40.3	36.2	38.1	48.3
Slovakia	4.9	4.6	36.9	34.4	58.2	61.0
Slovenia	5.1	3.6	38.1	37.5	56.8	58.9
The former Yugoslav Republic of Macedonia[b]	10.3	11.0	30.4	31.1	59.3	57.8
Yugoslavia	..	18.1	..	38.9	..	43.0
Estonia	11.0	5.7	31.1	25.3	57.9	69.1
Latvia	11.8	4.5	35.0	27.0	53.2	68.5
Lithuania	14.2	8.4	39.3	30.8	46.5	60.8
Armenia	50.8	28.3	26.6	32.1	22.6	39.6
Azerbaijan	26.7	23.1	31.7	35.1	41.6	41.8
Belarus	16.8	14.3	35.0	37.7	48.2	48.0
Georgia	69.7	25.7	9.3	22.1	21.0	52.2
Kazakhstan	16.4	10.4	36.8	34.6	46.8	55.0
Kyrgyzstan	40.0	37.6	31.2	26.7	28.7	35.7
Republic of Moldova	30.3	26.2	41.0	21.4	28.7	52.4
Russian Federation	8.2	6.9	42.3	37.8	49.6	55.3
Tajikistan	22.2	18.7	44.2	24.7	33.6	56.7
Turkmenistan	19.2	26.0	61.0	43.0	19.8	31.0
Ukraine	20.0	14.2	34.1	37.5	45.9	48.4
Uzbekistan	29.9	33.5	33.6	24.3	36.6	42.2

Source: National and CIS Statistical Committee data; direct communications from national statistical offices to the UN/ECE secretariat.

Note: GDP represents the sum of value added at basic prices by all producers in the economy. Agriculture includes forestry and fishing except in certain CIS countries.

[a] 1995 instead of 1993.
[b] 1998 instead of 1999.

CHART 3.3.3

Gross output in the electrical and optical equipment industry in Hungary by branch, 1996-2000
(1996=100)

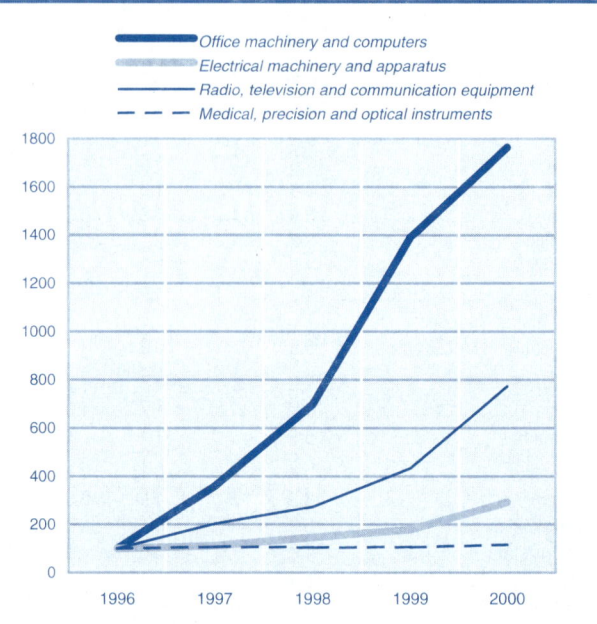

Source: Hungarian Statistical Office.

as the growth of private consumption decelerated from over 4 per cent in the first quarter to less than 1 per cent in the second half of the year. As in the other central European economies, foreign owned enterprises are playing an increasingly prominent role in Poland's manufacturing production and exports.[234] Output in Slovenia continued to grow steadily for the eighth successive year, GDP increasing by about 5 per cent in 2000 and gross industrial output by more than 6 per cent. External demand was the main factor behind the growth of manufacturing output, but the strong recovery in the Slovenian tourist industry also boosted aggregate output and contributed to the robust growth in retail sales.

Exports[235] were also the key factor behind the rapid economic recovery in Estonia with industrial production increasing by 9 per cent and GDP growing by over 6 per cent. Much of this growth is due to subcontracting from foreign (mostly Scandinavian) high-tech firms, which are an important catalyst for technology transfer.[236] After a decline in 1999, final consumer demand in Estonia also recovered strongly in 2000, giving a further push to domestic output. Rapid growth in Latvia's exports of goods and services helped to spur growth rates of 6.6 per cent in GDP in 2000, but a continuing recovery of domestic demand also helped to maintain a steady rate of expansion throughout the year. GDP increased much less in Lithuania, by 3.3 per cent in 2000 despite a strong export-led recovery in a number of manufacturing industries. The uneven pace of output was partly caused by disruptions to the delivery of crude oil from Russia;[237] the resumption of deliveries in the fourth quarter helped to boost total manufacturing output in the final months of the year.

The strength of external demand also created a favourable economic environment for manufacturers in the

---

[234] In 1999 foreign owned enterprises accounted for more than 20 per cent of total domestic sales in manufacturing and almost 35 per cent of manufacturing exports. In 1998 they accounted for 67 per cent of total transport equipment and almost 90 per cent of motor vehicle production. WIIW Database ..., op. cit.

[235] In January-September 2000, real merchandise exports from Estonia increased by almost 35 per cent (year-on-year), the highest rate of all the east European and Baltic countries (table 3.6.5).

[236] In 2000, output of electrical and optical equipment increased by 28 per cent in Estonia, 22 per cent in Latvia and almost 19 per cent in Lithuania.

[237] Lukoil, Russia's leading oil producer, broke off shipments to Mazeikiu Nafta, after failing to reach an agreement on prices in late 1999.

TABLE 3.4.1

Consumer prices in eastern Europe, the Baltic states and the CIS, 1999-2000
(Percentage change)

	Annual average		December over December		2000, year-on-year			
	1999	2000	1999	2000	QI	QII	QIII	QIV
Albania	-0.1	–	-1.0	4.2	-1.6	-0.5	-0.4	2.6
Bosnia and Herzegovina	-0.6	1.7	-0.4	3.4	0.5	–	2.7	3.7
Bulgaria	0.4	10.0	6.2	11.2	8.9	10.2	9.8	11.0
Croatia [a]	4.3	6.4	4.6	7.5	5.0	6.2	6.9	7.6
Czech Republic	2.1	3.9	2.5	4.1	3.6	3.8	4.1	4.3
Hungary	10.1	9.9	11.3	10.1	10.0	9.2	9.9	10.5
Poland	7.4	10.2	9.9	8.6	10.4	10.1	10.9	9.2
Romania	45.9	45.7	54.9	40.7	53.8	44.6	44.9	41.6
Slovakia	10.5	12.0	14.2	8.3	15.6	15.8	8.8	8.5
Slovenia	6.3	9.0	8.1	9.0	8.5	9.5	8.8	9.3
The former Yugoslav Republic of Macedonia [a]	-1.4	10.1	2.3	10.8	4.3	12.7	12.6	10.9
Yugoslavia	44.1	77.5	54.0	115.1	53.7	59.8	73.3	110.5
Estonia	3.5	3.8	3.9	4.9	3.0	2.9	4.2	5.2
Latvia	2.4	2.8	3.3	1.9	3.4	3.2	2.8	2.0
Lithuania	0.8	1.0	0.3	1.5	0.8	0.9	0.9	1.4
Armenia	0.7	-0.8	2.1	0.4	0.1	-1.5	-1.0	-0.7
Azerbaijan	-8.6	1.8	-0.5	2.1	1.7	1.8	1.7	1.9
Belarus	293.7	168.9	251.3	108.0	227.4	196.1	175.8	124.0
Georgia	20.8	4.2	11.1	4.6	4.4	1.2	5.5	5.7
Kazakhstan	8.4	13.4	18.1	10.0	20.4	13.7	10.1	10.4
Kyrgyzstan	35.7	18.7	39.8	9.5	36.7	20.5	11.6	9.9
Republic of Moldova	39.3	31.3	43.8	18.5	40.0	35.1	29.4	23.1
Russian Federation	85.7	20.8	36.6	20.1	25.4	19.9	18.8	19.8
Tajikistan	27.5	32.9	30.1	60.6	28.1	29.6	19.6	52.8
Turkmenistan	..	..	..	..	..	..	..	..
Ukraine	22.7	28.2	19.2	25.8	25.1	27.4	31.1	28.9
Uzbekistan	29.0	..	26.0	..	25.1	22.9	24.2	..

Source: UN/ECE secretariat estimates, based on national statistics.

[a] Retail price index.

February, disinflation resumed in March and accelerated in the rest of 2000. The year-on-year rate of inflation in December was nearly half of its level a year earlier, a reflection of depressed demand[267] and a fairly firm exchange rate of the koruna. In the last quarter, weaker energy prices also contributed to the lower rate of inflation. Not only was disinflation significant, but it was realized in spite of large price adjustments, which had been postponed for several years by the previous government. Regulated prices increased by more than 20 per cent in 2000. Core inflation excluding these adjustments rose by 4.6 per cent compared with 10.8 per cent in 1999.[268]

In Poland the monetary authorities, concerned at the widening current account deficit, tried to curb domestic demand with an extremely tight monetary policy. The inflation rate started to fall from mid-2000 and decelerated substantially in the last quarter, thanks to a further weakening of demand and the easing of international oil prices. Surprisingly weak food prices pulled down the inflation rate further in the early months of 2001, the year-on-year rate falling from 8.6 per cent in December to 7.5 per cent in January and 6.6 per cent in February. The central bank's inflation target (6-8 per cent, year-on-year, by December 2001) may be undershot if the strength of the zloty and the current easing of food prices, which had contributed significantly to the overall inflation in 2000,[269] continue in the coming months. However, if the real economy continues to be squeezed too hard, a sharp slowdown in productivity may lead to a hardening of the core inflation rate even if rising unemployment lowers wage demands.

In Hungary the consumer price inflation in 2000, measured over the 12 months to December, was only slightly lower than a year ago and it overshot the government's target (6-7 per cent, annual average) by a large margin.[270] The rate of inflation would have been even

---

[267] Private consumption fell by more than 5 per cent in the first three quarters of 2000.

[268] National Bank of Slovakia, *Monetary Survey*, December 2000, p. 5.

[269] Food prices rose by 8.6 per cent and contributed 2.6 percentage points to consumer price inflation measured over the 12 months to December 2000. The corresponding statistics in 1999 were 6 per cent and 1.9 percentage points. The net inflation rate, which excludes food and fuel, in fact fell over the first three quarters of 2000 to 4.6 per cent from 5.2 per cent in the same period of 1999. National Bank of Poland, Monetary Policy Council, *Inflation Report, Third Quarter 2000* (Warsaw), December 2000.

[270] The Ministry of Finance revised the target in the spring to 7-8 per cent and in mid-August to 8-9 per cent. The government's original projection, incorporated in the budget, was based on two basic assumptions: an average crude oil price of $18 per barrel, and an average increase in nominal wages of 8.25 per cent, both of which turned out to be much below actual developments.

CHART 3.4.1

Consumer prices in eastern Europe, the Baltic states and the CIS, 1997-2001
(Year-on-year, monthly percentage change)

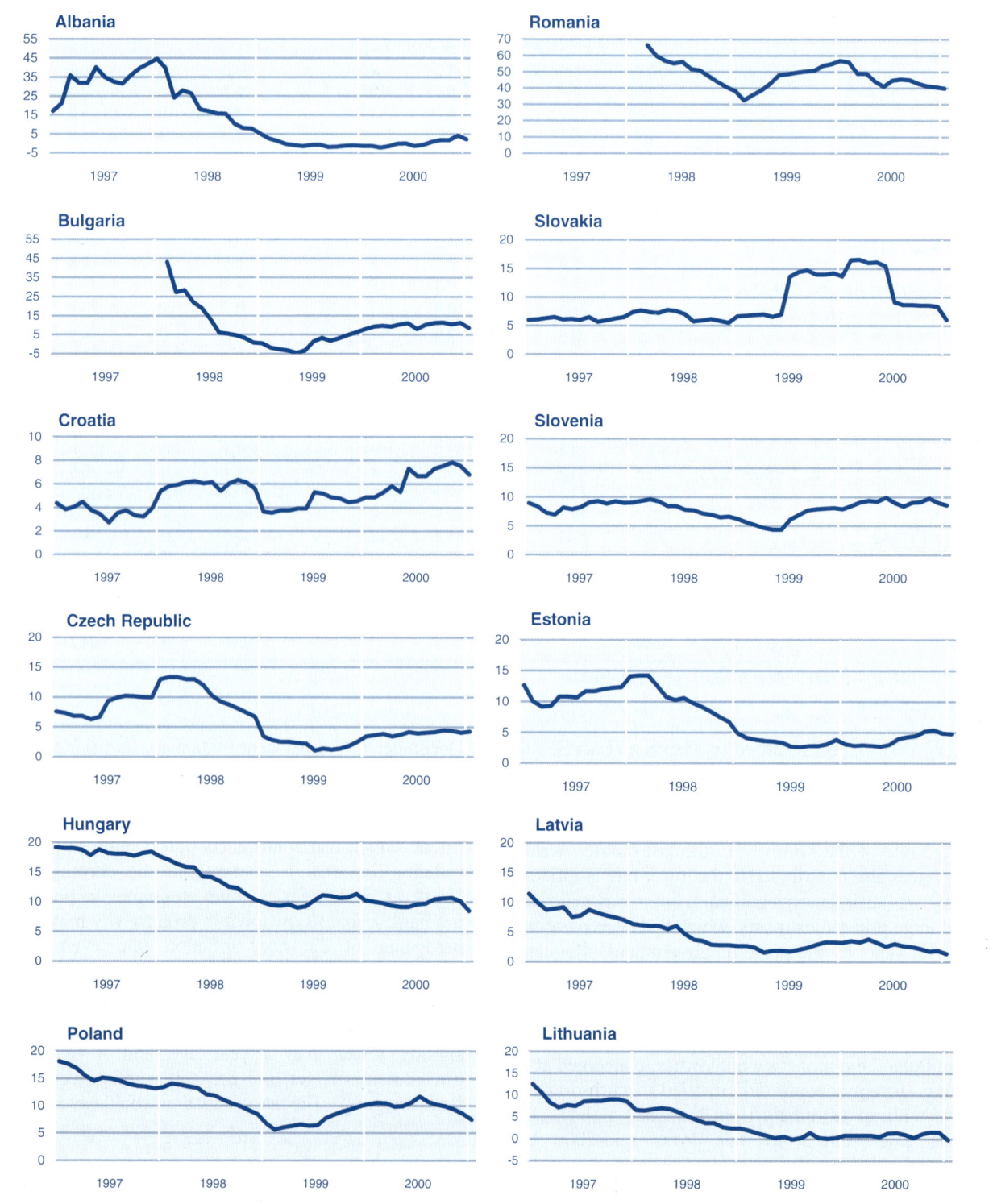

(For source and notes see end of chart.)

CHART 3.4.1 (concluded)

Consumer prices in eastern Europe, the Baltic states and the CIS, 1997-2001
(Year-on-year, monthly percentage change)

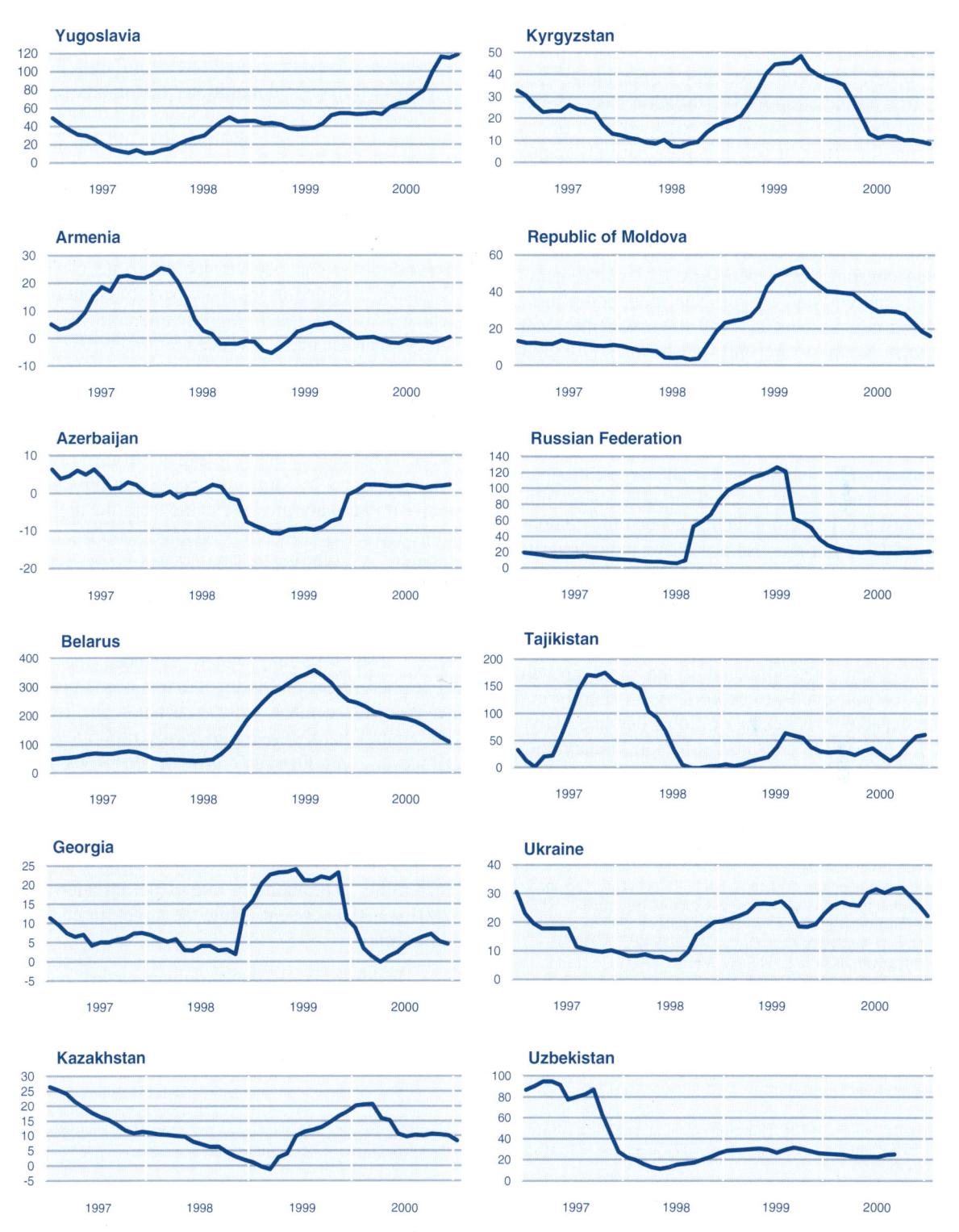

Source: National statistics and UN/ECE secretariat estimates.

higher if the government had not intervened to control the increase in the prices of natural gas and pharmaceuticals.[271] This stubborn inflation rate was mainly due to sharp increases in food and oil prices and by the weakness of the euro vis-à-vis the dollar. The year-on-year core rate of inflation, in contrast to the headline CPI, was higher in December 2000 than 12 months earlier, 9.8 and 8.7 per cent, respectively.[272] This was the first acceleration in core inflation since 1995. In addition to the one-off rise in unprocessed food prices in the autumn, the effect of which is only partially removed from the core index, the persistent increase in the price of services[273] since July "warns of the danger of inflation inertia and the associated long-term interruption in disinflation".[274] However, given an only modest increase in private consumption expenditure (3.7 per cent in the first three quarters) and a significant moderation in retail trade (from 6.5 per cent in 1999 to some 2 per cent in 2000), there seems to be only rather weak inflationary pressure coming from the side of consumer demand. Furthermore, the surge in labour productivity in industry (nearly 20 per cent year-on-year) and the relatively modest growth in real wages despite a significant improvement in the labour market all suggest that part of these price changes reflect structural adjustments related to the transition process which are not only temporary and unavoidable but are also a positive indication of the progress of reforms in Hungary.[275] Nevertheless, short-term remedies such as the capping of prices may slow the process of getting inflation down to single-digit rates, particularly if fiscal policy[276] remains lax in the run up to the 2002 general elections and if the rapid growth of industrial output, thanks to exports, slows sharply in line with the expected weakening of global demand. Given a rise of 1.5 per cent in consumer prices in January and 1.4 per cent in February 2001, the official forecast of a 6-7 per cent increase by the end of the year may prove to be optimistic.

Consumer prices also rose more slowly in 2000 compared with 1999 in Romania, but the year-end rate of some 40 per cent was the fourth highest among the transition economies after Yugoslavia, Belarus and Tajikistan. Thus, the actual rate of inflation did not only overshoot the original ambitious year-end target of 27 per cent but also the revised and more plausible target of 40 per cent despite weak consumer demand. In addition to a series of tariff and tax increases,[277] the nominal depreciation of the leu and higher oil prices, a poor harvest led to a large increase in food prices,[278] which account for some 60 per cent of total household expenditure. The persistently high rate of inflation in Romania is rooted in the slow pace of economic reform, which leaves it much more vulnerable to supply-side shocks than the more advanced reformers.

In the Czech Republic the inflation rate increased slightly during 2000 but remained low at around 4 per cent year-on-year in December, thanks to still relatively weak consumer demand[279] and a strong koruna, which was supported by large inflows of foreign capital. The major inflationary pressure came from the higher costs of imported energy, which weakened somewhat in the last quarter. A large rise in food prices (3.6 per cent year-on-year in December 2000 compared with a fall of 0.4 per cent in 1999) and increases in administered prices also contributed to the acceleration in the headline inflation rate. Net inflation, which excludes the impact of controlled prices and indirect taxes, was 3 per cent year-on-year in December, which was below the lower limit of the central bank's year-end target (3.5-5.5 per cent).[280] However, productivity growth in Czech industry remained much lower than in most of its neighbours and the rapid growth of producer prices relative to consumer prices in 2000, with the gap growing significantly in the second half, suggests that cost pressures are gradually increasing. The monthly rate of net inflation in January 2001 was 0.6 per cent, while the target for end-2001 is 2-4 per cent.

In Slovenia, despite a tight monetary policy, rising oil prices and the depreciation of the tolar[281] exerted

---

[271] This capping of natural gas prices has become an important source of controversy between the government and the business sector. MOL (the oil and gas monopoly) declared a fall of 45 per cent in net income in 2000. "Operating profits excluding gas almost quadrupled, while gas operations fell from a profit of 12 billion forints in 1999 to a loss of 117 billion", *Oxford Analytica East Europe Daily Brief*, 15 February 2001. These recent government interventions in price setting are seen as one of the reasons for the reluctance of some foreign investors despite the generally good macroeconomic performance and environment for FDI.

[272] National Bank of Hungary, *Quarterly Report on Inflation* (Budapest), December 2000 (www.mnu.hu). The National Bank describes the trend of inflation in terms of a core inflation index calculated according to the Bank's own methodology: namely, the consumer price index excluding seasonal foods, non-regulated fuels, motor fuels, and pharmaceutical goods. The Hungarian central statistical office also publishes a core inflation index, which excludes unprocessed foodstuffs.

[273] The year-on-year rate of increase in service prices rose from 8.8 per cent in July to 10.6 per cent in December, while for non-food manufactured goods prices fell from 11.3 per cent in June to 8.2 per cent in December.

[274] National Bank of Hungary, op. cit., p. 24.

[275] See sect. 3.2(iii) above and also chap. 2.6 on the experience of Ireland in this respect.

[276] The government promised to raise public sector salaries by 16 per cent in 2001 (after a 12 per cent increase in 2000) and the minimum wage by nearly two thirds. PlanEcon, *Monthly Report* (Washington, D.C.), 26 January 2001.

[277] For example, the unification and extension of VAT rates in January and April, respectively, and large increases in natural gas and electricity charges in June, August and September, contributed strongly to the overall increase in consumer prices.

[278] During the course of 2000, food prices increased by some 46 per cent compared with less than 37 per cent in 1999.

[279] In the first three quarters of 2000 private consumption rose by 1.8 per cent after falling 2.6 per cent in 1998 and more or less stagnating in 1999.

[280] Czech National Bank, *Inflation Report January 2001* (Prague), 2001.

[281] In order to maintain the competitiveness of exports to the euro and euro-related areas, the tolar was allowed to depreciate against the euro in nominal terms by some 7 per cent over the 12 months to December 2000, while it depreciated some 20 per cent against the dollar during the same period.

strong upward pressure on consumer prices, which rose 9 per cent for the year as a whole, the highest rate since 1999. However, the deterioration in the terms of trade effect was not the only cause of the acceleration in inflation, particularly in the second half of the year. To compensate for faster than expected inflation in the first half (the initial official annual target was 4.5 per cent), public sector wages and pensions were re-indexed in July.[282] In addition, with increased employment added to the improvement in disposable incomes, the growth of private consumption resumed an upward trend in the first quarter. Although core inflation (excluding food and energy) over the 12 months to December was nearly 2 percentage points lower than the headline inflation in 2000, it nevertheless accelerated much faster over the year.[283] The narrowing of the difference between the two rates of inflation, particularly in the second half of 2000, may point to growing pressures on prices, other than food and energy, which may at least be partly linked to rising labour costs. This risk of a wage-price spiral, combined with a simultaneous slowdown in productivity gains, may pose a major dilemma for the conduct of monetary policy in 2001.

In Croatia, there was a sharp rebound in inflation in 2000. In the first three quarters of the year a large increase in revenues from tourism largely offset the fall in real household incomes caused by sharply declining industrial employment and falling real wages, and private consumption recovered rather strongly.[284] Nevertheless, the acceleration in consumer prices was kept in check by the strong kuna and the government's decision to lower fuel taxes to cushion the rise in import prices for oil. However, in the last quarter the kuna started to weaken rapidly, and the government, among other administered price adjustments, allowed the household electricity prices to rise by 25 per cent. In December the year-on-year rate of inflation reached 7.5 per cent, the largest increase since the end of the hyperinflation in 1993. However, if the government cuts import tariffs as required by the terms of its accession to the WTO and is able to resist the rising social discontent over falling real wages and soaring unemployment, then inflation in 2001 can be expected to moderate. On the other hand, the rapid growth of producer prices in the closing months of 2000 suggest that disinflation at the retail level may prove difficult, at least in the first half of 2001.

In Bulgaria inflation fell from a peak in triple digits in 1997 to a single digit in 1999, but in 2000 it nearly doubled to reach 11 per cent at the end of the year, overshooting by a large margin the revised mid-year target of 6 per cent. However, this acceleration was mainly due to external and one-off factors such as higher import prices for energy, a bad harvest and frequent adjustments to regulated prices.[285] Soaring unemployment and only moderate growth in real wages dampened household consumption during 2000.

After falling in 1999, consumer prices in Albania and Bosnia and Herzegovina rose in 2000, albeit at much lower rates than in the other east European countries. In both of them economic recovery strengthened in 2000 but, with very high rates of unemployment and widespread, war-induced poverty, consumer price inflation remained subdued.

In The former Yugoslav Republic of Macedonia inflation rose strongly over the course of 2000 to reach double digits after several quarters when prices had fallen. The acceleration was mainly due to the increase in energy prices and the introduction of VAT in April; although the economy started recovering from the Kosovo crisis in late 1999, demand remained weak in the face of high unemployment rates and falling real wages.

In Yugoslavia, direct and indirect price controls, combined with an artificially low official exchange rate of the dinar, had kept inflation rates at around 50 per cent in the two and a half years to mid-2000. The government devalued the dinar in June and liberalized some prices in October. The monthly inflation rate soared during the second half and the cumulative 12-month inflation rate moved into triple digits. Further substantial increases in prices are expected partly as a result of the second devaluation of the dinar in December but also from the price liberalization process announced in the new government's annual programme; at present, major public utility prices, for example, are still controlled.

In the *Baltic economies* inflation rates in 2000 were again much lower than those in the majority of east European countries. In both Latvia and Lithuania 12-month inflation rates remained below 2 per cent, and in Estonia just below 5 per cent. The relatively higher rate of inflation in Estonia, despite its prudent fiscal policy and significant gains in labour productivity, reflects in the main the depreciation of the currency[286] and stronger consumer demand (the latter supported by the economic upturn and credit expansion). In Latvia the relatively strong exchange rate[287] offset part of the inflationary

---

[282] In May 1999, a minimum wage agreement was reached between the government, the employers and the trade unions, which linked increases in base wages to the rate of inflation from December 1999. According to this agreement, if prices rose more than 5 percentage points above their December 1999 level, base wages would be fully indexed in line with inflation. In July 2000 consumer prices were 5.3 per cent higher than in December 1999. However, while most public sector wages are linked to base wages, those in the "economic sector", which includes manufacturing wages, are also linked to other factors such as real GDP growth, which makes them less responsive to change in the base wage.

[283] Core inflation measured over the 12 months to December was 4.4 per cent in 1999 and 7.2 per cent in 2000. Institute of Macroeconomic Analysis and Development, *Slovenian Economic Mirror* (Ljubljana), January 2001, p. 10.

[284] In the first three quarters of 2000, private consumption expenditure and retail trade volume increased by 4.3 per cent and 15.3 per cent, respectively, after both had fallen in 1999.

[285] In 2000, the government raised natural gas prices twice by 17.5 per cent and 16.4 per cent. *Reuters News Service*, 9 March 2001.

[286] The kroon is pegged to the euro.

[287] The lat is pegged to the SDR, which has appreciated against the euro and depreciated against the dollar at a more moderate rate than in most other transition economies.

effect of rising oil prices. In Lithuania, tight fiscal and monetary policies, soaring unemployment, and, above all, the fixed exchange rate against the dollar, have kept the inflation rate very low.

In contrast to most east European economies, inflation fell sharply in most of the CIS economies in 2000 as the effects of the 1998 Russian financial crisis began to recede. Large increases in commodity export revenues and improved tax collection have helped to reduce some of the major imbalances in most of these economies. Improvements in the design and conduct of macroeconomic policy[288] have helped to lower inflation. In addition, given the much slower pace of reforms in these countries, price controls continue to be used extensively at the retail level in many of them, albeit to varying degrees. In the second half of 1999 a great deal of the moderation in inflation rates was due to the collapse of real household incomes and increased job insecurity which had negative effects on consumer demand. In 2000, in many CIS countries, household consumption improved, reflecting in the main, the recovery of real wages from mid-1999 and, in a few of them, some improvement in employment.[289] Nevertheless, on the supply side, large productivity gains and moderated increases in input prices, reflecting to a large extent the relative stability of their exchange rates, played a major role in containing pressures.

Among the CIS economies consumer price inflation in the 12 months to December 2000 was higher than in December 1999 only in Tajikistan, Ukraine and, to a much lesser extent, in Azerbaijan. However, the highest rate of inflation was again in the shortage-ridden Belarus economy even though price increases were held back by the extensive use of direct price controls. Nevertheless, there was also an effort to tighten monetary policy in 2000.

In Ukraine, inflation was relatively modest compared with most of the other CIS economies in 1998 and 1999, but it rose rather steadily in the first three quarters of 2000. This upturn was mainly due to a revival of real household incomes[290] and consumption,[291] supported by large increases in wages, pensions and social support payments. There was also faster growth in small business activity and above all a sharp recovery of agricultural output and incomes despite a severe drought in the spring. In addition, the central bank's purchases of hard currency in the interbank market to meet debt servicing obligations also added to inflationary pressures. Nevertheless, improved labour productivity absorbed much of the wage cost pressure, and a stable hryvnia, thanks to strong export earnings and tight controls on the domestic market, kept imported inflation at bay.

In Russia the rate of inflation over the 12 months to December 2000 rose by just over 20 per cent, some 2 percentage points above the official target, but almost half the rate in 1999. However, growing cost-pressures and the rapid growth of the money supply, due to large unsterilized foreign exchange inflows, started to have an impact on the monthly inflation rate in early 2001. The monthly rate of increase in consumer prices changes surged to 2.8 per cent in January and 2.3 per cent in February, which means that the prices index in two months has already reached more than one third of the way to the government's year-end target of 12-14 per cent. Part of the January increase is the result of seasonal factors (food prices rose by more than 3 per cent) and increases in regulated prices (fares for public transport, residential water and heating). But the rise in February was mainly due to increases for private services, which suggests the recent acceleration in unit labour costs (large wage increases accompanied by weakened productivity growth) and monetary expansion is feeding through to the non-tradeables sector. Therefore the end of year target is likely to be exceeded, and probably by a large margin if the recent weakening of output growth and the pressure on the rouble intensify in the coming months. Thus, without an acceleration in the pace of microeconomic reforms to eliminate excess labour in enterprises and to stimulate new investment (both domestic and foreign), the recent improvements in macroeconomic stabilization in Russia, and even more so in most of the other CIS economies, may prove to be short-lived once the external environment becomes less favourable.

(iii) Producer prices and labour costs in industry in 2000

Industrial producer price inflation, which picked up sharply in 1999, continued to accelerate in 2000 in eastern Europe and the Baltic countries (table 3.4.2), reflecting in the main soaring prices of energy and, albeit at much lower rates, imported industrial raw materials, particularly metals.[292]

In eastern Europe producer price inflation decelerated only in Poland and Romania. In Poland, prices stagnated in November and fell by nearly 1 per cent in December reflecting not only lower oil prices and the strong zloty but also weaker domestic demand. Weak domestic demand also checked the rate of increase of industrial output prices in Romania, although it remains very high due to supply-side shocks which have been amplified by very slow progress in enterprise restructuring.

---

[288] See sect. 3.2.

[289] According to the preliminary official statistics, real household incomes in Russia grew 9.1 per cent in 2000, after falling 14.2 per cent in 1999. Bank of Finland, *Russian and Baltic Economies, The Week in Review*, 23 February 2001.

[290] Real household disposable incomes increased by nearly 12 per cent between January and October 2000. PlanEcon, *Monthly Report* (Washington, D.C.), 19 January 2001.

[291] Retail trade volume increased by 5.6 per cent in 2000 after falling some 10 per cent in 1998-1999.

[292] See sect. 2.1.

TABLE 3.4.2

Producer prices in industry a in eastern Europe, the Baltic states and the CIS, 1999-2000
(Percentage change)

	Annual average		December over December		2000, year-on-year			
	1999	2000	1999	2000	QI	QII	QIII	QIV
Albania	..	..	..	..	..	..	..	..
Bosnia and Herzegovina	4.3	0.9	-0.7	-0.2	-0.7	1.8	2.8	–
Bulgaria	3.2	16.9	12.5	14.9	16.4	18.0	16.2	17.1
Croatia	2.5	9.6	5.9	11.2	8.6	10.1	8.9	10.7
Czech Republic	1.1	5.1	3.6	5.1	4.7	4.7	5.2	5.7
Hungary	5.0	11.4	7.3	12.0	9.3	11.7	12.3	12.3
Poland	5.7	7.8	8.0	5.6	7.8	7.9	8.4	6.9
Romania	42.2	51.7	63.0	47.8	59.3	48.8	50.7	49.6
Slovakia	3.7	9.8	7.6	9.2	9.5	11.5	9.4	8.9
Slovenia	2.2	7.7	3.5	9.3	5.3	7.1	9.0	9.3
The former Yugoslav Republic of Macedonia	-0.2	9.0	4.2	7.9	7.4	10.7	9.8	8.2
Yugoslavia	43.3	105.4	61.1	142.9	70.0	99.1	112.1	128.8
Estonia	-1.3	4.9	2.1	6.1	3.7	4.6	5.3	6.0
Latvia	-4.0	0.8	-0.9	1.1	0.8	1.1	0.8	0.6
Lithuania	3.0	17.8	23.2	2.2	26.0	22.2	16.3	8.7
Armenia	4.1	-0.4	2.9	-1.8	0.1	0.4	-0.7	-1.4
Azerbaijan	-1.3	9.4	0.6	8.6	4.7	18.4	6.5	8.1
Belarus	355.7	185.7	245.0	167.6	179.6	177.2	201.3	182.2
Georgia	..	..	..	..	..	..	..	..
Kazakhstan	19.0	38.0	57.5	19.4	65.3	44.0	31.9	21.2
Kyrgyzstan	52.2	24.2	47.4	15.5	43.3	24.4	18.1	15.5
Republic of Moldova	47.1	33.6	58.6	24.2	40.6	39.8	31.6	25.0
Russian Federation	59.1	46.5	67.3	31.6	60.1	52.0	45.3	33.7
Tajikistan	45.6	39.0	64.0	33.9	67.5	40.7	26.9	30.9
Turkmenistan	..	..	..	..	..	..	..	..
Ukraine	31.1	20.8	15.7	20.6	19.9	22.4	20.6	20.4
Uzbekistan	38.0	..	34.5	..	41.4	57.0	71.4	..

Source: UN/ECE secretariat estimates, based on national statistics.

a Industry = mining + manufacturing + utilities.

In the Baltic region producer prices accelerated only in Estonia reflecting stronger demand, which allowed producers to pass on cost increases to retailers, and its relatively weaker exchange rate against the dollar.[293]

Following the rouble crisis in mid-1998 and the subsequent reactive currency devaluations, imported input prices soared in most of the CIS countries. This imported inflation, combined with a collapse in labour productivity, led to a significant acceleration of industrial output prices in 1999. However, in 2000, and in contrast to most of the east European and Baltic economies, producer price inflation moderated considerably. Nevertheless, the rates of increase in most of them remain much higher than in eastern Europe. Furthermore, in most of them, industrial producer prices have risen much more than consumer prices. The large difference reflects both the extensive use of price controls at the retail level (the extreme cases being Belarus and Uzbekistan) and the very slow rate of progress with microlevel restructuring, which prevents a faster growth of labour productivity by encouraging overmanning in the majority of enterprises in these economies.

In most of the east European economies industrial wages continued to grow strongly in 2000 (table 3.4.3). However, in contrast to the past several years, their growth was less than the increase in producer prices in many of these economies, particularly in the second half of the year, with the major exception of Slovenia. Labour productivity surged as a result of strong output growth, falling employment, the latter reflecting the deepening of enterprise restructuring in some. Unit labour costs thus fell almost everywhere, the main exceptions being Croatia, Slovenia and particularly Romania. However, even in these countries, the rates of increase were considerably lower than in 1999. Given the surge in energy-related input costs, however, the fall in real unit labour costs does not imply an increase in profit margins, even in those branches where the exports account for a large share of total production.[294]

In the Baltic and CIS economies, in contrast to most of eastern Europe, unit labour costs continued to rise sharply and in some at a faster rate than in 2000. They declined

---

[293] In Lithuania, the average inflation rate in 2000, compared with 1999, shows a surge in industrial output prices due to a base period effect. The index rose nearly 7 per cent in December 1999 as a result of a 25 per cent increase in the prices of refined petroleum products, which account for more than 30 per cent of total industrial production.

[294] Chap. 3.6(ii).

TABLE 3.4.3

Wages and unit labour costs in industry [a] in eastern Europe, the Baltic states and the CIS, 1999-2000
(Annual average percentage change)

	Nominal wages [b]		Real product wages [c]		Labour productivity [d]		Unit labour costs [e]		Real unit labour costs [f]	
	1999	2000	1999	2000	1999	2000	1999	2000	1999	2000
Albania	..	..	..	..	..	..	..	..	..	..
Bosnia and Herzegovina [g]	15.4	10.3	10.7	9.8	10.1	14.3	4.8	-3.5	0.5	-4.0
Bulgaria	5.5	11.0	2.3	-5.1	-3.7	16.9	9.5	-5.1	6.1	-18.8
Croatia	5.7	5.5	3.2	-3.7	1.4	4.1	4.3	1.3	1.8	-7.5
Czech Republic	6.6	7.0	5.5	1.9	0.1	8.4	6.5	-1.2	5.4	-6.0
Hungary	13.4	15.0	8.1	3.2	9.4	19.7	3.7	-4.0	-1.2	-13.8
Poland	9.0	10.9	3.1	2.9	9.6	14.8	-0.6	-3.4	-5.9	-10.3
Romania	44.0	41.7	1.3	-6.6	-1.7	16.3	46.4	21.8	3.0	-19.7
Slovakia	7.9	9.2	4.0	-0.5	-0.7	12.6	8.6	-3.0	4.7	-11.7
Slovenia	9.3	12.0	7.0	4.0	1.2	7.0	7.9	4.7	5.6	-2.8
The former Yugoslav Republic of Macedonia [g]	1.2	5.7	1.3	-3.1	-1.7	6.8	2.9	-1.0	3.1	-9.3
Yugoslavia	23.1	97.8	-14.0	-3.7	..	..	..	..	..	..
Estonia	10.6	10.6	12.0	5.4	4.3	5.7	6.0	4.6	7.3	-0.3
Latvia	14.3	13.5	19.1	12.6	-5.1	2.9	20.4	10.3	25.4	9.4
Lithuania	6.5	1.2	3.4	-14.1	-10.0	9.2	18.3	-7.3	14.8	-21.3
Armenia	20.1	13.4	15.3	13.9	13.0	7.5	6.2	5.5	2.0	6.0
Azerbaijan	5.8	15.0	7.2	5.1	0.4	6.9	5.4	7.6	6.8	-1.7
Belarus	326.4	201.9	-6.4	5.7	9.4	8.4	289.8	178.6	-14.5	-2.5
Georgia	..	..	..	..	..	..	..	..	..	..
Kazakhstan	12.3	25.9	-5.7	-8.8	3.3	..	8.7	..	-8.7	..
Kyrgyzstan	23.4	21.7	-18.9	-2.0	3.9	7.5	18.8	13.2	-21.9	-8.8
Republic of Moldova	23.9	31.2	-15.8	-1.8	3.2	9.5	20.1	19.8	-18.4	-10.3
Russian Federation	42.6	43.1	-10.3	-2.3	8.9	6.7	31.0	34.1	-17.6	-8.5
Tajikistan	41.6	30.7	-2.8	-6.0	22.6	18.9	15.4	9.9	-20.7	-21.0
Turkmenistan	..	..	..	..	..	..	..	..	..	..
Ukraine	16.1	30.2	-11.5	7.8	13.9	15.5	1.9	12.8	-22.3	-6.7
Uzbekistan [g]	62.4	56.7	17.7	4.9	5.2	..	54.5	..	11.9	..

Source: UN/ECE secretariat estimates, based on national statistics and direct communications from national statistical offices.

Note: Annual averages are calculated on the basis of monthly data, except for employment which are quarterly.

[a] Industry = mining + manufacturing + utilities.

[b] Average gross wages in industry except in Bosnia and Herzegovina and The former Yugoslav Republic of Macedonia: net wages in industry; in Bulgaria, Estonia and all the CIS economies: gross wages in total economy; in Yugoslavia: net wages in total economy.

[c] Nominal wages deflated by producer price index.

[d] Gross industrial output deflated by industrial employment.

[e] Nominal wages deflated by productivity.

[f] Real product wages deflated by productivity.

[g] Data for 2000 are for the first half of the year.

only in Lithuania where nominal wages were virtually unchanged while productivity gains were large. Elsewhere, unit labour costs generally increased at double-digit rates, due to continued rapid wage growth in most countries combined with a slowdown in industrial productivity, as was the case in Russia, mainly in the last quarter.

(iv) Structure and change in manufacturing industry wages during transition

(a) Introduction

Since the beginning of the 1990s, the transition economies have been undergoing a massive process of structural change, albeit at different speeds dictated by various country-specific conditions and the differential impact of external factors. One aspect of this process, which is closely related to that of catching up with the mature market economies, is the changing pattern of industrial production including changes in the quality of products. This adjustment, in turn, has led to significant changes in the wage spread among industries, to a large extent reflecting the different skill intensities required by new production technologies. In some countries this process has been much more rapid than in others. The speed of the transfer and diffusion of new technology and organizational forms from the advanced market economies is frequently linked to the scale of foreign direct investment although domestic capacities (the level of education of the work force, the state of existing technologies and specialization, etc.) also play a crucial role.[295] Changes in the structure of relative wages can be

---

[295] See chap. 5 of this *Survey* on the role of FDI in the transition process and, in particular, for a discussion of the evidence relating to spillovers from FDI to the rest of the host economy.

considered, *grosso modo*, as a summary indicator of changes in employment and output structures.

This note examines some of the characteristics of the industrial distribution of wages and their evolution during the 1990s in selected east European and Baltic countries by asking three sets of questions:[296]

- How similar was the branch structure of relative wages among the transition economies at the end of the 1990s? *and* What changes occurred in the degree of similarity during the first decade of transition?

- In which countries was the branch distribution of wages most equal (unequal) at the end of the 1990s? *and* Has there been a shift towards more or less "egalitarianism" within countries over the last decade?

- To what extent have changes in branch wage differentials been influenced by differential trends in branch labour productivity and output growth?

The principal data used in this note[297] are the statistics of average monthly gross wages per person employed in each of the NACE 2-digit branches of manufacturing industry.[298] However, neither the country nor the period coverages are uniform because of data limitations. Furthermore, due to the lack of value added data at the manufacturing branch level, gross industrial output is used as a proxy. In addition, the time series for some of the countries contain breaks which may influence the results.[299] The statistics and estimates in this note should therefore be interpreted with more than the usual degree of caution.

Keeping in mind the data limitations and the small sample of countries, it is still possible to suggest some answers to the questions raised above. Except for a few branches (mainly those with the highest and the lowest wages per head) there does appear to be a large degree of uniformity among the transition economies in the branch structure of relative wages. Nevertheless, mainly because of the range between the highest and lowest paid branches, the degree of wage dispersion within countries varies more greatly from country to country, reflecting not only their different rates of reform but also the differences in the structure and level of their foreign trade and the intensity of investment, both domestic and foreign.

Over the period 1993-1999, the branch structure of relative wages across countries increased little if measured by the 14 NACE subsections, but the change was more significant at a higher degree of branch disaggregation (23 NACE divisions). The branch dispersion of wages increased substantially in some countries during the 1990s, as the branches which initially had the highest wages recorded the largest rates of increase and the lowest paid received the smallest wage increases.

There is a positive relationship between the wage growth and the growth rates of labour productivity and output and these relationships are stronger at the more disaggregated branch structure.

Finally, the changes in the transition economies are then compared with those in Germany, representing a mature market economy which serves as a reference point, towards which the transition economies are trying to converge, although at significantly different rates.

(b) Branch wage structure in 1999

The branch distribution of average gross wages relative to the average for total manufacturing for 11 transition economies in 1999 is shown in table 3.4.4.[300] Taking the average distribution for the 11 countries (column 12, subsections breakdown), the branch differentials fall within a rather narrow range. Excluding the highest paid branch[301] (petroleum products) the second highest level of wages (chemicals) is less than double the lowest (leather products). This relatively "egalitarian" distribution of average wages between the manufacturing branches is much the same in almost all 11 countries, as suggested by the low coefficients of variation in the last column of the table, which range between some 7 and 19 per cent. Furthermore, the dispersion among countries exceeds that for the all-country average, by some 15 per cent or more, in only three of the 14 branches, namely petroleum products (18.7 per cent), paper and publishing (16 per cent) and wood products (15.7 per cent). Wages in the petroleum products branch are higher than the manufacturing average in all 11 countries, but in Romania, and particularly in Bulgaria, they are much higher, nearly or more than twice the average, respectively, while the margin is only about 10 per cent in Slovenia, Estonia and Latvia. Wages in paper and publishing are also above the manufacturing average in all 11 countries. Their relatively large dispersion, however, is mainly due to the effect of much higher wages in the publishing and printing division (22) in all of the countries, but particularly in Hungary and Estonia, where wages are about twice the manufacturing average. These deviations may reflect different product composition *within* each branch.[302] Towards the other end of the scale, the relative

---

[296] This note basically draws upon the analysis included in an earlier UN/ECE study carried out for nine west European countries for the 1960s. UN/ECE, *Structure and Change in European Industry* (United Nations publication, Sales No. E.77.II.E.3).

[297] The main sources are the national statistics officially published and/or obtained by the UN/ECE secretariat through direct communication with the national statistical offices.

[298] See box 3.4.1 for the branch codes and descriptions.

[299] See footnotes to table 3.4.5.

[300] In this table there are two levels of branch disaggregation: NACE 2-digit 14 subsections (alphabetic codes) for 11 countries and NACE 2-digit 23 divisions (numeric codes) for 8 countries. The different sample sizes for countries is dictated by data availability.

[301] In order not to repeat long branch names, abbreviated names will be used in this section. See box 3.4.1 for full names of the branches.

[302] Publishing covers a very wide range of products from cheap newspapers and pulp fiction to high-class colour printing of art books. Hungary certainly produces the latter and western publishers were sending books for printing in Hungary before 1989.

> **BOX 3.4.1**
>
> **NACE Rev. 1¹ classification of economic activities in manufacturing**
>
> | Codes | | |
> |---|---|---|
> | Subsections | Divisions | Description |
> | DA | | Food products, beverages and tobacco |
> | | 15 | Food products and beverages |
> | | 16 | Tobacco products |
> | DB | | Textiles and textile products |
> | | 17 | Textiles |
> | | 18 | Wearing apparel; dressing and dyeing of fur |
> | DC | | Leather and leather products |
> | | 19 | Tanning and dressing of leather; manufacture of luggage, handbags, saddlery, harness and footwear |
> | DD | | Wood and wood products |
> | | 20 | Wood and products of wood and cork, except furniture; articles of straw and plaiting materials |
> | DE | | Pulp, paper and paper products; publishing and printing |
> | | 21 | Pulp, paper and paper products |
> | | 22 | Publishing, printing and reproduction of recorded media |
> | DF | | Coke, refined petroleum products and nuclear fuel |
> | | 23 | Coke, refined petroleum products and nuclear fuel |
> | DG | | Chemicals, chemical products and man-made fibres |
> | | 24 | Chemicals and chemical products |
> | DH | | Rubber and plastic products |
> | | 25 | Rubber and plastic products |
> | DI | | Other non-metallic mineral products |
> | | 26 | Other non-metallic mineral products |
> | DJ | | Basic metals and fabricated metal products |
> | | 27 | Basic metals |
> | | 28 | Fabricated metal products, except machinery and equipment |
> | DK | | Machinery and equipment n.e.c. |
> | | 29 | Machinery and equipment n.e.c. |
> | DL | | Electrical and optical equipment |
> | | 30 | Office machinery and computers |
> | | 31 | Electrical machinery and apparatus n.e.c. |
> | | 32 | Radio, television and communication equipment and apparatus |
> | | 33 | Medical, precision and optical instruments, watches and clocks |
> | DM | | Transport equipment |
> | | 34 | Motor vehicles, trailers and semi-trailers |
> | | 35 | Other transport equipment |
> | DN | | Manufacturing n.e.c. |
> | | 36 | Furniture; manufacturing n.e.c. |
> | | 37 | Recycling |
>
> ¹ Nomenclature générale des activités économiques dans les Communautés européennes (General Industrial Classification of Economic Activities within the European Communities), 1996.

wage in the wood products branch is one of the lowest in all 10 countries (except in Hungary where it is some 15 per cent above the average manufacturing wage), but it ranges from less than 70 per cent of the manufacturing average in Bulgaria and Croatia to nearly 100 per cent in Estonia. Again, these variations may be due to differences in the detailed product composition, including the extent to which the various products are finished. Despite these significant differences among countries in relative wages in some branches, when the 11 economies are taken together the manufacturing sector falls into three distinct groups with respect to relative wages:

- Those branches which pay well above (30 per cent or more) the average manufacturing wage, namely petroleum products, chemicals and paper and publishing (mainly division 22);

- Those which pay significantly below (some 20-30 per cent less) the average, namely textiles/clothing, leather products, wood products, furniture and recycling;

- Those which pay about or some 10 per cent more than the average wage in total manufacturing industry.

In conventional theory, interindustry wage differentials should reflect different skill intensities and, occasionally, compensation for special hardship or hazard in working conditions. However, in practice, due to differences, *inter alia*, in labour market conditions and structures, in institutions and traditions, the determinants

TABLE 3.4.4

Relative average gross wages in manufacturing branches in selected east European and Baltic economies, 1999
(Total manufacturing = 100)

NACE Rev.1 Subsections	Divisions	Bulgaria	Croatia	Czech Republic	Hungary[a]	Poland	Romania	Slovakia	Slovenia	Estonia	Latvia	Lithuania	Unweighted average of countries[b]	Standard deviation[b]	Coefficient of variation[b] (per cent)
DA		100.0	117.9	96.3	94.6	93.6	93.4	96.3	115.1	104.3	111.4	101.1	102.2	8.8	8.7
	15	88.1	116.6	96.3[c]	93.6	91.2	90.6	..	114.3	104.3	110.4	..	88.1	12.5	14.1
	16	191.2	150.9	96.3[c]	152.8	194.3	212.9	..	200.0	..	237.3	..	167.4	31.0	18.5
DB		65.2	65.0	68.9	57.8	65.9	75.6	66.7	72.8	77.3	92.7	82.8	71.9	9.5	13.2
	17	74.9	62.1	74.0	64.1	78.2	76.1	..	76.8	78.7	107.2	..	68.2	13.7	20.1
	18	61.6	66.0	61.1	54.3	59.6	75.5	..	69.2	76.3	81.4	..	58.7	8.9	15.2
DC	19	65.0	55.6	67.7	55.4	68.6	69.0	70.0	76.2	80.0	64.0	77.8	68.1	8.0	11.7
DD	20	67.7	68.4	84.3	114.6	79.9	70.8	81.1	85.0	95.7	87.3	71.8	82.4	13.0	15.7
DE		102.1	121.2	116.7	172.2	132.4	101.5	122.3	123.0	164.3	140.5	123.4	129.1	20.6	16.0
	21	94.9	93.2	105.9	124.9	117.6	98.1	..	102.3	125.0	97.4	..	92.7	11.4	12.2
	22	110.8	138.8	126.0	201.5	140.7	104.6	..	141.7	181.9	146.8	..	123.4	29.6	24.0
DF	23	237.4	144.8	146.7	181.6	184.4	197.0	153.9	112.8	107.4[d]	109.5	150.6[d]	163.1	30.5	18.7
DG	24	141.8	143.2	123.0	135.0	138.9	138.3	115.3	151.0	107.4	95.9	150.6	130.9	17.8	13.6
DH	25	94.1	76.2	106.3	106.9	102.6	107.3	117.8	103.1	87.2	80.3	86.7	97.1	13.0	13.4
DI	26	113.9	103.2	107.0	98.9	104.2	106.3	109.2	101.7	121.6	91.4	107.4	105.9	7.4	6.9
DJ		138.3	84.1	105.6	120.7	108.7	117.9	119.8	99.6	108.5	110.0	89.3	109.3	11.8	10.8
	27	165.2	80.8	114.6	100.8	124.4	138.7	..	102.4	..	156.7	..	109.3	29.1	26.6
	28	86.3	86.9	98.7	132.3	96.7	92.1	..	98.3	113.2	86.3	..	86.4	15.1	17.5
DK	29	101.6	82.5	104.2	106.7	102.5	111.1	97.3	97.1	97.4	94.9	94.7	99.1	7.5	7.6
DL		95.3	125.9	99.4	98.7	117.8	119.9	97.6	103.0	109.3	99.1	113.7	107.3	9.8	9.1
	30	98.1	99.8	103.8	119.4	184.1	115.3	..	129.1	..	88.2	..	104.2	30.0	28.8
	31	95.1	125.3	102.4	88.7	111.8	114.2	..	101.7	125.6	95.7	..	92.7	12.0	12.9
	32	102.5	130.6	91.2	95.2	128.0	155.3	..	103.9	95.6	90.0	..	99.6	23.4	23.5
	33	88.6	114.6	98.7	139.1	115.3	115.4	..	101.2	104.9	126.3	..	99.9	16.1	16.1
DM		115.6	105.3	120.7	103.9	115.8	121.0	116.6	104.8	120.8	89.2	126.0	112.7	10.7	9.5
	34	95.1	93.2	125.6	105.0	115.1	113.5	..	106.7	..	71.5	..	91.7	16.6	18.1
	35	122.8	107.0	106.9	99.1	116.6	129.8	..	100.2	114.3	90.9	..	97.0	13.0	13.4
DN		69.2	69.2	83.0	96.7	81.1	78.8	86.6	86.3	88.5	83.6	91.2	83.1	7.1	8.5
	36	69.1	67.4	81.8	94.1	79.0	78.2	..	84.1	89.0	84.4	..	70.9	8.6	12.1
	37	80.9	99.4	96.4	100.0	128.0	89.8	..	120.1	..	74.6	..	87.7	18.1	20.7
Standard deviation															
Subsections		44.9	29.8	21.6	35.3	31.2	33.2	23.4	20.1	22.7	17.9	22.3	25.2		
Divisions		42.3	28.8	20.4	35.3	35.7	36.9	..	28.0	..	36.6	..	25.5		
Coefficient of variation (per cent)															
Subsections		41.7	30.6	21.1	32.0	29.2	30.8	22.6	19.6	21.7	18.6	22.1	24.1		
Divisions		39.8	28.7	20.2	31.7	30.8	32.7	..	25.9	..	35.6	..	26.7		

Source: UN/ECE secretariat estimates, based on national statistics and direct communications from national statistical offices.

[a] 1998.

[b] Statistics calculated on the basis of 11 countries for NACE subsections (alphabetic, 14 branches) and 8 countries for NACE divisions (numeric, 23 branches); Slovakia, Estonia and Lithuania are excluded from the statistics computed for NACE divisions.

[c] 15 and 16 are assumed to be equal to DA.

[d] DF is assumed to be equal to DG.

of wage differentials are complex. Nevertheless, despite the various economic and social factors affecting wage behaviour, it is clear from the data presented here that the traditional, relatively slow-growing and unskilled labour-intensive branches (textiles/clothing, leather/footwear, wood/furniture) have the lowest relative wages, while skill-intensive industries (such as engineering) and relatively fast-growing and physical capital-intensive industries (petroleum products, chemicals) generally have the highest.

Chart 3.4.2 compares the average branch structure of wages in the transition economies with that in Germany at the end of the 1990s. There are only two significant differences between the two structures. Food, beverages and tobacco is the lowest paid manufacturing branch in Germany (nearly 40 per cent below the manufacturing average) whereas in the transition economies it is slightly better paid than the average. These variations may well reflect the product heterogeneity within the NACE branches.[303] The second

---

[303] The heterogeneity of these branches also refers to relative factor intensity, so that the within-branch variance of wages per head may straddle the average level for manufacturing industry as a whole. See, for example, P. Rayment, "The homogeneity of manufacturing industries with respect to factor intensity: the case of the United Kingdom", *Oxford Bulletin of Economics and Statistics*, Vol. 38, No. 3, August 1976, pp. 203-209. The food processing industry (like tobacco) is both physical capital and unskilled labour intensive, so German food products may be produced with a lot of machines and relatively low-paid labour.

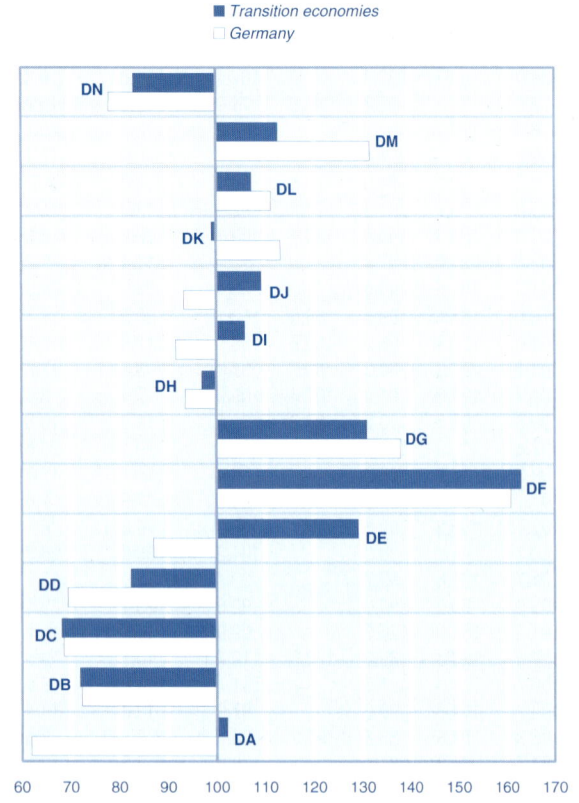

CHART 3.4.2

Relative average gross wages in manufacturing branches: unweighted average of 11 east European and Baltic economies and Germany,[a] 1999
(Total manufacturing = 100)

Source: See table 3.4.4, column 12 "Unweighted average of countries"; UN/ECE Common Database.

[a] 1998.

branch with a large relative wage difference between the transition economies and Germany is the paper and publishing branch. While in Germany it is again one of the lowest paying branches, in the transition economies the average wages in this branch reach nearly 30 per cent above the average wage in manufacturing. Also for transport equipment the difference reaches nearly 20 percentage points, although both are above the manufacturing average, albeit in Germany by some 30 per cent versus 13 per cent, given its much advanced automotive industry where the product is not only partly manufactured or assembled but is also designed, tested, etc., which requires much more engineering skill and capital investment. All the other branches occupy a somewhat similar relative position in the transition economies and in Germany, differences not exceeding some 15 percentage points.

Although branch structure of relative wages is similar among the transition economies, they do differ in respect of the spread of wages between branches. The coefficients of variation at the bottom of table 3.4.4 show that, in terms of the NACE subsections, the largest wage dispersion is in Bulgaria where the coefficient exceeds 40 per cent. The second group of countries, with a dispersion coefficient of around 30 per cent consists of Croatia, Hungary, Poland and Romania. The third group, with the least dispersion of around 20 per cent, consists of the Czech Republic, Slovakia, Slovenia and the three Baltic economies.[304]

Interindustry average wage differentials are usually assumed to broadly reflect differences in productivity and, therefore, in a developed market economy, a declining dispersion of branch wages may indicate a maturing of the economy.[305] However, in a transition economy, the same phenomenon may imply a slow pace of reforms and a postponement of enterprise restructuring since, in general, the dispersion of labour incomes in the centrally planned economies had been greatly compressed.

The structure of relative wages in 1999, and its rate of change over the last decade may therefore reflect, *ceteris paribus*, the different pace of reform in individual transition economies. However, there are many other factors which may influence the degree of dispersion both over time and across countries, such as initial conditions in terms of the extent of labour hoarding, the interindustry structure of production, the degree of capital intensity, etc. Furthermore, a distinction has to be made between the early reformers and the laggards. For example, a comparison of the wage structure in 1999 in Bulgaria with those of the central European early reformers must take into consideration the delayed start of real reforms in the former. The comparison of Bulgaria with Romania, however, indicates a relatively deeper restructuring in the former during the late 1990s.

(c) Change in the branch wage structure between 1993 and 1999

Has the branch structure of relative wages become *more* or *less* similar during the last 10 years, both among and within countries?[306] Comparing the averages for the

---

[304] Among the eight countries for which the breakdown by NACE divisions is available, it is only in Latvia that there is a significant (nearly double) difference between the coefficients of variation and 23 divisions. In Slovenia also the difference between the two coefficients of variation (some 6 percentage points) is much larger than in the other east European countries.

[305] N. Kaldor, "Causes of the slow rate of economic growth in the United Kingdom" in F. Targetti and A. Thirwall (eds.), *The Essential Kaldor* (London, Duckworth, 1989). In this article, originally delivered as an Inaugural Lecture at the University of Cambridge in 1966, Kaldor identifies the stage of "economic maturity" as the point where the difference between productivity in agriculture and industry had been largely eliminated and therefore the resource-allocation from agriculture to industry had been diminished. In a more recent article, P. Rayment, "Structural change in manufacturing industry and the stability of the Verdoorn Law", *Economia Industriale*, Vol. 34, No. 1, February 1981, extends this argument to the manufacturing sector: "There is no particular reason to suppose that similar interindustry flows will not take place within the *manufacturing sector* in response to interindustry productivity differences, given that average wage differences between industries broadly reflect differences in productivity and that output in the more productive sectors is expanding. An economy in which such resource allocation failed to take place might be described as senile, a condition more serious than maturity", p. 107.

[306] The data for this section are only available for 1993-1999 and therefore do not capture the full transition effect on branch wage structures since 1989.

TABLE 3.4.5

Relative average gross wages in manufacturing branches in selected east European and Baltic economies, 1993 and 1999

(Total manufacturing = 100)

NACE Rev.1					1993							1999		
Subsections	Divisions	Czech Republic	Hungary[a]	Poland	Romania	Slovakia	Slovenia	Latvia	Unweighted average of countries[b]	Standard deviation[b]	Coefficient of variation[b] (per cent)	Unweighted average of countries[b]	Standard deviation[b]	Coefficient of variation[b] (per cent)
DA		100.6	96.0	97.7	105.2	98.8	124.3	122.9	106.5	12.0	11.3	100.1	9.1	9.1
	15	100.6[c]	95.1	96.7	104.6	..	..	122.5	104.7	12.5	12.0	96.5	9.4	9.7
	16	100.6[c]	143.9	134.5	131.9	..	..	162.7	143.2	14.0	9.7	199.3	35.7	17.9
DB		77.6	63.4	79.8	76.8	76.5	85.6	87.5	78.2	7.8	10.0	71.5	10.9	15.3
	17	78.0	68.0	84.0	75.5	..	..	89.9	79.1	8.3	10.5	79.9	16.2	20.2
	18	76.3	59.4	77.0	78.6	..	..	82.6	74.8	8.9	11.9	66.4	11.5	17.3
DC	19	83.0	57.5	75.3	81.5	77.9	84.7	93.2	79.0	11.1	14.0	67.3	6.4	9.5
DD	20	89.0	104.6	86.3	88.7	87.9	90.3	94.7	91.7	6.3	6.9	86.1	13.6	15.8
DE		105.0	166.2	120.8	102.5	108.6	127.8	109.4	120.0	22.2	18.5	129.8	22.3	17.2
	21	96.1	123.6	110.3	98.9	..	..	76.9	101.1	17.4	17.2	108.8	12.1	11.1
	22	117.2	184.8	126.3	106.2	..	..	126.8	132.3	30.5	23.1	143.9	36.1	25.1
DF	23	125.3	161.8	197.1	161.0	145.1	140.9	238.0	167.0	38.5	23.1	155.2	34.8	22.4
DG	24	113.4	119.1	118.3	120.4	118.0	142.4	104.6	119.5	11.5	9.6	128.2	18.3	14.3
DH	25	106.0	109.7	108.1	113.3	118.6	111.1	111.0	111.1	4.1	3.7	103.5	11.4	11.0
DI	26	105.1	94.3	95.3	104.4	107.5	101.0	96.0	100.5	5.4	5.3	102.7	6.0	5.9
DJ		112.6	95.7	109.8	113.3	126.5	92.5	105.8	108.0	11.5	10.6	111.8	8.0	7.1
	27	123.7	85.7	120.9	132.0	..	..	131.9	118.8	19.2	16.1	127.0	21.6	17.0
	28	100.2	101.9	98.1	93.2	..	..	89.0	96.5	5.3	5.5	101.2	18.0	17.8
DK	29	100.4	114.0	100.2	104.1	95.9	94.5	88.2	99.6	8.1	8.2	102.0	5.9	5.7
DL		96.9	119.1	108.8	93.9	95.0	100.1	80.3	99.1	12.2	12.3	105.1	9.6	9.1
	30	84.3	111.5	130.4	85.5	..	..	122.7	106.9	21.2	19.8	122.2	36.7	30.0
	31	103.3	141.5	109.9	96.6	..	..	100.9	110.5	18.0	16.3	102.5	10.7	10.5
	32	84.3	89.2	105.7	86.8	..	..	70.7	87.3	12.5	14.3	111.9	28.8	25.8
	33	94.6	118.7	108.2	92.8	..	..	83.8	99.6	13.8	13.8	119.0	15.0	12.6
DM		106.5	94.8	109.0	108.9	96.4	96.3	118.4	104.3	8.8	8.4	110.3	11.6	10.5
	34	108.9	92.4	107.5	111.6	..	..	110.5	106.2	7.9	7.4	106.1	20.7	19.5
	35	103.1	106.4	110.3	106.1	..	..	122.0	109.6	7.4	6.8	108.7	15.1	13.9
DN		88.6	80.3	88.5	92.3	86.1	89.2	102.6	89.7	6.8	7.6	85.1	5.8	6.8
	36	85.9	79.3	86.7	91.7	..	..	99.7	88.7	7.6	8.5	83.5	6.4	7.7
	37	116.5	100.0	134.1	106.1	..	..	184.9	128.3	34.1	26.6	97.8	19.5	19.9
Standard deviation														
Subsections		12.9	30.9	29.4	20.4	19.3	20.1	38.5	21.9			23.3		
Divisions		14.7	30.7	25.5	19.7	..	..	38.2	22.8			29.8		
Coefficient of variation (per cent)														
Subsections		12.8	29.3	27.5	19.5	18.8	19.0	34.7	20.8			22.4		
Divisions		14.7	28.7	23.3	19.1	..	..	33.7	21.3			27.2		

Source: UN/ECE secretariat estimates, based on national statistics and direct communications from national statistical offices.

Note: Data coverage – Czech Republic: enterprises with 20 employees or more in 1999 and 25 or more in 1993; Hungary: average gross wages are estimated by dividing the wage-fund of each branch by the employment of that branch. Enterprises with more than 10 employees in 1998 and with more than 20 in 1993; Poland: economic entities employing more than nine persons in 1999 and five persons in 1993; Slovakia: enterprises with 20 or more employees; Estonia: enterprises with more than 49 employees.

[a] 1993 and 1998.

[b] Statistics calculated on the basis of seven countries for NACE subsections (alphabetic, 14 branches) and five countries for NACE divisions (numeric, 23 branches).

[c] Divisions 15 and 16 are assumed to be equal to DA.

seven transition economies[307] in 1993 and 1999 (table 3.4.5 and chart 3.4.3) it can be seen that, in relative terms, average wages in the lowest paid branches at the start of the period fell further during the 1990s (namely, textiles/clothing, leather products, wood products and furniture, and recycling). Those which were originally around or above the manufacturing average have increased further, the main exceptions being petroleum products, rubber and plastics, and food, beverages and tobacco. Nevertheless, in 1999 petroleum products remained by far the highest paid of all the 14 branches.

A comparison of charts 3.4.2 and 3.4.3 suggests that during the 1990s, the relative wage distribution in the transition economies was moving towards the structure of Germany in 1998. In general, relative wages in the transition economies declined in those branches that were the lowest paid in Germany in 1998 and they increased in those which were the highest paid in German manufacturing industry. There were few exceptions, however, namely metal products and particularly paper

---

[307] Bulgaria, Croatia, Estonia and Lithuania are not included in this part of the analysis due to the lack of comparable data for the early 1990s.

CHART 3.4.3

Relative average gross wages in manufacturing branches: unweighted average of seven east European and Baltic economies, 1993 and 1999

(Total manufacturing = 100)

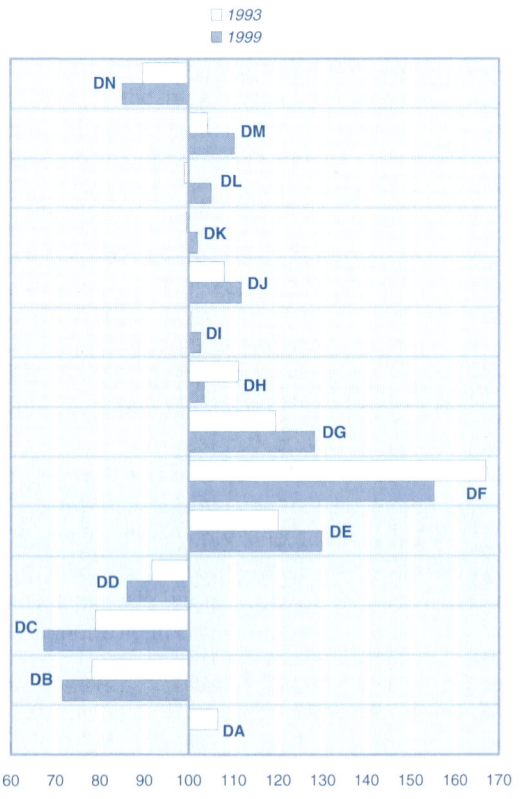

Source: See table 3.4.5, columns 8 and 11 "Unweighted average of countries".

and publishing. In these branches relative wages have increased to well above the manufacturing average while they are below average in Germany. In contrast, in food, beverages and tobacco, branches which include the lowest paid industrial jobs in Germany, relative wages in the transition economies have declined slightly although still remaining around the manufacturing average.

Another point emerging from table 3.4.5 is that while the all-country coefficient of variation for electrical and optical equipment branch shows a decline of some 3 percentage points between 1993 and 1999, at the more disaggregated level (divisions 30-33), the same statistic, even though calculated on a smaller sample of five countries, suggests that the relative wage dispersion across countries during the transition rose significantly in division 30 (office machinery and computers, from less than 20 to 30 per cent) and in division 32 (radio, television and communication equipment and apparatus from some 14 to nearly 26 per cent), which may reflect different rates of technological change and of increasing demand for special skills and/or significant changes in the commodity composition of exports influenced in certain cases by FDI, particularly in Hungary.

To sum up, dissimilarities in the dispersion of relative wages in seven transition economies have increased, reflecting in the main differences in the rate of technological change combined with changes in the patterns of specialization brought about by price liberalization, international trade and foreign investment. Another conclusion, albeit tentative, given the limited sample size, is that in terms of wage structures, the transition economies are moving towards the western economies' pattern, represented here by Germany.

As for the branch structure of relative wages in individual countries, on the other hand, it is only in Latvia that relative wages became more similar across branches. The coefficient of variation by NACE subsections in this country fell from 34.7 per cent in 1993 (table 3.4.5) to 18.6 per cent in 1999 (table 3.4.4). However, calculated on the basis of NACE divisions the coefficient of variation increases from 33.7 per cent in 1993 to 35.6 per cent in 1999, the highest rates of dispersion of all the countries in both years, except Bulgaria in 1999. This relatively large difference between the two measures in Latvia is mainly due to the disaggregation of the NACE subsections of food/tobacco, metals and electrical/optical equipment. A similar picture, albeit less significant, emerges also in Poland (in 1993) and Slovenia (in 1999). In the other four countries the degrees of dispersions are similar under both breakdowns, both in 1993 and 1999, and both show enlarged wage differences between manufacturing branches during the 1990s. Wage inequality increased sharply in the Czech Republic and Romania but in the former, it remained at around 20 per cent in 1999 (at both levels of disaggregation), the lowest rate of dispersion of all 11 transition economies which, *inter alia*, probably reflects the slow pace of microlevel restructuring in Czech industry.

An increasing dispersion of branch wages implies a positive relationship between the rate of increase in wages and the initial level of relative wages, in this case in 1993. In fact, chart 3.4.4, which shows the total increase in branch wages relative to a similar change in the average wage in total manufacturing industry, illustrates this development clearly for the seven transition economies during the 1990s. The lowest paid jobs in 1993 (i.e. those where wages were less than 90 per cent of the manufacturing average) generally received the smallest increases between 1993 and 1999. In contrast, initially the highest paid jobs (i.e. those where wages were at least 20 per cent more than the manufacturing average) generally received the largest increases. A similar pattern is also apparent in Germany between 1993 and 1998, albeit at much slower rates of change, reflecting the conditions in a mature market economy where adjustments tend to be marginal in comparison with those in the transition economies.[308]

---

[308] Rates of change would probably be even slower for Germany excluding the former GDR.

CHART 3.4.4

Change in relative average gross wages by manufacturing branches in selected east European and Baltic economies and Germany, 1993 and 1999

(Percentages)

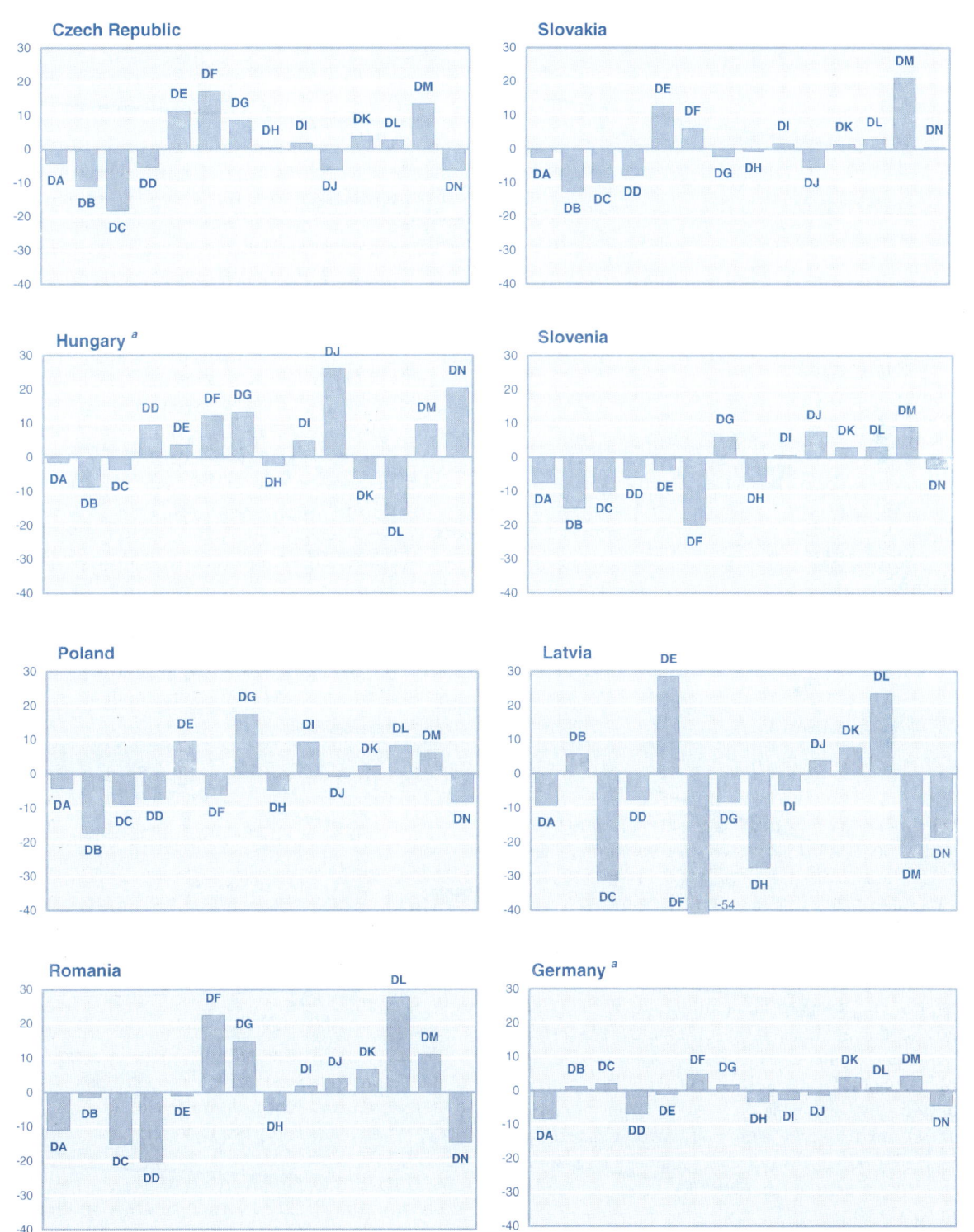

Source: UN/ECE secretariat estimates, based on national statistics and direct communication from national statistical offices.

Note: The zero-line is the cumulative per cent change in total manufacturing industry between 1993 and 1999. The change in the relative average wage in each branch is calculated as follows: $[(W_j \div W_t)-1]*100$, where W is the wage index in 1999 with 1993=100, j refers to the branch and t to total manufacturing.

[a] 1993-1998.

CHART 3.4.5

Growth rates of wages, labour productivity and output, by manufacturing branch, in selected east European and Baltic economies, 1993-1999
(Percentages)

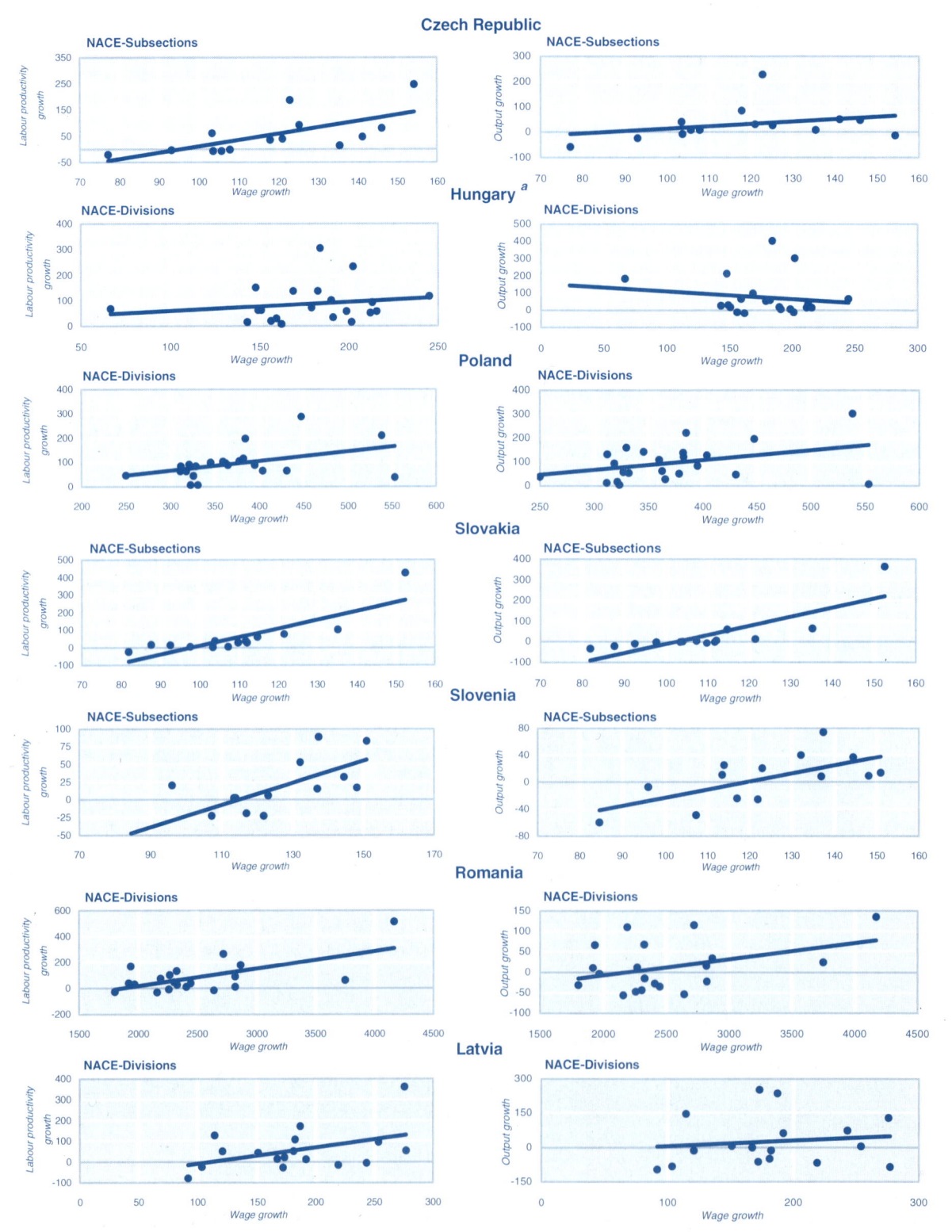

Source: UN/ECE secretariat estimates, based on national statistics and direct communication from national statistical offices.

[a] NACE division 30 is excluded from these charts where cumulative output growth is nearly 5,000 per cent and productivity is some 3,000 per cent between 1993 and 1998.

(d) Relationship between wage, labour productivity and output growth rates

Do the differential growth rates of average wages in manufacturing branches reflect differential growth rates of output and labour productivity in the transition economies? Given the limitations of the data, the relationships shown in chart 3.4.5 in terms of scatter diagrams should not be interpreted as indicating more than general tendencies. Nevertheless, the diagrams do suggest that there is a positive relationship between the growth rates of wages and those of output and labour productivity in the majority of countries.[309] The major exception is Hungary where, although the growth rates of labour productivity and wages are positively correlated, albeit less significantly than in the other countries, there seems to be a negative relationship between the growth rates of wages and output. This negative relationship may be due to a "rationalization effect" in some slow-growing, traditional industries where employment falls rapidly, leading to relatively faster growth in labour productivity. This is the case for some branches in almost all the countries (chart 3.4.5), but in Hungary it is much more significant in branches such as metals and non-electrical machinery where the output growth rate was similar to the manufacturing average while productivity and wages grew nearly two thirds faster than in manufacturing as a whole. In contrast, in electrical machinery, electronics, etc., output growth far outpaced both productivity and wage growth. In Hungary, many completely new (greenfield) industries were established during the second half of the 1990s so that comparisons between 1993 and 1998 reflect almost completely different sets of firms in some branches.

3.5 Labour markets – employment and unemployment

(i) Changes in employment in 2000

Despite the continued strong recovery in the majority of *east European countries* there was little improvement in most of the labour markets. The decline in employment, which emerged in 1999, has continued and even accelerated in several countries during the first three quarters of 2000. However, unlike the period immediately following the Russian crisis, when employment started falling as a result of the general economic slowdown, the main reason for the decline in 2000 appears to be the deepening of the process of enterprise restructuring in many countries, which has often been accompanied by sizeable job cuts and a faster rate of closure of loss-making enterprises. Rapidly growing labour productivity also contributed to the sluggish short-term labour demand in many economies.[310]

In the first three quarters of 2000, the decline in employment accelerated in the region as a whole (from about 1 per cent in 1999 to nearly 2 per cent), although the changes in individual countries reflect the diversity of their macroeconomic situation (table 3.5.1). There were relatively large increases in employment only in Hungary and Slovenia (although in both cases they were considerably less than in 1999), and employment was flat in The former Yugoslav Republic of Macedonia. There was some small recovery from very low levels in Bosnia and Herzegovina, but elsewhere the declines were general with a considerable deterioration in Bulgaria and Poland.

In the Czech Republic, where the fall in employment in 1999 accelerated sharply as a result of measures aimed at the deepening of the process of enterprise restructuring, employment continued to decline in 2000. However, as the economy started a gradual but sustained recovery driven by strong exports and capital investment, the rate of decline slowed somewhat in 2000 as well. In the first three quarters employment fell by some 2 per cent; all major sectors of the economy including services were affected, with the largest falls in agriculture and construction (in both cases more than 7 per cent).

In Hungary, a relatively high rate of employment growth was maintained for a third consecutive year, although at a lower pace than in the previous two years. The pattern of employment growth in 2000, was similar to that in 1999: the main sectors providing new jobs were construction and, especially, services (almost 80 per cent of the total gains), while in manufacturing employment stagnated and in agriculture it continued to fall.

In Slovenia, where economic activity also remained strong in 2000, employment continued to grow for the third consecutive year, although, as in Hungary, there were signs of deceleration in the second half of the year. The expansion of employment was due to a small increase in construction and large gains in services, whereas employment in agriculture and industry continued to decline slightly.

In Poland, employment grew steadily between 1993 and 1998, but as a result of the short-term negative effect of the Russian crisis, combined with the acceleration of industrial restructuring and the closure of loss-making enterprises, it fell by nearly 3 per cent in 1999. The situation appears to have deteriorated further in 2000: in the third quarter, *paid employment* fell by more than 3 per cent, year-on-year (compared with less than 1 per cent in 1999).[311] The largest falls were in agriculture, and mining and quarrying (in both cases above 10 per cent).[312]

---

[309] These relationships are, in fact, stronger at the more disaggregated level of NACE divisions in those countries where both levels are available, i.e. Hungary, Poland, Romania and Latvia.

[310] For recent changes in productivity see sect. 3.4.

[311] Quarterly estimates of employment changes in 2000 are somewhat uncertain as the labour force survey – the most comprehensive source for quarterly employment in this country – has a lacuna in the second and third quarters of 1999 when GUS (the Polish National Statistical Office) stopped conducting the quarterly labour force survey. Another series produced by GUS – average paid employment – which is used for the analysis, accounts for some 60 per cent of the labour force data and does not include private agriculture, which accounts for more than 20 per cent of the labour force.

[312] GUS, *Biuletyn Statystyczny*, No. 12 (Warsaw), January 2000, p. 46.

TABLE 3.5.1

Total and industrial employment in eastern Europe, the Baltic states and the CIS, 1999-2000
(Percentage change over the same period of preceding year)

	Total employment [a]						Employment in industry [a]					
	1999			2000			1999			2000		
	Annual	QIII	QIV	QI	QII	QIII	Annual	QIII	QIV	QI	QII	QIII
Eastern Europe [b]	-2.0	-1.1	-1.1	-1.9	-2.1	-1.7	-5.9	-4.6	-4.5	-5.4	-5.5	-5.0
Albania	-1.8	-2.2	-2.0	-1.7	-1.7	-1.5	-2.1	..	..	..	..	..
Bosnia and Herzegovina [c]	3.1	2.8	0.5	1.0	1.3	1.2	0.2	–	2.3	0.6	0.9	0.6
Bulgaria	-2.6	-6.6	-6.8	-10.3	-9.7	-10.7	-8.1	-12.2	-7.2	-14.9	-12.8	-10.2
Croatia	-0.4	-1.0	-1.2	-2.1	-2.3	-1.8	-2.8	-3.1	-2.1	-2.5	-2.5	-1.7
Czech Republic	-3.6	-3.7	-3.6	-2.7	-1.9	-2.1	-3.2	-4.1	-4.1	-4.7	-3.4	-2.0
Hungary	3.1	3.1	2.0	0.9	0.6	1.1	0.9	1.8	0.2	-1.7	-2.0	-1.3
Poland	-2.7	-0.7	-1.4	-3.6	-3.6	-3.2	-7.3	-4.5	-5.3	-6.5	-6.4	-5.9
Romania [d]	-0.6	-0.6	0.3	0.3	-1.2	-0.4	-6.4	-6.5	-6.4	-5.0	-6.9	-7.7
Slovakia [e]	-4.7	-2.3	-2.9	-2.4	-1.9	–	-2.9	-2.9	-2.4	-5.2	-3.6	-2.2
Slovenia	1.8	2.1	3.4	1.9	2.1	0.9	-1.6	-2.0	-2.3	-1.8	-0.6	-0.2
The former Yugoslav Republic of Macedonia	1.8	-0.9	-0.9	0.5	0.4	0.4	5.5	-0.9	–	3.7	3.5	-2.6
Yugoslavia [f]	-8.2	-9.4	-9.3	..	..	-1.5	-12.1	-11.0	-11.6	..	..	-4.7
Baltic states	-1.2	-1.0	-1.4	-1.6	-1.7	-2.0	-3.2	-3.1	-2.6	-1.2	0.4	0.3
Estonia	-4.1	-3.9	-3.7	-2.5	-1.7	1.0	-5.8	-6.2	-6.2	-5.9	4.4	8.9
Latvia	-0.5	-0.1	0.8	0.9	0.4	-0.8	-4.2	-3.6	-2.6	1.1	0.5	-0.5
Lithuania	-0.5	-0.5	-1.8	-2.9	-3.0	-3.8	-1.4	-1.2	-0.7	-0.1	-1.5	-3.3
CIS	-0.4	..	..	..	..	..	..	..	..	..	..	..
Armenia	-2.9	-3.8	-4.2	-0.2	-1.2	-1.4	-6.8	-5.7	-8.1	–	-1.5	-1.5
Azerbaijan	–	0.1	-0.2	–	0.1	0.1	3.1	3.6	5.3	–	–	–
Belarus	0.6	0.4	-0.4	0.2	–	-0.2	0.8	0.7	0.2	-0.3	–	-0.2
Georgia	-8.9	..	..	..	..	..	..	..	..	..	..	..
Kazakhstan	-0.4	-0.2	-0.4	..	..	..	0.1	-0.6	-1.2	..	..	..
Kyrgyzstan	3.5	3.3	3.9	-0.1	0.4	0.9	-5.5	-0.6	-0.6	2.6	-0.6	-1.9
Republic of Moldova	-9.0	-8.6	-11.8	..	..	..	-12.1	-13.8	-5.1	..	..	..
Russian Federation	0.5	1.6	1.3	0.6	0.8	0.9	-0.6	–	1.4	2.1	2.1	2.1
Tajikistan	-3.9	-3.7	-5.5	-8.0	-7.0	-5.2	-14.6	-13.7	-12.8	-9.1	-6.9	-7.6
Turkmenistan	0.7	..	..	..	..	..	1.8	..	..	..	..	..
Ukraine	-2.3	-2.2	-2.3	-0.8	-1.6	-1.8	-8.3	-8.4	-8.4	-2.8	-2.7	-1.9
Uzbekistan	1.0	0.9	0.9	1.1	0.9	..	0.9	0.7	1.4	0.2	1.1	..
Total above	-1.1	..	..	..	..	..	..	..	..	..	..	..
Memorandum items:												
CETE-5	-2.1	-0.8	-1.3	-2.2	-2.0	-1.7	-4.7	-3.1	-3.7	-5.0	-4.6	-3.7
SETE-7 [b]	-1.9	-1.4	-0.9	-1.4	-2.3	-1.8	-6.8	-6.9	-5.7	-6.2	-7.0	-7.2

Source: National statistics and direct communications from national statistical offices to UN/ECE secretariat.

[a] Changes in employment based on quarterly statistics are not always fully comparable with those based on annual data due to differences in coverage.

[b] Regional quarterly aggregate of total employment exclude Yugoslavia; that of industrial employment excludes in addition Albania.

[c] Data reported by the statistical office of the Federation; these exclude the area of Republika Srpska.

[d] Labour force survey data.

[e] End of year data.

[f] Data exclude Kosovo and Metohia.

Employment in construction and manufacturing also fell significantly (by some 4 and 6 per cent, respectively). Employment in services, which until recently has been the main source of new jobs, started falling for the first time since 1995.

In Slovakia, as a result of a marked slowdown in the growth of output and the start of a long-delayed process of enterprise restructuring, total employment fell in 1999 by nearly 5 per cent, the largest fall since 1992 and the highest rate of decline in the region. In the first three quarters of 2000, as a result of an economic recovery which became visible in the second half of the year, and some special measures to stop rising unemployment,[313] the employment situation improved. The rate of decline decelerated considerably, and employment stopped falling in the third quarter of the year. In all the main

---

[313] In addition to the economic recovery, the improvement in employment was also due to the creation of temporary jobs in public works during the summer months. The programme of public works was launched by the government in response to the alarmingly high level of unemployment, which reached 19.5 per cent in February. As of 15 September, nearly 60,000 such temporary jobs had been created. *Reuters Business Briefing,* 4 October 2000.

sectors of the economy, employment stagnated during the first three quarters of 2000, except in services where, as in previous years, it continued to increase, although only slightly. It seems, however, that this improvement was only temporary, and although data for the fourth quarter were still not available at the time of writing this *Survey*, a sharp increase in unemployment in the last months of the year suggests that the fall in employment is likely to resume.

In Romania, where for the first time in three years an export-led recovery got underway, employment continued to fall slightly. In the first three quarters of 2000, the level of employment was basically flat in construction and services, but it declined by more than 6 per cent in industry, reflecting, *inter alia*, continued industrial restructuring and the closure of loss-making enterprises. However, most of these losses were offset by steadily growing employment in agriculture.[314]

In Bulgaria, despite a strong export-led expansion and some attempts by the government to create new jobs (mainly publicly-financed infrastructural projects), there was no improvement in employment in 2000. Continued lay-offs in industrial firms undergoing restructuring and large job losses caused by closure of loss-making enterprises resulted in a sharp decline in employment (the number of those employed under employment contracts dropped in 2000 by nearly 11 per cent). All sectors of the economy were affected by the decline, but there were particularly large falls in agriculture and industry (some 8 and 12 per cent, respectively). In the other countries of the region for which data are available, employment continued to decline at much the same rates as in 1999, although more so in Croatia, reflecting perhaps the steps undertaken by the new government to restructure the enterprise sector, accelerate privatization and implement a tougher bankruptcy policy. Data on employment in Yugoslavia for the first two quarters of 1999, the period of the Kosovo conflict, are not available. The resulting lacuna in the series does not allow any judgement on the employment changes in the first half of 2000. In the third quarter of 2000, employment continued to fall, but reflecting perhaps a robust recovery from the crisis caused by NATO bombing, the rate of decline decelerated considerably and did not exceed 2 per cent compared with more than 9 per cent in the same period of 1999.

In the *Baltic states,* reflecting their different economic performance, developments in the labour markets were more varied in 2000, with the changes in employment being particularly heterogeneous. In Estonia, where structural changes in the economy have increased competitiveness and resilience to external shocks, a strong recovery after the 1998 Russian financial crisis led to a notable deceleration in the decline of employment. In the third quarter of 2000, it started to grow again, rising by 1 per cent (year-on-year). The improvement was mainly due to manufacturing industry where employment started to grow rapidly in 2000, and by the third quarter was 12 per cent above its level of a year earlier. In Latvia, where output growth was also relatively strong, employment started to grow somewhat at the end of 1999 but despite the continued growth of output, it weakened in the first half of 2000 and was falling again by the third quarter. During the first three quarters of 2000, employment was actually flat in all the main sectors of the economy except industry, where it declined slightly. The Lithuanian economy has recovered more slowly than the other Baltic states from the recession caused by the Russian crisis, and the government has maintained a tight fiscal policy combined with enterprise restructuring and a faster rate of privatization. As a result the situation in the labour market has deteriorated, and by the third quarter of 2000 employment was nearly 4 per cent below its level of a year earlier. The decline affected all sectors of the economy, the largest falls occurring in services and particularly construction (some 3 and 14 per cent, respectively).

In the *CIS countries,* despite a widespread and strong economic recovery, there was also little improvement in employment. In the first three quarters of 2000, there were some small increases in Kyrgyzstan, Russia and Uzbekistan, but employment remained flat in Azerbaijan and Belarus, and elsewhere it continued to decline at much the same rates as in 1999 (except in Tajikistan, where the fall was much larger than in 1999). In Russia, employment rose by nearly 1 per cent, for the second consecutive year, and according to preliminary estimates, the rate accelerated in the last quarter.[315] The new jobs were mainly concentrated in services, but for the first time since the transition started there was also a substantial increase in industry where employment grew by more than 2 per cent.

(ii) Unemployment

In most of *eastern Europe*, given the accelerated decline in employment, registered unemployment rates generally remained high throughout 2000. Several countries (Bulgaria, Croatia, the Czech Republic, Romania and Slovakia) reported their highest unemployment rates since the transition started in 1989. Unemployment also reached a five-year high in Poland. In those cases where there was a fall in unemployment, it usually occurred in tandem with falling employment, suggesting departures from the labour force. Only in Hungary and Slovenia were falls in unemployment a result of net job creation.

In December 2000, the average rate of unemployment in eastern Europe reached 15.1 per cent, the highest regional rate since the transition started, with most countries falling within a range of just below 9 per cent (Czech Republic and Hungary) to nearly 23 per cent

---

[314] This suggests that agriculture, which accounts for nearly 45 per cent of total employment, continues to absorb, or reabsorb, workers displaced in other parts of the economy.

[315] To 1.4 per cent, year-on-year. Direct communications from the national statistical office to the UN/ECE secretariat.

TABLE 3.5.2

Registered unemployment in eastern Europe, the Baltic states and the CIS, 1999-2001

(Per cent of labour force, end of period)

	1999 Dec.	2000 Mar.	2000 Jun.	2000 Sept.	2000 Dec.	2001 Jan.
Eastern Europe	14.6	15.3	14.7	14.6	15.1	..
Albania	18.2	18.4	17.6	17.3	16.9	..
Bosnia and Herzegovina [a]	39.0	39.2	39.1	39.2	39.4	..
Bulgaria	16.0	18.8	18.2	17.8	17.9	18.5
Croatia	20.8	21.7	20.5	21.4	22.6	23.0
Czech Republic	9.4	9.5	8.7	8.8	8.8	9.1
Hungary	9.6	10.2	8.9	8.8	8.9	..
Poland	13.1	14.0	13.6	14.0	15.0	15.6
Romania	11.5	11.9	10.8	9.9	10.5	10.8
Slovakia	19.2	19.3	19.1	16.6	17.9	19.8
Slovenia	13.0	12.6	11.8	11.7	12.0	..
The former Yugoslav Republic of Macedonia [b]	43.8	44.5	43.6	44.6	44.9	..
Yugoslavia [c]	27.4	26.3	26.5	26.9	26.6	..
Baltic states	9.1	9.8	9.3	9.4	10.0	..
Estonia [d]	6.7	7.1	6.2	6.0	7.3	8.1*
Latvia	9.1	9.0	8.4	7.9	7.8	7.9
Lithuania	10.0	11.4	11.1	11.8	12.6	13.1
CIS [e]	8.3	7.9	7.2	7.0	6.9	..
Armenia	11.5	12.2	11.9	11.2	10.9	..
Azerbaijan	1.2	1.2	1.1	1.1	1.2	..
Belarus	2.0	2.1	2.0	2.2	2.1	..
Georgia	5.6	6.4	..	..	..	..
Kazakhstan	3.9	4.5	4.2	3.9	3.7	..
Kyrgyzstan	3.0	3.2	3.2	3.1	3.1	..
Republic of Moldova	2.1	2.2	2.0	2.1	1.8	..
Russian Federation [f]	12.2	11.4	10.1	9.8	9.6	9.6
Tajikistan	3.1	3.0	3.1	2.9	3.0	..
Turkmenistan	..	..	..	..	..	..
Ukraine	4.3	4.5	4.3	4.2	4.2	..
Uzbekistan	0.5	0.5	0.7	0.6	0.6	..
Memorandum items:						
CETE-5	12.5	13.1	12.6	12.6	13.3	..
SETE-7	16.5	17.3	16.5	17.4	17.8	..
Russian Federation [g]	1.7	1.6	1.4	1.3	1.4	1.3
Former-GDR	17.7	18.9	16.5	16.6	17.2	18.7

Source: National statistics; direct communications from national statistical offices to UN/ECE secretariat.

[a] Data reported by the Statistical Office of the Federation; these exclude the area of Republika Srpska.

[b] Estimates by the Ministry of Finance.

[c] Data exclude Kosovo and Metohia.

[d] Job seekers until October 2000. January's unemployment rate has been calculated on the basis of the labour force in the fourth quarter of 2000.

[e] Excluding Georgia and Turkmenistan.

[f] Based on monthly Russian Goskomstat estimates according to the ILO definition, i.e. including all persons not having employment but actively seeking work. The figures have been revised in line with the results of the labour force survey conducted in November 2000.

[g] Registered unemployment.

(Croatia)[316] (table 3.5.2). The total number of persons registered as unemployed was close to 8 million, nearly 4 per cent more than in December 1999.

In Hungary, strong output growth has nevertheless continued to generate a relatively strong demand for labour, with some branches reporting labour shortages of skilled workers.[317] The rate of unemployment has declined fairly steadily since February 2000, falling to 8.9 per cent in December (0.7 percentage points lower than a year earlier). In Slovenia there has been a gradual downward trend in unemployment since October 1998, reaching 12 per cent in December 2000.

In the Czech Republic, unemployment peaked at 9.8 per cent in January 2000 and then declined fairly steadily to 8.8 per cent in December, a development helped by special labour market policies.[318] Government officials hope that in 2001, new job opportunities arising from economic growth and from a significant inflow of FDI to greenfield projects will offset the losses caused by the restructuring of heavy industries, banking and some other state held companies. On these assumptions, the Finance Ministry has lowered its forecast for unemployment at the end of 2001, from 9.4 per cent (estimated in October 2000) to 8.4 per cent.[319] A new National Employment Action Plan is also expected to work in this direction.[320]

In Poland, after falling between 1995 and 1998 unemployment started to rise again at the end of 1998 and the situation continued to worsen through 2000, as the economy slowed from 6-7 per cent annual growth rates in the mid-1990s to just over 4 per cent in the last two years. Moreover, many analysts believe that taking into account the specific labour market conditions in Poland, even a growth rate of 5 per cent is insufficient to reverse the

---

[316] In Croatia, unemployment is exaggerated by the measure of "registered unemployment", which is considerably higher than that given in the labour force survey. The latter gives a rate of 15.1 per cent in the first half of 2000, as opposed to 21.2 per cent according to the registered figures. The phenomenon can be explained by the fact that in addition to the usual divergence between registered and labour force unemployment, which exists in most transition economies due to the general deficiencies of the former, the sizeable difference between the two measures in Croatia may be explained by the fact that a large number of those registered as unemployed work in the black economy or are self-employed in agriculture (according to the labour force survey data, there were some 273,000 unemployed people in the first half of 2000, while the registered statistics reported a much higher figure – 353,000 people – for the same period). The situation is further aggravated by the fact that the reported employment data do not include many of the self-employed, particularly in agriculture. Consequently, the labour force is underestimated and the unemployment rate is biased upwards. For similar reasons, caution is needed in interpreting the unemployment data in all the countries of the former SFR of Yugoslavia. For a more detailed discussion of the relationship between registered and labour force unemployment, see UN/ECE, *Economic Survey of Europe, 1999 No. 1*, pp. 131-134.

[317] PlanEcon, *Monthly Report: Hungary* (Washington, D.C.), 23 February 2001, p. 31.

[318] As employment continued to decline, although at a slower rate than in 1999, the fall in the unemployment rate in 2000 to a large extent was due to a new scheme providing incentives for early retirement in 2000. A slower pace of labour shedding in some large enterprises, especially in the steel and mining industries, which received financial support from the government, also helped to slow down the growth in unemployment. *CTK Business News*, 8 July 2000.

[319] According to the macroeconomic forecast made in February. *Interfax Czech Republic Business News Service*, 2 February 2001.

[320] Adopted by the Czech government in mid-February, this is a programme of support for the creation of new jobs in small- and medium-size businesses.

upward trend in unemployment.[321] The sharp rise was due to a number of factors. First, the restructuring of many unprofitable industries such as coal mining, steel, defence and public transport, combined with the ending of job guarantees in privatized firms,[322] led to a wave of mass lay-offs. Second, sharply rising labour productivity has also reduced the short-term demand for labour. Third, the situation has been aggravated by the fact that members of the demographic peak of the first half of the 1980s are beginning to enter the labour market.[323] In the 12 months to December 2000, the unemployment rate increased by nearly 2 percentage points to 15 per cent, its highest rate since 1994 (chart 3.5.1). However, the *registered* unemployment figures probably overstate the real situation, *inter alia*, as a result of the government's reform of state health-care services.[324] Polish unemployment reached a six-year high (15.6 per cent) in January 2001,[325] and it can be expected to worsen as corporate restructuring continues and manufacturers announce lay-offs amid signs of a slowdown in output growth.[326] The government has already raised its projection of unemployment at year's end from 14.9 per cent to 15.4 per cent, but many analysts believe it could reach 16-18 per cent.[327] Another specific problem which affects the Polish labour market and which will have to be dealt with by the government is restrictive labour regulations that limit the creation of new jobs.[328]

In Slovakia, the combination of austerity measures and a weaker economic performance, particularly in industry and public sector construction, led to a dramatic rise in unemployment in 1999. In the first half of 2000, the situation continued to deteriorate, mainly due to a more rapid rate of large-scale corporate restructuring. Unemployment reached 19.5 per cent in January and February and remained virtually unchanged until July. The rate subsequently fell to 16.1 per cent in October thanks to a new public works programme, but this is essentially a short-term measure and the effects have been transitory: unemployment started to increase again in November and by January 2001 it had reached a new record level of 19.8 per cent. According to national analysts, high rates of unemployment will probably continue to be the biggest economic and social problem facing policy makers in the next few years. A significant fall in the numbers unemployed is unlikely before the second half of this decade: in the meantime, it may decrease slowly but will probably remain above 14 per cent.[329] By the end of 2001 the unemployment rate is expected to fall to 18.2 per cent.[330]

There was no radical improvement in the labour markets in the south-east European transition economies. At the end of 2000, unemployment rates in all countries of the region except Romania, were some 17 per cent or more. In Albania, where GDP grew strongly (albeit from a very low base) and the government introduced several projects to boost employment,[331] the unemployment rate declined by more than 1 percentage point in the 12 months to December 2000, but it still stood at nearly 17 per cent.[332] In 2001, the economy is expected to continue to grow strongly, but unemployment is unlikely to fall much more, while roughly the same proportion of the labour force will continue to seek employment abroad, primarily in Greece and Italy.[333]

In Bulgaria, as a result of lay-offs in industrial firms undergoing restructuring, the unemployment rate surged in the early months of 2000, peaking at a 19 per cent rate in April. However, the effects of restructuring have been partly offset by strong service sector growth and by a number of job-creating infrastructure projects: the unemployment rate declined from May, reflecting also to some extent a mid-year seasonal improvement, but by December it was still at 17.9 per cent, nearly two percentage points higher than a year earlier. The rate rose again to 18.5 per cent in January and to 18.7 per cent in

---

[321] According to calculations by the central statistical office, the Polish economy would have to grow at a rate of 10 per cent to be able to absorb the net increase in the labour force. CreditanStalt, *Central Europe Quarterly*, II/2000 (Vienna).

[322] The privatization of many Polish companies in the mid-1990s included contractual clauses restricting lay-offs: these have now started to expire.

[323] The growth of the net working-age population in 2000 is estimated at around 240,000 (compared, for example, with some 150,000 in 1995) and is expected to increase further by some 270,000 in 2001 and 2002. *Polish News Bulletin* (Warsaw), 1 December 2000.

[324] The health-care reforms encouraged many of those who were unofficially employed in the grey economy to register as unemployed in order to maintain their eligibility for free state health insurance. Evidence that the registered unemployment figures have been affected by this change in the *incentive* to register is provided by the quarterly labour force survey, which estimates that unemployment rose by around 120,000 persons between the end of 1999 and the end of 2000. This is much less than the increase of around 350,000 in the registered measure. SG, *Weekly Financial Market Review* (Warsaw), 23 February 2000.

[325] The total number of unemployed exceeded 2.8 million people, but the problem is even more aggravated by the fact that almost 80 per cent of them have no rights to unemployment benefits.

[326] In the fourth quarter of 2000, GDP grew by an estimated 2.5 per cent compared with 6 per cent in the first quarter of the year. Stemming from the sagging consumer demand for new cars, lay-offs have been recently announced at manufacturers Daewoo and Fiat. *Warsaw Business Journal*, 26 February 2001.

[327] *Reuters Business Briefing*, 21 February 2001.

[328] In early March 2001, the government formulated a programme to fight rising unemployment by lowering taxes, loosening the labour code and encouraging investment. The appropriate bills are to be sent to parliament for approval in the next few weeks.

[329] Conference on *Prospects of Economy and Society* organized in February 2000 by the Slovak Statistics and Demographic Society. As cited by *Reuters Business Briefing*, 1 March 2001.

[330] *CTK Business News*, 26 February 2001.

[331] During 1999-2000, nearly 2 billion lek (some $14 million) were allocated for the creation of new jobs, mainly in public works. According to the Minister of Labour and Social Affairs, nearly 70,000 people were employed under these projects. *Reuters Business Briefing*, 4 October 2000.

[332] Generally, unemployment in the country has been also mitigated by temporary emigration, amounted to 430,000. EIU, *Country Profile: Albania*, 2000-01, p. 23.

[333] *Oxford Analytica Brief*, 3 January 2001.

CHART 3.5.1

Registered unemployment rates in selected east European, Baltic and CIS economies, 1993-2000
(Per cent of labour force, end of period)

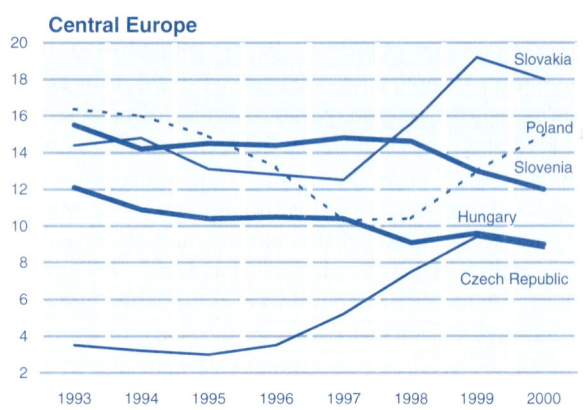

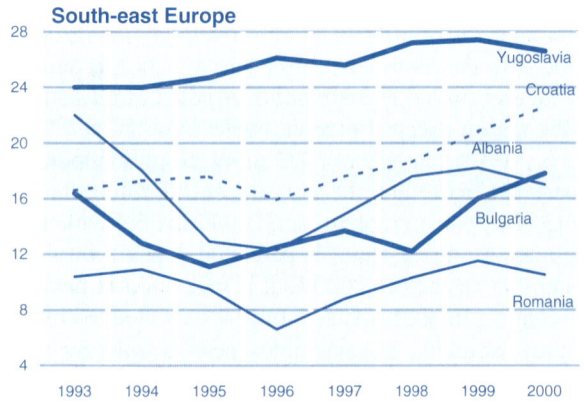

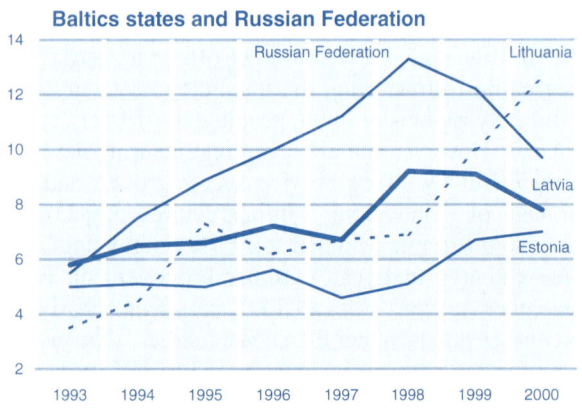

Source: National statistics; UN/ECE secretariat Common Database.

A faster rate of privatization and a more rigorous implementation of bankruptcy law led to a marked worsening of the labour market in Croatia in 2000. Unemployment continued to rise, reaching a record 21.7 per cent in March. After a seasonal fall in the summer, unemployment continued to rise to 22.6 per cent in December. It is likely to remain high in 2001 as the government plans to introduce some rapid reforms to lay the basis for an acceleration of economic development. This will eventually lead to lower unemployment, but not significantly before two to four years.[335]

In Romania, where the economy is emerging from a three-year recession, there was some improvement in the labour market after unemployment peaked at 12.2 per cent in February 2000. By the end of the year it stood at 10.5 per cent (1 percentage point lower than 12 months previously). The new government intends to boost the rate of economic growth to 4.5 per cent in order to raise employment by 1.5 per cent, and cut the unemployment rate to 9.9 per cent by the end of 2001.[336] To stimulate employment a programme of low-interest rate credits will also be launched.[337]

In Bosnia and Herzegovina, the unemployment rate was broadly unchanged in the 12 months to December 2000, but it remained at the very high level of 39 per cent of the labour force. The return of refugees is likely to add to the pressures on the labour market.[338] Regular and consistent data on unemployment are still not available for The former Yugoslav Republic of Macedonia, but it appears that there was no improvement in 2000.[339] Semi-official estimates show that the unemployment rate remained very high and in the 12 months to December 2000 increased by more than 1 percentage point to nearly 45 per cent.[340] In Yugoslavia, despite a strong recovery of output from the effects of NATO bombing in 1999, there was little improvement in the labour market in February 2001. As output growth is expected to remain high, and with foreign direct investment increasing rapidly[334] and restructuring of most state enterprises nearing completion, unemployment should fall slowly in 2001.

---

[334] In 2000, Bulgaria attracted the largest inflow of foreign direct investment (estimated at nearly $1 billion) among all the south-east European transition economies. *Bulgarian News Agency*, 27 December 2000.

[335] BBC Monitoring Service, *Central Europe and Balkans*, 1 February 2001.

[336] *Reuters Business Briefing*, 1 March 2001.

[337] About 1 trillion lei (some $37.5 million) is to be extended in the form of low-interest rate credits to small- and medium-sized enterprises by the Romania Unemployment Fund in 2001. Some 195,000 jobs are expected to be created as a result. *Romanian News Digest*, 6 February 2001.

[338] In July 2000, 3,600 refugees from ethnic minorities returned to their pre-war homes, almost four times as many as in the same month in 1999. *Oxford Analytica Brief*, 26 September 2000.

[339] The national statistical office of The former Yugoslav Republic of Macedonia has stopped reporting unemployment rates. The number of registered unemployed rose steadily in 2000 reaching some 367,000 persons in December 2000 (a more than 3 per cent increase over the same period of 1999).

[340] Direct communications to the UN/ECE secretariat from the Ministry of Finance. However, as in the case of Croatia, these figures exaggerate considerably the real unemployment, as accurately estimating the full number of economically active population in The former Yugoslav Republic of Macedonia is difficult given the high level of self-employment and a vast black economy not included in the official figures. The latest labour force survey, conducted in April 2000, puts the total labour force at 811,600 and the unemployment rate at 32.2 per cent, 0.2 percentage points less than in the same period of 1999.

2000. The official data show a slight fall in the unemployment rate from 27.4 per cent to 26.6 per cent in the 12 months to December 2000. However, once enterprise restructuring and large-scale reforms get underway in 2001 further increases in open unemployment will probably be unavoidable.

In the 12 months to December 2000, the total number of unemployed persons in the *Baltic states* increased by more than 10 per cent and the registered unemployment rate at the end of the year stood at 10 per cent, the highest rate since the transition started (table 3.5.2).[341] Unemployment continued to fall in Latvia, where it had peaked in April 1999 (at 10.2 per cent of the labour force), but in Estonia, unemployment continued to rise despite a more rapid rate of economic growth (chart 3.5.1). The unexpected rise in the unemployment rate in October, partly reflects the sharp fall in the growth of industrial output in the fourth quarter and possibly recent changes in the entitlement to unemployment benefits.[342]

Unemployment rose steadily in Lithuania during 2000 reaching a record 12.6 per cent in December, nearly 3 percentage points higher than 12 months earlier. Continued enterprise restructuring and a new bankruptcy law expected to be adopted by the parliament are likely to prevent unemployment from falling below 12 per cent in the near future.[343]

Registered unemployment in the *CIS countries*, the only available data series for most of them[344] did not change very much in the 12 months to December 2000. Unemployment rates remained very low, varying mostly between 0.6 per cent (Uzbekistan) and 4.2 per cent (Ukraine), the main exception being Armenia (nearly 11 per cent). These figures, however, are very misleading as to both the magnitude and the dynamics of unemployment since a large proportion of the jobless, although willing to work, do not register for various reasons.[345]

Instead, estimates of unemployment which try to be somewhat close to the ILO definition (i.e. *all* those who are out of work and actively searching for a job), suggest a marked reduction in the numbers unemployed.[346] The total number of unemployed in the CIS declined from an annual average of 14 million in 1999 to 12.5 million in 2000. The average unemployment rate in the region, on the basis of these more accurate figures, was 9.5 per cent (compared with 11 per cent in 1999).[347] This change mostly reflects the marked improvement in Russia where the rapid growth of output has led to employment growth and reduced the unemployment rate, which had been falling since February 1999, to below 10 per cent at the end of 2000. According to labour force survey data in 2000, unemployment stabilized in Ukraine, although at a relatively high level: the unemployment rate stood at 11.4 per cent in March and June, but increased slightly to 11.7 per cent in September, 1.4 percentage points higher than a year ago.[348]

3.6 Foreign trade and payments

(i) Current account developments

In 2000 the strong economic growth in the transition economies was accompanied by a general improvement in their current account balances[349] and other external financial indicators. In aggregate, their current account balances rose from near balance in 1999 to a record surplus of some $28 billion in 2000 (table 3.6.1), most of it being generated by fuel exporters and above all by the Russian Federation. A major reason for this huge surplus was the sharp increase in world prices of fuels and raw materials that boosted the earnings of commodity exporters in the region, but another factor was the broadly-based strength of demand in western Europe and among the transition economies themselves, including Russia (section ii). The increase in the volume of exports of goods and services spurred domestic output growth and led to improved current account balances, despite the rise in the price of imported fuels. In several east European and Baltic countries, the growth of net earnings from services was entirely responsible for the improvement in the current account (table 3.6.2).

The international financial crises of 1997-1998 continued to have repercussions on the balance of payments of the countries in the region, although their impact has been uneven. The strongest effects are still being felt by the CIS. With the principal exception of Russia, current account balances have been constrained by smaller or even negative capital inflows. However,

---

[341] The official figures for registered unemployment tend to underestimate considerably the actual levels in the Baltic countries. In the fourth quarter of 2000, unemployment rates derived from labour force surveys, based on the ILO definition of unemployment, were at 13.9 per cent in Estonia, 14.6 per cent in Latvia (November) and 16.1 per cent in Lithuania (November), whereas the registered rates were 7, 7.8 and 12.1 per cent, respectively.

[342] As of 1 October, the eligibility conditions were eased and the period for unemployment benefits payment extended from 180 days to 270 days. EIU, *Country Report: Estonia*, December 2000, p. 22. Labour force survey data confirm the increase in unemployment in the fourth quarter, up 1.1 percentage points from the third quarter to 13.9 per cent.

[343] *Reuters Business Briefing*, 7 February 2001.

[344] So far only the Russian Federation and Ukraine conduct regular quarterly labour force surveys.

[345] Among these reasons are low unemployment benefits (often paid in arrears), undeveloped employment services, strict and complicated rules of registration, etc. This proportion varies in different countries between 50 to 80 per cent of the total unemployment.

[346] CIS Statistical Committee, *Statistika SNG, Statistical Bulletin*, No. 2 (Moscow), January 2001, p. 75. These are rough estimates made by the committee and it is considered that they represent a more realistic picture of unemployment in the CIS region.

[347] The unemployment rates reflecting these more accurate figures varied between some 8-9 per cent in Azerbaijan and Kyrgyzstan, to 12-14 per cent in Georgia, Kazakhstan and the Republic of Moldova.

[348] Direct communications from the national statistical office.

[349] This section is based on national balance of payments statistics. The discussion of trade in sect. (ii) is based on customs data.

TABLE 3.6.1

Current account balances of eastern Europe, the Baltic states and the CIS, 1997-2000

(Million dollars, per cent)

	1997	1998	1999	January-September 1999	January-September 2000	2000	Per cent of GDP 1997	1998	1999	Jan.-Sept. 2000	2000
Eastern Europe [a]	-14 392	-17 611	-20 843	-13 340	-12 055*	-18 955*	-4.1	-4.6	-5.6	-4.5	-5.1
Albania	-254	-45	-155	-44	-320*	-500*	-11.1	-1.5	-4.2	-11.3	-13.4
Bosnia and Herzegovina	-1 060	-789	-971	-700*	-500*	-878[b]	-29.0	-18.6	-21.4	-13.5	-17.7
Bulgaria	1 046	-61	-652	-414	-364	-696	10.3	-0.5	-5.3	-4.2	-5.6
Croatia	-2 325	-1 530	-1 523	-720	-4	-750*	-11.5	-7.1	-7.6	–	-3.9
Czech Republic	-3 211	-1 336	-1 567	-773	-1 263	-2 369	-6.1	-2.4	-3.0	-3.4	-4.8
Hungary	-981	-2 298	-2 081	-1 296	-936	-1 754	-2.1	-4.9	-4.3	-2.7	-3.7
Poland	-4 312	-6 858	-11 569	-8 010	-7 890	-9 978	-3.0	-4.3	-7.4	-6.9	-6.3
Romania	-2 137	-2 968	-1 296	-739	-593	-1 400	-6.1	-7.2	-3.8	-2.4	-3.8
Slovakia	-1 952	-2 059	-1 083	-791	-169	-713	-9.6	-9.7	-5.5	-1.2	-3.7
Slovenia	11	-147	-783	-526	-393	-594	0.1	-0.8	-3.9	-2.8	-3.2
The former Yugoslav Republic of Macedonia	-276	-308	-135	-28	-124	-200*	-7.5	-8.8	-3.9	-4.6	-5.7
Yugoslavia	-1 845	-1 238	-1 421	-800*	-1 072	-1 400*	-9.4	-7.4	-8.7	-5.7	-5.6
Baltic states	-1 890	-2 426	-2 134	-1 329	-804	-1 432*	-9.5	-11.0	-9.5	-4.6	-6.2
Estonia	-563	-478	-294	-139	-184	-331	-12.2	-9.2	-5.7	-4.9	-6.8
Latvia	-345	-650	-646	-377	-290	-500*	-6.1	-10.7	-9.7	-5.5	-7.2
Lithuania	-981	-1 298	-1 194	-814	-330	-600*	-10.2	-12.1	-11.2	-4.0	-5.3
CIS	-4 092	-6 715	23 125	12 443*	35 367*	48 470*	-0.7	-1.7	8.3	14.8	14.3
Armenia	-307	-403	-307	-192	-203	-300*	-18.7	-21.3	-16.6	-16.0	-15.7
Azerbaijan	-916	-1 365	-600	-655	67	200*	-23.1	-30.7	-13.3	1.9	4.1
Belarus	-788	-866	-194	-36	-206	-162	-5.7	-7.3	-1.8	-2.8	-1.6
Georgia	-375	-416	-195	-159	-170*	-200*	-10.4	-11.4	-6.9	-7.5	-6.4
Kazakhstan	-799	-1 236	-233	-637	655	1 200*	-2.5	-5.6	-1.4	4.8	6.6
Kyrgyzstan	-138	-371	-185	-102	-36	-100*	-7.8	-23.2	-15.1	-4.0	-7.7
Republic of Moldova	-275	-327	-34	-14	-73	-120*	-14.2	-19.3	-2.9	-7.9	-9.3
Russian Federation	2 060	721	25 049	14 284	33 618	46 000*	0.5	0.3	13.4	19.3	18.6
Tajikistan	-56	-120	17	13*	70*	100*	-6.1	-9.1	1.6	10.4	10.2
Turkmenistan	-580	-934	-851	-557*	50*	100*	-21.6	-33.0	-26.0	1.5	2.3
Ukraine	-1 335	-1 296	834	767	1 579	1 700*	-2.7	-3.2	2.8	7.0	5.2
Uzbekistan	-584	-102	-176	-270	15	50*	-4.0	-0.7	-1.0	0.2	0.4
Total above [a]	-20 374	-26 752	148	-2 226*	22 507*	28 083*	-2.2	-3.4	–	4.3	3.8
Memorandum items:											
CETE-5	-10 445	-12 698	-17 083	-11 396	-10 650	-15 408	-3.7	-4.2	-5.8	-5.0	-5.3
SETE-7 [a]	-3 947	-4 913	-3 760	-1 944	-1 405*	-3 546*	-5.5	-6.0	-5.1	-2.6	-4.7
Asian CIS	-3 755	-4 947	-2 530	-2 559*	449*	1 051*	-6.2	-9.4	-5.2	1.3	2.2
Three European CIS [c]	-2 397	-2 489	606	718	1 300	1 419*	-3.6	-4.6	1.5	4.2	3.2

Source: National balance of payments statistics; press reports; IMF; UN/ECE secretariat estimates.

[a] Excludes Bosnia and Herzegovina and Yugoslavia.

[b] IMF projection.

[c] Belarus, Republic of Moldova and Ukraine.

some of the more chronic difficulties with external balance can be attributed to domestic policies that have failed to accelerate restructuring and, as a result, have deterred foreign investment.

(a) Eastern Europe and the Baltic states

In *eastern Europe* the aggregate current account deficit declined slightly in 2000 (to around 5 per cent of GDP), following a decade of more or less continuous increase. This long-lasting expansion of the deficit has been made possible by the availability of foreign finance, particularly of FDI, which has also contributed to the build-up of official reserves. Although several countries were adversely affected by the financial turmoil in 1997-1998, the inflow of finance was maintained, helping eastern Europe to reach the fastest rate of economic growth since the beginning of the transition. By contrast, many emerging market economies in other parts of the world have been faced with a sharp reduction in financial flows and a forced adjustment in their current accounts from large deficits to surplus.

After contracting in 1999, the dollar value of *central European* exports of goods and services recovered in 2000, rising by around 10 per cent. Import growth also recovered but at a somewhat slower pace.[350] As a result

---

[350] The growth rates of exports are considerably larger when measured in terms of euros and volumes (see sect. 3.6(ii) below).

natural resources, and have attracted little foreign private investment (chapter 5), making them dependent on official funds. All have been eligible for concessional loans through the IMF Poverty Reduction and Growth Facility (PRGF)[427] and the World Bank's IDA facility. Multilateral loans at low interest rates have increased from one third (Tajikistan) to two thirds (Armenia) of their total external debt. Nonetheless, they now face heavy debt repayments.

Very briefly, the IMF analysis shows that all five countries are likely to face a difficult fiscal and external outlook in the next decade. The base scenario envisages a favourable external environment and implementation of a strong reform programme, resulting in GDP growth of 4.5-6.5 per cent per annum throughout the 10 year projection period. In this case the external debt of four countries would be manageable (debt servicing would be difficult for the next five years because of possible cash flow problems[428] but should improve thereafter), but for Kyrgzstan the situation could remain very difficult for the whole decade.[429] Under the second scenario, the performance of these economies is weaker either because of their feeble response to reform policies, and/or because of a less favourable external environment. GDP then grows at only 2-3 per cent per annum and export growth expands only modestly, in line with projected increases in world trade. In this case, debt ratios deteriorate sharply in Georgia, Kyrgzstan and the Republic of Moldova and the risk increases of an unsustainable debt situation.

The impact of the peak debt servicing burden in 2001-2004 on national budgets is a serious concern in all countries except, possibly, Armenia.[430] Moreover, if these countries meet their external debt servicing obligations and fiscal targets, it is unlikely that adequate resources will be available to raise living standards. These five countries are currently among the poorest in the world, and they suffer from a high incidence of absolute poverty.[431] Even if they were to achieve the growth rates envisaged in the base scenario, it would take until 2005 to regain their 1991 levels of income. If lower growth rates were to prevail, sustainability would require larger amounts of external assistance in the form of highly concessional new money (or grants) and/or the restructuring of external obligations. An IMF simulation suggests that higher rates of growth and a restructuring of scheduled debt payments could create a sustainable situation. However, at lower growth rates (scenario two) some debt reduction would also be required to achieve sustainability, except possibly in Kyrgyzstan.[432] Armenia would probably not require debt relief.

Although the programmes of the four countries that have concluded PRGF agreements[433] are individually tailored, there is a large degree of commonality which is broadly consistent with the base scenario: adherence to macroeconomic stabilization targets, including an improvement in tax collection and overall fiscal consolidation; improvements in public and corporate governance and a reduction of corruption (both of which could also boost tax revenues); and an acceleration of economic restructuring, with priority given to large-scale privatizations. These measures are intended to raise economic efficiency and export performance and improve the business climate so as to boost investment. FDI is being counted on for restructuring and to help fill the financing gaps. The countries have also been advised to seek rescheduling agreements and negotiations have been completed or are underway with bilateral creditors.[434]

Most of these countries had already arranged IMF-backed programmes in the first half of the 1990s. Although there has been some progress in stabilization and restructuring, none has achieved the expected degree of policy reform or output and export growth (factors which contributed to the need for previous debt reschedulings). In part these disappointing outcomes are explained by the effects of armed conflict, political and religious turmoil, and natural disasters (including earthquakes and, more recently, severe drought) that have made reforms more difficult to implement and have contributed to the increase in poverty. However, it is also generally accepted that widespread policy slippage, pervasive problems of governance and corruption and the slow pace of restructuring have been equally or more important.[435] These chronic obstacles to development will have to be overcome if the new programmes are to achieve their growth and financial objectives.[436]

---

[427] The PRGF is a three-year concessional facility for low income countries which carries an annual interest rate of 0.5 per cent and a maturity of 10 years with a 5½ year grace period

[428] Debt servicing ratios are projected to peak in 2001-2004, due to rescheduled debt coming due and repayments of multilateral loans.

[429] In Kyrgyzstan the non-interest current account is projected to strengthen less than in the other countries because of a temporary fall in exports when gold production starts to wind down.

[430] Increasing external debt service payments and what is deemed to be the modest ability of government to enhance revenues suggests that fiscal sustainability indicators will remain in an undesirable range. Of all the transition economies, these countries rank among the lowest in their ability to raise tax revenues (table 3.2.5).

[431] In 1998, absolute poverty rates ranged from 45 per cent in Georgia to 68 per cent in Tajikistan. IMF and the World Bank, op. cit.

[432] Regarding Kyrgyzstan, the IMF has noted that "even with rescheduling of part of non-concessional debt, the debt service burden remains high, especially over the next few years and there is no clear prospect for finding a sustainable answer to the external debt situation". IMF, *Public Information Notice*, No. 00/87, 13 October 2000.

[433] The facility was approved for Georgia in January 2001, for Kyrgyzstan and Tajikistan in June 1998, and for the Republic of Moldova in December 2000. Negotiations on a PRGF are underway with Armenia.

[434] In March the Paris Club rescheduled Georgia's debt coming due in 2001-2002. Instead of $88 million, it has been reduced to $33 million, and creditors agreed in principle to consider further restructuring in the case of financing need. *Financial Times*, 8 March 2001. According to U. Sarbanov, chairman of the National Bank of Kyrgyzstan, Russia and Turkey are ready to restructure the country's debts and Russia has called upon other countries to take similar action. *BBC Summary of World Broadcasts*, SUW/0677 WE/3, 9 February 2001.

[435] Nevertheless, the international community, including the IFIs, generally underestimated the difficulties of transition and the gestation periods needed for structural and institutional reforms to be put into effect. But they also overestimated the authorities' willingness and ability to implement these reforms. IMF and the World Bank, op. cit.

[436] Many of the factors holding back growth in these countries are as, or even more, serious in some other less indebted members of the CIS. See, for example, the EBRD indices of economic reform. EBRD, *Transition Report 2000* (London). According to Transparency International, the members of the CIS rank above the transition economy average in perceptions of corruption (table 5.2.2).

PART TWO

ASPECTS OF STRUCTURAL CHANGE AND ADJUSTMENT IN TRANSITION ECONOMIES

CHAPTER 4

DOMESTIC SAVINGS IN THE TRANSITION ECONOMIES

There is widespread agreement that the mobilization of domestic resources is crucial for raising rates of economic growth and promoting development. Despite many ambiguities in the relationship, the body of empirical research supports the common-sense view that capital investment is a powerful engine of economic growth and that higher levels of domestic saving are associated with higher levels of investment. Although foreign investment can be important, its role is essentially complementary, and usually subsequent, to domestic efforts: historically, domestic private savings have played the major role in supporting investment in the industrialized countries. This chapter examines the aggregate savings-investment balances in a large group of transition economies, an exercise which is only possible now because of recent improvements in their statistics. Among the various determinants of savings in the transition economies, the analysis emphasizes the importance of the level of per capita income and the depth and strength of the financial system. The latter underlines the crucial importance of financial reform and the creation of sound institutions for encouraging higher levels of savings and investment.

4.1 Introduction

The economic transformation of the former centrally planned economies involves a fundamental re-allocation of resources and deep economic structural change. If these countries are to build modern economies based on up-to-date production technologies and, ultimately, catch up with the living standards in the industrialized countries, they need to sustain high rates of economic growth for a long period of time. However, the process of transformation during the past decade has been rather uneven and progress has often lagged behind expectations due to the unprecedented problems and policy challenges that these countries have been facing.

When assessing the experience of the past decade, it has sometimes been claimed that whereas the process of economic transformation and reindustrialization requires the mobilization of enormous resources and their channelling into efficient use, the transition economies, after several decades of economic mismanagement, are poorly endowed with domestic resources. It has been further argued that, given the restricted access of many transition economies to the international financial markets and the limited amounts of official assistance they have been getting, many of these countries face severe resource constraints – similar to those faced by many developing countries – which have hampered their economic recovery and, if unchecked, may continue to cause serious impediments to future development and growth.

While the debate about the determinants of (and constraints on) development and growth is not new – it has long been present in the development economics literature and in the old and still on-going policy debate on these issues – there has not been much empirical research on the actual pervasiveness of resource constraints in the transition economies, and of the extent to which such constraints may be narrowing their growth prospects. This can be partly explained by the absence of adequate data (or by its poor quality), in particular on domestic savings, which has effectively prevented in-depth research in this area. This chapter addresses some of the issues related to the financing of development and growth in the transition economies, and it focuses on their saving-investment balances and, in particular, on the role of domestic private savings. In defining its analytical focus, the chapter draws extensively on previous theoretical and empirical research in this area (section 4.2). Thanks to the progress in statistical reporting, especially in the last few years, it is now possible to re-constitute the aggregate saving-investment balances for a large group of transition economies (section 4.3). The availability of these data has allowed a more detailed empirical analysis of the saving and investment patterns in the transition economies as well as some of the main determinants of private savings (section 4.4).

4.2 Savings, investment and growth

The analysis of the relationships between saving and investment and between investment and growth occupies an important place both in economic theory and in empirical economic research. In view of the undisputed link between fixed investment and growth, these relationships are closely monitored by policy makers as well. Governments have traditionally been active in searching for ways and means of stimulating economic activity and achieving high and sustained rates of economic growth.

Economists – both in theoretical and in applied research – have for a long time been intrigued by the links between domestic savings and investment, on the one hand, and between investment and economic growth and development, on the other. The "conventional wisdom" about these links has been that thrift is a major determinant of growth, which in turn leads to the belief that in the long run there must exist a positive return on the invested capital, regarded as "the reward for parsimony".[437] In the main, empirical research has provided convincing evidence in support of this conjecture, in particular as regards long-run economic performance.[438]

Despite the indisputable fact of the existence of links between savings, investment and growth, there is an ongoing debate as to how, precisely, savings and investment affect economic performance and vice versa: different theoretical models provide different interpretations of the causal relations and transmission mechanisms, and many of the results in this area are quite ambiguous. Thus two important strands of economic theory – the neo-classical and the Keynesian – offer different interpretations of the role of savings and investment for economic growth; and, in addition, the results differ substantially according to whether the models refer to a closed or an open economy.

The relationship between savings, investment and growth has been closely scrutinized in the different growth models which comprise the corpus of economic growth theory, most of which are in the neo-classical tradition. These models incorporate some of the basic assumptions of the neo-classical economics: for example, the existence of perfect markets which clear instantaneously through adjustment in prices; a tendency towards the full utilization of production factors; social endowments of production factors (in accordance with their marginal product), etc. In general, neo-classical growth models are exclusively focused on the supply side and, consequently, output is determined by supply conditions alone.

Earlier (pre-neo-classical) growth models such as the Harrod-Domar model implied a direct link between the (short-run) rate of economic growth and the level of current investment.[439] As recognized by one of its authors, this model was not meant to be a long-run growth model; it was envisaged as a tool to analyse economic performance in the short run, particularly during the course of a business cycle.[440] However, in practice it has been extensively used – sometimes without justification – to analyse longer-term growth performance, especially in the context of designing aid programmes for developing countries.[441]

While very attractive for policy purposes because of its clear framework and ease of manipulation, the Harrod-Domar model – due to the simplicity of its assumptions – fails to capture some of the important links and relations that are widely believed to be part and parcel of actual economic life. Hence, both its empirical validity and its policy relevance have been widely questioned by economists.[442] One of the key underlying assumptions of the Harrod-Domar model is that both domestic and foreign savings (the latter often in the form of external assistance) are fully channelled into productive investment. Obviously, this is a very strong – and probably not always realistic – assumption, especially as regards a developing or transition economy. If it is to be adopted as a working guideline for policy making purposes (in the context of aid and development programmes), it needs to be tested against the actual absorptive capacity of the economy: that is, whether it is capable of fully putting into productive use the envisaged financial resources. In a developing country (as well as in transition economies), the actual absorptive capacity of the economy may be a constraint for the effective deployment of such resources because of institutional bottlenecks and/or a scarcity of profitable investment opportunities.

---

[437] S. Cesaratto, "Savings and economic growth in neo-classical theory", *Cambridge Journal of Economics*, Vol. 23, No. 6, 1999, pp. 771-793.

[438] For example, the Penn World Tables, containing comparable data on long-term economic performance (from 1950 onwards) for some 150 countries, provide evidence of a positive and relatively strong statistical association between average investment rates and long-run rates of growth of per capita GDP. R. Summers, I. Kravis and A. Heston, "International comparisons of real product and its composition: 1950-1977", *The Review of Income and Wealth*, Series 26, No. 1, 1980, pp. 19-66 and R. Summers and A. Heston, "The Penn World Tables (Mark 5): an extended set of international comparisons, 1950-1985", *The Quarterly Journal of Economics*, Vol. 106, No. 2, May 1991, pp. 327-368.

[439] The model assumes that the growth of output in the current year is proportional to the investment ratio (the share of investment in output) in the previous year.

[440] E. Domar, *Essays in the Theory of Economic Growth* (New York, Oxford University Press, 1957).

[441] In the framework of the Harrod-Domar growth model a targeted rate of growth of GDP implies a "required" investment rate, the "incremental capital output ratio". Hence, the difference between domestic savings and the "required investment rate" was interpreted as a "financing gap" which needed to be bridged by additional finance (in particular, foreign savings or aid). Most development assistance programmes of the 1950s-1970s were designed along this strand of economic thinking. W. Easterly, "The ghost of the financing gap: testing the growth model used in the International Financial Institutions", *Journal of Development Economics*, Vol. 60, No. 2, 1999, pp. 423-438.

[442] In his comprehensive study, W. Easterly tested the Harrod-Domar model on pooled cross-country data for 146 countries for the period 1950-1992 in an attempt to find out whether *ex post* there is any empirical justification of the underlying assumptions of the model. These results were profoundly negative both as regards the relation between aid and investment and the relation between investment and growth. Moreover, in 60 per cent of the countries studied he actually found a negative statistical association between foreign aid and domestic investment and in most of the others there was no statistically significant correlation between aid and investment. As regards the underlying assumption of a linear relation between lagged investment and growth, the sample data did not provide evidence of a statistically significant association either. He concluded that "there is no theoretical or empirical justification for assuming a short-term proportional relationship between investment and growth or between 'investment requirements' and saving", and that "there is no theoretical or empirical justification for using a 'financial gap' calculation to influence policy or the allocation of foreign aid". W. Easterly, loc. cit.

Another implication of the assistance policies derived from the Harrod-Domar growth model is that an economy has to have a positive and sufficiently large marginal saving rate (the share of savings in an incremental change of income) in order to embark on a path of self-sustained growth. If this condition is not met, official credit will fail to generate growth while foreign debt will continue to accumulate, driving the economy into a debt trap. Consequently, external aid in the form of debt finance (and its continued availability) should in principle be conditional on the country achieving higher domestic saving rates. However, even if this is done, there are no *ex-ante* guarantees of success in meeting such conditionality due to the complexity of private saving behaviour and the numerous factors that affect it (this issue is discussed in more detail in section 4.4). In addition – in a developing or transition economy – there are further limitations due to the limited absorptive capacity of the economy and institutional bottlenecks.

The neo-classical growth theory has relaxed some of the simplistic assumptions of the Harrod-Domar model but it still fails to offer a satisfactory account of the links between savings and growth, which would conform to the "conventional wisdom", that capital accumulation is the engine of growth. Indeed, one of the puzzling results of the mainstream growth models is the apparent lack of a direct link between the saving rate and the long-run rate of growth of the economy. In the growth model developed by Robert Solow, a rise in the saving rate only causes a one-time increase in the level of per capita income and does not affect the equilibrium rate of growth; it is only during the transition from one steady state to another that the rate of growth changes in response to a change in the saving rate.[443] These controversial results have not been supported by empirical evidence which, as noted earlier, suggests a positive correlation between the investment ratio and the long-run rate of growth.

Further extensions of neo-classical growth theory have attempted to circumvent the limitations of the Solow model. Thus, endogenous growth models incorporate an explicit link between variables which reflect different preferences regarding the allocation of output between present and future consumption (that is, savings) and future economic performance, in the first place growth. One strand of these models hinges on the introduction of a "human capital" variable which is an input in the production function and whose present value depends on past savings and investment decisions.[444] Other endogenous growth models assume a relation between investment and the level of productive efficiency (the rate of technological progress), which provides a link between savings/investment and the rate of growth.[445] A third group of models deviates from the standard neo-classical assumption of constant returns to scale and considers capital accumulation as a source of increasing returns to scale.[446] All these theoretical approaches imply an active role of savings in future growth, in line with the notion that capital accumulation is a fundamental source of growth.[447]

Keynesian economics interprets the role of savings and investment in promoting growth in a different context. In contrast to the basic neo-classical assumptions, in the Keynesian framework prices only change or adjust very slowly: in the short run they are taken as given and fixed ("sticky" prices); output is demand determined and suppliers produce what is demanded at the given price level; markets may be imperfect and adjustment may be costly; and there is not necessarily a general tendency towards the full utilization of production factors. In an economy that operates under these assumptions, any exogenous disturbance that changes aggregate effective demand (including investment) – which may be external or internal, or policy induced – affects growth as well. Obviously, a change in the consumption/saving patterns of economic agents (which may also be a response to a change in the environment or in expectations) directly affects the level of economic activity (and hence growth) through the disturbance generated in final demand. In the framework of an open economy (the so-called Mundell-Fleming model), the relationship between aggregate demand (and the implied policy mix) and growth becomes more complex due to the effect of the exchange rate regime: the same disturbance can produce different growth outcomes depending on the actual exchange rate regime.[448]

Regarding the relationship between investment and savings, a number of empirical studies in this area, based on comprehensive statistical data for various countries, have demonstrated the existence of a strong and statistically significant correlation between the two.[449]

---

[443] In the Solow model, the long-run (equilibrium, or steady-state) rate of growth only depends on the rates of growth of labour supply and the efficiency of the production technology ("technical progress"), both of which are taken as exogenously determined. R. Solow, "A contribution to the theory of economic growth", *Quarterly Journal of Economics*, Vol. 70, 1956, pp. 65-94. As observed by Cesaratto, this model implies that the savings decisions of the community (that is, its choices between present and future consumption) are irrelevant for the determination of the (long-run) rate of growth, an implication which breaks the direct link between thrift and economic growth. S. Cesaratto, loc. cit.

[444] Among the first models of this type is that suggested in R. Lucas, "On the mechanics of economic development", *Journal of Monetary Economics*, Vol. 22, No. 1, 1988, pp. 3-42.

[445] P. Romer, "Endogenous technological change", *Journal of Political Economy*, Vol. 98, No. 5, Part 2, 1990, pp. 71-102.

[446] P. Romer, "Increasing returns and long-run growth", *Journal of Political Economy*, Vol. 94, No. 5, 1986, pp. 1002-1037.

[447] However, as argued by some of their critics, the establishment of such a link in these extensions of the neo-classical growth model is in most cases achieved at the expense of deviations from the standard principles of the neo-classical theory. S. Cesaratto, loc. cit.

[448] While providing a useful framework for analysing short-term economic adjustment (given that the main assumptions are empirically valid), the models based on Keynesian principles do not address the long-run growth properties of the economy and the factors that affect them. The analytical power of these models as a policy-making tool diminishes when the underlying key assumptions are violated in reality (for example, in circumstances when prices do change rapidly or when supply constraints matter).

[449] M. Feldstein and C. Horioka, "Domestic saving and international capital flows", *Economic Journal*, Vol. 90, No. 358, 1980, pp. 314-329. Later, similar results were reported in A. Penati and M. Dooley, "Current account imbalances and capital formation in industrial countries, 1949-

Despite these relatively robust empirical findings there remains significant divergence in the interpretation of the results.[450] Martin Feldstein and Charles Horioka, the authors of the first and highly influential study in this area, assume that in a world of perfect capital mobility, domestic investment and saving rates should be completely independent of one another. Under the assumption of perfect capital mobility, investors from any part in the world should have an equal opportunity to invest in any country and thus the level of domestic investment should only depend on the expected rate of future returns.[451] Hence the authors interpret the observable correlation between investment and savings as a reflection of the existence of market imperfections and restrictions on the free flow of capital. Subsequently this interpretation (the so-called Feldstein-Horioka puzzle) was widely debated – and challenged – in the literature, especially as regards its policy implications. It has been argued that the existence of a strong statistical correlation between domestic investment and domestic savings, even in countries with no or very weak controls on capital mobility implies that in reality capital is not truly perfectly mobile and cannot be expected to become so even if all formal restrictions are lifted.[452]

Whatever the interpretation, one of the main conclusions of these empirical findings is that, historically, countries have in the main relied mostly on domestically generated savings to finance domestic investment.[453] Moreover, various studies have shown that the statistical association between investment and savings is an inherent feature of economic performance both in the short and in the long run; this empirical relationship is general and is not restricted to a particular group of countries.[454]

Although there is still considerable debate regarding the theoretical modelling of the relationship between savings, investment and growth, empirical research has produced much less ambiguous results in this area: in general, empirical economics has come up with rather strong results emphasizing the importance of domestic savings and investment for the development and growth of individual countries and nations. In fact, recent theoretical research seeking to reflect the role of capital accumulation as an engine of growth has partly been a response to such empirical findings. While economic theory has so far not been fully successful in reflecting the underlying economic interactions in consistent, closed form models, the notion that savings and investment play a fundamental role in the process of economic development continues to dominate present day economic thinking.

4.3 The patterns of savings and investment in the ECE transition economies

Savings and investment are essential for development and growth, and even more so for those countries with economies undergoing an unprecedented transition from plan to market. The legacy of communism was a group of economies characterized by inefficient production technologies and employing obsolete physical assets. Building modern and competitive market economies requires, among other things, a complete overhaul of practically all industries. For this to materialize enormous amounts of resources need to be mobilized and channelled into productive fixed investment. Indeed, the experience during a decade of economic transformation provides convincing evidence that the most successful transition economies have been those where the economic environment stimulated domestic savings and business fixed investment. Some of the leading reformers among the transition economies have experienced in recent years an investment boom, often led by FDI and involving large multinational companies, that has laid the foundations of a number of new, modern and competitive industries.

The available data on recent economic performance in the transition economies support the view that capital accumulation is essential for achieving high rates of economic growth. Despite the inevitable caveat related to the short observation period,[455] the pooled data shown in chart 4.3.1 are in line with the findings of other empirical studies which, as noted earlier, support the existence of a positive statistical association between the level of investment and the rate of economic growth. The relatively high dispersion in the scatter diagram in chart 4.3.1 (indicating a relatively weak correlation between the two variables) is not surprising given the fact that the transition economies are still undergoing fundamental structural change, which inevitably involves a high degree of instability in structural relationships.

Analysing the determinants of capital accumulation, as well as its two-way relationship with development and growth, requires in the first place a detailed knowledge of

---

81", *IMF Staff Papers*, Vol. 31, No. 1, 1984, pp. 1-24 and L. Tesar, "Savings, investment and international capital flows", *Journal of International Economics*, Vol. 31, No. 1-2, 1991, pp. 55-78.

[450] Later studies have explored the existence of possible sample biases in the cross-country analysis of the statistical association between investment and savings. For example, it has been argued that this correlation is much weaker in developing countries than in industrialized ones; in addition it has been pointed out that small economies tend to experience larger fluctuations in capital flows than large ones, which would also weaken the saving-investment correlation. M. Dooley, J. Frankel and D. Mathieson, "International capital mobility: what do saving-investment correlations tell us?", *IMF Staff Papers*, Vol. 34, No. 3, 1987, pp. 503-530.

[451] This interpretation has sometimes been used as an argument in favour of the rapid liberalization of international capital flows. However, the available empirical evidence does not provide strong support for this hypothesis. For example, Feldstein and Horioka obtain results which are equivalent to the statistical rejection of the hypothesis of perfect international mobility of capital.

[452] A central argument is scepticism as to the possibility of ever eliminating the numerous market and informational imperfections that characterize real economic life and which imply additional costs and risks associated with the international movement of capital.

[453] Thus, for the industrialized countries it has been estimated that domestic savings are responsible for some 85-95 per cent of domestic investment. M. Feldstein and C. Horioka, loc. cit.

[454] L. Tesar, loc. cit.

[455] The fundamental association between capital accumulation and growth is essentially a long-run relation, whereas the relevant data for the transition economies are only available for a relatively short period of time.

Domestic Savings in the Transition Economies 171

CHART 4.3.1

Investment ratios and rates of growth of GDP per capita in selected east European, Baltic and CIS economies, 1995-1999
(Per cent)

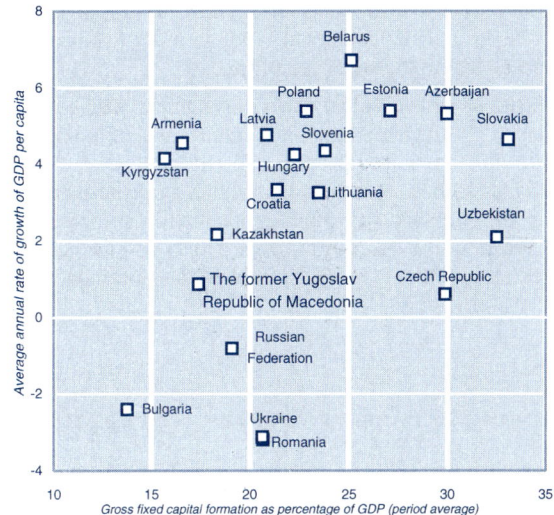

Source: UN/ECE secretariat, based on national statistics.

the actual patterns of savings and investment. Until recently, due to the absence of adequate statistical data, it was not possible to analyse in detail, and on a comparative basis, the components of saving-investment balances in the transition economies. Owing to the progress in statistical reporting in these countries, and especially to the almost universal adoption of the System of National Accounts (although practical application varies widely among countries), it is now possible to calculate the saving-investment balances for a large number of ECE transition economies in recent years. The method used in compiling these balances is described in box 4.3.1 and the actual results (in terms of percentage shares in GDP) are shown in tables 4.3.1 and 4.3.2.[456]

The data indicate a very high degree of variation in all the components of the saving-investment balances of the transition economies. Cross-country variation in itself cannot be regarded as atypical,[457] since it mirrors existing differences in the levels of industrialization and per capita income,[458] as well as traditional and historical patterns. In addition, the on-going process of deep structural change in the transition economies has probably also added to the divergence; moreover, the speed of this process differs considerably among countries.

The balances presented in tables 4.3.1 and 4.3.2 show the saving-investment patterns of the private sectors and of governments in the transition economies over the last five years or so. While private savings are analysed in more detail in section 4.4, the remainder of this section is mostly devoted to changes in the aggregate gross saving and gross investment ratios.

Each individual ratio can be interpreted both in terms of its absolute level and of its change over time, with the latter indicating the degree of stability of the underlying structural relation. The significant variability over time in many cases is yet another indication of the instability of structural relations in many of the transition economies. In general, the dynamics of the saving and investment ratios in most countries are non-monotonic year-on-year, even during the recent phase of recovery, which suggests that the process of deep structural change in these countries is still underway.

Given the great cross-country diversity of the saving patterns in the transition economies, it is instructive to compare them with the saving patterns in other countries and regions as such a perspective allows a better assessment of the level of domestic savings in individual countries. For example, during the period 1994-1997, the unweighted average gross domestic saving ratio in the EU member states was 19.5 per cent; the variation among countries was also substantial (though not as much as among the transition economies) with the saving ratio ranging between 14.4 per cent of GDP in the United Kingdom and 25.6 per cent of GDP in the Netherlands.[459] Among the industrialized countries Japan has traditionally had the highest gross domestic saving rates (usually above 30 per cent of GDP). On a global scale, during the period 1983-1992, the highest average gross domestic saving ratios were in the newly industrialized economies of southeast Asia (an average of 24.5 per cent of GDP), followed by the industrialized countries (20.4 per cent average rate) while the gross saving ratios in Latin America and Africa were 15.3 per cent and 16.8 per cent, respectively.[460] From such a perspective the domestic saving ratios in the central European transition economies such as the Czech Republic, Hungary, Poland, Slovakia and Slovenia (which are also in general quite advanced in the transformation reforms), as well as the Russian Federation (which is a special case) fall into the high category. The rest of the transition economies are characterized by saving ratios which are in the low to medium range.

---

[456] As a word of caution, despite the notable progress in statistical reporting, the quality of the available statistical data for the transition economies is uneven and sometimes questionable. In particular, due to recurrent discrepancies in the reporting of the balance of trade and services in the national accounts of a number of countries, the current account balance as reported in the national balance of payments statistics has been used in the actual calculations of the saving-investment balances. For the sake of internal consistency and the comparability of the estimates, this has been done for all the transition economies. The reliability of other statistical data used in the computations (such as the fiscal statistics but also the balance of payments data themselves) may also be questioned. Due to these limitations, the components of the saving-investment balances in tables 4.3.1 and 4.3.2 should be regarded as tentative.

[457] The heterogeneity of the saving-investment patterns across countries has been observed in other empirical studies as well. See S. Edwards, *Why Are Saving Rates So Different Across Countries?: An International Comparative Analysis*, NBER Working Paper, No. 5097 (Cambridge, MA), April 1995.

[458] For an assessment of convergence and divergence in per capita income levels among the transition economies see UN/ECE, *Economic Survey of Europe*, 2000 No. 1, pp. 155-188.

[459] *OECD Economic Outlook*, No. 66 (Paris), December 1999, p. 219.

[460] The average ratios reported above are calculated for representative samples of countries. S. Edwards, op. cit.

BOX 4.3.1
The arithmetic of the national saving-investment balance

Although closely related, savings and investment denote different economic categories. At the level of individual economic agents, "savings" denote that part of income from the current period which the agent sets aside for future consumption, while "investment" refers to the expenditure actually made by the agent during this period for the acquisition of various types of assets. Each economic agent, among other things, strikes a balance between the amounts of savings and of investment expenditure. When investment expenditure exceeds savings, the agent has to borrow additional funds in order to finance the deficit; conversely, in the case of a positive balance the excess amount can be lent to those in need of funds.

The annual saving-investment balance of a country represents the aggregate of the individual saving-investment balances of all the economic agents that are entitled to identify themselves with the country. While there may be different ways of looking at a national saving-investment balance, it is usually recognized that there are two main categories of agent that need to be distinguished in the aggregate balance: the private sector (which incorporates all businesses and households) and the state (with all its bodies and institutions). Dis-aggregating the saving-investment balance this way requires identification of the three components (savings, investment expenditure and the ensuing balance) for the private sector, the government and the economy as a whole. It is this approach that has been followed in compiling the saving-investment balances for the transition economies.

At the microlevel the saving-investment account is derived from the individual income balances. Each economic agent i uses monetary income R_i either for consumption C_i or for saving S_i:

$$R_i = C_i + S_i \qquad \ldots (1)$$

On the other hand the agent incurs expenditure E_i which can be grouped into two major categories: consumption C_i and investment I_i:

$$E_i = C_i + I_i \qquad \ldots (2)$$

Subtracting (2) from (1) yields

$$D_i = R_i - E_i = S_i - I_i \qquad \ldots (3)$$

which implies a numerical equivalence between the balance of monetary income and the saving-investment balance.

In turn, the aggregated national saving-investment balance is derived from the national accounts identity:

$$Y = C + I + M - X \qquad \ldots (4)$$

where Y denotes total income (gross national product); C is total final consumption; I stands for gross capital formation; and M and X denote imports and exports, respectively.

Since aggregate income is either used for consumption or saved, it follows that:

$$Y = C + S \qquad \ldots (5)$$

where S denotes total gross domestic savings.

Substituting (5) into (4) yields the main accounting identity of the national saving-investment balance:

$$S - I = X - M \qquad \ldots (6)$$

where X – M is the balance of trade in goods and services. In the national saving-investment balance, a negative trade balance is interpreted as foreign savings attracted to finance domestic investment.

As both savings and investment have two components (private sector and government) (6) can be rewritten as:

$$(S_p + S_g) - (I_p + I_g) = (S_p - I_p) + (S_g - I_g) = X - M \qquad \ldots (7)$$

where subscripts p and g denote private sector and government, respectively.

Taking into account the definition of the saving-investment balance from the individual income accounts, (1) to (3), and substituting in (7) yields:

$$D_p + D_g = X - M \qquad \ldots (8)$$

where

$$D_p = R_p - E_p = S_p - I_p \qquad \ldots (9)$$

is the aggregated income balance of the private sector and

$$D_g = R_g - E_g = S_g - I_g \qquad \ldots (10)$$

is the income (fiscal) balance of the public sector (or, more precisely, general government).

These identities are sufficient to compile the saving-investment balance from the national accounts and the general government fiscal statistics. Knowing the values of the balance of trade in goods and services and of gross capital formation, the first step is to determine gross domestic savings from (6). (In the absence of sufficiently detailed national accounts, the balance of trade in goods and services is sometimes approximated by the current account of the balance of payments.) It follows from (10) that government savings (S_g) can be computed from the fiscal accounts as the sum of the fiscal balance D_g and capital expenditure by the government (I_g). Private savings (S_p) are then determined as the residual difference between total savings and government savings. Similarly, gross private investment (I_p) is the difference between gross capital formation and the government's capital expenditure.

TABLE 4.3.1

Saving-investment balances in selected east European and Baltic countries, 1994-1999
(Per cent of GDP)

	1994	1995	1996	1997	1998	1999		1994	1995	1996	1997	1998	1999
Bulgaria							**Slovakia**						
Gross domestic investment	9.4	15.7	8.4	11.4	16.9	19.0	Gross domestic investment	23.1	27.3	37.1	36.6	36.1	31.9
Budget	..	2.1	1.6	3.1	4.0	5.5	Budget	..	5.0	6.7	6.7	5.9	3.7
Private	..	13.5	6.8	8.3	12.9	13.5	Private	..	22.3	30.4	29.9	30.2	28.2
Gross domestic savings	9.1	14.6	7.8	15.0	16.4	13.7	Gross domestic savings	27.9	29.5	26.5	27.0	26.5	26.4
Budget	..	-3.9	-14.8	1.5	4.7	6.4	Budget	..	4.5	3.0	0.7	–	0.1
Private	..	18.5	22.6	13.5	11.7	7.3	Private	..	25.0	23.5	26.3	26.5	26.3
Foreign savings	0.3	1.1	0.6	-3.6	0.5	5.4	Foreign savings	-4.8	-2.1	10.6	9.6	9.7	5.5
Government balance	..	-6.0	-16.4	-1.6	0.7	0.9	Government balance	..	-0.5	-3.7	-6.0	-5.9	-3.6
Private sector balance	..	4.9	15.8	5.2	-1.2	-6.3	Private sector balance	..	2.6	-6.9	-3.6	-3.7	-1.9
Croatia							**Slovenia**						
Gross domestic investment	17.4	17.6	21.9	28.2	23.2	23.2	Gross domestic investment	20.9	23.3	23.4	24.1	25.6	28.2
Budget	..	4.5	6.8	6.0	6.9	9.4	Budget	..	4.5	4.7	4.8	5.2	6.4
Private	..	13.1	15.1	22.1	16.3	13.8	Private	..	18.8	18.7	19.3	20.4	21.8
Gross domestic savings	23.0	9.9	16.2	16.6	16.0	15.9	Gross domestic savings	25.1	23.2	23.6	24.3	25.6	25.3
Budget	..	2.8	5.0	3.8	5.4	5.8	Budget	..	4.2	4.5	2.9	3.7	5.8
Private	..	7.0	11.2	12.8	10.6	10.1	Private	..	19.0	19.2	21.4	21.9	19.5
Foreign savings	-5.7	7.7	5.8	11.5	7.1	7.3	Foreign savings	-4.2	0.1	-0.2	-0.2	–	2.9
Government balance	..	-1.7	-1.8	-2.2	-1.5	-3.6	Government balance	..	-0.3	-0.3	-1.9	-1.6	-0.6
Private sector balance	..	-6.0	-3.9	-9.4	-5.6	-3.7	Private sector balance	..	0.2	0.5	2.1	1.6	-2.3
Czech Republic							**The former Yugoslav Republic of Macedonia**						
Gross domestic investment	29.8	34.0	34.9	32.8	29.7	28.5	Gross domestic investment	15.5	20.8	20.1	22.4	23.0	21.0
Budget	..	7.1	6.4	5.5	5.2	5.7	Budget	..	2.8	2.5	1.3	1.9	2.6
Private	..	26.9	28.5	27.3	24.4	22.8	Private	..	17.9	17.6	21.0	21.1	18.4
Gross domestic savings	27.8	31.4	27.5	26.7	27.3	26.5	Gross domestic savings	10.8	15.8	13.6	14.9	14.2	17.0
Budget	..	5.1	4.0	3.0	2.3	1.6	Budget	..	1.8	1.5	1.0	–	1.0
Private	..	26.3	23.6	23.7	25.0	24.9	Private	..	14.0	12.1	13.9	14.2	16.0
Foreign savings	1.9	2.6	7.4	6.1	2.4	2.0	Foreign savings	4.7	5.0	6.5	7.5	8.8	4.0
Government balance	..	-2.0	-2.4	-2.6	-2.9	-4.1	Government balance	..	-1.0	-1.0	-0.4	-1.9	-1.6
Private sector balance	..	-0.6	-5.0	-3.5	0.5	2.1	Private sector balance	..	-3.9	-5.6	-7.1	-6.9	-2.4
Hungary							**Estonia**						
Gross domestic investment	22.2	23.9	26.8	27.4	29.7	28.8	Gross domestic investment	27.6	26.7	27.8	30.9	29.4	24.5
Budget	..	5.5	5.2	6.0	5.9	5.7	Budget	..	4.2	5.2	4.4	4.4	4.4
Private	..	18.4	21.6	21.4	23.8	23.1	Private	..	22.6	22.6	26.5	25.0	20.1
Gross domestic savings	12.8	18.4	23.1	25.2	24.8	24.5	Gross domestic savings	20.3	22.3	18.7	18.7	20.2	18.8
Budget	..	-2.2	1.0	0.5	-1.9	–	Budget	..	2.2	2.3	5.4	2.8	-0.9
Private	..	20.6	22.1	24.8	26.7	24.5	Private	..	20.1	16.4	13.3	17.4	19.6
Foreign savings	9.4	5.6	3.7	2.1	4.9	4.3	Foreign savings	7.3	4.4	9.1	12.2	9.2	5.7
Government balance	..	-7.7	-4.2	-5.5	-7.8	-5.6	Government balance	..	-2.0	-3.0	1.0	-1.6	-5.3
Private sector balance	..	2.1	0.5	3.4	2.9	1.3	Private sector balance	..	-2.4	-6.2	-13.2	-7.6	-0.5
Poland							**Latvia**						
Gross domestic investment	17.6	19.7	21.9	24.6	26.2	27.1	Gross domestic investment	19.1	17.6	18.8	22.8	27.6	26.3
Budget	..	2.7	3.1	3.5	3.7	3.2	Budget	..	0.9	2.2	2.5	4.1	5.0
Private	..	17.0	18.8	21.0	22.5	23.9	Private	..	16.7	16.6	20.3	23.5	21.3
Gross domestic savings	18.3	23.9	20.9	21.6	21.9	19.7	Gross domestic savings	24.6	17.2	13.4	16.7	16.9	16.0
Budget	..	-0.3	-0.6	0.1	0.5	-0.3	Budget	..	-2.4	0.7	2.3	3.0	1.5
Private	..	24.2	21.5	21.5	21.3	20.0	Private	..	19.6	12.7	14.4	13.9	14.5
Foreign savings	-0.7	-4.2	1.0	3.0	4.3	7.4	Foreign savings	-5.5	0.4	5.4	6.1	10.7	10.3
Government balance	..	-3.0	-3.7	-3.5	-3.2	-3.5	Government balance	..	-3.3	-1.5	-0.2	-1.1	-3.5
Private sector balance	..	7.2	2.7	0.5	-1.2	-3.9	Private sector balance	..	2.9	-3.9	-5.9	-9.6	-6.8
Romania							**Lithuania**						
Gross domestic investment	24.8	24.3	25.9	20.6	21.4	19.9	Gross domestic investment	18.4	24.7	24.5	26.5	24.4	22.9
Budget	..	5.4	4.7	3.9	4.1	..	Budget	..	4.0	2.8	3.1	4.0	5.5
Private	..	18.9	21.1	16.7	17.3	..	Private	..	20.8	21.7	23.4	20.4	17.4
Gross domestic savings	23.4	19.3	18.6	14.6	14.3	16.1	Gross domestic savings	16.2	14.5	15.3	16.3	12.3	11.7
Budget	..	1.9	-0.4	-2.6	-2.4	..	Budget	..	-0.8	-1.0	1.0	3.7	-1.9
Private	..	17.4	18.9	17.1	16.7	..	Private	..	15.3	16.3	15.3	8.7	13.6
Foreign savings	1.4	5.0	7.3	6.1	7.2	3.8	Foreign savings	2.2	10.2	9.2	10.2	12.1	11.2
Government balance	..	-3.5	-5.1	-6.5	-6.5	..	Government balance	..	-4.8	-3.8	-2.1	-0.4	-7.4
Private sector balance	..	-1.5	-2.2	0.4	-0.6	..	Private sector balance	..	-5.4	-5.4	-8.1	-11.7	-3.8

Source: UN/ECE secretariat, based on national statistics.

TABLE 4.3.2
Saving-investment balances in selected countries of the CIS, 1994-1999
(Per cent of GDP)

	1994	1995	1996	1997	1998	1999		1994	1995	1996	1997	1998	1999
Armenia							**Kyrgyzstan**						
Gross domestic investment	23.5	18.4	20.0	19.1	19.1	19.5	Gross domestic investment	9.0	18.3	25.2	21.7	15.4	12.4
Budget	..	2.1	3.0	1.2	3.7	1.7	Budget	..	1.2	0.6	0.7	0.8	–
Private	..	16.3	17.0	17.9	15.4	17.8	Private	..	17.2	24.6	21.0	14.6	12.4
Gross domestic savings	6.8	1.0	1.8	0.4	-1.5	4.5	Gross domestic savings	1.4	2.6	1.5	13.8	-7.7	-2.8
Budget	..	-1.3	-1.9	-1.4	0.9	-2.4	Budget	..	-12.7	-8.2	-5.4	-2.7	-2.5
Private	..	2.3	3.8	1.8	-2.4	6.8	Private	..	15.3	9.7	19.2	-5.0	-0.3
Foreign savings	16.6	17.4	18.2	18.7	20.6	15.0	Foreign savings	7.6	15.7	23.7	7.8	23.2	15.2
Memorandum items:							*Memorandum items:*						
Government balance	..	-3.4	-5.0	-2.6	-2.8	-4.0	Government balance	..	-13.8	-8.8	-6.0	-3.6	-2.5
Private sector balance	..	-14.0	-13.2	-16.1	-17.8	-11.0	Private sector balance	..	-1.9	-14.9	-1.8	-19.6	-12.7
Azerbaijan							**Republic of Moldova**						
Gross domestic investment	15.3	23.8	29.0	34.2	33.4	30.2	Gross domestic investment	28.8	24.9	24.2	23.8	25.9	22.1
Budget	..	1.4	1.3	1.3	1.1	6.3	Budget	..	3.4	3.3	4.9	5.0	2.4
Private	..	22.4	27.7	32.9	32.3	23.9	Private	..	21.5	20.9	18.9	20.9	19.7
Gross domestic savings	6.8	7.2	-0.2	11.2	2.7	15.2	Gross domestic savings	21.8	18.3	12.3	9.0	5.4	20.1
Budget	..	-2.4	-1.0	0.4	-0.8	1.8	Budget	..	-4.3	-7.2	-5.3	0.8	-1.7
Private	..	9.5	0.8	10.8	3.5	13.5	Private	..	22.6	19.6	14.3	4.7	21.9
Foreign savings	8.5	16.6	29.2	23.1	30.7	15.0	Foreign savings	7.1	6.6	11.9	14.8	20.4	2.0
Memorandum items:							*Memorandum items:*						
Government balance	..	-3.7	-2.3	-1.0	-1.9	-4.5	Government balance	..	-7.7	-10.6	-10.2	-4.2	-4.2
Private sector balance	..	-12.9	-26.9	-22.1	-28.8	-10.5	Private sector balance	..	1.1	-1.3	-4.6	-16.2	2.2
Belarus							**Russian Federation**						
Gross domestic investment	32.9	25.1	24.5	27.6	27.8	24.0	Gross domestic investment	25.5	25.4	24.6	22.8	15.7	15.5
Budget	..	6.8	7.5	9.1	8.8	9.0	Budget	..	5.9	5.2	4.2	3.2	..
Private	..	18.2	17.0	18.6	18.9	15.0	Private	..	19.5	19.5	18.6	12.5	..
Gross domestic savings	23.2	20.7	20.7	21.7	20.2	21.6	Gross domestic savings	28.7	27.8	27.6	23.4	16.0	29.0
Budget	..	3.5	5.2	7.4	7.8	7.4	Budget	..	2.1	–	-1.6	-3.0	..
Private	..	17.2	15.5	14.3	12.4	14.1	Private	..	25.7	27.6	25.0	19.1	..
Foreign savings	9.7	4.4	3.8	5.9	7.6	2.4	Foreign savings	-3.2	-2.4	-3.0	-0.6	-0.4	-13.5
Memorandum items:							*Memorandum items:*						
Government balance	..	-3.4	-2.2	-1.7	-1.0	-1.6	Government balance	..	-3.9	-5.1	-5.8	-6.2	..
Private sector balance	..	-1.1	-1.5	-4.2	-6.5	-0.8	Private sector balance	..	6.2	8.1	6.4	6.6	..
Georgia							**Ukraine**						
Gross domestic investment	16.8	24.0	8.1	15.6	24.4	14.1	Gross domestic investment	35.3	26.7	22.7	21.4	20.8	19.8
Budget	..	1.9	3.0	1.9	1.4	..	Budget	..	3.2	3.2	3.1	1.6	1.3
Private	..	22.1	5.0	13.8	23.0	..	Private	..	23.5	19.4	18.3	19.2	18.5
Gross domestic savings	-8.7	16.5	1.5	8.1	15.9	7.0	Gross domestic savings	32.3	23.6	20.0	18.8	17.6	22.2
Budget	..	-4.8	-5.2	-3.2	-3.7	..	Budget	..	-2.3	-1.2	-3.2	0.4	-0.2
Private	..	21.3	6.7	11.3	19.6	..	Private	..	25.9	21.2	22.0	17.2	22.4
Foreign savings	25.5	7.5	6.5	7.6	8.5	7.0	Foreign savings	3.1	3.1	2.7	2.7	3.2	-2.4
Memorandum items:							*Memorandum items:*						
Government balance	..	-6.7	-8.2	-5.1	-5.0	–	Government balance	..	-5.5	-4.4	-6.3	-1.2	-1.5
Private sector balance	..	-0.8	1.7	-2.5	-3.4	–	Private sector balance	..	2.4	1.8	3.7	-2.0	3.9
Kazakhstan							**Uzbekistan**						
Gross domestic investment	28.7	23.3	16.1	15.6	17.2	15.4	Gross domestic investment	18.3	24.2	23.0	18.9	14.8	15.3
Budget	..	2.6	1.0	1.8	2.2	1.6	Budget	..	6.1	7.1	7.4	7.0	6.3
Private	..	20.7	15.1	13.8	15.0	13.8	Private	..	18.1	15.9	11.5	7.8	9.0
Gross domestic savings	21.1	22.0	12.6	12.0	11.6	14.3	Gross domestic savings	20.4	24.0	15.9	15.0	14.5	13.5
Budget	..	-1.3	-4.3	-5.6	-6.0	-4.2	Budget	..	2.0	-0.2	5.2	3.6	4.1
Private	..	23.3	16.9	17.6	17.6	18.5	Private	..	22.0	16.1	9.8	10.9	9.4
Foreign savings	7.6	1.3	3.6	3.6	5.5	1.1	Foreign savings	-2.1	0.2	7.1	4.0	0.3	1.8
Memorandum items:							*Memorandum items:*						
Government balance	..	-3.9	-5.3	-7.4	-8.2	-5.7	Government balance	..	-4.1	-7.3	-2.2	-3.4	-2.2
Private sector balance	..	2.6	1.7	3.8	2.6	4.6	Private sector balance	..	3.9	0.2	-1.8	3.1	0.4

Source: UN/ECE secretariat, based on national statistics.

Notwithstanding the substantial heterogeneity and variability of the saving-investment ratios, the saving-investment balances for the transition economies also suggest some similarities within groups of countries. Chart 4.3.2 portrays the dynamics of the (gross domestic) saving and (gross) investment ratios in two groups of transition economies, which are probably representative of two broad patterns of saving and investment behaviour during the past decade.

Domestic Savings in the Transition Economies 175

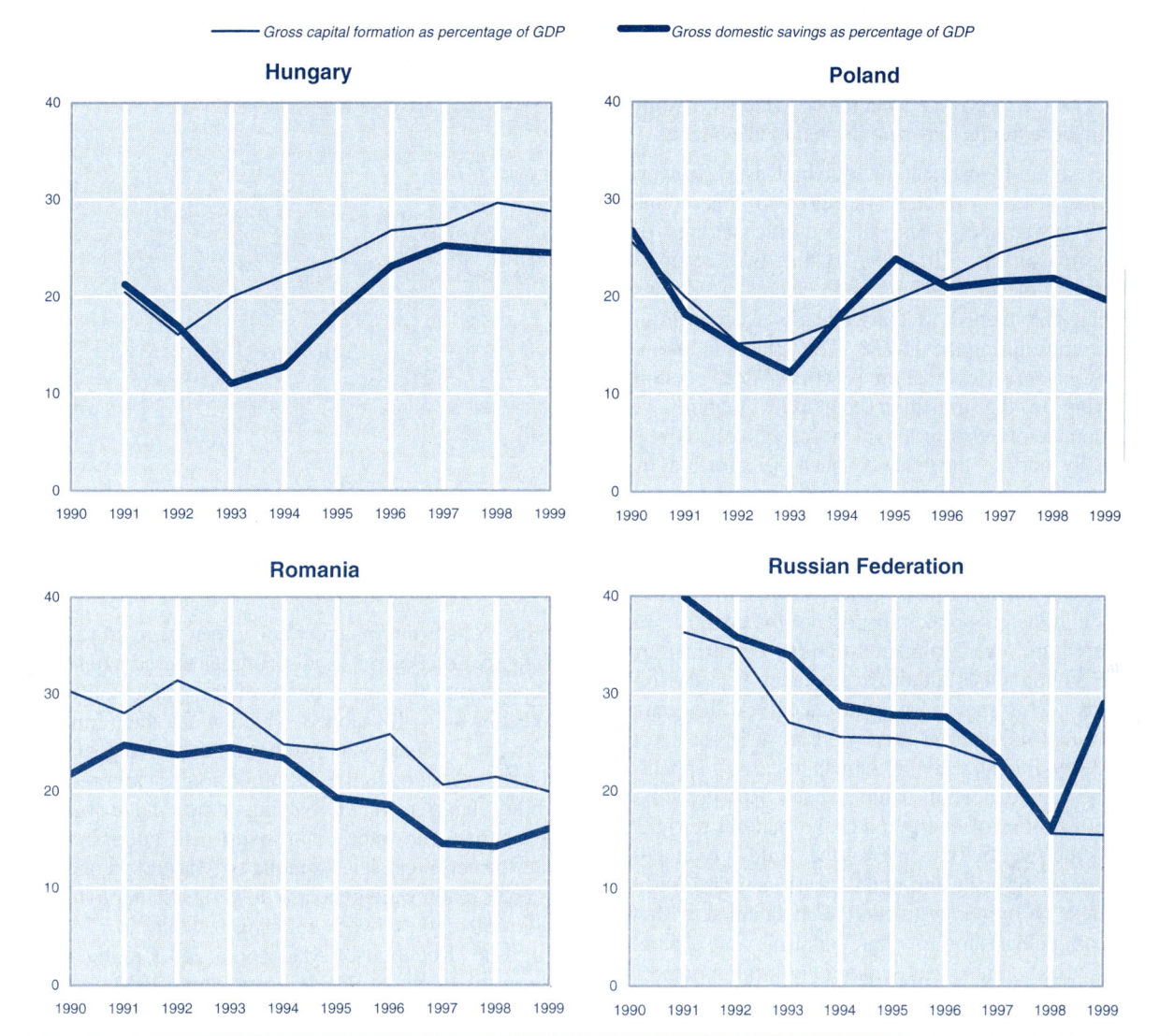

CHART 4.3.2

Saving and investment ratios in selected east European and CIS economies, 1990-1999
(Per cent)

Source: UN/ECE secretariat, based on national statistics.

The ratios for Hungary and Poland (chart 4.3.2) are probably typical of economies that have undergone a successful transformation in this period and their evolution falls into two distinctly different phases. In the initial phase, which corresponds to the period of transformational recession, there is a drop in the saving and investment ratios and this can be traced in all transition economies. While this was largely a consequence of the fall in real incomes (as consumption is much less elastic to changes in income than both savings and investment), it was also partly an adjustment from the abnormally high saving and investment ratios that characterized the centrally planned economies.[461]

In Hungary and Poland, this phase was followed by an upturn in the ratios around the mid-1990s, corresponding to the recovery and growth of output which is continuing in both countries. In both of them, the recovery in gross domestic investment has been stronger than in gross domestic savings, indicating that they have attracted foreign savings to support the rapid growth of domestic investment. In contrast, domestic saving ratios, after recovering somewhat, have stopped growing (in Hungary) or declined (in Poland), suggesting a relative shift in preferences towards present consumption.

---

[461] C. Denizer and H. Wolf, *The Savings Collapse During the Transition in Eastern Europe*, World Bank Working Papers Series, No. 2419 (Washington, D.C.), August 2000. Among the then centrally planned economies, Hungary was an exception with relatively lower saving and investment ratios.

The saving and investment ratios in Romania and Russia (the lower panel of chart 4.3.2) are probably symptomatic of countries that have experienced serious difficulties in the process of economic transformation. In both countries, the prevailing trend throughout the whole decade has been a decline in both savings and investment, a reflection of their prolonged transformational recessions.[462] But, given the experience of Hungary and Poland, when a recovery eventually occurs, a similar reversal in these trends may be expected to take place.

The saving-investment pattern in Russia, however, reveals one feature which is specific to this country, namely, a systematic excess of domestic savings over domestic investment. In most of the other transition economies domestic savings fell short of domestic investment, and there was consequently a net inflow of foreign savings during the decade. The latter is in line with the common-sense view that the process of deep economic restructuring in the transition economies requires very large amounts of resources which are not all available domestically and so the balance must be attracted from abroad.

The atypical pattern in Russia reflects the chronic outflow of capital from the country during the past decade and the combination of a general lack of investors' confidence in the economic prospects of the country[463] and a relatively high (even compared to other countries) gross domestic saving ratio, although the latter was declining until 1998. This may seem unusual, given the general decline in real incomes in Russia during the past decade. The abnormally high saving ratios, however, appear to reflect the abundance of natural rents (Russia being a major net exporter of energy and other natural resources) as well as the specific outcomes of the "wild" privatization which prevailed during the initial phase of transition. In the absence of proper regulation, and coupled with the widespread dismantling of state controls, a substantial share of these rents was unlawfully appropriated by profiteers and, due to the legally dubious nature of these profits, a large share of them ended up outside the Russian economy. Without this "excessive" component of gross domestic savings (which was concentrated in a handful of individuals), savings would probably have evolved in much the same way as in other transition economies with a similar output performance.

Although the saving-investment balances of the transition economies (tables 4.3.1 and 4.3.2) vary considerably, some of the general features outlined above can be traced in other countries as well. In particular, the saving-investment ratios in the rest of central Europe (the Czech Republic, Slovakia and Slovenia) as well as in the

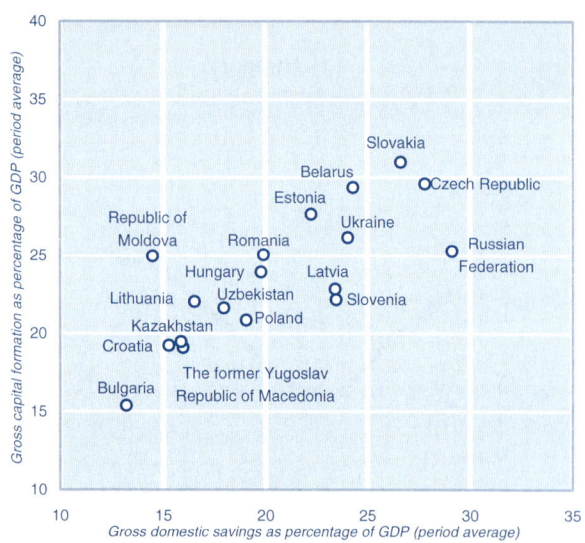

CHART 4.3.3

Gross domestic savings and gross investment in selected east European, Baltic and CIS economies, 1991-1999
(Per cent)

Source: UN/ECE secretariat, based on national statistics.

Baltic states are to a certain extent similar to those in Hungary and Poland: in all countries there were falls in the ratios during the initial phase of transition (these data are not shown in the tables) which were then followed by recovery. There has been some convergence in the investment ratios in this group of countries in recent years while changes in the saving ratios have been more divergent. The saving and investment ratios in Bulgaria, The former Yugoslav Republic of Macedonia and to some extent Croatia were generally lower, and although evolving differently (they were relatively stable in The former Yugoslav Republic of Macedonia and Croatia while the investment ratio in Bulgaria started rising after 1997), by 1999 they were comparable to those in Romania. The dynamics of the saving and investment ratios in most of the CIS countries (which in general are less advanced with market reforms than the central European transition economies) had some features in common with those in Russia and in the countries of south-east Europe.[464] Notably, the average gross domestic saving ratios in some of the CIS countries (Armenia, Azerbaijan, Georgia, Kyrgyzstan) have been much lower (in some years even negative) than those in other transition economies.

Despite the considerable variation across countries and over time in the individual saving and investment patterns, the data do suggest some empirical regularities. The pooled data shown in chart 4.3.3 indicate a strong positive correlation between the average gross saving and

---

[462] The down and upswings in the saving ratio in Russia in 1998-1999 probably reflect the distorting impact of the financial crisis of August 1998 on saving behaviour, as the crisis had deep and lasting economic repercussions, and probably can be regarded as outliers from the general trend.

[463] The strong economic recovery in Russia in 2000 has brought about some change in these ratios, in particular, an upturn in real investment. However, it remains to be seen whether this marks a reversal in the underlying trends.

[464] It should be noted that before the start of economic transformation, the Soviet Union had even higher saving and investment ratios than most of the other centrally planned economies. Thus in the successor states of the Soviet Union there was an even larger fall from this starting point during the initial phase of transition.

CHART 4.3.4

Private savings and fixed investment in selected east European, Baltic and CIS economies, 1995-1999
(Per cent)

Source: UN/ECE secretariat, based on national statistics.

gross investment ratios of individual countries between 1991 and 1999. This is in line with the conjecture (discussed in section 4.2) of the primordial role of domestic savings as a source for domestic investment.

The saving-investment balances of the transition economies also underscore the leading role of private savings as the main source of gross domestic savings: the private sector has systematically made a dominant net contribution to gross domestic savings while dis-saving is often a feature of government behaviour.[465] Private savings are positively correlated with fixed investment in the transition economies (chart 4.3.4) although, according to the available data, this relation is somewhat weaker than that between gross savings and gross investment.[466]

4.4 The determinants of private saving in the transition economies

The saving-investment balance is an accounting identity between groups of spending and financing items. It does not imply any specific causal relationships; moreover, the separate items that enter the balance are of a different economic nature and, accordingly, the underlying forces driving them may also vary. Because of this, the analysis of the determinants of saving is usually performed separately, and not necessarily in the context of the saving-investment balance, using specific methods and techniques. The main focus of the analysis that follows in this section is on the determinants of private saving.

The fact that private savings account for the dominant share of gross national savings suggests that ultimately they are a key factor affecting not only the levels of domestic investment but, following the discussion in the previous sections, long-run economic performance as well. The fundamental importance of private savings has long been acknowledged by economists and policy makers, who have focused attention on the main determinants of parsimonious behaviour. Understanding the motivation for saving (at the level of individuals and for the community as a whole) is not only of academic interest but is important in terms of its policy implications. Identifying the key determinants of saving may help policy makers to design policies to stimulate domestic savings and thus domestic investment.

The annual flow of national private savings (as documented in the previous section) reflects the aggregate outcome of all microlevel decisions concerning the allocation of current income to consumption and savings during a selected reference period (in this case, one year). To analyse the determinants of these flows requires an examination of both the motives for individual saving behaviour and the factors affecting the aggregation of the microlevel flows.

The main theoretical explanation of individual saving behaviour in the economic literature is based on the notion of the intertemporal allocation of resources: individual agents (households) decide what portion of their current income they should allocate for present consumption and what portion should be set aside for future consumption (saving). A number of theoretical models have been proposed to study the saving behaviour of individuals including those based on the optimization of an individual utility function over a life cycle.[467] During the life cycle, the patterns of individual saving behaviour may change (switching from saving to dis-saving), depending on the present level of income (precautionary savings being made in periods of above average income and drawing from past savings or borrowing in the opposite case). In addition, theoretical models suggest different types of saving behaviour depending on the availability of external finance: if the borrowing constraints are not binding, individuals may change their saving patterns in order to smooth consumption over time. Other assumptions or restrictions also affect the optimal saving patterns derived from theoretical models. For example, the system of taxation and the operation of the social security system, as well as changes in them, may influence the saving decisions of individuals and households. These facets of individual behaviour are not exhaustive but just outline some of the aspects that need to be addressed when analysing saving patterns at a microlevel.

---

[465] This also agrees with the empirical findings about saving patterns in other countries. B. Bosworth, *Saving and Investment in a Global Economy* (Washington, D.C., Brookings Institution, 1993).

[466] The available statistical data only allow a breakdown of savings and investment into "private sector" and "government" from 1995; hence the ratios shown in chart 4.3.4 are averaged over a much shorter period than those shown in chart 4.3.3.

[467] For a discussion see S. Edwards, op. cit.

At the microlevel it is not only households but also businesses that take decisions about saving. While some of the factors that affect the saving decisions of firms may be common to households, there are also firm-specific incentives to save or dis-save. Among them are the depth of the financial system and the access to various financial instruments; the access to resources from abroad (foreign savings); the prevailing opportunity costs of investing in various instruments; and so on. These are all factors that in principle should be taken into account when analysing the determinants of national private savings.

When savings are analysed at the macrolevel, the observable data on national private savings reflect the aggregate outcome of the varying behaviour of numerous individuals and households. When accounting for this economy-wide dimension, a number of additional factors need to be taken into consideration. For example, the aggregate saving pattern will be affected by demographic factors, such as the age structure of the population, and by the situation on the labour market. In addition, the structure of incomes in the economy, the distribution of wealth, the growth of incomes as well as other related factors are also important.

The literature on the determinants of saving in the transition economies is not very abundant, partly due to the unavailability (until recently) of adequate data for this type of analysis.[468] Despite their tentative nature and possible imperfections, the newly compiled saving-investment balances for the transition economies discussed in section 4.3 do provide an empirical basis for extending research in this area.

Given the wide range of factors that may affect saving behaviour, the technique most widely used in empirical research on the determinants of saving has been regression analysis. The selected reduced-form model takes into account (to the extent possible, given the availability of data) the considerations outlined at the beginning of this section.[469]

The independent variable in the model is private savings defined as a percentage of GDP (as reported in tables 4.3.1 and 4.3.2). The set of independent variables includes the following:

- Current account balance (as a percentage of GDP). When this is negative, it denotes the net amount of foreign savings which have been attracted, in addition to domestic savings. The sign of the estimated coefficient is interpreted in terms of the complementarity of the two flows: a positive sign (a negative correlation between the two flows) suggests substitutability between the two flows (with foreign savings potentially crowding out domestic), while a negative sign (a positive correlation between the two flows) would imply complementarity of the two (with foreign savings adding to domestic savings).

- *Government savings* (as a percentage of GDP – tables 4.3.1 and 4.3.2). The sign and the value of the estimated coefficient are also interpreted in terms of the complementarity/substitutability of the two flows. In principle a negative sign is expected, implying that changes in government savings are partly offset by opposite changes in private savings. The closer the estimated coefficient is to -1, the greater the degree of substitutability between private and public savings.

- *Social security expenditure* (as a percentage of GDP). This variable is a proxy for the generosity of the social security system. In principle, theory suggests a negative sign (substitutability of the two flows) because individuals may tend to save less if they expect more generous social security benefits.

- *Level of per capita GDP*.[470] This variable aims to capture the impact of the absolute level of income on saving behaviour. It is expected that the higher the level of per capita income, the greater the share of income that will be allocated to savings (positive coefficient).

- *Rate of growth of per capita income*. Different theoretical models imply different directions in this relationship, so that the sign of the coefficient is basically an empirical issue. Two different variables have been selected for this purpose: the rate of change of GDP per capita (as reported in the national statistics) and the rate of change of real gross consumer wages (nominal wages deflated by the CPI).

- *Level of monetization* (the share of broad money in GDP). This variable aims to capture the development of the financial system in the country and as such it should have a positive effect on savings (the expected sign of the coefficient is positive).[471]

- *Real interest rate*. Since a change in real interest rates may act either as an incentive or as a disincentive to save, the sign of the coefficient is again an empirical issue.

- *Rate of change of the CPI*. In the model this reflects macroeconomic stability and the expected sign is negative, macroeconomic instability leading to dis-saving.

---

[468] Among the relatively few empirical works in this area are two studies conducted at the World Bank: C. Denizer and H. Wolf, op. cit. and C. Denizer, H. Wolf and Y. Ying, *Household Savings in Transition Economies*, World Bank Working Papers Series, No. 2299 (Washington, D.C.), March 2000. The first of these studies analyses the determinants of saving during the initial period of transition (until 1995, using IMF estimates of savings) while the second is devoted to the more narrow aspect of household saving behaviour.

[469] The specification largely builds on the model suggested in S. Edwards, op. cit.

[470] As these data have to be comparable among countries in the estimations, per capita GDP has been taken at purchasing power parities (PPPs) and expressed in 1990 dollars. These estimates were based on UN/ECE, *International Comparisons of Gross Domestic Product in Europe, 1996* (United Nations publication, Sales No. E.99.II.E.13).

[471] This variable may also reflect borrowing constraints faced by consumers, which will reduce their ability to smooth consumption through borrowing (and will hence affect their saving behaviour). S. Zeldes, "Consumption and liquidity constraints: an empirical investigation", *Journal of Political Economy*, Vol. 97, No. 2, April 1989, pp. 305-346. In this case the expected sign will be negative. Such an interpretation, however, by itself implies the existence of a relatively developed financial system, which is not the case in most transition economies.

TABLE 4.4.1

The main determinants of private savings in eastern Europe, the Baltic states and the CIS, 1995-1998: descriptive statistics

Variable	Dimension	Eastern Europe, Baltic states and CIS		Eastern Europe and Baltic states		CIS countries	
		Unweighted average	Standard deviation	Unweighted average	Standard deviation	Unweighted average	Standard deviation
Private savings	Per cent of GDP	16.5	7.0	18.4	5.2	14.2	8.3
Current account balance	Per cent of GDP	-7.1	7.2	-5.2	4.3	-9.5	9.1
Government savings	Per cent of GDP	0.0	4.0	1.2	3.3	-1.5	4.2
Social security spending	Per cent of GDP	10.5	4.1	12.2	4.0	8.5	3.2
GDP per capita (at PPPs, international comparisons)	Thousand dollars [a]	5.0	2.8	6.7	2.5	2.9	1.4
Rate of growth of GDP per capita (national statistics)	Per cent	2.2	5.6	3.5	4.4	0.6	6.5
Rate of growth of real gross consumer wages	Per cent	7.3	17.2	3.4	9.2	12.0	22.7
Level of monetization (broad money)	Per cent of GDP	24.2	16.9	34.2	17.0	12.1	4.2
Ex-post real interest rate on short-term deposits	Per cent	-6.6	20.8	-3.3	14.6	-10.6	26.1
Annual rate of change of CPI	Per cent	59.9	147.7	43.3	155.8	79.7	136.6
Annual rate of change of the terms of trade ratio	Per cent	-0.5	11.4	-3.0	4.3	2.4	15.8
Age dependency ratio (non-working age population in proportion to working age population)	Per cent	52.4	8.2	47.9	2.1	57.7	9.5

Source: UN/ECE secretariat calculations, based on national statistics (ECE Common Database) and IMF data (*IMF Staff Country Reports*, various issues).

Note: The group "eastern Europe and the Baltic states" includes: Bulgaria, Croatia, Czech Republic, Hungary, Poland, Romania, Slovakia, Slovenia, The former Yugoslav Republic of Macedonia, Estonia, Latvia and Lithuania; the "CIS countries" include Armenia, Azerbaijan, Belarus, Georgia, Kazakhstan, Kyrgyzstan, the Republic of Moldova, the Russian Federation, Ukraine and Uzbekistan. The country coverage has been exclusively determined by the availability of statistical data.

[a] 1990 prices.

- *Rate of change in the terms of trade.*[472] This variable captures the gains from favourable changes in international prices (a positive change is equivalent to a windfall gain in resources) and as such the expected sign is positive.

- *Age dependency ratio* (defined as the proportion of the non-working age population to the working age population). The models of saving behaviour based on the lifetime cycle imply that individuals save more during their productive age and vice versa; hence the expected sign of the coefficient is negative.

Some general statistics (means and standard deviations) for the variables used in the regression analysis are shown in table 4.4.1.[473] As noted in section 4.3, while there is substantial cross-country variability in the saving-investment patterns, there are also groups of countries that reveal similar patterns or share common features. Different country sets reveal some notable divergence in the patterns prevailing in eastern Europe and the Baltic region, on the one hand, and in the CIS, on the other.[474] The corresponding statistics for the two subsets of variables are also given in table 4.4.1.[475]

These general statistics highlight some of the differences between these two groups of countries in terms of the average levels of the main variables. Thus during the period 1995-1998, "eastern Europe" on average was characterized by higher relative levels of private savings, government savings, social security spending and monetization but relatively smaller current account deficits. The absolute levels of GDP per capita in eastern Europe and the Baltic states were higher than those in the CIS and were growing faster while average CPI inflation and age dependency were lower.[476] The average rate of change in the terms of trade had different signs for the two groups, while the average real interest rate was negative in both cases but was smaller in absolute terms in eastern Europe and the Baltic states.

The statistical association between some of the regressors and the dependent variable (the private saving ratio) for the ECE transition economies in 1995-1998 is illustrated in charts 4.4.1, 4.4.2 and 4.4.3. Chart 4.4.1 indicates a positive correlation between the current account balance and private savings (that is, a negative correlation between the net inflow of foreign savings and the level of domestic private savings). This suggests that foreign savings tended to "crowd out" domestic savings

---

[472] In the actual estimation the terms of trade variable was approximated by the ratio PPI/CPI (the "domestic terms of trade").

[473] The period selected for the estimation (1995-1998) was determined by the availability of data.

[474] Other groupings of countries were also tested but they produced less significant differences.

[475] Throughout this paper (including the results shown in tables 4.4.1 and 4.4.2) the group "eastern Europe and the Baltic states" includes Bulgaria, Croatia, Czech Republic, Hungary, Poland, Romania, Slovakia, Slovenia, The former Yugoslav Republic of Macedonia, Estonia, Latvia

and Lithuania; the "CIS countries" include Armenia, Azerbaijan, Belarus, Georgia, Kazakhstan, Kyrgyzstan, the Republic of Moldova, the Russian Federation, Ukraine and Uzbekistan; while the "ECE transition economies" include all of the above. The country coverage has been exclusively determined by the availability of statistical data.

[476] The reported average rate of change in the CPI for eastern Europe and the Baltic states (43.3 per cent) may appear unusually high for the period 1995-1998 when there was notable disinflation in most of these countries, but the high average is almost exclusively due to the hyperinflationary episode in Bulgaria (when the annual inflation rate in 1997 averaged more than 1000 per cent).

CHART 4.4.1

Current account balance and private savings in selected east European, Baltic and CIS economies, 1995-1998
(Period averages, per cent)

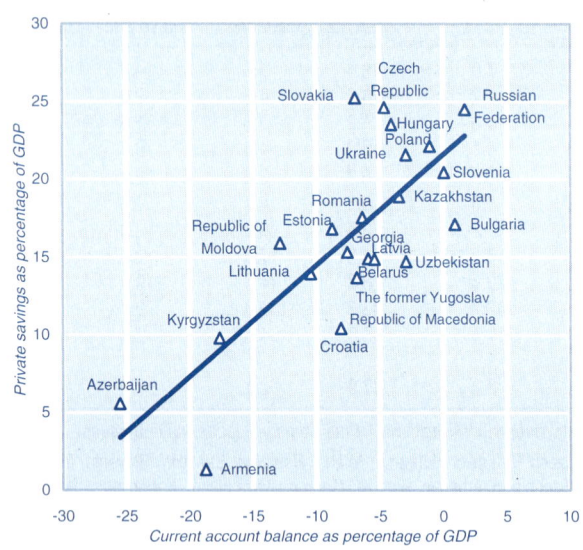

Source: UN/ECE secretariat, based on national statistics.

CHART 4.4.3

Monetization and private savings in selected east European, Baltic and CIS economies, 1995-1998
(Period averages, per cent)

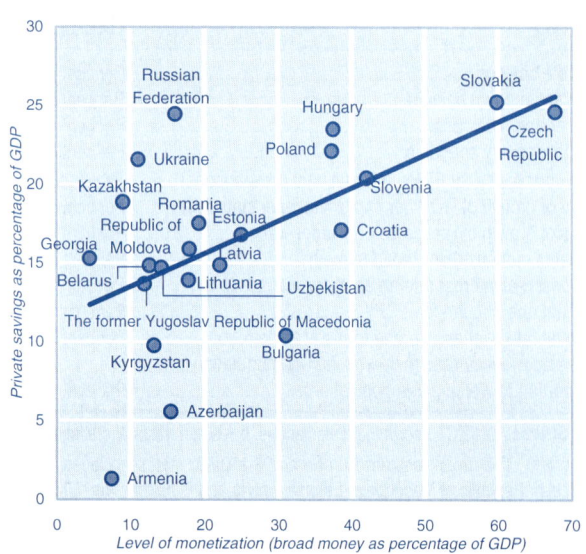

Source: UN/ECE secretariat, based on national statistics.

CHART 4.4.2

GDP per capita and private savings in selected east European, Baltic and CIS economies, 1995-1998
(Period averages, thousand dollars per capita, per cent)

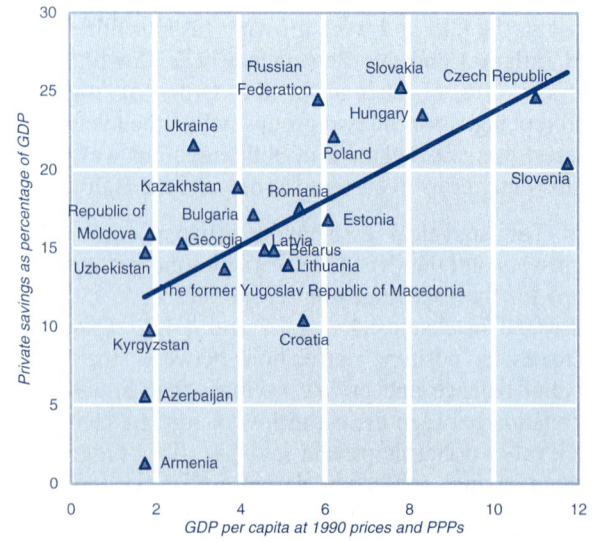

Source: UN/ECE secretariat, based on national statistics.

and in this sense the two were largely substitutable. Chart 4.4.2 points to a positive correlation between the level of per capita GDP and the intensity of private domestic savings, that is, countries with relatively higher per capita income tended to allocate a relatively higher share of their income for future consumption.

Chart 4.4.3 indicates that private savings in the transition economies were positively associated with the depth of the financial system (as approximated by the degree of monetization), that is, a more developed financial system tends to facilitate private savings. Moreover, a visual inspection of chart 4.4.3 confirms that the level of monetization of the economy is a realistic proxy for financial development and reform in the transition economies. Indeed, the transition economies that have made the most progress in reforming their financial systems (in terms of rehabilitation and privatization of the banking system, establishing and enforcing prudential banking regulations, introducing modern financial services and banking products, establishing functioning capital markets, etc.) are also among those with the highest monetization ratios; they are also among those that have mobilized a larger share of private domestic savings in recent years.

The actual results of the regression analysis (panel estimates using ordinary least squares for the groupings "eastern Europe and the Baltic states", "CIS countries" and "ECE transition economies") are shown in table 4.4.2. In general the model appears to be quite successful in explaining the variation in the dependent variable (the values of R-squared are quite high for panel estimates), while most of the estimated coefficients have the expected sign. These results confirm the above observations based on the visual inspection of the statistical relationships.

On average (judging from the results for the full sample of countries), the estimates imply that foreign savings attracted by the transition economies have been

TABLE 4.4.2

Regression analysis of the determinants of private savings in eastern Europe, the Baltic states and the CIS, 1995-1998: ordinary least squares estimations on panel data

(Dependent variable, private savings)

Independent variables	Eastern Europe, Baltic states and CIS		Eastern Europe and Baltic states		CIS countries	
Number of observations:	88	88	48	48	40	40
Current account balance	0.464 (6.34)	0.473 (6.49)	0.091 (.88)	0.082 (.79)	0.572 (5.40)	0.560 (5.73)
Government savings	-0.606 (-4.61)	-0.679 (-5.20)	-0.599 (-3.60)	-0.534 (-3.31)	-0.955 (-4.67)	-0.975 (-5.29)
Social security spending	0.309 (2.33)	0.337 (2.49)	0.336 (2.81)	0.369 (3.26)	0.373 (1.29)	0.376 (1.37)
GDP per capita (at PPPs, international comparisons)	1.224 (4.35)	1.188 (4.25)	0.669 (2.99)	0.650 (2.87)	1.926 (3.28)	1.963 (3.73)
Rate of growth of GDP per capita (national statistics)	-0.086 (-.91)		0.092 (.75)		0.079 (.46)	
Rate of growth of real gross consumer wages		0.024 (.71)		0.010 (.17)		0.049 (1.23)
Level of monetization (broad money)	0.058 (1.32)	0.063 (1.44)	0.137 (4.35)	0.139 (4.38)	0.427 (1.85)	0.450 (2.17)
Ex-post real interest rate on short-term deposits	-0.073 (-2.07)	-0.079 (-2.23)	-0.195 (-1.95)	-0.102 (-1.84)	-0.036 (-.72)	-0.052 (-1.03)
Annual rate of change of CPI	-0.008 (-1.53)	-0.006 (-1.30)	-0.008 (-1.52)	-0.008 (-1.55)	0.007 (.68)	0.004 (.45)
Annual rate of change of the terms of trade ratio	0.025 (.62)	0.011 (.24)	0.159 (1.60)	0.180 (1.88)	0.084 (1.63)	0.050 (.87)
Age dependency ratio (non-working age population in proportion to working age population)	0.174 (5.75)	0.162 (4.92)	0.133 (3.65)	0.133 (3.53)	0.051 (.89)	0.034 (.63)
Adjusted R-squared	0.688	0.686	0.786	0.783	0.740	0.751

Source: UN/ECE secretariat calculations, based on national statistics (ECE Common Database) and IMF data (*IMF Staff Country Reports*, various issues).

Note: t-statistics in parentheses. For the definition of country groups see the note to table 4.4.1.

substituting for rather than complementing domestic savings (positive and statistically significant coefficient). Private savings in the transition economies do tend to move in the opposite direction to government savings, partly offsetting changes in the latter (negative and statistically significant coefficient). The results support the notion that countries with higher per capita incomes tend to save relatively more than countries with lower income levels (positive and statistically significant coefficient). The estimated coefficients of the monetization, inflation and terms of trade variables all have the expected signs but are not statistically significant. Of the variables whose directions of impact are indeterminate, the real interest rate has a statistically significant and negative coefficient,[477] while the two variables reflecting income growth have coefficients with opposite signs but neither is statistically significant.

Two of the estimated coefficients (both of which are statistically significant) systematically have signs opposite to that expected: those for the social security and the age dependency variables. The emergence of a positive sign in the first case may reflect the radical overhaul in the social security system in many of the transition economies: due to the on-going reforms, the system is not stable enough to generate long-run expectations, and the actual social security benefits are probably regarded by individuals merely as complements to other income. A similar instability probably affects saving patterns over the life cycle and is reflected in the coefficient of the age dependency variable.

While there are no major dissimilarities between the regression results for the groupings "eastern Europe and the Baltic states" and "CIS countries", the separate estimates reveal some intriguing nuances in the patterns of saving in the two groups of transition economies. The most important differences are in the estimated coefficients on the current account balance, government savings, GDP per capita and monetization variables. The CIS coefficient for the current account variable is positive, large and statistically highly significant, implying the same interpretation as outlined above. The coefficient for eastern Europe and the Baltic states is also positive but much smaller in value and statistically non-significant, implying much weaker evidence of crowding out of private savings by foreign savings. The coefficient of the government savings variable in the CIS is very close to -1 (which suggests an almost complete offsetting of government savings by private dis-saving), while the coefficient of eastern Europe and the Baltic states is around -0.5). This suggests that total gross domestic savings in the CIS is largely insensitive to the saving stance of the

---

[477] This result, however, may also reflect distortions in saving behaviour caused by the endemic incidence of negative real interest rates in the transition economies.

government, which is not the case in eastern Europe and the Baltic states. The coefficients of the per capita income and monetization variables are both greater in absolute value for the CIS than for eastern Europe and the Baltic states, suggesting that private savings in the CIS are more sensitive to changes in these variables than in eastern Europe and the Baltic states. Hence, *ceteris paribus*, any further catching up in these variables (considering the fact that average per capita income levels and monetization in the CIS are below those in eastern Europe and the Baltic states) might be expected to produce an even faster rate of catching up in private savings. There is also a difference in the signs of the coefficient on the inflation variable but in the CIS case it is not statistically significant.

4.5 Policy implications and conclusions

Despite the existence of ambiguities and unsettled issues, both theoretical and empirical research in the main seems to support the long-held common-sense views that: 1) capital accumulation is an engine of economic growth, and 2) increased domestic savings lead to higher levels of investment and thus contribute to long-run growth. Although the conventional prescription, namely that economies' policies should encourage higher domestic savings in order to achieve higher rates of long-run growth, may not be universally valid nor always working in one direction, more often than not this does appear to fit the experience of many fast-growing economies.

Both theory and evidence are more ambiguous as to the assessment of the actual financing needs of developing or transition economies and to the actual mechanisms which are best suited to channel external financial assistance. Common sense suggests that if domestic savings and investment are low, then one approach to accelerating development would be to complement domestic resources with foreign savings, possibly through international financial assistance programmes. Indeed, this has been the implied logic of many developmental assistance programmes for several decades. There are, however, a number of inherent problems and unresolved issues in this approach. Reliable analytical tools to assess precisely the amount of external financing needs do not exist. The models that have been used for this purpose have proved to be inadequate and the *ex-post* performance of recipient countries has not validated either the prescriptions of the models or the amounts of resources that have been allocated for assistance. There may be numerous practical impediments, arising from the institutional environment and the actual absorptive capacity of the economy, to channelling external assistance into productive investment; if these are not eliminated, the outcome may be counterproductive. The main conclusion is that there are no "easy fixes" to the deep developmental problems that many of the economies in transition are facing. A comprehensive, long-term policy approach to these problems is needed, in which external assistance should be an integral component.

Judging from past experience, domestic savings (and in the first place private savings) have played the leading role as a source of investment and growth in most industrialized counties. Attracting external resources has been important for development and growth but for this to happen on a massive scale they usually consist of capital inflows attracted by gainful investment opportunities. Without disregarding the importance of external assistance, it seems more likely that the transition economies will follow this traditional path. Moreover, while external assistance may imply external policy conditionality, when dealing with private savings and improvements in the investment climate, domestic policy becomes endogenous, that is, policy can and does affect saving and investment behaviour. Hence, by applying appropriate public policies, it may be possible to generate and attract more resources for financing the process of economic transformation in the transition economies.

The empirical analysis of the determinants of private savings reported in this chapter reveals some of the important factors that have affected saving behaviour in these economies in recent years and allows some general conclusions to be drawn. The actual level of aggregate savings reflects the simultaneous impact of numerous factors that affect individual saving behaviour; some of these are subject to direct policy control, others can be indirectly affected by policy, and some may be policy neutral, at least in the short run (such as demographic factors). Among the policy-sensitive factors that have exerted a statistically significant effect (and can be expected to continue to do so) on the level of private savings in the transition economies, are the depth and level of development of the financial system, the level of government savings and the level of social security spending. The impact of monetary policy (in particular interest rate policy) has been more ambiguous. Among the statistically significant factors that may be indirectly influenced by policy are the size of the current account balance, the rate of inflation and the level of per capita income.

The estimated regression model highlights the importance of the level of per capita incomes and of the depth of the financial system as major determinants of private saving. The robust finding of a strong positive correlation between financial depth and the intensity of private saving has important policy implications in terms of prioritizing financial reforms in the transition economies. This conclusion is especially relevant for the CIS countries where there is a greater sensitivity of private savings to the depth of the financial system: a catching up in terms of financial deepening is likely to stimulate a more rapid growth in private savings.

Foreign capital that has been attracted to the transition economies in recent years has tended to crowd out domestic savings; this was especially the case in the CIS countries but less so in the countries of eastern Europe and the Baltic region. In turn, government savings in the CIS countries tended to be almost fully offset by private savings and vice versa, while this occurred only on a limited scale in the other transition economies. A high rate of substitutability between these flows may reduce the efficiency of policies aimed at promoting one particular type of savings. The model explored in this chapter does not identify the actual causes of substitutability, and further research will be needed in order to define them. However, one relevant conclusion is that policy needs to tackle first the issue of substitutability between different forms of savings, before attempting to address the level of aggregate domestic savings as such.

Savings and investment are not an unconditional panacea for development and growth. They only perform the role of engine in a healthy macroeconomic environment and in the framework of a coherent and consistent long-term policy. Only under these circumstances can a virtuous circle of "high savings – high investment – high growth" become a reality. The first signs of something emerging along these lines can be observed in recent years in some of the more advanced transition economies. While much more effort will be needed to sustain the rate of growth, this at least indicates that success is achievable and that policy efforts in this direction will be rewarded.

CHAPTER 5

ECONOMIC GROWTH AND FOREIGN DIRECT INVESTMENT IN THE TRANSITION ECONOMIES

Foreign direct investment (FDI) has long been seen – and strongly recommended – as a crucial instrument in the process of transforming the former centrally planned economies of eastern Europe and the former Soviet Union into vibrant market systems. This chapter looks at the actual performance of FDI in promoting economic growth and restructuring in the transition economies since 1990. The basic conclusion is that the record is a very mixed one and that the wider benefits of FDI are contingent on the domestic economic and institutional environment – there is nothing automatic about them. FDI in the transition economies since 1990 has largely flowed to just a few central European countries, which are also the leading candidates for EU membership. These have indeed benefited from significant FDI financing of the balance of payments, and enterprises with foreign investment, not surprisingly, have had high rates of growth of output, productivity and exports. However, the expected spillover benefits to purely domestic enterprises – which represent the broader advantages of FDI for economic development – are found to be few and far between, and indeed often appear to have been negative rather than positive. In the absence of positive spillovers – and a fortiori in the presence of negative ones – the restructuring and development of the domestic enterprise sector may be inhibited, thereby reinforcing fears that an "enclave" economy might be emerging where a technologically advanced FDI sector pulls ahead but has little if any positive impact on the rest of the economy. The chapter ends with a discussion of how national policy measures might be designed to prevent such an outcome, inter alia, by strengthening national innovation systems, improving the absorptive or adaptive capabilities of local enterprises, and by adopting a more strategic approach to FDI in order to strengthen its development impact.

5.1 Introduction: theoretical aspects of FDI and economic growth

Foreign direct investment is often seen as an important catalyst for the economic transformation of the ECE transition economies. Its importance is seen to be not only in providing finance for the acquisition of new plants and equipment, but also in the transfer of technology and organizational forms from relatively more technologically advanced economies. FDI can also result in positive "spillovers" to the local economy through linkages with local suppliers, competition, imitation and training. It can also result, however, in negative spillovers if it forces domestic enterprises to close down because they cannot obtain the necessary financing for upgrading their technology. Moreover, it is possible that spillovers to the rest of the economy may not occur at all if there are institutional obstacles or deficiencies in the absorptive capacity of domestic enterprises.

As finance, FDI represents an inflow of foreign resources that can raise domestic savings rates in the recipient countries. This finance can include purchases by the foreign direct investor of equity capital (including additional paid up capital) in the foreign investment enterprise (FIE), reinvestment of profits by the FIE and loans to the FIE from the parent firm. The FIE may also borrow abroad on its own account (although such funds are not classified as FDI). If the FIE uses these funds to build a new facility or upgrade an existing one, domestic fixed investment increases. Normally this involves a mix of domestic and imported inputs, especially foreign machinery and equipment. However, FDI also includes the acquisition of existing plants and equipment, in which case there is a transfer of title to existing assets rather than the creation of new ones. In the 1990s, most of these inflows were absorbed into the state budget since a large majority of the acquisitions involved the purchase of state assets. Also the profits of FIEs and funds from abroad may be placed in purely financial investments. In these cases, FDI does not have a direct impact on real investment, although an acquisition can result in the transfer of new technology and organizational forms over time.

The remainder of this section reviews the theoretical links between FDI and economic transformation. The determinants of FDI and the development of FDI in the transition economies are discussed in sections 5.2 and

5.3, respectively. Some economic consequences of FDI inflows, including their impact on the balance of payments and GDP growth, are discussed in sections 5.4 and 5.5. FDI as a channel of technology transfer and diffusion in the transition economies is explored further in sections 5.6 and 5.7. Conclusions and policy recommendations are made in section 5.8. An annex contains a discussion of the methodology for estimating technology transfer and spillovers.

(i) The role of transnational corporations (TNCs) in facilitating technological and organizational change

Technical change and technological learning are essential for the economic transformation of eastern Europe and the CIS. Since most research and development (R&D) takes place in TNCs located in the most advanced economies, these global enterprises can play an important role in transferring technology. The environment of the host country is also important for the diffusion of this technology to the local economy. These spillovers, as they are often called in growth theory, can occur directly through linkages with the local economy, through the labour market or through competitive pressure. But they can be negative if the FIE "crowds out" local enterprises through strong competitive pressures.

TNCs transfer technology in two ways: (1) directly, or internally, to FIEs under their ownership and control; and (2) indirectly, or externally, to other firms in the host economy. They can also have *direct* and *indirect* positive impacts on the diffusion of technology, irrespective of their ownership and control.[478] A TNC can encourage technical change and technological learning *directly* through the transfer of new technology and organizational skills to one of its affiliates (FIE). The absorptive capacity (knowledge, skills and experience) of the FIE will then determine the pace of technological accumulation within the enterprise. These direct effects can appear as changes in productivity, industrial structure, R&D expenditure and the composition of exports. At the same time the presence of TNCs in the host economy can increase the rate of technical change and technological learning *indirectly* through technology spillovers from their FIEs to local or domestically owned enterprises (DEs). Spillovers can occur as a consequence of a TNC upgrading the technology of its affiliates (FIEs) to a level that is typically better than in the rest of the host economy. The innovation system and social capabilities of the host economy, together with the absorptive capacity of other enterprises in the host economy, will then determine the pace of technological progress in the economy as a whole.

Technology spillovers can occur between firms that are vertically integrated with the TNC (interindustry spillovers) or in direct competition with it (intra-industry spillovers). They can increase technical change and technological learning in at least four ways.[479] First, *competition* with the foreign affiliate can increase intra-industry spillovers by stimulating technical change and technological learning. Greater competitive pressure faced by local firms induces them to introduce new products to defend their market share and adopt new management methods to increase productivity. This kind of spillover is most important in industries with relatively low actual and potential competition and high barriers to entry. Second, *cooperation* between FIEs and upstream suppliers and downstream customers increases technological spillovers. To improve the quality standards of their suppliers, TNCs often provide resources to improve the technological capabilities of both vertically and horizontally linked firms. Third, *human capital* can spill over from FIEs to other enterprises as skilled labour moves between employers. These spillovers are especially important for enterprises that lack the technological capabilities and managerial skills to compete in world markets. Finally, the proximity of local firms to FIEs can sometimes lead to *demonstration* or *imitation* spillovers. When FIEs introduce new products, processes and organizational forms, they provide a demonstration of increased efficiency to other local enterprises. Local enterprises may also imitate FIEs through reverse engineering, personal contact and industrial espionage. In addition, a concentration of related industrial activities may also encourage the formation of industrial clusters, which further encourage FDI and local spillovers.

Not all TNC activity leads to technology transfer and positive spillovers.[480] TNCs can have a negative impact on the direct transfer of technology to the FIE and reduce the spillovers from FDI in the host economy in several ways. They can provide their affiliates with too few, or the wrong kind of technological capabilities, or even limit access to the technology of the parent company. This type of behaviour may restrict the production of its affiliate to low-value activities and can also reduce the scope for technical change and technological learning within the affiliate. Even if the TNC transfers new technology to its affiliate, it can reduce the scope for technology spillovers by limiting downstream producers to low value added activities or eliminate them altogether by relying on foreign suppliers (including itself) for higher value added

---

[478] For a similar discussion, see UNCTAD, *World Investment Report 1992: Transnational Corporations as Engines of Growth* (United Nations publication, Sales No. E.92.II.A.24), pp. 141-156.

[479] For a similar classification, see A. Kokko, *Foreign Direct Investment, Host Country Characteristics and Spillovers* (Stockholm, Stockholm School of Economics, 1992), and T. Perez, *Multinational Enterprises and Technological Spillovers* (Amsterdam, Harwood Academic Publishers, 1998), pp. 24-27.

[480] See, for example, J. Dunning, "Re-evaluating the benefits of foreign direct investment", *Transnational Corporations*, Vol. 3, No. 1, 1994, pp. 23-51, and P. Bardham, "The contributions of endogenous growth theory to the analysis of development problems: an assessment", in F. Coricelli, M. di Matteo and F. Hahn (eds.), *New Theories in Growth and Development* (London, Macmillan, 1998). Dunning argues that TNCs can limit the access of affiliates to certain markets, the range of products they produce, the kinds of technology they adopt, the R&D activity they undertake and their pattern of networking with local enterprises. They can also reduce competition and taxes paid in the host country through market domination and transfer pricing. Bardham also suggests that TNCs can restrict domestic production when they set up affiliates with the main purpose of protecting existing property rights and taking out patents in the host country.

intermediate products. In some cases they can even eliminate competition by "crowding out" local producers. They may also limit exports to competitors and confine production to the needs of the TNC. This behaviour not only limits the scope for technology spillovers, but it may also lead to a decline in the overall growth rate of the host economy by reducing competition and worsening the balance of payments.

Technology spillovers from TNCs tend to occur more frequently when the social capabilities of the host country and the absorptive capacity of the firms in the economy are high. While relatively backward countries have a certain scope for catching up, it is often difficult for the country to build the necessary social capabilities and absorptive capacities that allow firms to take advantage of the technology spillovers that are potentially available to the economy. Countries (and firms) without the capability to assimilate new technology tend to attract mainly market-seeking or resource-seeking foreign investment, while countries with this capability tend to attract more efficiency-seeking and asset-seeking foreign investment.[481] Closing the technology gap will be difficult without the relevant capabilities. As a result, there appears to be a certain threshold of development that countries must cross before the potential for technological spillovers can be realized.[482]

It is also useful to distinguish the broad category of productivity spillovers from technological spillovers. Often both happen together since industrial and corporate restructuring are connected to the competitive environment. Technology spillovers occur when TNCs improve the technology of their affiliates and this in turn diffuses to other firms in the host economy. They tend to occur more frequently in countries with relatively high levels of "social capabilities" (e.g. education levels, technological capabilities, good legal systems, etc.). In contrast, productivity spillovers can occur without any transfer of technology. For example, a TNC can create competitive pressures that force less efficient firms to close, thus increasing the average productivity of the industry in the host economy.

(ii) The role of FDI in economic growth: theoretical and empirical considerations

Numerous empirical studies at the firm, industry and economy-wide levels confirm that technical change and technological learning are important determinants of economic growth.[483] TNCs are responsible for much of this technological accumulation, yet growth theory rarely acknowledges the important role that these organizations play. In neo-classical analysis, FDI does not influence the long-run growth rate, but only the level of income. An exogenous increase in FDI would increase the amount of capital (and output) per person, but this would only be temporary, as diminishing returns (on the marginal product of capital) would impose a limit to this growth. FDI can influence the long-run growth rate only through technological progress or growth of the labour force, which are both considered exogenous.

If FDI is not only finance but also a bundle of fixed assets, knowledge (codified and tacit) and technology, then it can be expected to generate growth endogenously. According to recent endogenous growth theory, FDI influences growth via variables such as R&D and education (or human capital).[484] Even if diminishing returns prevail inside the enterprise, various externalities (outside the enterprise) can provide the necessary positive feedback to sustain growth in the long run. TNCs create such positive externalities for the local economy when they transfer new technology and organizational forms directly to its affiliate. They can also create them indirectly through subcontracting, joint ventures and strategic alliances, technology licensing, imports of capital goods and migration. Through technology transfer and technology spillovers, these growth models suggest that FDI can speed up the development of new intermediate product varieties (the horizontally differentiated inputs model), raise product quality (the quality ladder model), facilitate international collaboration on R&D, and introduce new forms of human capital.[485] By providing firms in relatively backward countries with greater access to finance and a wider range of intermediate products, FDI can increase

---

[481] J. Dunning, loc. cit.

[482] A model of catching up by Verspagen shows why countries with a high learning capacity and/or small productivity gap are likely to catch up, while others will tend to fall further behind. Crossing this threshold requires improving the human capital in the country as well as its "national innovation system". B. Verspagen, "A new empirical approach to catching up or falling behind", *Structural Change and Economic Dynamics*, Vol. 2, 1991, pp. 359-380. For a discussion of this threshold from the point of view of TNCs, see A. Kokko, op. cit.

[483] J. Temple, "The new growth evidence", *Journal of Economic Literature*, Vol. 37, No. 1, March 1999, pp. 112-156, and S. Durlauf and D. Quah, "The new empirics of economic growth", in J. Taylor and M. Woodford (eds.), *Handbook of Macroeconomics* (Amsterdam, Elsevier Science, 1999), pp. 235-308.

[484] Romer includes a technology parameter in the production function that exhibits increasing returns to knowledge and constant returns in knowledge accumulation. Technical knowledge is generally public (or non-rival) and at least partly excludable, and tacit knowledge is private or firm-specific (rival) and is excludable in that it requires certain rights to access it. P. Romer, "Increasing returns and long-run growth", *Journal of Political Economy*, Vol. 94, 1986, pp. 1002-1037. Lucas introduced human capital as a parameter in the production function to generate increasing returns and endogenous growth. R. Lucas Jr., "On the mechanics of economic development", *Journal of Monetary Economics*, Vol. 22, No. 3, 1988, pp. 3-42.

[485] Some growth models suggest that the intensity of R&D determines the pace of economic growth by increasing the variety (and quality) of capital goods and inducing the necessary human capital for subsequent innovations. This product differentiation reflects the increased specialization of labour across an increasing variety of activities in the global economy. P. Romer, "Endogenous technological change", *Journal of Political Economy*, Vol. 98, 1990, pp. S71-102; G. Grossman and E. Helpman, *Innovation and Growth in the Global Economy* (Cambridge, MIT Press, 1991); and P. Aghion and P. Howitt, "A model of growth through creative destruction", *Econometrica*, Vol. 60, 1992, pp. 323-351. Grossman and Helpman represent the growth process as a quality ladder that firms climb depending on the stochastic nature of the R&D process. Aghion and Howitt describe how changing product variety leads to a process of creative destruction and explain how excessive R&D expenditures can have the opposite effect that Romer predicts.

productivity directly in the FIE and indirectly in local enterprises through knowledge spillovers. The existence of technology transfer and local spillovers prevent the unbounded decline of the marginal productivity of capital suggested in conventional growth theory and makes endogenously driven long-term growth possible.

Although the scope for externalities of various types and the influence they have on long-run growth is a common theme in most endogenous growth models, very few of them consider explicitly the role of FDI in generating these externalities.[486] A widely held view is that international trade (especially in new intermediate and capital goods) leads to R&D spillovers and higher productivity growth.[487] But while recent evidence shows that the composition of imports appears to influence productivity growth (especially in developing countries), it also reveals that domestic R&D has a greater influence on productivity growth than foreign R&D. The lack of sound evidence that international trade is an important channel of technology transfer has important policy implications for the creation of new free trade agreements. It also suggests that other channels of technology transfer should be examined more closely.[488] Recent studies based on endogenous growth theory indicate that the transfer of technology and technology spillovers from FDI encourage long-run growth, but the extent to which this occurs depends crucially on the stock of human capital and the absorptive capacity of firms in the host economy.[489] Scale effects found in industry data indicate that the direct transfer of technology to the FIE is more important than spillovers from the FIE to the domestic economy. But the dearth of statistically significant evidence suggests that no one channel of technology transfer is better than another and that these channels may be complementary rather than substitutes.

5.2 Principal determinants of FDI flows

There is widespread agreement on what determines the flow of FDI to one country rather than another. Countries attracting large amounts of FDI generally have good economic fundamentals, that is, they have achieved a high degree of macroeconomic and political stability and have favourable growth prospects.[490] They also tend to possess a good infrastructure and legal system (including enforcement of laws), a skilled labour force, and a foreign sector that has been liberalized to some extent (membership in free trade areas is a particular attraction). Location, country (market) size and natural endowments are generally important as well. In the former centrally planned economies, the degree of progress made in moving from plan to market has been a key explanation of FDI inflows (tables 5.2.1 and 5.2.2, charts 5.2.1 and 5.2.2 and appendix table B.17).[491] More generally, those transition economies that have attracted substantial amounts of FDI have followed policies that have created friendly investment environments (although they often possess certain natural advantages as well).

This section will first discuss some of the determinants of FDI flows into the first group of transition economies chosen as candidates for EU accession (Czech Republic, Hungary, Poland, Slovenia and Estonia). These countries have received the bulk of FDI in the transition economies during the past decade, never less than 60 per cent of the total annual inflow. The focus then switches to countries that have failed to attract much FDI. In some cases, they have been in a favourable position to do so, but domestic political and/or economic policies have discouraged investment. In others, the causes appear to be more fundamental and intractable.

The first wave of EU candidate countries were among the first to achieve macroeconomic stabilization and their economic reforms have been the most advanced of all the transition economies. Although there have been considerable policy differences between them, a key element of the reforms has been the privatization of state assets with the involvement of foreign strategic investors. These acquisitions, the timing of which has been determined by the political process and national timetables for the sale of specific assets, have accounted for a considerable share of total FDI. Exclusive of Slovenia (see below), the early investment promotion efforts of these countries not only signalled that foreign investment was welcome in the former state run economies, but they also capitalized on the enthusiasm of western investors. At various times, investment incentives have been introduced[492] which still seem to retain their attractiveness for individual countries competing for FDI.

---

[486] L. de Mello, Jr., "Foreign direct investment in developing countries and growth: a selective survey", *The Journal of Development Studies*, Vol. 34, No. 1, 1997, pp. 1-34. G. Grossman and E. Helpman, op. cit., incorporate FDI into their growth model, but only to the extent that it determines the international location of production.

[487] D. Coe and E. Helpman, "International R&D spillovers", *European Economic Review*, Vol. 39, 1995, pp. 859-887. They show that the total factor productivity of a country depends not only on its own R&D activity, but also the R&D activity of its trading partners.

[488] W. Keller, "Do trade patterns and technology flows affect productivity growth?", *The World Bank Economic Review*, Vol. 14, No. 1, January 2000, pp. 17-47.

[489] E. Borensztein, J. De Gregorio and J.-W. Lee, "How does foreign direct investment affect economic growth", *Journal of International Economics*, Vol. 45, 1998, pp. 115-135. Though not always statistically significant, the results show that FDI has a positive impact on economic growth, depending on the level of human capital in the host country. See also R. Baldwin, H. Braconier and R. Forslid, *Multinationals, Endogenous Growth and Technological Spillovers: Theory and Evidence*, Centre for Economic Policy Research (CEPR) Discussion Paper, No. 2155 (London), May 1999.

[490] Sections 5.2-5.5 are based on FDI data from the balance of payments (also see box 5.3.1).

[491] The relationship between the degree of economic reform and FDI inflows has been commented on previously. See, for example, EBRD, *Transition Report 1998* (London).

[492] G. Hunya, *International Competitiveness. Impacts of FDI in CEECs*, The Vienna Institute for International Economic Studies (WIIW) Research Reports, No. 268 (Vienna), August 2000.

TABLE 5.2.1

Foreign direct investment [a] in eastern Europe, the Baltic states and the CIS, 1990-2000
(Million dollars, per cent)

	Million dollars							FDI/GDP, nominal (per cent)					
	1990-1992	1993-1996	1997-1999	1998	1999	Jan.-Sept. 2000	2000	1990-1992	1993-1996	1997-1999	1999	Jan.-Sept. 2000	2000
Eastern Europe [b c]	6 583	31 655	44 848	15 502	18 865	..	..	1.0	2.6	4.0	4.9	..	..
Eastern Europe [b d]	5 936	24 930	40 982	14 270	17 373	11 569	21 502*	0.9	2.0	3.7	4.7	4.3	5.8
Albania	20	271	134	45	41	71	100	0.6	3.3	1.6	1.1	2.5	2.7
Bosnia and Herzegovina	–	–	160	100	60	90	117*	–	–	1.3	1.4	2.4	2.4
Bulgaria	101	345	1 848	537	806	504	975	0.3	0.8	5.3	6.5	5.9	7.9
Croatia	16	844	2 788	898	1 408	710	1 000*	–	1.3	4.5	7.0	4.9	5.2
Czech Republic [e]	1 649	5 513	9 128	2 720	5 108	3 265	4 595	1.9	3.0	5.7	9.6	8.8	9.3
Hungary	3 241	10 213	6 153	2 036	1 944	1 419	1 957	3.1	6.0	4.4	4.0	4.1	4.2
Poland (accrual basis)	1 058	11 747	18 543	6 365	7 270	..	..	0.5	2.6	4.0	4.7	..	..
Poland (cash basis)	411	5 022	14 677	5 129	6 471	3 674	9 461	0.2	1.1	3.2	4.2	3.2	6.0
Romania	117	1 117	4 287	2 031	1 041	587	998	0.1	0.9	3.9	3.1	2.4	2.7
Slovakia	200	949	999	508	330	1 151	2 075	0.5	1.5	1.6	1.7	7.8	10.8
Slovenia	180	612	804	248	181	63	181	0.4	0.9	1.4	0.9	0.5	1.0
The former Yugoslav Republic of Macedonia	..	44	164	118	30	125	160*	–	0.3	1.5	0.9	4.6	4.5
Yugoslavia	..	..	740	113	112	–	–*	..	..	..	..	–	–
Baltic states	119	1 836	4 144	1 863	1 138	811	1 148*	..	3.8	6.5	5.2	4.7	5.0
Estonia	82	729	1 152	581	305	288	398	..	6.2	7.7	5.9	7.7	8.1
Latvia	29	821	1 225	357	347	263	400*	..	5.3	6.8	5.6	5.0	5.7
Lithuania	8	286	1 767	926	486	260	350*	..	1.4	5.7	4.6	3.1	3.1
CIS	..	12 799	24 077	6 726	6 644	3 604	5 363*	..	0.8	2.0	2.4	1.5	1.6
Armenia	..	52	395	221	122	100	140*	..	1.2	7.3	6.6	7.9	7.3
Azerbaijan	..	1 039	2 648	1 023	510	-27	-30*	..	12.1	21.3	12.7	-0.8	-0.6
Belarus [e]	7	115	574	149	225	68	90	..	0.3	1.6	2.1	0.9	0.9
Georgia	..	54	551	265	82	75*	100*	..	0.6	5.7	3.0	3.3	3.2
Kazakhstan	100	2 964	4 056	1 144	1 629	897	1 099*	..	4.6	6.7	10.0	6.6	6.0
Kyrgyzstan	..	191	228	109	36	15*	20*	..	3.8	5.0	2.9	1.6	1.5
Republic of Moldova	42	116	195	81	34	95	120*	..	2.1	4.1	2.9	10.3	9.3
Russian Federation	1 554	6 346	12 709	2 762	3 309	1 781	3 000*	..	0.5	1.4	1.8	1.0	1.2
Tajikistan	..	66	75	24	21	15*	24*	..	2.0	2.3	1.9	2.2	2.4
Turkmenistan	11	523	267	64	60*	65*	100*	..	2.8	3.0	1.8	2.0	2.3
Ukraine	170	1 145	1 862	743	496	470	600*	..	0.8	1.5	1.7	2.1	1.8
Uzbekistan	9	187	518	140	121	50	100*	..	0.5	1.1	0.7	0.5	0.7
Total above [b c]	..	46 290	74 069	24 305	26 785	..	..	..	1.7	3.1	3.9	..	..
Total above [b d]	..	39 565	69 203	22 859	25 156	15 984	28 013*	..	1.5	2.9	3.8	3.0	3.8
Memorandum items:													
CETE-5 [d]	5 681	22 309	31 762	10 641	14 034	9 572	18 269	1.2	2.4	3.6	4.7	4.5	6.2
SETE-7 [b]	254	2 621	9 220	3 629	3 326	1 997	3 232*	0.1	1.0	4.1	4.5	3.7	4.3
Asian CIS	..	5 076	8 737	2 991	2 580	1 190*	1 553*	..	3.4	5.8	5.5	3.4	3.2
3 European CIS [f]	194	1 376	2 631	974	728	634	810*	..	0.7	1.6	1.8	2.1	1.8

Source: UN/ECE secretariat, based on national balance of payments statistics; IMF.

Note: In March 2001, a change in methodology in the Czech Republic resulted in a shift of intercompany loans from "other investment" in the balance of payments to "FDI". As a result FDI inflows in 1999 and 2000 have increased to $3,718 and $6,324 million, respectively. Belarus has revised upward its 1999 inflows to $444 million. The new data are not reflected in any part of chapter 5, but they have been incorporated in appendix table B.17.

[a] Inflows into the reporting countries.
[b] Excluding Bosnia and Herzegovina and Yugoslavia.
[c] Includes Poland on an accrual basis.
[d] Includes Poland on a cash basis.
[e] See note to this table.
[f] Belarus, Republic of Moldova and Ukraine.

TABLE 5.2.2

Foreign direct investment inflows in eastern Europe, the Baltic states and the CIS, 1988-2000
(Billion dollars, per cent)

	Cumulative FDI inflows 1988-1999						FDI inflows / GDFCF[a] (per cent)		FDI inflows / current account (per cent)		Secondary education[b]	Corruption index 2000	
	Billion dollars	Per cent of GDP[c]	Rank	Per cent of GDP (PPP)[c]	Rank	Per capita (dollars)	Rank	1993-1996	1997-1999	1993-1996	1997-1999	1997	Rank[d]	CPI score
Eastern Europe[e]	84.4	22.8	..	9.6	..	789	..	12	17	58[f]	86	80	51	3.8
Albania	0.4	11.8	18	4.1	16	126	16	..	..	104	28	38	..	..
Bosnia and Herzegovina	0.2	3.6	..	..	..	57	..	..	..	–	4	..	..	..
Bulgaria	2.3	18.5	14	5.5	11	279	12	6	39	26	488	77	52	3.5
Croatia	3.7	18.4	15	11.6	6	815	7	8	19	74	52	82	51	3.7
Czech Republic	16.5	31.1	7	12.3	5	1 609	2	10	20	92	164	99	42	4.3
Hungary	19.8	40.9	3	17.8	2	1 969	1	30	19	89	115	98	32	5.2
Poland (FDI: accrual basis)	32.1	20.6	12	10.0	7	830	5	14	17	-672	85	98	43	4.1
Romania	5.5	16.2	16	4.3	15	246	13	4	20	19	67	78	68	2.9
Slovakia	2.2	10.9	20	3.9	17	400	11	5	5	58	20	94	52	3.5
Slovenia	1.6	8.0	22	5.3	12	806	6	5	6	-88	88	92	28	5.5
The former Yugoslav Republic of Macedonia	0.2	6.1	24	2.1	21	103	19	2	9	7	23	63	..	..
Yugoslavia	0.7	4.2	..	1.7	..	70		..	..	–	21	62	89	1.3
Baltic states	6.1	27.7	..	12.0	..	805	..	18	26	97	64	91	42	4.4
Estonia	2.0	38.2	4	16.9	3	1 361	3	23	28	104	86	104	27	5.7
Latvia	2.1	33.2	6	14.2	4	853	5	34	29	-255	75	84	57	3.4
Lithuania	2.1	19.4	13	8.4	9	557	8	6	24	19	51	86	43	4.1
CIS	38.7	14.1	..	2.7	..	137	..	4	11	..	..	86	74	2.5
Armenia	0.4	24.2	10	5.1	13	117	17	7	45	8	41	90	76	2.5
Azerbaijan	3.6	91.0	1	19.7	1	456	10	51	61	62	92	77	87	1.5
Belarus	0.7	6.6	23	1.0	25	68	22	1	6	6	30	93	43	4.1
Georgia	0.6	21.8	11	3.1	19	111	18	4	46	5	56	77	..	..
Kazakhstan	7.1	44.9	2	9.7	8	477	9	20	55	131	185	87	65	3.0
Kyrgyzstan	0.4	34.4	5	3.7	18	86	21	21	41	23	33	79	..	..
Republic of Moldova	0.3	30.1	8	4.9	14	96	20	12	20	22	29	81	74	2.6
Russian Federation	20.6	11.2	19	2.1	22	141	15	2	8	-15	-45	96[f]	82	2.1
Tajikistan	0.2	13.8	17	2.4	20	24	25	12	..	12	39	78	..	..
Turkmenistan	0.8	24.5	9	5.7	10	165	14	9	24	-59	18	..	..	..
Ukraine	3.2	10.3	21	1.9	23	64	23	3	8	27	99	94[f]	87	1.5
Uzbekistan	0.7	4.1	25	1.2	24	28	24	2	3	14	77	94	79	2.4
Total above[e]	129.2	19.4	..	5.5	..	325	..	8	14	..	..	..	..	..
Memorandum items:														
CETE-5	72.2	24.3	..	11.1	..	1 088	..	14	16	174	92	96	39	4.5
SETE-7[e]	12.2	16.5	..	5.5	..	299	..	6	22	28	69	68	57	3.4
Asian CIS	13.9	29.8	..	6.7	..	191	..	14	29	66	84	83	77	2.4
European CIS[g]	24.8	10.9	..	2.0	..	118	..	3	8	..	..	91	72	2.6
Poland: cash basis	20.1	12.9	..	6.3	..	520	..	5.6	13	21	59	..	..	..

Source: UN/ECE secretariat, based on national balance of payments statistics. Transparency International, *Corruption Perceptions Index (CPI)*, (www.transparency.de). For data on secondary education, World Bank, *World Development Indicators 2000* (Washington, D.C.), 2000.

[a] GDFCF - gross domestic fixed capital formation, converted to dollars at current exchange rates.

[b] Per cent of the relevant age group.

[c] GDP in 1999, at current prices and exchange rates. GDP(PPP) is purchasing power parity GDP.

[d] Country rank out of 90 countries surveyed. The score ranges from 0-6, highest to lowest perceived corruption.

[e] Excluding Bosnia and Herzegovina and Yugoslavia.

[f] 1980.

[g] Belarus, Republic of Moldova and Ukraine.

CHART 5.2.1

Cumulative FDI inflows as a percentage of current year GDP in eastern Europe, the Baltic states and the CIS,[a] 1990-1999
(Per cent)

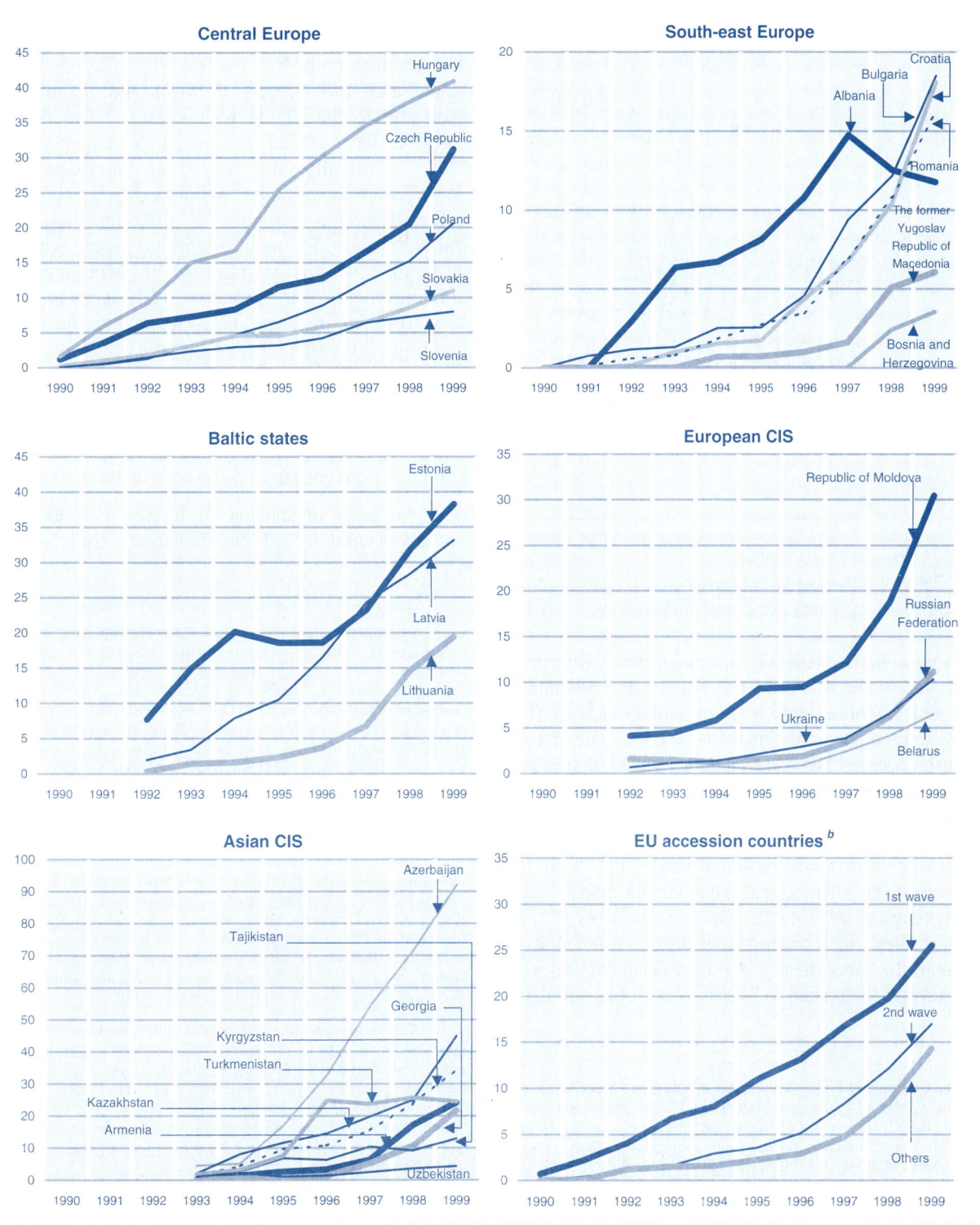

Source: UN/ECE secretariat, based on national account and balance of payments statistics. FDI inflows are cumulated from 1988.

[a] Nominal GDP, at current prices and exchange rates.

[b] First wave: Czech Republic, Hungary, Poland, Slovenia and Estonia; second wave: Bulgaria, Romania, Slovakia, Latvia and Lithuania. See text.

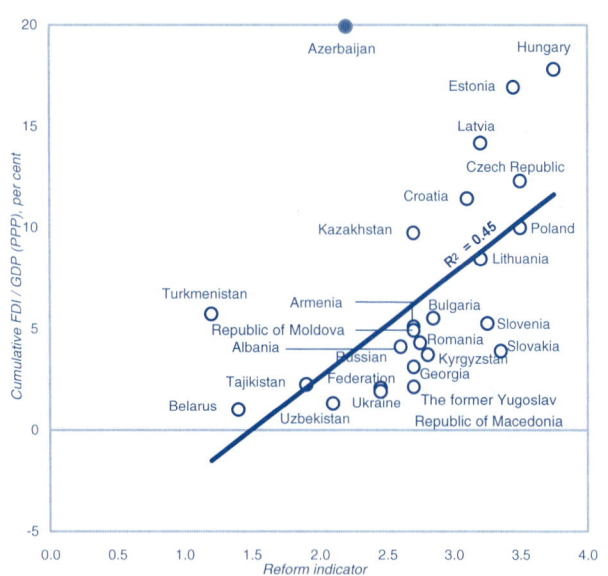

CHART 5.2.2

Ratio of cumulative FDI inflows to GDP(PPP) and progress in reform [a]
(Per cent)

Source: National balance of payments statistics and EBRD, *Transition Report 1999* (London) (for the reform indicator).

Note: Azerbaijan is excluded from the regression.

[a] FDI is cumulated from 1989-1999; GDP(PPP) refers to 1999.

Geographical proximity to major west European markets and production centres is also a major advantage for the four countries, which share borders with the EU while Estonia enjoys easy maritime access. The size of the Polish economy has contributed to its leading position as a domicile for FDI. Most of these countries embarked on the transition with poor market supporting institutions and physical infrastructure. However, considerable progress has been made in some areas, often with the assistance of the international development banks[493] and the involvement of foreign strategic investors.[494] In particular, these investments have been instrumental in upgrading the important telecommunications sector.[495] Local corruption appears to be less of a problem in these four countries than elsewhere in the region. Corruption is often cited by foreign business as a deterrent to FDI, and this appears to be the case in the transition economies as well.[496]

Prospects for (or actual) EU membership have often proved a magnet for FDI in the accession countries.[497] The acceleration of FDI into the EEC after the Treaty of Rome and into Greece, Portugal and Spain prior to accession to the EU is well known. The first wave countries have tended to have similar experiences with FDI.[498] Initially, the free trade provisions of the Association Agreements (negotiated in 1991) probably attracted foreign investors.[499] Although these accords did not promise EU membership, they were widely seen at the time as a first step towards it. More recently key announcements of the progress in EU accession seem to have resulted in larger FDI flows into the candidate countries, but much more so into the first wave than into the second (Bulgaria, Romania, Slovakia, Latvia and Lithuania).[500] From the very beginning of the decade, investors have differentiated between these two groups of countries (chart 5.2.1), although the official announcements began to do so only in 1997.

An asset of interest to foreign investors that is broadly shared by all the transition economies is the

---

[493] These countries have received the assistance of the EBRD, the World Bank, the EU (through PHARE and EIB loans) and, more generally, the G-24 programme (from the latter early in the reform process). Institution building has also been advanced through the process of the harmonization of national laws with the EU *Acquis Communautaire*.

[494] The EBRD has become the largest single investor in the transition economies. By mobilizing private investors, its influence on FDI inflows extends beyond its stake holdings.

[495] According to the Hungarian Institute of World Economics, the world ranking of the first wave of accession countries in telecommunications facilities has risen since 1990, and all except Poland were in the upper third of the sample in 1999. However, Bulgaria, Romania, Russia and Ukraine have lost ground. Similar differences were found in internet penetration. I. Berend (citing E. Erlich), "From regime change to sustained growth in central and eastern Europe", UN/ECE, *Economic Survey of Europe, 2000 No. 2/3*, chap. 2.

[496] According to the indices calculated by Transparency International, an average value of 5.0 for the first wave countries is much better than those for other groups of transition economies (table 5.2.2). The secretariat found a significant negative relationship between the corruption index and cumulated FDI inflows/GDP in the host transition economy. For a more general statistical analysis of corruption and FDI flows, see Shang-Jin Wei, *How Taxing is Corruption on International Investors?*, NBER Working Paper, Number 6030 (Cambridge, MA), May 1997.

[497] The potential benefits of EU membership, including for foreign investors, have been extensively discussed. Very briefly, accepting EU rules and regulations reduces investment risk by creating a business environment similar to that in western Europe. In particular, the risk of arbitrary policy changes in, for example, market access and taxation are diminished and property rights become more secure. There is also a reduction in the transaction costs of cross-border business. See, for example, R. Baldwin, J. Francois and R. Portes "The costs and benefits of eastern enlargement: the impact on the EU and central Europe", *Economic Policy*, Vol. 24, April 1997, pp. 127-170.

[498] This issue has received considerable attention. For instance, Havrylyshyn found that all potential EU accession countries, which he defined as all non-CIS economies, attracted more FDI than the non-accession group did. O. Havrylyshyn, "EU enlargement and possible echoes beyond the new frontiers", paper presented at the WIIW 25th Anniversary Conference, *Shaping the New Europe: Challenges of EU Eastern Enlargement – East and West European Perspectives* (Vienna), 11-13 November 1998.

[499] Under the interim arrangements of the Association Agreements between the EC and Czechoslovakia, Hungary and Poland, measures liberalizing trade in industrial products entered into force on 1 March 1992. UN/ECE, *Economic Survey of Europe in 1991-1992*, p. 188.

[500] A. Bevan and S. Estrin, *The Determinants of Foreign Direct Investment in Transition Economies*, London Business School, Centre for New and Emerging Markets Discussion Paper Series, No. 9 (London), October 2000. The EU accession-related announcements by the European Council were Copenhagen (June 1993), Essen (December 1994), Madrid (December 1995) and Agenda 2000 (July 1997). The first three announcements were not country specific, but the most recent defined the first and second wave countries.

relative abundance of well-educated but low-cost labour. The first wave of five candidate countries lead the region in terms of educational attainment,[501] and nominal wages are several times lower than in the lowest-wage EU economies. Wages in the first wave countries make them competitive as hosts for FDI even after adjustments are made for their lower productivity.[502] However, relatively rapid increases in unit labour costs seem to discourage foreign investors.[503]

Given their favourable location, educated labour forces and other assets, several other transition economies have been well placed to receive foreign investments, but the results have been largely disappointing (table 5.2.1 and chart 5.2.1). Slow economic reform and a lack of restructuring have been general features, but there have been specific factors as well. For example, in Slovakia until recently the political climate and official attitudes toward foreign investment were viewed unfavourably by foreign investors. Bulgaria and Romania were characterized for years by policy immobility and periodic economic crises, but subsequent changes in policy have led to their acceptance in the second wave of EU accession countries. FDI has increased mainly because privatization programmes have been accelerated.

The republics of the former SFR of Yugoslavia also possess assets of potential interest to foreign investors. However, risks associated with the breakup of the country have dominated foreign perceptions: regional and internal conflicts, financial difficulties (e.g. the former SFR of Yugoslavia's default on foreign debt, loss of official reserves, negotiations with foreign creditors) and, most recently, the Kosovo conflict (which adversely affected the entire Balkan region). Slow economic reform and the political situation (which disqualified Croatia from the PHARE programme) were also factors. However, investment in Croatia has increased following the cessation of hostilities and again after the election of a reform-minded government. On the other hand, peace and large amounts of foreign aid have done little to help attract FDI into Bosnia and Herzegovina, which for the time being remains a dysfunctional state subject to ethnic tensions. Yugoslavia has been viewed as a high-risk country, subject to a United Nations embargo and pursuing an inward-looking economic policy. Its only significant foreign investment has been the FDI-related privatization of the telecommunications enterprise. After the recent elections, however, the prospects for fundamental change have improved. Slovenia has attracted only modest amounts of investment (see below) despite the restoration of peace, a good location (bordering on two EU countries) and solid economic fundamentals. This is the result of a deliberate policy choice, however, which has become more welcoming in the past year.

Within the CIS, countries well endowed with natural resources – Azerbaijan, Kazakhstan and Turkmenistan (oil and gas) and Kyrgyzstan (gold) – have attracted relatively large amounts of FDI into the extractive industries. However, generally unfavourable investment climates (including, for example, slow rates of economic reform, high levels of corruption, poor records of enforcing existing laws and agreements, etc.), great distances from world markets and landlocked locations appear to have generally deterred investment in other sectors. Some of these same factors also help to explain the low levels of foreign investment in other CIS countries including Russia,[504] which has a huge natural resource base and great potential for foreign investment.[505]

Although a number of the factors discussed above appear individually to explain FDI inflows into the transition economies, they are in fact interrelated and it is doubtful that their separate contributions can be unravelled. The countries of central Europe (and the Baltics to a lesser extent) have benefited from their location, political history and initial economic conditions, which facilitated the early launching of economic reforms, the introduction of stabilization programmes and the achievement of political stability. These same factors also help to explain the development of various institutions (especially of the market supporting type), the relatively lower levels of corruption and the prospects for EU membership in the not too distant future. The confluence of all these factors, individually important to foreign investors, is likely to have created a virtuous circle of an improving investment climate, above average economic prospects and increasing FDI. Other transition countries, more distant from west European markets and with different political histories, have been less fortunate.

5.3 The development of FDI flows, 1990-2000

Foreign investment was generally prohibited during the period of central planning. Only Hungary, Poland and Romania permitted some FDI (in the form of joint ventures) and the amounts involved were small. The former SFR of Yugoslavia, which was considered a mixed economy, received only modest foreign investment in the 1980s. From this low base, FDI in the transition economies increased at a modest pace in the early 1990s. In fact, with the exception of Hungary, inflows were generally disappointing, falling far short of

---

[501] In general the transition economies rank very high by world standards, significantly above the average of developing countries (table 5.2.2).

[502] A. Bevan and S. Estrin, op. cit., have found that unit labour costs in a selection of transition economies are a significant determinant of FDI inflows. They note that nominal wages alone are not a good explanatory variable.

[503] Ibid.

[504] R. Ahrend, "Foreign direct investment into Russia - pain without gain? A survey of foreign direct investors", *Russian Economic Trends*, June 2000.

[505] A major reason for Russia's failure to attract much investment in the extractive sector is the lack of a comprehensive legal framework for production sharing agreements (PSAs) and protracted legislative procedures. UN/ECE, "A note on production sharing in Russia", *Economic Survey of Europe, 1998 No. 3,* chap. 5.

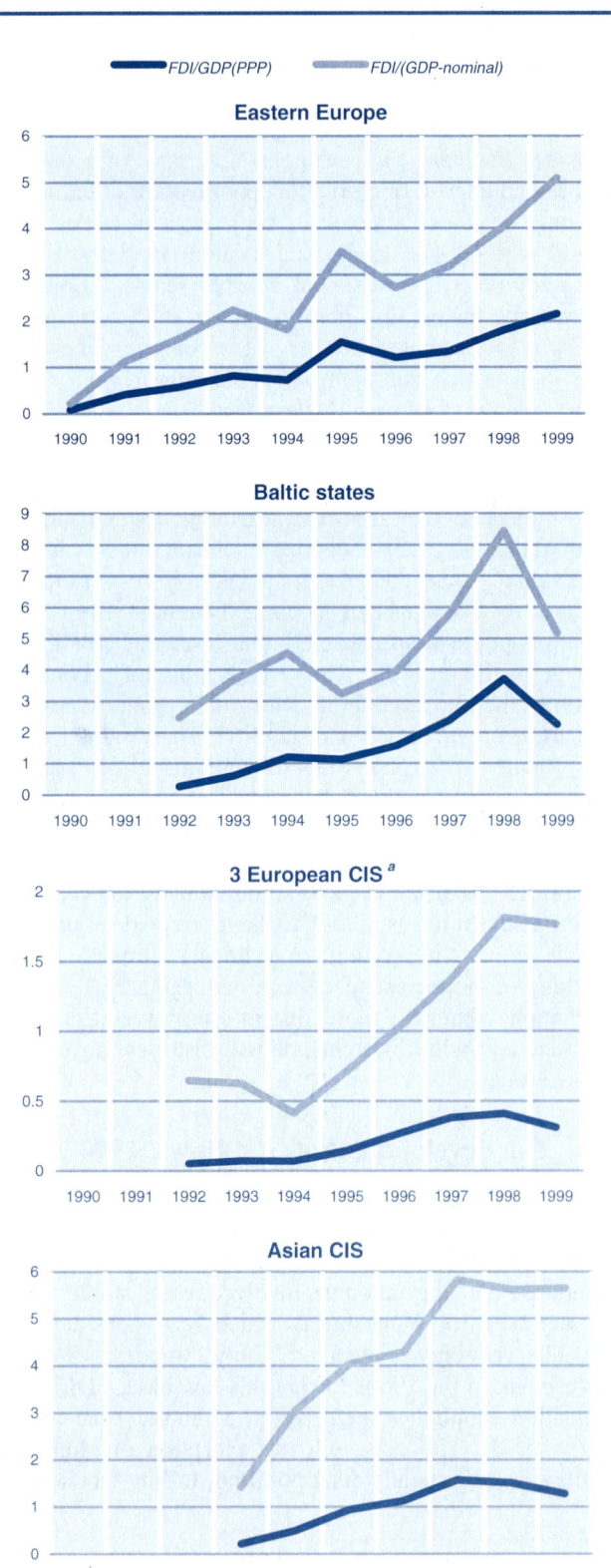

CHART 5.3.1

Annual FDI inflows as a percentage of GDP, 1990-1999
(Per cent)

Source: National balance of payments statistics; UN/ECE secretariat for GDP(PPP).

a Belarus, Republic of Moldova and Ukraine.

expectations.[506] However, in the second half of the decade, FDI flows accelerated (table 5.2.1 and charts 5.2.1 and 5.3.1). In 1999 annual investments reached nearly $28 billion (4 per cent of GDP),[507] and cumulated inflows amounted to some $130 billion. Preliminary data for 2000 suggest that annual FDI inflows continued to increase.[508]

Policy decisions in Hungary and Estonia gave them an early lead in attracting foreign investment. Their objective was to sell off state assets rapidly to foreign strategic investors and thus achieve increased economic efficiency and integration into world markets. In addition to Hungary, the Czech Republic[509] and Poland began to attract relatively large inflows from the middle of the decade, resulting in a high concentration of FDI in these three countries: they accounted for two thirds of the total annual flow to the ECE transition economies in 1995. The subsequent acceleration of privatization and the generally improving investment climate in other transition economies boosted their FDI inflows and resulted in a somewhat more even geographical distribution. However, in 1999-2000 the concentration increased again, due to the fast pace of investment in the three leading countries. Other noteworthy developments in the second half of the 1990s were:

- Poland became the main destination of FDI in 1996;

- An acceleration of flows into Latvia and, with a lag, into Lithuania (second wave countries), but their cumulative flows continue to lag behind those of Estonia;

- FDI in the Czech Republic surged following the passage of a new investment law in 1998 and accelerated privatization.[510] For two years the country has received FDI amounting to around 10 per cent of GDP, one of the highest ratios in the ECE region;

- Accelerated privatization in Bulgaria, Romania and Croatia significantly boosted inflows in 1996-1999. The sale of the national telecom companies in the latter two countries markedly raised FDI in 1998 and 1999, respectively;

---

[506] Early in the transition, some observers and policy makers expected a rush of FDI, which would play a major role in creating market systems, restructuring economies and stimulating economic growth.

[507] The interpretation of the indicators of FDI penetration (including FDI/gross domestic fixed capital formation) and the methodological issues surrounding them are discussed in box 5.3.1. It should be noted that the data for Poland (reported annually) are on an accrual and cash basis (tables 5.2.1 and 5.2.2), the accrual figures being somewhat higher than the cash figures (available monthly) published regularly in the *Economic Survey of Europe*.

[508] Chap. 3.6 of this *Survey*.

[509] Although Czech voucher privatization discouraged FDI in the affected enterprises, there were several large privatizations (e.g. Skoda involving VW) and greenfield investments involving foreign investors.

[510] According to R. Samek, a spokesperson for CzechInvest. Bureau of National Affairs (BNA), *Eastern European Reporter*, Vol. 10, No. 1 (London), January 2000.

> Box 5.3.1
>
> **FDI indicators and their interpretation**
>
> Direct investment is a category of international investment that reflects the objective of a resident entity in one country (the "direct investor") obtaining a lasting interest in an enterprise located in another country (the "direct or foreign investment enterprise").[1] A lasting interest implies the existence of a long-term relationship between the direct investor and the enterprise. A direct investment relationship is created when a foreign investor owns 10 per cent or more of the ordinary shares or voting power in the direct investment enterprise (incorporated or unincorporated).[2]
>
> FDI in the balance of payments comprises three components:
>
> - *Equity*: comprises equity in branches, all shares in subsidiaries and associates, and other capital contributions;
>
> - *Reinvested earnings*: consist of the direct investor's share (in proportion to direct equity participation) of earnings not distributed as dividends by subsidiaries and earnings of branches not remitted to the direct investor;
>
> - *Other direct investment capital*: covers the borrowing and lending of funds between direct investors and subsidiaries, including both short- and long-term investments.
>
> The transition economies have made good progress in reporting the components of FDI flows. By 1998, 12 of them reported reinvested earnings, several having done so for a number of years (see table below).[3] When the decision to report earnings is made there is invariably a break in the series. In most cases, this is not serious because reinvested profits were previously small, given the relatively recent establishment of direct investment enterprises. However, several countries have reported to have, or are believed to have, reinvested earnings of over 10 per cent of current equity investments. For those countries, failure to include reinvested profits (and inter-company loans) in total annual and cumulative FDI flows means the latter are underestimated and that the international comparability of the statistics is impaired. The largest underestimate is likely to have occurred in Hungary where non-reported reinvested earnings are estimated to have reached 1.3 per cent of GDP in 1997.[4]
>
> **Balance of payments components of FDI in eastern Europe, the Baltic states and the CIS as reported by the IMF,[a] 1991-1998**
>
> | | Equity capital | Reinvested earnings | Other capital | | Equity capital | Reinvested earnings | Other capital |
> |---|---|---|---|---|---|---|---|
> | Albania | 1992-1998 | .. | .. | Armenia | 1993-1998 | 1997-1998 | 1995; 1998 |
> | Bulgaria | 1990-1998 | 1998 | 1997-1998 | Azerbaijan | 1995-1998 | .. | 1995-1998 |
> | Croatia | .. | .. | .. | Belarus | 1993-1998 | 1997-1998 | 1996-1998 |
> | Czech Republic | 1993-1998 | .. | .. | Georgia | 1998 | .. | .. |
> | Hungary | 1991-1998 | .. | 1996-1998 | Kazakhstan | 1995-1998 | 1996-1998 | 1995-1998 |
> | Poland [b] | 1990-1998 | 1990-1998 | 1991-1998 | Kyrgyzstan | 1993-1998 | 1996-1998 | 1995-1998 |
> | Romania | 1991-1998 | .. | .. | Republic of Moldova | 1995-1998 | 1998 | 1995-1998 |
> | Slovakia | 1994-1998 | 1995-1998 | 1995-1998 | Russian Federation | 1997-1998 | 1998 | 1997-1998 |
> | Slovenia | 1992-1998 | .. | .. | Tajikistan | .. | .. | .. |
> | The former Yugoslav Republic of Macedonia | 1996-1998 | .. | 1996-1997 | Turkmenistan | 1996-1997 | .. | 1997 |
> | Estonia | 1992-1998 | 1992-1998 | 1992-1998 | Ukraine | 1994-1998 [c] | .. | .. |
> | Latvia | 1992-1998 | 1996-1998 | 1996-1998 | Uzbekistan | .. | .. | .. |
> | Lithuania | 1993-1998 | 1995-1998 | 1995-1998 | | | | |
>
> *Source:* IMF, *Balance of Payments Statistics Yearbook, Part 1: Country Tables* (Washington, D.C.), 1999.
>
> a Year for which data are reported.
>
> b Accrual basis (annual data only). Coverage of data on a monthly cash basis is less comprehensive.
>
> c Total FDI.
>
> Data on FDI inflows in the balance of payments generally begin in 1990, later for the CIS and the republics of the former SFR of Yugoslavia. Consequently any investments made prior to those dates are not reflected in the cumulative totals. For the reasons already mentioned, this is unlikely to be a problem except perhaps in Hungary and the republics of the former SFR of Yugoslavia.[5]
>
> Three types of ratios are typically used in the analysis of inward FDI: the FDI/GDP ratio, calculated from annual flows; the ratio of cumulated annual FDI flows[6] to GDP (using current year GDP); and the ratio of annual FDI flows to gross fixed capital formation. All three are measures of the penetration of FDI in the economy and give some idea of the potential economic impact of foreign investment.
>
> The GDP statistic generally used in these ratios is calculated at current prices and exchange rates (nominal GDP). One of its shortcomings stems from differences in the degree of undervaluation of national currencies relative to the dollar and from the often large depreciations of nominal exchange rates which, for example, occurred in several transition economies following the 1997-1998 financial crises. A partial solution is to use dollar GDP estimates at PPP exchange rates.[7] The latter raise the GDP of the transition economies, especially those of the CIS (whose exchange rates are the most undervalued). FDI/GDP ratios, including those based on GDP(PPP), are also sensitive to economic downturns, the resulting increases in the ratios implying (incorrectly) increases in FDI penetration. This is important because in some countries there have been falls in output from time to time, particularly in the early 1990s and again in 1997-1999.

> **Box 5.3.1 (concluded)**
>
> **FDI indicators and their interpretation**
>
> A variant of these measures replaces GDP with the population, yielding per capita flows or stocks. Population can be established accurately over time, which facilitates cross-country comparisons (problems not entirely solved by measuring GDP in PPPs), and it eliminates the problem of economic downturns. However, since per capita incomes vary considerably between countries, population figures are not likely to provide an accurate measure of economic size. Table 5.2.2 contains FDI ratios calculated using GDP (nominal), GDP(PPP) and population and country rankings based on each indicator.
>
> FDI indicators and their interpretation The FDI/domestic investment ratio is often analysed assuming (at least implicitly) that FDI contributes to local gross fixed capital formation. This can be justified if FDI inflows consist of capital goods in kind or if FDI cash flows are used to purchase capital equipment (as is typically the case with greenfield or follow-up investments in existing facilities). In both cases FDI increases the capital stock and productive capacity. The ratio loses this interpretation when FDI takes the form of mergers and acquisitions (M&As), which represent change in ownership rather than fixed investment. In many transition economies M&A activity has accounted for the bulk of FDI. The inter-company loan component of FDI may also be used for transactions other than the finance of capital goods (e.g. for financial speculation).[8] As privatization comes to an end, FDI should increasingly reflect capital investment (as is already the case in Hungary and Estonia).
>
> ---
>
> [1] The term "foreign investment enterprise" is used throughout this chapter but the IMF manual refers to "direct investment enterprise".
>
> [2] IMF, *Balance of Payments Manual*, Fifth Edition (Washington, D.C.), 1993.
>
> [3] By comparison, in 1991 only 11 industrial countries surveyed in the *Godeaux Report* compiled reinvested earnings. In 1997 an OECD survey concluded that about three fourths of OECD countries reported reinvested earnings. OECD, "Foreign direct investment: survey of implementation of methodological standards", *Financial Market Trends* (Paris), November 1998.
>
> [4] IMF, op. cit.
>
> [5] Slovenia is estimated to have inherited an FDI stock of $666 million which is not reflected in cumulated inflows. Estimates for the other republics are not available. UNCTAD, *World Investment Report, 1999: Foreign Direct Investment and the Challenge of Development* (United Nations publication, Sales No. E.99.II.D.3).
>
> [6] Cumulated annual FDI inflows are a measure of the country's stock of foreign assets.
>
> [7] UN/ECE, *International Comparisons of Gross Domestic Product in Europe, 1996* (United Nations publication, Sales No. E.99.II.E.13).
>
> [8] M&As can still positively affect economic efficiency (independently of new investment) if they lead to better management, better integration in global marketing networks, and so on.

- Azerbaijan, Kazakhstan and Turkmenistan (1994-1997) received relatively large investments in the natural resource extraction sectors;
- Changes in Slovak policy towards FDI were reflected in 2000 by the sale of Slovak Telecom (€1 billion) and the VSZ steelworks ($500 million plus $700 million in promised follow-up investments over 10 years).

The global financial crises of 1997-1998 had only a limited impact on foreign direct investment in the transition economies. In fact total inflows continued to rise, a reflection of both the long-term planning horizon of foreign direct investors and the more immediate opportunities presented by depressed asset prices. Foreign investors also remained interested in acquiring strategic assets, especially in telecommunications companies. However, FDI into Russia has fallen sharply in the wake of the rouble crisis, exacerbating a persistently unfavourable investment climate. Moreover, it has been reported that some new investments intended to supply the CIS market were postponed, particularly in the Baltic states. The Kosovo conflict also discouraged investment in south-east Europe, at least temporarily, but several key privatizations did go ahead.

Several major privatizations in 2000 (e.g. Poland=s TSPA for $4 billion; Slovak Telecom for €1 billion) show their continuing importance as a determinant of FDI. The experiences of Hungary and Estonia indicate that the winding down of privatization programmes results in a fall of receipts. In most east European and Baltic states, these programmes are due to be completed in 2001-2002, but in other countries the process is much further behind.

There are considerable differences in the amounts of FDI received by different transition economies. In 1999, the ratio of the cumulated inflows to GDP, a measure of the penetration of FDI in the host economy, was in the range of 30-40 per cent in the Czech Republic, Hungary,[511] Estonia and Latvia compared with around 10 per cent or less in many other countries (chart 5.2.1). However, this indicator is calculated using the nominal GDP and exchange rate of the host country, which is often undervalued (box 5.3.1). The FDI ratios calculated with GDP estimates based on PPPs are shown in table 5.3.1 and chart 5.3.1.[512] Although the regional average has increased from 0.5 per cent in 1993-1996 to 1 per cent in 1997-1999, the ranking of countries remained broadly similar. Several

---

[511] Hungary leads in the rankings despite the fact that its cumulated FDI is underestimated by the exclusion of reinvested profits (box 5.3.1).

[512] These ratios are lower because of the adjustment for exchange rate undervaluation. The inter-country variance is smaller than that of the ratios based on nominal GDP (also see table 5.2.2.)

TABLE 5.3.1

FDI inflows as a percentage of GDP(PPP), 1993-1999
(Period averages, per cent)

1993-1996		1997-1999	
Range 1.0-2.9		**Range 2.1-5.1**	
Hungary	2.9	Azerbaijan	5.1
Estonia	2.0	Estonia	3.4
Azerbaijan	1.7	Croatia	2.9
Latvia	1.7	Latvia	2.8
Poland	1.3	Lithuania	2.5
Czech Republic	1.2	Czech Republic	2.3
Kazakhstan	1.1	Poland	2.1
Turkmenistan	1.0	**Range 1.1-1.9**	
Range 0.5-0.9		Hungary	1.9
Albania	0.9	Kazakhstan	1.8
Croatia	0.8	Armenia	1.5
Slovakia	0.6	Bulgaria	1.5
Slovenia	0.6	Romania	1.1
Kyrgyzstan	0.5		
Transition economies average = 0.5		**Transition economies average = 1.0**	
Range 0.3-0.4		**Range 0.5-1.0**	
Lithuania	0.4	Georgia	1.0
Republic of Moldova	0.3	Slovenia	0.9
Range 0.1-0.2		Republic of Moldova	0.9
Armenia	0.2	Kyrgyzstan	0.7
Bulgaria	0.2	Turkmenistan	0.7
Romania	0.2	The former Yugoslav	
Russian Federation	0.2	Republic of Macedonia	0.6
Tajikistan	0.2	Slovakia	0.6
Belarus	0.1	Albania	0.5
Georgia	0.1	**Range 0.3-0.4**	
The former Yugoslav		Russian Federation	0.4
Republic of Macedonia	0.1	Tajikistan	0.4
Ukraine	0.1	Ukraine	0.4
Uzbekistan	0.1	Belarus	0.3
		Uzbekistan	0.3

Source: UN/ECE secretariat calculations, based on national balance of payments statistics and GDP(PPP) estimates.

CHART 5.3.2

Cumulative FDI inflows per capita and GDP(PPP) per capita, 1999
(Dollars)

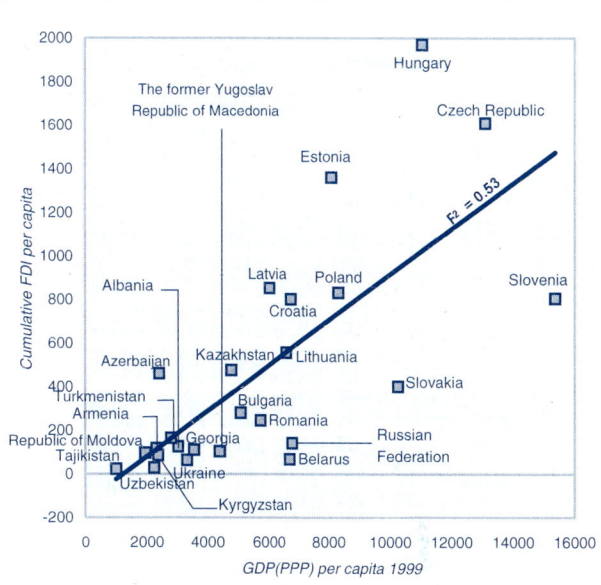

Source: National balance of payments statistics; UN/ECE secretariat for GDP(PPP).

Note: FDI inflows are cumulated from 1988 to 1999. Population refers to 1999.

CHART 5.3.3

Annual FDI inflows as a percentage of nominal GDP, 1985-1999
(Per cent)

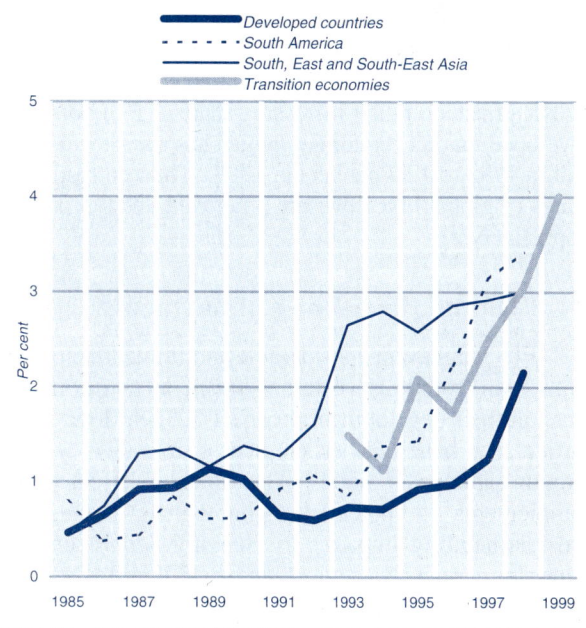

Source: UN/ECE secretariat for the transition economies; UNCTAD, *World Investment Report 2000*, for other areas.

east European and Baltic countries (and Azerbaijan) always rank near the top using this measure, while a number of CIS members occupy the lower ranks. In these CIS countries, the degree of FDI penetration has remained below the regional average. FDI has thus become another source of disparity in the region, with the highest income countries receiving most of the FDI (chart 5.3.2).

Attention is drawn to Slovenia, which has been considered one of the FDI leaders on the basis of cumulated inflows per capita (it ranked number 6 in 1999; table 5.2.2). However, taking the size of its economy into account, it ranks considerably lower (twelfth relative to GDP(PPP) and twenty-second relative to GDP-nominal). These latter ratios suggest a much smaller FDI penetration of the Slovene economy than is generally supposed. The ranking of Azerbaijan, Kazakhstan, Kyrgyzstan and the Republic of Moldova[513] also varies considerably depending on the indicator used (table 5.2.2).

From a global perspective several transition economies have become strong competitors for FDI. Even though they generally began to open up to such investment only early in the decade, by 1998 their average FDI/GDP (nominal) ratio had increased to 3 per cent, close to that of both east Asia and South America (chart 5.3.3). Given that the developing countries had decades of head start and

---

[513] The ratio of the Republic of Moldova was also raised by the collapse of output in 1998-1999 (box 5.3.1).

CHART 5.3.4

Cumulative FDI inflows as a percentage of current year GDP, 1985-1999
(Per cent)

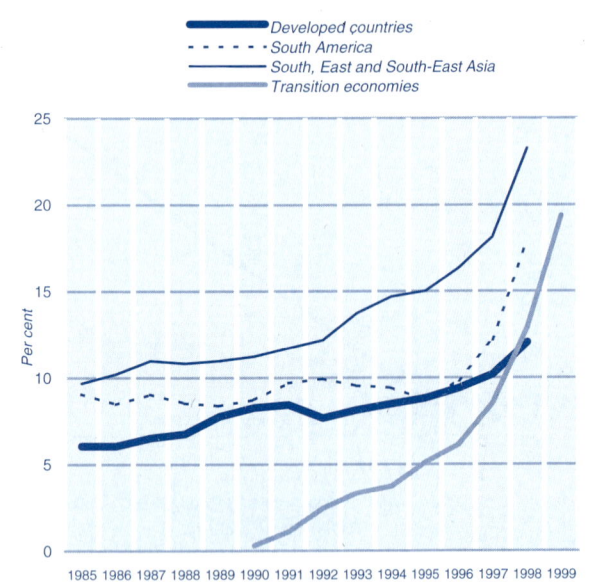

Source: UN/ECE secretariat for the transition economies; UNCTAD, *World Investment Report 2000*, for other areas.

received an accelerated inflow of FDI in the 1990s, their cumulative FDI/GDP ratios in 1998 still exceeded those of the transition economies by a considerable margin (chart 5.3.4). Nonetheless, FDI penetration of the Czech Republic, Hungary, Estonia, Latvia, Azerbaijan and Kazakhstan is roughly comparable to that in leading developing country recipients such as Chile and Malaysia. The growing attraction of the transition economies for FDI is also reflected in their increasing share of FDI outside the developed market economies, which has risen form 7.6 per cent in 1993 to 12.4 per cent in 1998. Their corresponding shares of global FDI flows are 3 per cent and 3.5 per cent, respectively.[514]

5.4 FDI and the balance of payments

FDI can have a considerable and immediate positive impact on countries' external financial positions and, thus, on their development prospects. Such flows can be particularly beneficial when access to other types of foreign capital is limited. The financial effect of FDI complements its potential technological, management and restructuring impact. In Hungary and Estonia, for example, early privatization-related FDI inflows helped to boost foreign exchange reserves and/or reduce external debt (i.e. net debt reduction). Indeed, reducing the high debt burden was a consideration determining Hungary's particular privatization strategy. Revenues increased

---

[514] The source of data on global flows is UNCTAD, *World Investment Report, 2000: Cross-border Mergers and Acquisitions and Development* (United Nations publication, Sales No. E.00.II.D.20).

TABLE 5.4.1

Ratio of FDI inflows to current account deficits, 1993-1999
(Per cent)

	1993-1996	1997-1999
Eastern Europe	58[a]	86
Baltic states	97	64
CIS[b]	45	77
of which:		
Asian CIS	66	84
European CIS[c]	21	59

Source: UN/ECE secretariat, based on national balance of payments statistics.

Note: The ratios are calculated as averages of cumulated FDI inflows to cumulated current account deficits.

[a] Excluding Poland, which had a large current account surplus in 1995.

[b] Excluding the Russian Federation.

[c] Belarus, Republic of Moldova and Ukraine.

official reserves and net debt fell in 1990-1993 and again in 1995 when privatization peaked. Estonia benefited comparably in 1992-1993. Toward the end of the decade, FDI-related privatization helped to strengthen the reserve positions of Bulgaria, Croatia, Romania and Lithuania. In 2000 Poland retired $940 million of Brady bond debt using some of the proceeds from the sale of the telecommunications enterprise, TSPA.

FDI also contributed to a loosening of balance of payments constraints in the region early in the decade. The growth of FDI has helped to finance increasing current account deficits. There was a fourfold increase in the combined current account deficit of eastern Europe in the 1990s, but 86 per cent of it was financed by FDI in 1997-1999 (table 5.4.1 and table 5.2.2). This means of finance is generally viewed favourably since it is relatively stable (see below), often promotes exports, and is largely non-debt creating.[515] Despite periods of sizeable current account deficits in the 1990s, the Czech Republic and Poland were able to forgo sovereign borrowing and hold down their external debt. On the other hand, there was a marked increase in the foreign indebtedness of several countries with large current account deficits and relatively low levels of inward FDI (e.g. Croatia, Romania, Slovakia and several Asian members of the CIS). FDI-related privatizations proved to be an attractive financing option for several countries nearing their debt ceiling.

FDI is generally considered more stable than other financial flows, because investments in fixed assets may be more difficult to liquidate (compared with financial investments) and because direct investors tend to make long-term commitments. Despite the lumpiness of privatization-related foreign investments, the volatility of

---

[515] Discussions of FDI as a source of finance, however, often overlook the fact that loans by a TNC to a foreign subsidiary count as part of the host country's foreign debt and that interest on the loans is counted as an outflow (in the current account).

TABLE 5.4.2

Coefficients of variation[a] of FDI inflows and other capital flows,[b] 1990-1999

(Standard deviation divided by the absolute means)

	1990-1999		1993-1999	
	FDI inflows	Other flows	FDI inflows	Other flows
Eastern Europe[c]	1.0	1.9	0.7	1.5
Albania	0.7	2.3	0.3	3.4
Bulgaria	1.2	1.6	1.0	2.6
Croatia	1.3	1.5	0.9	0.9
Czech Republic	0.9	2.9	0.7	1.7
Hungary	0.5	2.8	0.4	1.9
Poland (cash basis)	1.1	1.0	0.8	1.0
Romania	1.1	0.8	0.9	1.2
Slovakia	0.7	1.3	0.4	0.7
Slovenia	0.6	2.4	0.4	1.3
The former Yugoslav Republic of Macedonia	1.7	2.5	1.3	0.9
Baltic states	..	..	0.7	1.0
Estonia	..	..	0.6	1.5
Latvia	..	..	0.5	1.2
Lithuania	..	..	1.1	0.3
Total CIS	..	..	0.7	1.7
Armenia	..	..	1.3	0.5
Azerbaijan	..	..	0.8	0.7
Belarus	..	..	0.9	0.5
Georgia	..	..	1.2	0.5
Kazakhstan	..	..	0.4	1.4
Kyrgyzstan	..	..	0.6	0.5
Republic of Moldova	..	..	0.7	0.6
Russian Federation	..	..	0.7	2.3
Tajikistan	..	..	0.4	0.8
Turkmenistan	..	..	0.5	10.7
Ukraine	..	..	0.5	0.8
Uzbekistan	..	..	0.9	1.4
Total above	..	..	0.7	1.4
Memorandum items:				
CETE-5	0.8	2.1	0.6	1.3
SETE-7[c]	1.2	1.7	0.9	1.8
Asian CIS	0.9	5.0	0.8	2.1
3 European CIS[d]	0.8	0.8	0.7	0.6

Source: UN/ECE secretariat, based on national balance of payments statistics.

[a] Standard deviation divided by the mean, absolute annual dollar inflow.
[b] Excluding errors and omissions.
[c] Excluding Bosnia and Herzegovina and Yugoslavia.
[d] Belarus, Republic of Moldova and Ukraine.

FDI flows into the transition economies has been less than that of other types of capital. For example, in the wake of the global financial crises (1997-1998), FDI in these countries generally continued to rise, although most of them lost access to the international financial markets (at least temporarily) and suffered reversals of short-term and portfolio investments.[516] The notion of a relative stability of FDI flows is supported by the calculations in table 5.4.2,[517] particularly in the case of the east European and Baltic countries.[518] This shift to a more stable source of external financing has helped to strengthen the financial position of many transition economies.

These generally positive features of FDI, and its association with more dynamic export growth, may improve foreign perceptions of the host country's creditworthiness. Thus FDI may contribute to the creation of a virtuous circle, involving a reduction in borrowing costs, access to a broader range of financial instruments and more stable capital inflows. In Hungary, for example, the record ($4 billion) privatization-related FDI inflow at the end of 1995 contributed to the upgrading of its credit rating in 1996.[519] This rating and the continuation of a substantial, although reduced, inflow of FDI helped to maintain the country's access to the international capital markets in the aftermath of the global financial crises.

The potential financial benefits of FDI do not seem to have been widely appreciated by policy makers in the early stages of the transition. FDI, if it was considered important at all, was viewed as complementing domestic savings and as a source of technology and advanced management techniques. That is to say, it was seen largely as an element of industrial policy. More recently, and especially among the countries recently accelerating economic reforms, FDI-related privatization revenues have often been counted on as a means of financing current account (and fiscal) deficits and boosting official reserves.

It is often maintained that FDI will increase a country's exports and improve the current account balance. Thus, the argument goes, an increasing current account deficit financed by FDI should not be cause for concern. However, assessing the full impact of FDI on the balance of payments is difficult, not least because of data limitations. Four items in the balance of payments accounts deal specifically with the transactions of TNCs: FDI flows, including reinvested earnings, in the financial (capital) account and, in the current account, interest on intercompany debt, repatriated profits and reinvested earnings from direct (equity) investment (box 5.3.1).

---

[516] External bond issues were particularly affected, syndicated loans to a lesser extent.

[517] These results are similar to those obtained for the developing countries. UNCTAD, *World Investment Report, 1999: Foreign Direct Investment and the Challenge of Development* (United Nations publication, Sales No. E.99.II.D.3).

[518] Attention is drawn to the fact that the calculations in table 5.4.2 may not fully reflect the volatility of all FDI-related flows, i.e. those outside the identified FDI item in the financial (capital) account of the balance of payments. During a period of financial turbulence, for example, a TNC may accelerate (outward) profit remittances (a current account item) or it may borrow locally, using fixed assets as collateral, and transfer the funds abroad (perhaps selling the currency short). This latter transaction would be recorded in "other investment" in the balance of payments and thus would be excluded from the FDI volatility measure used here. However, the scope for such operations is a function of the sophistication of the financial system in the host country and the extent of controls on the capital account.

[519] More generally, A. Bevan and S. Estrin, op. cit., found that FDI inflows improved the credit ratings of a sample of transition economies with a lag. There was also evidence of a feedback effect whereby better credit ratings attracted more FDI.

A narrow measure of the direct impact of foreign investment enterprises is net transfers, calculated as the difference between FDI inflows and repatriated profits.[520] Repatriated earnings can be expected to increase as a function of the growth of the FDI stock and FIE profitability. (This outflow is a reminder that FDI is not a "free" source of finance, such as grants.) However, since earnings repatriation can only occur under conditions of FIE profitability, FDI is still likely to be preferable to debt, which requires servicing irrespective of the asset's performance. Data for the transition economies indicate that net inward transfers have been positive, owing to the small scale of profit repatriation so far (generally repatriated earnings have amounted to less than 10 per cent of net FDI inflows). This is likely to change as FDI stocks increase and FIEs move out of the start-up phase and become profitable. For example, in Hungary (the country with the most FDI) profit repatriation has risen steadily, the $920 million in 1998 representing nearly 60 per cent of net FDI inflows. In Azerbaijan, the first repatriation of earnings by foreign petroleum companies exceeded FDI in the first half of 2000 (tables 5.4.3 and 5.4.4).

A broader measure of direct FIE cross-border activity includes their exports and imports of goods and services. Typically a foreign direct investment finances the import of machinery and equipment,[521] which *ceteris paribus* causes a temporary deterioration of the current account balance. The current account will remain under pressure if the FIEs import merchandise for production or distribution. If the FIEs begin to export (as is generally assumed for investments in the tradeable goods sector) and/or if they replace imported inputs by local products (positive spillover effect), the current account balance will improve. However, even when FDI-linked activities lead to foreign exchange deficits, such investments may still improve the balance of payments if they create externalities that enhance the export potential of the whole economy.[522] Overall, the direct net balance of payments impact of the foreign investment and its contribution to economic integration depends on many factors including the eventual success of exports, the sector of operation (some sectors such as services export little or nothing at all), the development of downstream linkages, etc. Although the net effect is often assumed to be positive it can very well be negative in practice.

To take a specific example, Malaysia is one of the few countries for which data permit an evaluation of the direct balance of payments impact of FDI. Considered one of the most successful countries in attracting and using FDI, the impact of FIEs on the combined trade balance and income flows of the current account is estimated to have been negative in every year during 1980-1992.[523] The trade balance of the FIEs became positive in the late 1980s owing to their strong export growth. However, as their exports became more import intensive, the current account became negative. Eventually, in the late 1980s, these outflows on current account were offset by new FDI inflows on the capital account, but the cumulative impact during the whole period was negative. There are indications from other parts of the world that a negative trade impact of FDI is not unique to Malaysia.[524] In Austria, the aggregate merchandise trade balance of resident FIEs has been persistently negative during 1990-1997.[525] The case is interesting because Austria is a developed country where FIEs might have been expected to establish linkages with local suppliers, reduce dependence on imported intermediate inputs and generate a trade surplus.

In the transition economies the growth of total merchandise exports has been associated with FDI inflows (chart 5.4.1).[526] At the sectoral level the role of FDI as a driving force is suggested by the increases in the shares of FIEs in the exports of the manufacturing sector. They rose from zero at the beginning of the decade to substantial proportions by 1998 (table 5.4.5), in Hungary to 86 per cent. This high share suggests that virtually all the recent rapid export growth of Hungarian manufactures originates in FIEs. In the Czech Republic and Poland, the shares of FIEs are smaller, but their rapid expansion in the second half of the decade also suggests a powerful impact of FIEs on export growth. In all these countries FIEs have invested more heavily than domestic firms in new assets (e.g. relative to total sales, see table 5.4.5).[527]

A broader assessment of the balance of payment impact of FDI is possible only for Hungary and Azerbaijan, both of which have attracted large amounts

---

[520] The net transfer calculation excludes the following FDI related flows for which data are often lacking: royalties, license fees, wage remittances and net interest paid on loans to the parent firm. These, and the purchase of foreign services by FIEs, can be large.

[521] The FDI may also represent goods in kind imported for use in the FIE.

[522] UNCTAD, *Trade and Development Report, 1999* (United Nations publication, Sales No. E.99.II.D.1), p. 121.

[523] Ibid.

[524] A similar picture emerges for Thailand. Ibid., pp. 122-123. In the Mercosur FTA, FDI has also been associated with a deterioration of the trade balance. FIEs export to other Mercosur countries but they import capital goods and inputs from the United States. D. Chudnovsky, paper presented at UNCTAD's High-level Segment of the Trade and Development Board (Geneva), 16 October 2000.

[525] W. Altzinger, "A few data of Austrian FDI in CEE", paper presented at the UNCTAD Seminar on *Foreign Direct Investment and Privatization in Central and Eastern Europe* (Vienna), 2-3 March 2000. On the other hand Austria's FDI abroad has generated a trade surplus for the country, lending support to the notion that outward foreign investment is often undertaken to promote exports.

[526] This correlation is significant at the 5 per cent level. However, its robustness has not been tested with the addition of other potential explanatory variables. The correlation is much stronger in the smaller sample of east European and Baltic countries.

[527] The assumption here is that FIEs are more dynamic exporters than domestic firms. However, the increased export share of FIEs may also be explained by a compositional effect, as TNCs tend to become foreign investors in local export firms. While such a FIE/domestic firm shift has undoubtedly occurred, the relative investment intensity of FIEs is also likely to have increased export performance.

TABLE 5.4.3

Direct effect of FDI on the balance of payments in Hungary, 1996-1999

(Million dollars, per cent)

	1996	1997	1998	1999
Current account items (FIEs)	-350	-155	184	556
Trade balance	320	876	1 804	2 219
Exports	2 842	5 081	8 282	10 705
Imports	2 522	4 204	6 478	8 486
Income	-670	-1 032	-1 620	-1 663
Direct investment income	-261	-438	-920	-863
Reinvested earnings[a]	-409*	-594*	-700*	-800*
Capital account item:				
Net FDI (adjusted)[b]	2 687*	2 336*	2 255*	2 495*
Total above	2 337	2 181	2 439	3 051
Memorandum items:				
Non-FIE trade balance	-2 760	-3 010	-4 505	-5 215
Total net FDI (cash basis)	2 278	1 742	1 555	1 695
Total current account/GDP (cash basis)	-3.7	-2.1	-4.9	-4.3
Total current account/GDP (adjusted)[c]	-4.6	-3.4	-6.4	-6.0

Source: UN/ECE secretariat, based on national balance of payments statistics. For FIE exports and imports, K. Antaloczy and M. Sass, "Greenfield FDI in Hungary: is it better than privatization-related FDI?", paper presented at the UNCTAD Seminar on *Foreign Direct Investment and Privatization in Central and Eastern Europe* (Vienna), 2-3 March 2000. For estimates of reinvested earnings, 1996-1997, IMF Staff Country Report No. 99/27, *Hungary: Selected Issues* (Washington, D.C.), April 1999.

Note: The trade of FIEs is the trade of international free trade zones (IFTZs) only; see text.

[a] Reinvested earnings estimates: 1996-1997 are IMF estimates. 1998-1999 outflows are assumed to increase by $100 million annually.

[b] Net FDI on a cash basis plus estimates of reinvested earnings.

[c] Includes estimates of reinvested earnings (outflows).

TABLE 5.4.4

Direct effect of FDI on the balance of payments of the oil sector in Azerbaijan, 1995-2000

(Million dollars)

	1995	1998	1999	Jan.-Jun. 2000
Current account items (oil sector)	143	-228	258	467
Trade balance	227	78	476	702
Exports (oil and products)[a]	257	434	801	777
Imports	-30	-356	-325	-75
Services	-68	-286	-189	-62
Income	-16	-20	-29	-173
Compensation of employees[b]	-9	-20	-29	-20
Profit repatriation[b]	-7	–	–	-153
Capital account item:				
Net FDI[c]	130	757	350	11
Total above	273	529	608	478
Memorandum items:				
Total current account	-318	-1 363	-600	-49
Total net FDI inflows	282	1 024	510	85

Source: UN/ECE secretariat, based on balance of payments data reported to the IMF.

[a] Total exports of the oil sector, of which the oil consortia account for an increasing share, over two thirds in 1999.

[b] Oil consortia.

[c] Excludes signing bonuses paid to the government by foreign oil companies.

CHART 5.4.1

Export growth and ratio of cumulative FDI inflows to GDP(PPP)[a]

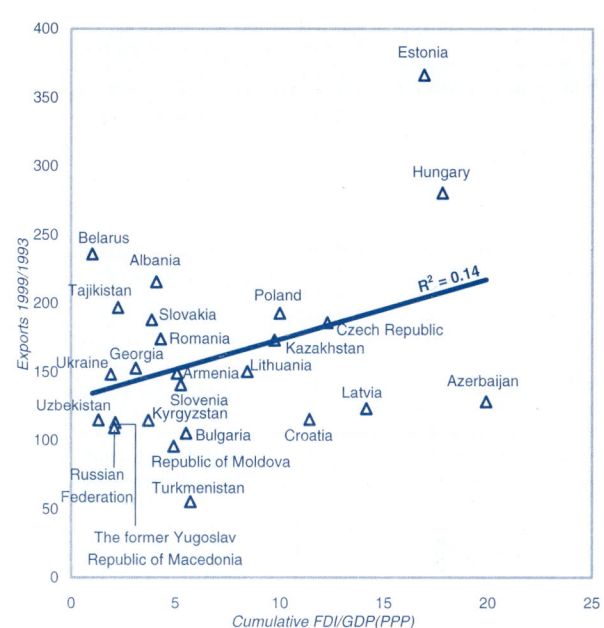

Source: UN/ECE secretariat, based on national balance of payments statistics and merchandise trade statistics.

[a] Ratio of exports (in current prices and dollars) in 1999 relative to 1993. FDI is cumulated from 1988 to 1999. GDP(PPP) refers to 1999.

of FDI (tables 5.4.3 and 5.4.4). In Hungary, the foreign trade balance of FIEs located in industrial foreign trade zones (IFTZs) worsened in the first half of the 1990s because of their imports of high-value machinery and inputs. However, between 1996 and 1999 IFTZs became net exporters, their aggregate trade surplus increasing from $0.3 billion to $2.2 billion.[528] This performance is noteworthy because many FIEs have been involved in assembly operations based on imported components. In consequence, the balance on FDI-associated current account items has moved into surplus, despite increased profit repatriation (direct investment income) and reinvestment of earnings by TNCs. This has helped to keep the total current account deficit in check (on a cash basis it fell to 3.5 per cent of GDP in the first half of 2000).[529] These estimates suggest an increasingly positive overall impact of FDI on the balance of payments, amounting to over $3 billion in 1999.

In Azerbaijan large foreign investments in the oil sector have helped to boost oil exports,[530] while oil-related

---

[528] IFTZs account for the bulk of foreign investment in Hungary, and thus their trade is a good proxy for the trade of all FIEs. The trade deficit of enterprises located in non-IFTZs (largely domestic enterprises) rose from $2.8 billion to $5.2 billion, respectively, which caused the total merchandise trade deficit to increase (table 5.4.3).

[529] UN/ECE, *Economic Survey of Europe, 2000 No. 2*.

[530] It is estimated that oil exports in 2000 will nearly double to 9 million tons. *Financial Times*, 4 July 2000. Receipts have also risen

TABLE 5.4.5

FDI penetration and exports in selected east European and Baltic economies, 1996-1998

(Per cent, ratios)

	Cumulative FDI/ GDP [a]	Share of FIEs in manufacturing				Total exports growth [b]		Contribution of exports to real GDP growth [c]				
		Investment 1998	Sales 1998	Exports				(1) Exports		(2) GDP		
				1996	1998			1996	1997	1998	1999	
Czech Republic	12.3	41.6	31.5	15.9	47.0	185	(1)	5.0	4.5	6.6	4.6
	..	..	..	..	..	..	(2)	4.8	-1.0	-2.2	-0.2
Hungary	17.8	78.7	70.0	77.5	85.9	280	(1)	3.1	10.4	8.0	7.0
	..	..	..	..	..	..	(2)	1.3	4.6	4.9	4.5
Poland	10.0	51.0	40.6	26.3	52.4	192	(1)	3.0	3.0	3.7	-0.4
	..	..	..	..	..	..	(2)	6.0	6.8	4.8	4.1
Slovenia	5.3	24.3	24.4	25.8	32.9	140	(1)	2.0	6.4	4.0	1.1
	..	..	..	..	..	..	(2)	3.5	4.6	3.8	5.0
Estonia	16.9	32.9	28.2	32.5	35.2	366	(1)	1.6	21.6	10.5	-2.1
	..	..	..	..	..	..	(2)	3.9	10.6	4.7	-1.1

Source: UN/ECE secretariat, based on national balance of payments, trade and national account statistics. For penetration of FIEs in manufacturing: G. Hunya, *International Competitiveness. Impacts of FDI in CEECs*, WIIW, Research Reports No. 268 (Vienna), August 2000.

[a] Cumulated FDI 1988-1999 and nominal GDP in 1999.

[b] Ratio of the dollar value of total exports in 1999 to 1993.

[c] Line (1) presents the rate of growth of exports of goods and services; line (2) presents the growth of GDP. All changes are at constant prices.

---

imports (presumably equipment funded by FDI) peaked in 1998 (table 5.4.4). However, imports of services by the oil sector and the compensation of foreign employees (associated with the oil consortia) have remained substantial. In the first half of 2000, the first (large) repatriation of profits occurred which caused the current account to remain in deficit. Overall, FDI in the oil sector made an annual net contribution of several hundred million dollars to the balance of payments in 1998-1999 and the first half of 2000.[531]

The evidence presented here suggests that FDI has so far had a positive impact on the balance of payments of these two transition economies. However, for some of the other countries less is known about the development of FIE imports than of exports (in general total export and import growth seem closely linked in the transition economies).[532] It should be noted that if the balance of payments outcome of TNC-related activities is a continuing deficit, the economy will need to generate net foreign exchange elsewhere, since financing such a deficit by relying on further inflows of FDI would amount to an unsustainable process of "Ponzi" financing.[533] Moreover, FDI may pose some of the same risks and financial management challenges as do other capital flows. Depending on the exchange rate system, capital inflows can cause an appreciation of nominal and/or real exchange rates and thus undermine export competitiveness.[534] This danger is accentuated if foreign investments flow into the non-tradeable sector (e.g. real estate), which, in addition, is unlikely to generate foreign currency receipts.

5.5 The direct effect of FDI on economic growth

Recent theories of economic growth emphasize the importance of knowledge and information as a determinant of growth. Empirical measures of knowledge generally focus on skill levels and R&D activity. But since almost all of the R&D activity takes place in the advanced economies of the ECE and Japan, the relatively less developed economies cannot catch up unless they can gain access to the new technology. Several different channels provide the opportunity for these economies to do this. The three most common channels of technology transfer include: (1) foreign direct investment; (2) international licensing agreements; and (3) international trade. Sections 5.5-5.7 focus on the

---

because of higher oil prices. Foreign investment in Azerbaijan has taken the form of production sharing agreements under which the government and the foreign partner share the costs and output.

[531] Note that the data for oil exports in table 5.4.4 include oil from domestic producers, but by 1999 they accounted for only one third of total export earnings from oil.

[532] At the enterprise level, the results of the UNCTAD survey of mainly import-oriented firms privatized through FDI (i.e. through Mergers and Acquisitions) show that import growth accelerated after privatization, boosting import surpluses. These results, of course, do not reflect the impact of any spillovers on the economy. The main reasons for growing imports were the increasing use of local affiliates as a distribution channel for imports, the substitution of suppliers from the TNC's own network for local sourcing, and the general increase in capital investment using imported capital goods. The sample consisted of 23 firms in seven central and east European countries. G. Hunya and K. Kalotay, "FDI and privatization in central and eastern Europe: trends, impact and policies", paper presented at the UNCTAD Seminar on *Foreign Direct Investment* …, op. cit.

[533] UNCTAD, *Trade and Development Report, 1999*, op. cit., p. 123.

[534] The anticipation of large inflows from planned privatizations led Czech and Polish authorities to create special foreign currency accounts to avoid disruption of the currency markets.

importance of FDI in transferring knowledge and stimulating economic growth. The remaining parts of this section look at the direct relationship between FDI and economic growth. Section 5.6 expands this analysis to include technology transfer and spillovers. The issue of catching up is then explored in section 5.7.

(i) Evidence from the developing economies

A growing number of studies have found a statistical relationship between FDI inflows and domestic economic activity in the host countries.[535] In many cases, they had received FDI for decades although the inflows accelerated in the early 1990s. In this section, some of these empirical findings, generally relating to developing countries in Asia and Latin America, are drawn on. Their experience may hint at the eventual macroeconomic impact of FDI in the transition economies (see below).

The empirical studies of the developing economies generally seek to establish a statistical relationship between FDI inflows and a measure of output growth and/or domestic investment. (Investment is most directly affected by FDI, but FDI may also impact GDP independently of fixed investment.) Such work is of interest because it attempts to capture the net effects of FDI in the economy as a whole. Negative effects may stem from various distortions in an economy – for example, those that offer profit opportunities to foreign investors without improving efficiency. These may occur, for example, if protectionist trade policies encourage TNCs to enter a country purely to obtain market share and monopolistic power.[536] Or, governments may attract FDI to strategic industries by offering investment incentives that offset any benefit the TNC may generate. Even FDI that is not motivated by these objectives may create negative spillovers (which affect aggregate output but may be difficult to identify from enterprise or sectoral data).

The three studies cited below have found a significant relation between FDI flows and economic growth in various samples of developing countries. The first, applying a model of endogenous economic growth, finds that FDI stimulated the long-term expansion of per capita GDP.[537] The contribution of FDI is likely to come from two effects. The more important seems to be that the productivity of FDI is higher than that of domestic investment.[538] This is because FDI embodies advanced technology and management skills and enhances access to world markets, factors that can stimulate the host country's efficiency and internal competition. However, it appears that the higher productivity occurs only when the host country has a minimum threshold stock of human capital (because there is an essential interaction between FDI/technology and human capital in the host economy). Second, FDI has the effect of increasing total domestic investment by more than one-for-one. Estimates of the "crowding in" phenomenon[539] put the total increase in investment at between 1.5 and 2.3 times the increase in the flow of FDI.[540] This increase in total capital accumulation occurs in addition to the positive impact of FDI on technological progress. Overall, in developing countries with an average stock of human capital, a 1 per cent increase in the FDI-GDP ratio is associated with a 0.4-0.7 per cent rise in long-term GDP per capita growth.[541]

In the second study[542] FDI flows were found to stimulate the long-run growth of China, Indonesia, Hong Kong, Japan and Taiwan, and the short-run growth of Singapore.[543] However, no relation between FDI and economic growth was found in South Korea and the Philippines. The third study, examining the impact of different types of capital flows in 18 countries, concluded that the most pronounced positive impact of FDI was on economic growth and domestic savings.[544] It had less of an effect in the Asian countries than in Latin America, presumably because domestic savings play a larger role in the Asian economies.

---

[535] For example, E. Borensztein et al., op. cit.; L. De Mello, Jr., op. cit.; and K. Zhang, "FDI and economic growth: evidence from 10 east Asian economies", *Economia Internationale*, November 1999.

[536] In an extreme case, a TNC may close down an acquired asset to reduce capacity in the region and increase its market power.

[537] E. Borensztein et al., op. cit. The data sample covers the years 1970-1989.

[538] Using a different sample of countries Kamin and Wood found a significant positive relation between FDI and real investment. The study covers the period 1983-1994, which includes the first years of the FDI boom. S. Kamin and P. Wood, *Capital Inflows, Financial Intermediation, and Aggregate Demand: Empirical Evidence from Mexico and other Pacific Basin Countries*, Board of Governors of the Federal Reserve System, International Finance Discussion Papers No. 583 (Washington, D.C.), June 1997.

[539] FDI may stimulate more domestic investment ("crowding in") if there is complementarity in production between FDI and domestic firms. In this case, the FIE may develop backward and forward linkages, perhaps even assisting partner firms (subcontractors or downstream customers) with technology and finance while holding out the prospects of a stable market for their output. On the other hand, FDI may "crowd out" equal amounts of investment by domestic entities through aggressive competition in local product or financial markets, especially in cases where domestic firms are already financially constrained.

[540] Estimates by UNCTAD suggest that there are marked regional differences among the developing countries with FDI tending to crowd in investment in much of Asia and crowding it out in Latin America. Also there are sectoral differences: mining and other raw material extraction projects, for example, generate little indirect investment because the FDI firms create few domestic linkages. UNCTAD, *World Investment Report 1999:...*, op. cit., pp. 172-173.

[541] GDP is measured at purchasing power parity (PPP). Human capital stock is measured by the average level of secondary school attainment in a sample of 69 developing countries.

[542] K. Zhang, op. cit., has noted two problems with the studies relying on cross-section analysis, applied by E. Borensztein et al. and S. Kamin and P. Wood. All presume a priori that FDI responds to or causes economic growth (see below) and do not consider the possibility of feedback effects and a long-run equilibrium relationship between FDI and economic growth. Second, there is evidence of considerable parametric variation across countries in regard to estimates of growth equations and FDI. In effect the methodology involves the imposition of a common (average) structure, thus masking these differences.

[543] Ibid. These countries appear to have experienced FDI-led growth, except for China and Indonesia, where the relationship was found to be bi-directional. The issue of causality is discussed below.

[544] W. Gruben and D. McLeod, "Capital flows, savings, and growth in the 1990s", *The Quarterly Review of Economics and Finance*, Vol. 38, No. 3, Fall 1998. There is no theoretical reason why FDI ought to increase domestic savings.

(ii) Direction of causation

It is usually assumed that FDI inflows stimulate growth (FDI-led growth). Such a relationship might be expected because FDI can enhance those factors which usually play an important role in promoting economic development: investment, technical progress, and, in the new growth theory, R&D, the accumulation of human capital and various positive externalities. However, the causation may run in the other direction, whereby rapid economic growth attracts FDI (growth-driven FDI). Very briefly, under this hypothesis, expanding domestic economic activity is likely to be associated with an improving investment environment and increased opportunity for boosting profits. The expansion of income and domestic markets makes it possible for TNCs to exploit economies of scale. In the longer term, growth-associated improvements in human capital, labour productivity and infrastructure are likely to increase the marginal return to capital and, thus, the demand for domestic and foreign investment.[545] Improved economic performance should also generate profits and encourage their reinvestment (reinvested earnings being a component of FDI). Evidence of a growth-led FDI relationship has been found in Malaysia and Thailand.[546]

Another possibility is a two-way causal process, in which FDI and growth have a reciprocal causal relationship. Evidence of such a virtuous circle has been found in China and Indonesia.[547]

In the transition economies, Hungary and Estonia showed early signs of FDI-led growth. In Hungary, there were significant inflows of FDI in the early 1990s (chart 5.5.1) before GDP started to recover (from the transition recession) in 1994. The output of FIEs was already expanding in 1992-1993 while that of domestic firms continued to decline (it was only later that the FIEs dominated economic performance). In Estonia, too, relatively large FDI inflows preceded the economic upturn in 1995. (A similar pattern may be observed somewhat later in Latvia.) In both cases, the governments' strategies involved an early infusion of FDI through the sale of strategic state assets. On the other hand, in Poland an economic recovery (starting in 1992) preceded the surge in FDI by several years. Due to its size, location etc., Poland was from the very beginning of the transition considered one of the most attractive countries for foreign investment. However, despite this and its early favourable economic performance, foreign direct investors essentially held off until 1996, when the country's large external debt was reduced in agreements with London and Paris Club creditors. Subsequently, FDI inflows and high rates of economic growth appear to have joined in a virtuous circle (as has probably also been the case in Hungary and the Baltic states). The fact that in Croatia, Slovakia and Slovenia there were extended periods of fairly rapid growth without attracting much FDI is explained by domestic policies (as already noted).[548] The experiences of Croatia and Slovakia underline the fact that FDI will only begin to flow after a commitment has been made to reform (including a privatization programme) and investor friendly policies are in place.

(iii) FDI and growth in the transition economies

Studies of the impact of FDI on GDP in the transition economies are lacking.[549] In most of these countries it might be difficult to find such a relation given the known importance of other factors: the degree of economic reform, the success of stabilization policies, the strength of import demand in major trade partners, and so on. The data in chart 5.5.2 do, however, suggest a positive association between FDI and economic growth, but the correlation falls slightly short of being significant.[550] As regards indirect evidence, in Hungary, FDI-driven export growth (see above) appears to have been largely responsible for the improvement in economic performance in the second half of the 1990s.[551] Exports were by far the most dynamic component of final demand, far exceeding the combined contribution of consumption and investment (chart 5.5.1).[552] This was also the case in the Czech Republic although GDP actually contracted due to falling domestic absorption. In all the countries in this sample, GDP and export growth were nearly always positively related and, given the role of foreign companies in exports (table 5.4.5), FDI is likely to have contributed significantly to this outcome. In Kyrgyzstan, FDI in gold production has contributed considerably to overall output growth, and gold is the only export that has increased in value between 1996 and 1999.[553] The contribution of foreign investment to output in Azerbaijan=s oil and gas industry has also been important (see section 5.6).

---

[545] See K. Zhang, op. cit., for a more systematic development of the growth-led FDI hypothesis.

[546] Ibid.

[547] Ibid.

[548] A. Bevan and S. Estrin, op. cit., found a strong relation between growth in GDP and FDI in their 11 country sample. Perhaps with the exception of Hungary, Poland and the Baltic states in the second half of the 1990s, their results seem at variance with the data presented in chart 5.5.1.

[549] The time series covering the transition years are still too short for the types of statistical test applied to the developing economies. At most, 10 years of data are available, less for all the countries of the former Soviet Union. The period includes falls in domestic output early in the transition and external shocks in the late 1990s, events independent of FDI activity. Moreover, in the early phase of the transition, inward FDI was small and, with the exception of Hungary and perhaps one or two other countries, could not have contributed much to economic growth. A recent study of growth factors in the transition economies (1990-1998) excludes FDI for this reason. O. Havrylyshyn et al., *Growth Experience in Transition Countries, 1990-1998*, IMF Occasional Paper, No. 184 (Washington, D.C.), April 2000.

[550] A preliminary statistical analysis suggests that whether or not a country experienced a serious economic crisis (i.e. resulting in a fall in output) is a much more important determinant of its average growth performance in the second half of the 1990s than is FDI. Large foreign investments in the natural resource sector are also important in this regard.

[551] Already in 1992-1993 the output of FIEs in the industrial sector increased by 9 per cent, in contrast to a 5 per cent decrease reported by domestic firms.

[552] Exports in the national accounts also include traded services such as tourism and transport that have benefited from FDI.

[553] National Bank of the Kyrgyz Republic, *Bulletin*, No. 7, 2000.

Economic Growth and Foreign Direct Investment in the Transition Economies

CHART 5.5.1
GDP growth and FDI flows as a per cent of nominal GDP in selected east European and Baltic economies, 1991-1999
(Per cent)

(For source see end of chart.)

CHART 5.5.1 (concluded)

GDP growth and FDI flows as a per cent of nominal GDP in selected east European and Baltic economies, 1991-1999
(Per cent)

Source: UN/ECE secretariat, based on national account and balance of payments statistics.

The results of the analysis of FDI inflows in certain developing countries suggest that it may also boost the long-term growth rate of the transition economies. Thus, the FDI/GDP ratio of eastern Europe increased from zero at the beginning of the decade to around 4 per cent in 1997-1999 (using nominal GDP) and to 1.8 per cent (using GDP at PPPs); applying the elasticities estimated by Borenzstein (0.4-0.7, based on GDP at PPPs) to the latter yields an increase of some 0.7-1.3 percentage points in the long-term per capita growth rate of the area, with larger increases in the Czech Republic, Hungary and the Baltic states. These elasticities reflect the human capital stock of an "average" developing country. However, the Borensztein study also found that the FDI-growth elasticity is directly related to a country's human capital. That is to say, a given FDI inflow has a greater impact in countries with a higher average level of human capital than a lower one. Since the transition economies are relatively well endowed in this regard, and generally rate much higher than the developing countries in terms of, say, secondary school attainment, it seems reasonable to argue that the impact of FDI in eastern Europe should be greater than the "average" elasticities would suggest.[554]

---

[554] See table 5.2.2. One caveat is that to be efficient human capital in these countries has to adjust to market conditions. In several of them concern is increasing about the apparent deterioration in the quality of education, adversely affected by years of tight budgets.

CHART 5.5.2

Growth of GDP and ratio of cumulative FDI inflows to GDP(PPP) [a]

Source: UN/ECE secretariat, based on national account and balance of payments statistics.

[a] Average growth of real GDP, 1997-2000 (estimates). FDI inflows are cumulated from 1988 to 1999. GDP(PPP) refers to 1999.

It is, of course, impossible to judge whether the Borensztein elasticities are applicable to the transition economies. Doubts arise simply because FDI in a transition economy may not have the same impact as in a developing country with a long-established market system (however rudimentary it may be). While examination of this question is beyond the scope of this chapter, it may be useful to raise the issue of mergers and acquisitions (M&As). Their share of total FDI in the region has been high, probably higher than in the developing countries covered by the studies mentioned above. A large share of M&As in FDI might suggest a smaller impact on economic growth because they represent a change of ownership rather than an injection of new fixed investment. However, the growth impulse could come, first of all, from better corporate governance and restructuring of the privatized firms, both reflecting possible efficiency gains without new investment. Second, the presence of these FIEs may generate positive spillovers. Finally, as time passes and M&As undertake new investments and restructure, they begin to look more and more like greenfield investments. In fact, statistical evidence from some transition economies indicates that the economic performance of manufacturing firms privatized through M&A is eventually as good as that of greenfield FDI.[555] Large foreign investments in telecommunications, financial and various business services may be expected to generate positive externalities and improve export efficiency.

5.6 FDI and productivity spillovers in the transition economies

There is a growing empirical literature on FDI as a channel for the diffusion of new technology and better organizational practice in host countries. Most of the evidence on productivity spillovers relies on enterprise and industry level panel data since they occur between enterprises. Panel data are derived directly from the income statements of individual enterprises and are usually obtained through industrial surveys carried out by national statistical offices. The data compiled at the firm level are often aggregated into industries to avoid breaching confidentiality rules.

One advantage of panel data is that they pick up certain country-specific factors that do not appear in cross-country time series data.[556] This may be important if host country characteristics matter. One limitation of industry level panel data, however, is that they do not measure interindustry spillovers adequately. The difficulty lies in identifying the relevant upstream suppliers (backward linkages) and downstream customers (forward linkages). By contrast, firm level panel data capture both intra-firm and inter-firm (or intra-industry) spillovers. These data measure not only intra-industry spillovers but also the movement of labour from FIEs to local firms, a positive externality of FDI.

Studies of R&D spillovers at the firm level that do not make explicit reference to FDI provide some indirect evidence of technology spillovers from FIEs to local enterprises in other industries. There is also some direct evidence of positive interindustry spillovers from a panel of individual firms in Venezuela and Indonesia.[557] In Venezuela, backward linkages appear less likely to facilitate spillovers than forward linkages because the FIEs have a high propensity to import, while in Indonesia spillovers are more likely to happen if the local firm is in close proximity to an FIE.

Evidence of productivity spillovers through FDI is mixed. Studies of Australian manufacturing in 1966, Canadian industry in 1972 and Mexico in the mid-1970s find significant intra-industry spillovers when a foreign presence (in employment or value added) is included as an explanatory variable among other firm and industry

---

[555] A. Zemplinerova and M. Jarolim, "FDI through M&A vs. greenfield FDI: the case of the Czech Republic", paper presented at the UNCTAD Seminar on *Foreign Direct Investment* ..., op. cit.

[556] L. de Mello, Jr., "Foreign direct investment-led growth: evidence from time series and panel data", *Oxford Economic Papers*, Vol. 51, 1999, pp. 133-151.

[557] For Venezuela see B. Aitken and A. Harrison, "Do domestic firms benefit from direct foreign investment? Evidence from Venezuela", *American Economic Review*, Vol. 89, No. 3, 1999, pp. 605-618. For Indonesia see F. Sjöholm, "Technology gap, competition and spillovers from direct foreign investment: evidence from establishment data", *The Journal of Development Studies*, Vol. 36, No. 1, 1999, pp. 53-73.

characteristics in total factor productivity.[558] Similar results were found in a study of United States FDI in France, Germany, Japan and the United Kingdom from 1968 to 1988 and in two studies of United Kingdom manufacturing enterprises covering the periods 1984-1992 and 1991-1995.[559] Using a dynamic approach to take into account the different economies of scale across industries, a second study of Mexico confirms that a foreign presence can have a significant influence on local productivity growth.[560] These spillover effects were large enough to assist local firms in Mexico to converge on United States productivity levels from 1965 to 1982.

Panel data from developing countries, however, provide little or no empirical support for positive net productivity spillovers from FDI. Panel data from Venezuela show significant technology transfer to the FIEs and some positive spillovers to domestic enterprises located near the FIE, but there were also negative spillovers to the local economy as a whole.[561] Other studies at the firm level also find positive spillovers, but they are limited to certain industries, such as those with relatively simple technology (Morocco) or which are export oriented (Indonesia).[562] There is also evidence that the presence of United States TNCs in Europe did not result in significant productivity spillovers in many industries, mainly because competitive pressure forced many local firms with small markets out of business.[563] A panel analysis of United Kingdom manufacturing firms from 1991 to 1996 also shows that the presence of foreign firms did not lead to wage and productivity spillovers.[564]

There is also little evidence of productivity spillovers in eastern Europe. Enterprise level panel data from Bulgaria, Poland and Romania covering the period 1993-1997 suggest that FDI may be important for transferring technology to an affiliate, but there is no evidence of positive productivity spillovers to local enterprises.[565] Instead, there is significant evidence of negative spillovers in Poland. Panel data for the Czech Republic between 1992 and 1996 also provide evidence of negative spillovers and suggest that there may not even have been much technology transfer to the FIEs.[566] This study also suggests that imports of capital goods appear to be the more important channel for technology transfer in the Czech Republic. A more recent study based on panel data covering 1995-1998 indicates that there are some spillovers in the Czech Republic, but they are limited to enterprises engaged in R&D or in the production of electrical equipment.[567] This study suggests that the absorptive capacity of enterprises is an important factor in determining the existence and extent of productivity spillovers. Studies of other transition economies at the firm and industry level find similar results to those in the Czech Republic over the same period.[568] Nevertheless, there is significant evidence that FDI is having a direct positive impact on the restructuring of former state enterprises in Hungary.

The rest of this section examines the extent to which TNCs facilitate technology transfer and

---

[558] However, none of these studies explain how these productivity spillovers take place. For the study on Australia, see R. Caves, "Multinational firms, competition and productivity in host-country markets", *Economica*, Vol. 41, 1974, pp. 176-193. For the study on Canada see S. Globerman, "Foreign direct investment and 'spillover' efficiency benefits in Canadian manufacturing industries", *Canadian Journal of Economics*, Vol. 12, 1979, pp. 42-56. For the study on Mexico, see M. Blomström and H. Persson, "Foreign investment and spillover efficiency in an underdeveloped economy: evidence from the Mexican manufacturing industry", *World Development*, Vol. 11, 1983, pp. 493-501.

[559] M. Nadiri, "US Direct Investment and the Production Structure of the Manufacturing Sector in France, Germany, Japan, and the UK", New York University, February 1992, mimeo. Using industry level panel data, Hubert and Pain show significant intra-industry and interindustry spillovers in United Kingdom manufacturing from 1984 to 1992. F. Hubert and N. Pain, *Inward Investment and Technical Progress in the UK Manufacturing Sector*, OECD Economics Department Working Paper, No. 268 (Paris), October 2000. Using panel data for 48 United Kingdom manufacturing industries, Liu et al., show significant intra-industry productivity spillovers to the domestic economy, the extent of which depends on the absorptive capacity of the domestic enterprises. X. Liu, P. Siler, C. Wang and Y. Wei, "Productivity spillovers from foreign direct investment: evidence from UK industry level panel data", *Journal of International Business Studies*, Vol. 31, No. 3, 2000, pp. 407-426.

[560] M. Blomström and E. Wolff, "Multinational corporations and productivity convergence in Mexico", in W. Baumol, R. Nelson and E. Wolff (eds.), *Convergence of Productivity: Cross-National Studies and Historical Evidence* (Oxford, Oxford University Press, 1994).

[561] B. Aitken and A. Harrison, op. cit. This study, first published in 1994 as a World Bank Research Paper, No. 1248, is one of the first empirical studies to use firm level panel data to test for spillovers.

[562] For Morocco, see M. Haddad and A. Harrison, "Are there positive spillovers from direct foreign investment? Evidence from panel data for Morocco", *Journal of Development Economics*, Vol. 42, 1993, pp. 51-74. For Indonesia, see M. Blomström and F. Sjöholm, "Technology transfer and spillovers: does local participation with multinationals matter?", *European Economic Review*, Vol. 43, 1999, pp. 915-923.

[563] J. Cantwell, *Technological Innovation and Multinational Corporations* (Oxford, Basil Blackwell, 1989).

[564] S. Girma, D. Greenaway and K. Wakelin, "Who benefits from foreign direct investment in the UK", University of Nottingham, 2000, mimeo.

[565] J. Konings, *The Effect of Direct Foreign Investment on Domestic Firms: Evidence from Firm Level Panel Data in Emerging Economies*, LICOS Discussion Paper, No. 86 (Leuven), 1999.

[566] S. Djankov and B. Hoekman, "Foreign investment and productivity growth in Czech enterprises", *The World Bank Economic Review*, Vol. 14, No. 1 (Washington, D.C.), 2000, pp. 49-64. By contrast, the study by A. Zemplinerova and M. Jarolim, op. cit., indicates the presence of some spillovers to local enterprises from 1994 to 1998.

[567] Y. Kinoshita, *R&D and Technology Spillovers via FDI: Innovation and Absorptive Capacity*, CERGE Working Paper, No. 163 (Prague), November 2000. The study by J. Damijan and B. Majcen, "Transfer of technology through FDI, spillover effects and recovery of Slovenian manufacturing firms", University of Ljubljana, 2000, mimeo, and J. Konings, op. cit., also indicate that spillovers in Slovenia are limited to enterprises engaged in R&D activity.

[568] A study of the Czech Republic, Hungary, Slovakia and Slovenia found few interindustry spillovers between 1993 and 1996. M. Knell, "FIEs and productivity convergence in central Europe", in G. Hunya (ed.), *Integration Through Foreign Direct Investment* (Cheltenham, Edward Elgar, 2000). Evidence from Slovenia also indicates no significant spillovers to the domestic economy as a whole, and that imports of capital goods are the most important channel of technology transfer. J. Damijan and B. Majcen, op. cit.

productivity spillovers in selected transition economies. This analysis is based on annual financial and operating data collected in the Czech Republic, Hungary, Poland, Slovenia and Estonia from 1993 to 1998. Primarily derived from statistical questionnaires or the income statements of individual enterprises, these data contain information on the overall operations of the enterprises, including total sales, export sales, value added, employment, wages, profits, exports, capital stock and R&D activity.[569] Depending on how the survey is structured, the data allow for either a comparison between enterprises with at least 10 per cent foreign ownership or with at least 50 per cent foreign ownership. The choice between the two measures will depend on whether less than 50 per cent ownership is also a controlling interest.

Data at the enterprise level provide the best way to test for productivity spillovers because the information is not confined to a particular industry. Rules concerning confidentiality create difficulties in obtaining these data even when they are collected by a statistical agency, but this can be overcome when they are available at the industry level. The Statistical Office of Estonia and the Ministry of Finance of Slovenia, however, have kindly provided enterprise level data so that the channels of technology transfer can be analysed in detail. The first two parts of the section therefore use data that are aggregated to the 2-digit ISIC, Rev.3 level and the remaining part uses the enterprise level data provided for Estonia and Slovenia.[570]

(i) FDI in east European manufacturing industry

During the first few years of the economic transition, there was a rapid decline of industrial output in virtually all the transition economies, with the technology intensive industries being most affected. When the recovery of industrial output occurred in the mid-1990s, the technology-intensive and scale-intensive industries had higher than average growth rates in almost every country.[571] This change in structure is shown in table 5.6.1 as the change in the distribution of total manufacturing sales (gross revenue minus changes in inventories) produced by firms in the five transition economies. There is considerable variation across countries, but the food and beverages industry continues to be the largest one in terms of sales. More importantly, there was a considerable structural change from 1993 to 1998. In every country there was higher than average growth in the electrical and precision instruments industries (ISIC 30-33), and in Hungary office machinery and equipment industry increased from 0.6 per cent of total manufacturing sales to 6.3 per cent. Motor vehicle production also increased significantly in every country except Estonia, and in Hungary its share increased from 4.4 per cent in 1993 to 13.4 per cent in 1998. In both industries, the share of sales by FIEs was also significantly above average.

There was also a major shift in the ownership structure of manufacturing industries from 1993 to 1998. Table 5.6.2 describes the structural change in terms of the percentage shares of manufacturing sales by FIEs. In all countries there was a large increase in the proportion of sales by FIEs, most of the change being due to the sale of former state owned enterprises to TNCs, except for the electrical and electronic industries which attracted considerable "greenfield" investment. In 1998, 70 per cent of manufacturing sales in Hungary were attributed to FIEs whereas in Slovenia their share was only about 24 per cent. This contrast mainly reflects differences in host country characteristics and, especially, in privatization strategies. The privatization authority in Hungary openly solicited TNCs as potential bidders whereas in Slovenia the strategy was to rely on corporate restructuring by existing management. The Czech Republic and Poland stepped up their encouragement of TNCs in the second half of the 1990s, and their success is reflected in the relatively large shift in ownership.

On average FIEs had significantly higher labour productivity than local enterprises in the region.[572] Labour productivity in local enterprises generally ranged from one third to two thirds of the productivity of FIEs, as measured by output per employee. (Output here is measured as revenue from sales of own products and implicitly includes changes in inventories.) In a few industries labour productivity was higher in domestically owned enterprises (DEs), including in basic metals and wearing apparel in the Czech Republic and Estonia, office machinery in Poland and Estonia and motor vehicles in Estonia. The acquisition of former state owned enterprises by foreign firms explains much of the variation in table 5.6.2. Foreign firms were mostly attracted to the most efficient and some of the largest DEs and this has an important impact on the comparison of relative labour productivity levels in domestic and foreign owned firms.

---

[569] The data used in this section were collected under the framework of PHARE-ACE Research Project P97-8112-R. The project studied the impact of FDI on the international competitiveness of east European manufacturing industries and on EU enlargement.

[570] It should be noted that the confidentiality problem can be overcome by stripping the data of its identifier and assigning it a number. In some cases, a researcher can negotiate with the statistical agency to do the calculations for a nominal fee.

[571] M. Knell and D. Hanzl, "Technology and industrial restructuring in central Europe", in D. Dyker and S. Radosevic (eds.), *Innovation and Structural Change in Post-Socialist Countries: A Quantitative Approach* (Amsterdam, Kluwer Academic Publishers, 1999).

[572] Empirical studies reviewed by UNCTAD suggest that foreign affiliates are usually more efficient in production than their domestic counterparts. This difference is partly due to economies of scale, but it also reflects the possession of superior technology, better organization of the firm, and to a lesser degree the introduction of new products and processes. Yet individual country-, industry- and firm-specific factors can create considerable difficulty in drawing conclusions from any empirical analysis. UNCTAD, *World Investment Report 1997: Transnational Corporations, Market Structure and Competition Policy* (United Nations publication, Sales No. E.97.II.D.10).

TABLE 5.6.1

Distribution of total manufacturing sales by industry in selected east European and Baltic economies, 1993 and 1998

(Per cent)

ISIC	Industry	Czech Republic 1993	Czech Republic 1998	Hungary 1993	Hungary 1998	Poland 1993	Poland 1998	Slovenia 1995	Slovenia 1998	Estonia 1996	Estonia 1998
D	Total manufacturing	100	100	100	100	100	100	100	100	100	100
15	Food and beverages	19.2	15.6	26.0	19.1	24.5	21.3	12.2	11.6	32.2	30.2
16	Tobacco	In 15	1.2	0.9	0.6	1.7	3.5	*	*	In 15	In 15
17	Textiles	4.7	3.7	2.7	2.1	3.6	2.3	4.5	4.6	6.9	6.6
18	Wearing apparel and fur	1.0	0.8	1.9	1.7	1.9	1.5	2.7	2.3	4.0	3.8
19	Leather products	2.2	0.7	1.3	0.8	1.0	0.6	*	1.6	1.3	1.2
20	Wood products	1.8	1.4	1.7	1.4	2.0	2.5	4.0	3.4	7.7	10.1
21	Pulp and paper products	2.5	2.8	1.8	1.8	1.9	2.3	4.4	3.9	1.5	1.7
22	Printing and publishing	1.4	1.7	4.6	3.4	2.3	2.7	4.6	4.4	4.6	4.8
23	Petroleum and coke	5.7	3.1	11.6	7.2	8.3	7.5	*	0.5	10.8	7.7
24	Chemicals and chemical products	6.3	7.3	10.2	7.5	8.6	8.0	9.7	9.9	In 23	In 23
25	Rubber and plastics	2.5	3.6	2.8	3.4	2.9	3.2	4.5	5.1	2.3	2.4
26	Non-metallic mineral products	5.4	5.9	3.4	3.1	4.3	4.4	3.9	4.0	4.3	5.2
27	Basic metals	12.2	12.8	4.7	4.4	9.4	7.7	5.8	4.5	5.5	6.9
28	Fabricated metals	4.7	5.5	5.4	4.3	3.1	4.0	6.6	7.6	In 27	In 27
29	Machinery and equipment	10.9	8.8	6.3	5.4	7.4	6.5	8.8	10.0	3.0	2.8
30	Office machinery and computers	0.1	–	0.8	6.3	0.1	0.3	0.9	*	5.3	6.0
31	Electrical machinery	3.9	5.0	3.0	4.5	3.1	3.4	4.7	4.4	In 30	In 30
32	Radio, telephone and communication equipment	0.6	1.3	2.2	5.9	1.6	2.6	2.1	2.5	In 30	In 30
33	Precision instruments	0.7	0.7	1.6	1.3	0.9	1.1	2.2	2.2	In 30	In 30
34	Motor vehicles	8.7	13.7	4.4	13.4	5.3	8.4	9.6	11.3	3.8	3.2
35	Other transport equipment	2.3	1.6	0.4	0.6	3.6	3.1	*	0.6	In 34	In 34
36	Furniture and miscellaneous manufacturing	2.6	2.5	1.9	1.3	2.4	2.8	3.5	3.5	6.8	7.3
37	Recycling	0.6	0.4	–	0.4	0.3	0.3	*	*	In 36	In 36

Source: WIIW Database on Foreign Investment Enterprises.

Note: Data for Estonia are for 1996 and data for Slovenia are for 1995. An * indicates sectors with less than three multinational firms that are included in total manufacturing. Slovenia's share of total manufacturing sales was 5.5 per cent in 1995 and 2.1 per cent in 1998.

TABLE 5.6.2

Share of FIEs in total sales by industry in selected east European and Baltic economies, 1993 and 1998

(Per cent)

ISIC	Industry	Czech Republic 1993	Czech Republic 1998	Hungary 1993	Hungary 1998	Poland 1993	Poland 1998	Slovenia 1995	Slovenia 1998	Estonia 1996	Estonia 1998
D	Total manufacturing	11.5	31.5	41.3	70.0	13.7	40.0	17.6	24.4	26.6	28.2
15	Food and beverages	13.9	22.1	48.1	55.7	12.5	37.6	7.2	10.2	20.0	19.3
16	Tobacco	In 15	94.6	99.4	95.7	3.5	95.3	*	*	In 15	In 15
17	Textiles	0.5	22.1	38.9	55.9	7.4	14.6	7.1	10.7	78.4	70.5
18	Wearing apparel and fur	1.6	15.6	39.6	47.2	23.3	40.1	2.0	1.1	10.5	9.8
19	Leather products	2.3	6.6	34.0	57.3	5.4	16.5	*	5.6	43.5	45.5
20	Wood products	4.7	36.5	31.8	45.5	12.9	43.6	2.5	2.6	11.5	16.3
21	Pulp and paper products	8.9	31.3	66.8	77.6	37.4	72.1	41.0	48.1	62.5	77.5
22	Printing and publishing	1.8	38.5	42.6	40.5	27.3	54.1	4.9	6.2	9.7	19.7
23	Petroleum and coke	–	–	2.1	100.0	–	0.4	*	*	37.0	44.4
24	Chemicals and chemical products	8.5	15.0	47.4	83.6	8.4	32.7	14.4	20.4	In 23	In 23
25	Rubber and plastics	21.8	45.2	58.1	51.7	17.4	56.7	13.6	20.1	28.0	26.3
26	Non-metallic mineral products	23.4	44.5	53.5	70.2	15.5	44.7	8.5	20.7	53.5	61.0
27	Basic metals	1.3	5.5	14.6	47.7	5.7	10.7	2.4	18.4	5.7	10.6
28	Fabricated metals	3.9	17.7	43.5	39.1	11.6	30.3	2.0	6.4	In 27	In 27
29	Machinery and equipment	2.0	14.4	32.9	52.6	8.1	18.5	20.4	26.1	16.9	20.3
30	Office machinery and computers	–	48.2	51.5	95.8	26.7	18.4	18.3	*	45.4	42.7
31	Electrical machinery	6.8	48.1	71.8	79.9	16.2	51.4	15.2	21.3	In 30	In 30
32	Radio, telephone and communication equipment	2.5	57.8	53.5	82.8	31.7	81.8	39.6	42.5	In 30	In 30
33	Precision instruments	9.4	15.9	47.7	40.6	9.0	38.0	11.9	22.6	In 30	In 30
34	Motor vehicles	58.5	82.1	64.0	96.8	53.2	89.9	72.3	83.1	10.6	13.7
35	Other transport equipment	2.2	1.8	60.1	48.6	3.5	7.6	*	0.9	In 34	In 34
36	Furniture and miscellaneous manufacturing	1.5	38.3	26.2	33.0	31.2	60.4	2.9	1.6	15.2	18.9
37	Recycling	–	45.6	27.9	31.6	22.4	20.6	*	*	In 36	In 36

Source: As for table 5.6.1.

Note: Data for Estonia are for 1996 and data for Slovenia are for 1995. An * indicates sectors with less than three multinational firms that are included in total manufacturing. Slovenia's share of FIEs in total manufacturing sales was 15 per cent in 1995 and 30.8 per cent in 1998

There is no clear trend of convergence in labour productivity between DEs and FIEs across industries (table 5.6.3). The aggregate productivity gap has narrowed slightly in the Czech Republic, Slovenia and Estonia, but there are many individual industries where it has increased. In Hungary and Poland the gap has widened significantly. Investment related to privatization and uncertainty about the prospects for institutional change explain some of the differences in relative productivity growth. Also, the timing of entry by TNCs plays a role: spillovers only occur over time as competition increases, backward and forward linkages develop and outsourcing becomes more prevalent.

The productivity gap between FIEs and DEs tends to be smaller when measured by value added per employee (table 5.6.4). On this basis, in 1993, the labour productivity of local enterprises was about two thirds of FIEs in the Czech Republic and Slovenia and more than 80 per cent in Poland. Moreover, the productivity gap appears to have widened significantly in the Czech Republic as a whole, a different conclusion from that based on the gross output measure. This may be due to different relative prices of intermediate goods or of factors of production between the FIEs and DEs. The parent firms may also be engaged in transfer pricing.

The difference between DEs and FIEs is especially marked in terms of capital intensity (table 5.6.5), although the interindustry variation across countries is considerable. Nevertheless, capital intensity in general was about two to three times higher in foreign firms than in domestically owned firms (except in Poland where the difference was much smaller in 1993), although there are numerous examples where the ratio is the other way around. This may reflect the fact that, in the centrally planned economies, industries were often *too* capital intensive – and market forces and TNCs should lower the ratios to more optimal levels. (However, there is probably a lot of noise in these data as there are also lags in the adjustment of employment levels.) By contrast, the difference in capital intensity between FIEs and domestic enterprises fell in the Czech Republic and Estonia indicating that the local enterprises have been increasing their fixed investment faster than the FIEs between 1993 and 1998.

Together, tables 5.6.3-5.6.5 show an uneven pattern of transnational activity that is nevertheless reflected in some rather large productivity differences across central Europe. Changes in the ratio of labour productivity levels between domestic and foreign enterprises in aggregate manufacturing from 1993 to 1998 suggest that there have not been enough intra-industry productivity spillovers for the local enterprises to catch up with the FIEs (chart 5.6.1). The rapidly widening productivity gap in Hungary and Poland illustrates this point. However, the elimination of the coke and petroleum sector reduces the gap between DEs and FIEs significantly in Hungary and shows how a sector with large changes in ownership can affect relative productivity.[573]

(ii) A simple test for productivity spillovers at the industry level

The data in tables 5.6.1-5.6.5 provide a basis for analysing the extent to which intra-industry productivity spillovers have taken place in all of the countries except Estonia. This can be done by relating the rate of convergence in labour productivity levels between the DEs and FIEs to the percentage share of sales in FIEs by industry and the initial gap in labour productivity between the two sets of enterprises in 1993.[574] The rate of convergence is measured by the ratio of the 1998 relative productivity levels between local enterprises and FIEs to those in 1993 (or the nearest year):

$$CONVERGE = \alpha + \beta_1 FIE + \beta_2 GAP + \varepsilon$$

where, for each industry in each country, FIE is the share of foreign owned enterprises in total sales, averaged between 1993 or 1995 and 1998, and GAP is the ratio of output per employee in domestically owned enterprises to the ratio of output per employee in foreign owned enterprises in 1993.[575] Evidence that TNCs are generating *enough* spillovers to stimulate productivity convergence is present when $\beta_1 > 0$, and evidence that the relative size of the productivity gap in 1993 leads to productivity convergence is present when $\beta_2 < 0$.

Table 5.6.6 summarizes the estimation results for the four countries. The negative signs for the coefficient on FIEs indicate that there are not enough productivity spillovers from FDI to close the productivity gap in central Europe. They also indicate that when there is productivity convergence between FIEs and DEs it is more likely to appear in those industries with a declining share of sales accounted for by FIEs. The coefficient, however, is not significant for either the Czech Republic or Poland. The negative sign for the Czech Republic suggests the evidence does not support the thesis that catching up is occurring in the manufacturing sector as a whole.[576] The negative signs for the GAP coefficient suggest that the initial size of the productivity gap influences the probability of productivity convergence in the transition economies. This coefficient is significant in all countries, except Poland.

---

[573] In 1993 the petroleum and coke sector was almost completely sold to foreign investors.

[574] This section adopts the method for testing for intra-industry productivity spillovers developed by M. Blomström and E. Wolff, loc. cit. In their study, Blomström and Wolff estimate productivity spillovers in two ways: (1) by the rate of labour productivity growth of DEs within an industry; and (2) by the rate of convergence in labour productivity levels between local and foreign firms within an industry. This chapter tests for productivity spillovers using the second approach because it avoids the need to construct price indices for each industry.

[575] As in the study by M. Blomström and E. Wolff, loc. cit., this chapter uses an income-based measure of output and productivity.

[576] This conclusion is supported by data at the enterprise level. S. Djankov and B. Hoekman, loc. cit., and Y. Kinoshita, op. cit.

TABLE 5.6.3

Convergence of gross output per employee in DEs and FIEs in selected east European and Baltic economies, 1993 and 1998
(Ratio of productivity levels between DEs and FIEs)

ISIC	Industry	Czech Republic 1993	Czech Republic 1998	Hungary 1993	Hungary 1998	Poland 1993	Poland 1998	Slovenia 1995	Slovenia 1998	Estonia 1996	Estonia 1998
D	Total manufacturing	0.48	0.53	0.66	0.35	0.67	0.53	0.44	0.47	0.56	0.67
15+16	Food, beverages and tobacco	0.95	0.66	0.58	0.52	0.80	0.55	0.78	0.78	0.50	0.48
17	Textiles	0.89	0.59	0.63	0.49	0.48	0.73	0.78	0.84	0.39	0.53
18	Wearing apparel and fur	1.09	0.88	0.64	0.55	0.64	0.58	0.58	0.82	1.31	1.53
19	Leather products	1.11	0.99	0.62	0.68	0.66	0.87	*	0.58	0.35	0.43
20	Wood products	0.62	0.41	0.46	0.36	0.75	0.42	0.67	0.93	0.84	0.68
21	Pulp and paper products	0.61	0.87	0.55	0.37	2.91	1.60	0.32	0.46	0.71	0.54
22	Printing and publishing	2.08	0.61	0.42	0.39	0.42	0.50	1.32	1.17	0.56	0.59
24	Chemicals and chemical products	0.68	0.95	0.86	0.51	0.58	0.70	0.67	0.65	0.32	0.46
25	Rubber and plastics	0.52	0.49	0.35	0.65	0.48	0.55	0.99	1.01	0.50	0.47
26	Non-metallic mineral products	0.44	0.43	0.59	0.43	0.46	0.49	0.52	0.45	0.38	0.39
27	Basic metals	0.70	0.81	0.75	0.64	0.83	0.63	1.78	0.82	1.13	1.41
28	Fabricated metals	1.24	0.81	0.42	0.70	0.55	0.43	0.70	0.95	In 27	In 27
29	Machinery and equipment	1.05	0.53	0.66	0.66	0.45	0.56	0.61	0.72	0.39	0.35
30	Office machinery and computers	..	1.38	1.13	0.15	0.33	1.64	0.43	*	0.32	1.35
31	Electrical machinery	0.67	0.74	0.76	0.51	0.75	0.69	0.74	0.76	In 30	In 30
32	Radio, telephone and communication equipment	0.31	0.45	0.34	0.18	0.57	0.19	0.44	0.58	In 30	In 30
33	Precision instruments	1.02	0.94	0.51	0.79	0.43	0.29	1.28	0.86	In 30	In 30
34	Motor vehicles	0.27	0.28	0.32	0.12	0.23	0.19	0.22	0.19	1.57	1.60
35	Other transport equipment	0.90	0.52	0.62	0.59	0.56	1.05	*	0.78	In 34	In 34
36	Furniture and miscellaneous manufacturing	0.63	0.31	0.75	0.70	0.61	0.54	0.72	0.70	0.53	0.56

Source: As for table 5.6.1.

Note: Data for Estonia are for 1996 and data for Slovenia are for 1995. An * indicates sectors with less than three multinational firms that are included in total manufacturing. Total manufacturing includes petroleum and coke (23) and recycling (37).

TABLE 5.6.4

Convergence of value added per employee in DEs and FIEs in selected east European and Baltic economies, 1993 and 1998
(Ratio of productivity levels between DEs and FIEs)

ISIC	Industry	Czech Republic 1993	Czech Republic 1998	Hungary 1997	Hungary 1998	Poland 1993	Poland 1998	Slovenia 1995	Slovenia 1998	Estonia 1996	Estonia 1998
D	Total manufacturing	0.66	0.54	0.31	0.36	0.80	0.65	0.66	0.70	0.70	0.70
15+16	Food, beverages and tobacco	0.70	0.67	0.44	0.51	0.83	0.52	0.64	0.71	0.51	0.44
17	Textiles	1.33	0.78	0.41	0.41	0.65	0.90	0.86	0.71	0.92	1.05
18	Wearing apparel and fur	1.05	1.00	0.59	0.56	0.81	0.70	1.49	0.72	1.08	1.16
19	Leather products	1.05	0.73	0.56	0.67	0.60	0.82	*	0.57	0.68	0.98
20	Wood products	0.47	0.40	0.33	0.35	0.96	0.71	1.08	0.53	1.09	0.75
21	Pulp and paper products	0.50	0.87	0.26	0.32	4.02	2.24	0.48	0.59	0.76	0.59
22	Printing and publishing	1.87	0.71	0.35	0.47	0.65	0.70	1.53	1.31	0.46	1.05
24	Chemicals and chemical products	0.49	0.57	0.33	0.33	0.62	0.58	0.89	1.05	0.27	0.28
25	Rubber and plastics	0.59	0.45	0.46	0.56	0.48	0.61	0.96	1.10	0.32	0.31
26	Non-metallic mineral products	0.62	0.42	0.36	0.41	0.44	0.69	0.47	0.49	0.55	0.40
27	Basic metals	0.75	0.72	0.48	0.70	0.99	0.81	0.99	0.70	1.19	1.07
28	Fabricated metals	0.86	0.70	0.53	0.64	0.56	0.57	0.76	0.93	In 27	In 27
29	Machinery and equipment	1.40	0.68	0.59	0.77	0.41	0.67	0.57	0.72	0.42	0.36
30	Office machinery and computers	..	1.06	0.08	0.12	0.12	0.96	0.52	*	0.61	1.03
31	Electrical machinery	1.15	0.72	0.41	0.48	0.81	0.77	0.67	0.77	In 30	In 30
32	Radio, telephone and communication equipment	0.10	0.54	0.48	0.44	0.59	0.39	0.40	0.58	In 30	In 30
33	Precision instruments	0.85	0.84	0.61	0.68	0.50	0.44	2.32	1.02	In 30	In 30
34	Motor vehicles	0.81	0.38	0.22	0.20	2.84	0.55	0.57	0.47	1.42	1.45
35	Other transport equipment	2.93	1.21	0.50	0.92	0.66	1.49	*	1.72	In 34	In 34
36	Furniture and miscellaneous manufacturing	1.18	0.68	0.43	0.63	0.76	0.75	0.97	1.63	0.67	0.59

Source: As for table 5.6.1.

Note: As for table 5.6.3. Data for Hungary are for 1997.

TABLE 5.6.5

Comparison of capital intensity (capital assets per employee) in DEs and FIEs in selected east European and Baltic economies, 1993 and 1998
(Ratio of capital intensity between DEs and FIEs)

ISIC	Industry	Czech Republic 1994	Czech Republic 1998	Hungary 1993	Hungary 1998	Poland 1993	Poland 1998	Slovenia 1995	Slovenia 1998	Estonia 1996	Estonia 1998
D	Total manufacturing	0.67	0.70	0.56	0.31	0.84	0.70	0.66	0.60	0.24	0.41
15+16	Food, beverages and tobacco	0.90	0.53	0.42	0.28	0.74	0.53	0.94	0.71	0.21	0.25
17	Textiles	1.47	0.68	0.72	0.49	0.90	1.08	0.92	0.97	2.85	0.54
18	Wearing apparel and fur	3.92	1.13	0.63	0.39	0.90	0.99	0.45	0.46	1.58	1.82
19	Leather products	3.39	2.06	0.51	0.83	2.56	1.64	*	0.92	0.14	0.28
20	Wood products	0.83	0.81	0.64	0.24	0.84	0.29	0.89	0.61	0.35	0.45
21	Pulp and paper products	0.74	0.97	0.91	0.52	0.45	0.23	0.23	0.30	0.31	0.26
22	Printing and publishing	0.62	0.95	0.55	0.44	0.94	0.73	0.98	0.85	0.79	2.33
24	Chemicals and chemical products	0.37	0.74	0.95	0.48	1.30	1.21	1.01	0.87	0.12	0.17
25	Rubber and plastics	0.91	0.52	0.31	0.48	1.24	0.63	1.66	0.87	0.21	0.27
26	Non-metallic mineral products	0.36	0.34	0.41	0.27	0.50	0.31	0.51	0.29	0.09	0.17
27	Basic metals	0.81	1.03	0.36	0.29	1.80	1.32	3.05	0.97	0.33	0.89
28	Fabricated metals	0.86	1.09	0.34	0.23	0.72	0.51	0.77	1.06	In 27	In 27
29	Machinery and equipment	1.08	0.98	0.56	0.47	2.10	0.72	0.83	0.86	0.39	0.70
30	Office machinery and computers	..	2.14	0.63	0.84	3.50	0.94	0.65	*	0.23	0.89
31	Electrical machinery	0.67	0.89	0.36	0.31	0.92	0.77	0.76	0.71	In 30	In 30
32	Radio, telephone and communication equipment	1.39	0.55	1.21	0.47	0.70	0.52	0.28	0.41	In 30	In 30
33	Precision instruments	0.71	0.82	1.27	0.82	0.72	0.85	1.19	1.07	In 30	In 30
34	Motor vehicles	0.59	0.61	0.54	0.15	0.37	0.37	1.17	1.09	0.52	0.99
35	Other transport equipment	0.67	3.41	0.71	0.43	1.35	0.80	*	0.32	In 34	In 34
36	Furniture and miscellaneous manufacturing	0.66	0.75	0.62	0.48	1.33	0.84	0.65	0.55	0.47	0.49

Source: As for table 5.6.1.

Note: As for table 5.6.3. For Hungary, nominal capital; for Estonia and Poland, total fixed assets; for the Czech Republic and Slovenia, total assets.

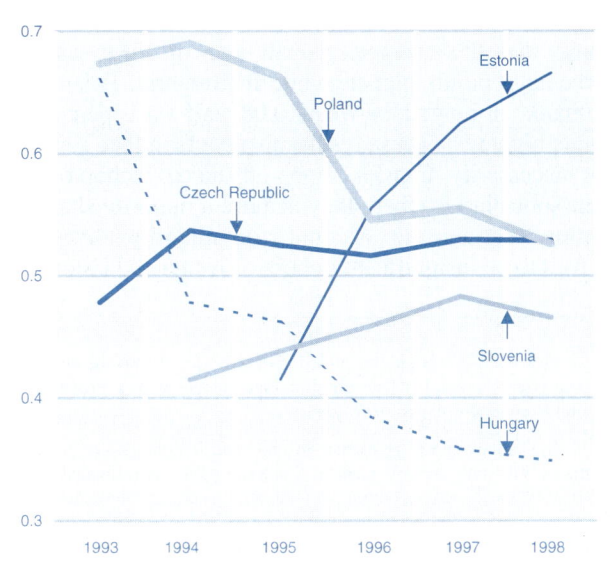

CHART 5.6.1

Productivity convergence between DEs and FIEs in total manufacturing in selected east European and Baltic economies, 1993-1998
(Per cent)

Source: WIIW Database on Foreign Investment Enterprises.

Another approach is to include an additional variable in the regression equation, namely one that represents the relative change in capital intensity (K/L) between FIEs and local enterprises from 1993 to 1998:

$$CONVERGE = \alpha + \beta_1 FIE + \beta_2 GAP + \beta_3 K/L + \varepsilon$$

In this equation, $\beta_3 > 0$ represents a reduction in the difference between the capital-labour ratios between the two years. In table 5.6.7 this coefficient is positive and significant for both Hungary and Slovenia and is negative and insignificant for both the Czech Republic and Poland. This suggests that FIEs in Hungary and Slovenia are becoming relatively more capital intensive than local enterprises, making it more difficult for the latter to incorporate the new technology transferred from abroad. This trend may also explain some of the divergence between FIEs and DEs in these two countries. If, as a result, sales by existing FIEs increase relative to the local enterprises, the gap between the two will be reinforced.

(iii) Testing for productivity spillovers at the enterprise level

By using the panel data that underlie the estimates in tables 5.6.1-5.6.5, it is possible to examine the channels of technology transfer and spillovers in more detail. Two datasets are used for the analysis: one comprises a sample of 363 manufacturing enterprises in Estonia for the period 1995 to 1998; and the other, 1093 enterprises in Slovenia from 1994 to 1998. The Slovenian sample includes all manufacturing firms with more than 10 employees. About 30 per cent of the Estonian enterprises are foreign owned (106 enterprises

TABLE 5.6.6

Regression analysis I of productivity convergence between DEs and FIEs in selected east European economies, 1993-1998

Independent variables	Dependent variable: convergence			
	Czech Republic	Hungary	Poland	Slovenia
Constant	1.388[a]	2.142[a]	1.819[a]	1.654[a]
	(6.40)	(6.38)	(3.95)	(11.75)
FIE	-0.242	-1.369[a]	-1.412	-0.624[b]
	(-0.52)	(-2.84)	(-1.12)	(-2.39)
GAP	-0.560[a]	-0.867[b]	-0.343	-0.629[a]
	(-3.14)	(-2.32)	(-0.85)	(-4.73)
R^2	0.41	0.46	0.13	0.62
F-statistic	5.65	7.24	1.28	11.19
Sample size	19	20	20	17

Source: UN/ECE secretariat.

Note: Absolute values of the t-statistic shown in parentheses. Data do not include the petroleum and coke sector. Dependent variable convergence is defined as the ratio of 1998 relative of productivity levels between DEs and FIEs to their 1993 relative level. Data for the dependent variables is given in table 5.6.3.

[a] Denote significance at 1 per cent level.

[b] Denote significance at 5 per cent level.

TABLE 5.6.7

Regression analysis II of productivity convergence between DEs and FIEs in selected east European economies, 1993-1998

Independent variables	Dependent variable: convergence			
	Czech Republic	Hungary	Poland	Slovenia
Constant	1.445[a]	1.849[a]	2.858[a]	1.170[a]
	(5.89)	(5.99)	(3.99)	(5.21)
FIE	-0.307	-1.220[a]	-1.132	-0.631[a]
	(-0.63)	(-2.92)	(-0.95)	(-2.84)
GAP	-0.563[a]	-1.144[a]	-0.498	-0.463[a]
	(-3.09)	(-3.40)	(-1.28)	(-3.54)
K/L	-0.0351	0.497[a]	-1.415[b]	0.393[a]
	(-0.55)	(2.66)	(-1.82)	(2.54)
R^2	0.43	0.63	0.28	0.74
F-statistic	3.70	8.90	2.07	12.54
Sample size	19	20	20	17

Source: UN/ECE secretariat.

Note: As for table 5.6.6.

[a] Denote significance at 1 per cent level.

[b] Denote significance at 5 per cent level.

in the sample) against 10 per cent in Slovenia (116 enterprises). However, in Estonia the share of FDI in fixed assets, sales and exports is about 50 per cent. Foreign firms are also more engaged in R&D as they account for more than 70 per cent of total R&D expenditures: on average a foreign firm invests three times as much in R&D capital as domestic firms. Although only about 10 per cent of enterprises in Slovenia are foreign owned, they account for 27 per cent of total sales, 35 per cent of total exports and 42 per cent of total imports. These enterprises also export twice as much as domestic enterprises and they purchase significantly more inputs abroad. On average a Slovenian firm with FDI invests more in R&D than one without, although the difference is not very large (3.5 versus 2.5 per cent of total sales). However, compared with Estonia, the share of R&D expenditures in the sales of Slovenian enterprises was five times higher if they were foreign owned and 10 times higher if they were domestically owned.

This subsection considers three important influences on productivity spillovers: (1) foreign direct investment; (2) absorptive capacity of domestic enterprises; and (3) international trade. The first and third influences provide the opportunity for technology transfer and spillovers and the second provides for their realization. In this section, productivity spillovers are defined in terms of total factor productivity (TFP) growth. (The annex to this chapter describes the model in detail.) However, since the number of enterprises is very large and the time period very small, the OLS estimating procedure is likely to provide biased and inconsistent results because of problems of heterogeneity. The best solution is to use either a fixed effects model or a random effects model. The basic difference between the two is that the first considers TFP growth to be fixed over time and the second considers it to be variable. Since the objective of this analysis is to examine the impact of different factors on changes in TFP growth, the random effects model is more appropriate even if it does not provide the most efficient estimates.[577]

The results in table 5.6.8 indicate that FDI is an important channel for the transfer of technology to FIEs located in Slovenia and Estonia. However, this evidence only appears after the regression is corrected for the initial selection bias of foreign investors for particular domestic enterprises with high potential. Foreign ownership contributes to the average TFP growth rate of FIEs in Slovenia by 0.57 percentage points and by 0.66 percentage points in Estonia. These figures are much higher than those obtained by previous studies for other transition countries. A study of the Czech Republic found that the average growth rate of FIEs was 0.3 percentage points higher, while in Bulgaria, Poland and Romania it ranged between 0.08 and 0.11 percentage points higher.[578] These results also confirm that TNCs do not necessarily transfer more advanced technology to their subsidiaries where they acquire a majority share. A dummy variable to account for majority ownership proved to be insignificant in both Slovenia and Estonia.[579]

---

[577] However, it should be added that a major disadvantage of the random effects model is the assumption that changes in TFP growth at the firm level are uncorrelated over time.

[578] S. Djankov and B. Hoekman, loc. cit., and J. Konings, op. cit. Their estimates refer only to TFP growth. Since the model is estimated in first differences the changes in output are related to the changes in factor inputs. This means that the foreign owned firms are expected to perform better due to enhanced technology, but it leaves aside the possibility that this may also be due to better utilization of the "old" factor inputs. In contrast to other studies, the model used in this chapter differentiates between factor inputs used by foreign and domestic firms. However, because this approach is indirect, it cannot directly account for changes in the efficiency of "old" inputs.

[579] Another study has also failed to find significant differences between majority and minority owned foreign firms in Slovenia. M. Rojec, J. Damijan and B. Majcen, "Export propensity of foreign subsidiaries in Slovenian manufacturing sector", University of Ljubljana, 2000, mimeo.

TABLE 5.6.8

Impact of FDI: direct effects and spillovers in Slovenia (1994-1998) and Estonia (1995-1998)

(Regression results in selected DEs and FIEs)

	Slovenia		Estonia	
Constant	-0.012	-0.295[a]	0.115[a]	-0.256[a]
	(-0.753)	(-5.354)	(3.002)	(-2.669)
FDI	0.052[b]	0.572[a]	0.030	0.662[a]
	(1.729)	(5.631)	(0.455)	(4.045)
Majority share	-0.022	-0.029	0.032	0.001
	(-0.831)	(-1.099)	(0.627)	(0.025)
Spillovers-domestic	-0.001	-0.001	0.001	0.0001
	(-0.517)	(-0.514)	(0.189)	(0.080)
Spillovers-domestic (FDI)[b]	0.000	0.001	-0.003	-0.002
	(0.215)	(0.449)	(-1.526)	(-1.080)
Spillovers-exports	-0.001	-0.001	0.001	0.002
	(-0.917)	(-0.909)	(0.295)	(0.433)
Spillovers-exports (FDI)[b]	0.000	-0.001	0.002	0.001
	(-0.291)	(-0.619)	(1.200)	(0.652)
1996	0.023[b]	0.023[b]		
	(2.124)	(2.095)		
1997	0.039[a]	0.037[a]	-0.003	-0.005
	(3.583)	(3.396)	(-0.132)	(-0.197)
1998	0.010	0.008	-0.117[a]	-0.126[a]
	(0.862)	(0.656)	(-3.695)	(-4.016)
Lambda		-0.334[a]		-0.409[a]
		(-5.358)		(-4.207)
Sector dummies	Yes	Yes	Yes	Yes
Number of observations	4 372	4 372	1 119	1 119
Adjusted R²	0.733	0.729	0.809	0.810

Source: UN/ECE secretariat.

Note: t-statistics in parentheses.

[a] Denote significance at 1 per cent level.

[b] Denote significance at 5 per cent level.

These regressions also indicate there are no significant spillovers to other firms in the same industry in Slovenia and Estonia, and this was true for both domestic and export markets. Nor were there any differences between foreign and domestic firms in the capability to adapt to spillovers. Evidence from Bulgaria and Romania also indicates the absence of significant spillovers and in Poland there were even negative ones.[580] The lack of spillovers in Slovenia and Estonia is not due to the absence of TNCs since FIEs account for 27 and 50 per cent of total sales in Slovenia and Estonia, respectively. The extent of spillovers is more likely to be a function of the ability of individual enterprises to realize technological opportunities in the market.

Table 5.6.9 summarizes the results when the innovative and absorptive capacity of domestic enterprises is taken into account.[581] There is no indication, however, of significant innovation effects in Slovenia and Estonia, i.e. there appears to be no interdependence between enterprises' R&D stocks and TFP growth. The results also reveal an insignificant absorptive capacity (interaction term of R&D and spillovers) of domestic firms for exploiting knowledge spillovers at the sector level. This may be because there is very little R&D activity in the domestic firms in relative and absolute terms, but it may also be that R&D stocks are not properly measured at the firm level.

Evidence for the other transition countries is mixed. The results for the Czech Republic indicate negative spillovers to local enterprises, but only when the enterprises' innovative and absorptive capacity is not taken into account.[582] There is also evidence that the innovative capacity of Czech domestic firms is not correlated with their TFP growth and there are no significant spillovers when measured as the share of foreign owned firms in a sector's total employment. On the other hand, the absorptive capacity of Czech domestic enterprises appears to have a significant positive impact on TFP growth of domestic enterprises.[583] Similarly, in Bulgaria, Poland and Romania the innovative capacity of domestic enterprises appears to have no significant impact on TFP growth, but the absorptive capacity of these enterprises appears have a positive impact in Bulgaria and Poland.[584]

Estimates based on panel data suggest that there may be alternative paths for the diffusion of technology to domestic firms. International trade can be an important source of international R&D spillovers.[585] Foreign R&D spillovers to domestic firms are measured by the share of imports in total costs of materials (capital equipment and intermediate goods) and by the share of exports in total sales (indicating the ability of firms to meet high quality standards in western markets).

Table 5.6.10 summarizes the results when international trade is taken into account. Since there are no data on imports at the firm level for Estonia, technology diffusion can only be detected through exports. The estimates reveal no significant technology spillovers to Estonian domestic firms through their export performance. This may be due to the relatively small export orientation of Estonian firms to western markets.

---

[580] J. Konings, op. cit.

[581] According to Cohen and Levinthal, R&D can be thought of as having two complementary effects on firm's productivity growth. First, R&D directly expands a firm's technology level by innovations, which is called the *innovation effect*. It also increases the firm's absorptive capacity – its ability to identify, assimilate and exploit outside knowledge, which is usually called the *learning* or *absorption effect*. These two effects are separated in the model by considering R&D alone (the innovative effect on the firm) and in interaction with spillovers at the sector level indicating the ability of the firm to exploit knowledge spillovers at the sector level. W. Cohen and D. Levinthal, "Innovation and learning: the two faces of R&D", *Economic Journal*, Vol. 99, September 1989, pp. 569-596.

[582] S. Djankov and B. Hoekman, loc. cit.

[583] Y. Kinoshita, op. cit.

[584] J. Konings, op. cit.

[585] D. Coe and E. Helpman, loc. cit., provide evidence of such beneficial effects of international R&D spillovers through international trade on domestic productivity in 21 OECD countries. D. Coe, E. Helpman and A. Hoffmaister, "North-South R&D spillovers", *The Economic Journal*, Vol. 107, January 1997, pp. 134-149 extend this analysis to show that there are substantial R&D spillovers from these OECD countries to 77 developing countries.

TABLE 5.6.9

Impact of R&D: importance of innovative and absorptive capacity in Slovenia (1994-1998) and Estonia (1995-1998)

(Regression results in selected DEs)

	Slovenia [a]	Estonia [b]
Constant	-0.505 [c]	-0.426 [c]
	(-4.752)	(-3.434)
R&D	-0.0004	-0.009
	(-0.677)	(-0.455)
Spillovers-domestic	0.00005	0.001
	(0.106)	(0.262)
Spillovers-exports	-0.0001	0.00006
	(-0.411)	(0.013)
R&D spillovers-domestic [d]	0.0001	-0.0004
	(1.411)	(-0.453)
R&D spillovers-exports [d]	-0.00005	0.001
	(-1.176)	(1.030)
1996	0.030 [c]	0.130 [c]
	(2.708)	(3.610)
1997	0.039 [c]	0.123
	(3.538)	(3.867)
Sector dummies	Yes	Yes
Number of observations	2 943	815
Adjusted R^2	0.659	0.605

Source: UN/ECE secretariat.

Note: t-statistics in parentheses.

[a] Spillovers measured at NACE 5-digit sectors for Slovenia.

[b] Spillovers measured at NACE 2-digit sectors for Estonia.

[c] Denote significance at 1 per cent level.

[d] Denote significance at 5 per cent level.

TABLE 5.6.10

Impact of R&D and international knowledge spillovers through trade in Slovenia and Estonia

(Regression results on sample DEs)

	Slovenia		Estonia	
	Without R&D	With R&D	Without R&D	With R&D
Constant	-0.542 [a]	-0.542 [a]	-0.403 [a]	-0.404 [a]
	(-5.139)	(-5.117)	(-3.497)	(-3.498)
R&D		-0.00004		0.002
		(-0.062)		(0.196)
Exports/sales	0.0006 [a]	0.0006 [a]	0.0001	0.0001
	(3.841)	(3.674)	(0.259)	(0.282)
Imports/material costs	0.00003 [b]	0.00003 [b]		
	(2.159)	(2.062)		
R&D exports		-0.000004		-0.00004
		(-0.191)		(-0.146)
R&D imports		0.0000003		
		(-0.190)		
1996	0.033 [a]	0.033 [a]	0.120 [a]	0.120 [a]
	(2.930)	(2.922)	(4.139)	(4.125)
1997	0.041 [a]	0.040 [a]	0.114 [a]	0.114 [a]
	(3.658)	(2.624)	(4.049)	(4.043)
Sector dummies	Yes	Yes	Yes	Yes
Number of observations	2 943	2 943	815	815
Adjusted R^2	0.668	0.665	0.602	0.602

Source: UN/ECE secretariat.

Note: t-statistics in parentheses.

[a] Denote significance at 1 per cent level.

[b] Denote significance at 5 per cent level.

In contrast, there are positive international R&D spillovers, both through exports and imports, in Slovenia. The estimates also reveal a significant positive impact of R&D and significant negative spillovers from FDI on domestic enterprises. These results indicate that technology spillovers occur in Slovenia either through direct foreign linkages or through arm's-length trade.[586]

The analysis of panel data from Slovenia and Estonia suggest that FDI plays an important role in transferring technology to the transition economies, but there appears to be no significant intra-industry spillovers from foreign owned to domestically owned enterprises. Even after controlling for the absorptive capacity of domestic enterprises there were not only no significant spillovers, but actually evidence of negative intra-industry spillovers.[587] The relatively high productivity growth of domestic enterprises suggests that R&D spillovers are occurring through other channels, but the evidence that international trade is important for the diffusion of technology is somewhat mixed.

5.7 Does FDI facilitate catching up with the European Union?

A recent ECE study analysed the income gaps between the transition economies and western Europe.[588] Even with the surge in growth in 2000, only a few central European countries have made any progress in narrowing this gap in the past decade and, in many cases (especially in the CIS), income differences have actually widened. The economic growth literature of the past decade has highlighted the role of the technology available in the more advanced countries as a factor in the process of "catching up". An important component of this process is FDI as a major channel of international technology transfer. This raises the question whether FDI can be instrumental in moving countries from the "economic periphery" into the group of economically advanced nations.[589] Within western Europe FDI is credited with helping to sharply narrow the income difference between Ireland and the EU.

---

[586] S. Djankov and B. Hoekman, loc. cit., find a significant positive impact of large import penetration on TFP growth of domestic firms in the Czech Republic. However they consider import penetration at the sector level (indicating intra-sector spillovers from imports), which is not directly comparable to the approach taken in this chapter.

[587] S. Djankov and B. Hoekman, loc. cit., also found this to be the case in the Czech Republic, for which they give three reasons. First, the magnitude of technology transfers via FDI might be too small. Small foreign investments in absolute and relative terms provide little scope for productivity growth in the host firm as well as for spillovers to other firms. Second, it might be due to selection bias. FDI flows might be directed into the better performing domestic enterprises in the first place, which in turn provides less scope for productivity increases relative to other domestic firms. Third, firms without foreign participation might be successful in acquiring and employing new technology independently of FDI, mainly through international trade.

[588] UN/ECE, "Catching up and falling behind: economic convergence in Europe", *Economic Survey of Europe, 2000 No. 1,* chap. 5.

[589] For example, Berend argues that an appropriate response to the challenge of the structural crisis of the periphery is impossible without massive western investments. I. Berend, loc. cit.

TABLE 5.7.1
International comparisons of labour productivity, 1998
(Value added per person employed)

NACE	ISIC		EU-15 average (ecu)	Czech Republic FIE	Czech Republic DE	Hungary FIE	Hungary DE	Poland FIE	Poland DE	Slovenia FIE	Slovenia DE	Estonia FIE	Estonia DE
D		Total manufacturing	50 048	0.82	0.45	0.76	0.27	0.49	0.31	0.72	0.51	0.28	0.20
DA	15	Food products and beverages	45 223	0.84	0.57	0.62	0.31	0.63	0.33	1.01	0.72	0.52	0.23
DB	17-18	Textiles and textile products	28 636	0.61	0.50	0.49	0.23	0.44	0.35	0.87	0.57	0.26	..
DC	19	Leather and leather products	25 115	0.55	0.41	0.41	0.27	0.44	0.36	0.95	0.54	0.34	0.34
DD	20	Wood and wood products	34 739	1.12	0.45	0.74	0.26	0.53	0.38	1.11	0.59	0.33	0.25
DE	21-22	Pulp, paper, publishing and printing	55 572	0.73	0.57	0.88	0.34	0.47	0.51	0.74	0.64	0.30	0.23
DG	24	Chemicals and man-made fibres	80 154	0.90	0.51	0.71	0.23	0.47	0.27	0.59	0.62	0.20	0.06
DH	25	Rubber and plastic products	46 557	1.00	0.45	0.71	0.40	0.62	0.38	0.62	0.68	0.73	0.23
DI	26	Other non-metallic mineral products	46 966	1.24	0.52	0.76	0.31	0.50	0.34	1.09	0.54	0.65	0.26
DJ	27-28	Basic and fabricated metals	44 758	0.69	0.53	0.57	0.37	0.60	0.39	0.66	0.53	0.27	0.28
DK	29	Machinery and equipment n.e.c.	49 556	0.57	0.39	0.43	0.33	0.42	0.28	0.67	0.48	0.43	0.16
DL	30-33	Electrical and optical equipment	55 820	0.52	0.35	0.82	0.27	0.54	0.32	0.68	0.50	0.19	0.20
DM	34-35	Transport equipment	55 164	1.01	0.36	1.24	0.30	0.41	0.30	0.73	0.31	0.26	0.38
DN	36	Furniture; manufacturing n.e.c.	33 961	0.78	0.53	0.48	0.31	0.45	0.34	0.35	0.57	0.39	0.23
		Average annual growth rate relative to EU-15 growth rate, 1993-1998											
D		Total manufacturing	..	6.77	2.60	7.73[a]	-1.83[a]	10.50	4.70	5.05[b]	7.38[b]	4.80[c]	4.77[c]

Source: Eurostat Cronos Database and WIIW Database on Foreign Investment Enterprises.

Note: Eurostat estimates of EU average for manufacturing firms with 20 or more employees. Calculations based on 1996 producer prices and 1996 PPPs. DA excludes tobacco and DN excludes recycling. Total manufacturing includes tobacco (16), petroleum and coke (23) and recycling (37).

[a] Hungarian growth rate relative to EU-15 growth rate of industrial production.
[b] 1995-1998.
[c] 1996-1998.

In Portugal and Spain, the effects of the surge in FDI inflows in the first half of the 1980s appears to have been more modest in this regard. In Greece FDI seems to have had little impact, apparently because other policies were not supportive.[590] Evidence from Asia also indicates that FDI does not automatically lead to improved economic performance in the host country.

Undoubtedly, FDI *can* be a catalyst for catching up with the EU through both the transfer and diffusion of technology. Although the evidence suggests that there are not enough spillovers for local enterprises to catch up with the FIEs, technology may still be transferred from TNCs to their affiliates more rapidly than the spillover rate to local enterprises. Thus, catching up can occur not only between the FIEs and enterprises in the EU, but also between local enterprises in transition economies and those in the EU. Table 5.7.1 shows that this is generally true, except for local enterprises in Hungary, which have fallen behind at an average rate of about 2 per cent per year. The average annual productivity growth of FIEs in the region exceeded the EU average by just over 5 per cent in Estonia and well over 10 per cent in Poland. Productivity growth exceeded the EU average by more than 15 per cent in specific industries such as transport equipment (Czech Republic, Hungary and Poland), machinery and equipment (Czech Republic), electrical and optical equipment (Hungary), pulp and paper, etc. (Poland), textiles and textile products (Slovenia) and wood and wood products (Slovenia). In all countries except Estonia productivity growth in machinery and equipment was higher than the EU average and higher than in the FIEs in each transition economy. This indicates that productivity spillovers may be occurring but, as in Indonesia, Morocco and Venezuela, they are limited to certain industries.

The average labour productivity of FIEs and local enterprises in total manufacturing was still well below the average EU productivity level in 1998. When measured in terms of 1996 PPPs, the labour productivity of FIEs in the Czech Republic, Hungary and Slovenia was about three fourths of the EU average in 1998, although it exceeded it in some industries. In contrast, the average productivity level of FIEs in Poland and Estonia was about one half and one fourth of the EU average, respectively. Of the industries that exceeded the EU average the most notable is transport equipment in the Czech Republic and Hungary. Some enterprises within the electrical and optical equipment industry were also above the EU average. In both cases domestic outsourcing has become an important potential source of productivity spillovers.[591] For example,

---

[590] Ireland's income rose from 42 to 74 per cent of EU income between 1986 and 1998. Comparable figures for Portugal and Spain are 37 to 45 per cent and 47 to 52 per cent, respectively. UN/ECE, *Economic Survey of Europe, 2000 No. 1*, chart 5.3.1. All three countries, of course, also benefited from the single market. Also see B. Larre and R. Torre, "Is convergence a spontaneous process? The experience of Spain, Portugal and Greece", *OECD Economic Studies*, No. 16 (Paris), Spring 1991.

[591] S. Radosevic and U. Hotopp, "The product structure of central and eastern European trade: the emerging patterns of change and learning", *MOCT-MOST*, Vol. 9, 1999, pp. 171-199.

Volkswagen owns a majority share of Skoda Automotive, but often outsources production to Skoda General Manufacturing, a domestic firm. A prominent example of domestic outsourcing is office machinery and computer equipment in Hungary. A concentration of FDI in computing equipment by several well-known European and American firms has resulted in considerable outsourcing to domestically owned firms, especially Videoton.[592] These case studies suggest that, despite the limited success so far, there may be considerable scope for the transfer of technology and technology spillovers in central Europe.

By using the data in table 5.7.1, together with the corresponding data for 1993 or thereabouts, it is possible to analyse whether TNCs are an important catalyst for catching up with the EU. This can be done by relating the rate of convergence in labour productivity levels between the FIEs and DEs in the transition economies and all enterprises in the EU, to the percentage share of employment in FIEs by industry and the initial productivity gap in 1993.[593] The rate of convergence is defined as the ratio of the 1998 and 1993 values of productivity (value added per employee) in each transition economy industry relative to the corresponding EU average:

$$EUCONVERGE = \alpha + \beta_1 FIE + \beta_2 EUGAP + \varepsilon$$

where FIE is value added in foreign owned firms as a share of total value added and EUGAP is the labour productivity gap between the transition economy and EU industries in 1993. The estimates suggest that TNCs have played an important role in the catching-up process in the Czech Republic, Hungary and Poland, but it is statistically insignificant in the case of Estonia (table 5.7.2). TNCs thus appear to be transferring technology, but the evidence of spillovers is inconclusive. TNCs do not appear to be playing an important role in transferring technology to Slovenia, but there is strong evidence that the productivity gap itself is stimulating technical change and technological learning. Other channels of technology transfer may thus be more significant in Slovenia. The initial productivity gap appears to be an important stimulus in all the other countries, but is insignificant in the case of Hungary.

It is difficult to assess fully the role of FDI in the transition economies because the time series are so short. In the case of Hungary, FDI-driven exports and export-led growth appear to be key factors helping to narrow the gap with the EU. It may also be playing an important

---

[592] A. Szalavetz, *Sailing Before the Wind of Globalization: Corporate Restructuring in Hungary*, Hungarian Academy of Sciences, Institute for World Economics Working Paper, No. 78, 1997.

[593] This section adopts the method for testing for productivity convergence developed by M. Blomström and E. Wolff, loc. cit. The authors estimate productivity convergence in two ways: (1) annual rate of growth of value added per employee in Mexican industry; and (2) the rate of convergence in labour productivity levels between corresponding Mexican and United States industries. This paper tests for productivity convergence using the second approach because it avoids constructing price indices for each industry.

TABLE 5.7.2

Regression analysis of productivity convergence between selected east European and Baltic economies and EU industries, 1993-1998

	Dependent variable: EUCONVERGE				
	Czech Republic	Hungary	Poland	Slovenia	Estonia
Constant	1.804[a]	0.385	1.867[a]	2.218[a]	2.129[a]
	(7.44)	(0.836)	(8.36)	(9.85)	(3.48)
FIE	1.219[a]	2.792[a]	0.590[b]	-0.423[c]	0.125
	(3.29)	(4.44)	(1.78)	(-1.64)	(0.13)
GAP	-1.837[a]	-1.274[c]	-2.169[a]	-1.843[a]	-4.126[b]
	(-3.61)	(-1.50)	(-2.56)	(-4.11)	(-1.97)
R^2	0.71	0.67	0.43	0.67	0.29
F-statistic	12.22	9.97	3.79	9.23	2.02
Sample size	13	13	13	12	13

Source: UN/ECE secretariat.

Note: Absolute value of the t-statistic shown in parentheses. Data based on NACE Rev.1 classification and does not include the petroleum and coke sector. EUCONVERGE is defined as the ratio of the 1998 ratio of value added per employee in the transition economy industry to value added per employee in the corresponding average EU industry to their 1993 ratio. FIE for Hungary is the share of sales by foreign owned enterprises in total sales. The starting year for Estonia and Slovenia is 1995 and for the FIE average in Estonia, 1996.

[a] Denote significance at 1 per cent level.
[b] Denote significance at 5 per cent level.
[c] Denote significance at 10 per cent level.

role in other countries. In Poland, however, where the catch-up process started earlier and has been the most significant,[594] it is likely that domestic resources have played the leading role. Whatever the impact of FDI, fundamental economic reform has been a precondition for attracting it and using it efficiently. At both the firm and industry levels, the evidence shows that FIEs in the transition economies have been closing the productivity gap with their EU counterparts, generally at a faster pace than domestic firms have been able to. However, there is little evidence that spillovers from FIEs to domestic firms have been important in this process.

5.8 Concluding comments and policies

A number of transition economies have attracted significant amounts of FDI, and several now rank quite high in this regard by global standards. However, large disparities in the distribution of FDI have emerged in the region, and there are signs that the differences are increasing. In particular, the low-income transition economies have lagged behind central Europe in their ability to attract FDI, and it is likely that the current pattern of FDI will exacerbate the income gaps among the transition economies, especially as economic growth and FDI can interact in a virtuous circle.

This chapter has shown that FDI has had a significant direct impact on the exports and economic growth of several transition economies, mostly those that have received *substantial* amounts of FDI. The analysis provides new evidence that the growth of labour

---

[594] UN/ECE, *Economic Survey of Europe, 2000 No. 1*, chart 5.3.1

productivity of FIEs in the manufacturing sector has generally been faster than that of DEs, although that was not the case in Slovenia. However, even in the countries where the impact of FDI appears to have been greatest, growth rates of GDP are still not sufficient to rapidly narrow income gaps with the EU. Studies of developing countries, however, suggest that FDI has a long-term impact on growth, and the same may be expected in the transition economies.

Despite the case for the importance of positive spillovers made by proponents of FDI, the statistical evidence for their existence in the market economies is mixed. The analysis presented here suggests that there have been few or no positive productivity spillovers from FDI in the transition economies. In manufacturing sectors, the presence of FIEs tends to be associated with relatively poor productivity growth in domestic enterprises. Moreover, on average, DEs perform poorly compared with FIEs in Hungary, the country with the greatest penetration of FDI. By contrast, in Slovenia, which has attracted comparatively little FDI, DEs have outperformed FIEs. Although these results need to be examined further, it is possible that a large FIE presence may hinder the adaptation of domestic enterprises to the market system (i.e. negative spillovers) by a premature intensification of domestic competition. Slovene domestic enterprises seem to have been relatively more successful in coping with this pressure. Determining an optimal degree of FDI penetration – large enough to create positive spillovers, but not so great as to inhibit adaptation by domestic enterprises – deserves greater attention.

It is important to bear in mind the limitations of the methodologies and data used in the analysis of FDI spillovers. Most of the cross-sectoral regressions presented above tested for intra-industry spillovers, but they may be of limited validity if the potential for significant spillovers is sector specific. Case studies may be a more appropriate way to explore this issue. Spillovers from FIEs to upstream and/or downstream DEs (interindustry spillovers) are potentially more important as channels for technology transfer, but it is not possible to test for interindustry spillovers using only sectoral data. Detailed enterprise data are needed, but, even in this case, the application of the necessary econometric techniques requires assumptions about enterprises which are unlikely to have been met, at least during the early stages of the transition. Statistical analyses of FDI spillovers also typically exclude those stemming from the non-manufacturing sectors – agriculture, extraction, financial services and telecommunications (the latter having attracted considerable amounts of FDI through privatization). The impact of service sectors may be particularly important given their underdevelopment during the period of central planning.

Even though FDI spillovers are not always found in long-established market economies, there are particular reasons why they might be absent in the transition economies. Linkages take time to develop and FDI is still a relatively new phenomenon in these countries. More generally the transition environment has not always been conducive to their creation. With the collapse of central planning, managers focused on keeping enterprises afloat, dealing with payments arrears, beginning restructuring and, in some cases, preparing companies for privatization. To different degrees, enterprises were suddenly exposed to foreign competition when local trade regimes were liberalized with very little time to adjust. Many DEs are likely to have been too weak to respond to the competition from FIEs or to take advantage of the opportunities offered by FIEs as partners. To do so would require effective corporate governance (including managers used to strategic planning in a market environment) and sufficient resources to support adaptation to the new circumstances. Enterprises' financial difficulties and the rudimentary state of the financial sector have often made it impossible to obtain bank credits, which either were not available or could be had only at high interest rates and short maturities (unlike the finance available to FIEs). Finally, some traditional (foreign) suppliers of FIEs have followed them into their new countries of operation, essentially pre-empting the development of potential domestic partnerships (in fact the FIEs may have actively encouraged traditional suppliers to do so).

Although dynamic FIEs can help to underpin economic growth, the absence of positive spillovers can lead to the emergence of an "enclave" economy, divided between high productivity FIEs and lagging domestic enterprises. Among other things, payment of above average wages by FIEs can lead to increasing income and regional inequalities. At the same time, attempts to match the wage rates of FIEs by domestic enterprises tends to undermine their competitiveness (because of their lower productivity) and increase the risks of bankruptcy. The exit of domestic firms from the market also increases the opportunities for monopolistic behaviour by FIEs.

In addition to their efforts to attract FDI, policy makers might consider more active measures to help maximize the long-term benefits of FDI, particularly those that facilitate the development of backward and forward linkages. Given the international commitments undertaken by many transition economies, the scope for policies to support the development of domestic firms is increasingly limited (e.g. by national treatment clauses). However, the promotion of positive spillovers involves sound stabilization policies (fostering lower domestic interest rates), improving the functioning of the banking system and capital markets, educational reforms to increase the supply of appropriate skills, the provision of new infrastructure, etc. Effective competition policies could help to protect domestic firms from unfair FIE competition (predatory practices). In particular domestic firms may need to be strengthened so that they can compete more effectively with FIEs (i.e. to avoid negative spillovers including the bankruptcy of potentially viable domestic firms) or become more attractive partners for FIEs in upstream and downstream operations. Additional steps might also be taken to improve both the national innovation system and the absorptive capacities of local enterprises. Since FDI is only one among several channels of technology transfer, such a policy is likely to attract the kinds of FDI that would result in technological spillovers. Small and medium enterprise development programmes, often partially funded by the development banks, including multilateral institutions, could also adopt the potential for spillovers as a criterion for the selection of projects. Overall, such measures could help to avoid the emergence of FDI enclaves.

FDI inflows have helped to ease balance of payments constraints and thus increase the availability of resources for development. As noted above in section 3.6(iv), countries with low levels of FDI (which is usually symptomatic of other problems) have been prone to external payments problems. In recent years, policy makers have often counted on FDI as a major source of external financing, a preference which is likely to continue. However, as large-scale privatization winds down, FDI inflows are expected to diminish – other things being equal.

Although the short-term impact of FDI is often positive, it is possible to overlook the fact that it can eventually have a negative effect on the balance of payments if export revenues fail to offset FDI-related imports and profit repatriation. Estimates for Hungary and Azerbaijan indicate a positive effect of FDI so far, but for different reasons these two countries may not be representative. An issue for policy makers is whether it is possible and desirable to discriminate in favour of FDI, which is likely to have positive rather than negative balance of payments consequences. The issue may be particularly important for the majority of transition economies, which already have structural current account deficits.

A related question is how to channel foreign capital into productive investment and exports, as opposed to, for example, real estate speculation.[595] Recent experience has shown that a concentration of FDI in the non-tradeable sector may weaken export performance (due to real exchange rate appreciation) and make the host country more vulnerable to economic crises.[596]

The current economic situation in the ECE region seems favourable to further increases of FDI in the transition economies. With improved growth prospects for western Europe (the main source of FDI in the transition economies), increased FDI can be expected as part of the continuing process of economic integration and "internationalization" of production processes.

To varying degrees all the transition economies wish to promote FDI. There is considerable international experience of how to do this, but global competition for FDI is now intense (more so than in the 1970s and 1980s). Moreover, in coping with the legacy of industrial development under central planning, the transition economies are often in competition for FDI among themselves, including for large strategic investments.

A general policy approach to FDI promotion necessarily involves strengthening domestic economic fundamentals.[597] These include political and macroeconomic stability, long-term growth prospects, market access, the availability of skilled workers and the state of infrastructure. In the transition economies they also include necessary market reforms and structural transformation. While success in these areas may not necessarily result in more foreign investment, they are nevertheless necessary conditions for growth based on domestic resources.[598] In the end, domestic and foreign investors tend to be motivated by similar factors.

With the tendency to focus on central Europe in discussions of the transition process, sight is sometimes lost of the fact that about one third of the transition economies have yet to achieve macroeconomic stabilization (as indicated by their very high inflation rates) or to make much progress with structural transformation. Beyond stabilization and the economic "fundamentals", policies toward FDI do seem to be important. The mode of privatization (via vouchers or management buyouts: Czech Republic, Slovakia, Russia), the discouragement of foreign investors (Slovenia), the introduction of investment incentives (recently the Czech Republic), the nature of science and technology policy (Hungary) can all make a difference as to whether FDI flows into a country or not. In a number of natural resource-rich countries, a workable production-sharing agreement (PSA) law appears to be important: this has attracted foreign investment to large projects in several countries, but in Russia the PSA framework still needs to be improved.

As part of a strategy to attract FDI, some countries have used business surveys to identity and, where possible, eliminate specific obstacles to foreign investment. The experience of Estonia is of particular interest because it has long been one of the most successful countries in this regard. Nevertheless, the survey results indicate that there is still room for improvement (table 5.8.1). This approach may be especially important for countries seeking to maintain FDI as privatization revenues become exhausted: as this occurs, there will be an increasing emphasis on greenfield (and follow-up) investments which may be more sensitive to the types of obstacles listed in table 5.8.1 than are large strategic FDI privatizations.

For the countries that have received very little FDI, fundamental economic and institutional reform is essential (and not only for the sake of attracting FDI), but often the commitment of the authorities (including parliaments) is

---

[595] Thailand, for example, tried to curb foreign speculation in the real estate market by taxing foreign investment.

[596] Work by UNCTAD has shown that in the later stages of South-East Asia's expansion, FDI flows had a reduced impact on export growth because they were directed to the non-tradeable goods sectors. UNCTAD, *Trade and Development Report, 1999*, p. 122.

[597] Interviews with corporate managers indicate that investors, when selecting the site for a major investment project, tend to attach more importance to the "fundamentals", than to fiscal or financial incentives provided by the prospective host government. C. Oman, "Policy competition for direct foreign investment", *OECD Development Centre Studies* (Paris), 2000.

[598] Ibid.

TABLE 5.8.1

Obstacles to foreign direct investment in Estonia, 1997 and 1998

(Index, range 0-5)[a]

	1997	1998
Bureaucracy[b]	..	3.22
Corruption	2.86	3.05
Labour quality	3.09	2.89
VAT payments/rebates	3.19	2.81
Customs procedures	2.82	2.76
Project finance	2.69	2.69
Work and residence permits	2.70	2.69
Tax rates[b]	..	2.66
Gaps in legislation	3.08	2.62
Slow land reform	2.83	2.59
Unfair competition	2.79	2.41
Land acquisition	2.56	2.22
Raw material availability	2.10	1.95
Absence of tariffs	2.03	1.65

Source: T. Ziacik, *An Assessment of the Estonian Investment Climate: Results of a Survey of Foreign Investors and Policy Implications*, Bank of Finland Institute for Economies in Transition (BOFIT), Discussion Papers No. 3 (Helsinki), 2000.

[a] A 1 denotes "no problem" and a 5 denotes a "serious problem".

[b] Not included in the 1997 survey.

doubtful. This is largely a domestic matter and there is often little the international community can do until a change in thinking occurs. Pervasive corruption (often at both the centre and local levels) and political tensions (including ethnic conflict) may stifle both economic reform and the prospect of FDI. Nonetheless, some countries rich in natural resources have attracted large foreign investments and more are in the pipeline. However, one of the pre-conditions appears to be a workable law on production sharing agreements. Although FDI can boost the output and exports of primary materials, and so improve the external financial situation, the spillovers from this sector are generally small[599] (in part because of the producing country's limited capacity to produce the required capital goods). Moreover such a pattern of investment can perpetuate dependence on primary material exports, and domestic policy makers may be tempted to view the large revenues as a substitute for necessary reform.

Even if a country gets its economic fundamentals right, progresses with reforms and otherwise follows the standard recommendations for promoting investment, it may still fail to attract much FDI. According to one view, these countries are fundamentally disadvantaged by geography because they are:[600]

- at great distances from major world markets and primary sea routes;
- land-locked, often remote mountainous regions (i.e. as opposed to the coastal areas preferred by foreign investors, especially for manufacturing);
- poor in infrastructure (which is also expensive to build given local conditions and distances); and
- small, with only limited possibilities of market growth.

All these factors tend to raise transport costs, increase travel time and raise the risk of disruptions to transport links (especially if the neighbours are unstable or uncooperative). Several transition economies (especially in central Asia) face one or more of these challenges. The problem is highlighted by the challenge of attracting FDI into China's western regions (adjoining several Asian members of the CIS), despite their mineral wealth and the availability of various investment incentives. Yet, China is well known to international investors, having received more FDI than any other developing economy (over $40 billion annually in the late 1990s). However, foreign investors are deterred by the remoteness of the regions, their weak infrastructure and communications links, inefficient state industries, corruption and ethnic unrest.[601]

In a number of countries that have been slow in undertaking reforms and introducing FDI promotion programmes there is concern that they will fall permanently behind in the global competition for FDI. In part these fears stem from the notion that competition for at least certain types of FDI may be a zero sum game. Countries which attracted FDI early in the transition process have gained advantages which are difficult for others to overcome: for example, investor friendly reputations, stronger financial positions (which reduce the risk of doing business), etc. Second, these advantages are reinforced if not totally overshadowed by the status of the first wave of EU accession countries.[602] Third, there is room (at least in eastern Europe) for only a few large foreign companies in key sectors such as automobiles. Once established in a country, the TNC will tend to make any additional investment there, for reasons of scale economies, etc. Moreover, such strategic investments will also attract foreign suppliers or downstream firms (as VW has done in the Czech Republic).[603] These concerns receive some support from the findings presented here which show that the ranking of countries according to FDI inflows has remained broadly similar (i.e. there has been no closing of the FDI gap) and that the concentration of FDI flows in the three leading countries has recently increased. What is more, there is evidence of a virtuous circle whereby FDI improves credit ratings, which in turn attract more FDI, thus increasing the difference between leaders and laggards.[604]

---

[599] UNCTAD, *World Investment Report, 1999*.

[600] J. Sachs, "A new map of the world", *The Economist*, 24 June 2000.

[601] Report on a government investment promotion conference, Chengdu, China. *International Herald Tribune*, 31 October 2000.

[602] The issue of diversion of FDI to potential EU candidates was raised by O. Havrylyshyn, "EU enlargement ...", op. cit.

[603] However, an argument against this pessimistic view is that countries can increase their attractiveness to foreign investors by creating a stable and predictable institutional framework and expectations of a competitive rate of return to fixed investment.

[604] A. Bevan and S. Estrin, op. cit.

Among other things, transition economies beyond central Europe may currently suffer from a locational disadvantage – the combination of distance from west European markets and inadequate infrastructure. However, this problem should not be insurmountable. The Bulgarian Black Sea coast (as well as all the states of the former SFR of Yugoslavia, the Baltic states, Belarus, the Republic of Moldova, most of Ukraine and parts of Russia) is 1500 kilometres from the centre of Germany, much less than the dimensions of the current EU and the United States single markets. These outlying countries could therefore become more attractive to foreign investors if they were connected with western Europe by an efficient and integrated telecommunications and transport infrastructure (for example, clearing the Danube waterway will help in the short run). The international investment banks (EBRD, EIB and World Bank) are all engaged in upgrading the infrastructure of the transition economies, but it remains questionable whether the infrastructure plans are sufficiently coherent – and on a sufficient scale – to overcome the locational disadvantages of these economies and integrate them more closely into the broader European economy.

ANNEX TO CHAPTER 5

MEASURING TECHNOLOGY TRANSFER AND SPILLOVERS

Section 5.6 examined technology transfer and spillovers through the use of panel data. The analysis of the data starts from a standard growth accounting approach,[605] the objective of which is to study the various factors that affect overall productivity, including the diffusion of technology. This is done by decomposing total factor productivity (TFP) growth into factors internal and external to the firm, including R&D investments and human capital, and different sources of international technology transfer, respectively.

The model assumes that the production function of enterprise i has the following form:

$$Y_{it} = A_{it} K_{it}^{\alpha} L_{it}^{\beta} N_{it}^{\gamma} \qquad \ldots (1)$$

where Y_{it} is gross output, K_{it}, L_{it} and N_{it} represent capital stock, labour input and materials, respectively, and A_{it} is TFP. The production function is homogenous of degree r in K, L and N, so that $r = \alpha+\beta+\gamma \neq 1$.[606] To get the TFP of each enterprise, it is necessary to differentiate the equation with respect to time. Under the assumption that the marginal product of each input is equal to its factor price, the equation can be rewritten as:

$$y_{it} = a_{it} + \alpha k_{it} + \beta l_{it} + \gamma n_{it} \qquad \ldots (2)$$

where $y_{it} = \log(Y_{it+1}/Y_{it})$, $a_{it} = \log(A_{it+1}/A_{it})$, $k_{it} = \log(K_{it+1}/K_{it})$, $l_{it} = \log(L_{it+1}/L_{it})$, and $n_{it} = \log(N_{it+1}/N_{it})$. TFP growth, or technological progress, is therefore the difference between the growth of output and the weighted sum of the growth of inputs, the weights being the individual shares of the factors in total output.

Estimating these equations at an aggregate level will lose some information concerning the average technology stock and average TFP growth. Since the technology parameter is the residual, i.e. that part of the change in output that cannot be explained by the variance of factor inputs, it says nothing about the factors that influence TFP growth. In reality this residual may capture a number of factors that may have little in common with technology levels or TFP growth. In this specification the technology parameter depends crucially on the goodness of fit of the model. This is especially true in transition economies, in which this estimation approach – due to an inefficient utilization of production factors – may return incorrectly high parameters for technology level or TFP growth.[607]

Ideally the model should include those factors that determine the level of technology or its growth. This is difficult since technology embodies skills and knowledge that are not easy to measure. The model used in section 5.6 assumes that the firm's technology level A_{it} is determined as:

$$A_{it} = G_i(RD_{it}, H_{it}, F_i, S_{jt}, X_{it}, M_{it}, d_j, d_t) \qquad \ldots (3)$$

where RD_{it} and H_{it} capture the sources of technology internal to the firm, and factors F_i through M_{it} capture the sources external to the firm, i.e. international technology spillovers. RD_{it} represents annual R&D expenditures (relative to output), H_{it} indicates accumulated human capital (measured as average labour costs per employee), F_i is a dummy variable for foreign ownership, S_{jt} measures intra-industry R&D spillovers stemming from foreign owned firms (measured as the share of foreign owned firms in industry j's domestic sales and exports), X_{it} and M_{it} refer to the export propensity (exports to sales ratio) and import propensity (ratio of imports to material costs) of the firm, respectively, while d_j and d_t are sector and time dummies.

---

[605] R. Solow, "Technical change and the aggregate production function," *Review of Economics and Statistics*, Vol. 39, August 1957, pp. 312-320.

[606] S. Basu and J. Fernald, *Aggregate Productivity and the Productivity of Aggregates*, NBER Working Paper, No. 5382 (Cambridge, MA), December 1995.

[607] J. Damijan and S. Polanec, "Is Vintage Capital Important? Efficiency of Foreign vs. Domestic Firms in Slovenia," University of Ljubljana, 2000, mimeo. They show that foreign owned firms in Slovenia had significantly lower parameters of technology level as compared with domestic firms from 1994 to 1998.

The term R&D (RD_{it}) captures the absorptive capacity of the enterprise. This factor reflects both the innovation effect and the learning or absorption effect of R&D activity. These two knowledge effects are separated in the model by considering RD_{it} as internal to the firm and $RD_{it}S_{jt}$ as external to it. The stock of human capital (H_{it}) represents the skills of the workforce, improvements in which raise the overall productivity of the firm. Enterprises employ labour of different skills, which employees acquire through education and training both inside and outside the firm. Human capital is assumed to lie within the firm's scope in this model since it indicates the firm's eagerness to enhance its technology level by engaging skilled workers. Inter-firm diffusion of labour (job reallocation) is captured by the variable S_{jt}, which represents intra-industry spillovers from foreign to domestic firms. The model assumes that some workers trained by foreign firms migrate to domestic firms. Labour costs per employee proxy the human capital stock of the enterprise, which assumes that, on average, firms with higher average per capita labour costs employ relatively more skilled labour. Human capital will thus have a differential impact on TFP growth in foreign relative to domestic firms.

If FDI is an efficient channel of technology transfer, it is reasonable to infer that the "foreign ownership factor" (F_i) not only shifts the technological constant A_{it} of the host firm but also affects the efficiency of its factor utilization. As a consequence, it is not possible to assume identical production functions across firms: allowance has to be made for the differences in efficiency with which foreign owned and domestic firms use capital, labour and materials. This is allowed for by multiplying K, L and N by foreign ownership dummys (F_ik_{it}, F_il_{it}, F_in_{it}) to obtain different parameters for foreign and domestic firms. A dummy variable is also included in the model to separate majority owned foreign firms from minority owned foreign firms. This is to find out whether majority foreign ownership facilitates the transfer of more complex technology and management skills to local firms.

For firms without foreign participation, knowledge spillovers (S_{jt}) from foreign firms in the same industry may be important. These externalities, however, may not always be positive, as local enterprises may be "crowded out" by foreign enterprises if they do not have the capability to adapt quickly enough. Foreign enterprises create externalities by demonstrating new technologies and management methods, enhancing competition, and creating backward and forward linkages with local suppliers and by workforce training. Previous studies control for these effects either by taking the foreign share of aggregate employment in an industry or the aggregate foreign share of total output. The model tests for these externalities by including two variables that control for crowding out caused by relatively large domestic sales of foreign enterprises and for the imitation and agglomeration effects stimulated by the export orientation of foreign enterprises. These variables are the share of domestic sales by foreign firms in an industry's total domestic sales ($S.D_{jt}$) and the share of foreign exports in an industry's total exports ($S.X_{jt}$). Finally, the model also tests for the importance of international trade by including the export propensity (X_{it}, the export to output ratio) and import propensity of the firm (M_{it}, the ratio of imports to material costs).

In addition to allowing foreign and domestic firms to differ in terms of the efficiency with which they use factor inputs, sector specific effects are captured in dummy variables d_j. In the transition economies it is also necessary to assume that the efficiency of enterprises will improve over time as more productive capital and skilled labour are employed. The model controls for this by including a time variable d_t. In the absence of other proxies, the time variable is also intended to capture time-specific aggregate shocks to the whole economy, shocks which are inherent to transition economies.

The results of three different tests are presented in tables 5.6.8-5.6.10. Table 5.6.8 considers the importance of direct transfers of technology through FDI to selected local firms. The equation supporting this table can be written as:

$$y_{it} = b_{it} + \delta F_i + \alpha k_{it} + \beta l_{it} + \gamma n_{it} + \chi F_i k_{it} + \phi F_i l_{it} + \varphi F_i n_{it} + \kappa H_{it} + \lambda F_i H_{it} + \mu S.D_{jt} + \nu S.X_{jt} + \theta_j d_j + \psi_t d_t + \varepsilon_{it} \quad \ldots (4)$$

where b_{it} is a log of a constant term (the residual that accounts for alternative sources of TFP growth not accounted for in the model), δ measures the difference in TFP growth rates between domestic and foreign firms, α, β, γ, and χ, ϕ, φ represent shares of factor inputs in domestic and foreign firms, respectively, κ and λ represent the impact of human capital in domestic and foreign firms, μ and ν measure intra-industry spillovers from foreign to domestic firms in domestic and export markets, respectively, θ and ψ are parameters of sector and time dummies, while ε is the error term.

Table 5.6.9 analyzes the associated, indirect intra-industry spillovers from FDI to other firms in the economy. The equation supporting this table considers only domestic firms and can be written as:

$$y_{it} = b_{it} + \delta F_i + \alpha k_{it} + \beta l_{it} + \gamma n_{it} + \chi F_i k_{it} + \phi F_i l_{it} + \varphi F_i n_{it} + \kappa H_{it} + \lambda F_i H_{it} + \eta RD_{it} + \mu S.D_{jt} + \nu S.X_{jt} + \rho RD_{it} S.D_{jt} + \tau RD_{it} S.X_{jt} + \theta_j d_j + \psi_t d_t + \varepsilon_{it} \quad \ldots (5)$$

where η is the rate of return on firms' R&D investments (the parameter of innovative capacity), and ρ and τ measure absorptive capacity to technology shocks in domestic and exports markets.

Table 5.6.10 investigates the importance of alternative sources of technology for firms without FDI, including imports of capital and intermediate goods and learning by exporting. The equation supporting this table also considers only domestic firms and can be written as:

$$y_{it} = b_{it} + \delta F_i + \alpha k_{it} + \beta l_{it} + \gamma n_{it} + \chi F_i k_{it} + \phi F_i l_{it} + \varphi F_i n_{it} + \kappa H_{it} + \lambda F_i H_{it} + o X_{it} + \pi M_{it} + \eta RD_{it} + \upsilon RD_{it} X_{it} + \omega RD_{it} M_{it} + \theta_j d_j + \psi_t d_t + \varepsilon_{it} \quad \ldots (6)$$

where, in addition to (4), o and π represent international R&D spillovers via firms' exports and imports, η is the rate of return on firms' R&D investments, υ and ω measure the absorptive capacity of domestic firms to technology shocks through exports and imports. International R&D spillovers to domestic firms are measured by the share of imports in total costs of materials (imports of capital equipment and intermediate goods) and by the share of exports in total sales (indicating capability of firms to meet high quality standards in western markets).

The estimates in tables 5.6.8-5.6.10 use a random effects model to deal with the changes in TFP over time. The reason for this choice is that OLS estimators may give biased and inconsistent estimates of TFP because they suffer from probable correlation between the productivity effects and the output variable.[608] As there are no suitable firm-specific instruments to control for this problem, it is necessary to use either the random or fixed effects model to take firm-specific effects into account.[609] Though preferable to OLS, neither technique is absolutely accurate for estimating the above equations. Fixed effects models assume constant TFP growth over time for a single firm. Even though the Hausman test shows that the fixed effects model provides a better specification of equations (4)-(6), the assumptions of this model are inappropriate given that the aim of this study is to examine the impact of different factors on changes in TFP. However, the assumption that changes in TFP at the firm level are uncorrelated over time is a major disadvantage of the random effects model.

---

[608] S. Djankov and B. Hoekman, "Foreign investment and productivity growth in Czech enterprises", *The World Bank Economic Review*, Vol. 14, No. 1 (Washington, D.C.), 2000, pp. 49-64.

[609] For a discussion on the use of different panel data techniques see C. Hsiao, *Analysis of Panel Data* (Cambridge, Cambridge University Press, 1986), and H. Baltagi, *Econometric Analysis of Panel Data* (Chichester, John Wiley and Sons, 1995).

CHAPTER 6

ECONOMIC TRANSFORMATION AND REAL EXCHANGE RATES IN THE 2000s: THE BALASSA-SAMUELSON CONNECTION

In a developing economy, one which is catching up with the income levels in the more economically advanced countries, productivity in the sectors producing tradeable goods will tend to rise faster than in those producing non-tradeables. Since wage increases tend to be more or less the same in all sectors, inflation will be relatively higher in the non-tradeables sector, an effect that will be strengthened if demand in a growing economy is biased towards services. The result is that relatively faster productivity growth in the tradeables sector will lead not only to an unavoidably higher inflation rate for non-tradeables but also to a real appreciation of the exchange rate. This hypothesis, known as the Balassa-Samuelson effect, is tested against the experience of the transition economies since 1990 and is found to hold. This is an ineluctable process for a developing economy, which has particularly important implications for those transition economies about to join the EU since it may create a serious conflict between the EMU targets for exchange rate stability and inflation.

6.1 Introduction

Since they embarked on the construction of new political and economic systems, the transition economies have adopted very different exchange rate regimes. Some have chosen the hardest version of pegs, a currency board, while others have opted for flexibility, and many have changed course along the way. There has also been great diversity in the extent to which they have chosen to liberalize the capital account, which is intimately related to the exchange rate regime.

The era of diversity is likely to come to an end for a substantial number of them in the near future. By the middle of the 2000s, several countries from central and eastern Europe will have joined the European Union, and the enlargement process is likely to continue. Barring surprises, by the end of the decade, 10 or more of them will have completed the process. EU membership imposes a number of obligations in this respect. In the long run, they must become members of the monetary union. Along the way, they must "converge", which implies a substantial degree of exchange rate flexibility. Before getting there, they are expected to eliminate all restrictions on capital flows. The not-too-distant future is therefore one of full capital mobility and the most extreme and irreversible form of exchange rate fixity.

This evolution raises a number of critical questions. To start with, a generally held view is that the differences in the exchange rate regime reflect in part the varied political-economic equilibria that have emerged following the collapse of the Soviet bloc.[610] Such equilibria, once established, only change very slowly. Undoubtedly, EU membership will exert a powerful influence in this respect, but the experience with the earlier EU members suggests that it would be unrealistic to expect rapid changes.

The conditions attached to EU membership, the *acquis communautaire*, have always been shaped to fit the particular characteristics of the existing members. In many respects, the transition countries are fundamentally different from previous entrants to the EU. For example, table 6.1.1, which refers to the per capita GDP of previous entrants at their date of entry and to similar 1998 figures for the transition countries, shows that the transition countries, with the exception of Slovenia, are considerably poorer than any of the previous new entrants to the Union. This comparison barely scratches the surface, as it ignores the larger differences in terms of economic structure, the welfare state, gender gaps, the development of the banking and financial systems, etc. Importantly, the EU has become more cohesive as economic and financial integration has deepened. Much of today's *acquis communautaire* would have been impossible to agree upon 20 years ago, when diversity

---

[610] See, e.g. S. Fischer and R. Sahay, *The Transition Economies After Ten Years*, IMF Working Paper WP/00/30 (Washington, D.C.), February 2000; and C. Wyplosz, "Macroeconomic lessons from ten years of transition", in B. Pleskovic and J. Stiglitz (eds.), *Annual World Bank Conference on Development Economics 1999* (Washington, D.C.), 2001.

TABLE 6.1.1

Per capita GDP (PPP-adjusted) in relation to the EU average, 1991 and 1998

(Per cent)

	1991	1998
Czech Republic	60.2	55.4
Hungary	44.9	45.9
Poland	29.3	34.2
Slovakia	41.7	43.5
Slovenia	55.7	64.1
Estonia	40.5	34.4
	\multicolumn{2}{c}{Year of accession to EU}
Greece		62.4
Portugal		60.8
Spain		73.7

Source: World Bank; IMF.

within the Union was wider than it is today, and yet much less than it will be when the transition economies have joined.

An implication of the relative backwardness of the transition economies is that they are expected to catch up with the EU – indeed, this is a key economic objective. Faster growth and continuing structural changes are bound to affect the exchange rate. In particular, the Balassa-Samuelson hypothesis implies a continuous real appreciation. Here again, previous new entrants to the EU faced a similar process but, as table 6.1.1 indicates, it is likely to have been significantly more moderate than what is in store for the transition economies.

In this chapter, the focus is on the Balassa-Samuelson effect, which is potentially important for the future exchange rate policies of the EU candidate countries. Countries which join the European Union will have to agree on an exchange rate regime within the EMS framework and, eventually, they will join the European Monetary Union. The presence of a sizeable Balassa-Samuelson effect will affect both the choice of the exchange rate path and their inflation performance once they are in the monetary union. Those countries which currently peg their currencies may already be facing a situation where inflation is influenced by this effect. As the candidate countries will have to meet the convergence targets of the EU, the presence of a sizeable Balassa-Samuelson effect is therefore potentially problematic. For those countries which operate a flexible exchange regime, the evolution of the nominal exchange rate may become a key policy instrument for meeting the convergence criteria.

The next section briefly looks at the restrictions that accession may impose on exchange rate policies. Section 6.3 presents the theoretical building blocks of the catch-up process and of the Balassa-Samuelson effect. Section 6.4 examines graphically whether these hypotheses are verified in the transition countries. Having confirmed their likely presence, section 6.5 proceeds formally to estimate and measure them. Section 6.6 draws some conclusions from the implications of the empirical findings.

This chapter tries to cover all the transition countries. However, data availability is a serious constraint. It may seem that too much emphasis is put on the issue of EU accession, but the process involved offers a unique insight into how countries with different exchange rate regimes will converge towards monetary union and on the relationships between different exchange rate regimes and the catch-up process and the associated Balassa-Samuelson effect. Their experience is also instructive for countries for which EU membership is not at present on their agenda.

6.2 The choice of an exchange rate regime in the 2000s

(i) General principles

A number of countries from eastern Europe are likely to join the EU by 2004-2005. It has not yet been fully decided what restrictions will apply to their exchange rate regimes, but a number of principles have already been put forward. The whole situation is dominated by the fact that the end-point is known, namely, that they will eventually adopt the euro.[611] Two periods need to be distinguished: the first before joining the EU and the second before joining the monetary union.

Logically, since the final destination is known, the discussion must proceed backwards in time. The ECOFIN Council[612] has recently affirmed the principle of equal treatment of all member states. *Inter alia*, this implies the application of the convergence criteria to new members. According to the Treaty of the European Union, prior to joining the monetary union, a country must have achieved a high and sustainable degree of nominal convergence with the euro area. This is to be assessed on the basis of the convergence criteria laid down in Article 121 and the Protocol on the Convergence Criteria. In particular a candidate country must have remained in the ERM-2 for at least two years with its exchange rate within the prescribed fluctuation band, without significant tensions in its foreign exchange market, and without a change in the central parity of its currency against the euro as a result of an initiative by the non-euro state.

Prior to joining ERM-2, countries are required by the treaty to "regard their exchange rate policies as a matter of common interest". This essentially means that competitive devaluations are ruled out but the choice of exchange rate regime remains free. However, the rules of accession to the monetary union imply that new member states will be expected to join the revised exchange rate mechanism ERM-2, which is summarized in box 6.2.1.

---

[611] In principle, a country can ask for an opt-out clause, as was offered to Denmark and the United Kingdom. In practice, however, such a request is likely to be turned down and, anyway, there has been no suggestion that any of the current candidates are interested in this option.

[612] ECOFIN Council, *ECOFIN Council Conclusions on Exchange Rate Strategies for Accession Countries* (Brussels), 7 November 2000.

> **Box 6.2.1**
>
> **The exchange rate mechanism-2**
>
> The arrangements for the new ERM-2 were set out by the Amsterdam Council Resolution of 16 June 1997 and the Agreement between the ECB and the national central banks of non-euro area member states of 1 September 1998. Central rates are to be set and adjusted jointly by the ECB and the relevant non-euro area national central banks (NCBs). Adjustments to central rates should be timely to avoid misalignments. The standard band of fluctuation is ±15 per cent around the central rate. Intervention at the limits is in principle automatic and unlimited and supported by very short-term financing. However, the ECB and the NCB concerned can suspend intervention if price stability is endangered. Narrower bands can be declared as a unilateral commitment by a non-euro area central bank or formally agreed at the request of a non-euro member state. In the latter case, the decision will be taken jointly by the ministers of the euro area member states, the ECB, and the minister and the NCB of the non-euro area state.
>
> Thus, ERM-2 is compatible with a fairly broad range of exchange rate arrangements. The ECOFIN Council (2000) only excluded three regimes: any regime without a mutually agreed central rate to the euro, crawling pegs and pegs to currencies other than the euro. Entering the EU with a currency board arrangement tied to the euro is compatible with the ERM-2 in the sense that it could be regarded as a unilateral commitment by the acceding member state, with no obligations for the ECB beyond those implied by the regular rules of the system. It is understood that the currency board must have been in operation for a substantial period of time to prove the viability of its target exchange rate with the euro in order to be accepted by the ECB.

There is no rule concerning the timing of entry into ERM-2 but that decision, and the choice of a central parity, requires agreement between the ECB and the country in question.

(ii) Historical overview of exchange rate arrangements

The types of exchange rate regime adopted since the early 1990s by a number of central and east European countries and Russia are summarized in table 6.2.1. It follows the IMF classification, which is based on official statements about exchange rate policies. At the beginning of the 1990s, conventional pegs with or without drift (regimes 3 to 6) were the most common exchange rate regime. The choice of this option was driven by the wish to use the exchange rate as the nominal anchor in the initial period of macroeconomic stabilization. Since the mid-1990s, there has been a tendency to move towards exchange rate regimes that are either relatively flexible or very rigid. The Czech Republic, Poland, Russia and the Slovak Republic have abandoned their crawling pegs or bands in favour of more or less managed floats. Romania and Slovenia have retained floating regimes since the early years of transition, although in practice Slovenia limits exchange rate movements severely. According to this classification, Hungary is the only country still maintaining a conventional crawling band. In contrast, Bulgaria and the Baltic states operate hard pegs: currency boards in Bulgaria, Estonia and Lithuania, a conventional peg with a zero fluctuation band in Latvia. While Bulgaria's and Estonia's currency boards are tied to the euro, Lithuania's currency board is tied to the dollar and Latvia's peg to the SDR.

Interestingly, the two countries that still operate conventional peg regimes, Hungary and, de facto, Slovenia, also maintain restrictions on short-term capital flows. According to the European Commission's most recent Progress Reports, the Czech Republic and Poland, which recently adopted more flexible managed floats, are now about to remove their last remaining restrictions on short-term capital flows. The countries with rigid pegs, Bulgaria, Estonia, Latvia and Lithuania, have already completed, or almost completed, the liberalization of short-term capital flows. That the accession states will enter the EU with practically full liberalization of capital movements makes the next enlargement markedly different from previous ones. In the enlargement of the 1980s, Spain and Portugal entered the EU with the possibility of retaining their restrictions on capital flows for a period that lasted more than 10 years.

(iii) The challenges of accession to the European Union

The principles described in section 6.2(i) imply that most of the candidate countries will have to reverse the recent direction of their exchange rate policies. In order to be admitted into the euro area, those which currently allow for a float will need to reduce the range of variability of their exchange rates; and those which have adopted hard pegs (currency boards or zero fluctuation bands, or narrow bands in the case of Hungary) will have to adopt some degree of flexibility.

(a) From flexibility to ERM-2

Regarding the first group of countries, those that will have to give up the no-commitment floating regime, it might be argued that the regime change will be largely formal since the ERM-2 allows for wide fluctuation bands (±15 per cent). There are, however, two reasons to doubt whether the change will be entirely benign. First, these countries will most likely be required to remove all remaining capital account restrictions on entering the EU. The experience with conventional pegs and free capital movement is not encouraging. From Latin America to Asia, and including the Czech Republic and Russia, and

TABLE 6.2.1

Exchange rate arrangements in eastern Europe, the Baltic states and the Russian Federation, 1990-2000

	1990	1991	1992	1993	1994	1995	1996	1997	1998	1999	2000
Bulgaria	3	8	8	8	8	8	8	2	2	2	2
Czech Republic	3	3	3	3	3	3	6	7	7	7	7
Hungary	3	3	3	3	3	6	6	6	6	6	6
Poland	3	5	5	5	5	6	6	6	6	6	8
Romania	3	7	7	7	7	7	7	7	7	7	7
Slovakia	3	3	3	3	3	3	6	6	7	7	7
Slovenia	..	..	7	7	7	7	7	7	7	7	7
Estonia	..	..	2	2	2	2	2	2	2	2	2
Latvia	..	..	8	8	3	3	3	3	3	3	3
Lithuania	..	..	8	8	2	2	2	2	2	2	2
Russian Federation	..	..	8	8	6	6	6	6	8	8	8

Source: J. von Hagen and Jizhong Zhou, "The choice of exchange rate regimes of transition economies", Zentrum für Europäische Integrationsforschung (Bonn), 2001, mimeo.

Note: Exchange rate regime description:

1. Dollarization: no separate legal tender;
2. Currency board: currency fully backed by foreign exchange reserves;
3. Conventional fixed pegs: peg to another currency or currency basket within a band of at most ±1 per cent;
4. Horizontal bands: pegs with bands larger than ±1 per cent;
5. Crawling pegs: pegs with central parity periodically adjusted in fixed amounts at a fixed, pre-announced rate or in response to changes in selected quantitative indicators;
6. Crawling bands: crawling pegs combined with bands of more than ±1 per cent;
7. Managed float with no pre-announced exchange rate path: active intervention without precommitment to a pre-announced target or path for the exchange rate;
8. Independent float: market-determined exchange rate and monetary policy independent of exchange rate policy.

more recently Turkey, capital inflows have tended to surge only to be abruptly reversed.[613] While in some cases the reversals can be blamed on unsustainable macroeconomic policies, they have also occurred in countries with impeccable macroeconomic policy credentials. *Ex post*, the reversals have been associated with microeconomic weaknesses, but it is fair to say that these shortcomings had long gone undetected, and most of them were only identified after the crises had erupted. It is also likely that, in spite of all the monitoring associated with the accession process, the new EU members will remain vulnerable in a number of ways specific to the transition process which, while known, may not be recognized *ex ante* as a potential source of severe financial instability.

Second, the relative economic backwardness of the transition countries suggests that their equilibrium real exchange rates will be appreciating. If this is absorbed through a nominal appreciation, the fluctuation margin could become much more uncomfortable than is commonly assumed on the basis of the experience with ERM-1, which brought together a much more homogeneous group of countries. If the real appreciation is absorbed through inflation, the risk is that the acceding countries will find it difficult to meet the convergence criteria. A possibly aggravating factor in this case is that the markets might conclude that EMU membership will be delayed and that the high inflation rate calls for a depreciation, thus triggering an exchange rate crisis. The optimistic view is that the magnitude of this effect is small enough to be contained within the large fluctuation bands of ERM-2. A key purpose of this chapter is to provide estimates of the effect in order to judge which outcome is the more likely.

(b) From quasi-EMU to ERM-2 (and EMU)

Bulgaria and the Baltic countries now have a regime almost equivalent to full EMU membership. Their central banks perform essentially mechanical tasks with no macroeconomic policy content. Unless they are allowed to bypass the ERM-2 requirement, they will have to re-establish a degree of flexibility which they have rejected in the past, and seem content to have done so. Such a step could be a source of potentially serious difficulties.

Even if it is assumed that the monetary authorities will not want to abandon the strong discipline that they have established in recent years, they will have to convince their political authorities and the financial markets that this is still their determination. With a regime of high capital mobility, false steps will quickly attract speculative pressure. A necessary condition is that Maastricht-type independence be given to the central

---

[613] The literature on this issue, started by C. Diaz-Alejandro, "Goodbye financial repression, hello financial crash", *Journal of Development Economics*, Vol. 19, No. 1-2, 1985, pp. 1-24, has been growing fast. Useful references are B. Eichengreen, A. Rose and C. Wyplosz "Exchange market mayhem: the antecedents and aftermaths of speculative attacks," *Economic Policy*, Vol. 21, 1995, pp. 249-312; A. Demirguç-Kunt and E. Detragiache, "The determinants of banking crises in developing and developed countries", *IMF Staff Papers*, Vol. 45, No. 1, March 1998, pp. 81-109; and C. Wyplosz, *How Risky is Financial Liberalization in the Developing Countries?*, CEPR Discussion Paper No. 2724, March 2001.

CHART 6.2.1

Consumer price inflation in Estonia and the euro area, January 1994-January 2001

Source: Bank of Estonia, *Bulletin* (Tallinn); ECB, *Monthly Bulletin* (Frankfurt am Main).

banks, but that may not be enough.[614] Vulnerabilities will have to be kept to a minimum.

A likely resolution of the problem is for these countries to adopt unilaterally a tight version of the ERM, allowing for no fluctuation band, in effect retaining a currency board arrangement. This is entirely possible within the framework of ERM-2. An even tougher solution would be to unilaterally euroize, but this is considered to be a different arrangement from ERM-2 and would therefore require the agreement of the ECB and the European Union.

Even if such a solution were adopted, the combination of a hard peg and a Balassa-Samuelson effect would result in a higher inflation rate than in the euro area. If this effect is strong, it is entirely possible that some of the convergence criteria would be missed (inflation, the nominal interest rate). Here again, it is necessary to determine the order of magnitude of the effect. A preliminary, partial indication is provided by the case of Estonia, a country that from June 1993 tied its currency to the deutsche mark and, therefore, since 1999 to the euro. Chart 6.2.1 compares the inflation rates in Estonia and the euro area since 1994. Two facts stand out. First, the disinflation process has been slow since 1994, taking over four years to get the rate down from around 50 per cent to just under 10 per cent; this was partly because the kroon may have been initially undervalued, and partly because many administered prices were only gradually liberalized.[615] Second, the inflation gap has increased since mid-2000. This development partly reflects the rise in oil prices, which is also visible in the euro area inflation rate. On average, inflation has been higher in Estonia by 5.6 percentage points over the period January 1997-February 2001, and by 2.1 percentage points from January 1999 to January 2001. This is a rough indication of how matters could develop.

6.3 The implications of catch up

The theoretical background used to analyse the real exchange rate appreciation inherent in the catch-up process is the Balassa-Samuelson effect. This can be described as follows. Trade integration implies that most of the productivity gains appear in the traded goods sector. This is not entirely correct, of course, as non-traded goods and services enter as intermediate inputs in the production of traded goods and are therefore facing indirect competition.[616] In addition, to the extent that many services – the bulk of non-traded goods – are superior goods, rising standards of living will be accompanied by increasing demand for them. In this sector as well, there are bound to be some economies of scale and scope, although their magnitude should not be overestimated.

There is, however, little doubt that productivity will rise faster in the traded than in the non-traded goods sector. Since rising productivity usually translates into rising wages, relatively faster productivity growth in the traded goods sector means that wages in this sector will tend to outpace those in the non-traded goods sector. The central assumption of the Balassa-Samuelson theory is that wage increases tend to be equalized across sectors. Two main reasons are advanced to justify this assumption. First, in the labour market, it is expected that supply will shift towards the better-paid jobs and thus will exert pressure towards wage equalization, even though inter-sectoral labour mobility is limited (skills, geographical location). Second, considerations of fairness or solidarity, possibly backed by trade union pressure, will act to limit large differences.

The non-traded goods sector, facing smaller productivity increases than in the traded goods sector, however, cannot remain profitable if it accommodates such wage increases. The solution is to raise prices faster for non-traded goods. Thus, the supply-side's reaction to the larger productivity increases in the traded goods sector is to generate a higher rate of price inflation in the non-traded sector.

What about the demand side? Rising productivity induces increases in income and wealth, hence rising consumption. If the demand for both traded and non-traded goods grows at the same rate, demand is neutral

---

[614] A particular difficulty is that, while Bulgaria's and Estonia's currency boards are tied to the euro, Lithuania's is tied to the dollar and Latvia's peg to the SDR. The last two countries will have to shift to the euro, always a delicate transition.

[615] The liberalization of administered prices is still not complete.

[616] The idea of the Balassa-Samuelson effect was initially developed to take into account technological progress that is biased towards the traded goods sector. This chapter focuses on a different interpretation more relevant to the transition countries, namely, that growth is largely driven by the catch-up process.

and the supply-side effect dominates in the sense that it does not skew inflation towards non-traded goods and services. Only if demand growth were to be biased towards traded goods could the supply side effect be offset, partly or completely. If, as is usually thought to be the case, demand is biased towards services, which constitute the bulk of non-traded goods, the demand side effect reinforces that on the supply side.

The last step in the reasoning concerns the exchange rate. The ratio of non-traded to traded goods prices is often taken as a measure of the real exchange rate. In which case, the conclusion must be that faster productivity growth in the traded goods sector leads to a real appreciation.

If a wider definition of the real exchange rate is used, based for example on the consumer price index, one more step is needed. This starts with the observation that, for a small economy, the prices of traded goods are driven by world prices and the nominal exchange rate. Under the assumption that the nominal exchange rate is constant, the conclusion is that the change in the prices of traded goods is the same at home and abroad.

Non-traded goods price inflation is equal to the rise in prices for traded goods *plus* a measure of asymmetric productivity growth; it is therefore higher in countries where productivity is rising more rapidly. Catching-up countries, in this case the transition economies, are therefore expected to have higher rates of inflation in non-traded goods prices. This conclusion applies to the consumer price index, an average of the prices of traded and non-traded goods. The result is real appreciation of the exchange rate.

If the exchange rate is not constant, the result still holds as domestic traded goods prices rise at the same rate as the foreign traded good prices *plus* the rate of depreciation. When computing the real exchange rate, this effect is automatically taken into account.[617]

In conclusion, it is important to note that the Balassa-Samuelson effect is an equilibrium phenomenon, not an undesirable transitory effect that ought to be counteracted through policy actions. In fact policy is unable to check this process, at least without resorting to distortionary price controls. The real appreciation reflects the natural evolution of the economy, which has to be translated into relative price changes. It is also one channel through which standards of living – e.g. as proxied by wages – rise towards those in more advanced economies.

6.4 A first look at the evidence

(i) Relative wages

Before turning to direct econometric estimates of the Balassa-Samuelson effect, it will be useful to first look at the basic statistics for each of the various steps in the above reasoning. First, is the assumption that wages tend to be equalized across sectors or, at least, that their relative position remains constant. Chart 6.4.1 shows relative gross wages in industry and the services sector in 12 countries for the period 1992-1999, depending on data availability (note that the scale differs from one country to another).[618]

The two first rows provide evidence for the countries of central and eastern Europe as well as the three Baltic countries. In view of the considerable structural changes that have been underway, the margin of variation is typically quite small, usually no more than 15 per cent. In addition, the ratios typically display no trend, and where there is one it is towards unity, i.e. towards full equalization. The last row includes four CIS countries where the ratio has been changing more widely and not always towards unity. This is not surprising given that the market mechanism is far from being well-established in these countries. The conclusion is that a key assumption of the Balassa-Samuelson mechanism, namely, stability in relative wages across sectors, tends to be confirmed in the transition economies where markets have been developed most.

(ii) Relative productivity

The second assumption to be checked is whether productivity has been rising faster in the traded than in the non-traded goods sector. There is no direct measure of these sectors but it is customary to consider that much of the industrial sector produces traded goods, while most services are non-traded. In principle total factor productivity should be compared, but this requires estimation of production functions for each country which is impossible given the short time series available and the lack of capital stock data. Instead, the general practice in the literature of measuring labour productivity, the ratio of output to employment, is followed.

Chart 6.4.2 brings together the evidence for the six countries for which the data are available for enough years to produce meaningful graphs. After some irregular behaviour in the early years of transition, productivity is definitely growing faster in industry than in the services sector. The average annual difference from the trough to the last observation ranges from 4.6 percentage points in Slovenia to 11.1 percentage points in the Czech Republic. These are large numbers.

---

[617] Let π^T and π^N be traded goods price inflation at home, π^{T*} and π^{N*} abroad, and ε the rate of nominal exchange rate depreciation, so that $\pi^T = \varepsilon + \pi^{T*}$. Then the evolution of the real exchange rate is:

$$\varepsilon - (\alpha \pi^T + (1-\alpha) \pi^N) + (\alpha \pi^{T*} + (1-\alpha) \pi^{N*})$$

where α is the share of traded goods in consumption, assumed to be same at home and abroad for simplicity. The real exchange rate changes as:

$$-(1-\alpha)[(\pi^N - \pi^T) - (\pi^{N*} - \pi^{T*})].$$

It appreciates when $\pi^N - \pi^T > \pi^{N*} - \pi^{T*}$.

[618] This procedure disregards differences in the structure of employment in different sectors. It is obvious that skill, gender, seniority, firm size, ownership, location, etc. affect wage differences.

CHART 6.4.1

Relative wages in industry and services, 1992-1999

Source: UN/ECE Common Database.

CHART 6.4.2

Relative productivity in industry and services, 1992-1998

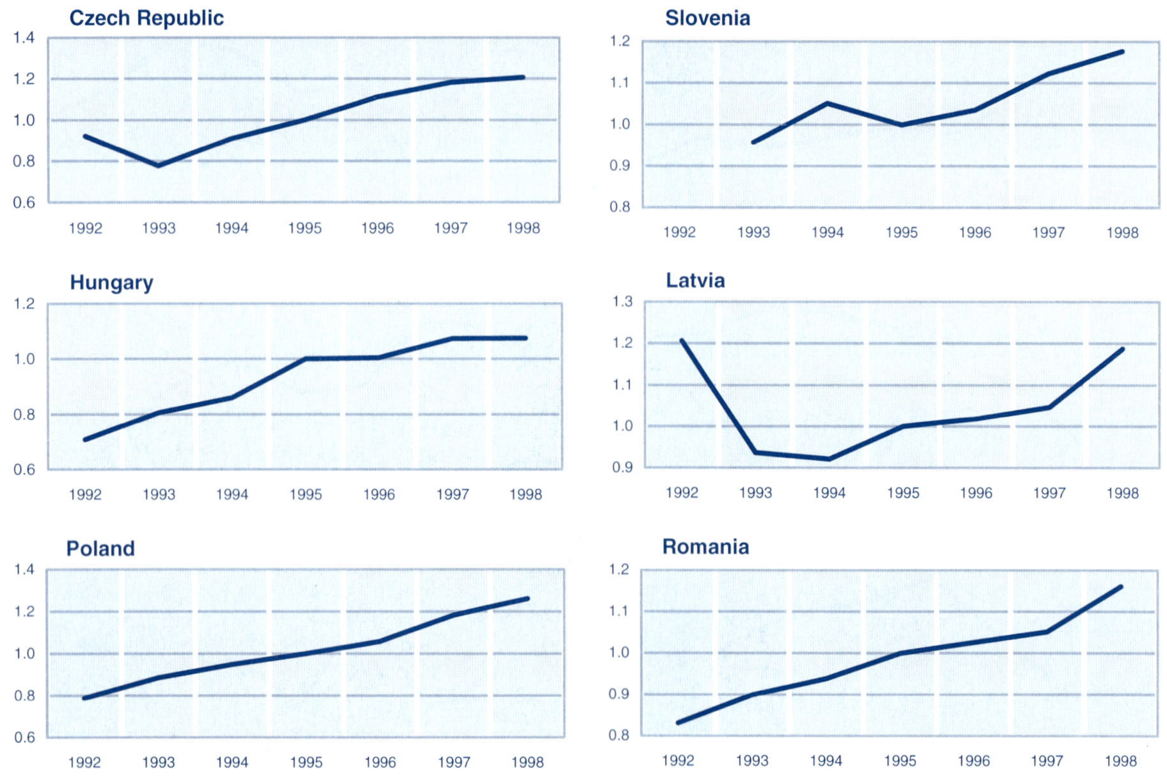

Source: UN/ECE Common Database.

(iii) Relative prices

Finally, as an approximation of the ratio of non-traded to traded goods prices, the evolution of the price of services relative to the producer price index for industrial goods is examined. Chart 6.4.3 presents the available information for 16 countries. Occasional sudden declines in the price ratio are related to sharp devaluations, often following a period of overvaluation. Over the whole period, however, a clear trend is discernible in all countries. The chart suggests that it is indeed worth undertaking a formal test of the Balassa-Samuelson effect in the transition countries.

6.5 Formal evidence

The visual examination of the data suggests that each step of the reasoning that leads to the Balassa-Samuelson effect is empirically verified. The accumulated evidence is strong, but it remains largely circumstantial as a number of other factors are likely to interfere with the postulated mechanism. For example, demand factors – including exchange rate changes – are likely to interfere with the Balassa-Samuelson effect. This could come about as a structural effect either associated with the luxury good nature of many services, or with a drop in demand for domestic production relative to previously unavailable traded goods. There could also be an adjustment effect if, through price moderation and possibly public subsidies, large manufacturing firms were able to overcome the drop in incomes and spending associated with the transition shock.

The analysis proceeds in several steps, following the same logic as in the previous section: since the Balassa-Samuelson effect rests on a number of mechanisms, the presence of each of them is checked before testing directly for the complete effect. First the behaviour of labour productivity is investigated, in order to confirm that it is driven by supply-side factors. Next, real product wages in industry and in services are related to productivity, gross and net wages being examined separately. The following step examines what has been driving growth in industry and in the services sectors. Importantly, these steps are not regarded as structural estimations, but simply as additional ways of exploring the statistical properties of the data and of detecting possible heterogeneity among countries in this process. The steps from productivity to real product wages, to real consumer wages and to growth allow the Balassa-Samuelson effect to be disentangled. The effect of these factors on inflation has not been included as the necessary assumptions would have been rather heroic. Finally, direct estimates of the Balassa-Samuelson effect are made, using the methodology developed by De Gregorio et al.,[619] which allows for demand factors as suggested by Bergstrand.[620]

---

[619] J. De Gregorio, A. Giovannini and H. Wolf, "International evidence on tradeables and nontradeables inflation", *European Economic Review*, Vol. 38, No. 6, June 1994, pp. 1225-1244.

[620] J. Bergstrand, "Structural determinants of real exchange rates and national price levels: some empirical evidence", *The American Economic Review*, Vol. 81, No. 1, 1991, pp. 327-334.

Economic Transformation and Real Exchange Rates in the 2000s: The Balassa-Samuelson Connection 235

CHART 6.4.3

Relative prices of services and non-food manufactures, 1989-1999

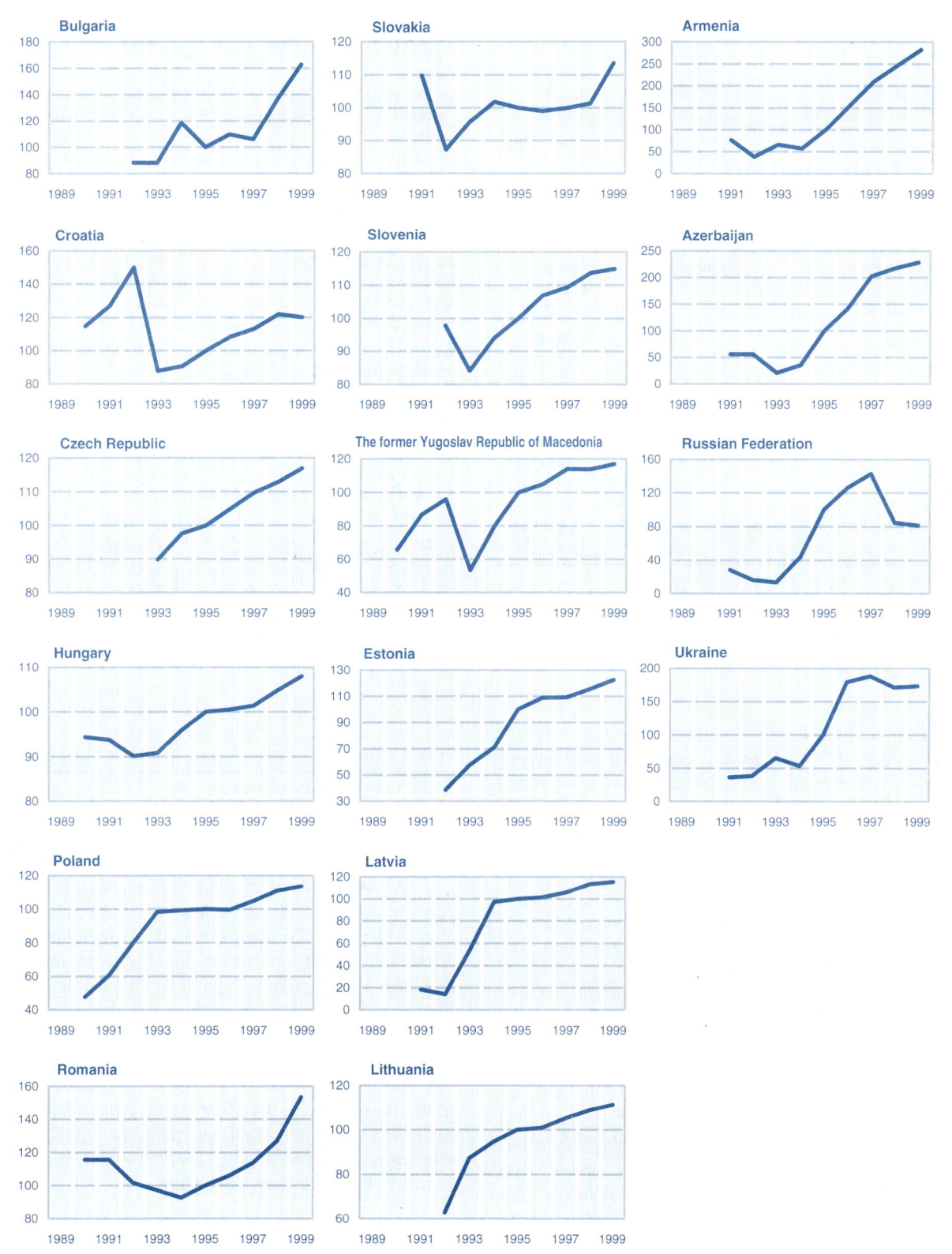

Source: UN/ECE Common Database.

TABLE 6.5.1

Estimated regressions results for sectoral productivity
(Dependent variable: productivity)

Variables	Industry	Service
Constant	1.348217***	2.955725***
Productivity lagged	0.753621***	0.399006***
Total FDI/total GDP	0.024500***	0.066109***
Sectoral investment/sectoral GDP	0.050157*	0.015964***
Sample	1991-1998	1992-1998
Included observations	8	7
Number of cross-sections used	11	10
Total panel (unbalanced) observations	60	55
Adjusted R-squared	0.617728	0.483132
Standard error of regression	0.109048	0.042949
Mean of dependent variable	4.643807	4.608888
Standard deviation of dependent variable	0.176373	0.059740
Estimation method	GLS[a]	GLS[a]
Czech Republic	1992-1998	1992-1998
Hungary	1992-1998	1993-1998
Poland	1993-1998	1993-1998
Romania	1991-1998	1992-1998
Slovakia	1996-1998	1994-1997
Slovenia	1994-1997	..
Estonia	1994-1997	1994-1997
Latvia	1992-1998	1992-1998
Lithuania	1993-1998	1993-1998
Kyrgyzstan	1994-1998	1994-1998
Russian Federation	1996-1998	1996-1998

Source: Basic data from UN/ECE Common Database.

Note: Variables are in logs (net capital inflow was always positive for the observations used for estimation). Significance tests at the 10, 5 and 1 per cent level, respectively, are indicated by *, ** and ***.

[a] Cross-section weights.

TABLE 6.5.2

Estimated regressions results for sectoral real product wages
(Dependent variable: gross sectoral wage deflated by producer price index)

Variables	Industry	Service
Constant	-1.532179***	..
Country effect	..	..
Czech Republic	..	-0.063584
Hungary	..	-0.011136
Poland	..	-0.009449
Slovakia	..	0.025473
Estonia	..	0.059634
Latvia	..	0.180058
Lithuania	..	0.031741
Real product wage lagged	0.641248***	0.125584***
Productivity	0.283233***	0.479235***
Employment	-0.301050***	3.273128***
Unemployment rate	-0.023311***	..
Sample	1991-1999	1991-1998
Included observations	9	8
Number of cross-sections used	11	7
Total panel (unbalanced) observations	68	42
Adjusted R-squared	0.501623	0.892094
Standard error of regression	0.407117	0.184464
Mean of dependent variable	0.244320	0.183151
Standard deviation of dependent variable	0.576688	0.561551
Estimation method	GLS[a]	GLS[a]
Czech Republic	1991-1998	1991-1998
Hungary	1993-1998	1993-1998
Poland	1993-1998	1993-1998
Romania	1993-1998	..
Slovakia	1993-1998	1995-1998
Slovenia	1995-1998	..
Estonia	1994-1998	1994-1998
Latvia	1992-1998	1993-1998
Lithuania	1992-1998	1993-1998
Kyrgyzstan	1992-1999	..
Russian Federation	1995-1998	..

Source and note: As for table 6.5.1.

[a] Cross-section weights.

Panel data are used for all the transition countries for the period 1991-1999. However, due to many missing observations, the panel is unbalanced. Each table shows which countries and years are included in the regression equations.

(i) Sectoral productivity

Table 6.5.1 reports regressions of sectoral productivity (industry and services separately, in logs) on two explanatory variables: sectoral investment as a ratio to sectoral GDP, and total foreign direct investment as a ratio to total GDP.[621] It could be argued that foreign direct investment is subsumed in total investment. However, if foreign direct investment is an important channel for transfers of technology, it should play an additional role. An allowance is also made for slow adjustment by introducing lagged productivity. The sample includes 10 or 11 countries, depending on the sector under investigation. Various robustness checks (fixed and random effects, varying coefficients, different estimation methods, etc.) were conducted and these confirmed the substance of the results wherever they were found to be meaningful.

---

[621] It would have been preferable to use sectoral foreign direct investment, of course, but the data are not disaggregated by sector. If spillover effects dominate sector-specific effects the approach here is appropriate but this may not be the case (chap.5).

All the explanatory variables are significant at the conventional confidence levels and have the expected sign. Only for the investment ratio in industry is the coefficient significant at more than the 1 per cent level. It is worth noting that foreign direct investment adds to investment, and that this effect is significantly larger in the services sector. More detailed analysis is required to determine where exactly this additional effect is strongest; it could be in the banking sector or in retail trade, two sectors where foreign investments are known to have been important in building up know-how. Unsurprisingly, productivity has been adjusting faster in industry than in the services sector.

(ii) Sectoral real product wages

Critical to the Balassa-Samuelson effect is the link from labour productivity to wages. Does it exist in the transition economies? The relationship is explored in table 6.5.2 for a sample of eight or nine countries between 1991 and 1999, with variations depending on data availability. The dependent variable is the real gross product wage (in log form). The impact of productivity on the real product wage is found to be highly significant. Interestingly, reflecting the gradual process of retooling in industry, the effect is slower and initially smaller in this sector than in the services sector. In the long run, however, the impact is larger (the implied long-run coefficient being 0.79 in industry and 0.55 in the services sector).

The estimation also allows for labour market characteristics to affect real product wages. Unemployment is found to hold down wages, but only in industry. This surprising result in fact provides further support to the Balassa-Samuelson hypothesis, which sees wages in the services sector being driven not by labour market conditions in this sector but by a tendency towards equalization across sectors. Actually, the attempt to find empirical support for this proposition failed.

Sectoral employment has also been included as an explanatory variable. Employment affects the real product wage negatively in industry, positively in the services sector, both effects being highly significant. This finding supports the view developed by Grafe and Wyplosz,[622] according to which, in the transition phase, productivity is driven by the sectoral reallocation of labour from industry to services. Only when industry releases its inefficiently used labour force – or excess employment – inherited from central planning can the process of deep restructuring develop.

(iii) Sectoral real wages[623]

The wage equalization assumption really concerns net consumer wages, but unfortunately data on these do not exist for most transition countries. Accordingly, the estimates that follow, which includes only four or six countries, should be considered as very tentative or merely illustrative. A simple check is made for the transmission of real product wages and taxes (which create a wedge between gross and net wages) to net real wages.

The results reported in table 6.5.3 confirm the presence of such a transmission channel. All the coefficients have the correct sign and are significant at the conventional confidence levels, the effect from real product wages to real wages being weakest in industry.

(iv) Sectoral growth

The last check on the data concerns the annual growth of output (GDP) in each sector. The main purpose of this exercise is to determine the roles of demand and supply factors. Recall that the Balassa-Samuelson effect is presumed to originate in the supply

---

[622] C. Grafe and C. Wyplosz, "The real exchange rate in transition economies", in M. Blejer and M. Skreb (eds.), *Balance of Payments, Exchange Rate and Competitiveness in Transition Economies* (Kluwer Academic Publishers, 1999).

[623] Net wages in each sector deflated by the consumer price index.

TABLE 6.5.3

Estimated regressions results for sectoral real wage
(Dependent variable: net sectoral wage deflated by consumer price index)

Variables	Industry	Service
Constant	0.007912**	-0.029594***
Real wage lagged	0.671040***	0.687206***
Real product wage increase	0.061037*	0.529754***
Tax *(ratio of gross to net wages)* increase	-0.234936***	-0.310088***
Time	0.006196***	0.008691***
Sample	1993-1999	1993-1999
Included observations	7	7
Number of cross-sections used	6	4
Total panel *(unbalanced)* observations	38	23
Adjusted R-squared	0.449795	0.862067
Standard error of regression	0.126439	0.023095
Mean of dependent variable	0.068505	0.026499
Standard deviation of dependent variable	0.170459	0.062185
Estimation method	GLS[a]	GLS[a]
Hungary	1993-1999	1993-1999
Poland	1993-1998	1993-1998
Romania	1993-1999	
Slovenia	1993-1999	1994-1998
Latvia	1994-1999	1995-1999
Lithuania	1995-1999	

Source and note: As for table 6.5.1.

[a] Cross-section weights.

---

side of the economy but that, under plausible conditions, demand-side effects should not work against it. At any rate, it is useful to evaluate the respective roles of these two channels.

Table 6.5.4 reports the result of the estimated regressions of sectoral growth. The supply side is captured via employment and productivity, lagged to reduce the problem of reverse causality. Data availability allows the inclusion of eight countries in the (unbalanced) panel. The presence of supply-side factors is strongly confirmed by the data, although employment is not found to affect growth significantly in the services sector. A possible reason for this is that the services sector does not face a manpower constraint: it offers equally attractive wages as industry but is seen as providing more desirable occupations. Another possibility is that the services sector is quite heterogeneous, with a larger share of unskilled workers who may have nowhere else to go.

The other variables include demand-side factors, total domestic consumption and exports, both lagged. Consumption enters positively, as expected, and is highly significant. Exports do not affect growth in the services sector, confirming the non-tradeable characteristics of this sector.

(v) The Balassa-Samuelson effect

Having tested the presumptions concerning the different components of the Balassa-Samuelson hypothesis, its presence can now be tested directly. The purpose is to determine whether the relative prices of non-traded to traded goods respond positively to different

TABLE 6.5.4

Estimated regressions results for sectoral output growth
(Dependent variable: sectoral GDP at constant prices)

Variables	Industry	Service
Constant	-4.507638***	0.413191*
Sectoral employment lagged	0.511320***	..
Sectoral productivity lagged	0.459751***	0.723927***
Consumption lagged	0.783707***	0.182189***
Exports lagged	0.227025***	..
Time	..	0.018402***
Sample	1992-1999	1992-1999
Included observations	8	8
Number of cross-sections used	11	10
Total panel (unbalanced) observations	62	58
Adjusted R-squared	0.785472	0.324213
Standard error of regression	0.091454	0.068647
Mean of dependent variable	4.710958	4.628120
Standard deviation of dependent variable	0.197452	0.083506
Estimation method	GLS[a]	GLS[a]
Czech Republic	1992-1999	1992-1999
Hungary	1993-1998	1993-1998
Poland	1993-1998	1993-1998
Romania	1992-1999	1992-1999
Slovakia	1996-1998	..
Slovenia	1994-1999	1994-1999
Estonia	1996-1999	1996-1999
Latvia	1997-1999	1997-1999
Lithuania	1992-1999	1992-1999
Kyrgyzstan	1993-1999	1994-1999
Russian Federation	1996-1998	1996-1998

Source and note: As for table 6.5.1.

[a] Cross-section weights.

TABLE 6.5.5

Estimation results on service-to-consumer goods price ratio

Variables	Base version	Exchange rate regime effect
Constant	2.060734***	1.108583***
Service-to-consumer goods price ratio lagged	0.444020***	0.446326***
Productivity in industry	0.242327***	0.174235***
Exchange rate effect[a]		0.007960***
Productivity in services	-0.184074*	0.128094*
GDP/capita (PPP)	0.027596**	0.006321
Inflation acceleration		
Country effect		
Czech Republic	-0.001539**	-0.002185***
Hungary	0.001177**	0.002089***
Poland	-0.003233**	-0.003756**
Romania	0.000553	0.000522*
Slovenia	0.003063***	0.003482***
Estonia	0.001503**	0.001395**
Latvia	-0.004271***	-0.004174***
Lithuania	-0.000796**	-0.000586***
Russian Federation	-0.006278**	-0.006452**
Sample	1991-1998	
Included observations	8	
Number of cross-sections used	9	
Total panel (unbalanced) observations	56	
Adjusted R-squared	0.954151	0.954108
Means of dependent variable	4.567562	0.065078
Standard error of regression	0.065048	4.567562
Standard deviation of dependent variable	0.303785	0.303785
Estimation method	GLS[b]	GLS[b]
Czech Republic	1994-1998	
Hungary	1992-1998	
Poland	1992-1998	
Romania	1991-1998	
Slovenia	1993-1998	
Estonia	1993-1998	
Latvia	1992-1998	
Lithuania	1993-1998	
Russian Federation	1995-1998	

Source and note: As for table 6.1.1 and table 6.5.1, except that inflation acceleration is not in logs. (The consumer goods prices refer to the consumer price index less food and less services.)

[a] Exchange rate regimes of own currency without any formal commitment.

[b] Cross-section weights.

---

secular trends in the two sectors, with a possible additional role for demand factors.[624]

As before, all the available data are used to build a panel of nine countries over the nine years 1991-1999. The relative price change is shown in chart 6.4.3, i.e. the ratio of the services price index to the non-food manufacturing producer price index. Labour productivity is displayed in chart 6.4.2. Following Bergstrand,[625] demand-side effects are captured by two variables, GDP per capita (PPP-adjusted) and the change in the rate of inflation.

The basic regression is reported in the first column of table 6.5.5. Crucially, the two productivity coefficients are significant and have the correct sign, confirming the presence of the Balassa-Samuelson effect: productivity growth in industry leads to a real appreciation, productivity growth in services to a real depreciation. The former enters with a larger coefficient, as expected given that the services sector is usually more labour intensive than industry. If productivity rises by 10 per cent in the industrial sector alone, the relative price of non-traded to traded goods increases by 2.4 per cent in the short run and by 4.4 per cent in the long run.

GDP per capita also enters the equation significantly and positively, suggesting the possibility of a bias towards non-traded goods. The inflation acceleration term differs from one country to another, as reported in table 6.5.5.

This regression equation survived a variety of robustness checks. Different estimation methods (fixed and random effects, OLS and GLS regressions) were tested; allowance was made for a potential bias in government spending; the possibility that the relationship may have changed over time was explored by allowing for additive and multiplicative dummy variables to capture the number of years since the beginning of

---

[624] Following the formulation in J. De Gregorio et al., op. cit., pp. 1225-1244, the Balassa-Samuelson equation can be written as follows:

$$\log(P_N/P_T) = a_0 + a_1[\alpha_N/\alpha_T \log(\pi_T) - \log(\pi_N)] + \text{demand factors},$$

where P_N/P_T is the ratio of non-traded to traded goods prices, α_N and α_T are the shares of labour in, respectively, the non-traded and traded goods sectors, and π_T and π_N is productivity in each sector.

[625] J. Bergstrand, op. cit, pp. 327-334.

reforms (using the dating proposed by Fischer and Sahay).[626] Since productivity in industry, in some cases, declined in the early transformation period, a check was made to see if there were different coefficient values during these years. None of these potential effects turned out to be significant, and none had any substantial effect on the results.

The only variation that seems to matter is the exchange rate regime. This possibility is suggested by the behaviour of relative prices as shown in chart 6.4.3. Using the classification shown in table 6.2.1, three categories of exchange rate regime were established: hard pegs (regimes 1 to 3 in table 6.2.1), exchange rate commitment (regimes 4 to 6) and no explicit commitment (regimes 7 and 8). The resulting dummy variables were used to test for an effect on the productivity coefficients. Table 6.5.5 shows that the only exchange rate regime to make a difference is the no-commitment one. The second column indicates that the effect of productivity in the traded goods sector (industry) increases under this regime while it changes sign in the non-traded goods sector (services), being marginally significant. In the third column, the effect of productivity in the non-traded goods sector is again found to be negative, as predicted by the Balassa-Samuelson assumption, while the role of productivity in the traded goods sector remains enhanced under the no-commitment exchange rate regime. We conclude that a floating rate regime strengthens the Balassa-Samuelson effect. This is not surprising: if the exchange rate is free to absorb some of the equilibrium real appreciation in the form of a nominal appreciation rather than forcing adjustment through absolute price changes, the effect is bound to appear faster, which makes a difference given the short time series. Of course, with a longer data series, such nominal short-term rigidities should vanish. The result therefore essentially confirms the robustness of the evidence regarding the Balassa-Samuelson effect. In particular, the estimate of the all-important coefficient of productivity in industry remains unchanged.

6.6 Policy implications

The likely continuing presence of a Balassa-Samuelson effect is a serious complicating factor for the process of integration of the transition countries into ERM-2 and, eventually, EMU. In this respect, the next accession round raises more serious challenges than previous ones.

First, the economic distance for the new entrants to catch up is much larger than for any previous entrants to the European Union, as documented in table 6.1.1. The scope for catch up of the largest transition country, Poland, is about twice that facing Greece or Portugal when they joined. By 2004, they will have moved further ahead, of course. Another message from the table, is that the 30 per cent average real appreciation (as measured by the ratio of non-traded to traded goods prices) between 1995 and 1999 corresponds to only a minute closing of the initial gap. Even if growth remains rapid until 2004, the scope for catch up and real appreciation will still be considerably larger than was ever the case in previous accessions.

Second, previous accessions allowed for a larger menu of options. ERM membership was not required, EMU was not in existence. Even if the transition economies elect to move slowly, an option discussed below, the fact that eventually they must first join the ERM, and then EMU, is an important constraint which affects both the behaviour of forward-looking financial markets and the authorities. Finally, at the time of previous accessions, capital controls were not actively disallowed. Greece, Portugal and Spain all made extensive use of this possibility. (Whether it helped to stabilize their exchange markets remains another, and controversial, issue, however.)

A number of policy implications emerge from the analysis of this chapter. A sizeable real appreciation will characterize the transition countries for a long time to come, and most likely for long after they have joined EMU. This means either a trend appreciation of their nominal exchange rates, or an inflation rate in excess of the EMU average. The estimates in table 6.5.5 allow a "guesstimate" of the size of this effect. Assuming a continuation of the average rates of growth of trend productivity in both sectors over the last five years for the countries displayed in chart 6.4.2 (8.6 per cent a year for industry and 1.9 per cent for services) and ignoring the per capita GDP term which reinforces the Balassa-Samuelson effect, the implied average annual rate of real appreciation lies between 2.9 and 3.1 per cent – say 3 per cent.[627]

During the two-year ERM membership period, which is required prior to EMU entry, there will be a trade-off between exchange rate stability and the inflation target. Keeping the nominal exchange rate stable, as required for accession to EMU, could lead to an inflation rate 3 percentage points above that in the euro area. Preventing such an inflation rate, which is also required for entry into the monetary union, will require the nominal exchange rate to appreciate each year by 3 percentage points. Over two years, this would represent about half of the ERM-2 bandwidth.

This may seem comfortable but it is not. Indeed, the tendency for real appreciation could be reinforced by capital inflows. In fact, the inflows will affect the real exchange rate both via the nominal rate and via the Balassa-Samuelson effect as foreign investment has been found to significantly raise productivity growth more in industry, and less in the services sector. Such an outcome could absorb the remaining half of the bandwidth. The risk of currency crises in the acceding countries is therefore far from negligible.

---

[626] S. Fischer, and R. Sahay, op. cit.

[627] It is assumed that there is no real appreciation elsewhere; otherwise these results would be modified.

PART THREE

STATISTICAL APPENDIX

For the user's convenience, as well as to lighten the text, the *Economic Survey of Europe* includes a set of appendix tables showing time series for the main economic indicators over a longer period. The data are presented in two sections, following the structure of the text: *Appendix A* provides macroeconomic indicators for the market economies in western Europe, North America and Japan for 1986-2000, *Appendix B* does the same for the east European countries, the Baltic states and the Commonwealth of Independent States for 1980-2000.

Re-estimated historical series are not yet available for all the transition economies, and longer time series could in some instances be obtained only by splicing older data with the new statistics (as explained in the notes to the tables). For the economies of western Europe and North America data for the more recent years may also be subject to revision as more comprehensive benchmark figures become available.

Data were compiled from international and national statistical sources. Details on recent changes in national accounts methodology were provided in chapter 7 of the *Economic Survey of Europe, 2000 No. 1*. Aggregates are UN/ECE secretariat calculations, using PPPs obtained from the 1996 European Comparison Programme. Greece has become a member of the euro area at the beginning of 2001. In order to ensure continuity of time series and comparability with the text tables, Greece has been included in the euro area aggregates for all years shown in the appendix tables.

The figures for 2000 are based on data available at mid-March 2001.

APPENDIX TABLE A.1

Real GDP in western Europe, North America and Japan, 1986-2000
(Percentage change over preceding year)

	1986	1987	1988	1989	1990	1991	1992	1993	1994	1995	1996	1997	1998	1999	2000
France	2.4	2.5	4.6	4.2	2.6	1.0	1.5	-0.9	2.1	1.7	1.1	1.9	3.3	3.2	3.2
Germany[a]	2.3	1.5	3.7	3.6	5.7	5.1	2.2	-1.1	2.3	1.7	0.8	1.4	2.1	1.6	3.0
Italy	2.5	3.0	3.9	2.9	2.0	1.4	0.8	-0.9	2.2	2.9	1.1	2.0	1.8	1.6	2.9
Austria	2.3	1.7	3.2	4.2	4.7	3.3	2.3	0.4	2.6	1.6	2.0	1.3	3.3	2.8	3.3
Belgium	1.8	2.7	4.6	3.6	2.8	1.9	1.6	-1.5	3.0	2.6	1.2	3.4	2.4	2.7	3.9
Finland	2.5	4.2	4.7	5.1	–	-6.3	-3.3	-1.1	4.0	3.8	4.0	6.3	5.3	4.2	5.7
Greece	1.6	-0.5	4.5	3.8	–	3.1	0.7	-1.6	2.0	2.1	2.4	3.5	3.1	3.4	4.0
Ireland	-0.4	4.7	5.2	5.8	8.5	1.9	3.3	2.7	5.8	9.7	7.7	10.7	8.6	9.8	10.0
Luxembourg	7.8	2.3	10.4	9.8	2.2	6.1	4.5	8.7	4.2	3.8	2.9	7.3	5.0	7.5	8.1
Netherlands	2.8	1.4	2.6	4.7	4.1	2.3	2.0	0.8	3.2	2.3	3.0	3.8	4.1	3.9	3.9
Portugal	4.1	6.4	7.5	5.4	4.8	2.4	1.9	-1.4	2.5	3.9	3.6	3.7	3.6	3.0	3.2
Spain	3.2	5.6	5.2	4.7	3.7	2.3	0.7	-1.2	2.3	2.7	2.4	3.9	4.3	4.0	4.1
Euro area[b]	2.5	2.6	4.2	3.9	3.7	2.6	1.5	-0.8	2.4	2.3	1.5	2.4	2.8	2.6	3.4
United Kingdom	4.2	4.4	5.2	2.1	0.7	-1.5	0.1	2.3	4.4	2.8	2.6	3.5	2.6	2.3	3.0
Denmark	4.1	-0.3	-0.7	0.2	1.0	1.1	0.6	–	5.5	2.8	2.5	3.0	2.8	2.1	2.4
Sweden	2.3	3.1	2.3	2.4	1.4	-1.1	-1.4	-2.2	4.1	3.7	1.1	2.1	3.6	4.1	3.6
European Union[c]	2.8	2.9	4.2	3.5	3.1	1.8	1.2	-0.4	2.8	2.4	1.7	2.6	2.8	2.6	3.3
Cyprus	3.8	7.0	8.5	7.9	7.4	0.6	9.8	0.7	5.9	6.1	1.9	2.5	5.0	4.5	4.9
Iceland	6.3	8.5	-0.1	0.3	1.1	1.2	-3.3	0.9	3.6	0.6	5.7	5.3	4.5	4.3	3.6
Israel	3.6	6.2	3.4	1.4	6.3	5.7	6.8	3.4	6.9	8.3	4.6	2.9	2.2	2.3	3.0
Malta	3.9	4.1	8.4	8.2	6.3	6.3	4.7	4.5	5.7	6.2	4.0	4.9	3.4	4.0	4.3
Norway	3.6	2.0	-0.1	0.9	2.0	3.1	3.3	2.7	5.5	3.8	4.9	4.7	2.0	0.9	2.2
Switzerland	1.6	0.7	3.1	4.3	3.7	-0.8	-0.1	-0.5	0.5	0.5	0.3	1.7	2.3	1.5	3.3
Turkey	7.0	9.5	2.1	0.3	9.3	0.9	6.0	8.0	-5.5	7.2	7.0	7.5	3.1	-5.0	7.0
Western Europe	3.0	3.1	4.0	3.3	3.4	1.7	1.4	0.1	2.4	2.6	1.9	2.8	2.8	2.2	3.5
Canada	2.6	4.1	4.9	2.5	0.3	-1.9	0.9	2.3	4.7	2.8	1.5	4.4	3.3	4.5	4.7
United States	3.4	3.4	4.2	3.5	1.8	-0.5	3.0	2.7	4.0	2.7	3.6	4.4	4.4	4.2	5.0
North America	3.4	3.5	4.2	3.4	1.6	-0.6	2.9	2.6	4.1	2.7	3.4	4.4	4.3	4.3	5.0
Japan	3.0	4.5	6.5	5.3	5.3	3.1	0.9	0.4	1.0	1.6	3.5	1.8	-1.1	0.8	1.7
Total above	3.1	3.5	4.5	3.7	3.0	1.0	2.0	1.2	2.9	2.5	2.8	3.3	2.8	2.8	3.8
Memorandum items:															
4 major west European economies[d]	2.8	2.7	4.3	3.3	3.1	1.9	1.3	-0.3	2.7	2.2	1.3	2.1	2.4	2.1	3.0
Western Europe and North America	3.2	3.3	4.1	3.4	2.5	0.6	2.1	1.4	3.3	2.7	2.7	3.6	3.6	3.2	4.2

Source: Eurostat; OECD; national statistics.

Note: All aggregates exclude Israel. Growth rates of regional aggregates have been calculated as weighted averages of growth rates in individual countries. Weights were derived from 1996 GDP data converted from national currency units into dollars using 1996 purchasing power parities. 1993 SNA/ESA95 definitions except for Iceland, Malta, Switzerland and Turkey.

[a] West Germany 1986-1991.

[b] Twelve countries above.

[c] Fifteen countries above.

[d] France, Germany, Italy and the United Kingdom.

APPENDIX TABLE A.2

Real private consumption expenditure in western Europe, North America and Japan, 1986-2000
(Percentage change over preceding year)

	1986	1987	1988	1989	1990	1991	1992	1993	1994	1995	1996	1997	1998	1999	2000
France	3.6	3.0	2.7	3.0	2.7	0.7	0.9	-0.4	1.2	1.2	1.3	0.2	3.6	2.7	2.4
Germany[a]	3.5	3.4	2.7	2.8	5.4	5.6	2.7	0.1	1.0	2.0	1.0	0.7	2.0	2.6	1.6
Italy	4.0	3.8	4.0	3.7	2.1	2.9	1.9	-3.7	1.5	1.7	1.2	3.2	3.1	2.3	2.2
Austria	2.2	2.9	3.3	4.3	4.5	2.5	3.0	0.8	2.4	2.6	3.2	1.4	2.9	2.3	2.7
Belgium	3.1	1.8	3.7	3.9	3.2	3.0	2.2	-1.0	2.0	1.0	0.7	2.1	3.3	1.9	2.9
Finland	4.0	5.1	5.3	4.6	-0.6	-3.8	-4.4	-3.1	2.6	4.4	4.2	3.5	5.1	3.7	3.0
Greece	0.7	1.2	3.6	6.1	2.6	2.8	2.4	-0.8	2.0	2.8	2.4	2.8	3.1	2.9	2.9
Ireland	2.0	3.3	4.5	6.5	1.4	1.8	2.9	2.9	4.4	4.1	6.4	7.5	7.8	7.8	9.1
Luxembourg	5.7	4.6	4.6	5.1	5.7	6.3	-0.9	1.7	2.4	2.4	4.4	3.8	2.3	4.1	3.5
Netherlands	2.6	2.7	0.8	3.5	4.2	3.1	2.5	1.0	2.2	2.0	4.0	3.0	4.4	4.4	3.7
Portugal	5.6	5.3	6.9	3.1	6.0	3.6	3.6	0.9	2.2	5.2	3.9	3.3	6.0	4.8	3.3
Spain	3.3	5.8	4.9	5.7	3.6	2.9	2.2	-2.2	0.9	1.6	2.2	3.1	4.5	4.7	4.0
Euro area[b]	3.5	3.5	3.3	3.6	3.6	3.2	2.0	-1.0	1.4	1.9	1.7	1.8	3.3	3.0	2.5
United Kingdom	6.6	5.3	7.5	3.2	0.7	-1.7	0.5	2.9	2.9	1.7	3.6	3.9	4.0	4.4	3.6
Denmark	5.9	-2.2	-2.1	-0.1	0.1	1.6	1.9	0.5	6.5	1.2	2.5	2.9	3.6	0.5	0.2
Sweden	4.4	4.6	2.4	1.2	-0.4	0.9	-1.4	-3.1	1.8	0.6	1.4	2.0	2.7	3.8	3.0
European Union[c]	4.0	3.7	3.9	3.4	3.0	2.3	1.7	-0.4	1.7	1.8	2.0	2.1	3.4	3.2	2.6
Cyprus	1.7	5.5	10.5	6.9	9.0	9.9	3.2	-4.8	5.0	10.3	3.5	4.0	8.4	3.1	5.5
Iceland	6.9	16.2	-3.8	-4.2	0.5	4.1	-4.5	-4.5	1.9	4.2	6.4	6.0	10.0	6.9	4.0
Israel	15.1	8.9	4.5	0.4	5.6	7.2	8.0	7.3	9.5	5.8	5.4	4.2	3.6	3.4	3.6
Malta	1.4	0.5	9.0	9.2	3.8	3.8	4.3	0.8	2.3	10.5	7.1	1.6	2.5	5.9	5.8
Norway	5.0	-0.8	-2.0	-0.6	0.7	1.5	2.2	2.2	4.0	3.4	5.3	3.6	3.3	2.4	2.1
Switzerland	2.3	2.2	1.7	2.3	1.2	1.6	0.1	-0.9	1.0	0.6	0.7	1.4	2.2	2.2	2.3
Turkey	5.8	-0.3	1.2	-1.0	13.1	2.7	3.2	8.6	-5.4	4.8	8.5	8.4	0.6	-3.1	6.0
Western Europe	4.1	3.5	3.6	3.1	3.4	2.3	1.7	–	1.4	2.0	2.3	2.4	3.2	2.9	2.8
Canada	4.0	4.1	4.4	3.6	1.3	-1.4	1.8	1.8	3.1	2.1	2.5	4.4	2.9	3.5	4.0
United States	4.2	3.3	4.0	2.7	1.8	-0.2	2.9	3.4	3.8	3.0	3.2	3.6	4.7	5.3	5.3
North America	4.2	3.4	4.1	2.7	1.8	-0.3	2.8	3.2	3.7	2.9	3.1	3.6	4.6	5.1	5.2
Japan	3.2	4.1	5.1	4.7	4.4	2.7	2.6	1.8	2.6	1.4	2.4	0.8	0.1	1.2	0.5
Total above	4.0	3.5	4.1	3.2	2.9	1.3	2.3	1.7	2.6	2.3	2.7	2.7	3.3	3.6	3.4
Memorandum items:															
4 major west European economies[d]	4.3	3.8	4.1	3.2	3.0	2.3	1.7	-0.2	1.6	1.7	1.7	1.8	3.1	3.0	2.3
Western Europe and North America	4.1	3.4	3.9	2.9	2.6	1.0	2.3	1.6	2.6	2.4	2.7	3.0	3.9	4.0	4.0

Source: Eurostat; OECD; national statistics.

Note: See appendix table A.1.

[a] West Germany 1986-1991.

[b] Twelve countries above.

[c] Fifteen countries above.

[d] France, Germany, Italy and the United Kingdom.

APPENDIX TABLE A.3

Real general government consumption expenditure in western Europe, North America and Japan, 1986-2000
(Percentage change over preceding year)

	1986	1987	1988	1989	1990	1991	1992	1993	1994	1995	1996	1997	1998	1999	2000
France	2.4	2.2	3.2	1.6	2.5	2.7	3.8	4.6	0.7	-0.1	2.3	2.1	0.3	2.5	1.5
Germany [a]	2.5	1.5	2.1	-1.6	2.2	0.4	5.0	0.1	2.4	1.5	1.8	-0.9	0.5	-0.1	1.4
Italy	2.6	4.8	4.0	0.2	2.5	1.7	0.6	-0.2	-0.9	-2.2	1.0	0.2	0.3	1.5	1.6
Austria	1.8	0.2	1.1	1.7	2.3	3.2	3.5	3.7	3.0	1.3	1.2	-1.4	2.8	3.2	2.5
Belgium	1.3	2.7	-0.7	1.1	-0.3	3.6	1.5	-0.1	1.4	1.2	2.4	0.1	1.4	3.4	2.1
Finland	3.4	4.4	1.9	2.2	4.0	2.1	-2.4	-4.2	0.3	2.0	2.5	4.1	1.7	2.0	0.4
Greece	-0.8	0.9	5.7	5.5	0.6	-1.5	-3.1	2.6	-1.1	5.7	0.9	3.0	1.7	-0.1	0.8
Ireland	2.6	-4.8	-5.0	-1.3	5.4	2.7	3.0	0.1	4.1	3.8	3.2	5.6	5.3	5.2	4.5
Luxembourg	2.7	4.7	4.9	3.9	3.1	3.9	1.5	3.7	2.0	2.2	4.4	2.1	2.8	12.8	3.9
Netherlands	3.6	2.6	1.4	1.5	1.6	1.5	1.7	1.5	0.6	0.8	-0.4	3.2	3.4	2.5	3.1
Portugal	7.2	3.8	8.6	6.6	5.4	10.3	1.1	0.9	2.1	2.7	-0.3	2.6	3.0	3.4	3.0
Spain	5.4	8.9	4.0	8.3	6.6	5.6	4.0	2.4	-0.3	1.8	1.3	2.9	3.7	2.9	2.6
Euro area [b]	2.8	3.2	2.9	1.2	2.8	2.2	3.0	1.4	0.9	0.6	1.5	0.9	1.2	1.6	1.8
United Kingdom	1.6	–	–	0.8	2.5	2.9	0.5	-0.8	1.4	1.6	1.7	-1.4	1.1	4.0	2.6
Denmark	0.9	2.2	-0.1	-0.8	-0.2	0.6	0.8	4.1	3.0	2.1	3.4	0.8	3.1	1.4	0.8
Sweden	1.3	1.0	0.6	2.1	2.6	2.8	–	0.2	-0.9	-0.6	0.9	-1.2	3.2	1.7	0.1
European Union [c]	2.6	2.6	2.3	1.1	2.7	2.3	2.5	1.0	1.0	0.7	1.6	0.5	1.3	2.0	1.8
Cyprus	3.6	5.3	10.5	1.9	17.4	3.9	13.8	-14.3	4.1	2.9	11.7	4.9	7.3	-5.0	2.8
Iceland	7.3	6.5	4.7	3.0	4.3	3.2	-0.8	2.3	3.7	1.3	1.0	3.1	3.4	4.9	3.5
Israel	-9.7	18.3	-2.5	-8.6	7.7	4.1	1.4	4.2	-0.2	1.8	5.1	1.9	2.0	2.9	2.1
Malta	4.4	9.1	6.0	12.7	5.7	10.9	8.9	6.0	6.4	8.5	8.4	-1.1	-4.0	-1.1	3.6
Norway	1.9	4.6	-0.1	1.9	4.9	4.3	5.3	2.2	1.4	0.3	2.8	1.9	3.8	2.7	1.4
Switzerland	3.4	1.7	4.5	5.4	5.4	3.5	0.7	-0.1	2.0	-0.1	2.0	–	0.7	-0.4	0.5
Turkey	9.2	9.4	-1.1	0.8	8.0	3.7	3.6	8.6	-5.5	6.8	8.6	4.1	7.8	6.5	5.0
Western Europe	2.9	2.9	2.2	1.2	3.0	2.4	2.5	1.4	0.7	1.0	1.9	0.7	1.6	2.1	2.0
Canada	1.9	1.4	4.6	2.8	3.7	2.8	1.0	0.1	-1.2	-0.5	-1.4	-1.2	1.6	1.3	2.4
United States [d]	5.4	3.0	1.2	2.8	3.3	1.2	0.5	-0.8	0.1	0.4	1.1	2.4	2.1	3.3	2.8
North America	5.1	2.8	1.5	2.8	3.3	1.3	0.5	-0.7	–	0.4	0.9	2.1	2.1	3.2	2.8
Japan	4.8	3.5	3.4	2.9	2.5	3.2	2.7	3.2	2.9	4.3	2.8	1.3	1.9	4.0	3.6
Total above	4.1	3.0	2.1	2.1	3.1	2.1	1.7	0.8	0.7	1.2	1.6	1.4	1.9	2.9	2.6
Memorandum items:															
4 major west European economies [e]	2.3	2.1	2.3	–	2.4	1.8	2.7	0.8	1.1	0.3	1.7	-0.1	0.6	1.7	1.7
Western Europe and North America	4.0	2.9	1.8	2.0	3.2	1.9	1.5	0.3	0.3	0.7	1.4	1.4	1.8	2.7	2.4

Source: Eurostat; OECD; national statistics.

Note: See appendix table A.1.

[a] West Germany 1986-1991.

[b] Twelve countries above.

[c] Fifteen countries above.

[d] Includes also government gross investment expenditures.

[e] France, Germany, Italy and the United Kingdom.

APPENDIX TABLE A.4

Real gross domestic fixed capital formation in western Europe, North America and Japan, 1986-2000
(Percentage change over preceding year)

	1986	1987	1988	1989	1990	1991	1992	1993	1994	1995	1996	1997	1998	1999	2000
France	6.0	6.0	9.5	7.3	3.3	-1.5	-1.6	-6.4	1.5	2.0	–	-0.1	6.6	7.3	6.7
Germany[a]	3.3	1.8	4.4	6.3	8.5	6.0	4.5	-4.5	4.0	-0.7	-0.8	0.6	3.0	3.3	2.4
Italy	2.3	4.2	6.7	4.2	4.0	1.0	-1.4	-10.9	0.1	6.0	3.6	2.1	4.3	4.6	6.1
Austria	2.4	4.4	6.8	4.1	6.2	6.6	0.6	-0.9	4.6	1.3	2.2	1.0	2.7	3.2	3.7
Belgium	3.2	6.2	15.7	12.6	8.5	-4.1	1.7	-3.1	-0.1	4.9	0.8	6.7	4.6	4.8	4.2
Finland	1.0	4.9	11.0	13.0	-4.6	-18.6	-16.7	-16.6	-2.7	10.6	8.4	11.9	9.3	2.7	4.8
Greece	-6.2	-5.1	8.9	7.1	5.0	4.8	-3.2	-3.5	-2.7	4.2	8.4	13.2	8.0	7.3	7.8
Ireland	-2.8	-1.1	5.2	10.1	13.4	-7.0	–	-5.1	11.8	13.3	16.5	17.8	14.7	12.5	11.0
Luxembourg	31.0	17.9	15.0	7.0	2.7	31.6	-9.0	28.4	-14.9	3.5	-3.5	10.5	1.5	26.6	0.1
Netherlands	6.9	0.9	4.5	4.9	1.6	0.2	0.6	-2.8	2.2	4.8	6.3	6.6	4.1	6.5	4.3
Portugal	10.9	18.0	14.8	4.2	8.2	3.5	4.8	-5.8	3.5	-4.0	6.2	10.6	8.8	6.0	5.8
Spain	9.9	14.0	13.9	13.6	6.6	1.6	-4.4	-10.5	2.5	8.2	2.1	5.0	9.7	8.9	5.9
Euro area[b]	4.4	4.8	7.9	7.0	5.7	1.8	0.1	-6.6	2.1	3.1	1.8	2.7	5.3	5.5	4.9
United Kingdom	2.1	8.9	14.8	5.9	-2.3	-8.7	-0.7	0.8	3.6	2.9	4.9	7.5	10.1	5.4	2.3
Denmark	16.7	-0.9	-6.2	-0.8	-2.1	-3.3	-2.0	-4.0	7.6	11.6	4.0	10.9	7.6	1.5	8.4
Sweden	0.3	8.2	6.6	11.3	1.3	-8.9	-10.8	-17.2	6.1	9.4	5.0	-1.1	8.5	8.1	4.5
European Union[c]	4.2	5.5	8.7	6.8	4.2	-0.2	-0.3	-5.7	2.5	3.4	2.4	3.5	6.1	5.5	4.6
Cyprus	-7.1	4.5	10.6	20.0	-2.8	-1.6	16.2	-12.8	-2.5	-1.7	7.4	-4.5	8.0	-1.2	2.9
Iceland	-1.6	18.8	-0.2	-7.9	3.0	2.0	-11.3	-11.4	-1.1	-2.8	27.4	10.5	26.6	-0.8	11.1
Israel	7.4	6.1	1.6	-2.2	25.3	41.9	5.2	5.3	8.4	6.6	7.7	-2.4	-4.0	0.6	-2.6
Malta	-8.7	30.7	6.1	1.0	17.9	–	-0.2	11.1	8.5	17.8	-8.4	-4.5	-3.4	0.8	18.7
Norway	7.6	0.3	-1.8	-6.9	-10.8	-0.4	-3.1	4.3	4.5	3.4	9.9	13.9	5.8	-5.6	-2.7
Switzerland	5.4	4.0	8.1	5.3	3.8	-2.9	-6.6	-2.7	6.5	1.8	-2.4	1.5	4.5	1.8	4.7
Turkey	8.4	45.1	-1.0	2.2	15.9	0.4	6.4	26.4	-16.0	9.1	14.1	14.8	-3.9	-16.0	16.2
Western Europe	4.4	7.2	8.1	6.4	4.5	-0.2	-0.2	-4.0	1.8	3.6	3.0	4.1	5.6	4.2	5.0
Canada	5.4	10.7	9.8	5.9	-3.6	-3.5	-1.3	-2.7	7.4	-1.9	5.8	15.4	3.4	10.1	11.2
United States[d]	..	..	3.6	2.7	-1.8	-6.9	6.5	8.1	9.1	6.1	9.3	9.6	11.8	9.2	9.2
North America	..	..	4.2	3.0	-2.0	-6.7	5.8	7.2	9.0	5.4	9.0	10.0	11.1	9.2	9.4
Japan	5.1	9.4	12.0	8.6	8.8	2.2	-2.5	-3.1	-1.4	0.3	6.8	1.0	-4.0	-0.9	1.2
Total above	..	..	7.0	5.3	2.4	-2.6	2.0	0.9	4.3	3.8	6.1	6.1	6.4	5.5	6.3
Memorandum items:															
4 major west European economies[e]	3.4	4.8	8.3	6.0	4.0	–	0.7	-5.2	2.5	2.2	1.6	2.3	5.6	5.0	4.2
Western Europe and North America	..	..	6.1	4.7	1.3	-3.5	2.8	1.6	5.4	4.5	6.0	7.1	8.4	6.7	7.2

Source: Eurostat; OECD; national statistics.

Note: See appendix table A.1.

[a] West Germany 1986-1991.

[b] Twelve countries above.

[c] Fifteen countries above.

[d] Private sector only. See appendix table A.3.

[e] France, Germany, Italy and the United Kingdom.

APPENDIX TABLE A.5

Real total domestic expenditures in western Europe, North America and Japan, 1986-2000

(Percentage change over preceding year)

	1986	1987	1988	1989	1990	1991	1992	1993	1994	1995	1996	1997	1998	1999	2000
France	3.7	3.2	4.6	3.7	2.9	0.5	0.8	-1.6	2.1	1.6	0.7	0.7	4.0	3.2	3.2
Germany[a]	3.3	2.4	3.6	2.9	5.2	4.7	2.8	-1.1	2.3	1.7	0.3	0.6	2.4	2.4	2.1
Italy	3.1	4.3	4.1	3.1	2.7	2.1	0.9	-5.1	1.7	2.0	0.9	2.7	3.1	3.0	2.3
Austria	2.1	2.6	3.2	3.7	4.4	3.5	2.3	0.6	3.5	2.6	1.9	1.3	2.5	2.6	2.7
Belgium	2.6	3.5	4.8	4.3	2.9	1.7	1.8	-1.5	2.1	1.9	0.9	2.6	3.9	2.1	3.1
Finland	2.8	5.1	6.5	6.9	-1.5	-8.5	-5.8	-5.7	3.7	4.4	2.9	6.0	5.8	2.5	3.0
Greece	-1.2	-1.5	7.3	5.3	2.8	3.7	-1.7	-0.9	1.1	4.2	3.3	3.6	4.7	3.0	3.7
Ireland	1.2	-0.2	2.1	7.3	6.4	0.2	-0.1	1.0	5.1	6.4	7.3	9.3	10.2	6.0	9.0
Luxembourg	8.7	5.4	6.7	8.6	3.2	8.7	-1.5	9.7	-0.5	3.2	2.7	5.5	2.4	11.3	2.5
Netherlands	3.8	1.4	1.8	4.7	3.5	1.9	1.6	-1.1	3.1	2.4	2.8	3.9	4.2	4.2	3.5
Portugal	8.2	9.9	10.7	3.9	5.9	3.8	3.7	-1.4	2.9	3.1	3.0	4.6	6.1	4.7	3.7
Spain	5.4	8.1	7.0	7.8	4.8	2.9	1.0	-4.2	1.3	3.2	1.9	3.4	5.6	5.5	4.1
Euro area[b]	3.5	3.6	4.5	4.0	3.9	2.6	1.4	-2.3	2.1	2.1	1.1	2.0	3.6	3.2	2.9
United Kingdom	4.7	4.9	8.0	2.8	-0.3	-2.7	0.8	2.2	3.4	1.8	3.0	3.8	4.6	3.7	3.7
Denmark	6.6	-2.3	-1.6	-0.1	-0.7	-0.1	0.9	-0.3	7.0	4.2	2.2	4.9	4.5	-0.6	2.4
Sweden	2.1	4.3	2.8	3.7	0.9	-2.1	-1.8	-5.2	3.1	2.0	0.7	0.9	4.2	3.4	2.7
European Union[c]	3.7	3.7	4.9	3.7	3.1	1.6	1.3	-1.6	2.4	2.1	1.4	2.3	3.8	3.2	3.0
Cyprus	-1.5	5.6	11.3	9.7	6.3	5.1	9.3	-9.5	7.4	7.8	4.6	1.4	8.8	0.7	4.7
Iceland	4.9	15.5	-1.1	-4.1	1.5	4.7	-5.3	-4.2	1.6	3.0	7.8	6.2	12.2	4.6	5.3
Israel	5.4	9.0	2.5	-2.8	9.3	12.1	5.3	6.8	5.3	6.7	5.5	1.2	0.8	5.1	1.7
Malta	–	3.5	11.5	8.3	7.6	4.9	0.1	4.8	5.9	9.5	2.8	-0.1	-1.1	5.0	11.9
Norway	7.4	-0.8	-3.0	-2.0	-0.5	0.8	1.5	3.1	4.0	4.3	4.2	6.4	5.4	-1.0	1.6
Switzerland	4.5	2.0	2.6	4.1	3.9	-0.6	-2.7	-1.0	2.7	1.8	0.4	1.3	4.3	1.4	2.5
Turkey	7.0	8.9	-1.3	1.5	14.6	-0.6	5.6	14.2	-12.5	11.4	7.6	9.0	0.6	-4.0	8.0
Western Europe	3.9	3.9	4.4	3.5	3.6	1.4	1.4	-0.8	1.8	2.6	1.7	2.6	3.7	2.8	3.2
Canada	3.4	4.7	5.3	4.1	–	-1.4	0.9	1.4	3.2	1.7	1.4	6.2	2.2	4.2	5.5
United States	3.8	3.7	3.2	2.9	1.4	-1.1	3.1	3.2	4.4	2.4	3.7	4.7	5.5	5.2	5.7
North America	3.7	3.7	3.4	3.0	1.3	-1.1	2.9	3.0	4.3	2.4	3.5	4.8	5.3	5.1	5.7
Japan	3.8	5.3	7.3	5.6	5.3	2.7	0.6	0.3	1.2	2.1	4.0	0.9	-1.5	0.9	1.3
Total above	3.8	4.0	4.4	3.6	2.9	0.6	1.9	1.0	2.8	2.4	2.8	3.3	3.6	3.5	4.0
Memorandum items:															
4 major west European economies[d]	3.7	3.6	4.9	3.1	2.9	1.6	1.5	-1.4	2.3	1.8	1.1	1.8	3.4	3.0	2.8
Western Europe and North America	3.8	3.8	3.9	3.3	2.4	0.2	2.1	1.1	3.0	2.5	2.6	3.7	4.5	3.9	4.5

Source: Eurostat; OECD; national statistics.

Note: See appendix table A.1.

[a] West Germany 1986-1991.

[b] Twelve countries above.

[c] Fifteen countries above.

[d] France, Germany, Italy and the United Kingdom.

APPENDIX TABLE A.6

Real exports of goods and services in western Europe, North America and Japan, 1986-2000
(Percentage change over preceding year)

	1986	1987	1988	1989	1990	1991	1992	1993	1994	1995	1996	1997	1998	1999	2000
France	-0.4	3.4	8.7	10.0	4.8	5.9	5.4	–	7.7	7.7	3.5	11.8	7.7	4.0	13.6
Germany [a]	-0.6	0.4	5.5	10.2	11.0	12.6	-0.8	-5.5	7.6	5.7	5.1	11.3	7.0	5.1	13.2
Italy	0.8	4.5	5.1	7.8	7.5	-1.4	7.3	9.0	9.8	12.6	0.6	6.4	3.6	–	10.2
Austria	-2.3	3.1	10.2	9.7	7.8	5.2	1.5	-1.4	5.6	6.7	6.2	9.9	5.5	7.6	7.5
Belgium	2.8	5.0	9.6	8.3	4.6	3.1	3.7	-0.4	8.4	5.7	1.2	6.7	4.4	5.2	10.6
Finland	0.7	2.9	3.5	1.6	1.2	-7.3	10.3	16.7	13.1	8.6	5.8	14.1	8.9	7.1	17.7
Greece	14.0	16.0	9.0	4.6	-4.0	3.7	10.5	-3.5	6.3	0.9	3.5	18.2	5.9	6.5	12.5
Ireland	2.9	13.7	9.0	10.3	8.7	5.7	13.9	9.7	15.1	20.0	12.2	17.4	21.4	12.4	16.2
Luxembourg	3.3	4.4	11.7	8.1	3.4	6.7	4.8	2.8	4.4	4.4	4.0	10.5	9.9	7.9	15.0
Netherlands	1.8	4.0	9.0	6.7	5.3	4.7	2.9	1.5	6.7	6.7	4.6	8.8	7.4	5.6	9.1
Portugal	6.8	11.2	8.2	13.0	10.0	2.6	5.0	-3.6	8.7	13.5	7.1	8.5	7.6	4.8	8.9
Spain	1.9	6.3	5.1	3.0	3.2	7.9	7.4	8.5	16.7	10.0	10.4	15.3	8.3	6.6	10.8
Euro area [b]	0.8	3.7	6.7	8.4	7.0	6.1	4.1	1.3	9.1	8.3	4.4	10.7	6.7	4.3	12.0
United Kingdom	4.5	5.9	0.6	4.8	4.9	-0.2	4.1	3.9	9.2	9.5	7.5	8.6	2.6	4.0	7.4
Denmark	0.5	4.5	7.6	4.2	6.2	6.1	-0.9	-1.5	7.0	2.9	4.3	4.1	2.4	9.7	5.4
Sweden	3.7	4.3	2.5	3.1	1.6	-2.3	2.3	7.6	14.1	11.3	3.5	13.7	8.4	5.9	9.8
European Union [c]	1.4	4.1	5.6	7.7	6.5	4.9	4.0	1.8	9.2	8.4	4.8	10.3	6.0	4.3	11.1
Cyprus	-1.7	13.7	13.5	16.8	7.9	-8.4	18.7	-1.3	7.9	4.6	4.1	0.8	-2.4	6.5	6.6
Iceland	5.9	3.3	-3.6	2.9	–	-5.9	-1.9	7.0	9.9	-3.3	10.0	6.0	2.2	5.5	2.6
Israel	5.6	10.2	-1.5	4.0	2.0	-2.6	14.1	9.9	12.8	8.4	6.6	7.7	6.3	10.1	9.5
Malta	7.0	12.6	6.1	10.7	13.3	7.5	9.7	5.3	7.1	5.4	-5.9	4.0	8.1	8.1	5.6
Norway	2.2	1.1	6.4	11.0	8.6	6.1	5.2	3.2	8.7	4.3	9.3	6.1	0.3	1.7	2.8
Switzerland	-0.4	2.3	6.5	6.6	2.1	-2.1	3.0	1.5	1.8	1.6	2.5	8.6	5.0	5.9	8.4
Turkey	-5.1	26.4	18.4	-0.3	2.5	3.7	11.0	7.7	15.2	8.0	22.0	19.1	12.0	-7.0	15.0
Western Europe	1.1	5.1	6.3	7.3	6.3	4.7	4.3	2.1	9.3	8.2	5.6	10.6	6.2	3.8	11.1
Canada	5.2	3.3	9.5	1.3	4.7	2.3	7.9	10.9	13.1	9.0	5.9	8.8	8.9	10.0	9.6
United States	7.4	11.2	16.1	11.8	8.7	6.5	6.2	3.3	8.9	10.3	8.2	12.3	2.3	2.9	9.2
North America	7.2	10.6	15.5	10.9	8.4	6.2	6.3	4.0	9.3	10.2	8.0	12.0	2.8	3.5	9.2
Japan	-5.5	-0.5	5.9	9.1	7.0	4.1	3.9	-0.1	3.5	4.1	6.5	11.2	-2.3	1.4	12.0
Total above	2.6	6.5	10.1	9.1	7.3	5.2	5.1	2.5	8.4	8.4	6.8	11.3	3.4	3.3	10.4
Memorandum items:															
4 major west European economies [d]	0.9	3.2	5.1	8.4	7.5	5.2	3.5	1.1	8.5	8.5	4.2	9.7	5.4	3.4	11.4
Western Europe and North America	4.1	7.8	10.9	9.1	7.3	5.4	5.3	3.0	9.3	9.2	6.8	11.3	4.5	3.7	10.1

Source: Eurostat; OECD; national statistics.

Note: See appendix table A.1.

[a] West Germany 1986-1991.

[b] Twelve countries above.

[c] Fifteen countries above.

[d] France, Germany, Italy and the United Kingdom.

APPENDIX TABLE A.7

Real imports of goods and services in western Europe, North America and Japan, 1986-2000
(Percentage change over preceding year)

	1986	1987	1988	1989	1990	1991	1992	1993	1994	1995	1996	1997	1998	1999	2000
France	6.5	7.7	8.8	8.0	5.5	3.1	1.8	-3.7	8.2	8.0	1.6	6.9	11.3	4.0	14.7
Germany[a]	2.7	4.2	5.1	8.3	10.3	13.1	1.5	-5.5	7.4	5.6	3.1	8.4	8.6	8.1	10.2
Italy	4.0	12.2	5.9	8.9	11.5	2.3	7.4	-10.9	8.1	9.7	-0.3	10.1	9.0	5.1	8.3
Austria	-2.9	5.4	10.4	8.0	6.9	5.8	1.4	-1.1	8.2	9.3	5.8	9.7	3.7	7.1	6.3
Belgium	4.5	6.7	10.4	9.6	4.8	2.8	4.1	-0.4	7.2	5.0	0.8	5.7	6.5	4.5	9.9
Finland	1.5	9.2	10.9	9.0	-0.8	-13.5	0.6	1.3	12.8	7.8	6.4	11.3	8.5	4.3	12.8
Greece	3.8	16.6	8.0	10.6	8.7	6.0	-2.8	0.2	1.2	9.3	7.0	13.9	11.3	3.9	8.7
Ireland	5.6	6.2	4.9	13.5	5.1	2.4	8.2	7.5	15.5	16.4	12.5	16.8	25.8	8.7	16.3
Luxembourg	3.8	7.5	8.2	6.6	4.5	9.0	-0.8	2.8	-0.1	3.8	4.0	9.3	8.3	11.2	11.2
Netherlands	3.5	4.2	7.6	6.7	4.2	4.1	2.1	-2.1	6.7	7.5	4.4	9.5	8.0	6.3	8.9
Portugal	16.9	23.1	18.0	6.1	14.0	7.3	10.7	-3.3	9.0	9.1	4.9	10.6	13.8	8.8	8.7
Spain	14.4	20.1	14.4	17.3	7.8	9.0	6.9	-5.2	11.3	11.0	8.0	13.3	13.4	11.9	10.4
Euro area[b]	5.2	9.1	7.9	9.3	8.5	6.5	3.6	-5.2	8.1	7.9	3.0	9.2	9.8	6.6	10.6
United Kingdom	6.9	7.9	12.8	7.4	0.5	-5.0	6.8	3.2	5.4	5.5	9.1	9.2	8.8	8.1	8.9
Denmark	9.7	-2.8	5.3	4.1	1.2	3.0	-0.4	-2.7	12.3	7.3	3.5	10.0	7.4	2.2	5.8
Sweden	4.5	7.7	5.3	7.4	0.7	-4.9	1.1	-2.5	12.2	7.2	3.0	12.5	11.2	4.3	9.7
European Union[c]	5.5	8.7	8.6	8.9	6.9	4.4	4.0	-3.8	7.9	7.5	3.9	9.3	9.7	6.7	10.2
Cyprus	-11.0	5.5	13.4	20.4	5.8	2.2	18.2	-18.1	8.2	11.5	6.7	-0.5	7.5	-3.3	5.4
Iceland	0.9	23.3	-4.6	-10.3	1.3	5.4	-8.0	-8.6	4.2	3.8	16.7	8.6	23.3	6.1	7.0
Israel	11.2	19.6	-2.8	-5.0	9.5	16.0	8.8	14.1	10.9	4.5	8.2	1.9	1.7	14.6	4.8
Malta	0.1	12.3	11.1	11.1	15.7	5.4	3.0	5.9	7.5	10.0	-5.9	-1.7	2.5	9.1	13.9
Norway	11.8	-6.5	-2.4	2.2	2.5	0.2	0.7	4.4	4.9	5.6	8.0	11.3	9.3	-3.1	1.2
Switzerland	8.1	6.2	5.2	5.9	2.6	-1.6	-4.2	0.1	7.9	5.1	2.7	7.6	9.6	5.5	6.4
Turkey	-3.5	23.0	-4.5	6.9	33.0	-5.2	10.9	35.8	-21.9	29.6	20.5	22.4	2.3	-3.7	18.0
Western Europe	5.2	9.1	7.7	8.6	8.0	3.7	4.1	-1.8	6.4	8.5	4.8	9.9	9.3	6.1	10.4
Canada	8.5	5.6	13.7	6.3	2.3	3.2	6.2	7.4	8.3	6.2	5.8	15.1	6.1	9.4	12.0
United States	8.4	6.1	3.8	4.0	3.8	-0.5	6.6	9.1	12.0	8.2	8.6	13.7	11.9	10.7	13.7
North America	8.4	6.0	4.6	4.2	3.7	-0.2	6.6	8.9	11.7	8.0	8.4	13.8	11.4	10.6	13.5
Japan	3.2	11.3	19.5	15.7	7.0	-1.1	-0.7	-1.4	7.8	12.8	13.2	1.2	-6.8	3.0	9.7
Total above	6.2	8.1	8.3	7.9	6.0	1.3	4.4	2.8	8.9	9.0	7.6	10.2	7.6	7.5	11.6
Memorandum items:															
4 major west European economies[d]	4.8	7.6	7.8	8.2	7.3	4.4	4.1	-4.4	7.3	7.0	3.3	8.6	9.3	6.5	10.5
Western Europe and North America	6.8	7.6	6.2	6.4	5.8	1.8	5.3	3.6	9.1	8.3	6.6	11.9	10.3	8.3	11.9

Source: Eurostat; OECD; national statistics.

Note: See appendix table A.1.

[a] West Germany 1986-1991.

[b] Twelve countries above.

[c] Fifteen countries above.

[d] France, Germany, Italy and the United Kingdom.

APPENDIX TABLE A.8

Industrial output in western Europe, North America and Japan, 1986-2000
(Percentage change over preceding year)

	1986	1987	1988	1989	1990	1991	1992	1993	1994	1995	1996	1997	1998	1999	2000
France	0.6	1.2	4.6	3.7	3.2	-0.2	-1.1	-3.7	3.9	2.5	0.8	3.8	5.2	2.1	3.2
Germany [a]	1.8	0.4	3.6	4.9	5.2	2.4	-2.3	-7.6	3.6	1.2	0.6	3.5	4.2	1.5	6.6
Italy	4.1	2.6	6.9	3.9	6.3	-0.4	-1.3	-2.1	6.2	5.0	-1.9	3.8	1.1	–	4.8
Austria	1.2	1.0	4.4	5.8	6.8	1.9	-1.2	-1.5	4.0	4.9	1.0	6.4	8.2	6.0	9.1*
Belgium	0.8	2.1	5.8	3.4	1.5	-1.9	-0.4	-5.1	2.1	6.5	0.5	4.7	3.4	0.9	5.3
Finland	1.8	5.0	3.2	3.6	-0.6	-8.7	1.3	5.6	11.3	7.3	3.6	10.2	7.4	5.4	11.5
Greece	-0.3	-1.2	5.1	1.8	-2.5	-1.0	-1.1	-2.9	1.3	1.8	1.2	1.3	7.1	3.9	-1.3*
Ireland	2.1	8.9	10.7	11.6	4.7	3.3	9.1	5.6	11.9	20.5	8.1	17.5	19.8	14.8	15.1
Luxembourg	1.9	-0.6	8.7	7.8	2.6	0.4	-0.8	-4.3	5.9	2.0	0.1	5.8	-0.1	11.5	4.1*
Netherlands	0.2	1.1	0.1	5.1	2.4	1.8	-0.2	-1.1	4.9	4.6	2.4	0.2	2.4	2.2	2.9
Portugal	7.3	4.4	3.8	6.7	9.0	–	-2.3	-5.2	-0.2	11.6	5.3	2.6	5.7	3.0	0.5
Spain	3.3	4.6	3.1	5.1	-0.3	-0.7	-3.1	-4.7	7.7	4.8	-1.3	6.9	5.5	2.6	4.4
Euro area [b]	2.2	1.8	4.5	4.6	4.2	0.5	-1.5	-4.3	4.7	3.7	0.3	4.2	4.2	1.9	5.2
United Kingdom	1.4	4.1	5.2	2.1	–	-3.3	0.4	2.1	5.2	1.8	1.0	1.0	0.8	0.5	1.5
Denmark	7.3	-3.0	2.2	2.0	3.1	–	3.4	-2.6	10.0	4.6	2.0	5.6	2.2	2.5	6.4
Sweden	0.2	2.8	2.9	2.9	0.3	-5.2	-1.7	-0.4	11.5	9.8	1.0	6.5	4.2	3.0	10.0
European Union [c]	2.1	2.1	4.5	4.1	3.5	-0.2	-1.2	-3.3	5.0	3.6	0.4	3.8	3.7	1.7	4.8
Israel	3.6	4.9	-3.1	-1.6	8.0	6.8	8.2	6.9	7.4	8.4	5.4	1.8	2.8	1.4	...
Norway	4.1	6.6	2.9	9.3	2.5	2.5	5.6	3.6	7.0	5.9	5.4	3.4	-0.6	-0.2	2.9
Switzerland	3.8	1.2	7.8	1.5	4.8	0.5	-1.0	-1.8	4.3	2.0	–	4.7	3.6	3.4	8.1
Turkey	11.7	10.5	1.6	3.6	9.5	2.7	5.0	8.0	-6.2	12.7	7.5	10.7	1.2	-3.7	7.0
Western Europe	2.5	2.4	4.4	4.1	3.7	0.1	-0.9	-2.8	4.4	3.9	0.8	4.2	3.5	1.5	5.1
Canada	-0.6	4.4	6.1	-0.4	-2.8	-3.8	1.1	4.5	6.5	4.5	1.4	4.4	2.4	4.4	5.6
United States	1.2	4.6	4.5	1.8	-0.2	-2.0	3.1	3.5	5.4	4.8	4.6	6.8	4.9	4.2	5.7
North America	1.0	4.6	4.7	1.6	-0.4	-2.1	3.0	3.6	5.5	4.8	4.3	6.7	4.7	4.2	5.7
Japan	-0.2	3.4	9.4	5.8	4.2	1.9	-5.7	-3.5	1.3	3.3	2.3	3.5	-6.5	0.8	5.6
Total above	1.4	3.4	5.4	3.5	2.3	-0.4	-0.5	-0.6	4.3	4.1	2.5	5.1	2.2	2.5	5.4
Memorandum items:															
4 major west European economies [d]	2.0	1.8	4.8	3.9	4.0	0.2	-1.3	-3.8	4.6	2.5	0.1	3.2	3.0	1.1	4.5
Western Europe and North America	1.8	3.4	4.5	2.9	1.8	-0.9	0.8	0.1	4.9	4.3	2.5	5.4	4.1	2.9	5.4

Source: National statistics; OECD, *Main Economic Indicators* (Paris), various issues; UN/ECE secretariat estimates.

Note: Growth rates of regional aggregates have been calculated as weighted averages of growth rates in individual countries. Weights were derived from 1995 gross value added originating in industry converted from national currency units into dollars using 1995 GDP.

[a] West Germany 1986-1991.
[b] Twelve countries above.
[c] Fifteen countries above.
[d] France, Germany, Italy and the United Kingdom.

APPENDIX TABLE A.9

Total employment in western Europe, North America and Japan, 1986-2000
(Percentage change over preceding year)

	1986	1987	1988	1989	1990	1991	1992	1993	1994	1995	1996	1997	1998	1999	2000
France	0.4	0.8	0.9	1.7	1.0	0.1	-0.5	-1.2	-0.1	0.8	0.3	0.3	1.2	1.8	1.9
Germany[a]	1.4	0.7	0.8	1.5	3.0	2.5	-1.5	-1.4	-0.2	0.2	-0.3	-0.2	0.9	1.1	1.5
Italy	0.7	0.2	1.1	0.7	1.6	1.9	-0.5	-2.5	-1.5	-0.1	0.6	0.4	1.0	1.2	1.4
Austria	0.4	–	0.6	1.3	1.6	1.4	0.2	-0.6	-0.2	–	-0.6	0.5	0.8	1.4	0.9
Belgium	0.6	0.6	1.7	1.2	0.9	0.1	-0.5	-0.8	-0.4	0.7	0.4	0.8	1.2	1.3	1.3
Finland	-0.4	0.5	1.0	0.9	-0.5	-5.7	-7.2	-6.2	-1.1	1.6	1.4	3.3	2.1	2.1	1.5
Greece	0.4	-0.1	1.6	0.4	1.3	-2.3	1.5	0.9	1.9	0.9	-0.4	-0.3	3.4	-0.7	1.2
Ireland	0.5	0.6	0.3	-0.1	3.3	-0.1	3.1	1.5	3.2	5.4	3.8	5.6	5.0	6.4	5.0
Luxembourg	2.5	2.7	-7.0	1.5	1.6	1.3	0.2	-0.5	0.7	0.9	2.3	3.2	4.4	5.1	5.2
Netherlands	2.5	1.6	2.3	1.8	3.0	2.6	1.6	0.7	-0.1	2.4	2.3	3.2	3.0	2.8	2.7
Portugal	2.7	2.3	2.2	1.9	1.7	2.8	-1.6	-2.0	-1.0	-0.2	2.3	1.7	2.7	1.8	1.5
Spain	2.2	3.1	2.9	4.1	2.6	0.2	-1.9	-4.3	-0.9	1.8	1.3	2.8	3.7	3.5	3.1
Euro area[b]	1.1	0.9	1.3	1.6	2.0	1.3	-0.9	-1.7	-0.4	0.7	0.5	0.8	1.7	1.7	1.8
United Kingdom[c]	0.2	2.0	3.6	3.2	1.0	-3.2	-2.6	-1.3	0.6	1.1	1.0	2.0	1.2	1.0	0.6
Denmark	2.3	0.4	-0.7	-0.7	-0.7	-0.6	-0.8	-1.5	1.4	0.5	0.7	1.2	1.2	1.1	0.9
Sweden	0.6	0.8	1.4	1.5	0.9	-1.5	-4.4	-5.1	-0.8	1.3	-0.6	-1.1	1.2	2.3	2.0
European Union[d]	1.0	1.1	1.6	1.8	1.8	0.4	-1.3	-1.8	-0.2	0.7	0.6	1.0	1.6	1.6	1.6
Cyprus[e]	1.1	3.1	4.7	3.9	2.8	0.6	4.5	-0.1	2.3	3.4	1.0	-0.2	1.2	0.8	..
Iceland[e]	3.2	5.8	-3.0	-1.5	-1.1	-0.1	-1.4	-0.8	0.5	0.9	3.1	1.0	3.4	2.7	2.0
Israel	1.4	2.6	3.5	0.5	2.1	6.1	4.2	6.1	6.9	5.2	2.4	1.4	1.6	3.1	4.0
Malta[f]	2.1	5.9	2.5	0.9	0.8	2.5	1.0	0.5	-1.3	3.3	1.0	0.5	0.4	0.6	2.1
Norway	3.3	2.0	-0.5	-2.8	-0.8	-0.7	-0.3	0.2	1.3	2.1	2.1	2.9	2.3	0.7	0.5
Switzerland	2.3	2.5	2.6	2.7	3.2	1.8	-1.6	-0.7	-0.3	0.3	0.3	-0.3	1.2	0.6	1.4
Turkey	1.9	2.3	1.5	2.6	1.7	1.7	0.2	0.2	2.8	3.7	2.0	-2.5	2.8	2.2	2.7
Western Europe	1.1	1.3	1.6	1.9	1.8	0.6	-1.1	-1.4	0.2	1.1	0.8	0.6	1.7	1.6	1.7
Canada	3.1	2.8	3.2	2.2	0.8	-1.8	-0.7	0.8	2.0	1.9	0.8	2.3	2.6	2.8	2.6
United States	2.3	2.6	2.2	2.1	1.2	-0.9	0.7	1.5	2.3	1.5	1.4	2.2	1.5	1.5	1.3
North America	2.4	2.6	2.3	2.1	1.2	-1.0	0.5	1.4	2.3	1.5	1.4	2.3	1.6	1.7	1.4
Japan	0.5	0.4	1.2	1.5	1.7	2.0	1.1	0.4	0.1	0.2	0.5	1.1	-0.7	-0.8	-0.5
Total above	1.4	1.6	1.8	1.9	1.5	0.3	-0.2	-0.1	0.9	1.1	0.9	1.3	1.2	1.2	1.3
Memorandum items:															
4 major west European economies[g]	0.7	0.9	1.6	1.8	1.8	0.4	-1.3	-1.6	-0.2	0.5	0.3	0.6	1.1	1.2	1.3
Western Europe and North America	1.6	1.8	1.9	2.0	1.5	-0.1	-0.4	-0.2	1.1	1.3	1.0	1.3	1.6	1.6	1.6

Source: OECD, *Main Economic Indicators* and *Quarterly Labour Force Statistics*, latest issues; Eurostat, New Cronos Database; national statistics.

Note: Total employment is defined as the number of persons engaged in some productive activity within resident production units (national accounts concept). The labour force survey concept (based on resident household surveys) is used for Canada, Israel, Turkey, United Kingdom, United States; Austria (up to 1987); Portugal (up to 1990); Ireland, Netherlands and Spain (up to 1994). All aggregates exclude Israel.

[a] West Germany 1986-1991.

[b] Twelve countries above.

[c] Number of jobs.

[d] Fifteen countries above.

[e] Full-time equivalent.

[f] Full-time occupied at the end of the year.

[g] France, Germany, Italy and the United Kingdom.

APPENDIX TABLE A.10

Standardized unemployment rates[a] in western Europe, North America and Japan, 1986-2000
(Per cent of civilian labour force)

	1986	1987	1988	1989	1990	1991	1992	1993	1994	1995	1996	1997	1998	1999	2000
France	10.3	10.5	10.0	9.4	9.0	9.5	10.4	11.7	12.3	11.7	12.4	12.3	11.8	11.2	9.5
Germany[b]	6.5	6.3	6.2	5.6	4.8	4.2	6.6	7.9	8.4	8.2	8.9	9.9	9.3	8.6	8.1
Italy	9.0	9.8	9.8	9.8	9.0	8.6	8.8	10.2	11.1	11.6	11.7	11.7	11.8	11.3	10.5
Austria	3.1	3.8	3.6	3.1	3.2	3.5	3.6	4.0	3.8	3.9	4.3	4.4	4.5	4.0	3.7
Belgium	10.3	10.1	9.0	7.5	6.7	6.6	7.2	8.8	10.0	9.9	9.7	9.4	9.5	8.8	7.0
Finland	6.7	4.9	4.2	3.1	3.2	6.6	11.7	16.3	16.6	15.4	14.6	12.7	11.4	10.2	9.8
Greece	6.6	6.7	6.8	6.7	6.4	7.0	7.9	8.6	8.9	9.2	9.6	9.8	10.9	11.7	11.1*
Ireland	16.8	16.6	16.2	14.7	13.4	14.7	15.4	15.6	14.3	12.3	11.7	9.9	7.5	5.6	4.2
Luxembourg	2.6	2.5	2.0	1.8	1.7	1.7	2.1	2.6	3.2	2.9	3.0	2.7	2.7	2.3	2.2
Netherlands	8.3	8.1	7.6	6.9	6.2	5.8	5.6	6.5	7.1	6.9	6.3	5.2	4.0	3.3	2.8
Portugal	8.8	7.3	5.9	5.2	4.8	4.2	4.3	5.7	6.9	7.3	7.3	6.8	5.2	4.5	4.2
Spain	21.2	20.6	19.5	17.2	16.3	16.4	18.4	22.7	24.2	22.9	22.2	20.8	18.8	15.9	14.1
Euro area[c]	9.9	9.9	9.5	8.8	8.1	8.2	9.1	10.8	11.5	11.2	11.5	11.5	10.9	10.0	9.1
United Kingdom	11.6	10.6	8.7	7.3	7.1	8.8	10.0	10.5	9.6	8.7	8.2	7.0	6.3	6.1	5.6
Denmark	5.4	5.4	6.1	7.3	7.7	8.4	9.2	10.2	8.2	7.2	6.8	5.6	5.2	5.2	4.7
Sweden	2.7	2.2	1.8	1.5	1.7	3.1	5.6	9.1	9.4	8.8	9.6	9.9	8.3	7.2	5.9
European Union[d]	9.9	9.7	9.1	8.3	7.7	8.2	9.2	10.7	11.1	10.7	10.8	10.6	10.0	9.2	8.3
Cyprus[e]	3.7	3.4	2.8	2.3	1.8	3.0	1.8	2.6	2.7	2.6	3.1	3.4	3.3	3.8	3.5*
Iceland	0.6	0.5	0.6	1.6	1.8	2.6	4.3	5.3	5.4	4.9	3.8	3.9	2.7	2.1	2.3
Israel[f]	7.1	6.1	6.4	8.9	9.6	10.6	11.2	10.0	7.8	6.9	6.7	7.7	8.5	8.9	8.8
Malta[g]	6.9	4.4	4.0	3.7	3.8	3.6	4.0	4.5	4.1	3.8	4.4	5.0	5.1	5.3	4.5
Norway	2.0	2.1	3.2	5.0	5.3	5.6	6.0	6.1	5.5	5.0	4.9	4.1	3.3	3.3	3.5*
Switzerland	0.8	0.7	0.6	0.5	0.5	2.0	3.1	4.0	3.8	3.5	3.9	4.2	3.5	3.0	2.7
Turkey[f]	7.9	8.3	8.4	8.7	8.2	7.9	7.9	7.6	8.1	6.9	6.1	6.4	6.8	7.6	6.6
Western Europe	9.4	9.2	8.7	8.1	7.6	8.0	8.9	10.1	10.5	10.0	10.0	9.9	9.4	8.8	7.9
Canada	9.6	8.8	7.8	7.6	8.1	10.3	11.2	11.4	10.4	9.4	9.6	9.1	8.3	7.6	6.8
United States	7.0	6.2	5.5	5.3	5.6	6.7	7.4	6.8	6.1	5.6	5.4	4.9	4.5	4.2	4.0
North America	7.3	6.5	5.7	5.5	5.9	7.1	7.8	7.3	6.5	6.0	5.8	5.3	4.9	4.5	4.3
Japan	2.8	2.9	2.5	2.3	2.1	2.1	2.2	2.5	2.9	3.1	3.4	3.4	4.1	4.7	4.7
Total above	7.5	7.2	6.6	6.2	6.1	6.7	7.4	7.9	7.8	7.4	7.4	7.2	6.9	6.6	6.1
Memorandum items:															
4 major west European economies[h]	9.3	9.2	8.6	7.9	7.3	7.3	8.7	9.8	10.1	9.7	10.0	10.1	9.6	9.1	8.3
Western Europe and North America	8.5	8.1	7.4	7.0	6.8	7.6	8.4	8.9	8.8	8.3	8.2	7.9	7.4	7.0	6.4

Source: OECD, *Main Economic Indicators* and *Quarterly Labour Force Statistics*, latest issues; Eurostat, New Cronos Database; national statistics.

Note: All aggregates exclude Israel. Comparisons with previous years are limited by changes in methodology in Austria (1993), Finland (1984), Iceland (1991), Israel (1995), Norway (1989), Portugal (1983), Switzerland (1991) and the United States (1994).

[a] Eurostat-OECD definition except for Austria (1982-1992), Cyprus, Finland (1982-1983), Iceland (1982-1990), Israel, Malta, Switzerland (1982-1990) and Turkey.

[b] West Germany 1986-1990.

[c] Twelve countries above.

[d] Fifteen countries above.

[e] Registered unemployment rate, average of monthly data.

[f] Definitions comply with ILO guidelines but do not follow the Eurostat-OECD standards.

[g] Registered unemployment rate at the end of the year.

[h] France, Germany, Italy and the United Kingdom.

APPENDIX TABLE A.11

Consumer prices in western Europe, North America and Japan, 1986-2000
(Percentage change over previous year)

	1986	1987	1988	1989	1990	1991	1992	1993	1994	1995	1996	1997	1998	1999	2000
France	2.7	3.1	2.7	3.6	3.3	3.2	2.4	2.1	1.7	1.7	2.0	1.2	0.7	0.5	1.5
Germany [a]	-0.2	0.3	1.2	2.8	2.7	3.6	5.1	4.5	2.7	1.8	1.5	1.8	0.9	0.6	1.9
Italy	5.8	4.8	5.1	6.3	6.5	6.3	5.3	4.6	4.1	5.2	3.9	1.7	1.8	2.2	2.5
Austria	1.7	1.4	2.0	2.5	3.2	3.4	4.0	3.7	3.0	2.2	1.9	1.3	0.9	0.6	2.3
Belgium	1.3	1.5	1.1	3.2	3.4	3.2	2.4	2.8	2.4	1.5	2.0	1.6	1.0	1.1	2.6
Finland	2.9	4.1	5.1	6.6	6.2	4.3	3.0	2.1	1.1	1.0	0.6	1.2	1.4	1.2	3.4
Greece	23.0	16.4	13.5	13.7	20.4	19.5	15.9	14.4	10.7	8.8	8.3	5.5	4.8	2.6	3.1
Ireland	3.8	3.1	2.1	4.1	3.3	3.2	3.1	1.4	2.4	2.5	1.7	1.4	2.4	1.6	5.6
Luxembourg	0.3	-0.1	1.4	3.4	3.3	3.1	3.2	3.6	2.2	1.9	1.3	1.4	1.0	1.0	3.1
Netherlands	0.2	-0.8	0.7	1.1	2.5	3.1	3.2	2.6	2.7	2.0	2.0	2.2	2.0	2.2	2.6
Portugal	11.8	9.4	9.7	12.6	13.4	10.5	9.5	6.7	5.4	4.2	3.1	2.3	2.8	2.3	2.9
Spain	8.8	5.2	4.8	6.9	6.7	5.9	5.9	4.6	4.8	4.6	3.6	2.0	1.8	2.3	3.4
Euro area [b]	3.7	3.1	3.3	4.6	4.8	4.9	4.8	4.1	3.3	3.0	2.6	1.8	1.4	1.3	2.3
United Kingdom	3.4	4.1	4.9	7.8	9.5	5.9	3.7	1.6	2.4	3.5	2.4	3.1	3.4	1.5	3.0
Denmark	3.6	4.0	4.6	4.8	2.7	2.4	2.1	1.3	2.0	2.1	2.0	2.2	1.9	2.5	3.0
Sweden	4.2	4.2	5.8	6.5	10.4	9.4	2.2	4.7	2.2	2.5	0.5	0.5	-0.1	0.4	1.0
European Union [c]	3.7	3.3	3.6	5.2	5.6	5.1	4.5	3.7	3.1	3.1	2.5	2.0	1.7	1.3	2.4
Cyprus	1.2	2.8	3.4	3.8	4.5	5.0	6.5	4.9	4.7	2.6	2.9	3.6	2.2	1.7	4.3
Iceland	22.7	18.8	19.1	20.8	15.4	6.8	3.7	4.1	1.5	1.7	2.3	1.8	1.7	3.2	5.2
Israel	48.1	19.9	16.3	20.2	17.2	19.0	12.0	11.0	12.3	10.1	11.3	9.0	5.4	5.2	1.1
Malta	2.0	0.5	0.9	0.9	3.0	2.5	1.6	4.1	4.1	4.0	2.5	3.2	2.2	2.1	2.3
Norway	7.2	8.7	6.7	4.6	4.1	3.4	2.3	2.3	1.4	2.4	1.3	2.6	2.3	2.3	3.1
Switzerland	0.8	1.4	1.9	3.2	5.5	5.8	4.1	3.3	0.8	1.8	0.8	0.5	–	0.8	1.5
Turkey	34.3	37.8	69.4	63.3	60.3	65.8	70.1	66.2	105.2	88.0	79.8	84.8	86.2	64.9	48.8
Western Europe	3.6	3.3	3.6	5.1	5.6	5.1	4.5	3.7	3.0	3.0	2.4	2.0	1.7	1.3	2.4
Canada	4.1	4.4	4.0	5.0	4.8	5.6	1.5	1.8	0.2	2.2	1.6	1.6	0.9	1.7	2.7
United States	1.9	3.6	4.1	4.8	5.4	4.2	3.0	3.0	2.6	2.8	3.0	2.3	1.6	2.2	3.4
North America	2.0	3.7	4.1	4.8	5.4	4.3	2.9	2.9	2.4	2.8	2.9	2.2	1.5	2.2	3.3
Japan	0.7	–	0.7	2.4	3.1	3.2	1.7	1.3	0.7	-0.1	0.1	1.8	0.6	-0.3	-0.7
Total above	2.4	3.0	3.4	4.6	5.1	4.4	3.3	3.0	2.4	2.5	2.3	2.1	1.4	1.5	2.4
Memorandum items:															
4 major west European economies [d]	2.6	2.8	3.2	4.9	5.2	4.6	4.2	3.3	2.7	2.9	2.4	2.0	1.6	1.2	2.2
Western Europe and North America	2.7	3.5	3.9	5.0	5.5	4.7	3.6	3.2	2.7	2.9	2.7	2.1	1.6	1.8	2.9

Source: National statistics.

Note: All aggregates exclude Israel and Turkey. Growth rates of regional aggregates have been calculated as weighted averages of growth rates in individual countries. Weights were derived from 1996 private final consumption expenditure converted from national currency units into dollars using 1996 purchasing power parities.

[a] West Germany 1986-1991.

[b] Twelve countries above.

[c] Fifteen countries above.

[d] France, Germany, Italy and the United Kingdom.

APPENDIX TABLE B.1

Real GDP/NMP in eastern Europe, the Baltic states and the CIS, 1980, 1987-2000
(Indices, 1989=100)

	1980	1987	1988	1989	1990	1991	1992	1993	1994	1995	1996	1997	1998	1999	2000
Eastern Europe	88.7	99.4	100.8	100.0	93.2	82.9	79.3	79.0	82.1	86.9	90.3	92.1	93.8	95.0	98.7
Albania	79.4	92.4	91.0	100.0	90.0	64.8	60.1	65.9	71.4	80.9	88.2	82.0	88.6	95.0	102.6
Bosnia and Herzegovina	..	..	..	..	..	..	..	..	..	..	..	..	..	..	..
Bulgaria	76.2	99.3	101.9	100.0	90.9	83.3	77.2	76.1	77.5	79.7	71.6	66.6	68.9	70.6	74.1
Croatia [a]	99.0	102.5	101.6	100.0	92.9	73.3	64.7	59.5	63.0	67.3	71.3	76.2	78.1	77.8	80.7
Czech Republic	..	93.7	95.7	100.0	98.8	87.3	86.9	86.9	88.8	94.1	98.7	97.7	95.5	94.8	97.7
Hungary	86.3	99.4	99.3	100.0	96.5	85.0	82.4	81.9	84.4	85.6	86.8	90.7	95.1	99.3	104.5
Poland	91.1	95.9	99.8	100.0	88.4	82.2	84.4	87.6	92.1	98.6	104.5	111.7	117.1	121.8	126.8
Romania	88.5	106.7	106.2	100.0	94.4	82.2	75.0	76.2	79.2	84.8	88.2	82.8	78.3	75.8	77.0
Slovakia	..	97.1	99.0	100.0	97.5	83.3	77.9	75.1	78.7	84.0	89.2	94.8	98.6	100.5	102.7
Slovenia	98.9	103.5	100.5	100.0	91.9	83.7	79.1	81.4	85.7	89.3	92.4	96.6	100.3	105.5	110.6
The former Yugoslav Republic of Macedonia	93.3	101.4	98.1	100.0	89.8	84.3	78.7	72.8	71.6	70.8	71.6	72.6	74.8	76.8	80.7
Yugoslavia [a]	95.7	100.2	98.8	100.0	92.1	81.4	58.7	40.6	41.7	44.2	46.8	50.3	51.5	41.6	45.7
Baltic states	67.8	89.0	96.0	100.0	97.8	89.9	67.9	58.2	55.2	56.4	58.8	63.7	66.7	65.3	68.5
Estonia	74.5	89.2	93.8	100.0	91.9	82.7	71.0	65.0	63.7	66.4	69.0	76.3	79.9	79.0	84.1
Latvia	68.5	89.0	93.6	100.0	102.9	92.2	60.1	51.1	51.5	51.0	52.7	57.3	59.5	60.1	64.1
Lithuania	64.7	88.9	98.4	100.0	96.7	91.2	71.8	60.2	54.3	56.1	58.7	63.0	66.2	63.4	65.3
CIS [b,c]	77.5	93.9	98.1	100.0	96.8	90.9	78.0	70.4	60.3	56.9	55.0	55.6	54.0	55.7	59.8
Armenia	73.5	94.5	92.2	100.0	94.5	83.4	48.6	44.3	46.7	49.9	52.8	54.6	58.6	60.5	64.1
Azerbaijan	79.6	105.1	109.7	100.0	88.3	87.7	67.9	52.2	41.9	37.0	37.4	39.6	43.6	46.8	52.1
Belarus	65.7	91.3	92.4	100.0	98.1	96.9	87.6	81.0	70.8	63.4	65.2	72.6	78.7	81.4	86.1
Georgia	79.4	96.8	103.6	100.0	84.9	67.0	36.9	26.1	23.4	24.0	26.7	29.5	30.4	31.3	31.9
Kazakhstan	87.0	92.1	100.1	100.0	99.0	88.2	83.5	75.8	66.2	60.8	61.1	62.1	61.0	62.6	68.6
Kyrgyzstan	69.1	84.7	95.6	100.0	104.8	96.5	83.2	70.3	56.2	53.1	56.9	62.5	63.9	66.2	69.5
Republic of Moldova	72.1	90.3	91.9	100.0	97.6	80.5	57.2	56.5	39.0	38.5	36.2	36.8	34.4	33.2	33.9
Russian Federation	78.1	94.2	98.4	100.0	97.0	92.2	78.8	71.9	62.8	60.2	58.2	58.7	55.8	57.8	62.2
Tajikistan	80.8	93.9	106.9	100.0	100.2	91.7	62.1	52.0	40.9	35.8	29.8	30.3	32.0	33.1	35.9
Turkmenistan	80.7	97.1	107.5	100.0	101.8	97.0	82.5	83.7	69.2	64.2	68.5	60.7	63.8	74.0	87.0
Ukraine	75.0	93.4	95.2	100.0	96.4	88.0	79.3	68.0	52.5	46.1	41.5	40.2	39.4	39.3	41.6
Uzbekistan	76.0	88.4	97.0	100.0	99.2	98.7	87.7	85.7	81.2	80.5	81.9	86.1	89.9	93.9	97.6
Total above	80.3	95.2	98.7	100.0	95.9	88.8	78.2	72.4	65.9	64.8	64.3	65.4	64.7	66.2	70.2
Memorandum items:															
CETE-5	88.6	97.3	99.6	100.0	93.3	84.1	83.8	85.0	88.5	93.5	98.0	102.4	105.7	108.8	113.1
SETE-7	88.8	103.1	102.9	100.0	93.1	80.8	71.4	68.5	70.9	75.3	76.7	74.1	72.9	70.7	73.3
Czechoslovakia [b]	84.9	97.0	99.3	100.0	98.5	84.4	78.8	..	..	..	..	..	..	..	..
Yugoslavia (SFR) [a]	97.7	101.0	99.4	100.0	92.4	..	..	..	..	..	..	..	..	..	..
Former Soviet Union [b]	77.3	93.8	98.0	100.0	96.8	90.9	77.7	70.1	60.2	56.9	55.1	55.9	54.3	55.9	60.1
Former GDR	..	..	..	100.0	84.5	68.3	73.6	80.4	88.2	92.0	95.0	96.6	98.5	..	..

Source: UN/ECE Common Database, derived from national and CIS statistics.

Note: Data for the east European countries are based on a GDP measure, except where otherwise mentioned. For the countries of the former Soviet Union, NMP data for 1980-1990 were chain-linked to GDP data from 1990. Country indices were aggregated with previous year PPP-based weights obtained from the European Comparison Programme for 1996.

[a] Gross material product (1980-1989 for Croatia).

[b] Sum of individual country data for former members.

[c] Net material product for 1980-1990 (until 1992 in the case of Turkmenistan).

APPENDIX TABLE B.2

Real total consumption expenditure in eastern Europe, the Baltic states and the CIS, 1980, 1987-2000

(Indices, 1989=100 or earliest year available thereafter)

	1980	1987	1988	1989	1990	1991	1992	1993	1994	1995	1996	1997	1998	1999	2000
Bulgaria	..	..	..	100.0	100.6	92.3	89.4	86.2	82.3	80.7	75.3	64.0	68.8	72.0	..
Croatia	..	..	..	..	..	100.0	87.2	85.3	92.0	106.6	106.5	117.1	118.2	116.2	119.3
Czech Republic	..	91.3	93.1	100.0	104.9	85.5	88.4	90.2	94.5	97.2	103.0	104.6	102.3	102.7	103.7
Hungary	92.2	104.9	102.0	100.0	97.3	92.2	92.8	97.9	95.6	89.3	86.6	88.6	91.7	95.6	98.6
Poland	108.0	111.8	114.7	100.0	88.3	94.9	98.2	103.0	107.0	110.5	118.4	125.6	130.8	136.8	139.6
Romania	83.9	88.7	90.6	100.0	108.9	96.0	90.7	91.8	95.3	105.5	112.9	108.1	103.7	99.1	100.7
Slovakia	..	89.2	92.1	100.0	103.3	76.9	75.6	74.2	71.5	73.9	82.4	86.5	91.1	89.2	86.8
Slovenia	..	..	..	..	100.0	91.6	88.8	99.1	102.6	110.2	112.7	116.3	120.9	127.7	129.5
The former Yugoslav Republic of Macedonia	..	..	..	..	100.0	93.9	84.2	89.7	95.9	94.2	96.4	98.4	101.9	102.4	..
Estonia	..	..	..	..	..	..	..	100.0	101.2	110.4	116.5	124.4	131.3	131.6	..
Latvia	..	..	..	..	100.0	76.7	49.2	46.5	47.4	47.0	50.8	52.7	56.0	58.4	..
Lithuania	..	..	..	..	..	..	..	..	..	100.0	108.2	116.4	125.4	120.2	..
Armenia	..	..	..	..	100.0	97.4	84.9	66.4	68.9	74.5	76.8	81.7	85.4	85.7	..
Azerbaijan	..	..	..	..	..	..	100.0	77.4	62.2	60.4	65.3	72.2	80.4	..	..
Belarus	..	..	..	..	100.0	93.5	84.1	78.8	70.0	63.4	65.7	72.3	80.9	87.7	..
Georgia	..	..	..	..	100.0	79.2	77.1	45.4	42.4	46.1	..	..	..	..	..
Kazakhstan	..	..	..	..	100.0	96.8	96.2	84.9	67.7	55.0	51.3	51.8	50.4	53.6	..
Kyrgyzstan	..	..	..	..	100.0	83.5	72.8	64.3	51.8	43.4	46.2	42.4	48.8	49.3	..
Republic of Moldova	..	..	..	..	..	..	..	100.0	82.6	90.3	99.7	111.5	109.3	92.0	100.5
Russian Federation	..	..	..	..	100.0	93.9	89.0	88.1	85.8	83.3	80.7	82.7	76.7	72.6	78.1
Ukraine	..	..	..	..	100.0	94.3	88.6	72.0	65.0	62.6	57.4	56.4	56.3	55.6	..

Source: UN/ECE Common Database, derived from national and CIS statistics.

APPENDIX TABLE B.3

Real gross fixed capital formation in eastern Europe, the Baltic states and the CIS, 1980, 1987-2000

(Indices, 1989=100 or earliest year available thereafter)

	1980	1987	1988	1989	1990	1991	1992	1993	1994	1995	1996	1997	1998	1999	2000
Bulgaria	..	..	..	..	100.0	80.0	74.1	61.2	61.9	71.8	56.6	43.0	57.2	71.7	..
Croatia	..	..	..	..	..	100.0	88.5	94.5	93.6	108.2	148.8	183.5	189.1	187.0	180.5
Czech Republic	..	93.4	99.4	100.0	97.9	71.1	82.8	83.0	90.5	108.5	117.3	113.9	109.4	104.6	110.1
Hungary	114.7	110.7	100.6	100.0	92.9	83.1	81.0	82.6	92.9	88.9	94.8	103.6	117.3	125.0	133.3
Poland	124.6	116.5	126.5	100.0	75.2	71.9	73.6	75.7	82.6	96.2	115.2	140.1	160.0	170.5	175.7
Romania	163.7	161.0	157.6	100.0	64.4	44.0	48.9	52.9	63.9	68.3	72.2	73.4	69.6	62.1	65.5
Slovakia	..	..	..	..	100.0	74.8	71.5	67.7	64.6	68.0	89.7	100.4	111.6	90.6	90.0
Slovenia	..	..	..	..	100.0	88.5	77.1	85.4	97.4	113.8	123.9	138.2	153.9	183.2	186.1
The former Yugoslav Republic of Macedonia	..	..	..	..	100.0	95.8	79.9	73.6	67.3	74.1	79.0	75.6	76.7	77.6	..
Estonia	..	..	..	..	..	..	..	100.0	106.2	110.5	123.1	144.6	161.0	136.5	..
Latvia	..	..	..	..	100.0	36.1	25.7	21.6	21.8	23.7	29.0	35.0	50.4	47.2	..
Lithuania	..	..	..	..	..	..	..	..	..	100.0	117.6	143.6	157.8	149.0	..
Armenia	..	..	..	..	100.0	67.0	8.6	7.9	11.5	9.5	10.5	10.7	12.0	12.1	..
Azerbaijan	..	..	..	..	..	..	100.0	61.0	115.3	94.5	199.8	333.7	483.9	..	..
Belarus	..	..	..	..	100.0	104.2	84.8	78.3	67.6	47.6	46.1	56.2	61.8	59.3	..
Georgia	..	..	..	..	100.0	67.3	49.2	18.5	133.4	219.9	..	..	..	..	..
Kazakhstan	..	..	..	..	100.0	74.2	61.9	44.2	39.2	24.4	18.5	19.2	16.1	16.2	..
Kyrgyzstan	..	..	..	..	100.0	89.4	63.2	49.4	35.1	56.4	49.1	34.6	34.0	43.6	..
Republic of Moldova	..	..	..	..	..	..	..	100.0	56.5	50.8	63.8	60.4	66.0	50.8	53.4
Russian Federation	..	..	..	..	100.0	84.5	49.4	36.7	27.1	24.6	20.4	18.9	17.7	17.4	20.0
Ukraine	..	..	..	..	100.0	81.6	69.3	48.2	28.4	19.7	15.2	15.5	15.9	15.9	..

Source: UN/ECE Common Database, derived from national and CIS statistics.

APPENDIX TABLE B.4

Real gross industrial output in eastern Europe, the Baltic states and the CIS, 1980, 1987-2000
(Indices, 1989=100)

	1980	1987	1988	1989	1990	1991	1992	1993	1994	1995	1996	1997	1998	1999	2000
Eastern Europe	82.8	98.5	100.6	100.0	85.9	70.2	63.0	61.5	65.5	70.3	73.9	77.5	78.6	78.5	85.0
Albania	77.0	93.3	95.2	100.0	86.7	50.4	35.2	31.7	25.8	23.9	18.1	18.6	22.7	26.3	29.4
Bosnia and Herzegovina	106.0	101.1	98.1	100.0	101.8	76.9	25.5	2.0	1.7	2.8	5.2	7.0	8.7	9.6	10.5
Bulgaria	71.3	98.0	101.1	100.0	83.2	66.4	54.2	48.8	54.0	56.4	59.3	53.4	49.1	43.1	44.1
Croatia	88.7	102.0	100.6	100.0	88.7	63.4	54.2	51.0	49.6	49.7	51.3	54.8	56.8	56.0	57.0
Czech Republic	81.5	96.5	98.5	100.0	96.6	75.7	69.8	66.1	67.4	73.3	74.8	78.1	79.4	76.9	80.9
Hungary	92.9	106.4	105.3	100.0	90.7	74.0	66.8	69.5	76.2	79.7	82.4	91.5	103.0	113.7	134.5
Poland	86.3	95.5	100.5	100.0	75.8	69.7	71.7	76.3	85.5	93.8	101.6	113.3	117.3	122.9	131.6
Romania	76.9	99.2	101.9	100.0	81.9	63.3	49.4	50.1	51.7	56.6	60.1	55.8	48.1	44.3	47.9
Slovakia	76.7	98.6	100.8	100.0	94.0	75.9	68.6	66.1	69.3	75.1	76.9	77.9	80.9	78.0	85.1
Slovenia	90.3	101.6	98.9	100.0	89.5	78.4	68.1	66.1	70.4	71.8	72.5	73.2	75.9	75.6	80.2
The former Yugoslav Republic of Macedonia	72.1	97.3	95.6	100.0	89.4	74.0	62.3	53.7	48.0	42.9	44.3	45.0	47.0	45.8	47.4
Yugoslavia	80.0	97.6	98.4	100.0	88.0	72.5	57.0	35.7	36.2	37.6	40.4	44.2	45.8	35.2	39.1
Baltic states	72.1	92.7	96.6	100.0	98.6	95.1	64.7	44.4	36.3	37.1	38.9	42.1	44.6	41.2	43.9
Estonia	78.5	96.3	99.3	100.0	100.0	92.8	59.8	48.6	47.1	48.0	49.4	56.6	59.0	58.0	63.2
Latvia	72.5	93.7	97.1	100.0	100.8	100.2	65.6	44.6	40.1	38.7	40.8	46.4	47.9	45.3	46.7
Lithuania	70.0	91.2	95.6	100.0	97.4	94.0	65.8	43.2	31.7	33.4	35.0	36.2	39.2	34.8	37.2
CIS [a]	73.4	94.5	98.2	100.0	99.9	93.1	78.2	68.4	53.6	50.7	49.0	50.2	48.7	52.2	57.2
Armenia	76.3	110.3	109.1	100.0	92.5	85.4	44.2	39.5	41.6	42.2	42.8	43.2	42.3	44.5	47.4
Azerbaijan	76.1	96.1	99.4	100.0	93.7	85.4	59.4	47.7	35.9	28.2	26.3	26.4	27.0	28.0	29.9
Belarus	61.1	89.9	95.6	100.0	102.1	101.1	91.8	83.2	71.0	62.7	64.9	77.1	86.7	95.6	103.2
Georgia	70.6	96.2	99.3	100.0	94.3	73.0	39.6	25.0	15.2	13.2	14.1	15.2	15.0	16.1	17.1
Kazakhstan	72.4	94.1	97.6	100.0	99.2	98.3	84.7	72.2	51.9	47.7	47.8	49.7	48.5	49.8	57.1
Kyrgyzstan	66.7	89.0	95.1	100.0	99.4	99.1	73.5	56.3	35.5	26.7	27.8	38.8	40.9	39.1	41.4
Republic of Moldova	68.7	91.6	94.6	100.0	103.2	91.7	66.9	67.1	48.5	46.6	43.6	43.6	37.0	32.7	33.5
Russian Federation	74.4	95.0	98.6	100.0	99.9	91.9	75.4	64.7	51.2	49.5	47.5	48.5	46.0	49.7	54.2
Tajikistan	72.9	93.1	98.2	100.0	101.2	97.6	73.9	68.1	50.8	43.9	33.4	32.7	35.4	37.4	41.2
Turkmenistan	75.4	92.9	96.9	100.0	103.2	108.2	92.0	95.7	72.1	67.5	79.5	53.8	54.0	62.0	79.8
Ukraine	72.6	93.4	97.3	100.0	99.9	95.1	89.0	81.9	59.5	52.4	49.7	49.6	49.1	51.2	57.8
Uzbekistan	68.5	93.4	96.5	100.0	101.8	103.3	96.4	99.9	101.5	101.6	104.2	108.5	112.4	119.2	126.9
Total above	76.5	95.8	99.0	100.0	95.2	85.4	72.7	65.5	57.2	57.0	57.1	59.2	58.7	60.8	66.3
Memorandum items:															
CETE-5	85.4	98.3	100.7	100.0	87.0	73.3	69.8	70.6	76.3	82.4	86.5	93.7	97.8	100.7	109.5
SETE-7	78.6	98.8	100.6	100.0	84.1	65.4	52.0	47.0	48.3	51.1	53.9	51.8	48.0	43.3	46.1
Czechoslovakia	80.5	97.2	99.2	100.0	96.5	75.2	67.6	..	..	..	..	..	..	..	..
Yugoslavia (SFR) [a]	86.9	99.7	98.7	100.0	88.3	71.7	..	..	..	..	..	..	..	..	..
Former Soviet Union	73.4	94.5	98.2	100.0	99.8	93.2	77.7	67.5	53.0	50.2	48.6	49.9	48.6	51.8	56.8
Former GDR	75.2	94.7	97.7	100.0	72.7	37.0	34.8	36.8	42.0	44.4	45.9	49.1	52.8	55.3	..

Source: UN/ECE Common Database, derived from national and CIS statistics.

Note: Data for former Czechoslovakia and the former SFR of Yugoslavia for 1980 until the breakup obtained as sum of individual country data for former members. For the countries of the former Soviet Union, data for 1980-1990 were chain-linked to national or CIS data from 1990. Country indices were aggregated with previous year PPP-based weights on the basis of data obtained from the European Comparison Programme for 1996.

[a] Generated from components.

APPENDIX TABLE B.5

Total employment in eastern Europe, the Baltic states and the CIS, 1980, 1987-2000
(Indices, 1989=100)

	1980	1987	1988	1989	1990	1991	1992	1993	1994	1995	1996	1997	1998	1999	2000
Eastern Europe	96.7	100.0	99.9	100.0	97.1	90.7	85.4	82.6	82.6	82.2	82.7	82.7	83.0	80.7	..
Albania	77.9	95.9	97.6	100.0	99.2	97.5	76.0	72.7	80.7	79.0	77.5	76.9	75.3	74.0	..
Bosnia and Herzegovina	..	..	..	100.0	97.1	58.1	22.1	9.9	9.1	10.1	22.5	34.4	36.4	37.6	38.0
Bulgaria	100.0	102.8	102.4	100.0	93.9	81.6	75.0	73.8	74.3	75.2	75.3	72.3	72.2	70.4	..
Croatia	87.4	100.6	100.4	100.0	97.1	89.2	79.3	76.6	74.8	73.9	74.5	73.9	78.8	78.5	..
Czech Republic	95.3	98.9	99.4	100.0	99.1	93.6	91.2	89.7	90.4	92.8	93.4	91.6	90.1	86.9	..
Hungary[a]	104.2	101.7	100.7	100.0	96.7	86.7	78.1	73.2	71.8	70.4	69.8	69.8	70.7	72.9	73.6
Poland	102.0	100.8	100.1	100.0	95.8	90.1	86.3	84.3	85.1	86.7	88.3	90.8	92.9	90.4	..
Romania[b]	94.6	97.9	98.7	100.0	99.0	98.5	95.5	91.9	91.5	86.7	85.7	82.4	80.5	76.9	..
Slovakia[b]	90.8	99.0	99.8	100.0	98.2	85.9	86.8	84.6	83.7	85.7	84.5	82.6	81.8	78.0	..
Slovenia[c]	84.0	101.9	101.3	100.0	96.1	88.7	83.8	81.3	79.3	79.1	78.7	78.6	78.7	80.2	81.1
The former Yugoslav Republic of Macedonia	81.2	99.9	99.7	100.0	98.2	90.7	86.4	81.5	76.6	69.0	65.8	61.8	60.1	61.1	60.4
Yugoslavia	83.4	99.0	99.8	100.0	97.0	94.1	90.9	88.3	86.5	85.3	84.8	89.9	89.7	82.4	..
Baltic states[d]	94.9	99.4	99.6	100.0	98.5	98.9	94.4	89.0	83.2	80.6	80.1	80.9	80.5	79.5	..
Estonia	..	97.6	97.6	100.0	98.6	96.4	91.4	84.5	82.7	78.3	77.0	77.4	76.4	73.3	72.6
Latvia	97.0	100.4	100.5	100.0	100.1	99.3	92.0	85.6	77.0	74.3	72.3	73.7	74.1	73.8	..
Lithuania	93.4	99.5	99.8	100.0	97.3	99.7	97.5	93.4	88.0	86.4	87.2	87.7	87.0	86.6	..
CIS	93.8	98.4	98.8	100.0	100.2	98.9	96.6	94.2	91.4	90.5	89.8	88.5	87.5	87.2	..
Armenia	86.6	99.5	101.4	100.0	102.4	105.0	99.2	97.0	93.5	92.8	90.2	86.2	84.0	81.6	80.6
Azerbaijan	62.7	74.7	75.2	100.0	100.9	101.7	101.4	101.2	98.9	98.4	100.5	100.7	100.9	100.9	100.9
Belarus	95.4	99.0	99.5	100.0	99.1	96.6	94.1	92.9	90.4	84.8	84.0	84.1	85.0	85.5	85.4
Georgia	92.7	101.0	101.1	100.0	102.3	93.3	73.5	66.4	64.8	79.0	79.1	82.7	84.6	77.0	..
Kazakhstan	86.2	94.7	96.0	100.0	101.3	100.1	98.3	89.9	85.4	85.0	84.6	84.0	79.5	79.2	79.9
Kyrgyzstan	81.9	97.9	98.7	100.0	100.5	99.6	105.6	96.6	94.6	94.4	95.0	97.1	98.0	101.5	101.6
Republic of Moldova[e]	97.3	99.7	98.9	100.0	99.1	99.0	98.0	80.7	80.4	80.0	79.4	78.7	78.5	71.5	72.0
Russian Federation	96.9	99.7	99.9	100.0	99.6	97.7	95.3	93.7	90.6	87.9	87.2	85.5	84.2	84.6	85.5
Tajikistan	76.7	94.5	96.9	100.0	103.2	104.9	101.6	98.7	98.7	98.6	92.1	95.3	95.6	91.9	85.9
Turkmenistan	79.8	98.5	101.2	100.0	103.4	107.0	110.5	114.0	118.5	122.5	124.7	127.2	128.8	129.7	..
Ukraine	99.6	100.3	99.9	100.0	99.9	98.3	96.3	94.1	90.5	93.3	91.3	88.8	87.9	85.8	84.9
Uzbekistan	75.4	93.2	95.9	100.0	104.2	109.2	108.7	108.5	109.9	110.8	112.3	113.8	115.4	116.5	117.8
Total above	94.6	98.8	99.1	100.0	99.3	96.6	93.4	90.9	88.8	88.0	87.6	86.8	86.1	85.2	..
Memorandum items:															
CETE-5	99.7	100.5	100.1	100.0	96.7	89.8	85.8	83.3	83.5	84.7	85.5	86.4	87.4	85.5	..
SETE-7	92.3	99.2	99.7	100.0	97.6	91.9	84.9	81.5	81.4	78.9	78.8	77.7	77.0	74.0	..
Former Soviet Union	93.8	98.4	98.8	100.0	100.2	98.9	96.5	94.0	91.2	90.2	89.5	88.3	87.3	87.0	..

Source: UN/ECE Common Database, derived from national and CIS statistics.

[a] End of year, up to 1992; since 1992, annual average.

[b] End of year.

[c] Self-employed excluded until 1987.

[d] Excluding Estonia until 1985.

[e] Excluding Transdniestria since 1993.

APPENDIX TABLE B.6

Employment in industry in eastern Europe, the Baltic states and the CIS, 1989-2000
(Indices, 1989=100)

	1989	1990	1991	1992	1993	1994	1995	1996	1997	1998	1999	2000
Eastern Europe[a]	100.0	95.6	86.7	76.7	71.9	69.5	68.6	68.3	66.2	65.2	60.9	..
Albania	..	..	..	..	..	..	..	..	..	..	..	..
Bosnia and Herzegovina	100.0	98.3	60.3	23.3	8.3	9.2	18.7	22.0	26.8	28.9	28.9	28.4
Bulgaria	100.0	91.0	74.7	64.8	59.5	57.3	56.0	55.4	53.0	50.8	46.7	..
Croatia	100.0	102.4	84.8	70.3	70.4	67.3	59.5	59.0	56.6	60.0	58.3	..
Czech Republic	100.0	95.8	92.2	85.1	80.9	76.6	77.0	76.4	76.1	75.8	73.4	..
Hungary	100.0	97.0	85.4	77.3	69.1	66.0	62.5	61.9	63.0	65.9	66.4	65.6
Poland	100.0	93.7	86.1	76.7	74.4	73.8	76.2	75.6	75.8	75.0	69.5	..
Romania[b]	100.0	96.5	91.6	79.5	73.0	69.4	65.4	66.0	59.0	55.8	49.5	..
Slovakia	100.0	95.7	88.2	78.7	74.0	71.7	71.6	71.6	70.2	67.3	65.4	..
Slovenia	100.0	95.1	85.2	84.6	78.1	75.1	72.2	71.5	68.5	67.8	66.7	..
The former Yugoslav Republic of Macedonia	100.0	95.3	87.3	81.6	77.5	72.9	63.1	59.0	54.4	52.5	55.4	52.9
Yugoslavia	100.0	100.9	92.1	87.2	85.0	82.7	80.6	78.8	76.3	74.2	65.3	..
Baltic states	100.0	96.8	95.5	87.0	74.2	63.0	60.8	58.0	57.7	55.8	54.0	..
Estonia	100.0	96.9	93.0	85.8	73.6	70.7	76.4	73.0	68.8	67.5	63.6	..
Latvia	100.0	97.0	92.1	81.4	69.0	56.3	53.1	50.1	51.9	47.6	45.7	..
Lithuania	100.0	96.7	99.0	91.4	78.0	64.5	59.5	57.0	57.1	56.5	55.7	..
CIS	100.0	98.2	96.7	91.8	88.3	79.7	73.3	69.2	63.8	62.6	..	..
Armenia	100.0	102.6	95.0	84.0	75.2	73.7	62.8	52.9	47.5	43.4	40.5	40.0
Azerbaijan	100.0	97.1	94.9	88.9	81.1	77.4	72.9	58.6	50.1	52.0	53.6	53.6
Belarus	100.0	98.6	96.9	92.1	88.5	84.4	75.2	74.4	74.5	75.5	76.2	75.9
Georgia	100.0	104.2	92.6	66.0	56.5	51.6	46.8	33.6	25.8	26.4	..	..
Kazakhstan	100.0	98.5	99.9	96.2	83.6	76.9	69.6	66.9	59.0	57.8	57.9	..
Kyrgyzstan	100.0	99.9	92.7	89.5	80.5	72.0	61.2	54.6	51.2	50.1	47.4	46.6
Republic of Moldova[c]	100.0	102.4	95.1	93.1	55.0	52.1	44.7	43.9	42.9	40.8	35.9	33.7
Russian Federation	100.0	97.7	96.1	91.3	89.8	80.7	74.1	70.4	64.5	63.0	62.6	64.0
Tajikistan	100.0	102.5	100.8	98.2	86.1	81.9	71.9	71.1	62.5	60.1	51.4	47.2
Turkmenistan	100.0	104.2	100.8	101.0	110.7	110.5	115.4	119.9	132.9	150.2	152.9	..
Ukraine	100.0	98.1	97.3	92.7	87.9	78.3	72.2	66.8	61.2	59.3	54.4	..
Uzbekistan	100.0	101.5	102.5	101.5	103.2	90.1	92.3	93.5	93.7	94.1	94.9	..
Total above[a]	100.0	97.4	93.5	86.9	82.8	76.1	71.5	68.7	64.5	63.2	..	..
Memorandum items:												
CETE-5	100.0	94.9	87.5	79.1	75.1	73.0	73.6	73.1	73.1	72.8	69.4	..
SETE-7[a]	100.0	96.5	85.9	73.8	68.2	65.3	62.5	62.4	58.1	56.0	50.7	..
Former Soviet Union	100.0	98.2	96.7	91.6	87.9	79.2	72.9	68.9	63.6	62.3	..	..

Source: UN/ECE Common Database, derived from national and CIS statistics.

[a] Excluding Albania.

[b] End of year.

[c] Excluding Transdniestria since 1993.

APPENDIX TABLE B.7

Registered unemployment in eastern Europe, the Baltic states and the CIS, 1990-2000
(Per cent of labour force, end-of-period)

	1990	1991	1992	1993	1994	1995	1996	1997	1998	1999	2000
Eastern Europe	..	9.6	12.4	14.0	13.6	12.5	11.7	11.9	12.6	14.6	15.1
Albania	9.5	9.2	27.0	22.0	18.0	12.9	12.3	14.9	17.6	18.2	16.9
Bosnia and Herzegovina	..	..	..	..	..	..	..	39.0	38.7	39.0	39.4
Bulgaria	1.8	11.1	15.3	16.4	12.8	11.1	12.5	13.7	12.2	16.0	17.9
Croatia [a]	..	14.1	17.8	16.6	17.3	17.6	15.9	17.6	18.6	20.8	22.6
Czech Republic	0.7	4.1	2.6	3.5	3.2	2.9	3.5	5.2	7.5	9.4	8.8
Hungary	1.7	7.4	12.3	12.1	10.9	10.4	10.5	10.4	9.1	9.6	8.9
Poland	6.5	12.2	14.3	16.4	16.0	14.9	13.2	10.3	10.4	13.1	15.0
Romania	1.3	3.0	8.2	10.4	10.9	9.5	6.6	8.8	10.3	11.5	10.5
Slovakia	1.6	11.8	10.4	14.4	14.8	13.1	12.8	12.5	15.6	19.2	17.9
Slovenia	..	10.1	13.3	15.5	14.2	14.5	14.4	14.8	14.6	13.0	12.0
The former Yugoslav Republic of Macedonia [a]	..	24.5	26.2	27.7	30.0	36.6	38.8	41.7	41.4	43.8	44.9
Yugoslavia [a,b]	..	21.0	24.6	24.0	23.9	24.7	26.1	25.6	27.2	27.4	26.6
Baltic states	..	..	2.1	4.5	5.3	6.6	6.4	6.3	7.3	9.1	10.0
Estonia [c]	..	..	1.6	5.0	5.1	5.0	5.6	4.6	5.1	6.7	7.3
Latvia	..	..	2.3	5.8	6.5	6.6	7.2	7.0	9.2	9.1	7.8
Lithuania	..	..	3.5	3.4	4.5	7.3	6.2	6.7	6.9	10.0	12.6
CIS	..	..	2.7	3.6	4.4	5.8	6.6	7.6	9.0	8.3	6.9
Armenia	..	..	3.5	6.3	6.0	8.1	9.7	11.0	8.9	11.5	10.9
Azerbaijan	..	..	0.2	0.7	0.9	1.1	1.1	1.3	1.4	1.2	1.2
Belarus	..	..	0.5	1.3	2.1	2.7	4.0	2.8	2.3	2.0	2.1
Georgia	..	..	0.3	2.0	3.8	3.4	3.2	8.0	4.2	5.6	..
Kazakhstan	..	..	0.4	0.6	1.0	2.1	4.1	3.9	3.7	3.9	3.7
Kyrgyzstan	..	..	0.1	0.2	0.8	3.0	4.5	3.1	3.1	3.0	3.1
Republic of Moldova	..	..	0.7	0.7	1.0	1.4	1.5	1.7	1.9	2.1	1.8
Russian Federation [d]	..	..	5.2	6.1	7.8	9.0	10.0	11.2	13.3	12.2	9.6
Tajikistan	..	..	0.4	1.1	1.8	1.8	2.4	2.8	2.9	3.1	3.0
Turkmenistan	..	..	..	..	..	..	..	..	..	..	..
Ukraine	..	..	0.3	0.4	0.3	0.6	1.5	2.8	4.3	4.3	4.2
Uzbekistan	..	..	0.1	0.2	0.3	0.3	0.3	0.3	0.4	0.5	0.6
Memorandum items:											
CETE-5	..	9.7	11.3	13.3	12.9	12.0	11.2	9.8	10.2	12.5	13.3
SETE-7	..	9.3	14.2	15.1	14.6	13.7	12.5	14.3	15.4	16.5	17.8
Russian Federation [e]	..	0.1	0.8	1.1	2.1	3.2	3.4	2.8	2.7	1.7	1.4
Former-GDR	..	..	13.5	15.4	13.5	14.9	15.9	19.4	17.4	17.7	17.2

Source: National statistics and direct communications from national statistical offices to UN/ECE secretariat.

[a] The data reported on employment cover only the social sector in agriculture, hence unemployment rates are biased upwards.

[b] Since 1999, excluding Kosovo and Metohia.

[c] Job seekers till 2000.

[d] Based on Russian Federation Goskomstat's monthly estimates according to the ILO definition, i.e. including all persons not having employment but actively seeking work.

[e] Registered unemployment.

APPENDIX TABLE B.8

Consumer prices in eastern Europe, the Baltic states and the CIS, 1990-2000
(Annual average, percentage change over preceding year)

	1990	1991	1992	1993	1994	1995	1996	1997	1998	1999	2000
Albania	..	35.5	193.1	85.0	21.5	8.0	12.7	33.1	20.3	-0.1	–
Bosnia and Herzegovina	594.0	116.2	64 218.3	38 825.1	553.5	-12.1	-21.2	11.8	4.9	-0.6	1.7
Bulgaria	23.8	338.5	91.3	72.9	96.2	62.1	123.1	1 082.6	22.2	0.4	10.0
Croatia[a]	609.5	123.0	663.6	1 516.6	97.5	2.0	3.6	3.7	5.9	4.3	6.4
Czech Republic	9.9	56.7	11.1	20.8	10.0	9.1	8.9	8.4	10.6	2.1	3.9
Hungary	28.9	35.0	23.0	22.6	19.1	28.5	23.6	18.4	14.2	10.1	9.9
Poland	585.8	70.3	45.3	36.9	33.2	28.1	19.8	15.1	11.7	7.4	10.2
Romania	5.1	170.2	210.7	256.2	137.1	32.2	38.8	154.9	59.3	45.9	45.7
Slovakia	10.4	61.2	10.2	23.1	13.4	10.0	6.1	6.1	6.7	10.5	12.0
Slovenia	551.6	115.0	207.3	31.7	21.0	13.5	9.9	8.4	8.1	6.3	9.0
The former Yugoslav Republic of Macedonia[a]	608.4	114.9	1 505.5	353.1	121.0	16.9	4.1	3.8	1.1	-1.4	10.1
Yugoslavia	580.0	122.0	8 926.0	2.2E+14	7.9E+10	71.8	90.5	23.2	30.4	44.1	77.9
Estonia	18.0	202.0	1 078.2	89.6	47.9	28.9	23.1	11.1	10.6	3.5	3.8
Latvia	10.9	172.2	951.2	109.1	35.7	25.0	17.7	8.5	4.7	2.4	2.8
Lithuania	9.1	216.4	1 020.5	410.1	72.0	39.5	24.7	8.8	5.1	0.8	1.0
Armenia	6.9	174.1	728.7	3 731.8	4 964.0	175.5	18.7	13.8	8.7	0.7	-0.8
Azerbaijan	6.1	106.6	912.6	1 129.7	1 663.9	411.5	19.8	3.6	-0.8	-8.6	1.8
Belarus	4.7	94.1	971.2	1 190.9	2 219.6	709.3	52.7	63.9	73.2	293.7	168.9
Georgia	4.2	78.7	1 176.9	4 084.9	22 286.1	261.4	39.4	7.1	3.5	19.3	4.2
Kazakhstan	5.6	114.5	1 504.3	1 662.7	1 880.1	176.3	39.2	17.5	7.3	8.4	13.4
Kyrgyzstan	5.5	113.9	854.6	1 208.7	278.1	42.9	31.3	23.4	10.3	35.7	18.7
Republic of Moldova	5.7	114.4	1 308.0	1 751.0	486.4	29.9	23.5	11.8	7.7	39.3	31.3
Russian Federation	5.2	160.0	1 528.7	875.0	309.0	197.4	47.8	14.7	27.8	85.7	20.8
Tajikistan	5.9	112.9	822.0	2 884.8	350.3	682.1	422.4	85.4	43.1	27.5	32.9
Turkmenistan	5.7	88.5	483.2	3 128.4	2 562.1	1 105.3	714.0	83.7	16.8	..	..
Ukraine	5.4	94.0	1 485.8	4 734.9	891.2	376.7	80.2	15.9	10.6	22.7	28.2
Uzbekistan	5.8	97.3	414.5	1 231.8	1 550.0	76.5	56.3	73.2	17.7	29.0	..

Source: UN/ECE Common Database, derived from national statistics.

Note: From 1992 onwards indices derived from monthly data except for Armenia, Georgia, Hungary, Slovenia, Yugoslavia (from 1993); Turkmenistan (from 1995); Uzbekistan (from 1996).

[a] Retail prices.

APPENDIX TABLE B.9

Producer price indices in eastern Europe, the Baltic states and the CIS, 1990-2000
(Annual average, percentage change over preceding year)

	1990	1991	1992	1993	1994	1995	1996	1997	1998	1999	2000
Albania	..	..	..	..	..	..	..	..	..	..	..
Bosnia and Herzegovina	..	129.5	68 034.0	9 254.5	1 203.3	42.7	-5.3	4.5	3.4	3.9	-0.2
Bulgaria	14.7	296.4	56.1	28.3	75.7	53.4	137.7	948.8	16.9	3.3	..
Croatia	455.3	146.3	825.2	1 512.4	77.6	0.7	1.4	2.3	-1.2	2.6	9.7
Czech Republic	2.5	70.3	10.0	9.2	5.3	7.6	4.8	4.9	4.9	1.0	4.9
Hungary	22.0	32.6	12.3	10.8	11.3	28.9	21.8	20.4	11.3	5.1	11.7
Poland	622.4	40.9	34.5	31.9	25.3	25.4	12.4	12.2	7.3	5.7	..
Romania	26.9	220.1	184.8	165.0	140.5	35.1	49.9	152.7	33.2	42.2	51.6
Slovakia	5.2	68.9	5.3	17.2	10.0	9.0	4.1	4.5	3.3	3.8	9.8
Slovenia	390.4	124.1	215.7	21.6	17.7	12.8	6.8	6.1	6.0	2.1	..
The former Yugoslav Republic of Macedonia	394.0	112.0	2 198.2	258.3	88.9	4.7	-0.3	4.2	4.0	-0.1	..
Yugoslavia	468.0	124.0	8 993.0	1.4E+13	7.9E+10	57.7	90.1	19.5	25.5	44.2	..
Estonia	19.3	208.4	1 208.0	75.2	36.3	25.6	14.8	8.8	4.2	-1.2	4.9
Latvia	..	192.0	1 310.0	117.1	16.9	11.9	13.7	4.1	1.9	-4.0	0.6
Lithuania	..	148.2	1 510.0	391.7	44.8	28.3	17.2	6.0	-3.9	3.0	18.0
Armenia	..	120.0	947.0	892.0	4 714.0	275.0	22.4	19.0	13.4	2.3	0.8
Azerbaijan	..	179.5	7 453.6	1 974.0	3 779.0	384.9	67.7	11.4	-12.4	-9.3	25.0
Belarus	2.1	151.1	1 939.2	1 536.3	2 171.0	461.5	33.6	88.0	72.0	355.8	186.0
Georgia	..	..	..	..	..	..	..	..	2.3	15.7	6.0
Kazakhstan	..	193.0	2 465.1	1 042.8	2 920.4	139.8	23.8	15.5	0.8	18.8	38.0
Kyrgyzstan	..	160.0	1 664.0	831.0	228.0	43.0	32.0	30.0	9.0	54.0	32.0
Republic of Moldova	..	130.0	1 210.9	1 078.5	893.7	53.7	32.2	20.0	9.7	44.0	28.0
Russian Federation	3.9	240.0	3 280.0	900.0	230.0	170.0	25.6	7.5	23.2	67.3	31.6
Tajikistan	..	163.0	1 316.5	1 080.0	327.8	276.1	255.2	77.5	30.2	43.6	44.0
Turkmenistan	..	211.0	994.0	1 610.0	911.0	893.8	2 391.8	261.0	-30.5	..	..
Ukraine	..	..	2 491.7	4 698.3	1 134.5	488.9	52.0	7.7	13.0	31.1	21.0
Uzbekistan	..	147.0	1 296.0	1 119.0	1 066.0	834.0	133.0	54.0	41.0	38.0	60.9

Source: UN/ECE Common Database, derived from national statistics.

Note: From 1994 onwards indices derived from monthly data except: Bosnia and Herzegovina, Croatia, Czech Republic, Poland, The former Yugoslav Republic of Macedonia (from 1992); Hungary, Romania, Slovakia, Slovenia (from 1993); Turkmenistan, Yugoslavia (from 1995).

APPENDIX TABLE B.10

Nominal gross wages in industry in eastern Europe, the Baltic states and the CIS, 1990-2000

(Annual average, percentage change over preceding year)[a]

	1990	1991	1992	1993	1994	1995	1996	1997	1998	1999	2000
Albania[b]	..	..	..	69.5	34.5	29.3	..	..	20.4	10.4	..
Bosnia and Herzegovina[c]	..	..	..	..	..	4.1	249.4	50.8	31.1	15.4	..
Bulgaria	20.8	175.5	132.8	55.1	53.9	57.7	90.4	882.9	34.5	..	..
Croatia[c]	453.7	40.7	466.7	1 444.1	130.5	44.0	11.8	16.3	10.6	10.1	..
Czech Republic	3.0	16.5	21.0	22.6	16.9	18.3	17.7	11.9	10.7	6.8	7.2
Hungary[b]	27.2	33.4	24.3	24.9	23.3	19.1	21.7	21.8	16.6	13.5	15.0
Poland[c]	365.5	64.0	41.2	37.8	39.8	30.1	25.8	19.9	14.1	10.5	..
Romania[c]	9.7	125.0	173.5	210.7	139.4	55.3	56.7	99.5	49.3	40.7	48.7
Slovakia[b]	4.3	15.0	16.9	23.1	17.7	15.2	14.6	11.1	8.0	7.9	9.4
Slovenia	361.5	68.4	196.7	45.1	27.1	17.1	14.0	12.1	10.7	9.3	..
The former Yugoslav Republic of Macedonia[c]	433.6	79.2	1 083.7	454.0	105.8	11.1	3.6	2.3	3.1	1.5	..
Yugoslavia[c]	400.0	100.6	4 886.4	-62.5	229.6	74.1	74.5	41.7	39.6	24.6	113.5
Estonia[d]	..	122.2	570.3	93.3	71.3	34.6	23.8	19.7	13.2	0.9	..
Latvia	..	104.5	609.8	112.0	60.0	24.1	14.9	21.6	6.5	4.0	3.2
Lithuania	15.3	183.9	632.5	246.1	70.0	43.2	34.0	21.7	12.0	-0.4	..
Armenia	5.9	31.8	352.3	739.1	3 640.2	210.9	62.3	41.7	20.5	15.2	25.2
Azerbaijan	4.4	82.9	870.4	700.8	575.7	354.8	53.0	36.8	22.0	..	..
Belarus	14.1	112.1	910.9	1 073.8	69.6	618.7	58.5	96.8	109.4	323.9	..
Georgia	6.0	33.9	457.3	2 114.7	23 327.5	87.5	145.4	12.7	26.8	..	..
Kazakhstan	11.0	80.5	1 053.1	993.1	1 542.5	178.2	30.9	22.5	2.7	12.3	..
Kyrgyzstan	0.5	62.1	638.3	745.6	176.3	54.8	29.1	60.3	20.0	43.2	..
Republic of Moldova	14.2	90.1	815.0	773.0	284.4	43.8	32.2	24.9	16.6	22.5	..
Russian Federation	13.0	94.9	1 065.7	798.2	260.2	131.4	64.3	21.6	14.3	52.2	..
Tajikistan	8.0	76.2	550.2	917.5	142.2	145.2	425.3	71.9	96.4	26.4	28.4
Turkmenistan	..	83.8	1 010.1	1 467.7	622.2	686.2	915.3	121.5	27.1	..	..
Ukraine	39.0	107.9	1 419.0	2 286.1	737.8	408.5	71.5	13.5	5.9	18.1	..
Uzbekistan	..	82.3	706.1	1 159.3	806.8	278.4	99.8	76.3	60.3	50.0	..

Source: UN/ECE Common Database, derived from national statistics.

[a] Calculated from reported annual average wages.

[b] Gross wages in total economy. For Hungary for 1990-1992; for Slovakia for 1990-1991.

[c] Net wages in industry. For Poland and Romania for 1990-1992.

[d] Manufacturing for 1991-1993.

APPENDIX TABLE B.11

Merchandise exports of eastern Europe, the Baltic states and the CIS, 1980, 1988-2000

(Billion dollars)

	1980	1988	1989	1990	1991	1992	1993	1994	1995	1996	1997	1998	1999	2000
Eastern Europe	56.367	65.020	63.850	61.733	57.241	59.333	62.675	72.937	94.777	100.206	107.428	119.174	117.769	132.926*
Albania	0.320	0.230	0.302	0.231	0.101	0.072	0.123	0.139	0.202	0.213	0.137	0.207	0.265	0.239*
Bulgaria	7.160	7.554	6.651	5.232	3.433	3.992	3.769	3.935	5.345	4.890	4.940	4.194	4.006	4.808
Czechoslovakia	10.475	12.381	11.988	10.728	11.319	..	..	..	..	..	..	..	..	..
Czech Republic	..	..	..	..	..	8.767	14.463	15.882	21.273	22.180	22.779	26.351	26.242	28.979
Slovakia	..	..	..	..	..	3.500	5.458	6.714	8.585	8.822	9.640	10.775	10.277	11.905
Hungary	8.609	9.999	9.673	9.731	10.226	10.681	8.921	10.701	12.867	15.704	19.100	23.005	25.015	28.092
Poland	13.071	14.573	14.665	18.291	14.912	13.187	14.202	17.240	22.887	24.440	25.756	28.229	27.404	31.651
Romania	9.217	8.971	8.076	4.570	4.266	4.363	4.892	6.151	7.910	8.085	8.431	8.302	8.504	10.367
Yugoslavia (SFR)	7.514	11.311	12.496	12.950	12.984	14.772	..	..	..	..	..	..	..	..
Bosnia and Herzegovina	..	1.550	2.100	1.850	..	..	..	..	0.024	0.058	0.193	0.352	0.518	0.675
Croatia	..	2.300	2.600	4.020	3.310	4.353	3.709	4.260	4.633	4.512	4.171	4.541	4.303	4.432
Slovenia	1.836	3.278	3.408	4.118	3.874	6.681	6.083	6.828	8.316	8.310	8.369	9.050	8.546	8.731
The former Yugoslav Republic of Macedonia	..	..	0.654	1.113	1.095	1.199	1.055	1.086	1.204	1.147	1.237	1.311	1.191	1.326*
Yugoslavia	..	4.298	4.461	4.651	4.704	2.539	..	..	1.531	1.846	2.677	2.858	1.498	1.723
Baltic states	..	..	..	..	..	2.139	4.197	4.324	5.844	6.877	8.467	8.759	7.665	8.867
Estonia	..	..	..	..	..	0.444	0.802	1.305	1.838	2.079	2.934	3.236	2.938	3.157
Latvia	..	..	..	..	..	0.843	1.401	0.988	1.304	1.443	1.673	1.812	1.723	1.863
Lithuania	..	..	..	..	..	0.852	1.994	2.031	2.705	3.355	3.860	3.711	3.004	3.848
CIS: total	..	..	..	..	..	..	..	89.991	110.622	121.936	122.913	104.266	103.904	143.786*
CIS: non-CIS	..	..	..	..	..	51.242	52.547	62.652	80.007	87.897	88.698	76.840	82.169	114.930*
Armenia	..	..	..	..	..	..	0.156	0.216	0.271	0.290	0.233	0.221	0.232	0.298
Non-CIS	..	..	..	..	..	0.026	0.029	0.058	0.101	0.162	0.138	0.140	0.176	0.225
Azerbaijan	..	..	..	..	..	1.484	0.725	0.653	0.637	0.631	0.781	0.606	0.929	1.745
Non-CIS	..	..	..	..	..	0.754	0.351	0.378	0.352	0.341	0.403	0.374	0.718	1.510
Belarus	..	..	..	..	..	..	..	2.510	4.707	5.652	7.301	7.070	5.922	7.380
Non-CIS	..	..	..	..	..	1.194	0.789	1.031	1.777	1.888	1.922	1.910	2.286	2.926
Georgia	..	..	..	..	..	..	..	0.156	0.154	0.199	0.240	0.193	0.238	0.330
Non-CIS	..	..	..	..	..	0.068	0.069	0.039	0.057	0.070	0.102	0.085	0.131	0.194
Kazakhstan	..	..	..	..	..	..	..	3.231	5.250	5.911	6.497	5.436	5.592	9.140
Non-CIS	..	..	..	..	..	1.398	1.501	1.357	2.366	2.732	3.515	3.266	4.131	6.749
Kyrgyzstan	..	..	..	..	..	0.317	0.396	0.340	0.409	0.505	0.604	0.514	0.454	0.505
Non-CIS	..	..	..	..	..	0.077	0.112	0.117	0.140	0.112	0.285	0.283	0.271	0.297
Republic of Moldova	..	..	..	..	..	0.470	0.483	0.565	0.746	0.795	0.875	0.632	0.462	0.472
Non-CIS	..	..	..	..	..	0.166	0.178	0.159	0.279	0.252	0.267	0.203	0.209	0.196
Russian Federation [a]	..	..	..	..	..	..	..	66.862	79.869	86.889	86.627	72.550	73.689*	102.796*
Non-CIS	..	..	..	..	..	42.376	44.297	53.001	65.607	70.975	69.959	58.883	62.800*	89.068*
Tajikistan	..	..	..	..	..	0.193	0.350	0.492	0.749	0.770	0.746	0.597	0.689	0.779
Non-CIS	..	..	..	..	..	0.109	0.227	0.399	0.497	0.439	0.473	0.394	0.374	0.411
Turkmenistan	..	..	..	..	..	..	..	2.145	1.881	1.682	0.751	0.594	1.187	2.506
Non-CIS	..	..	..	..	..	0.908	1.049	0.494	0.951	0.610	0.300	0.442	0.698	1.187
Ukraine	..	..	..	..	..	7.415	7.817	10.272	13.128	14.401	14.232	12.637	11.582	14.573
Non-CIS	..	..	..	..	..	3.297	3.223	4.653	6.168	6.996	8.646	8.435	8.329	10.075
Uzbekistan	..	..	..	..	..	..	..	2.549	2.821	4.211	4.026	3.218	2.928	3.265
Non-CIS	..	..	..	..	..	0.869	0.721	0.966	1.712	3.321	2.689	2.425	2.047	2.094
Former Soviet Union	57.942	62.016	62.286	59.056	46.660	..	..	..	..	..	..	..	..	..
Total	114.310	127.035	126.136	120.788	103.901	112.714	119.419	167.252	211.243	229.019	238.808	232.199	229.338	285.580*

Source: UN/ECE secretariat, based on national statistical publications and direct communications from national statistical offices.

Note: Trade flows reported include the "new trade" among members of the dissolved federal states: former Czechoslovakia (from 1993), the former SFR of Yugoslavia (from 1992) and the former USSR: for the Baltic states (from 1992) and for the CIS. Data excluding the "new trade" were shown in earlier issues of this publication. Changes in the method of recording trade are reflected from 1993 in data for the Czech Republic (inclusion of OPT transactions, etc.), from 1995 in Latvia (imports registered c.i.f.) and Lithuania (change from special to general system), from 1996 in Hungary (inclusion of trade flows of free trade zones) and from 1997 in Slovakia (inclusion of OPT transactions, etc.).

As from 1991, all trade values are expressed in dollars at prevailing market exchange rates. For earlier years, values reported in national currencies were adjusted by the ECE secretariat to remove distortions stemming from mutually inconsistent national rouble/dollar cross-rates in the valuation of the then important intra-CMEA trade flows. For details on the revaluation, see the note to table 2.1.3 and the discussion in box 2.1.1 in UN/ECE, *Economic Bulletin for Europe*, Vol. 43, 1991.

[a] Russian Goskomstat data excluding trade by physical persons (shuttle trade), but including trade flows not crossing the Russian borders such as off-board fish sales and natural gas deliveries under debt repayment agreements with former CMEA countries.

APPENDIX TABLE B.12

Merchandise imports of eastern Europe, the Baltic states and the CIS, 1980, 1988-2000
(Billion dollars)

	1980	1988	1989	1990	1991	1992	1993	1994	1995	1996	1997	1998	1999	2000
Eastern Europe	65.443	60.158	61.185	63.408	61.610	68.388	76.285	86.128	117.026	135.887	146.195	159.491	155.434	172.589*
Albania	0.320	0.280	0.385	0.381	0.409	0.524	0.421	0.549	0.650	0.913	0.620	0.795	0.885	1.009*
Bulgaria	6.321	8.131	7.325	5.584	2.700	4.530	5.120	4.272	5.638	5.074	4.932	4.957	5.515	6.487
Czechoslovakia	10.619	12.180	11.772	11.808	10.962									
Czech Republic	..	..	..	..	..	10.368	14.617	17.427	25.265	27.919	27.563	28.789	28.073	32.244
Slovakia	..	..	..	..	..	3.889	6.332	6.634	8.777	11.112	11.622	13.006	11.265	12.671
Hungary	9.188	9.372	8.863	8.797	11.449	11.123	12.648	14.554	15.466	18.144	21.234	25.706	28.017	32.080
Poland	14.705	12.987	12.941	12.619	15.531	16.141	18.758	21.566	29.043	37.137	42.314	47.054	45.901	48.940
Romania	11.061	5.361	5.834	6.889	5.793	6.260	6.522	7.109	10.278	11.435	11.280	11.838	10.394	13.055
Yugoslavia (SFR)	13.229	11.847	14.064	17.330	14.765									
Bosnia and Herzegovina	..	1.300	1.850	1.750	..	..	..	..	0.524	1.204	1.555	2.120	2.431	2.290
Croatia	..	2.900	3.750	5.133	3.811	4.346	4.166	5.229	7.510	7.788	9.104	8.383	7.799	7.923
Slovenia	2.463	2.914	3.216	4.727	4.131	6.141	6.501	7.304	9.492	9.421	9.367	10.098	10.083	10.115
The former Yugoslav Republic of Macedonia	..	..	0.934	1.531	1.274	1.206	1.199	1.484	1.719	1.627	1.779	1.915	1.776	2.066*
Yugoslavia	..	4.915	5.383	6.701	5.548	3.859	..	..	2.665	4.113	4.826	4.830	3.296	3.711
Baltic states	..	..	..	..	..	1.802	4.101	5.251	8.006	10.110	12.809	13.768	11.888	12.906
Estonia	..	..	..	..	..	0.406	0.896	1.659	2.540	3.231	4.441	4.786	4.108	4.258
Latvia	..	..	..	..	..	0.794	0.961	1.240	1.818	2.320	2.724	3.189	2.946	3.186
Lithuania	..	..	..	..	..	0.602	2.244	2.352	3.649	4.559	5.644	5.794	4.834	5.463
CIS: total	..	..	..	..	..	..	..	63.137	79.576	86.960	94.316	81.127	62.339	70.776*
CIS: non-CIS	..	..	..	..	..	42.297	33.696	36.743	45.678	49.205	57.780	50.763	37.873	38.658*
Armenia	..	..	..	..	..	..	0.255	0.394	0.674	0.856	0.892	0.902	0.802	0.885
Non-CIS	..	..	..	..	..	0.050	0.087	0.188	0.340	0.578	0.593	0.672	0.626	0.711
Azerbaijan	..	..	..	..	..	0.940	0.629	0.778	0.668	0.961	0.794	1.077	1.036	1.172
Non-CIS	..	..	..	..	..	0.333	0.241	0.292	0.440	0.621	0.443	0.673	0.711	0.797
Belarus	..	..	..	..	..	..	..	3.066	5.564	6.939	8.689	8.549	6.664	8.477
Non-CIS	..	..	..	..	..	0.843	1.119	0.974	1.887	2.369	2.872	2.995	2.381	2.476
Georgia	..	..	..	..	..	..	..	0.338	0.385	0.687	0.944	0.884	0.602	0.726
Non-CIS	..	..	..	..	..	0.228	0.167	0.066	0.231	0.417	0.603	0.617	0.377	0.479
Kazakhstan	..	..	..	..	..	..	..	3.561	3.807	4.241	4.301	4.350	3.683	5.052
Non-CIS	..	..	..	..	..	0.469	0.494	1.384	1.154	1.295	1.969	2.290	2.088	2.295
Kyrgyzstan	..	..	..	..	..	0.421	0.448	0.317	0.522	0.838	0.709	0.842	0.600	0.555
Non-CIS	..	..	..	..	..	0.071	0.112	0.107	0.168	0.351	0.273	0.401	0.341	0.256
Republic of Moldova	..	..	..	..	..	0.640	0.628	0.659	0.841	1.072	1.172	1.024	0.573	0.777
Non-CIS	..	..	..	..	..	0.179	0.184	0.183	0.272	0.420	0.567	0.584	0.344	0.517
Russian Federation [a]	..	..	..	..	..	..	..	38.661	46.709	47.373	53.568	43.980	31.552*	33.769*
Non-CIS	..	..	..	..	..	36.984	26.807	28.344	33.117	32.798	39.365	32.703	22.685*	22.171*
Tajikistan	..	..	..	..	..	0.254	0.630	0.547	0.810	0.668	0.750	0.711	0.663	0.674
Non-CIS	..	..	..	..	..	0.132	0.374	0.314	0.332	0.285	0.268	0.265	0.148	0.115
Turkmenistan	..	..	..	..	..	..	..	1.468	1.364	1.011	1.183	1.008	1.478	1.785
Non-CIS	..	..	..	..	..	0.030	0.501	0.782	0.619	0.450	0.531	0.530	0.978	1.105
Ukraine	..	..	..	..	..	6.892	9.533	10.745	15.484	17.603	17.128	14.676	11.846	13.956
Non-CIS	..	..	..	..	..	2.049	2.652	2.907	5.488	6.427	7.249	6.779	5.103	5.916
Uzbekistan	..	..	..	..	..	..	..	2.603	2.748	4.712	4.186	3.125	2.841	2.947
Non-CIS	..	..	..	..	..	0.929	0.958	1.202	1.630	3.195	3.047	2.256	2.091	1.822
Former Soviet Union	52.218	58.044	64.983	64.963	45.405	..	..	..	..	..	..	..	..	..
Total	117.661	118.202	126.168	128.371	106.901	112.487	114.082	154.516	204.609	232.957	253.320	254.386	229.662	256.271*

Source: UN/ECE secretariat, based on national statistical publications and direct communications from national statistical offices.

Note: See appendix table B.11.

[a] Russian Goskomstat data excluding trade by physical persons (shuttle trade), but including trade flows not crossing the Russian borders such as off-board fish sales and natural gas deliveries under debt repayment agreements with former CMEA countries.

APPENDIX TABLE B.13

Balance of merchandise trade of eastern Europe, the Baltic states and the CIS, 1980, 1988-2000

(Billion dollars)

	1980	1988	1989	1990	1991	1992	1993	1994	1995	1996	1997	1998	1999	2000
Eastern Europe	-9.076	4.861	2.665	-1.675	-4.369	-9.055	-13.610	-13.190	-22.250	-35.680	-38.767	-40.317	-37.665	-39.663*
Albania	–	-0.050	-0.083	-0.150	-0.308	-0.452	-0.298	-0.410	-0.448	-0.701	-0.483	-0.589	-0.620	-0.770
Bulgaria	0.839	-0.577	-0.674	-0.352	0.732	-0.538	-1.352	-0.336	-0.293	-0.184	0.008	-0.763	-1.509	-1.679
Czechoslovakia	-0.144	0.201	0.216	-1.080	0.356	..	..	..	..	..	..	..	..	..
Czech Republic	..	..	..	..	..	-1.601	-0.154	-1.545	-3.992	-5.739	-4.784	-2.438	-1.831	-3.265
Slovakia	..	..	..	..	..	-0.389	-0.874	0.080	-0.192	-2.290	-1.983	-2.231	-0.988	-0.766
Hungary	-0.579	0.627	0.810	0.934	-1.223	-0.442	-3.727	-3.853	-2.599	-2.440	-2.134	-2.701	-3.002	-3.988
Poland	-1.634	1.586	1.724	5.672	-0.619	-2.955	-4.555	-4.326	-6.156	-12.697	-16.558	-18.825	-18.497	-17.289
Romania	-1.844	3.610	2.242	-2.320	-1.528	-1.897	-1.630	-0.958	-2.368	-3.351	-2.849	-3.536	-1.890	-2.688
Yugoslavia (SFR)	-5.715	-0.536	-1.568	-4.380	-1.780	14.772	..	..	..	..	..	..	..	..
Bosnia and Herzegovina	..	0.250	0.250	0.100	..	..	..	..	-0.500	-1.146	-1.362	-1.768	-1.913	-1.615
Croatia	..	-0.600	-1.150	-1.113	-0.501	0.007	-0.457	-0.969	-2.877	-3.276	-4.933	-3.842	-3.496	-3.491
Slovenia	-0.626	0.365	0.192	-0.609	-0.257	0.540	-0.418	-0.476	-1.176	-1.111	-0.998	-1.048	-1.537	-1.384
The former Yugoslav Republic of Macedonia	..	..	-0.280	-0.418	-0.179	-0.007	-0.144	-0.398	-0.515	-0.480	-0.542	-0.604	-0.585	-0.740*
Yugoslavia	..	-0.617	-0.922	-2.050	-0.844	-1.320	..	..	-1.134	-2.267	-2.149	-1.972	-1.798	-1.988
Baltic states	..	..	..	..	..	0.337	0.096	-0.927	-2.162	-3.232	-4.343	-5.009	-4.224	-4.039
Estonia	..	..	..	..	..	0.038	-0.094	-0.353	-0.702	-1.152	-1.507	-1.550	-1.170	-1.101
Latvia	..	..	..	..	..	0.049	0.440	-0.252	-0.514	-0.877	-1.051	-1.377	-1.223	-1.323
Lithuania	..	..	..	..	..	0.250	-0.250	-0.322	-0.944	-1.204	-1.784	-2.083	-1.831	-1.615
CIS: total	..	..	..	..	..	..	..	26.854	31.046	34.975	28.597	23.140	41.565*	73.010*
CIS: non-CIS	..	..	..	..	..	8.945	18.851	25.909	34.329	38.692	30.919	26.077	44.296*	76.273*
Armenia	..	..	..	..	..	..	-0.099	-0.178	-0.403	-0.566	-0.660	-0.682	-0.569	-0.588
Non-CIS	..	..	..	..	..	-0.024	-0.058	-0.130	-0.239	-0.416	-0.455	-0.532	-0.450	-0.486
Azerbaijan	..	..	..	..	..	0.544	0.096	-0.125	-0.031	-0.330	-0.013	-0.471	-0.107	0.573
Non-CIS	..	..	..	..	..	0.421	0.110	0.086	-0.088	-0.280	-0.040	-0.299	0.008	0.713
Belarus	..	..	..	..	..	..	..	-0.556	-0.857	-1.287	-1.388	-1.480	-0.742	-1.097
Non-CIS	..	..	..	..	..	0.351	-0.330	0.057	-0.110	-0.481	-0.950	-1.085	-0.095	0.450
Georgia	..	..	..	..	..	..	..	-0.182	-0.231	-0.488	-0.704	-0.692	-0.364	-0.396
Non-CIS	..	..	..	..	..	-0.160	-0.098	-0.027	-0.174	-0.347	-0.501	-0.532	-0.246	-0.285
Kazakhstan	..	..	..	..	..	..	..	-0.330	1.443	1.670	2.196	1.086	1.910	4.087
Non-CIS	..	..	..	..	..	0.929	1.007	-0.027	1.212	1.437	1.547	0.976	2.043	4.455
Kyrgyzstan	..	..	..	..	..	-0.104	-0.052	0.023	-0.113	-0.333	-0.105	-0.328	-0.146	-0.050
Non-CIS	..	..	..	..	..	0.005	–	0.010	-0.028	-0.239	0.012	-0.118	-0.070	0.042
Republic of Moldova	..	..	..	..	..	-0.170	-0.145	-0.094	-0.095	-0.277	-0.297	-0.392	-0.111	-0.306
Non-CIS	..	..	..	..	..	-0.013	-0.006	-0.024	0.007	-0.168	-0.300	-0.381	-0.135	-0.321
Russian Federation[a]	..	..	..	..	..	..	..	28.201	33.160	39.516	33.059	28.570	42.137*	69.027*
Non-CIS	..	..	..	..	..	5.392	17.490	24.657	32.490	38.177	30.594	26.180	40.115*	66.897*
Tajikistan	..	..	..	..	..	-0.061	-0.280	-0.055	-0.061	0.102	-0.004	-0.114	0.026	0.105
Non-CIS	..	..	..	..	..	-0.023	-0.147	0.085	0.165	0.154	0.205	0.129	0.225	0.295
Turkmenistan	..	..	..	..	..	..	..	0.677	0.517	0.670	-0.432	-0.414	-0.291	0.721
Non-CIS	..	..	..	..	..	0.878	0.548	-0.288	0.332	0.160	-0.231	-0.088	-0.280	0.081
Ukraine	..	..	..	..	..	0.523	-1.716	-0.473	-2.356	-3.202	-2.896	-2.038	-0.265	0.617
Non-CIS	..	..	..	..	..	1.248	0.571	1.746	0.680	0.569	1.397	1.657	3.227	4.159
Uzbekistan	..	..	..	..	..	..	..	-0.054	0.073	-0.501	-0.159	0.093	0.087	0.317
Non-CIS	..	..	..	..	..	-0.060	-0.237	-0.236	0.082	0.126	-0.358	0.169	-0.045	0.272
Former Soviet Union	5.724	3.972	-2.697	-5.907	1.255	..	..	..	..	..	..	..	..	..
Total	-3.351	8.833	-0.032	-7.583	-3.000	0.227	5.337	12.736	6.634	-3.937	-14.512	-22.187	-0.324*	29.309*

Source: UN/ECE secretariat, based on national statistical publications and direct communications from national statistical offices.

Note: See appendix table B.11.

[a] Russian Goskomstat data excluding trade by physical persons (shuttle trade), but including trade flows not crossing the Russian borders such as off-board fish sales and natural gas deliveries under debt repayment agreements with former CMEA countries.

APPENDIX TABLE B.14

Merchandise trade of eastern Europe and the Russian Federation, by direction, 1980, 1988-2000
(Shares in total trade, per cent)

	1980	1988	1989	1990	1991	1992	1993	1994	1995	1996	1997	1998	1999	2000[a]
Eastern Europe, *to and from:*														
Exports														
World	100.0	100.0	100.0	100.0	100.0	100.0	100.0	100.0	100.0	100.0	100.0	100.0	100.0	100.0
ECE transition economies	48.5	46.5	44.4	38.1	28.5	23.0	28.2	26.3	25.8	26.1	26.1	22.5	18.7	18.8
Former Soviet Union	27.1	27.2	25.5	22.3	17.9	12.4	9.8	9.0	8.9	9.4	10.3	7.5	4.7	4.8
Eastern Europe	21.4	19.3	18.9	15.8	10.7	10.7	18.5	17.4	16.9	16.7	15.8	14.8	13.5	14.1
Developed market economies	35.7	38.7	42.6	49.5	59.8	63.0	58.0	62.5	64.5	65.0	66.4	71.4	75.2	75.1
Developing economies	15.8	14.8	13.0	12.4	11.7	14.0	13.8	11.2	9.7	8.9	7.5	6.0	6.0	6.1
Imports														
World	100.0	100.0	100.0	100.0	100.0	100.0	100.0	100.0	100.0	100.0	100.0	100.0	100.0	100.0
ECE transition economies	42.0	40.5	36.4	26.6	25.5	24.7	29.3	26.1	25.3	23.8	22.1	18.3	17.7	21.8
Former Soviet Union	26.8	26.3	23.5	18.3	20.2	17.9	16.5	14.1	13.2	12.7	11.2	8.6	8.4	11.6
Eastern Europe	18.8	19.6	18.7	14.3	8.1	6.8	12.8	12.0	12.1	11.1	10.9	9.6	9.1	10.2
Developed market economies	38.7	41.1	44.0	53.3	58.3	64.4	61.5	65.0	65.8	66.6	68.1	72.5	73.0	68.1
Developing economies	19.3	18.4	19.5	20.1	16.1	10.9	9.2	9.0	8.9	9.6	9.8	9.2	9.3	10.1
Former Soviet Union/Russian Federation, *to and from:*														
Exports														
World	100.0	100.0	100.0	100.0	100.0	100.0	100.0	100.0	100.0	100.0	100.0	100.0	100.0	100.0
ECE transition economies	34.5	29.4	26.6	21.8	25.9	22.3	18.1	15.1	16.8	18.2	19.5	18.1	18.1	19.9
Eastern Europe	34.5	29.4	26.6	21.8	25.9	20.7	16.8	11.7	13.2	14.3	14.9	14.2	13.5	14.5
Developed market economies	42.2	38.9	41.8	49.5	56.5	57.9	59.7	66.6	60.6	58.1	58.6	60.0	57.6	56.6
Developing economies	23.3	31.7	31.6	28.7	17.6	19.9	22.2	18.3	22.6	23.8	21.9	21.9	24.3	23.5
Imports														
World	100.0	100.0	100.0	100.0	100.0	100.0	100.0	100.0	100.0	100.0	100.0	100.0	100.0	100.0
ECE transition economies	31.5	32.4	27.6	24.7	26.0	15.9	10.6	14.1	15.5	12.6	13.7	11.9	9.6	10.5
Eastern Europe	31.5	32.4	27.6	24.7	26.0	15.0	10.0	11.7	12.4	10.6	11.1	9.8	8.3	9.1
Developed market economies	46.4	46.3	50.1	52.9	58.1	62.4	60.6	70.3	69.5	67.8	68.3	68.2	68.2	69.0
Developing economies	22.1	21.3	22.3	22.4	15.9	21.7	28.8	15.6	15.0	19.6	18.0	19.9	22.2	20.5

Source: UN/ECE Common Database, derived from national statistics.

Note: Data for 1980-1990 refer to the east European CMEA countries (Bulgaria, Czechoslovakia, German Democratic Republic, Hungary, Poland and Romania) and to the former Soviet Union. Trade data in national currencies were revalued at consistent rouble/dollar cross-rates (see the note to appendix table B.11). As from 1991, eastern Europe covers Bulgaria, former Czechoslovakia (from 1993, Czech Republic and Slovakia including their mutual trade), Hungary, Poland and Romania, and the second panel reflects non-CIS trade of the Russian Federation only.

Partner-country grouping has been recently revised with subsequent revisions back to 1980. Thus, the earlier reported "Transition economies" group is now replaced by "ECE transition economies", which covers the Baltic states, CIS and the east European countries including the successor states of the former SFR of Yugoslavia. The "Eastern Europe" partner-group now covers Albania, Bulgaria, the Czech Republic, Hungary, Poland, Romania, Slovakia and the successor states of the former SFR of Yugoslavia, which earlier were in the "Other socialist countries" subgroup. The rest of subgroup "Other socialist countries", which in previous series covered China, Cuba, Democratic People's Republic of Korea, Mongolia and Viet Nam, is now included in the "Developing countries" group.

[a] January-September 2000.

APPENDIX TABLE B.15

Exchange rates of eastern Europe, the Baltic states and the CIS, 1980, 1988-2000
(Annual averages, national currency units per dollar)

	Unit [a]	1980	1988	1989	1990	1991	1992	1993	1994	1995	1996	1997	1998	1999	2000
Albania	lek	..	..	..	8.90	24.20	75.03	102.06	94.62	93.14	104.33	148.93	150.63	137.69	143.71
Bulgaria	lev [b]	0.86	0.83	0.84	0.79	17.45	23.42	27.85	54.13	67.08	177.88	1681.87	1760.37	1.8364	2.1233
Czechoslovakia	koruna	5.37	14.37	15.06	18.56	29.56	28.30	..	..	..	..	..	..	..	..
Czech Republic	koruna	..	..	..	..	..	..	29.15	28.79	26.54	27.14	31.70	32.29	34.57	38.60
Slovakia	koruna	..	..	..	..	..	..	30.80	31.93	29.71	30.68	33.62	35.23	41.36	46.33
Hungary	forint	32.64	50.41	59.07	63.21	74.73	78.98	91.91	105.11	125.69	152.65	186.79	214.40	237.15	282.18
Poland	Zloty [c]	3.05	430.64	1439	9500	10576	13627	18136	22723	2.42	2.70	3.28	3.49	3.96	4.35
Romania	leu	4.47	16.00	16.00	22.43	71.84	307.98	760.12	1654	2033	3085	7183	8876	15333	21709
Yugoslavia (SFR)	dinar [d]	24.64	25239	28760	11.32	19.64	..	..	..	..	..	..	..	..	..
Bosnia and Herzegovina	dinar	..	..	..	..	..	..	..	..	..	..	..	..	..	..
Croatia	kuna [e]	..	..	..	..	18.80	264.30	3577.63	6.00	5.23	5.43	6.10	6.36	7.11	8.28
Slovenia	tolar	..	..	..	..	27.57	81.29	113.24	128.81	118.52	135.37	159.69	166.13	181.77	222.68
The former Yugoslav Republic of Macedonia	denar [f]	..	..	..	..	19.69	508.07	23.26	43.25	38.05	39.92	50.40	54.48	56.90	65.90
Yugoslavia	dinar [g]	..	..	..	10.65	19.73	750.00	..	1.55	4.74	4.96	5.72	9.23	10.94	16.09
Estonia	kroon [h]	..	..	..	..	..	12.11	13.22	12.98	11.46	12.03	13.88	14.07	14.68	16.97
Latvia	lats [i]	..	..	..	..	..	..	0.67	0.56	0.53	0.55	0.58	0.59	0.59	0.61
Lithuania	litas [j]	..	..	..	..	..	..	4.37	3.98	4.00	4.00	4.00	4.00	4.00	4.00
Armenia	dram	..	..	..	..	..	..	8.66	288.35	405.93	413.47	490.70	504.92	535.06	539.54
Azerbaijan	manat	..	..	..	..	..	..	..	1169	4417	4295	3987	3869	4119	4474
Belarus	rouble [k]	..	..	..	..	..	..	2177	4017	11538	13472	26729	58971	274512	882
Georgia	lari [l]	..	..	..	..	..	..	..	..	1.10	1.29	1.26	1.30	1.39	2.02	1.98
Kazakhstan	tenge	..	..	..	..	..	..	..	35.54	60.95	67.30	75.43	78.35	119.47	142.13
Kyrgyzstan	som	..	..	..	..	..	..	..	10.86	10.83	12.81	17.37	21.37	39.73	47.79
Republic of Moldova	leu	..	..	..	..	..	..	..	4.07	4.50	4.60	4.62	5.37	10.52	12.43
Russian Federation	rouble [m]	0.65	0.61	0.63	0.59	1.74	192.75	927.46	2204	4559	5121	5785	9.71	24.62	28.13
Tajikistan	rouble [n]	..	..	..	..	..	..	..	..	107.59	292.89	560.64	..	1235.57	1831.23
Turkmenistan	manat	..	..	..	..	..	..	..	..	19.50	110.42	3509	4143	5200	5200
Ukraine	hryvnia [o]	..	..	..	..	..	..	4796	31700	147314	1.83	1.86	2.51	4.13	5.44
Uzbekistan	sum [p]	..	..	..	..	..	..	932.15	9.96	29.81	40.15	66.43	..	124.64	236.58
Memorandum item:															
Former GDR	mark [q]	3.30	8.14	8.14	8.14	1.66	1.56	1.65	1.62	1.43	1.50	1.73	1.76	..	..

Source: UN/ECE Common Database, derived from national, IMF and CIS statistics. Annual averages are unweighted arithmetic averages of monthly values. Change or redenomination of currency is indicated by a vertical bar.

Note: Under the central planning system with its state foreign trade monopoly, exchange rates served primarily statistical and accounting purposes (notably the conversion of foreign trade values for statistics expressed in domestic currency), without direct impact on domestic price formation. Market-based exchange rates and a meaningful link to domestic currency values emerged only with the transformations from 1989 onward. The official exchange rates of the earlier period are therefore not suitable for the conversion to dollars of macroeconomic and other data of these countries expressed in domestic currency. These strictures should be kept in mind in the interpretation and use of the data for the 1980s shown above.

[a] Currency unit of the last period shown. For prior periods, see footnotes.

[b] The leva was redenominated at 1:1,000 from 5 July 1999.

[c] The zloty was redenominated at 1:10,000 from 1 January 1995.

[d] The dinar was redenominated at 1:10,000 from 1 January 1990.

[e] The kuna replaced the Croat dinar on 3 May 1994 at 1:1,000; the 1994 average is shown in kuna terms.

[f] The denar (which had replaced the Yugoslav dinar 1:1 on 26 April 1992) was redenominated 1:100 on 1 May 1993; the 1993 average is shown in terms of that unit.

[g] The dinar was further redenominated on 1 July 1992 (1:10), 1 October 1993 (1:1 million), 1 January 1994 (1:1 trillion) and 24 January 1994 (1:13 million). Average annual exchange rates not available for 1993-1994.

[h] The kroon replaced the Soviet rouble in June 1992 with a peg to the deutsche mark (8:1); the average shown for 1992 refers to June-December.

[i] The lats replaced an earlier Latvian rouble at 1:200 on 18 October 1993; the 1993 average is shown in lat terms.

[j] The litas replaced the earlier talonas at 1:100 on 1 June 1993; the 1993 average is shown in litas terms.

[k] The Belarus rouble was redenominated 1:10 on 10 August 1994; the 1994 average here assumes this applied to the entire year. The Belarus rouble was further redenominated at 1:1,000 since January 2000. Annual averages were calculated from end-of-period monthly rates.

[l] The lari replaced the lari-kupon on 25 September 1995; the annual average for 1994 is shown in million lari-kupon, and that for 1995 in lari.

[m] 1980-1991: Soviet rouble/dollar rate used in the conversion of foreign trade data for statistical purposes. The rouble was redenominated at 1:1,000 from 1 January 1998.

[n] A new currency, the somon, was put into circulation on 30 October 2000. Made up of 100 dirams, the somon would be used in parallel to the Tajik rouble for 5 months, with the exchange rate of 1,000 roubles to the somon.

[o] The hryvnia replaced the former karbovanets on 2 September 1996 at 1:100,000; the average for 1996 is shown in hryvnia terms.

[p] Sum-kupon in 1993.

[q] German Democratic Republic mark through 1990, deutsche mark thereafter.

APPENDIX TABLE B.16

Current account balances of eastern Europe, the Baltic states and the CIS, 1990-2000
(Million dollars)

	1990	1991	1992	1993	1994	1995	1996	1997	1998	1999	2000
Eastern Europe[a]	-5 639	-2 147	-909	-7 896	-2 705	-1 894	-13 303	-14 392	-17 611	-20 843	-18 955*
Albania	-118	-168	-51	15	-157	-12	-107	-254	-45	-155	-500*
Bosnia and Herzegovina	..	..	..	..	-177	-193	-748	-1 060	-789	-971	-878[b]
Bulgaria	-1 710	-77	-361	-1 098	-32	-198	164	1 046	-61	-652	-696
Croatia[c]	-621	-589	329	623	853	-1 442	-1 091	-2 325	-1 530	-1 523	-750*
Czech Republic	-122	1 708	-456	456	-787	-1 369	-4 292	-3 211	-1 336	-1 567	-2 369
Hungary[d]	127	267	324	-3 455	-3 911	-2 480	-1 678	-981	-2 298	-2 081	-1 754
Poland[d]	716	-1 359	-269	-2 868	677	5 310	-1 371	-4 312	-6 858	-11 569	-9 978
Romania	-3 254	-1 013	-1 506	-1 174	-428	-1 774	-2 571	-2 137	-2 968	-1 296	-1 400
Slovakia	-767	-786	173	-601	665	391	-2 098	-1 952	-2 059	-1 083	-713
Slovenia[c]	518	129	926	192	573	-99	31	11	-147	-783	-594
The former Yugoslav Republic of Macedonia[c]	-409	-259	-19	15	-158	-222	-289	-276	-308	-135	-200*
Yugoslavia	..	..	..	..	-400	-1 037	-1 670	-1 845	-1 238	-1 421	-1 400*
Baltic states	..	..	548	353	-59	-788	-1 400	-1 890	-2 426	-2 134	-1 432*
Estonia	..	..	36	22	-167	-158	-398	-563	-478	-294	-331
Latvia	..	..	191	417	201	-16	-279	-345	-650	-646	-500*
Lithuania	..	..	321	-86	-94	-614	-723	-981	-1 298	-1 194	-600*
CIS	..	..	-538	10 267	5 212	4 326	6 139	-4 092	-6 715	23 125*	48 470*
Armenia	..	..	-50	-67	-104	-218	-291	-307	-403	-307	-300*
Azerbaijan	..	153	488	-160	-121	-401	-931	-916	-1 365	-600	200*
Belarus	..	..	131	-435	-444	-458	-516	-788	-866	-194	-162
Georgia	..	..	-248	-354	-277	-216	-275	-375	-416	-195	-200*
Kazakhstan	..	-1 300	-1 900	-641	-905	-213	-751	-799	-1 236	-233	1 200*
Kyrgyzstan	..	..	-61	-88	-84	-235	-425	-138	-371	-185	-100*
Republic of Moldova	..	..	-152	-155	-82	-95	-192	-275	-327	-34	-120*
Russian Federation[e]	-6 300	2 500	1 142	12 792	8 360	7 401	11 753	2 060	721	25 049	46 000*
Tajikistan	..	..	-53	-208	-170	-89	-70	-56	-120	17*	100*
Turkmenistan	-308	447	926	776	84	23	0	-580	-934	-851*	100*
Ukraine	..	..	-526	-765	-1 163	-1 152	-1 184	-1 335	-1 296	834	1 700*
Uzbekistan	..	..	-236	-429	118	-21	-980	-584	-102	-176	50*
Total above[a]	..	..	-900	2 724	2 448	1 644	-8 564	-20 374	-26 752	148*	28 083*
Memorandum items:											
CETE-5	473	-41	698	-6 277	-2 783	1 753	-9 408	-10 445	-12 698	-17 083	-15 408
SETE-7[a]	-6 112	-2 106	-1 607	-1 619	78	-3 647	-3 895	-3 947	-4 913	-3 760	-3 546*
Asian CIS	..	..	-1 133	-1 170	-1 459	-1 370	-3 723	-3 755	-4 947	-2 530*	1 051*
Three European CIS[f]	..	..	-547	-1 355	-1 689	-1 705	-1 892	-2 397	-2 489	606	1 419*

Source: National balance of payments statistics; IMF.

[a] Totals excluding Bosnia and Herzegovina and Yugoslavia.

[b] IMF projection.

[c] Excludes transactions with the republics of the former SFR of Yugoslavia: Croatia (1990-1992), Slovenia (1990-1991) and The former Yugoslav Republic of Macedonia (1990-1992).

[d] Convertible currencies. Hungary until 1995; Poland until 1992.

[e] 1990-1992 excluding transactions with the Baltic and CIS countries.

[f] Belarus, Republic of Moldova and Ukraine.

APPENDIX TABLE B.17

Inflows of foreign direct investment[a] in eastern Europe, the Baltic states and the CIS, 1990-2000
(Million dollars)

	1990	1991	1992	1993	1994	1995	1996	1997	1998	1999	2000
Eastern Europe[b]	479	2 332	3 124	4 165	3 575	9 230	7 974	9 399	15 268	18 615	21 502*
Albania[c]	–	–	20	58	53	70	90	48	45	41	100*
Bosnia and Herzegovina	..	..	..	..	–	–	–	–	100	90	117
Bulgaria[c]	4	56	42	40	105	90	109	505	537	819	975
Croatia	–	–	16	120	117	115	506	530	898	1 408	1 000*
Czech Republic	132	513	1 004	654	869	2 562	1 428	1 300	3 718[d]	6 324[d]	4 595
Hungary	311	1 459	1 471	2 339	1 146	4 453	2 275	2 173	2 036	1 970	1 957
Poland (cash basis)[c]	10	117	284	580	542	1 132	2 768	3 077	5 129	6 471	9 461
Romania	–	40	77	94	341	419	263	1 215	2 031	1 041	998
Slovakia	18	82	100	168	250	202	330	161	508	330	2 075
Slovenia	4	65	111	113	128	177	194	375	248	181	181
The former Yugoslav Republic of Macedonia[c]	–	–	–	–	24	9	11	16	118	30	160*
Yugoslavia	..	..	..	..	..	..	–	740	113	112	–*
Baltic states	..	..	119	238	460	454	685	1 142	1 863	1 139	1 148
Estonia	..	..	82	162	215	202	151	267	581	305	398
Latvia	..	..	29	45	214	180	382	521	357	347	400*
Lithuania	..	..	8	30	31	73	152	355	926	486	350*
CIS	..	..	1 777	1 875	1 770	4 064	5 288	8 842	6 726	6 886*	5 363*
Armenia[c]	..	..	–	1	8	25	18	52	221	122	140*
Azerbaijan[c]	..	..	–	60	22	330	627	1 115	1 023	510	-30*
Belarus	..	..	7	18	11	15	73	200	149	444	90
Georgia[c]	..	..	–	–	8	6	40	203	265	82	100*
Kazakhstan[e]	..	..	100	228	635	964	1 137	1 321	1 144	1 632	1 099*
Kyrgyzstan[c]	..	..	–	10	38	96	47	83	109	36	20*
Republic of Moldova	..	25	17	14	12	67	24	75	81	34	120*
Russian Federation[c]	–	100	1 454	1 211	690	2 065	2 579	4 865	2 762	3 309	3 000*
Tajikistan[c]	..	..	9	9	12	20	25	30	24	21*	24*
Turkmenistan[c]	–	–	11	79	103	233	108	108	64	80*	100*
Ukraine	..	..	170	198	159	267	521	623	743	496	600*
Uzbekistan[c]	..	..	9	48	73	-24	90	167	140	121	100*
Total above[b]	..	..	5 020	6 278	5 806	13 748	13 947	19 383	23 857	26 640*	28 013*
Memorandum items:											
CETE-5	475	2 236	2 970	3 853	2 935	8 526	6 995	7 087	11 639	15 276	18 269
SETE-7[b]	4	96	155	312	640	704	979	2 313	3 629	3 339	3 232*
Asian CIS	..	..	129	435	899	1 651	2 092	3 079	2 991	2 604*	1 553*
Three European CIS[f]	..	..	194	229	181	349	617	898	974	974	810*
Poland (accrual basis)	89	291	678	1 715	1 875	3 659	4 498	4 908	6 365	7 270	..

Source: National balance of payments statistics; IMF.

Note: Changes in coverage are available in chap. 5, box 5.3.1.

[a] Inflows into the reporting country.

[b] Excluding Bosnia and Herzegovina and Yugoslavia.

[c] Net of residents' investments abroad. Bulgaria, 1990-1994; Poland, 1990-1992.

[d] The Czech data for 1998-1999 have recently been revised to incorporate inter-company loans, increasing FDI inflows from $2,720 and $5,108 million, respectively. Both figures also reflect reinvested profits which is not the case for the preceding years. Also see the note.

[e] Drawings less repayments.

[f] Belarus, Republic of Moldova and Ukraine.

OTHER RECENT PUBLICATIONS FROM
THE UNITED NATIONS ECONOMIC COMMISSION FOR EUROPE

IN THE FIELD OF ECONOMIC ANALYSIS

- *Economic Survey of Europe, 2000 No. 2/3*, Sales No. E.00.II.E.28 (December)

    The papers presented at the Spring Seminar of May 2000 on "The Transition Process After Ten Years", are gathered in this issue, together with the comments of discussants and a summary of the general discussion. The papers cover long-run developments (Ivan Berend), macroeconomic policies and achievements (Stanislaw Gomulka), changes in production structures (Michael Landesmann) and the social costs and consequences (Michael Ellman).

- *Economic Survey of Europe, 2000 No. 1*, Sales No. E.00.II.E.12 (April)

    This issue reviews developments in 1999 and discusses the outlook for 2000. The "new economy", south-east Europe and capital inflows into the transition economies since 1989 are among the topics included in the current analysis, while there are special chapters on "Economic Convergence in Europe" and "The Fertility Decline in the Transition Economies, 1989-1998.

- *Economic Survey of Europe, 1999 No. 3*, Sales No. E.99.II.E.4 (November)

    This issue contains the proceedings of the 1999 Spring Seminar on the Reform of Pension Systems in the ECE Region. Included are papers by John Eatwell, Lawrence Thompson and Maria Augusztinovics, together with discussants' comments, and an introduction and summary of the day's discussion by the secretariat.

- *Economic Survey of Europe, 1999 No. 2*, Sales No. E.99.II.E.3 (July)

    In addition to an updated summary of economic developments in Europe, the CIS and North America to mid-1999, this issue contains the secretariat's analysis of "Postwar Reconstruction and Development in South-East Europe" which has received considerable attention in the course of the year.

- *Economic Survey of Europe, 1999 No. 1*, Sales No. E.99.II.E.2 (April)

    This issue provides a detailed survey of economic developments in Europe, the CIS and North America in 1998 and early 1999. There are special sections dealing with the start of EMU, monetary policy in the transition economies, a review of economic adjustment problems in Romania and a chapter devoted to the decline of fertility in the transition economies between 1982 and 1997.

- *Economic Survey of Europe, 1998 No. 3*, Sales No. E.98.II.E.25 (November)

    This issue brings the survey of economic developments in the ECE region up to November 1998 and pays special attention to the aftermath of the Russian crisis, both in Russia itself and in other transition economies. A special study looks at the difficulties of reaching production sharing agreements in Russia while emphasizing their potential role in attracting foreign investment in the country.

* * * * *

More details about other publications and activities of the United Nations Economic Commission for Europe, which pay special attention to issues concerning the transition economies, can be found at the secretariat's website: http://www.unece.org

* * * * *

To obtain copies of publications contact:

Publications des Nations Unies	United Nations Publications
Section de Vente et Marketing	2 United Nations Plaza
Organisation des Nations Unies	Room DC2-853
CH-1211 Genève 10	New York, NY 10017
Suisse	USA
Tel: (4122) 917 2612 / 917 2606 / 917 2613	Tel: (1212) 963 8302 / (1800) 253 9646
Fax: (4122) 917 0027	Fax: (1212) 963 3489
E-mail: unpubli@unog.ch	E-mail: publications@un.org